Suffixes
and Other Word-Final Elements of English

*A Compilation of More Than 1,500 Common and
Technical Free Forms, Bound Forms, and Roots
That Frequently Occur at the Ends of Words,
Accompanied by a Detailed Description of Each,
Showing Its Origin, Meanings,
History, Functions, Uses and Applications,
Variant Forms, and Related Forms,
Together with Illustrative Examples,
the Whole Uniquely Arranged in Reverse Alphabetical
Order for Ease of Use, Supplemented by a Detailed
Index, in Normal Alphabetical Order, Containing
Entries for All of the Foregoing.*

Laurence Urdang
EDITORIAL DIRECTOR

Alexander Humez
EDITOR

Howard G. Zettler
ASSOCIATE EDITOR

LAURENCE
URDANG
REFERENCE
BOOK

Gale Research Company
BOOK TOWER • DETROIT, MICHIGAN

Library of Congress Cataloging in Publication Data

Main entry under title:

Suffixes and other word-final elements of English.

"A Laurence Urdang reference book."
Includes index.
1. English language--Suffixes and prefixes.
2. English language--Word formation. I. Urdang,
Laurence. II. Humez, Alexander. III. Zettler, Howard G.
PE1175.S9   422   81-20259
ISBN 0-8103-1123-2   AACR2

Contents

v

Introduction and
How To Use This Book

Speakers of English are aware that the words of the language fall into several categories. They may occur as free-standing roots, like *take, run, house,* and many others, almost all of which can occur in close combination with other words or word elements, as in *intake, uptake, take-off, rerun, runabout, housekeeping, lighthouse, greenhouse,* and so on. Another category includes word elements that appear frequently or solely as combining forms, like *re-, pre-, -ing, -ful, -ly,* and so on. Some of these were words that could stand alone (free forms) in an earlier stage of the language: *-ful* is easily recognizable as a suffixal form of *full; -ly,* however, has lost most of its resemblance to *like* 'similar,' with which it is cognate, both going back to Germanic *lich* 'body,' the meaning 'similar' having arisen through the semantic development 'of the (same) body or kind; similar.'

In *Suffixes* we have listed more than 1500 forms that are either always or frequently encountered in combination with other words or word elements. Some of these, like *-amoeba, -cornea, -chorea,* occur as words in the language; these are listed and described for convenience, chiefly because they often occur in combination with other elements or words. The rest, which rarely or never occur in isolation (*-a, -theca, -ica*) are the mainstay of this book.

It will be noted that certain formulaic terminology to which precisionists may object has been employed in the descriptions for uniformity and clarity of treatment. The phrase "[noun-forming, with variants for other parts of speech] word-final element" has been adopted to describe what people loosely refer to as "suffixes," mainly because a suffix is properly a form that cannot stand on its own, and *Suffixes* lists many forms that function as independent words. The element to which the "word-final element" is attached is called the "combining root," despite the fact that "root" is a misnomer in those instances where the "suffix" is attached to a "prefix." This terminology has been used for the sake of simplicity of presentation and, in certain cases, to avoid a specific commitment as to the classification of the element.

With few exceptions, the suffixes described were selected because the editors found at least five examples of their use—albeit often in technical language. In certain instances, forms appearing in word-final position in fewer than five words were included because of the comparatively high frequency of the words in which they do occur. For example, *-mare*, which appears only in *nightmare* (and the considerably rarer *daymare*), is in; so is *-stress* (as in *seamstress*), which, though a combination of *-ster* and *-ess*, was felt to be more conveniently treated in its own entry.

Many word-final elements appear in combinations, for instance *-ic*, which can be seen in *-ical* and *-ically*. All of these are listed, but the last two are mere cross references to the main entries where their components (respectively *-ic* and *-al*, and *-ic*, *-al*, and *-ly*) are described.

There are a fair number of homographs shown. These are word-final elements which, though spelt identically, have different origins. Examples are *-a¹*, *-a²*, *-a³*, *-ica¹*, *-ica²*, *-ia¹*, *-ia²*, and so forth.

Each entry consists of the following information:

(1) a sequential number for each word-final element, in **bold** type;

(2) the entry itself, in **bold** type;

(3) descriptive text detailing the origin (in *italic* type), meaning(s) (enclosed in single quotation marks), and use(s) of the form;

(4) examples, in **bold** type, illustrating actual words in which the combining form appears in attested sources;

(5) variant forms or spellings, in **bold** type;

(6) related forms, in **bold** type, usually those showing the element in combination with other elements.

Important: It will be seen that the elements are listed in what may appear at first to be a rather curious order; on closer examination, it will be found that the main entries have been alphabetized from the *right end:* that is, **232 -somatia** comes before **233 -hepatia** (since, alphabetizing from the right, **"-matia"** comes before **"-patia"**). This was done because not all users of this book were expected to know, in all cases, where a suffix begins. For those who can always identify an entire suffix, the Index provides a complete listing of all forms in bold type alphabetized normally, from the *left*. The Index also includes all examples, variant forms, and related forms in bold type, all origins in italic type, and all meanings in single quotation marks, just as they appear in the main part of the book.

Users of *Suffixes* will undoubtedly find some omissions. For example, the word-final element *-aholic*, which leapt into prominence in recent times, arrived too late for inclusion in the main text of the book. It has its origin in the ending of *alcoholic* (hence *-aholic* is a "folk" spelling) and has acquired the meaning 'one who is addicted to' whatever is described by the preceding element. Examples are **workaholic, drugaholic.** Of course, there is no such form as **-aholic* (or even **-oholic* or **-holic*), and, in any event, it would not carry the meaning ascribed to it: *alcohol* comes from Arabic *al-kuhul,* in which *al* means 'the' and *kuhul* 'powdered antimony; distillate.'

We should be grateful for information from readers regarding omissions, which we shall be pleased to consider for inclusion in a subsequent edition of this book.

Laurence Urdang

Essex, Connecticut
September 1981

SUFFIXES
and Other Word-Final Elements
of English

1 **-a^1** A word-final element, used to form the plurals of nouns of two
varieties borrowed from Latin:
   1. Neuter nouns of the second declension whose singulars end in
   -um: **strata, data, addenda.**
   2. Neuter nouns of the third declension (whose singulars display a
   variety of endings): **genera, opera, lumina.**

2 **-a^2** A word-final element used to form the plurals of nouns of two
varieties borrowed from Greek:
   1. Neuter nouns of the second declension whose singulars end in
   -on: **protozoa, taxa, phenomena;**
   2. Neuter nouns of the third declension (whose singulars display a
   variety of endings): **schemata, chromata, somata.**

3 **-a^3** A word-final element, derived from the Greek and Latin neuter
plural ending **-a,** used to form collective nouns in taxonomic
nomenclature denoting classes of animals and plants as specified by
the combining root: **Fissipeda, Scorpionida, Pinnigrada.** Compare **-ae.**

4 **-a^4** A word-final element, used to form the singulars of nouns of two
varieties borrowed from Latin:
   1. Feminine nouns of the first declension: **pupa, nova, roseola.**
   2. Feminine nouns borrowed into Latin from the first declension of
   Greek: **basilica, amoeba, bibliotheca.** This suffix has two further
   analogical uses in English:
   1. To form feminine proper names: **Georgia, Roberta, Alexandra.**
   2. In chemical terminology, to designate the oxide of the element
   named by the combining root: **berylia, ceria, alumina.** Related
   forms: **-ae, -as** *(plurals).*

5 **-amoeba** A word derived from Greek *amoib(ē)* 'change' through Latin
that also acts as the word-final element in many combinations used to
designate 'a protozoan of particular type or location': **iodoamoeba,
hemamoeba, macramoeba.** Also, **-ameba.** Related forms: **-am(o)ebic,**

-am(o)eban, -am(o)ebid, -am(o)eboid, -am(o)ebiform, -am(o)ebous; -amoebas, -amoebae *(plurals)*.

6   **-ostraca**   A noun-forming word-final element, derived from Greek *ostrak(on)* '(hard) shell' and -a³, used in zoological taxonomic nomenclature to designate 'creatures having or characterized by a type of shell' specified by the combining root: **Leptostraca, Arthrostraca, Conchostraca**. Related form: **-ostracan**.

7   **-cocca**   A noun-forming word-final element, derived through Latin from Greek *kokk(os)* 'grain, berry' and -a³, used in naming botanical genera of shrubs 'possessing or characterized by berries' as specified by the combining root: **Melicocca, Sarcococca, Chiococca**. Compare **-coccus**.

8   **-theca**   A noun-forming word-final element, derived from Greek *thēk(ē)* 'case, container' and -a⁴, used in zoological and botanical terminology to designate 'a sheath, covering, or receptacle' for that which is specified by the combining root: **spermatheca, dactylotheca, sarcotheca**. Also, **-teca, -thec, -tec**. Related forms: **-thecal, -thecium, -thecial; -thecae, -thecas, -thecs, -tecs** *(plurals)*.

9   **-ica¹**   A word-final element, derived either from Latin *-ic(us)* '-ic²' or (through Latin) from Greek *-ik(os)* '-ic²' and -a³, used to form collective nouns meaning 'a collection of something (as information) concerning or relating to' the subject indicated by the combining form. Many of the terms, esp. those in medical terminology, are currently obsolete: **Judaica, Thebaica, ischiopubica**.

10   **-ica²**   A word-final element, derived from Latin *-ic(us)* '-ic²' or (through Latin) from Greek *-ik(os)* '-ic²' and -a⁴, used in forming singular nouns meaning 'a disability or that which refers to the thing, state, or condition' identified by the combining root: **lethologica** *(obs.)*, **monocyclica** *(arch.)*, **basilica**. Related forms: **-icas, -icae** *(plurals)*.

11   **-(r)rhoeica**   A word-final element, derived through Latin from Greek *rhe(in)* 'to flow' and **-ica²**, previously used in medical terminology to denote 'a fluid discharge or that which relates to it' as specified by the combining root: **seborrhoeica, dysmenorrhoeica, gonorrhoeica**. Also, **-(r)rhea, -(r)rhoea**.

12   **-cerca**   A noun-forming word-final element, derived from Greek *kerk(os)* 'tail' and -a³, used in zoological taxonomy to designate

creatures 'having a tail' of a sort specified by the combining root: **Onchocerca, Spirocerca, Schistocerca.** Related form: **-cercal.**

13   **-grada**   A collective noun-forming word-final element, derived from Latin *grad(us)* 'step, pace' and **-a³**, used formerly in zoological taxonomy to designate genera of 'creatures going or walking by the means or in the manner' specified by the combining root: **Pinnigrada, Digitigrada, Laevigrada.** Related form: **-grade.**

14   **-ida**   A noun-forming word-final element, derived through Latin from the Greek patronymic suffix *-id(es)* and **-a³**, used in zoological taxonomy to designate higher orders (classes) of taxa, with the sense of 'creatures of the form or taxa' specified by the combining root: **Scorpionida, Acarida, Beroida.** Related forms: **id¹, -id⁵, -idae, -idan.**

15   **-gravida**   A noun, often found as a word-final element of nouns, derived from the feminine singular of Latin *gravid(us)* 'heavy' and used in medical terminology to mean 'pregnant woman'; it is combined with terms or figures to specify the quantity of pregnancies experienced: **secundigravida, primigravida, 3-gravida.** Compare **-para.** Related forms: **-gravidic; -gravidas** *(plural).*

16   **-poda**   A noun-forming word-final element, derived from Greek *pous, pod-* 'foot' and **-a³**, used in zoological taxonomy to name 'creatures having or characterized by a type or number of feet' specified by the combining root: **Arthropoda, Gastropoda, Decapoda.** Related forms: **-pod, -pode, -podia, -podium, -pus, -podal, -podial, -podous, pody.**

17   **-chorda**   A noun, more often found as a noun-forming word-final element, derived from Greek *chord(ē)* 'catgut, string, chord, cord' and **-a³**, used in zoological taxonomy to denote 'a member of a division of the phylum or subfamily Chordata, possessing a notochord' of a type specified by the combining root: **Hemichorda, Cephalochorda, Protochorda.** Compare **-chord, -cord.** Related forms: **-chordata, -chordate; -chordae** *(plural).*

18   **-gaea**   A noun-forming word-final element, derived through Latin from Greek *gaia* 'land, earth,' used to mean 'the geographical or bio-geographical area' identified by the combining root: **Palaeogaea, Afrogaea, Dendrogaea.** Also, **-gea.** Related forms: **-gaeic, -geic, -gaean, -gean; gaeas** *(plural).*

19   **-acea**   A noun-forming word-final element, derived from Latin *-ace(us), -ace(a), -ace(um)* 'having the nature or qualities of' and **-a³**, used in

zoological taxonomy to name higher taxa of animals with the qualities or characteristics specified by the combining root: **Crustacea, Gorgonacea, Cetacea.** Compare **-aceae.** Related forms: **-acean, -acial, -aceous; -aceum** *(singular).*

20   **-oidea** A noun-forming word-final element, derived from scientific Greco-Latin **-oid** plus *-ea* (that is, the Latin suffix *-e(us), -e(a), -e(um)* 'of' and **-a³**), used in zoological taxonomy to name animal super-families with the meaning 'having the qualities or characteristics of that which is specified by the combining root': **Silicoidea, Ostracoidea, Molluscoidea.** Also, **-oida, -oides, -oidei.** Compare **-oideae.**

21   **-(r)rhea** A noun-forming word-final element, derived through Latin *-(r)rhoea* from Greek *-(r)rhoia* (from the verb *rhe(in)* 'to flow' and *-ia¹*), used chiefly in medical terminology to denote 'a fluid discharge' of a sort named by the combining root: **diarrhea, gonorrhea, pyorrhea.** Also, **-(r)rhoea, -(r)rhoeica.** Related forms: **-(r)rheic, -(r)rhoeic, -(r)rheal, -(r)rhetic; -(r)rheas, -(r)rhoeas** *(plurals).*

22   **-glea** A noun-forming word-final element, derived through Latin from Greek *glia, gloia* 'glue, cement,' used in medical terminology to denote 'a gelatinous medium binding' something specified by the first root: **ooglea, zooglea, mesoglea.** Also, **-gloea.** Related forms: **-glia, -glial, -gleic, -gloeal; -gleas, -gloeas** *(plurals).*

23   **-genea** A collective noun-forming element derived through Latin from Greek *gen(os)* 'race, kind, descent' and **-ea,** used formerly in zoological taxonomy to form the names of taxa (now acting as synonyms for more recent labels) with the meaning 'creatures descended in a manner or of a group' specified by the combining root: **Digenea, Pterygogenea, Monogenea.** Related form: **-geneous.**

24   **-pnea** A noun-forming word-final element, derived through Latin from (Attic) Greek *pnoē* 'air, breath, breathing' (cf. Ionic Greek *pnoiē*), used in medical terminology to designate 'breath or breathing' of a sort specified by the combining root: **hyperpnea, polypnea, oligopnea.** Also, **-pnoea.** Related forms: **-pneic, -pnoeic; -pneas** *(plural).*

25   **-cornea** A noun, often found as a noun-forming word-final element, derived from the substantive use of the feminine singular form of the Latin adjective *corne(us)* 'horny' (from Latin *cornu* 'horn'), and used in medical terminology to denote 'state, condition, or layer of the cornea (i.e. the horny outer layer of the eye)' as specified by the

combining root: **megalocornea, sclerocornea, ectocornea.** Related forms: **-corneal; -corneas** *(plural).*

26 **-chorea** A noun, more often a noun-forming word-final element derived through Latin from Greek *choreia* 'dance' and used in medical terminology to denote 'a nervous disorder of organic or infectious origin' in the place or of the type specified by the first root: **labiochorea, pseudochorea, orchichorea.** Related forms: **-choreal, -choreatic, -choreic; -choreas** *(plural).*

27 **-urea** A noun and a noun-forming word-final element, derived through French and Latin from Greek *our(on)* 'urine' and **-a⁴**, used in biochemical terminology to denote 'a compound containing $CO(NH_2)_2$' especially in the urine of man and other mammals: **oxalylurea, acetylurea, sulfourea.** Related forms: **-ureal, -uria, -uric; -ureas** *(plural).*

28 **-thyrea** A noun-forming word-final element, derived from Greek *thyre(os)* 'shield' (whence *thyroid* 'shield-shaped gland') and **-ia¹**, used in medical terminology to denote 'a condition of the thyroid gland' specified by the combining root: **athyrea, hypothyrea, hyperthyrea.** Also, **-thyreosis, -thyroidism.** Related forms: **-thyroid; thyreas, -thyreoses, -thyroidisms** *(plurals).*

29 **-phaga** A noun-forming word-final element, derived from Greek *phag(ein)* 'to eat' and **-a³**, used in zoological taxonomy to designate 'creatures who eat' either a thing or in a manner specified by the combining root: **Glossophaga, Lithophaga, Xylophaga.** Related forms: **-phag, -phage, -phagi, -phagia, -phagy, -phagic, -phagically, -phagism, -phagist, -phagous.**

30 **-tricha** A noun-forming word-final element, derived from Greek *thrix, trich-* 'hair' and **-a³**, used in zoological taxonomy in generic names for 'a creature or creatures having a ciliation' specified by the combining root: **Oxytricha, Peritricha, Gastrotricha.** Related forms: **-thrix, -trichous, -trichan, -trichic, -trichia.**

31 **-(r)rhyncha** A noun-forming word-final element, derived from Greek *rhynch(os)* 'snout, beak, proboscis' and **-a³**, used in zoological taxonomy to denote divisions of creatures according to the shape or qualities of their muzzles, as specified by the combining root: **Menorhyncha, Kinorhyncha, Oxyrrhyncha.** Related form: **-(r)rhyn-chous.**

32 **-trocha** A noun-forming word-final element, derived from Greek *troch(os)* '(circular) race track, wheel, hoop' and **-a⁴**, used in zoological terminology to name larval annelids 'having a ciliated band' of a sort (i.e., in a location) specified by the combining root: **amphitrocha, cephalotrocha, telotrocha**. This element (with **-a³**) appears with a different (though etymologically related) meaning in the names of two zoological divisions, with the sense of 'having a number of trochanters (i.e., runners)' specified by the combining root: **Monotrocha, Ditrocha**. Related forms: **-troch, -trochal; -trochas, -trochae** *(plurals)*.

33 **-grapha** A collective noun-forming word-final element, derived from Greek *graph(ein)* 'to write, mark' (literally, 'engrave'), and **-a³**, used in forming two types of combination.

    1. 'A collection of writings' as specified by the first root: **pseudepigrapha, agrapha, hagiographa**. Related forms: **-graphic, -graphical, -graphal, -graphous, -graphist, -graphia, -graphy, -grapher**.

    2. In biological taxonomy, denoting genera in terms of the markings their presence causes: **Opegrapha, Calligrapha**.

34 **-morpha** A noun-forming word-final element, derived through Latin from Greek *morph(ē)* 'form, shape' and **-a³**, used in the terminology of zoological nomenclature to name taxa higher than genus with the meaning 'creature or creatures possessing or characterized by the form' specified by the combining root: **Cynomorpha, Coccidiomorpha, Hystricomorpha**. Compare **-morph**.

35 **-glypha** A collective noun-forming word-final element, derived from Greek *glyph(ein)* 'to carve' and **-a³**, used in zoological taxonomy to name groups of venomous snakes, that is, 'creatures having grooved or hollowed fangs,' as further specified by the combining root: **Opisthoglypha, Protyroglypha, Solenoglypha**. Related forms: **-glyph, -glyphic, -glyphous**.

36 **-gnatha** A noun-forming word-final element, derived from Greek *gnath(os)* 'jaw' and **-a³**, used in zoological taxonomy to denote 'a creature (a class of creatures) having or characterized by a jaw' of the sort specified by the combining root: **Agnatha, Chaetognatha, Desmognatha**. Also, **-gnath, -gnathus, -gnathi, -gnathae**. Related forms: **-gnathous, -gnathic, -gnathan**.

37 **-ia¹** A noun-forming word-final element, variously construed as a singular or a collective, derived from the Latin and Greek stem and joining vowel *-i-* and *-a*, that is, **-a¹, -a², -a³**, and **-a⁴**, used in English with several specific meanings (in zoology, medicine, and botany), all related to one or the other of this element's more general meanings of 'a condition or state' or 'a class or collection' as particularized by the combining root:

1. Used in medicine to describe specific diseases, either physical or mental: **pneumonia, hysteria, phobia.**

2. Used in botany to denote a specific plant genus: **Wisteria, Buddleia, Fuchsia.**

3. Used generally to denote things derived from, belonging to, or related to a specified thing or person: **Marylandia, tabloidia, Einsteinia.**

4. Used in the names of taxonomic divisions to indicate classes or orders of plants or animals: **Amphibia, Mammalia, Cryptogamia.** Compare -a^1, -a^2, -a^3, -a^4. Related forms: **-ian, -ial; -ias** (*plural, senses 1 and 2*).

38   **-ia^2**   A noun-forming word-final element, variously construed as a plural or a collective, derived from the neuter plural of two kinds of Latin noun and adjective:

1. Those of the second declension, with singulars ending in *-ium* (some of which represent Latin or Latinate borrowings of neuter Greek nouns and adjectives of the second declension, with singulars in *-ion* and plurals in *-ia*): **media, sporangia, polyphonia.**

2. Those of the third declension, with genitive singulars ending in *-is* (the nominative having no specific marker): **animalia, marginalia, memorabilia.** By abstraction, certain Latin or Latinate *masculine* nouns, with singulars ending in *-ius* (Greek *-ios*), have been borrowed into English with plural forms ending in **-ia^2**, virtually always in a collective sense, most frequently in taxonomic nomenclature: **Mammalia, Cryptogamia, Allotheria.** Compare **-ia^1, -a^1, -a^2, -a^3.** Related forms: **-ian, -ial; -ium, -ius, -ion, -ios** (*singulars*).

39   **-bia**   A noun-forming word-final element, derived from the homographic Latin feminine singular and neuter plural inflections of *-bius* 'having a mode of life' from Greek *bios* 'life,' used as a singular or a collective in zoological generic names: **Byrobia, Dermatobia, Cordylobia** or as a plural or a collective in biological group names: **aerobia, anaerobia, coenobia.** In both cases, the ending conveys the meanings 'creature or creatures possessing a mode of life' specified by the combining root. Related forms: **-bian; -bium, -bion, -biont** (*singulars*).

40   **-phobia**   A noun-forming word-final element, derived from Greek *phob(os)* 'fear' and **-ia¹**, used in combinations meaning 'fear or dread of' that which is named by the combining root: **agoraphobia, claustrophobia, ochlophobia.** Related forms: **-phobe, -phobiac, -phobist, -phobism, -phobic, -phobous, -phobically; -phobias** *(plural).*

41   **-malacia**   A noun and a word-final element of nouns, derived through Latin from Greek *malakia* 'softness' (from *malak(os)* 'soft' and **-ia¹**), used in medical terminology to denote 'the softening or softness of a tissue, often pathological' as specified by the combining root: **gastromalacia, osteomalacia, pneumomalacia.** Related form: **-malacias** *(plural).*

42   **-oecia**   A noun-forming word-final element, derived from Greek *oik(os)* 'house, dwelling' and **-ia²**, used in botanical taxonomy to name species according to the number of separate plants on which male, female, and hermaphrodite flowers appear: **Monoecia, Dioecia, Trioecia.** Related forms: **-oecian, -ecian, -oecious, -ecious, -oecism, -ecism, -oecium, -ecium.**

43   **-tocia**   A noun-forming word-final element derived from Greek *tok(os)* 'birth' and **-ia¹**, used in medical terminology to form two types of combinations:
   1.   'Conditions of labor or parturition' as qualified by the combining root: **dystocia, bradytocia, oxytocia.** Also, **-toky, -tokia** *(obs.).*
   2.   'The product of parturition or of a particular mother,' as specified by the combining root: **thelytocia, arrhenotocia, embryotocia.** Related form: **-tocias** *(plural).*

44   **-pedia¹**   A noun-forming word-final element, derived from Latin *pēs, ped-* 'foot' and **-ia²**, used in zoological taxonomy to designate 'creatures possessing or characterized by a foot or feet' of the type or number specified by the combining root: **Pinnipedia, Cirripedia, Fissipedia.** Related forms: **-ped, -pede.**

45   **-pedia²**   A noun-forming word-final element, derived through Latin from Greek *paideia* 'education' (cf. *pais, paid-* 'child, youth'), used in older medical terminology to designate 'a treatise or compendium of knowledge on a subject' specified by the combining root: **orthopedia, pharmacopedia, logopedia.** Also, **-paedia.** Related forms: **-pedic, -paedic, -pedics, -paedics, -pedist, -paedist; -pedias, -paedias** *(plurals).*

46   **-ophidia**   A noun and an infrequent noun-forming word-final element, derived from Greek *ophis, ophid-* 'snake' and **-ia²**, formerly used in zoological taxonomy to name the division of *Squamata* comprising snakes—**Ophidia**—and currently found chiefly in medical terminology as a quasi-taxon designating 'venomous snakes': **thanatophidia, toxicophidia.**

47 **-podia** A noun-forming word-final element, derived from Greek *pous, pod-* 'foot' and **-ia**[1], used to denote 'a condition of the feet' or 'the state of possessing a sort or number of feet' specified by the combining root: **dipodia, micropodia, megalopodia.** Related forms: **-pod, -pode, -poda, -pus, -podal, -podial, -podous, -podium, -pody; -podias** *(plural).*

48 **-cardia** A noun-forming word-final element, derived through Latin from Greek *kardia* 'heart,' used in the terminology of medicine and the life sciences in several related senses, each specified by the combining root:
   1. 'A specific type of heart action or location': **dextrocardia, bradycardia, tachycardia.**
   2. In generic names, 'animal or animals possessing a specified type of heart': **Diplocardia, Leptocardia, Distocardia.**
   3. In generic names of plants and animals, 'possessing a heartlike shape or part': **Oxycardia, Isocardia, Gynocardia.** Related forms: **-cardiac; -cardias** *(plural).*

49 **-poeia** A noun-forming word-final element, derived from Greek *poi(ein)* 'to make, produce, create' and **-ia**[1], used in the sense of 'the making, production of' that which is specified by the combining root: **onomatopoeia, pharmacopoeia, pathopoeia.** Also, **-peia, -poiesis, -poesis.** Related forms: **-poeic, -poetic, -poietic, -poetical, -poietical, -poetically, -poietically; -poeias, -peias, -poeses, -poieses** *(plurals).*

50 **-phagia** A noun-forming word-final element, derived from Greek *phag(ein)* 'to eat' and **-ia**[1], used in two senses:
   1. In biomedical terminology, 'an eating of a substance or a manner of eating' specified by the combining root: **homophagia, brady-phagia, geophagia.**
   2. In medical terminology, 'a desire for food' specified by the combining root: **hyperphagia, polyphagia, aphagia.** Also, **-phagy.** Related forms: **-phag, -phage, -phagi, -phagic, -phagically, -phagous, -phagist, -phagism; -phagias, -phagies** *(plurals).*

51 **-(r)rhagia** A noun-forming word-final element, derived from Greek *rhag(as)* 'a break, tear, bursting' (cf. the verb *rhēx(ai)* 'to burst, break, tear'), used in medical terminology to denote 'a fluid discharge of excessive quantity' specified by the combining root: **colonorrhagia,**

myelorrhagia, seborrhagia. Compare -(r)rhea, -(r)rhage. Related forms: -(r)rhagic, -(r)rhagenic, -(r)rhexis; -(r)rhagias *(plural)*.

52 **-pragia** A noun-forming word-final element, derived from Greek *prass(ein)*, *pratt(ein)* 'to do, accomplish,' used in medical terminology to denote 'a quality of action or performance' specified by the combining root: **bradypragia, miopragia, tachypragia.** Related forms: **-praxia, -praxis, -praxic, -practic, -practics, -practice; -pragias** *(plural)*.

53 **-plegia** A noun-forming word-final element, derived from Greek *plēg(ē)* 'blow, stroke, wound' and -ia[1], used in medical terminology to denote 'a paralysis' of a sort specified by the combining root: **paraplegia, cardioplegia, gastroplegia.** Also, **-plegy.** Compare **-plexia, -plexy.** Related forms: **-plegic; -plegias, -plegies** *(plurals)*.

54 **-stegia** A noun-forming word-final element derived from Greek *steg(ē)* 'roof' and -ia[2], used in botanical terminology to name genera of plants whose flowers reveal a 'cover' of the type or in the location denoted by the first root: **Physostegia, Cryptostegia, Calystegia.**

55 **-algia** A noun-forming word-final element, derived through Greek *-algia* from *alg(os)* 'pain' and -ia[1], used in medical terminology to denote 'pain, painful condition' in the area or part of the body specified by the combining root: **neuralgia, podalgia, odontalgia.** Also, **-algy.** Related forms: **-algic; -algias, -algies** *(plurals)*.

56 **-phalangia** A noun-forming word-final element, derived from Greek *phalanx, phalang-* 'line of battle, a bone between two joints of a finger or toe' and -ia[1], used in medical terminology to denote 'a condition of the bones of the fingers or toes' as specified by the combining root: **triphalangia, symphalangia, brachyphalangia.** Related forms: **-phalangism; -phalangias** *(plural)*.

57 **-phthongia** A noun-forming word-final element, derived from Greek *phthong(os)* 'voice, sound, utterance' and -ia[1], used in medical terminology in a few words denoting 'a condition of speech' specified by the combining root: **aphthongia, diphthongia, heterophthongia.** Related forms: **-phthong; -phthongias** *(plural)*.

58 **-spongia** A noun-forming word-final element, derived from Greek and Latin *spong(ia)* 'sponge' and -ia[1], used in zoological taxonomy to designate genera of sponges: **Astylospongia, Hyalospongia, Euspongia.** Related forms: **-spongium, -spongiae.**

59 **-(r)rhachia**   A noun-forming word-final element, derived from Greek *rhach(is)* 'spine' and **-ia**[1], used in medical terminology to denote 'the presence in the spinal fluid of a foreign chemical substance' specified by the combining root: **glycorrachia, calciorrhachia, polypeptidorrhachia**. Related forms: **-(r)rhachitic; -(r)rhachias** *(plural)*.

60 **-brachia**   A noun-forming word-final element, derived from Greek *brachi(on)* 'arm' and **-ia**[1], used in medical terminology to denote 'an anatomical condition, usu. anomalous, involving an arm or arms' specified by the combining root: **abrachia, dibrachia, macrobrachia**. Compare **-brachium**. Related forms: **-brachial; -brachias** *(plural)*.

61 **-echia**   A noun-forming word-final element derived from Greek *ech(ein)* 'to have, hold' and **-ia**[1], used in medical terminology to mean 'a condition of holding, retaining, or adhesion' specified by the combining root: **synechia, asynechia, glycohistechia**. Related form: **-echiae** *(plural)*.

62 **-histechia**   A noun-forming word-final element, derived from Greek *hist(os)* 'tissue,' *ech(ein)* 'to hold,' and **-ia**[1], used in medical terminology to denote 'a tissue retaining' something specified by the combining root: **glycohistechia, cholesterohistechia, chlorhistechia**. Related form: **-histechias** *(plural)*.

63 **-trichia**   A noun-forming word-final element, derived from Greek *thrix, trich-* 'hair' and **-ia**[1], used in medical terminology in two senses:
  1. 'A pathological condition of the hair' as specified by the combining root: **oligotrichia, hypotrichia, lissotrichia**. Also, **-trichy**.
  2. 'Hairiness' of a sort specified by the combining root: **glossotrichia, polytrichia**. Also, **-trichosis**. Related forms: **-trichi, -trichias, -trichies** *(plurals)*.

64 **-stichia**   A noun-forming word-final element, derived from Greek *stix(os)* 'row, line,' used in medical terminology to denote 'an abnormal condition involving rows of eyelashes' of a sort or in a number specified by the combining root: **distichia, tristichia, polystichia**. Compare **-stich**. Related forms: **-stichal, -stichous; -stichias** *(plural)*.

65 **-branchia**   A noun-forming word-final element, derived from Greek *branchia* 'gills,' used in zoological terminology to form two types of combinations.
  1. As a plural, in taxonomic labels designating 'creatures having a

gill or a number of gills' specified by the combining root: **Filibranchia, Cryptobranchia, Tetrabranchia.**

2. As a singular, 'a gill or gill-like organ': **pulmobranchia, parabranchia, podobranchia.** Related forms: **-branch, -branchiate, -branchiata, -branchial; -branchiae** (*plural*, sense 2).

66 **-ischia** A noun-forming word-final element, derived from Greek *ischi(on)* 'hip joint' and **-ia²**, used in zoological taxonomy to denote 'creatures having hip joints' of a sort specified by the combining root: **Ornithischia, Saurischia.** Related forms: **-ischial, -ischian, -ischiac, -ischiatic.**

67 **-suchia** A noun-forming word-final element, derived from Greek *souch(os)* 'crocodile,' and **-ia²**, used in zoological taxonomy to name 'armored reptiles': **Parasuchia, Mesosuchia, Ensuchia.** Related form: **-suchian.**

68 **-onychia** A noun-forming word-final element, derived from Greek *onych(ion)* 'small claw' and **-ia¹**, used in medical terminology to denote 'a condition of the finger- or toenails' specified by the combining root: **leukonychia, paronychia, eponychia.** Related forms: **-onychial, -onychium; -onychias** (*plural*).

69 **-aphia** A noun-forming word-final element, derived from Greek *haph(ē)* 'sense of touch' (from *haptein* 'to fasten, grasp') and **-ia¹**, used in biomedical terminology to denote 'a condition of the sense of touch' specified by the combining root: **pseudaphia, anaphia, dysaphia.** Also, **-haphia.** Related forms: **-haptic; -haphias, -aphias** (*plurals*).

70 **-graphia** A noun-forming word-final element, derived from Greek *graph(ein)* 'to write' and **-ia¹**, used in two senses:
    1. Generally, 'writing on a topic' specified by the combining root: **biographia, blastographia, stomatographia.** Also, **-graphy.**
    2. In medical terminology, 'a psychological abnormality revealed through writing' as indicated by the combining root: **dysgraphia, pseudographia, palingraphia.** Related forms: **-graph, -grapher, -graphist, graphy, -graphic, -graphical, -graphous, -graphically; -graphias, -graphies** (*plurals*).

71 **-atrophia** A noun-forming word-final element, derived from Greek *atroph(os)* 'unfed' (from *a-* 'not' and *troph(os)* 'food') and **-ia²**, used in medical terminology in two senses:
    1. 'A condition of malnutrition' specified by the combining root: **metratrophia, metatrophia, pantatrophia.**

2. 'A progressive decline of a part of the body' specified by the combining root: **pedatrophia, neuratrophia, gastratrophia.** Also, **-atrophy.** Compare **-trophy.** Related forms: **-atrophic; -atrophias, -atrophies** *(plurals).*

72 **-morphia** A noun-forming word-final element, derived from Greek *morph(ē)* 'form, shape' and **-ia**[1], used in medical terminology to denote 'a condition of shape or form' specified by the combining root: **amorphia, orthomorphia, stasimorphia.** Also, **-morphy.** Related forms: **-morph, -morphic, -morphous, -morphically, -morphously, -morphi, -morphae, -morphism, -morphosis; -morphias, morphies** *(plurals).*

73 **-gnathia** A noun-forming word-final element, derived through Latin from Greek *gnath(os)* 'jaw' and **-ia**[1], used in medical terminology to denote 'a condition of the jaw' as specified by the combining root: **agnathia, orthognathia, micrognathia.** Related forms: **-gnath, -gnatha, -gnathus, -gnathae, -gnathi, -gnathan, -gnathous, -gnathal, -gnathic; -gnathias** *(plural).*

74 **-phakia** A noun-forming word-final element, derived from Greek *phak(os)* 'lentil, something lentil-shaped' and **-ia**[1], used in medical terminology to mean 'a lens' specified by the combining root: **pseudophakia, microphakia, aphakia.** Related form: **-phakias** *(plural).*

75 **-plakia** A noun-forming word-final element, derived from Greek *plax, plak-* 'a thing which is flat or plane,' used in medical terminology to designate 'a patch or patches, often of fungus, on mucous membrane' specified by the combining root: **malacoplakia, leukoplakia, melano-plakia.**

76 **-alia** A collective noun ending, derived through Latin from Greek *halia* 'assembly, group,' used in two types of combination:
   1. In the terminology of biology and ecology, to name biogeographic realms: **Antarctalia, Arctalia, Bassalia.**
   2. In biological terminology, to name various classes, especially genera: **Placentalia, portunalia** *(obs.),* **condalia.** Related form: **-alian.**

77 **-cephalia** A noun-forming word-final element, derived through Latin from Greek *kephal(ē)* 'head' and **-ia**[1], used in medical terminology to denote 'a condition of the head' specified by the combining root: **acephalia, hemicephalia, notancephalia.** Related forms: **-cephala, -cephalan, -cephaloid, -cephalism, -cephalic, -cephalous, cephaly; -cephalias** *(plural).*

78 **-encephalia** A noun and a noun-forming word-final element, derived from Greek *enkephal(os)* 'that which is within the head, the brain' and **-ia¹**, used in medical terminology to denote 'a condition of the brain' specified by the combining root: **atelencephalia, deranencephalia, pantencephalia.** Also, **-encephaly.** Related forms: **-encephalic, -encephalous, -encephalus; -encephalias, encephalies** *(plurals).*

79 **-sialia** A noun-forming word-final element, derived from Greek *sial(on)* 'spittle' and **-ia¹**, used in medical terminology to describe 'a condition of the saliva' specified by the combining root: **asialia, glycosialia, oligosialia.** Related form: **-sialias** *(plural).*

80 **-lalia** A noun-forming word-final element, derived from Greek *lal(ein)* 'to babble' and **-ia¹**, used chiefly in medical terminology to denote 'a disorder of speech, especially articulatory' specified by the combining root: **echolalia, dyslalia, bradylalia.** Also, **-laly** *(rare).* Related forms: **-lalic; -lalias, -lalies** *(plurals).*

81 **-placentalia** A noun-forming word-final element, derived through scientific Latin **-placenta** and **-alia**, used in zoological terminology to designate creatures 'having a placenta' of a sort specified by the combining root: **Villiplacentalia, Discoplacentalia, Zonoplacentalia.** Related form: **-placentalian.**

82 **-scelia** A noun-forming word-final element, derived from Greek *skel(os)* 'leg' and **-ia¹**, used in medical terminology to denote 'a condition of a leg or legs' specified by the combining root: **rhaeboscelia, macroscelia, polyscelia.** Related form: **-scelias** *(plural).*

83 **-thelia** A noun-forming word-final element, derived from Greek *thēl(ē)* 'nipple' and **-ia¹**, used in medical terminology to denote 'a condition of the nipple or nipples' specified by the first root: **polythelia, microthelia, athelia.** Related forms: **-thelism; -thelias** *(plural).*

84 **-melia** A noun-forming word-final element, derived through Latin from Greek *mel(os)* 'limb' and **-ia¹**, used in medical terminology to denote 'a state or condition of the limbs' specified by the combining root: **cacomelia, megalomelia, ectromelia.** Related forms: **-melic, -melus; -melias** *(plural).*

85 **-myelia** A noun-forming word-final element, derived from Greek *myel(os)* 'marrow' and **-ia¹**, used in biomedical terminology in two related senses, both 'a condition of the bone marrow' and 'a condition

of the bone marrow of the spinal cord,' hence, 'a condition of the spinal cord,' as specified by the combining root: **micromyelia, hematomyelia, diastomyelia.** Related forms: -myelic, -myeletic; -myelias *(plural)*.

86 **-abilia** A word-final element, used in forming collective and plural nouns, borrowed from Latin with the meaning 'able, fit for, capable of' that which is particularized by the combining root: **educabilia, memorabilia, notabilia.** Compare -able. Related form: -abilis *(singular)*.

87 **-cheilia** A noun-forming word-final element, derived from Greek *cheil(os)* 'lip' and -ia[1], used in medical terminology to denote 'a condition of the lip or lips' specified by the combining root: **acheilia, ankylocheilia, macrocheilia.** Also, -chilia. Related forms: -cheilias, -chilias *(plurals)*.

88 **-philia** A noun-forming word-final element, derived from Greek *phil(ein)* 'to love, have an affinity for' and -ia[1], used chiefly in medical terminology in two related senses:
   1. 'A tendency towards an action or activity' specified by the combining root: **spasmophilia, hemorraphilia, chromatophilia.**
   2. 'An abnormal liking or appetite for a thing' specified by the combining root: **necrophilia, gatophilia, alcoholophilia.** Also, -phily. Related forms: -phil, -phile, -philiac, -philous, -philism, -philist, -philite; -philias, -philies *(plurals)*.

89 **-symbolia** A noun-forming word-final element, derived from Greek *symbol(on)* 'a sign, signal, token, covenant' (from the verb *symball(ein)* 'to throw together, put together, compare, interpret') and -ia[1], used in medical terminology to denote 'a condition involving the ability to interpret symbols, i.e., to connect signs with that which they represent': **asymbolia, strephosymbolia, dyssymbolia.** Also, -symboly. Related forms: -symbolias, -symbolies *(plurals)*.

90 **-cholia** A noun-forming word-final element, derived from Greek *chol(ē)* 'bile' and -ia[1], used in medical terminology to designate 'a condition of the bile' as specified by the combining root: **melancholia, bactericholia** *(obs.)*, **hypercholia.** Also, -choly. Related forms: -choliac, -cholic, -choleic, -cholically, (*British* -cholily), -choliness, -cholish, -cholist, -cholize; -cholias, -cholies, -choliae *(plurals)*.

91 **-bulia** A noun-forming word-final element, derived through Latin from Greek *boul(ē)* 'will' and -ia[1], used in medical terminology to denote 'a condition of the will' specified by the combining root: **abulia,**

parabulia, hyperbulia. Also, -boulia. Related forms: -bulic, -boulic; -bulias, -boulias *(plurals)*.

92 **-chylia** A noun-forming word-final element, derived from *chyl(os)* 'juice, chyle' and **-ia¹**, used in medical terminology to mean 'a condition of the digestive juices' specified by the combining root: **achylia, oligochylia, hypochylia.** Compare **-chymia.** Related form: **-chylias** *(plural)*.

93 **-dactylia** A noun-forming word-final element, derived from Greek *daktyl(os)* 'digit, i.e., finger or toe,' and **-ia¹**, used in medical terminology to denote 'a condition of the fingers or toes' of the type or number indicated by the combining root: **adactylia, hexadactylia, megalodactylia.** Also, **-dactyly.** Related forms: **-dactyl, -dactylic, -dactylism, -dactylous, -dactyloid; -dactylias, -dactylies** *(plurals)*.

94 **-gamia** A noun-forming word-final element, derived from Greek *-gam(os)* 'marriage' and **-ia²**, used chiefly in botanical taxonomy to name classes of plants according to 'possession of reproductive organs or a mode of fertilization' described by the combining root: **Phanerogamia, Cryptogamia, apogamia.** Also, **-gamy.** Related forms: **-gam, -gamae, -gamic, -gamous, -gamist, -gamistic, -gametism; -gamias, -gamies** *(plurals)*.

95 **-dynamia** A noun and a noun-forming word-final element derived through Latin from Greek *dynam(is)* 'power' and **-ia¹**, used in medical terminology to denote 'a condition of strength' qualified by the combining root: **adynamia, neuradynamia, hypodynamia.** Also, **-dynamy.** Related forms: **-dyne, -dynamic; -dynamias, -dynamies** *(plurals)*.

96 **-emia** A noun-forming word-final element, derived from Greek *haima, haimat-* 'blood' and **-ia¹** (the initial etymological *h* generally being lost in combination with a preceding element), used in biomedical terminology in two closely related senses, particularized by the combining root:
   1. 'A specified condition of the blood': **anemia, ischemia, hyperemia.**
   2. 'A condition of the blood involving a specified substance in the blood': **uremia, hypoglycemia, alcoholemia.** Also, **-aemia, -hemia, -haemia.** (The spelling with the digraph *-ae* is chiefly British.) Related forms: **-emic, -aemic, -hemic, -haemic; -emias, -aemias, -hemias, -haemias** *(plurals)*.

97 **-septicemia** A noun, often employed as a noun-forming word-final

element, derived through Latin *septic(us)* 'putrefied' (from Greek *sēpsis* 'rot, putrefaction') and **-emia,** used in medical terminology to denote 'a condition caused by the entrance into the blood of virulent microorganisms' as specified by the combining root: **pneumosepti-cemia, autosepticemia, pyosepticemia.** Also, **-septicaemia.** Compare **-sepsis.** Related forms: **-septicemic, -septicaemic; -septicemias, -septi-caemias** *(plurals).*

98 **-glycemia** A noun, often used as a noun-forming word-final element, derived through Latin from Greek *gluk(us)* 'sweet' and **-(h)emia** (from *haim(a)*, *haimat-* 'blood' and **-ia¹**), used in medical terminology to denote 'a condition of sugar in the blood' as specified by the combining root: **normoglycemia, hypoglycemia, pathoglycemia.** Also, **-glycaemia.** Compare **-emia.** Related forms: **-glycemic; -glycemias** *(plural).*

99 **-acidemia** A noun and a noun-forming word-final element, derived from **-acid** and **-emia,** used in medical terminology to denote 'a condition of increased hydrogen-ion concentration in the blood': **hypacidemia, uricacidemia, aminoacidemia.** Related form: **-acidemias** *(plural).*

100 **-phemia** A noun-forming word-final element, derived from Greek *phēm(a)* 'speech, utterance' (from the verb *pha(nai)* 'to speak, utter' and the noun-forming suffix **-ma**) and **-ia¹**, used in medical terminology to denote 'a disorder of speech, especially one related to articulation or fluency' as specified by the combining root: **aphemia, ataxiophemia, bradyphemia.** Compare **-phasia.** Related forms: **-phemic; -phemias** *(plural).*

101 **-cythemia** A noun-forming word-final element, derived through Latin from Greek *kyt(os)* 'hollow, vessel, cell' and **-(h)emia** 'a condition of the blood,' used in medical terminology to denote 'a condition involving cells in the blood' of a type or quantity specified by the first root: **leukocythemia, microcythemia, myelocythemia.** Also, **-cythaemia.** Related forms: **-cythemic, -cythaemic; -cythemias, -cythaemias** *(plurals).*

102 **-leukemia** A noun, often employed as a noun-forming word-final element, derived through Latin from Greek *leuk(os)* 'white' and **-emia,** used in medical terminology to mean either 'an increase of the number of leukocytes in the tissues and/or in the blood' or to differentiate among varieties of the disease, as specified by the first root: **aleukemia, lymphsarcoleukemia, pseudoleukemia.** Also,

-leukaemia, -leucemia, -leucaemia. Related forms: -leukemic, -leukaemic, -leucemic, -leucaemic; -leukemias, -leukaemias, -leucemias, -leucaemias *(plurals)*.

103   **-volemia**   A noun-forming word-final element, developed from *vol(ume)* 'volume' and **-emia**, used in medical combinations to mean 'a condition of the volume of plasma in the body' specified by the combining root: **hypovolemia, normovolemia, hypervolemia.** Related forms: **-volemic; -volemias** *(plural)*.

104   **-chromemia**   A noun-forming word-final element, derived from Greek *chrōma, chrōmat-* 'color' and **-emia**, used in medical terminology to mean 'a condition of hemoglobin in the blood' specified by the combining root: **oligochromemia, hypochromemia, polychromemia.** Related form: **-chromemias** *(plural)*.

105   **-anemia**   A noun-forming word-final element, derived from Greek *an-* 'without, lacking' and **-emia**, a combining form of Greek *haim(a)*, *haim(at-)* 'blood,' and **-ia**[1], used in medical terminology to designate 'a condition of red blood cell deficiency or its remedy' as specified by the combining root: **pseudoanemia, antianemia, spanemia.** Also, **-anaemia, -nemia** *(rare)*. Compare **-emia.** Related forms: **-anemic; -anemias** *(plural)*.

106   **-cnemia**   A noun-forming word-final element, derived from Greek *knēm(ē)* 'shin, part of the leg below the knee' and **-ia**[1], used in medical terminology to denote 'a condition of the leg below the knee' as specified by the combining root: **acnemia, macrocnemia, platycnemia.** Also, **-cnemy** *(rare)*. Related forms: **-cnemial, -cnemic; -cnemias, -cnemies** *(plurals)*.

107   **-oxemia**   A noun-forming word-final element, formed from *ox(ygen)* and **-emia**, used in medical terminology to denote 'a state of oxygen in the blood' specified by the combining root: **anoxemia, hyperoxemia, hypoxemia.** Related forms: **-oxemic; -oxemias** *(plural)*.

108   **-toxemia**   A noun, often employed as a noun-forming word-final element, derived from Greek *tox(ikon)* 'poison' and **-emia**, used in medical terminology to denote 'a toxic substance in the blood' specified by the combining root: **ophiotoxemia, lymphoidtoxemia, bacteriotoxemia.** Also, **-toxaemia.** Compare **-toxia.** Related forms: **-toxemic, -toxaemic; -toxemias, -toxaemias** *(plurals)*.

109   **-sphygmia**   A noun-forming word-final element, derived from Greek

sphygm(os) 'pulse' and -ia[1], used in medical terminology to denote 'a condition of the pulse' specified by the combining root: **asphygmia, microsphygmia, bradysphygmia.** Related forms: -sphygmic; -sphygmias *(plural).*

110   **-(r)rhythmia**   A noun-forming word-final element, derived through Latin from Greek *rhythm(os)* 'regular motion, pulse' and -ia[1], used in medical terminology to denote 'a condition of the heartbeat or the pulse' specified by the combining root: **arrhythmia, allorhythmia, eurhythmia.** Related forms: -(r)rhythmic, -(r)rhythmical; -(r)rhythmias *(plural).*

111   **-mimia**   A noun-forming word-final element, derived through Latin from Greek *mimia* 'mimicry,' used in medical terminology to denote 'a condition of ability to express thought through gestures' specified by the combining root: **amimia, dysmimia, echomimia.** Related forms: -mime, -mimic, -mimesis, -mimetic, -mimical, -mimically; -mimias *(plural).*

112   **-ophthalmia**   A noun-forming word-final element, derived from Greek *ophthalm(os)* 'eye' and -ia[1], used in medical terminology to denote 'a pathological or anatomical condition of the eyes' specified by the combining root: **periophthalmia, heterophthalmia, synophthalmia.** Related forms: -ophthalmic; -ophthalmias *(plural).*

113   **-nomia**   A noun-forming word-final element, derived from Greek *(o)nom(a)* 'name' and -ia[1], used in medical terminology to denote 'an aphasia involving names or the ability to name phenomena' as specified by the combining root: **anomia, paranomia, dysnomia.** Related forms: -nomic; -nomias *(plural).*

114   **-chromia**   A noun-forming word-final element, derived from Greek *-chrom(a)* 'color' and -ia[1], used in medical terminology to denote 'a state or condition of pigmentation' specified by the combining root: **anisochromia, achromia, xanthochromia.** Also, -chromy. Related forms: -chrome, -chromic, -chromous, -chromatic, -chromatism; -chromias, -chromies *(plurals).*

115   **-somia**   A noun-forming word-final element, derived from Greek *sōma, sōmat-* 'body' and -ia[1], used in medical terminology to denote 'a condition of possessing a body' of a sort specified by the combining root: **celosomia, polysomia, nanosomia.** Compare -somatia. Related forms: -some[3], -soma, -somus, -somal, -somic, -somatic, -somatous, -somatically, -somite; -somias *(plural).*

116 **-stomia**[1] A noun-forming word-final element, derived from Greek *stom(a)*, *stom(at-)* 'mouth' and **-ia**[1], used in medical terminology to denote 'a condition of the mouth' specified by the combining root: **stenostomia, hypostomia, cacostomia.** Compare **-stoma**[1]. Related form: **-stomias** *(plural)*.

117 **-stomia**[2] A noun-forming word-final element, derived from Greek *stom(a)*, *stom(at-)* 'mouth' and **-ia**[2], used in zoological taxonomy to name higher taxa of 'creatures possessing a mouth' of a sort specified by the combining root: **Aulostomia, Plagiostomia, Deuterostomia.** Compare **-stoma**[2].

118 **-dermia** A noun-forming word-final element, derived through Latin from Greek *derma* 'skin' and **-ia**[1], used in medical terminology to denote 'a skin condition' specified by the combining root: **adermia, leukoderma, gerodermia.** Also, **-derma** (sense 2). Related forms: **-derm, -dermis, -dermal, -dermic, -dermatic, -dermoid, -dermatoid, -dermatous; -dermias, -dermas, -dermata** *(plurals)*.

119 **-thermia** A noun-forming word-final element derived from Greek *therm(ē)* 'heat' and **-ia**[1], used in medical terminology in two related senses:
   1. 'A state of body temperature' specified by the combining root: **normothermia, hyperthermia, hypothermia.**
   2. 'Generation of body heat' as specified by the combining root: **diathermia, transthermia, azothermia.** Also, **-thermy.** Related forms: **-thermic, -thermal, -thermous, -therm; -thermias, -thermies** *(plurals)*.

120 **-spermia** A noun-forming word-final element, derived from Greek *sperm(a)*, *sperm(at-)* 'germ, seed' (from the verb *speir(ein)* 'to sow seed' and the noun-forming suffix **-ma**) and **-ia**[1], used in biomedical terminology to denote 'the condition of possessing or producing seed (sperm)' of a sort or quantity specified by the combining root: **nematospermia, azoospermia, polyspermia.** Also, **-spermy.** Related forms: **-sperm, -sperma, -spermal, -spermic, -spermous, -spermatism; -spermias** *(plural)*.

121 **-cormia** A noun-forming word-final element, derived through Latin from Greek *korm(os)* 'trunk' and **-ia**[1], used in medical terminology to denote 'an abnormal development of the trunk of the body' specified by the first root: **nanocormia, camptocormy, schistocormia.** Also, **-cormy.** Related forms: **-cormias, -cormies** *(plurals)*.

122 **-osmia** A noun-forming word-final element, derived from Greek *osm(ē)* 'an odor, smell' and **-ia¹**, used in medical terminology to denote 'a condition of the sense of smell' specified by the combining root: **cacosmia, anosmia, hemiosmia.** Related forms: **-osmic; -osmias** *(plural).*

123 **-dymia** A noun-forming word-final element, derived through Latin from Greek *didym(os)* 'twin' and **-ia¹**, used in medical terminology to denote 'an abnormal condition in which anomalous twins are joined at a part of their bodies' specified by the combining root: **sternodymia, cephalodymia, ischiodymia.** Related forms: **-dymus; -dymias** *(plural).*

124 **-chymia** A noun-forming word-final element, derived from Greek *chym(os)* 'juice' and **-ia¹**, now rarely found in medical terminology referring to 'a condition of partly digested food in the duodenum' specified by the combining root; all but the first example are obsolete or obsolescent: **achymia, oligochymia, leptochymia.** The ending is also found in one word pertaining to the humors of the body, esp. the blood: **cacochymy.** Also, **-chymy.** Compare **-chylia.** Related forms: **-chymias, -chymies** *(plurals).*

125 **-thymia** A noun-forming word-final element, derived from Greek *thalm(os)* 'mind, spirit' and **-ia¹**, used in medical terminology to denote 'a condition of the mind or will' specified by the combining root: **parathymia, schizothymia, cyclothymia.** Related forms: **-thymic; -thymias** *(plural).*

126 **-plania** A noun-forming word-final element, derived from Greek *plan(os)* 'a wandering, a going astray' and **-ia¹**, used in medical terminology to denote 'the deviation from its normal location' of something named by the combining root: **arterioplania, uroplania, leukocytoplania.** Related forms: **-plane², -planetary; -planias** *(plural).*

127 **-mania** A noun, derived from Greek *mania* 'madness' (derived from *men(os)* 'mind, rage, strength' and **-ia¹**), also used as a noun-forming word-final element in two related senses, the one technical and the other popular, each as specified by the combining root:
   1. 'A specified state of mental disorder': **pyromania, erotomania, narcosomania.**
   2. 'An infatuation or craze, often shortlived': **Francomania, Anglomania, bibliomania.** Related forms: **-maniac, -maniacal, -maniacally, -manic, -manically; -manias** *(plural).*

128 **-crania** A noun-forming word-final element, derived from Latin

cran(ium) 'skull' and **-ia**[1], used in medical terminology to denote 'a condition of the skull or head' specified by the combining root: **meroacrania, pneumocrania, rhaebocrania.** Note that this element is not to be confused with *-crania*, the plural of **-cranium** (q.v.). Related forms: **-cranic, -cranial; -cranias** *(plural).*

129 **-adenia** A noun-forming word-final element, derived through Latin from Greek *aden* 'gland' and **-ia**[1], used in forming two groups of terms:

    1. A singular noun in medical terminology using **-ia**[1], denoting 'a condition of the glands' with the first root either naming the gland or specifying the condition: **lymphadenia, hypoadenia, fibroadenia.**

    2. In botanical taxonomy, a collective noun using **-ia**[2] naming taxa according to 'glands' specified by the combining root: **Dipladenia, Gymnadenia, Piptadenia.** Related forms: **-adenic; -adenias** *(plural, sense 1).*

130 **-genia** A noun-forming word-final element, derived from Greek *gen(ys)* 'jaw' and **-ia**[1], used in medical terminology to denote 'a condition of the jaw or of the development of the jaw' as specified by the combining root: **opisthogenia, microgenia, progenia.** Related forms: **-genic; -genias** *(plural).*

131 **-sthenia** A noun-forming word-final element, derived from Greek *sthen(ēs)* 'strength' and **-ia**[1], used in medical terminology to denote 'power, strength' as specified by the combining root: **hypersthenia, amyosthenia, adenohypersthenia.** Compare **-asthenia.** Related forms: **-sthenic; -sthenias** *(plural).*

132 **-asthenia** A word and a noun-forming word-final element, derived from Greek *a* 'without,' *sthen(ēs)* 'strength,' and **-ia**[1], used extensively in medical terminology to denote 'a condition of depleted vitality' specified by the combining root: **neurasthenia, angioasthenia, cardiasthenia.** Compare **-sthenia.** Related forms: **-asthenic; -asthenias** *(plural).*

133 **-splenia** A noun-forming word-final element, derived from Greek *splēn* 'spleen' and **-ia**[1], used in medical terminology to denote 'a condition of the spleen' specified by the combining root: **asplenia, megalosplenia, hypersplenia.** Related forms: **-splenic, -splenism; -splenias** *(plural).*

134 **-menia** A noun-forming word-final element, derived from Greek

mēn(iaia) 'menses' (from *mēniaios, mēniaia, mēniaion* 'monthly' from *mēnē* 'moon') and -ia[1], used in biomedical terminology to denote 'a condition of menstrual activity' specified by the combining root: **paramenia, amenia, myelomenia.** Related form: **-menias** *(plural).*

135 **-penia** A noun-forming word-final element, derived from Greek *penia* 'poverty, lack,' used in medical terminology to mean 'a deficiency' specified by the combining root: **calcipenia, thrombopenia, lymphopenia.** Related forms: **-penic; -penias** *(plural).*

136 **-adrenia** A noun-forming word-final element, derived from Latin *ad* 'near, at,' *ren(es)* 'kidneys,' and -ia[1], used in medical terminology to denote 'a degree or condition of adrenal activity' specified by the combining root: **hypoadrenia, dysadrenia, hyperadrenia.** Related forms: **-adrenal, -adrenalism; -adrenias** *(plural).*

137 **-phrenia** A noun-forming word-final element, derived from Greek *phrēn* 'midriff, diaphragm, seat of the intellect and emotions' and -ia[1], used in medical terminology to denote 'a disordered condition of mental activity' specified by the combining root: **schizophrenia, toxiphrenia, cataphrenia.** Compare **-phasia.** Related forms: **-phrenic, -phrenically; -phrenias** *(plural).*

138 **-lagnia** A noun-forming word-final element, derived through Latin from Greek *lagneia* 'lust,' used in medical terminology in its etymological sense to denote 'a sexual predilection' specified by the combining root: **algolagnia, zoolagnia, urolagnia.** Also, **-lagny.** Related forms: **-lagnias, -lagnies** *(plurals).*

139 **-(r)rhinia** A noun-forming word-final element, derived from Greek *rhis, rhin-* 'nose' and -ia[1], used in medical terminology to denote 'a condition of the nose' specified by the combining root: **arhinia, atretorrhinia, macrorhinia.** Related forms: **-(r)rhine; -(r)rhinias** *(plural).*

140 **-crinia** A noun-forming word-final element, derived by shortening of the word *endocrine*, (itself derived from Greek *krin(ein)* 'to separate, judge'), used actively in medical terminology to denote 'a condition of endocrine secretion' as specified by the combining root: **hemocrine, hypocrine, neurocrine.** Compare **-crisia** *(sense 2).* Related forms: **-crine, -crinism; -crinias** *(plural).*

141 **-somnia** A noun-forming word-final element, derived from Latin *somn(us)* 'sleep' and -ia[1], used in medical terminology to denote 'a

condition of or like sleep' specified by the combining root: **insomnia, parasomnia, dyssomnia.** Related forms: **-somniac; -somnias** *(plural).*

142 **-conia** A noun-forming word-final element, derived from Greek *konia* 'dust,' used in medical terminology to denote 'small particles or granules' in the part or fluid of the body specified by the combining root: **hemoconia, chondroconia, statoconia.** Related form: **-coniae** *(plural).*

143 **-hedonia** A noun-forming word-final element derived from Greek *hēdon(ē)* 'pleasure' and **-ia¹,** used in medical terminology to denote 'a condition of pleasure, cheerfulness' as qualified by the combining root: **anhedonia, hyphedonia, hyperhedonia.** Related forms: **-hedonic; -hedonias** *(plural).*

144 **-clonia** A noun-forming word-final element, derived from Greek *klon(os)* 'tumult' (not to be confused with Greek *klōn* 'twig, shoot,' whence English *clone* and *clonal*) and **-ia¹,** used in medical terminology to denote 'a condition involving spasms' of a sort specified by the combining root: **logoclonia, opsoclonia, myoclonia.** Also, **-klony.** Related forms: **-clonus, -clonism, -clonic; -clonias, -klonies** *(plurals).*

145 **-pneumonia** A noun and a noun-forming word-final element, derived from Greek *pneumōn* 'lung' and **-ia¹,** used in medical terminology to denote 'an inflammation of the lungs' of a type or in a particular area specified by the combining root: **peripneumonia, bronchopneumonia, pleuropneumonia.** Compare **-pnea.** Related forms: **-pneumonic; -pneumonias** *(plural).*

146 **-chronia** A noun-forming word-final element, derived from Greek *chron(os)* 'time' and **-ia¹,** used mostly in medical terminology to form three groups of combinations:
1. 'A condition of processes with respect to time.'
2. 'A condition of chronaxy between muscle and nerve.'
3. 'The time of formation of a part or tissue': **isochronia** (senses 1 and 2), **heterochronia** (senses 1 and 3), **synchronia** (senses 1 and 3). Also, **-chrone.** Related forms: **-chronic, -chronism; -chronias, -chrones** *(plurals).*

147 **-tonia** A noun-forming word-final element, derived through scientific Latin *ton(us)* 'normal muscle contraction, tension' (from Greek *ton(os)* 'that which stretches or is stretched, tension') and **-ia¹,** used in medical terminology to denote 'a condition or degree of tonus of a sort or in a region of the body' specified by the combining root: **hypotonia,**

catatonia, somatotonia. Also, -tony. Related forms: -tone, -tonic, -tonous; -tonias, -tonies *(plurals)*.

148   -axonia   A plural noun and a noun-forming word-final element, derived from Greek *axōn* 'axis' and -ia², used in zoological taxonomy to label 'creatures possessing a distinct axis or axes' as specified by the first root: **Podaxonia, Anaxonia, Tetraxonia.** Related forms: **-axon, -axone.**

149   -zonia   A noun-forming word-final element, derived from Greek *zōn(ē)* 'belt, girdle' and -ia², used in zoological taxonomy to designate creatures 'having a band' as specified by the combining root: **Aglaozonia, Phanerozonia, Cryptozonia.** Related forms: **-zone, -zonal.**

150   -capnia   A noun-forming word-final element, derived through Latin from Greek *kapn(os)* 'smoke' and -ia¹, used in medical terminology to denote 'a condition of carbon dioxide content in the blood' specified by the combining root: **acapnia, hypocapnia, eucapnia.** Related forms: **-capnial, -capnic; -capnias, -capniae** *(plurals)*.

151   -sternia   A noun-forming word-final element, derived from Greek *stern(on)* 'chest, breastbone, sternum' and -ia¹, used in medical terminology to denote 'a condition of the sternum' specified by the combining root: **asternia, koilosternia, schistosternia.** Related forms: **-sternum, -sternal; -sternias** *(plural)*.

152   -odynia   A noun-forming word-final element, derived from Greek *odyn(ē)* 'pain' and -ia¹, used in medical terminology to denote 'a state of pain' in a location specified by the first root: **neurodynia, thoracodynia, ophthalmodynia.** Compare **-algia.** Related forms: **-odyne, -odynic; -odynias** *(plural)*.

153   -gynia   A noun-forming word-final element, variously construed as a plural and a collective, derived from Greek *gyn(ē), gynaik-* 'woman' and -ia¹, used in the terminology of Linnaean botanical classification to designate taxa of plants by their number of pistils: **digynia, pentagynia, octogynia.** Related forms: **-gyne, -gyn, -gynious, -gynous, -gynic, -gyny.**

154   -ecoia   A noun-forming word-final element, derived through Latin from Greek *ako(ē)* 'hearing' and -ia¹, used in medical terminology to denote 'a condition of the sense of hearing' specified by the combining root: **oxyecoia, dysecoia, bradyecoia.** Compare **-acousia.** Related form: **-ecoias** *(plural)*.

155 **-noia** A noun-forming word-final element, derived through Latin from Greek *no(os)*, *no(ys)* 'mind' and **-ia¹**, used in medical and popular terminology to denote 'a condition of the mind or will' specified by the combining root: **paranoia, anoia, hypnoia.** Related forms: **-noiac, -noid, -noic, -noetic; -noias** *(plural)*.

156 **-chroia** A noun-forming word-final element, now obsolete and largely replaced by **-chromia,** derived from Greek *chro(os)* *(chrōs)* 'the surface of the skin, the color of the skin, color' and **-ia¹**, used in medical terminology to denote 'a condition of coloration' specified by the combining root: **parachroia, cacochroia, xanthochroia.** Compare **-chromia.** Related forms: **-chroic, -chroism, -chroous, -chrous; -chroias** *(plural)*.

157 **-therapia** A noun and a noun-forming word-final element, both now archaic, derived from Greek *therapeia* 'a service done to someone, especially to a sick person' (from the verb *therapeu(ein)* 'to serve, attend, take care of'), used in the sense of 'medical care' of a sort specified by the combining root: **therapia, balneotherapia, odontotherapia.** Also, **-therapy.** Related forms: **-therapist, -therapeutic, -therapeutics; -therapias, -therapies** *(plurals)*.

158 **-opia** A noun-forming word-final element, derived from Greek *ops*, *op-* 'eye, face' and **-ia¹**, used widely in medical terminology to denote 'a visual condition' specified by the combining root: **diplopia, myopia, amblyopia.** Also, **-opy, -opsia, -opsy.** Related forms: **-ope, -opic, -opical, -opically; -opias, -opies, -opsias, -opsies** *(plurals)*.

159 **-copia** A noun and a noun-forming word-final element, derived from Latin *cōpia* 'plenty, abundance,' used in the single term **Cornucopia** 'horn of plenty.' Related forms: **-copious, -copiously; -copias** *(plural)*.

160 **-scopia** A noun-forming word-final element derived from Greek *-skopia* 'viewing, observation' (from the verb *skop(ein)* 'to look at, observe' and **-ia¹**), once widely used in medical terminology but now almost entirely replaced by **-scopy,** still found in combinations in its etymological sense: **aknephascopia, cinemascopia, mixoscopia.** Related forms: **-scope, -scopic, -scopical, -scopist, -scopically; -scopias** *(plural)*.

161 **-diplopia** A noun, derived from Greek *diplo(us)* 'double,' *ops*, *op-* 'eye,' and **-ia¹**, used as a noun-forming word-final element in medical terminology denoting 'a condition of double vision' specified by the

combining root: **monodiplopia, amphodiplopia, amphoterodiplopia.**
Related forms: **-diplopic; -diplopias** *(plural).*

162 **-anopia** A noun, derived from Greek *an-* 'without,' *ops, op-* 'eye,' and
-ia[1], used as a noun-forming word-final element in medical terminology
in two senses:
1. 'A condition involving nonuse or arrested development of the
   eye' as specified by the combining root: **hemianopia, quadrantanopia, hesperanopia.**
2. 'A condition of defective color vision' specified by the combining
   root: **tritanopia, protanopia, tetartanopia.** Also, **-anopsia.** Related
   forms: **-anopic; -anopias, -anopsias** *(plurals).*

163 **-tropia** A noun-forming word-final element, derived from Greek
trop(os), trop(e) 'a turning, turn, deviation' and **-ia**[1], used in medical
terminology to denote 'a condition of deviation in the visual axis' as
specified by the combining root: **hypertropia, anatropia, catatropia.**
Related forms: **-tropal, -tropic; -tropias** *(plural).*

164 **-metropia** A noun-forming word-final element, derived through Latin
from Greek *metr(on)* 'measure' and **-opia,** used in medical terminology
to denote 'a condition of the refraction of the eye' specified by the
combining root: **brachymetropia, heterometropia, ametropia.** Also,
occasionally, **-metropy.** Related forms: **-metropic, -metropical;
-metropies, -metropias** *(plurals).*

165 **-prosopia** A noun-forming word-final element, derived from Greek
prosōp(on) 'face' and **-ia**[1], used in medical terminology to denote 'a
condition of the face' specified by the combining root: **aprosopia,
leptoprosopia, schizoprosopia.** Related form: **-prosopias** *(plural).*

166 **-topia** A noun-forming word-final element, derived from Greek *top(os)*
'place, location' and **ia**[1], used chiefly in medical terminology to denote
'a condition of placement of organs in the body' as specified by the
combining root: **skeletopia, normotopia, heterotopia.** Also, **-topy.**
Related forms: **-topism, -topic; -topias, -topies** *(plurals).*

167 **-ectopia** A noun and a noun-forming word-final element, derived from
Greek *ek* 'out, out of' plus *top(os)* 'place' and **-ia**[1], used in medical
terminology to denote 'a condition in which an organ or part is out of
its normal place' as specified by the combining root: **neurectopia,
myectopia, osteectopia.** Also, **-ectopy.** Related forms: **-ectopic;
-ectopias, -ectopies** *(plurals).*

168 -typia A noun-forming word-final element, derived from Greek *typ(os)* 'model, type' and -ia¹, used in medical terminology to denote 'a condition of conformity to type' specified by the first root: **atypia, ectypia, zelotypia.** Related forms: **-type, -typal, -typism; -typias** *(plural).*

169 -aria A noun-forming word-final element, plural or singular depending upon context, derived from the homographic Latin feminine singular and neuter plural of *-ari(us)* '-ary¹,' and extensively used, especially in botanical taxonomy, to designate 'plants (or creatures) like or related to' that specified by the combining root: **Campanularia, Ficaria, cercaria.** Related forms: **-arian, -ary; -arium** *(singular).*

170 -blepharia A noun-forming word-final element derived through Latin from Greek *blephar(on)* 'eyelid' and -ia¹, used in medical terminology to denote 'a condition of the eyelid' specified by the combining root: **ablepharia, macroblepharia, atretoblepharia.** Related forms: **-blepharal; -blepharias** *(plural).*

171 -filaria A noun and a noun-forming word-final element, derived from Latin *fīl(um)* 'thread' and -aria, used in zoological and medical terminology to denote 'filamentous nematodes of the superfamily Filarioidea' either in taxonomic names or in general descriptive combinations: **Agamofilaria, Stephanofilaria, microfilaria.** Related forms: **-filarial; -filariae** *(plural).*

172 -paria A noun-forming word-final element, derived through Latin from Greek *parei(a)* 'cheek' and -a³, used in zoological taxonomy to label genera and orders of trilobites according to the form of their cheeks specified by the combining root: **Ptychoparia, Opisthoparia, Proparia.** Related forms: **-pariid, -parian.**

173 -ovaria A noun-forming word-final element, derived from Latin *ōvāri(um)* 'ovary' (cf. *ōvum* 'egg') and -ia¹, used in medical terminology to denote 'a condition of the ovary or of ovarial activity' specified by the combining root: **anovaria, hypovaria, hyperovaria.** Related forms: **-ovarial, -ovarism; -ovarias** *(plural).*

174 -andria A noun-forming word-final element, derived from Greek *anēr, andr-* 'man' and -ia², formerly used in naming Linnaean botanical classes to denote 'plants having stamens' of types or quantities specified by the combining root: **Polyandria, Gynandria, Tetrandria.** Related forms: **-ander, -andric, -andrism, -andra, -andrian, -androus, -andry; -andries** *(plural).*

175 **-dendria** A noun-forming word-final element, derived through Latin from Greek *dendr(on)* 'tree' and **-ia¹**, occasionally used in medical terminology to describe the twiglike branching of nerve fibers: **oligodendria, telodendria, zoodendria.** Compare **-dendron.**

176 **-chondria** A noun-forming word-final element, derived from Greek *chondr(os)* 'grain; gristle, cartilage' (the latter having the appearance of washed grain) and **-ia¹**, used in medical terminology in two senses, as specified by the combining root:
  1. 'A condition involving granules in the composition of cells' as specified by the combining root: **mitochondria, plastochondria, lipochondria.**
  2. In the word *hypochondria*, its derivatives, and related combining forms, 'relating to cartilage' as specified by the combining root. *Hypochondria* 'an abnormal condition characterized by preoccupation with worry about disease' is derived from Greek *hypo-* 'below' *-chondr(os)* in its sense of 'cartilage'—specifically, 'the cartilage of the rib-cage, that is, the area thought to be the seat of the emotions—and **-ia¹**. Related forms: **-chondriac; -chondrias** *(plural).*

177 **-hydria** A noun-forming word-final element, derived from Greek *hydōr, hydat* 'water' (of which the usual combining form is *hydr-*) and **-ia¹**, used in medical terminology to denote 'a level of water or other fluid in the body' as specified by the combining root: **oligohydria, histohydria, isohydria.** In certain forms, such as **achlorhydria,** the *-hydr-* element may be construed in the specialized sense 'hydrogen' (itself from *hyd(ō)r-* 'water,' the joining vowel **-o-**, and **-gen** in the sense of 'producer,' so named because this element produces water when combined with oxygen). Related forms: **-hydrous; -hydrias** *(plural).*

178 **-theria** A noun-forming word-final element, derived from Greek *thēr(ion)* 'wild beast' and **-ia²**, used in zoological taxonomy to name higher mammalian taxa, especially the prehistoric: **Prototheria, Metatheria, Allotheria.** Related forms: **-there, -therium, -theridae.**

179 **-meria** A noun-forming word-final element, derived from Greek *mer(os)* 'part, portion' and either **-ia¹** or **-a²**, used to form two kinds of combination:
  1. In botanical taxonomy, a collective ending indicating genera classed by 'parts' specified by the first root: **Micromeria, Cryptomeria, Schizomeria.** Related form: **-meral.**
  2. In medical terminology, 'a condition of parts' specified in the

combining root: **platymeria, polymeria.** Compare **-mer.** Related forms: **-meric; -merias** *(plural).*

180   **-bacteria**   A noun and an active noun-forming word-final element, derived through Latin from Greek *bakteri(on)* 'little stick, rod' (as bacteria are characteristically twig-shaped) and **-ia²**, used in the terminology of microbiology to denote subclasses of 'the genus of microscopic plants forming the class Schizomycetes' as specified by the combining root: **coccobacteria, trichobacteria, gymnobacteria.** Related forms: **-bacterial, -bacterially; -bacterium** *(singular).*

181   **-arthria**   A noun-forming word-final element, derived from Greek *arthr(oun)* 'to articulate, utter distinctly' and **-ia¹**, used in medical terminology to denote 'a condition involving the ability to articulate' specified by the first root: **dysarthria, mogiarthria, bradyarthria.** Related form: **-arthrias** *(plural).*

182   **-chiria**   A noun-forming word-final element, derived from Greek *cheir* 'hand' and **-ia¹**, used in medical terminology to form two groups of combinations.
1.   'A condition involving hands' specified by the first root: **microcheiria, acheiria, tricheiria.**
2.   'A condition involving stimulus and its perception' specified by first root: **allochiria, synchiria, dyschiria.** Also, especially in sense 1, **-cheiria.** Related forms: **-chirias, -cheirias** *(plurals).*

183   **-coria¹**   A noun-forming word-final element, derived through Latin from Greek *kor(os)* 'satiety' and **-ia¹**, used in medical terminology to denote 'a condition of the sense of satiety,' the quality or object of that sense specified by the combining root: **acoria, saccharocoria, hypercoria.** Also, **-koria.** Related form: **-corias** *(plural).*

184   **-coria²**   A noun-forming word-final element, derived through Latin from Greek *kor(ē)* 'pupil' and **-ia¹**, used in medical terminology to denote 'a condition of a pupil' specified by the combining root: **microcoria, asthenocoria, dicoria.** Related form: **-corias** *(plural).*

185   **-phoria**   A noun-forming word-final element, derived from Greek *phor(ein)* (the frequentative form of *pher(ein)* 'to bear, carry') and **-ia¹**, used in medical terminology in two senses:
1.   'A condition of the visual axes of the eye' specified by the combining root: **cyclophoria, hypophoria, cataphoria.**
2.   'An emotional state or tendency' specified by the combining root:

ideaphoria, euphoria, dysphoria. Related forms: **-phore, -phor, -phora, -phoric, -phorous; -phorias** *(plural)*.

186 **-moria** A noun-forming word-final element, derived from Greek *mōr(os)*, *mōr(a)*, *mōr(on)* 'dull, stupid' and **-ia**[1] or from Greek *mōria* 'folly, silliness,' used in two medical combinations to mean 'a condition of dementia' specified by the combining root: **monomoria, phantasmatomoria.**

187 **-metria**[1] A noun-forming word-final element, derived through Latin from Greek *metr(on)* 'measure' and **-ia**[1], used in medical terminology to denote 'a condition of the ability to measure muscular acts' specified by the combining root: **hypermetria, dysmetria, hypometria.** Compare **-meter.** Related form: **-metrias** *(plural)*.

188 **-metria**[2] A noun-forming word-final element, derived from Greek *mētr(a)* 'uterus,' used in medical terminology to designate 'a condition of the uterus' specified by the combining root: **ametria, dimetria, atretometria.** Related forms: **-metrium; -metrias** *(plural)*.

189 **-gastria** A noun-forming word-final element derived from Greek *gaster*, *gast(e)r-* 'stomach, belly' and **-ia**[1], used in medical terminology to denote 'a condition of possessing a stomach or stomachs' specified by the first root: **agastria, dextrogastria, microgastria.** Related forms: **-gaster, -gastric; -gastrias** *(plural)*.

190 **-uria** A noun-forming word-final element, derived from Greek *our(on)* 'urine' and **-ia**[1], used in medical terminology in two senses:
  1. 'The presence of a substance in urine' specified by the combining root: **acetonuria, albuminuria, hemoglobinuria.**
  2. 'The condition of possessing urine' of a type specified by the combining root: **polyuria, paruria, pyuria.** Compare **-urea.** Related forms: **-uric; -urias** *(plural)*.

191 **-sauria** A noun and a plural word-final element, derived through Latin from Greek *saur(os)* 'horse mackerel, lizard' and **-ia**[2], used widely in zoological nomenclature for names of higher taxa of 'lizards or animals resembling lizards (often extinct)' as specified by the combining root: **Pterosauria, Ankylosauria, Dinosauria.** Related forms: **-saur, -saurus, -saurian.**

192 **-neuria** A noun-forming word-final element, derived through Latin from Greek *neur(on)* 'sinew, tendon, fiber,' hence 'nerve' and **-ia**[1], formerly used widely in medical terminology to denote 'a condition involving nerves' specified by the combining root; currently, only two combinations are actively used: **acystineuria, ovariodysneuria.** Compare **-neurosis.** Related form: **-neurias** *(plural).*

193　**-sthenuria**　A noun-forming word-final element, derived from Greek *sthen(s)* 'strength' and **-uria,** used in medical terminology to denote 'a condition of urination or of the specific gravity of urine' specified by the combining root: **normosthenuria, hyposthenuria, isosthenuria.** Related form: **-sthenurias** *(plural).*

194　**-globinuria**　A noun-forming word-final element, derived from *globin* 'the protein in hemoglobin (the oxygen-carrying part of red blood cells)' (from Latin *glob(us)* 'ball' and **-in**) and **-uria** 'a condition of the urine,' used in medical terminology to denote 'a condition involving the presence of globin or other complex proteins in the urine': **myoglobinuria, methemoglobinuria, hemoglobinuria.** Related form: **-globinurias** *(plural).*

195　**-albuminuria**　A noun and a noun-forming word-final element, derived from *albumin* (a common protein) and **-uria** 'a condition of the urine,' used in medical terminology to denote 'a condition characterized by an excess of serum (simple) proteins in the urine' as specified by the combining root: **pseudalbuminuria, noctalbuminuria, nyctalbuminuria.** Related form: **-albuminurias** *(plural).*

196　**-gyria**　A noun-forming word-final element, derived through Latin from Greek *gyr(os)* 'ring' and **-ia[1],** used in medical terminology to denote 'a condition of the development of the convolutions of the cerebral cortex' specified by the combining root: **agyria, ischogyria, schizogyria.** Related forms: **-gyric; -gyrias** *(plural).*

197　**-basia**　A noun-forming word-final element, derived from Greek *bas(is)* 'step' and **-ia[1],** used in medical terminology to denote 'ability to walk' or 'a condition of that ability' specified by the combining root: **abasia, dysbasia, brachybasia.** Related forms: **-base, -basis, -bat, -batic, -basic; -basias** *(plural).*

198　**-ergasia**　A noun and a noun-forming word-final element, derived through Latin from Greek *ergaz(esthai)* 'to work, labor' and **-ia[1],** used actively in medical terminology to denote 'interfunctioning of the mind and body' or 'a condition of that organismic functioning' specified by the combining root: **oligergasia, pathergasia, hypoergasia.** Related forms: **-ergastic; -ergasias** *(plural).*

199 **-phasia** A noun-forming word-final element, derived from Greek *-phas(is)* 'speech, utterance' (cf. *phanai* 'to speak') and **-ia**[1], used in medical terminology to denote 'a speech disorder' of a sort specified by the combining root: **aphasia, bradyphasia, dysphasia**. Also, **-phasy, -phemia, -phasis**. Related forms: **-phasic**[1]**, -phatic; -phasias, -phasies, -phemias, -phases** *(plurals)*.

200 **-clasia** A noun-forming word-final element, derived from Greek *klas(is)* 'crushing, breaking' (from Greek *klān* 'to break') and **-ia**[1], used in medical terminology to denote 'a condition involving crushing, breaking, or breaking up' specified by the combining root: **phreniclasia, arthroclasia, periodontoclasia**. Also, **-clasis**. Related forms: **-clase, -clast, -clastic; -clasias, -clases** *(plurals)*.

201 **-plasia** A noun-forming word-final element, derived from Greek *plas(is)* 'a molding, formation' (from the verb *plass(ein)*, *platt(ein)* 'to mold, form, shape' and the resultative abstract noun-forming suffix **-sis**) and **-ia**[1], used in medical terminology to denote 'a condition of formation or development' specified by the combining root: **dysplasia, heteroplasia, homoplasia**. Also, **-plasy**. Related forms: **-plasis, -plastia, -plasty, -plasma, -plastic, -plasmatic, -plasmic; -plasias, -plasies** *(plurals)*.

202 **-dysplasia** A noun and a noun-forming word-final element, derived from Greek *dys-* 'bad, difficult,' *plass(ein)* 'to form,' and **-ia**[1], used extensively in medical terminology to indicate 'a condition of abnormal development' as specified by the combining root: **encephalodysplasia, myelodysplasia, arthrodysplasia**. Related forms: **-dysplastic; -dysplasias** *(plural)*.

203 **-onomasia** A noun-forming word-final element, derived from Greek *onomaz(ein)* 'to call, name' (cf. *onoma, onomat-* 'a name') and **-ia**[1], used in two combinations in the terminology of rhetoric to mean 'to name' as specified by the first root: **paronomasia, antonomasia**. Related form: **-onomasias** *(plural)*.

204 **-chromasia** A noun-forming word-final element, derived through Latin from Greek *chrōmat-* (the oblique case stem of *chrōma* 'color') and **-ia**[1] (the *-t-* changing to *-s-* upon combination), used in medical terminology in two senses:
1. 'A condition of color (as cells, skin)' specified by the combining root: **achromasia, hypochromasia, metachromasia**.
2. 'A condition of the stainability of tissues' specified by the combining root: **basichromasia, homochromasia, metachromasia**.

Many combinations, such as **metachromasia**, carry both meanings. Related forms: **-chrome, -chromia, -chromy, -chromatism, -chromatic, -chromatically; -chromasias** *(plural)*.

205 **-thanasia** A noun-forming word-final element, derived from Greek *thanat(os)* 'death' and **-ia¹**, used to denote 'a variety of death' specified by the combining root: **euthanasia, cacothanasia, electrothanasia**. Related forms: **-thanasic; -thanasias** *(plural)*.

206 **-crasia** A noun-forming word-final element, derived through Latin from Greek *krasia* 'mixture' (from *krat(os)* 'mixed' and **-ia¹**), used in medical terminology to form two groups of combinations.
   1. 'A condition of a mixture, good or bad' specified by the first root: **orthocrasia, eucrasia, spermacrasia**.
   2. 'A condition involving loss of control' specified by the combining root: **uracrasia, copracrasia**. Related forms: **-crasic; -crasias** *(plural)*.

207 **-phrasia** A noun-forming word-final element, derived from Greek *phras(is)* 'a speaking, way of speaking' (from the verb *phrazein* 'to tell, explain') and **-ia¹**, used in medical terminology to denote 'an abnormal condition of speech' specified by the combining root: **dysphrasia, bradyphrasia, angiophrasia**. Compare **-phasia, -phemia**. Related forms: **-phrase, -phrastic; -phrasias** *(plural)*.

208 **-ectasia** A noun and a noun-forming word-final element, derived from Greek *ektas(is)* 'an extension, a stretching out' (from the verb *ektein(ein)* 'to stretch out' and **-sis**) and **-ia¹**, used in medical terminology to denote 'a condition of dilation, extension, or distension of an organ' specified by the combining root: **aortectasia, arteriectasia, desmectasia**. Also, **-ectasis, -ectasy**. Related forms: **-ectatic; -ectasias, -ectases, -ectasies** *(plurals)*.

209 **-stasia** A noun-forming word-final element, derived from Greek *stas(is)* 'a standing still, stoppage, inhibition' (from the verb *hista(nai)*, *stē(nai)* 'to stand, make stand') and **-ia¹**, used in medical terminology in two senses:
   1. 'A condition involving the ability to stand' as specified by the combining root: **astasia, ananastasia, amyostasia**.
   2. 'A condition of stoppage or inhibition' of a sort specified by the combining root: **cholestasia, phlebostasia, hemostasia**. Also, **-stasis**. Related forms: **-stasic, -state², -static, -statics, -stat; -stasy; -stasias, -stases** *(plurals)*.

210 **-algesia** A noun and a noun-forming word-final element, derived through Latin and Greek *algēs(is)* 'sense of pain' and **-ia**[1], used actively in medical terminology to denote 'a condition of sensitivity to pain' specified by the combining root: **haphalgesia, thermalgesia, analgesia.** Compare **-algia.** Related forms: **-algesic, -algetic; -algesias** *(plural).*

211 **-pselaphesia** A noun and a noun-forming word-final element, derived from Greek *psēlaphēs(is)* 'touch, touching' (from the verb *psēlaph(ān)* 'to touch, grope' and **-esis**) and **-ia**[1], used in medical terminology to denote 'a condition of the tactile sense' specified by the combining root: **apselaphesia, hypopselaphesia, hyperpselaphesia.** Also, **-pselaphesis.** Related forms: **-pselaphesias, -pselapheses** *(plurals).*

212 **-aesthesia** A noun and a noun-forming word-final element, derived through Latin from Greek *aisthēs(is)* 'feeling' and **-ia**[1], used extensively in medical terminology to denote 'a condition of feeling, perception, or sensation' specified by the combining root: **anaesthesia, seismaesthesia, trichaesthesia.** Also, **-esthesia.** Related forms: **-aesthetic, -esthetic; -aesthesias, -esthesias** *(plurals).*

213 **-genesia** A noun-forming word-final element, derived from Greek *genes(is)* 'origin, birth, formation' and **-ia**[1], currently used occasionally in medical terminology to form two groups of compounds.
   1. 'A condition concerning formation' specified by the first root: **agenesia, paragenesia, mitogenesia.** Also, **-genesis** (currently the more active ending).
   2. 'The production or procreation of something' specified by the first root: **algogenesia, syngenesia, dysgenesia.** Also, **-genesis** (currently the most active ending) and **-geny.** Related forms: **-genesian, -genesious, -genetic; -genesias, -geneses** *(plurals).*

214 **-kinesia** A noun and a noun-forming word-final element derived from Greek *-kinēsia* 'motion,' actively used in medical terminology to mean 'a motion or movement' specified by the combining root: **bradykinesia, telokinesia, diadochokinesia.** Also, **-cinesia; -kinesis, -cinesis.** Related forms: **-kinetic, -cinetic; -kinesias, -cinesias, -kineses, -cineses** *(plurals).*

215 **-mnesia** A noun-forming word-final element, derived from Greek *mnēs(is)* 'remembering, memory' and **-ia**[1], used largely in medical terminology to denote 'a condition or type of memory' specified by the combining root: **amnesia, cryptomnesia, automnesia.** Also, **-mnesis.** Related forms: **-mnesiac, -mnesic, -mnestic; -mnesias, -mneses** *(plurals).*

216   **-osphresia**   A noun-forming word-final element, derived from Greek *osphrāsia* and *osphrēsis* and **-ia¹**, both 'a smelling, smell,' used in medical terminology to denote 'a condition of the sense of smell' specified by the combining root: **oxyosphresia, hyposphresia, anosphresia.** Also, **-osphrasia.** Related forms: **-osphresis, -osphretic; -osphresias, -osphrasias, -osphreses** *(plurals).*

217   **-tresia**   A noun-forming word-final element, derived from Greek *-trēs(is)* 'perforation' and **-ia¹**, used occasionally in medical terminology to form combinations in its literal sense, the point of perforation being specified by the first root: **proctotresia, sphenotresia, atresia.** Related forms: **-tresic, -tretic; -tresias** *(plural).*

218   **-atresia**   A noun and a noun-forming word-final element, derived from *a-* 'not,' Greek *-trēs(is)* 'perforation, hole,' and **-ia¹**, used in medical terminology to denote 'a condition of occlusion,' the organ affected being specified by the combining root: **colpatresia, proctatresia, gynatresia.** Compare **-tresia.** Related forms: **-atresic, -atretic; -atresias** *(plural).*

219   **-aphrodisia**   A noun and a noun-forming word-final element, derived from Greek *aphrodis(ia)* 'sacred to Aphrodite (the goddess of love)' and **-ia¹**, used in medical terminology in two combinations denoting 'a condition of sexual arousal, especially excessive' as specified by the combining root: **anaphrodisia, hypaphrodisia.** Related forms: **-aphrodisiac, -aphroditic; -aphrodisias** *(plural).*

220   **-crisia**   A noun-forming word-final element, derived through Latin from Greek *kris(is)* 'judgment, separation' (from *krin(ein)* 'to judge, separate') and **-ia¹**, used with low frequency in medical terminology to form two groups of combinations:
   1.   'A diagnosis' specified by the first root: **acrisia** *(obs.),* **urocrisia.**
   2.   'A condition of endocrine secretion' (now being replaced by **-crinia**) specified by the combining root: **hypercrisia, hypoendocrisia, hyperendocrisia.** Compare **-crinia.** Related form: **-crisias** *(plural).*

221   **-gnosia**   A noun-forming word-final element, derived from Greek *gnōs(is)* 'knowledge, knowing' (cf. Greek *gnōnai* 'to know, perceive') and **-ia¹**, used in medical terminology to denote 'a condition involving the faculty of perceiving or recognizing' specified by the combining root: **macrostereognosia, atopognosia, dysgnosia.** Also, **-gnosis, -gnosy.** Related forms: **-gnostic, -gnomic, -gnomonic; -gnosias, -gnosies, -gnoses** *(plurals).*

222   **-agnosia**   A noun and a noun-forming word-final element, derived through Latin from *a-* (negative), Greek *gnōs(is)* 'knowledge,' and **-ia¹**, used actively in medical terminology to denote 'a condition of the loss of the faculty to perceive' specified by the first root: **logagnosia, dysanagnosia, pragmatagnosia.** Also, **-agnosis.** Compare **-gnosia.** Related forms: **-agnosias, -agnoses** *(plurals).*

223   **-blepsia**   A noun-forming word-final element, derived through modern Latin from Greek *bleps(is)* 'sight' and **-ia¹**, used in medical terminology to denote 'a condition of sight' specified by the first root: **ablepsia, monoblepsia, oxyblepsia.** Also, **-blepsy.** Related forms: **-blepsias, -blepsies** *(plurals).*

224   **-pepsia**   A noun-forming word-final element derived from Greek *peps(is)* 'digestion' (cf. *pessein, peptein* 'to cook') and **-ia¹**, used in medical terminology to denote 'a condition or state of the digestion' specified by the combining root: **dyspepsia, bradypepsia, eupepsia.** Also, **-pepsy.** Related forms: **-peptic; -pepsias, -pepsies** *(plurals).*

225   **-dipsia**   A noun-forming word-final element, derived from Greek *dip(sa)* 'thirst' and **-ia¹**, used in medical terminology to denote 'a condition of thirst' specified by the combining root: **adipsia, anadipsia, dysdipsia.** Also, **-dipsy.** Related forms: **-dipsias, -dipsies** *(plurals).*

226   **-opsia**   A noun-forming word-final element, derived from Greek *ops(is)* 'vision' (cf. *ops, op-* 'eye') and **-ia¹**, used in medical terminology to denote 'a condition or type of vision' specified by the combining root: **cyanopsia, anopsia, chloropsia.** Also, **-opsy, -opia, -opy.** Related forms: **-opsis, -optic, -optical, -optically; -opsias, -opsies, -opias, -opies** *(plurals).*

227   **-anopsia**   A noun and a noun-forming word-final element, derived from Greek *an-* 'without,' *ops(is)* 'vision' (cf. *ops, op-* 'eye'), and **-ia¹**, used in medical terminology in two senses:
   1. 'A condition involving nonuse or suppression of vision' as specified by the combining root: **psychanopsia, hemianopsia, quadrantanopsia.**
   2. 'Defective color vision' of a type specified by the combining root: **deuteranopsia, tritanopsia, cyanopsia.** Also, **-anopia.** Compare **-opsia.** Related forms: **-anopsias, -anopias** *(plurals).*

228   **-glossia**   A noun-forming word-final element, derived from Ionic Greek *gloss(a)* (cf. Attic Greek *glotta*) 'tongue' and **-ia¹**, used in two related senses, each particularized by the combining root:

1. 'The possession of a specified type or condition of tongue':
    bradyglossia, macroglossia, trichoglossia.
2. In two terms, 'the possession of a specified number of tongues':
    aglossia, diglossia. Related forms: **-glossa, -glossal, -glot, -glottal,
    -glottic; -glossias** *(plural).*

229   **-geusia**   A noun-forming word-final element, derived from Greek
      geus(is) 'sense of taste' (from Greek *geuein* 'to taste') and **-ia**[1], used in
      medical terminology to denote 'a condition of the sense of taste'
      specified by the combining root: **ageusia, cacogeusia, hypogeusia.**
      Also, **-geustia.** Related forms: **-geusic; -geusias** *(plural).*

230   **-ousia**   A noun-forming word-final element, derived from Greek *ōn,
      ous(a), on,* 'being' and **-ia**[1], used in theological terminology to denote
      'the essence or substance of something' (esp. in explanations of the
      nature of Christ) as specified by the combining root: **homoousia,
      homoiousia, heteroousia.** Related forms: **-ousian; -ousias** *(plural).*

231   **-acousia**   A noun-forming word-final element, derived through Latin
      from Greek *akous(is)* 'hearing' and **-ia**[1], used in medical terminology
      to denote 'a particular condition of the hearing' specified by the
      combining root: **hyperacousia, anacousia, presbyacousia.** Also,
      -acusia, -acusis, -akusis. Compare **-acoustic, -ecoia.** Related forms:
      -acousiae, -acusiae, -acuses, -akuses *(plurals).*

232   **-somatia**   A noun-forming word-final element, derived from Greek
      sōma, sōmat- 'body' and **-ia**[1], used in medical terminology to denote 'a
      condition of the body, especially concerning size' specified by the
      combining root: **diplosomatia, macrosomatia, microsomatia.** Related
      forms: **-soma, -some**[2]**, -somia, -somus, -somal, -somic, -somatic,
      -somatous, -somatically, -somite; -somatias** *(plural).*

233   **-hepatia**   A noun-forming word-final element, derived through Latin
      from Greek *hēpar, hēpat-* 'liver' and **-ia**[1], used in medical terminology
      to denote 'a condition of the liver or its functioning' specified by the
      combining root: **microhepatia, hyperhepatia, megalohepatia.** Related
      forms: **-hepatic; -hepatias** *(plural).*

234   **-cratia**   A noun-forming word-final element, derived through Latin
      from Greek *krat(os)* 'power, strength' and **-ia**[1], occasionally used in
      medical terminology to form two groups of combinations:
      1. 'A condition of power and strength': **acratia** *(obs.).*
      2. 'A condition of incontinence (i.e., loss of the power of continence)'

specified by the first root: **gonacratia, uracratia.** Related form: **-cratias** *(plural).*

235   **-galactia**   A noun-forming word-final element, derived from Greek *gala, galakt-* 'milk' and **-ia**[1], used in medical terminology to denote 'a condition involving secretion of milk' specified by the combining root: **agalactia, oligogalactia, hypergalactia.** Related form: **-galactias** *(plural).*

236   **-proctia**   A noun-forming word-final element, derived from Greek *prōkt(os)* 'anus' and **-ia**[1], used in medical terminology to denote 'a condition of the anus' specified by the combining root: **aproctia, hemoproctia, enteroproctia.** Related form: **-proctias** *(plural).*

237   **-sitia**   A noun-forming word-final element, derived through Latin from Greek *sit(os)* 'grain, food' and **-ia**[1], used occasionally in medical terminology to denote 'a condition of appetite for food' specified by the initial root: **asitia, apositia** *(obs.),* **eusitia.**

238   **-mantia**   A noun-forming word-final element, derived from Greek *manteia* 'divination, prophecy,' used in medical terminology to denote 'prognosis after examination' of something specified by the first root: **glossomantia, uromantia.** Also, with greater frequency, **-mancy.** Related forms: **-mantic, -mancer; -mantias, -mancies** *(plurals).*

239   **-mentia**   A noun-forming word-final element, derived from Latin *mens, ment-* 'mind' and **-ia**[1], used in medical terminology to denote 'a condition of the mind' specified by the combining root: **amentia, dementia, deprementia.** Related forms: **-mential; -mentias** *(plural).*

240   **-odontia**[1]   A noun-forming word-final element, derived through Latin from Greek *odōn, odont-* 'tooth' and **-ia**[2], used in zoological taxonomy to denote 'an animal or class of animals possessing teeth of a nature' specified by the first root: **Anomodontia, Aplodontia, Decynodontia.** Compare **-odon.**

241   **-odontia**[2]   A noun-forming word-final element, derived from Greek *odōn, odont-* 'tooth' and **-ia**[1], used in medical terminology to denote 'a form, condition, or mode of treatment of the teeth' specified by the combining root: **macrodontia, pathodontia, orthodontia.** Related forms: **-odontic, -odontics; -odontias** *(plural).*

242   **-otia**   A noun-forming word-final element, derived through Latin from

Greek *ous, ōt-* 'ear' and **-ia**[1], used in medical terminology to denote 'a condition of the ear' specified by the combining root: **melotia, ankylotia, pleonotia.** Related forms: -otic[1]; -otias *(plural).*

243 **-plastia** A noun-forming word-final element, derived from Greek *plast(os)* (the past participle of the verb *plass(ein), platt(ein)* 'to mold, form, shape') and **-ia**[1], used in medical terminology to denote 'a condition of cell or tissue formation or development' specified by the combining root: **anaplastia, mastoplastia, macroplastia.** Also, -plasia. Related forms: -plastic; -plasias, -plastias *(plurals).*

244 **-mastia** A noun-forming word-final element, derived through Latin from Greek *mast(os)* 'breast' and **-ia**[1], used in medical terminology to denote 'a condition of the breast or breasts' specified by the combining root: **amastia, gynecomastia, polymastia.** Related forms: -mazia, -masty, -mastoid; -mastias *(plural).*

245 **-privia** A noun-forming word-final element, derived from Latin *prīv(ātus, -a, -um)*—the past participle of the verb *prīv(āre)* 'to rob, bereave'—and **-ia**[1], used in medical terminology to denote 'a condition of loss or deprivation' of that which is specified by the combining root: **calciprivia, hormonoprivia, thyroprivia.** Related forms: -privic, -privous; -privias *(plural).*

246 **-praxia** A noun-forming word-final element, derived from Greek *prax(is)* 'action, conduct' (from the verb *prass(ein), pratt(ein)* 'to do, accomplish') and **-ia**[1], used in medical terminology to denote 'a condition concerning the performance of movements' as specified by the combining root: **echopraxia, apraxia, hyperpraxia.** Related forms: -praxis, -pragia, -practice, -praxic, -practic, -practics; -praxias *(plural).*

247 **-taxia** A noun-forming word-final element, derived from Greek *tax(is)* 'an ordering, arrangement' (from the verb *tass(ein), tatt(ein)* 'to order, arrange' and **-sis**) and **-ia**[1], used in medical terminology in two major senses:
1. 'A condition of impaired mental or physical control' specified by the combining root: **ataxia, diataxia, amyotaxia.**
2. 'A condition of internal arrangement or ordering' specified by the combining root: **heterotaxia, asyntaxia, prostaxia.** Also, -taxis, -taxy. Related forms: -taxic, -tactic; -taxias, -taxes, -taxies *(plurals).*

248 **-lexia** A noun-forming word-final element, derived through Latin from

Greek *lex(is)* 'a way of speaking' and **-ia¹**, used in medical terminology to denote 'an impairment of reading ability' specified by the combining root: **alexia, dyslexia, bradylexia**. (Originally, the Indo-European verb **leg-*, found in Greek as *legein*, in Latin as *legere*, and in English as *lie, lay*, seems to have meant 'to lie, lay, lay in order' and later, by extension, 'to speak, say, read (aloud),' that is, 'to produce or reproduce linguistic elements in (proper) order.') Also, **-lexis**. Related forms: **-lexic, -lectic; -lexias** *(plural)*.

249   **-plexia**   A noun-forming word-final element, derived from Greek *plēx(is)* 'stroke, wound' (cf. the noun *plēgē* 'blow, stroke, wound' and the verb *plēss(ein), plētt(ein)* 'to strike, wound'), used in medical terminology to denote 'a condition resulting from a stroke' as specified by the combining root: **pagoplexia, apoplexia, selenoplexia**. Also, **-plexy**. Compare **-plegia, -plegy**. Related forms: **-plectic, -plexic; -plexias, -plexies** *(plurals)*.

250   **-orexia**   A noun and a noun-forming word-final element, derived from Greek *orex(is)* 'desire, appetite' (from the verb *oregein* 'to stretch, to stretch out one's hand, reach for') and **-ia¹**, used in medical terminology to denote 'a condition of the appetite' specified by the combining root: **anorexia, parorexia, lycorexia**. Related forms: **-oretic, -orectic, -orexic; -orexias** *(plural)*.

251   **-pyrexia**   A noun and a noun-forming word-final element, derived from Greek *pyress(ein), pyrett(ein)* 'to have a fever' (cf. *pyretos* 'fever' and *pyr* 'fire') and **-ia¹**, used in medical terminology to denote 'a febrile condition' specified by the combining root: **apyrexia, hyperpyrexia, eupyrexia**. Related form: **-pyrexias**.

252   **-oxia**   A noun-forming word-final element, derived from the word *ox(ygen)* and **-ia¹**, used in medical terminology to denote 'a condition of oxygenation' specified by the combining root: **anoxia, hypoxia, asthenoxia**. (The word *oxygen* is derived from French *oxygène*, coined by Lavoisier from Greek *oxy(s)* 'sharp, acid' and **-gen** in its sense of 'producer' as a result of his observation that when (some) substances are burned with oxygen, the resulting oxides are acidic.) Related forms: **-oxic; -oxias** *(plural)*.

253   **-toxia**   A noun-forming word-final element, derived from Greek *tox(ikon)* 'poison,' originally, 'poison for smearing on arrows' (cf. Greek *toxa* 'bow and arrow') and **-ia¹**, used in medical terminology to denote 'a condition resulting from a poison' in a region of the body named by the combining root: **neurotoxia, thyrotoxia, urotoxia**. Also,

-toxy, -toxis, -toxicosis. Related forms: -toxic, -toxical, -toxically, -toxicity, -toxin, -toxism; -toxias, -toxies, -toxes, -toxicoses *(plurals)*.

254 **-myia** A noun-forming word-final element, derived from Greek *my(ia)* 'fly' and -ia^2, used in entomological taxonomy to label 'fly' genera: **Hylemyia, Wyeomyia, Stegomyia.**

255 **-mazia** A noun-forming word-final element, derived from Greek *maz(os)* 'breast' and -ia^1, used in medical terminology to denote 'a condition of the breast or breasts' specified by the combining root: **tetramazia, gynecomazia, pleomastia.** Also, **-mastia, -masty.** Related form: **-mazias** *(plural)*.

256 **-chezia** A noun-forming word-final element, derived from Greek *chez(ein)* 'to defecate' and -ia^1, used in medical terminology to denote 'a condition of defecation, especially involving the discharge of foreign substances' as specified by the combining root: **pyochezia, hematochezia, dyschezia.** Also, **-chesia.** Related forms: **-chezias, -chesias** *(plurals)*.

257 **-cephala** A noun-forming word-final element, derived through Latin from Greek *kephal(ē)* 'head' and -a^3, used in zoological taxonomy to classify genera according to the 'headedness' specified by the combining root: **Acephala, Globicephala, Anaplocephala.** Related forms: **-cephalic, -cephalan, -cephalus, -cephaloid, -cephalous, -cephalia, -cephaly.**

258 **-chela** A noun-forming word-final element, derived through Latin from Greek *chēl(ē)* 'claw' and -a^4, used in zoological terminology to denote 'a claw or grasping organ of some marine species' as specified by the combining root: **subchela, isochela, anisochela.** Related forms: **-chelate; -chelae** *(plural)*.

259 **-tela** A noun-forming word-final element, derived from Latin *tēla* 'something woven, web,' used formerly in medical terminology to denote 'a weblike membrane' specified by the combining root; most of the resulting combinations are now obsolete: **epitela, metatela** *(obs.)*, **diatela** *(obs.)*. Related form: **-telae** *(plural)*.

260 **-phila** A noun-forming word-final element, derived from Greek *phil(ein)* 'to love, have an affinity for' and -a^3, used in zoological taxonomy to name 'creatures attracted to, preferring to live or grow in' that which is specified by the combining root: **Nemophila, Ammophila, Anthophila.** Compare **-phil, -phile.**

261 **-coralla**   A noun-forming word-final element, derived from Latin *corall(ium)* 'coral' and -a³, used in some classifications of invertebrate zoology for subclasses of corals: **tetracoralla, hexacoralla, octacorallia.** Also, **-corallia.**

262 **-ella**   A noun-forming word-final element, by far the most frequently attested relic in English of the Latin diminutive ending *-ellus, -ella, -ellum,* used in its etymological sense in a variety of combinations, some borrowed directly from Latin, others from modern Italian and Spanish. (Thus, a noun ending in *-ella* in English can come from Spanish, Italian, or Latin *-ella*—the feminine singular form in all cases of this perennially productive suffix—or from Latin *-ella*, the neuter plural form, or from Latin *-ell(us, -a, -um)* plus -a³:
1.   'Small one': **pulcinella, fabella, Cinderella.**
2.   Usu. in generic names, 'small one resembling something specified by its combining root': **Phacella, Terebella, Zookanthella.**
3.   In generic names, 'small one belonging to a group that its combining root names': **Monardella, Klebsiella, Moluccella.** Related forms: **-el, -elle, -ellus, -ellum; -els, -elles, -ellas, -ellae, -elli, -ella** *(plurals).*

263 **-cella**   A noun-forming word-final element, derived from the Latin diminutive *-cella,* used in a plural sense for generic names in zoology and in a singular sense for other lower-level taxonomic terms: **navicella, Vermicella, Rocella.** Compare **-ella.** Related forms: **-cel, -cellate; -cellas** *(plural).*

264 **-bdella**   A noun-forming word-final element, derived from Greek *bdella* 'leech,' used in the taxonomical names of helminthology to designate genera of leeches: **Malacobdella, Macrobdella, Trachybdella.** Unlike the majority of taxonomic labels, which tend to be plurals or collectives, this one is singular. Related forms: **-bdellae, -bdellas** *(plurals).*

265 **-illa**   A diminutive ending, derived from late Latin *-illa,* from earlier Latin *-ella* 'small one,' used to form two groups of combinations:
1.   'Small one' in quasi-taxonomic terms, especially in the common names of plants and their seeds: **escobilla, algarobilla, abadilla.**
2.   'Small one' in nontaxonomic compounds: **cedilla, spadilla, fibrilla.** Compare **-ella.** Related forms: **-illas, -illae** *(plurals).*

266 **-maxilla**   A noun and a frequent noun-forming word-final element, derived from Latin *maxilla* 'cheek, jaw,' used in medical terminology to denote 'the upper jaw or the bones composing it' as specified by the combining root: **supramaxilla, premaxilla, intermaxilla.** Related forms: **-maxillar, -maxillary; -maxillae, -maxillas** *(plurals)*.

267 **-psylla** A noun-forming word-final element, derived from Greek *psyll(a)* 'flea' and **-a**[3], used in entomological taxonomy to designate genera of fleas: **Cediopsylla, Sarcopsylla, Xenopsylla.**

268 **-ola** A word-final element, functioning as a 'diminutive' of nouns, derived from Latin, used to form two groups of combinations:
1. In taxonomic terms employed by biology and zoology, a collective or plural ending meaning 'small one' as specified by the initial root: **Gladiola, Corrigiola, Miliola.**
2. In medical terminology, a singular diminutive: **vacciniola, arteriola, variola.** Compare **-ole**[1]. Related form (sense 2): **-olae** *(plural)*.

269 **-bola** A noun-forming word-final element, derived from Greek *ball(ein)* 'to cast, throw, strike, cast off,' used to form two groups of combinations:
1. In the terminology of geometry, 'a plane curve, cast' as specified by the initial prepositional root: **hyperbola, parabola.**
2. In taxonomic names in zoology and botany, 'something cast or cast off' as specified by the combining prepositional root: **Metabola, Amphibola, Carambola.** Related forms: **-bolic; -bolas** *(plural)*.

270 **-metabola** A noun and a noun-forming word-final element, derived through Latin from Greek *metabol(os)* 'changeable' and **-a**[3], used in some taxonomic classifications to designate insects according to 'a degree or type of metamorphosis' specified by the combining root: **Ametabola, Hemimetabola, Paurometabola.** Compare **-bola, -bolic.** Related forms: **-metabolism, -metabolic, -metaboly.**

271 **-cola** A noun-forming word-final element, derived from Latin *col(ere)* 'to inhabit' and **-a**[3], used in the terminology of botanical and zoological taxonomy to designate genera of plants and organisms 'having or characterized by a habitat' specified by the combining root: **Petricola, Hepaticola, Arenicola.** Compare **-cole.**

272 **-ula**[1] A noun-forming word-final element, derived from the feminine singular form of the Latin diminutive suffix *-ul(us), -ul(a), -ul(um)*, found in scientific terminology and in learned borrowings in its etymological sense of 'small one' of a sort specified by the combining root: **fibula, blastula, spatula.** Also, **-ule.** Compare **-cule.** Related

forms: -ulus, -ulum, -uli, -ula², -ular, -ulate, -ulic, -ulous; -ulae, -ulas *(plurals)*.

273 **-ula²** A noun-forming word-final element, derived from the neuter plural form of the Latin diminutive suffix *-ul(us)*, *-ul(a)*, *-ul(um)*, found in scientific terminology and learned borrowings in its etymological sense and grammatical function: **ovula, coagula, incunabula**. Related forms: **-ula¹, -ulus, -ulum, -uli, -ulae, -ule**.

274 **-cuticula** A noun and a noun-forming word-final element, derived from Latin *cut(is)* 'skin' and **-(c)ula¹**, used to denote 'a horny skin layer, especially the outer body walls of insects' specified by the combining root: **epicuticula, endocuticula, exocuticula**. Related forms: **-cuticular; -cuticulas, -cuticulae** *(plurals)*.

275 **-planula** A noun and a noun-forming word-final element, derived from Latin *plān(us)* 'flat' and **-ula¹**, used in entomological terminology to denote 'a flattened larva of a coelenterate' specified by the combining root: **coeloplanula, hydroplanula, stereoplanula** *(obs.)*. Related forms: **-plane¹, -planular; -planulae** *(plural)*.

276 **-scapula** A noun and a noun-forming word-final element, derived from Latin *scapula* 'shoulder-blade,' used in anatomical terminology to denote 'a shoulder-blade or a part of it' as specified by the combining root: **suprascapula, prescapula, proscapula**. Related forms: **-scapular; -scapulae, -scapulas** *(plurals)*.

277 **-morula** A noun and a noun-forming word-final element, derived from Latin *mōr(us)* 'mulberry' and **-ula¹**, used in medical terminology to denote 'a clump of blastomeres formed by cleavage of a fertilized ovum' as specified by the combining root: **archimorula, amphimorula, pseudomorula** *(obs.)*. Related forms: **-morular; -morulae** *(plural)*.

278 **-gastrula** A noun and a noun-forming word-final element, derived from Greek *gaster, gast(e)r-* 'stomach' and **-ula¹**, used in medical terminology to denote 'an embryonic stage following the blastula' as qualified by the combining root: **metagastrula, archigastrula, exogastrula**. Related forms: **-gastrular; -gastrulas, -gastrulae** *(plurals)*.

279 **-blastula** A noun and a noun-forming word-final element, derived through Latin from Greek *blast(os)* 'sprout, bud' and **-ula¹**, used in medical terminology to denote 'an early embryonic stage in the development of a fertilized egg' as qualified by the initial root:

diblastula, amphiblastula, discoblastula. Compare -blast. Related forms: -blastular; -blastulas, -blastulae *(plurals)*.

280   **-dactyla**   A noun-forming word-final element, derived through Latin from Greek *daktyl(os)* 'finger, toe' and -a³, used in zoological taxonomy to label creatures according to their form of 'fingers, toes, hands, and feet' as specified by the initial root: **Artiodactyla, Ancylodactyla, Perissodactyla.** Related forms: **-dactylic, -dactylous, -dactyly.** Compare **-dactyl.**

281   **-ma**   A noun-forming word-final element, derived from Greek *-ma*, an abstract-noun-forming suffix, generally added to verbal roots, and found in English as *-ma, -me,* and *-m* in borrowings from Greek, both direct and through Latin and French, in its etymological sense of 'the result of an action; a state or condition' specified by the combining root: **drama, stigma, plasma.** (This ubiquitous suffix may also be identified in the word-final elements -ism, -asm, and -oma.) Also, **-me, -m.** Related forms: **-matic, -matical, -maticist, -matically, -matism; -mas, -matas, -mes, -ms** *(plurals)*.

282   **-drama**   A noun and a noun-forming word-final element, derived through Latin from Greek *drama* 'deed, action on the stage,' used to form two groups of combinations:
1.   'A written composition for the stage' performed or accompanied as specified by the initial root: **melodrama, monodrama, mimodrama.**
2.   'An action, with or without dialogue, usually extempore, for psychotherapeutic purposes': **psychodrama, sociodrama.** Related forms: **-dramatic, -dramatically; -dramas** *(plural)*.

283   **-orama**   A noun-forming word-final element, derived from Greek *horāma* 'sight, view' (from the verb *horā(n)* 'to see' and the noun-forming suffix **-ma**), used to designate 'a scene or view of something constructed, depicted, projected, or natural' as specified by the combining root: **panorama, cyclorama, diorama.** Related forms: **-oramic; -oramas** *(plural)*.

284   **-laema**   A noun-forming word-final element, derived through Latin from Greek *laim(os)* 'throat, gullet' and -a³, used in the taxonomy of invertebrate zoology to designate classes of creatures 'having a throat or gullet' of the sort specified by the combining root: **Gymnolaema, Phylactolaema, Megalaema.** Also, **-laima.** Related forms: **-laemata, -laematous.**

285   **-dema**   A noun-forming word-final element, derived through Latin from Greek *dem(as)* 'body, body build,' (not to be confused with *dēm(os)* 'populace') used in entomological terminology to denote, especially in the generic names of insects, 'creature or creatures having a body' of a form specified by the initial root: **Dasydema, Diadema, apodema.**

286   **-edema**   A noun, derived through Latin from Greek *oidēma* 'swelling, tumor,' also used as a noun-forming word-final element in medical terminology describing specific types of locations of 'swelling resulting from an excessive accumulation of serous fluid in the tissues of the body': **arthredema, lymphedema, staphyledema.** Also, **-oedema.** Related forms: **-edemic, -edematous; -edemas, -edemata, -oedemas, -oedemata** *(plurals).*

287   **-anthema**   A noun-forming word-final element, derived from Greek *anthēma* 'a flowering,' used in medical terminology to denote 'an eruption, rash' of a type identified by the initial root: **enanthema, eisanthema, exanthema.** Compare **-anth.** Related forms: **-anthemata, -anthemas** *(plurals).*

288   **-nema**   A noun-forming word-final element, derived from Greek *nēma* 'thread', used to form five groups of combinations, each denoting 'possessing, being, or resembling a thread':
   1.   In biological taxonomy, 'a threadlike nematode': **Dipetalonema, Agamonema, Rhabdonema.**
   2.   In the taxonomy of microorganisms, 'having a thread shape': **Treponema, Uronema, Pleuronema.**
   3.   In medical terminology, 'a threadlike stage in the development of chromosomes': **diplonema, strepsinema, leptonema.**
   4.   In botanical taxonomy, 'a class of threadlike algae': **Zygnema, Zymonema, Actinonema.**
   5.   In botanical taxonomy, 'a plant species, with threadlike qualities' as specified: **Aglaonema, Gymnema, Steironema.** Related forms: **-neme; -nemes, -nemas, -nemata** *(plurals).*

289   **-trema**   A noun-forming word-final element, derived from Greek *trēma, trēma(t-)* 'hole,' used in medical terminology in two senses:
   1.   'A hole, orifice, opening' specified by the combining root: **helicotrema, peritrema, gonotrema.**
   2.   As a collective noun in generic names for 'creatures possessing an opening' specified by the combining root: **Eurytrema, Monorchotrema, Troglotrema.** Related forms: **-tremata, -tremas** *(plurals).*

290   **-blastema**   A noun and a noun-forming word-final element, derived from Greek *blastēma* 'offspring,' used in medical terminology to denote 'a mass of living substance' specified by the initial root: **mesoblastema, cytoblastema, epiblastema** *(obs.).* Compare **-blast.** Related forms: **-blastemal, -blastematic, -blastemic; -blastemas** *(plural).*

291   **-empyema**   A noun and a noun-forming word-final element, derived from Greek *empyēma* 'an abcess, suppuration,' used in medical terminology to denote 'an accumulation of pus, especially thoracic,' as qualified by the combining root: **typhloempyema, pneumoempyema, arthroempyema.** Related forms: **-empyesis, -empyemic; -empyemas, -empyemata** *(plurals).*

292   **-phragma**   A noun and a noun-forming word-final element, derived from Greek *phragma* 'fence, wall,' used in medical and entomological terminology to denote 'a septum or musculomembranous barrier between cavities' as specified by the combining root: **diaphragma, mesophragma, prephragma.** Also, **-phragm.** Related forms: **-phragmas, -phragmata, -phragms** *(plurals).*

293   **-stigma**   A noun and a noun-forming word-final element, derived from Greek *stigma* 'mark, tattoo,' used to denote 'a distinguishing marking or feature' especially in botanical and zoological taxonomic labels: **Chlorostigma, pterostigma, Pleurostigma.** Related forms: **-stigmatic, -stigmatism, -stigmal; -stigmas, -stigmata** *(plurals).*

294   **-asthma**   A noun and a noun-forming word-final element, derived through Latin from Greek *asthma, asthma(t-)* 'panting,' used in medical terminology to denote 'a condition of labored breathing' as specified by the initial root: **cardioasthma, pseudoasthma, acetonasthma** *(obs.).* Related forms: **-asthmatic; -asthmas** *(plural).*

295   **-gramma**   A collective noun-forming word-final element, derived from Greek *gramm(a)* 'letter, line of a drawing' and a³, used in botanical and entomological taxonomic names to denote 'having a line' as specified by the initial root: **Trichogramma, Pityrogramma, Cryptogramma.** Compare **-gram.**

296   **-lemma¹**   A noun and a noun-forming word-final element, derived through Latin from Greek *lēmma* 'thing received or taken, an assumption' (from Greek *labein* 'to seize, take' and the abstract-noun-forming suffix **-ma**), often used in the terminology of logic and mathematics to denote 'a proposition (often with sub-propositions) or

theorem' as qualified by the combining root: **dilemma, tetralemma, polylemma.** Related forms: **-lemmas, -lemmata** *(plurals).*

297   **-lemma**[2] A noun-forming word-final element, derived from Greek *lemma* 'rind, husk,' used in medical terminology to denote 'a confining membrane' specified by the combining root: **neurolemma, glandilemma, sarcolemma.** Related forms: **-lemmal; -lemmas, -lemmata** *(plurals).*

298   **-comma** A noun-forming word-final element, derived from Greek *komma* 'fragment,' used in medical terminology to denote 'a piece or member of a structure' designated by the initial root: **osteocomma, myocomma, inocomma.** Related form: **-commas** *(plural).*

299   **-oma** A noun-forming word-final element, probably derived by abstraction from Greek *onkōma, onkōmat-* 'a swelling' (from the verb *onko(un)* 'to swell, bulge' and the abstract-noun-forming suffix *-ma*), used in medical terminology to denote 'a tumor' of the sort or in the location specified by the combining root: **melanoma, fibroma, nephroma.** Related forms: **-ome, -omatoid; -omas, -omata** *(plurals).*

300   **-coloboma** A noun-forming word-final element, derived through Latin from Greek *kolobōma* 'an imperfection' (from *kolob(oun)* 'to stunt, maim' and *-ma*), used in medical terminology to denote 'the absence or defect of an ocular tissue affecting function, especially of the iris' as specified by the combining root: **iridocoloboma, pseudocoloboma, blepharocoloboma** *(obs.).* Related forms: **-colobomas, -colobomata** *(plurals).*

301   **-coma**[1] A noun and a noun-forming word-final element, derived through Latin from Greek *kōma* 'deep sleep,' used occasionally in medical terminology to form two groups of combinations:
   1. 'A condition of profound unconsciousness' defined by the initial root: **semicoma, narcoma.**
   2. 'A condition of torpor' specified by the first root: **agrypnocoma.**
   Related forms: **-comatose; -comas** *(plural).*

302   **-coma**[2] A noun-forming word-final element, derived from Greek *kom(ē)* 'hair' and *-a*[3], used in taxonomic nomenclature to designate genera 'possessing or characterized by hair' as specified by the combining root: **Pyncnocoma, Abrocoma, Acoma.**

303   **-sarcoma** A noun and a noun-forming word-final element, derived from Greek *sarkōma* 'fleshy growth' (from *sarx, sark-* 'flesh' and

-oma), used in medical terminology to designate 'a malignant neoplasm' specified by the combining root: **osteosarcoma, fibrosarcoma, lymphosarcoma.** Related forms: **-sarc, -sarcomatous, -sarcomatoid; -sarcomas, -sarcomata** *(plurals)*.

304   **-osteoma** A noun and a noun-forming word-final element, derived from Greek *osteo(n)* 'bone' and **-oma**, used actively in medical terminology to denote 'a tumor composed of bone tissue, usually benign' specified by the combining root: **periosteoma, chondrosteoma, myosteoma.** Related forms: **-osteon, -osteum, -osteomatoid, -osteomatous; -osteomas, -osteomata** *(plurals)*.

305   **-lymphoma** A noun and a noun-forming word-final element, derived from Latin *lymph(a)* 'lymph' and **-oma**, used in medical terminology to denote 'a tumor or neoplastic disorder of lymphoid tissue' as specified by the combining root: **adenolymphoma, angiolymphoma, cystadenolymphoma.** (Current medical practice is to substitute **-oma** for **-lymphoma** in combinations; *cystadenoma* is thus a replacement for *cystadenolymphoma.*) Related forms: **-lymphomatoid, -lymphomatous; -lymphomas, -lymphomata** *(plurals)*.

306   **-angioma** A noun and a noun-forming word-final element, derived from Greek *angei(on)* 'vessel' and **-oma**, used actively in medical terminology to denote 'a tumor composed chiefly of blood and lymph vessels' specified by the first root: **hemangioma, lymphangioma, phlebangioma.** Related forms: **-angiomatous; -angiomas, -angiomata** *(plurals)*.

307   **-thelioma** A noun-forming word-final element, derived from scientific Latin *theli(um)* 'nipple, layer of cellular tissue' and **-oma**, used in medical terminology to denote 'a tumor in a cellular tissue' as specified by the combining root: **endothelioma, epithelioma, mesothelioma.** Related forms: **-thelium, -theliomatous; -theliomas, -theliomata** *(plurals)*.

308   **-epithelioma** A noun and a noun-forming word-final element, derived from scientific Greco-Latin *epitheli(um)* 'layer of cellular tissue covering the outer surfaces of the body and its organs' (from Greek *epi-* 'on' and *-theli(um)* '-thelium') and **-oma**, used in medical terminology to denote 'a tumor of epithelial tissue' as specified by the combining root: **lymphepithelioma, chorioepithelioma, neuroepithelioma.** Compare **-endothelioma.** Related forms: **-epitheliomas, -epitheliomata** *(plurals)*.

309   **-endothelioma**   A noun and a noun-forming word-final element,
      derived from scientific Greco-Latin *endotheli(um)* 'layer of cellular
      tissue lining the inner surface of certain organs' (from Greek *endo-*
      'within' and *-theli(um)* '-thelium') and **-oma**, used in medical
      terminology to denote 'a tumor of endothelial tissue' specified by the
      combining root: **periendothelioma, reticuloendothelioma, lymph-
      angioendothelioma.** Compare **-epithelioma.** Related forms: **-endotheli-
      omas, -endotheliomata** *(plurals).*

310   **-glioma**   A noun and a noun-forming word-final element, derived
      through Latin from Greek *glia, gloia* 'glue' and **-oma**, used in medical
      terminology to denote 'a tumor arising from the neuroglia' as
      qualified by the initial root: **ganglioma, angioglioma, fibroglioma.**
      Related forms: **-gliomatous; -gliomas, -gliomata** *(plurals).*

311   **-loma**   A noun-forming word-final element, derived from Greek *lōm(a)*
      'fringe, hem' and **-a³**, used in botanical taxonomy to designate plants
      'having a fringe' of a sort specified by the combining root: **Tricholoma,
      Isoloma, Entoloma.**

312   **-myeloma**   A noun and a noun-forming word-final element, derived
      from Greek *myel(os)* 'marrow' and **-oma**, used occasionally in medical
      terminology to designate 'a tumor composed of cells normally found
      in bone marrow' as qualified by the initial root: **chloromyeloma,
      orchiomyeloma, chlorosarcomyeloma** (*obs.,* now **chloronoma**).
      Compare **-myelia.** Related forms: **-myelomatoid, -myelomatous;
      -myelomas, -myelomata** *(plurals).*

313   **-papilloma**   A noun and a noun-forming word-final element, derived
      from Latin *papill(a)* 'nipple, nipple-shaped protuberance' and **-oma**,
      used in medical terminology to denote 'an epithelial tumor' of a sort
      specified by the combining root: **fibropapilloma, myxopapilloma,
      polypapilloma.** Related forms: **-papillomatous; -papillomata, -papil-
      lomas** *(plurals).*

314   **-granuloma**   A noun and a noun-forming word-final element, derived
      from Latin *grānul(um)* 'particle, grain' and **-oma**, used in medical
      terminology to designate 'a tumor-like mass or nodule of granulation
      tissue' as specified by the combining root: **paragranuloma, oleo-
      granuloma, lipogranuloma.** Related forms: **-granulomatous; -granulo-
      mas, -granulomata** *(plurals).*

315   **-dermoma**   A noun and a word-final noun-forming element, derived
      from Greek *derm(a)* 'skin' and **-oma**, used in medical terminology to

denote 'a tumor of the skin layers,' the number of layers specified by the combining root: **bidermoma, didermoma, monodermoma.** Compare **-dermia.** Related form: **-dermomas** *(plural).*

316 **-noma** A noun and a noun-forming word-final element, derived from Greek *nom(ē)* 'pasturage, spread, spreading sore' and -a⁴, used in a few medical terms denoting 'a spreading, invasive gangrene' specified by the combining root: **noma, müllerianoma, pelidnoma.** Related form: **-nomas** *(plural).*

317 **-adenoma** A noun and a noun-forming word-final element, derived through Latin from Greek *adēn* 'gland' and **-oma,** used widely in medical terminology to designate 'a tumor composed of glandular tissue or glandlike in structure' as qualified by the initial root: **lymphadenoma, chorioadenoma, nephradenoma.** Related forms: **-adenomatous; -adenomas, -adenomata** *(plurals).*

318 **-carcinoma** A noun and a noun-forming word-final element, derived through Latin and Greek *karkin-* 'crab' and **-oma,** used frequently in medical terminology to denote 'a malignant tumor composed of epithelial cells, with a tendency to metastasize' specified by the combining root: **sarcocarcinoma, mastocarcinoma, psammacarcinoma.** Related forms: **-carcinomatoid, -carcinomatous; -carcinomas, -carcinomata** *(plurals).*

319 **-lipoma** A noun also found as a noun-forming word-final element, derived through Latin from Greek *lip(os)* 'fat' and **-oma,** used in medical terminology to denote 'a tumor made up of fatty tissue' as qualified by the combining root: **osteolipoma, angiolipoma, fibrolipoma.** Related forms: **-lipid, -lipoid, -lipomatous; -lipomas, -lipomata** *(plurals).*

320 **-fibroma** A noun also widely found as a noun-forming word-final element, derived from Latin *fibr(a)* 'fiber' and **-oma,** used in medical terminology to denote 'a benign tumor made up of fibrous tissue' of a type or in an area specified by the combining root: **angiofibroma, myxofibroma, osteofibroma.** Also, **-inoma** *(rare).* Related forms: **-fibrous, -fibromatous; -fibromas, -fibromata** *(plurals).*

321 **-chondroma** A noun, also widely found as a noun-forming word-final element, derived from Greek *chondr(os)* 'grain; gristle, cartilage' and **-oma,** used in medical terminology to denote 'a benign cartilaginous tumor' of a type or in a location designated by the combining root:

angiochondroma, perichondroma, enchondroma. Related forms: -chondromatous; -chondromas, -chondromata *(plurals)*.

322 **-scleroma** A noun and a noun-forming word-final element, derived from Greek *sklēr(os)* 'hard' and **-oma**, used in medical terminology to denote 'an induration, a hardening of tissues' whose location is specified by the combining root: **pharyngoscleroma, rhinoscleroma, laryngoscleroma.** Related forms: -scleromas, -scleromata *(plurals)*.

323 **-nephroma** A noun and occasionally a noun-forming word-final element, derived through modern Latin from Greek *nephr(os)* 'kidney' and **-oma**, used in medical terminology to denote 'a tumor of the kidney or area of the kidney' as designated by the combining root: **paranephroma, epinephroma** (*obs.,* now **hypernephroma**). **mesonephroma.** Related forms: -nephromas, -nephromata *(plurals)*.

324 **-stroma** A noun and occasionally a noun-forming word-final element, derived from Greek *strōma, strōma(t)* 'bed, bed covering,' used in medical terminology to denote 'the supporting tissue of an organ' as specified by the combining root: **mesostroma, blastostroma, myostroma.** Related forms: -stromal, -stromatal, -stromatic; -stromata, -stromas *(plurals)*.

325 **neuroma** A noun and occasionally a noun-forming word-final element, derived from Greek *neur(on)* 'sinew, fiber,' hence 'nerve,' and **-oma**, used in medical terminology to denote 'a tumor made up of nerve cells and fibers' as specified by the combining root: **glioneuroma, fibroneuroma, ganglioneuroma.** Related forms: -neuromas, -neuromata *(plurals)*.

326 **-soma** A noun and a noun-forming word-final element derived from Greek *sōma, sōmat-* 'body,' used in two major senses:
1. In the terminology of zoological and botanical taxonomy, 'having a body' of a sort specified by the combining root: **Malacosoma, Dolichosoma, Trypanosoma.**
2. In biomedical terminology, 'a body or portion of a body' specified by the combining root: **mesosoma, actinosoma, prosoma.** Related forms: -some[3], -somus, -somia, -somic, -somal, -somatic, -somatous, -somatia, -somatically, -somite; -somi, -somas, -somata *(plurals)*.

327 **-toma** A noun-forming word-final element, derived from Greek *tom(os)*, *tom(ē)*, *tom(on)* 'cut, segmented' and -a[3], used in zoological taxonomy to name genera, especially of insects, with the meaning

'creatures possessing or characterized by a kind of segmentation' specified by the combining root: **Triatoma, Diatoma, Neotoma.** Related form: **-tomic.**

328   **-hematoma**   A noun and occasionally a noun-forming word-final element, derived from Greek *haima, haimat-* 'blood' and **-oma,** used in medical terminology to denote 'a swelling containing blood, usu. because of a break in a blood vessel wall,' the location designated by the combining root: **meninghematoma, cephalhematoma, othematoma.** Compare **-emia.** Related forms: **-hematomas, -hematomata** *(plurals).*

329   **-stoma¹**   A noun-forming word-final element, derived from Greek *stoma, stoma(t-)* 'mouth,' used in biomedical terminology to designate 'a mouth' of a sort specified by the combining root: **hypostoma, pseudostoma, protostoma.** Related forms: **-stoma², -stomus, -stomum, -stome, -stomia¹, -stomia², -stomate, -stomous, -stomatous, -stomy; -stomas, -stomata** *(plurals).*

330   **-stoma²**   A noun-forming word-final element, derived from Greek *stoma, stoma(t-)* 'mouth' and **-a³,** used in zoological taxonomy to name genera of 'creatures possessing a mouth' of a sort specified by the combining root: **Bdellostoma, Gnathostoma, Melastoma.** Also, **-stomata.** Compare **-stoma¹.**

331   **-cystoma**   A noun, and frequently a noun-forming word-final element, derived through Latin from Greek *kyst(is),* 'sack, bladder' and **-oma,** used in medical terminology to denote 'a cystic tumor' of a type or location specified by the combining root: **osteocystoma, syringocystoma, fibrocystoma.** Related forms: **-cystomatous; -cystomas, -cystomata** *(plurals).*

332   **-myxoma**   A noun and occasionally a noun-forming word-final element, derived from Greek *myx(a)* 'nasal slime' and **-oma,** used in medical terminology to designate 'a soft tumor made up of primitive connective tissues' of a type or in a location specified by the first root: **lymphomyxoma, angiomyxoma, fibromyxoma.** Related forms: **-myxomas, myxomata** *(plurals).*

333   **-derma**   A noun-forming word-final element, derived from Greek *derma, dermat-* 'skin,' used in biomedical terminology in several related senses, each as qualified by the combining root:
   1.   'A specified skin or covering': **sauroderma, sarcoderma, epiderma.**
   2.   'A skin ailment or skin of a specified type': **toxicoderma, leucoderma, xanthoderma.**

3. In generic names, 'creatures possessing a specified type of skin': **Mycoderma, Trichoderma, Heloderma.** Related forms: **-derm, -dermis, -dermal, -dermic, -dermoid, -dermatoid, -dermatic, -dermatous; -dermas, -dermata** *(plurals).*

334 **-sperma** A noun-forming word-final element, derived from Greek *sperm(a), sperm(at-)* 'germ, seed, that which is sown' (from the verb *speir(ein)* 'to sow seed' and the noun-forming suffix -ma) and -a³, used in botanical taxonomy to name genera of plants 'possessing a seed or germ' specified by the combining root: **Lepidosperma, Aspidosperma, Ptychosperma.** Compare **-sperm.**

335 **-plasma** A noun and, in two senses, a noun-forming word-final element, derived through German and Latin from Greek *plasma, plasmat-* 'something formed or molded':
1. In biological and some medical terminology, 'the fluid part of cytoplasm or protoplasm,' as indicated by the combining root: **endoplasma, hyaloplasma, ectoplasm.** Also, **-plasm.**
2. In botanical and biological names for genera, 'one formed' as specified by the combining root: **Anaplasma, Histoplasma, Toxoplasma.** Related forms: **-plasmic, -plasmatic; -plasmas, -plasmata** *(plurals).*

336 **-desma** A noun-forming word-final element, derived from Greek *desm(os)* 'bond, band, ligament,' used in biological and medical terminology to mean 'something bridging or connecting' as specified by the combining root: **cytodesma, plasmodesma, lithodesma.** Also, **-desm.** Related forms: **-desmic; -desms, -desmata** *(plurals).*

337 **-osma** A noun-forming word-final element, derived from Greek *osm(ē)* 'an odor, smell' and -a³, used in botanical taxonomic nomenclature to designate genera as 'having a characteristic odor' specified by the combining root: **Agathosma, Xylosma, Barosma.**

338 **-trauma** A noun also occasionally found as a noun-forming word-final element, derived from Greek *trauma, trauma(t-)* 'wound,' used in medical terminology to denote 'a wound or injury, psychic or physical' as specified by the combining root: **barotrauma, microtrauma, neurotrauma.** Related forms: **-traumatic, -traumatically; -traumas, -traumata** *(plurals).*

339 **-enchyma** A noun and a noun-forming word-final element, derived from Greek *enchyma, enchyma(t-)* 'infusion' (cf. *ench(ein)* 'to pour in, infuse' and *chymos* 'liquid, juice'), used in medical terminology to

denote 'the liquid that nourishes tissue, or tissue itself' as specified by the combining root: **collenchyma, cystenchyma, chlorenchyma.** Related forms: **-enchyme; -enchymas, -enchymata** *(plurals).*

340 **-phyma** A noun widely used as a noun-forming word-final element, derived from Greek *phyma, phymat-* 'a swelling, tumor,' used in medical terminology in its etymological sense as qualified by the combining root: **osteophyma, syphilophyma, arthrophyma.** Related forms: **-phymatic; -phymas, -phymata** *(plurals).*

341 **-ana** A collective suffix, which also occurs as **-iana,** derived from the Latin neuter nominative plural word-final element *-(i)ana,* meaning 'assembled items of bibliographical or anecdotal data concerning a person, place, or activity' as specified by the combining root: **Shakespeareana, Americana, Shaviana.** Also, **-iana.**

342 **-ina**[1] A noun-forming word-final element, derived from the feminine form of the Italian diminutive suffix *-ina* from Latin *-in(us), -in(a), -in(um),* used in borrowings from Italian generally designating 'a musical instrument or device' specified by the combining root: **ocarina, aeolina, concertina.** Also, **-ine.** Related forms: **-inas, -ines** *(plurals).*

343 **-ina**[2] A noun-forming word-final element, both singular and plural, derived from the homographic feminine singular and neuter plural of the Latin suffix *-in(us)* 'of, belonging to,' used in botanical and biological taxonomy to name higher taxa of creatures or plants 'related to, like, or characterized by' that which is specified by the combining root: **Oleacina, Acarina, Monadina.** Compare **-inae.**

344 **-monadina** A noun-forming word-final element, derived through scientific Latin from Greek *monad* 'minute simple organism' (from *mon(o)* 'one, single' and **-ad**) and **-ina**[2], used in the terminology of microbiological taxonomy to designate orders of flagellate protozoa: **Chrysomonadina, Protomonadina, Cryptomonadina.**

345 **-mastigina** A noun-forming word-final element, derived from Greek *mastix, mastig-* 'whip' and **-ina**[2], used in marine biology to name orders and sub-orders of flagellates, particularized by the combining root: **Rhizomastigina, Phytomastigina, Polymastigina.** Related forms: **-mastix, -mastigine.**

346 **-angina** A noun, derived from Latin *ang(ere)* 'to strangle' that, as a free form, refers chiefly to 'angina pectoris;' used as a word-final

element in medical terminology, it refers to a specified kind of 'severe ulceration, usu. of the throat or mouth': **staphyloangina, herpangina, monocytangina**. Related forms: -anginal; -anginas *(plural)*.

347 **-fauna** A collective noun designating 'the animal life in a particular region,' derived from Latin *Fauna*, a Roman nature goddess, and also used as a collective noun-forming word-final element to designate 'the animals or animal life of a sort or in a region or period' specified by the combining root: **paleofauna, microfauna, avifauna**. Related forms: **-faunal, -faunally; -faunas, -faunae** *(plurals)*.

348 **-zoa** A noun-forming word-final element, derived from Greek *zōa*, the nominative-accusative plural of *zōon* 'living being, animal' (cf. the verb *za(ein)* 'to live'), used in zoological terminology to name lower divisions of the animal kingdom containing one-celled creatures: **Protozoa, Sporozoa, Metazoa**. Related forms: **-zoon, -zoal, -zoan, -zoid, -zooid, -zoite.**

349 **-campa** A noun-forming word-final element, derived through Latin from Greek *kamp(ē)* 'caterpillar' and -a³, used in the nomenclature of zoological taxonomy to designate type genera of the caterpillar family: **Lasiocampa, Olisiocampa, Hemerocampa.**

350 **-para** A noun-forming word-final element, derived from Latin *par(ere)* 'to bring forth (children)' and -a⁴, used in biomedical terminology in two senses:
  1. 'A woman who has given birth to children in a number of pregnancies' specified by the combining root: **primipara, secundipara, nullipara.**
  2. 'A female of any species producing a number or type of egg or offspring' specified by the combining root: **pupipara, pluripara, ovovivipara**. Related forms: **-parous, -parity, -parously; -paras, -parae** *(plurals)*.

351 **-cera** A noun-forming word-final element, derived from Greek *ker(as)*, *ker(at-)* 'horn' (not to be confused with Greek *kēr(os)* 'wax' which appears as the homographic combining form *cer-* in English) and -a³, used in zoological taxonomy to mean 'possessing or characterized by a horn or hard, hornlike growth' as specified by the combining root: **Cladocera, Rhopalocera, Blepharocera**. Related forms: **-ceran, -ceratoid, -keratoid, -ceratosis, -keratosis, -cerite, -ceros; -cerae** *(plural)*.

352 **-fera** A noun-forming word-final element, derived from Latin *fer(re)*

'to bear, carry, produce' and -a³, used in zoological taxonomic nomenclature to designate classes of 'creatures bearing or producing' that which is specified by the combining root: **tubulifera, conchifera, mangifera.** Related forms: **-fer, -ferae, -ferous.**

353   **-camera**   A noun and a noun-forming word-final element, derived from Latin *camera* 'room, chamber,' used in the specialized sense of 'a photographic device' of a sort specified by the combining root: **cinecamera, telecamera, gastrocamera.** Related forms: **-cameras, -camerae** *(plurals).*

354   **-ptera**   A noun-forming word-final element, derived from Greek *pter(on)* 'wing' and -a³, used in zoological taxonomy to name 'creatures possessing or characterized by wings' of a sort specified by the combining root: **Diptera, Lepidoptera, Trichoptera.** Related forms: **-pteron, -pter, -pteryx.**

355   **-agra**   A noun-forming word-final element, derived from Greek *agra* 'seizure,' denoting 'a pain or painful seizure' as specified by the combining root: **cephalagra, arteriagra, ophthalmagra.** Related form: **-agras** *(plural).*

356   **-dora**   A word-final element, derived from Greek *dor(on)* 'gift' and -a⁴, used in forming feminine personal names: **Isadora, Pandora, Theodora.**

357   **-phora**   A noun-forming word-final element, derived from Greek *phor(ein)* (the frequentative form of *pher(ein)* 'to bear, carry') and -a³, used in zoological taxonomy to name 'creatures that have or carry' that which is specified by the combining root: **Placophora, Thecophora, Rhabdophora.** Compare **-fera.** Related forms: **-phor, -phore, -phorae, -phori, -phoria, -phorous, -phoric.**

358   **-flora**   A collective noun and collective noun-forming word-final element, designating 'the plant life in a particular region' derived from Latin *flos, flor-* 'flower, flowering plant' and, by analogy to **-fauna,** with which it is frequently associated, *Flora,* the goddess of flowers. As a word-final element, **-flora** is used in two related senses:
1.   'The plant life of an area or type' specified by the joining root: **subflora, ethnoflora, microflora.**
2.   'Flowers of a size, condition, or quantity' indicated by the adjective acting as the first root: **grandiflora, nudiflora, multiflora.** Related forms: **-florate, -florous; -florae, -floras** *(plurals).*

359   **-pora**   A noun-forming word-final element, derived from Greek *por(os)* 'passage-way, means of passage' and -a³, used in zoological taxonomy to name 'creatures characteristically possessing or producing passageways or pores' as specified by the combining root: **Cellepora, Millepora, Retepora.** Related forms: **-pore, -poric, -porous.**

360   **-spora**   A noun-forming word-final element, derived from Greek *spor(os)* 'a sowing, a seed' (from the verb *speir(ein)* 'to sow seed,' whence also **-sperm**) and -a³, used in botanical taxonomy to name plants 'possessing reproductive elements (spores)' of a sort specified by the combining root: **Cercospora, Oospora, Spongospora.** Compare **-spore.**

361   **-vora**   A noun-forming word-final element, derived from Latin *vor(āre)* 'to swallow, swallow up, eat' (whence English *devour*) and -a³, used in zoological taxonomy to designate 'creatures that eat something' specified by the combining root: **Insectivora, Herbivora, Carnivora.** Related forms: **-vore, -vorous.**

362   **-ura**   A noun-forming word-final element, derived through scientific Latin from Greek *our(a)* 'tail' and -a³, used in zoological taxonomy to designate creatures 'having a tail' of a sort specified by the combining root: **Anura, Chelura, Xiphosura.** Related forms: **-uroid, -urus, -uridae.**

363   **-glossa**   A noun-forming word-final element, used variously as a plural and a singular, derived from Ionic Greek *glōssa* (cf. Attic Greek *glōtta*) 'tongue,' used in zoological taxonomy to name 'creatures having a tongue or tonguelike part' as denoted by the joining root: **Docoglossa, Eriglossa, Cheiroglossa.** Related forms: **-glossal, -glossia, -glot, -glottic, -glottal.**

364   **-ata**   A word-final element, derived from the homographic feminine nominative singular and neuter nominative plural endings of the past participle of the first conjugation of Latin: *-a* (theme vowel), *-t-* (past participle marker, comparable to English *-(e)d*), and -a[1, 4]. The use of this element in English is restricted to learned borrowings and scientific terminology—often resulting in the creation of doublets with words ending in *-ate* (cf -ate[1, 2]), e.g., **chordate, Chordata.** As in Latin, this element (and its related forms) may be used productively to create adjectives which may then be used substantively: **designata, vertebrata, data.** Note that this element is not to be confused with the *-ata* which appears word-finally in such Greek neuter plurals as *somata* and *chromata*, in which the *-at* is merely the combining form

of the stem and the *-a* is *-a²*. Compare *-ate*[1, 2, 3, 4]. Related forms: *-atus* (*masculine singular*, cf. *-us*), *-ati* (*masculine plural*, cf. *-i*), *-atum* (*neuter singular*, cf. *-um*), *-atae* (*feminine plural*, cf. *-ae*[1]).

365   **-branchiata**   A noun and a noun-forming word-final element, derived from Greek *branchi(a)* 'gills' and *-ata*, used in zoological taxonomy to designate 'creatures having gills' of a sort specified by the combining root: **Tubulibranchiata, Dorsibranchiata, Pygobranchiata.** Compare **-branchia.** Related forms: **-branch, -branchiate, -branchial.**

366   **-flagellata**   A noun and a noun-forming word-final element, derived from Latin *flagell(um)* 'a whip, stinger' and *-ata*, used in zoological taxonomy to designate 'creatures having a flagellum (i.e., a whiplike appendage)' of a sort specified by the combining root: **Cilioflagellata, Dinoflagellata, Lissoflagellata.**

367   **-tremata**   A noun-forming word-final element, derived from Greek *trēm(a)*, *trēm(at-)* 'hole' and *-ata*, used in zoological taxonomy to designate 'creatures with an orifice' of a sort specified by the combining root: **Monotremata, Hypotremata, Derotremata.** Compare **-trema.**

368   **-somata**   A noun-forming word-final element, derived from Greek *sōm(a)*, *sōm(at-)* 'body' and *-ata*, used in zoological taxonomy to designate 'creatures having a body' of a sort specified by the combining root: **Thecosomata, Podosomata, Holosomata.** Compare **-soma.**

369   **-stomata**   A noun-forming word-final element, derived from Greek *stom(a)*, *stom(at-)* 'mouth' and *-ata*, used in zoological taxonomy to designate 'creatures having a mouth or mouthlike opening' of a sort specified by the combining root: **Plagiostomata, Gnathostomata, Cryptostomata.** Compare **-stoma.**

370   **-procta**   A noun-forming word-final element, derived from Greek *prōkt(os)* 'anus' and *-a³*, used in zoological taxonomy to designate 'creatures having an anus of a sort or in a location' specified by the combining root: **Aprocta, Entoprocta, Dasyprocta.**

371   **-chaeta**   A noun, derived through Latin from Greek *chait(ē)* 'hair, bristle' and *-a⁴*, also used as a noun-forming word-final element (with *-a³*) in zoological taxonomy with the meaning 'possessing or characterized by bristles' as specified by the combining root: **Achaeta,**

Oligochaeta, Amphochaeta. Related forms: -chaete, -chete; -chaetes, -chetes *(plurals)*.

372 **-placenta** A noun and a noun-forming word-final element, derived through Latin from Greek *plak(ous)*, *plakent-* 'flat cake' (from *plax*, *plak-* 'flat'), used in medical terminology to denote 'an organ shaped like a flat cake (usually, the particular organ in the uterus that mediates between mother and fetus)': **subplacenta, ectoplacenta, discoplacenta.** Related forms: -placental; -placentas *(plural)*.

373 **-etta** A noun-forming word-final element, derived from the Italian feminine diminutive suffix *-etta* (from unattested Common Romance **-itta*, **-etta*), used in its etymological sense of 'small one': **Julietta, farcetta, operetta.** Also used, as a back formation with -a³, in the same sense to form taxonomic names: **Leucetta, Ascetta, Glaucionetta.** Compare **-etto** (the corresponding masculine form). Related forms: -et, -ette; -ettas *(plural)*.

374 **-phyta** A noun-forming word-final element, derived from Greek *phyt(os)* (the past participle of the verb *phyein* 'to grow, cause to grow, produce') and -a³, used in botanical taxonomy to designate 'plant phyla that produce or grow in or on' that which is specified by the combining root: **Pteridophyta, Bacillariophyta, Zoophyta.** Compare **-phyte.**

375 **-(r)rhiza** A noun-forming word-final element, derived from Greek *rhiza* 'root,' used in zoological terminology to designate 'a root' or, with -a³, 'plants having roots' of a sort specified by the combining root: **pseudorhiza, Saccorhiza, Xanthorrhiza.** Related form: -(r)rhizal.

376 **-iamb** A noun, derived through Latin from Greek *iamb(os)* 'a metrical foot consisting of a short syllable followed by a long syllable,' used as a noun-forming word-final element in literary terminology in combinations designating 'a metrical foot consisting of a short (or unstressed) syllable followed by a long (or stressed) syllable, a variant of this pattern, or a verse consisting of metrical feet of this sort,' as specified by the combining root: **diamb, choliamb, choriamb.** Also, **iambus.** Related forms: -iambic, -iambically; -iambs, -iambi, -iambuses *(plurals)*.

377 **-sorb** A verb-forming word-final element, derived from Latin *sorb(ēre)* 'to soak up,' used in its etymological sense as qualified by the combining root: **absorb, adsorb, chemisorb.** Principal parts: **-sorbing, -sorbed, -sorbed.** Related forms: -sorbative, -sorption.

378   **-ac** A word-final element, derived through Latin *-ac(us)* from Greek *-ak(os)*, used to form adjectives from the nouns to which it is added: **cardiac, iliac, Syriac.** A subset of the adjectives formed with this suffix are used substantively to designate, specifically, a sufferer from an ailment or a psychological compulsion as specified by the combining root: **maniac, phobiac, insomniac.** Related forms: **-acal, -acally, -acism; -acs** *(plural).*

379   **-cardiac** A noun, derived through Latin from Greek *kardia* 'heart' and **-ac**, also used in medical terminology as a word-final combining element in the formation of nouns and adjectives:

   1. To characterize types and locations of 'heart ailments': **pericardiac, paracardiac, pulmocardiac.**
   2. To identify 'heart ailment patients': **postcardiac, neurocardiac, myocardiac.** Related forms: **-cardia; -cardiacs** *(plural, meaning 2).*

380   **-iliac** An adjective and an adjective-forming word-final element, derived from Latin *īli(a)* 'groin, flanks' and **-ac**, used in medical terminology to refer to the *ilium* (flank, upper portion of the innominate bone), usually in relation to other regions of the body specified by the combining root: **sacroiliac, lumboiliac, transiliac.** Related form: **-ileal.**

381   **-maniac** A noun, derived from Greek *mania* 'madness' and **-ac**, also used as a word-final element in two related senses:

   1. In nouns, 'a person exhibiting a type of psychosis' named by the combining root: **toxicomaniac, narcomaniac, kleptomaniac.**
   2. In nouns, 'a person revealing an inordinate interest in something' specified by the combining root: **dipsomaniac, theomaniac, egomaniac.** Related forms: **-mania, -mane, -manic, -maniacal, -manically, -maniacally; -manes, -maniacs** *(plurals).*

382   **-aphrodisiac** An adjective (which may be used substantively) and an adjective-forming word-final element, derived from Greek *aphrodisi(a)* 'sacred to Aphrodite (the goddess of love)' and **-ac**, used in the sense of 'of or referring to an agent which arouses sexual desire' as specified by the combining root: **antiaphrodisiac, anaphrodisiac, antaphrodisiac.** These forms may be used substantively. Related forms: **-aphrodisia, -aphroditic; -aphrodisiacs** *(plural).*

383   **-ic**[1] A common adjective-forming word-final element, derived through Middle English *-ic, -ik, -ick* variously from Latin *-ic(us)*, Greek *-ik(os)*, and French *-ique* (the last being a semi-learned development

from the Greek and Latin cognates), used in a variety of related senses in combination with nouns as well as with other, non-freely-occurring stems:

1. 'Something having the form or character' denoted by the combining root: **dioramic, Alhambraic, vampiric.**
2. 'Consisting of or containing an ingredient' specified by the combining root: **alcoholic, hieroglyphic, boric.**
3. 'Of or relating to': **Hebraic, Icelandic, Arabic.**
4. 'Characteristic of or in the manner of the feature, culture, or procedure' named by the combining root: **Whitmanic, archaic, balletic.**
5. 'Associated or dealing with the concept' named in the combining root: **Mosaic, Koranic, Mozarabic.**
6. 'Utilizing the force, instrument, or process' named by the combining root: **electrophonic, hydroponic, orthopedic.**
7. 'Characterized by or affected with the concept' expressed by the root: **bubonic, chronic, paraplegic.**
8. 'Tending to bring about the condition' denoted by the combining root: **ataraxic, diuretic, antipyretic.**
9. 'Elements or compounds possessing the higher of two valences': **cupric, ferric, mercuric.**
10. In adjectives whose stems do not occur as words (usu. senses 2 or 3): **caloric, pubic, manic.** Compare -tic. Related forms: **-ical, -ically, -icly, -icate, -ication, -icism, -icist, -icity, -icize.** (Unless the etymologies of adjectives ending in -ic indicate that the suffix was directly borrowed from Greek, Latin, or French, it is to be assumed that the ending was added by English users of the initial root.)

384 **-ic²** A noun-forming word-final element, derived through the substantive use of adjectives ending in **-ic¹** or its various ancestors, Latin -ic(us), Greek -ik(os), and French -ique, used in several senses:

1. 'Something or someone possessing the character or nature' specified by the combining root: **critic, georgic, magic.**
2. 'An association' specified by the combining root: **music, psychic, logic.**
3. 'Something or someone exhibiting or affected by the concept' expressed by the combining root: **paraplegic, Gothic, vocalic.**
4. 'Something or someone effecting a specified result': **antispasmodic, diuretic, soporific.** Compare -ics.

385 **-syllabic** An adjective and an adjective-forming word-final element, derived from Greek syllab(ē) '-syllable' and **-ic¹**, used in combinations meaning 'having a number of syllables' specified by the combining

root: **decasyllabic, monosyllabic, parisyllabic.** Related forms: **-syllable, -syllabical** *(archaic)*, **-syllabically, -syllabicate, -syllabication, -syllabify, -syllabification.**

386 **-phobic** An adjective and an adjective-forming word-final element, derived from Greek *phob(os)* 'fear' and **-ic¹**, used in two main related senses:

　　1. 'Exhibiting or possessing an aversion for or fear of' something specified by the combining root: **Anglophobic, zoophobic, necrophobic.**

　　2. In chemical terminology, 'referring to the absence of a strong affinity' for the substance named by the combining root: **chromophobic, gentianophobic, osmiophobic.** Also, **-phobous.** Related forms: **-phobe, -phobia, -phobiac, -phobism, -phobist.**

387 **-microbic** An adjective, derived from English **microbe** and **-ic¹**, also used as an adjective-forming word-final element with the meaning 'referring to or consisting of microbes, i.e., small living organisms, especially ones that can cause disease,' as qualified by the combining root: **antimicrobic, polymicrobic, monomicrobic.** Also, **-microbial, -microbian.**

388 **-scorbic** An adjective-forming word-final element, derived from Latin *scorb(ūtus)* 'scurvy' and **-ic¹**, used in medical terminology to mean 'of or referring to the prevention or treatment of scurvy' as specified by the combining root: **ascorbic, antiscorbic, glucoascorbic.** Related forms: **-scorbutic, -scorbutical, -scorbutically.**

389 **-pubic** An adjective and an adjective-forming word-final element, derived from Latin *pūb(ēs)*, *pūb(is)* 'adult (i.e. sexually mature) males, genitalia' and **-ic¹**, used in medical terminology to mean 'of, referring, or relating to the pubis, i.e., frontal part of the pelvis,' as specified by the combining root: **suprapubic, subpubic, epipubic.**

390 **-thoracic** An adjective and an adjective-forming word-final element, derived from Greek *thōrax*, *thōrak-* 'armored breast-plate; that which is protected by an armored breast-plate, i.e., the chest' and **-ic¹**, used in medical terminology in the sense of 'of, referring, or relating to the chest' as specified by the combining root: **infrathoracic, scapulothoracic, subthoracic.** Also, **-thoracical** *(archaic)*.

391 **-pedic¹** An adjective-forming word-final element, derived from Latin *pes*, *ped-* 'foot' and **-ic¹**, used in combinations meaning 'referring or pertaining to the foot or feet' as specified by the combining root:

velocepedic, talipedic. Also, -pedal. Related forms: -ped, -pede, -pedia[1].

392   -pedic[2]   An adjective-forming word-final element, derived from Greek *pais, paid-* 'child, youth' and -ic[1], used in two senses:
1. 'Of or pertaining to children or their treatment': **orthopedic, gymnopedic.**
2. 'Of or pertaining to the education of children, or education in general': **encyclopedic, pharmacopedic.** Also, -paedic. Related forms: -pedia[2], -pedically, -pedics.

393   -odic[1]   An adjective-forming word-final element, derived from Greek *(h)od(os)* 'road, path, way' (cf. -ode[2]) and -ic[1], used in two related senses:
1. 'Of or referring to a particular way or path' specified by the combining root: **interelectrodic, exodic, kinesodic.**
2. 'Of or referring to an electrode, i.e. an electrical pathway': **interelectrodic, anodic, cathodic.** Related form: -odically.

394   -odic[2]   An adjective-forming word-final element, derived from Greek *ōid(ē)* 'song' (cf. -ode[1]) and -ic[1], used in the sense of 'of or referring to a particular kind of song or poem' specified by the combining root: **threnodic, palinodic, rhapsodic.** Related form: -odically.

395   -periodic   An adjective and an adjective-forming word-final element, derived from Greek *period(os)* 'way around, portion of time' (cf. Greek *(h)od(os)* 'way, road') and -ic[1], used in combinations in the sense of 'referring or relating to an interval or intervals of time' specified by the combining root: **unperiodic, photoperiodic, thermoperiodic.** Related forms: -period, -periodically, -periodicity.

396   -spasmodic   An adjective and an adjective-forming word-final element, derived from Greek *spasmōd(ēs)* 'convulsive, spasmlike' (from *spasm(a)* 'convulsion' and *-oeid(ēs)* '-like') and -ic[1], used in medical terminology in the sense of 'of, pertaining, or referring to a convulsion' as specified by the combining root: **antispasmodic, angiospasmodic, postspasmodic.** Also, -spasmodical. Related forms: -spasm, -spastic, -spasmodically.

397   -(r)rheic   An adjective-forming word-final element, derived through Latin from Greek *rhe(in)* 'to flow' and -ic[1], used chiefly in medical terminology in the sense of 'pertaining to a fluid discharge' of a sort specified by the combining root: **menorrheic, seborrheic, gonorrheic.**

Also, -(r)rhoeic, -(r)rheal, -(r)rhetic. Related forms: -(r)rhea, -(r)rhoea, -(r)rhoeica.

398 **-oleic** An adjective-forming word-final element, derived from Latin *ole(um)* 'oil' (cf. **-ole²**) and **-ic¹**, used in two related senses:
   1. 'Of or referring to materials derived from or involving oil' as specified by the combining root: **ricinoleic, linoleic, palmitoleic**.
   2. 'Of or referring to the products of oleic acid' as specified by the combining root: **gadoleic, sulfoleic, trioleic**.

399 **-poeic** An adjective-forming word-final element, derived from Greek *poi(ein)* 'to make, produce, create' and **-ic¹**, used in the sense of 'of, relating, or referring to the production or creation of' that which is named by the combining root: **mythopoeic, melopoeic, onomatopoeic**. Also, **-poetic, -poietic**. Related forms: **-poeia, -peia, -poetical, -poietical, -poetically, -poietically, -poesis, -poiesis**.

400 **-fic** An adjective-forming word-final element, derived from Latin *-fic(are)*, a combining form of the verb *fac(ere)* 'to do, make,' used to describe 'a kind of causation or production' specified by the preceding root, very often a verb ending in *-(i)fy* (q.v.): **acidific, pacific, odorific**. (Note that this suffix is preceded by the joining vowel *-i-* in combination.) Related forms: **-fice, -ficial, -ficient, -ficate, -fication, -ficative, -fy**.

401 **-scientific** An adjective and an adjective-forming word-final element, derived from Latin *sciens, scient-* (the present participle of the verb *scīre* 'to know') and *-ific* (see **-fic**), used in the sense of 'pertaining to a science' (i.e. a systematic body or method of knowledge) as specified by the combining root: **infrascientific, antiscientific, pseudoscientific**. Related forms: **-scient, -science, -scientifical, -scientifically**.

402 **-(r)rhagic** An adjective-forming word-final element, derived from Greek *rhag(as)* 'a break, tear, bursting' (cf. the verb *rhēx(ai)* 'to burst, break, tear') and **-ic¹**, used in medical terminology in the sense of 'of, pertaining, or referring to a kind or condition of excessive fluid discharge' specified by the combining root: **hemorrhagic, blennorrhagic, menorrhagic**. Related forms: **-(r)rhage, -(r)rhagia, -(r)rhexis**.

403 **-pelagic** An adjective and an adjective-forming word-final element, derived from Greek *pelag(os)* 'sea' and **-ic¹**, used in borrowings 'relating to the open sea' as specified by the combining root: **archipelagic, bathypelagic, myctipelagic**.

404 **-plegic** A word-final element, derived from scientific Greek *pleg(ia)* 'paralysis' (v. **-plegia**) and **-ic**[1] (in adjectives) or **-ic**[2] (in nouns), used in its etymological sense as qualified by the combining root:
1. In adjectives, 'of or pertaining to a specific paralysis': **hemiplegic, cephaloplegic, polyplegic.**
2. In nouns, 'a sufferer from a specific paralysis': **paraplegic, quadriplegic, monoplegic.** Related forms: **-plegia, -plegy, -plexia, -plexy, -plexic, -plectic.**

405 **-algic** An adjective-forming word-final element, derived from Greek *alg(os)* 'pain' and **-ic**[1], used in the sense of 'of, pertaining, referring, or related to pain' of a sort or in a location specified by the combining root: **neuralgic, otalgic, arthralgic.** Related forms: **-algia, -algy; -algias** *(plural)*.

406 **-logic** A noun, derived from the substantive use of the Greek adjective *logik(os)* 'pertaining to speech, discourse, reasoning' from *log(os)* 'word, speech, discourse' and **-ic**[1], also used as an adjective-forming word-final element in several related senses, each as specified by the combining root:
1. 'Pertaining to expression, either oral or written': **dialogic, phraseologic, tautologic.**
2. 'Pertaining to a collected body of theory, practice, science, or doctrine': **theologic, ecologic, etymologic.**
3. 'Pertaining to a treatise, written discourse, or the work on which it is based': **genealogic, pharmacologic, typologic.** Compare **-logetic, -logistic.** Related forms: **-logy, -logia, -logue, -log, -logical, -logically, -logism, -logist, -logian, -logician.**

407 **-ergic** An adjective-forming word-final element, derived from Greek *erg(on)* 'work' and **-ic**[1], used in two related senses:
1. 'Work': **synergic, monergic, neurergic.**
2. 'An effect of activity': **allergic, pathergic, telergic.** Also, **-ergetic.** Related forms: **-ergetical, -ergetically, -ergy; -ergies** *(plural)*.

408 **-urgic** An adjective-forming word-final element, derived through Latin from Greek *-ourg-*, a combining form of *erg(on)* 'work,' and **-ic**[1], used in two closely related senses:
1. 'Of or referring to work involving an agent or agents' specified by the combining root: **theurgic, thaumaturgic, neururgic.**
2. 'Of or referring to a technique of work or to a material worked with' as specified by the combining root: **dramaturgic, metallurgic, chemurgic.** Related forms: **-urgy, -urgia, -urgical, -urgically, -urgist, -urge.**

409 -machic   An adjective-forming word-final element, derived from Greek *mach(ē)* 'battle, fight' and -ic[1], used in combinations meaning 'of or pertaining to a type of fight or conflict' named by the combining root: **logomachic, tauromachic, monarchomachic.** Also, **-machical.** Related forms: **-mach, -machy, -machist; -machies** *(plural).*

410 -stichic   An adjective and an adjective-forming word-final element, derived from Greek *stix(os)* 'a row, line, line of verse' (from the verb *steix(ein)* 'to go in order, in a line'), used in combinations meaning 'of, pertaining, relating, or referring to verse having a number of lines' specified by the combining root: **tetrastichic, hexastichic, tristichic.** Related forms: **-stich, -stichically.**

411 -psychic   An adjective and an adjective-forming word-final element, derived from Greek *psych(ē)* 'mind, spirit' and -ic[1], used in a number of related senses:

1. In medical terminology, 'of, pertaining, or relating to the relation between mind and body' as specified by the combining root: **endopsychic, somatopsychic, neuropsychic.**
2. In the terminology of mysticism and parapsychology, 'of or pertaining to relations with a realm beyond the physical': **metapsychic, panpsychic, nonpsychic.** Related forms: **-psyche, -psychist, -psychical, -psychically.**

412 -graphic   An adjective and an adjective-forming word-final element, derived from Greek *graph(ein)* 'to write' and -ic[1], used in two related senses:

1. 'Concerning material written, printed, or otherwise transmitted in a manner' specified by the combining root: **mimeographic, radiographic, photographic.**
2. 'Concerning written or printed material in a field or on a topic' specified by the combining root: **demographic, hagiographic, lexicographic.** Also, **-graphical.** Related forms: **-graph, -grapher, -graphist, -graphy, -graphous, -graphically.**

413 -taphic   A word-final element, derived from Greek *taph(ē)* 'burial' and -ic[1], used in three English adjectives to describe 'a feature or condition related to burial': **epitaphic, bibliotaphic, cenotaphic.** Related forms: **-taph; -taphs** *(plural).*

414 -trophic   An adjective and an adjective-forming word-final element derived from Greek *troph(os)* 'that which feeds, food, nourishment' (from the verb *treph(ein)* 'to feed') and -ic[1], used in medical terminology in the sense of 'of, pertaining, or referring to a type of nutrition or nutritional requirement' specified by the combining root: **glycotrophic, hypertrophic, chemotrophic.** Also, **-trophous.** Related forms: **-troph, -trophy, -trophically.**

415   **-sophic**   An adjective-forming word-final element, derived from Greek *soph(os)* 'a wise, clever, skilled person' and **-ic¹**, used in a number of borrowings, all with the sense of 'wise in, knowledgeable about' that which is specified by the combining root: **theosophic, pansophic, physiosophic.** Related forms: **-soph, -sophist, -sopher, -sophical, -sophically, -sophy.**

416   **-morphic**   An adjective-forming word-final element, derived from Greek *morph(ē)* 'form, shape' and **-ic¹**, used in combinations meaning 'possessing or referring to the form or shape' specified by the combining root: **anthropomorphic, geomorphic, ichthyomorphic.** Also, **-morphous.** Related forms: **-morph, -morphia, -morphy, -morpha, -morphae, -morphi, -morphically, -morphously, -morphism, -morphosis.**

417   **-glyphic**   An adjective and an adjective-forming word-final element, derived from Greek *glyph(ein)* 'to carve' and **-ic¹**, used in combinations with two related meanings, each particularized by the combining root:
    1.   'Concerning a given method of carving, sculpture, or (early) writing': **anaglyphic, petroglyphic, lithoglyphic.**
    2.   'Concerning the product(s) of carving, sculpture, or (early) writing': **hieroglyphic, hermoglyphic, triglyphic.** Related forms: **-glyph; -glyphs** *(plural).*

418   **-bathic**   An adjective-forming word-final element, derived from Greek *bath(os)* 'depth' and **ic¹**, used in technical terminology to denote 'of or pertaining to a depth' as specified by the combining root: **isobathic, eurybathic, stenobathic.** Related forms: **-bath; -baths** *(plural).*

419   **-pathic**   An adjective-forming word-final element, derived from Greek *path(ein)* 'to suffer, be sensitive to' and **ic¹**, used in a variety of related senses:
    1.   'Referring or pertaining to an illness or affected part of the body' specified by the combining root: **psychopathic, cardiopathic, dermatopathic.**
    2.   'Referring or pertaining to feelings or emotions' as specified by the combining root: **empathic, sympathic, antipathic.**
    3.   'Referring or pertaining to a form or system of treatment' specified by the combining root: **osteopathic, allopathic, naturo-pathic.**
    4.   'Referring or pertaining to love or attraction (generally excessive)

for something' specified by the combining root: **anthropopathic, erotopathic, idiopathic.** Compare **-pathetic.** Related forms: **-path, -pathia, -pathy, -pathology.**

420 **-ornithic** An adjective and an adjective-forming word-final element, derived from Greek *ornis, ornith-* 'bird' and **-ic**[1], used in the sense of 'referring or pertaining to a bird or birds' of the sort specified by the combining root: **stereornithic, pholornithic, dinornithic.** Related forms: **-ornithoid, -ornithes.**

421 **-mythic** An adjective and an adjective-forming word-final element, derived from Greek *myth(os)* 'a telling, a story, a legend' and the general adjective-forming suffix **-ic**[1], used in the sense of 'of, referring, or relating to legends, myths, their nature, or their telling' as specified by the combining root: **stichomythic, polymythic, antimythic.** Related forms: **-myth, -mythical, -mythically.**

422 **-vocalic** An adjective and an adjective-forming word-final element, derived from Latin *vōcāl(is)* 'sounding, verbal, vocal' (cf. *vōx, vōc-* 'voice, sound') and **-ic**[1], used in the specialized sense of 'of or referring to a vowel or vowels' as specified by the combining root: **prevocalic, semivocalic, intervocalic.** Related form: **-vocalically.**

423 **-cephalic** An adjective and a frequently used adjective-forming word-final element, derived from Greek *kephal(ē)* 'head' and **-ic**[1], used in medical terminology to mean 'of, referring, or relating to the head' of a sort or with reference to a location specified by the combining root: **platycephalic, postcephalic, tapinocephalic.** Related forms: **-cephalism, -cephaly, -cephalia.**

424 **-cyclic** An adjective, derived from Greek *kykl(os)* 'circle, ring, wheel' and **-ic**[1], also used as an adjective-forming word-final element in general related senses:
1. 'Referring, relating, or belonging to a cycle' of the type denoted by the combining root: **acyclic, epicyclic, ontocyclic.**
2. 'Referring to a wheel or wheels': **bicyclic, tricyclic, hydrocyclic.**
3. In botany, 'referring to plant leaves or flowers arranged in a whorl': **dicyclic, hemicyclic, eucyclic.**
4. 'Involving a circle': **pericyclic, encyclic, geocyclic.**
5. In chemistry, 'referring, relating, or belonging to a ring of atoms': **carbocyclic, acyclic, azocyclic.** Related forms: **-cycle, -cyclical, -cyclically; -cycles** *(plural).*

425 **-angelic** An adjective and an adjective-forming word-final element,

derived through Latin from Greek *angel(os)* 'messenger' and -ic[1], used in ecclesiastical terminology in the specialized sense of 'of, referring or relating to, or resembling an angel' (i.e., a heavenly being in Christian theology, originally, 'messenger of God'): **archangelic, pseudoangelic, overangelic.** Also, **-angelical.** Related form: **-angelically.**

426 **-telic** An adjective and an adjective-forming word-final element, derived from Greek *tel(os)* 'end' and -ic[1], used in the sense of 'referring to an end or purpose' of a sort specified by the combining root: **uricotelic, autotelic, hypertelic.** Also, **-telical.** Related form: **-telically.**

427 **-philic** An adjective-forming word-final element, derived from Greek *phil(ein)* 'to love, have an affinity for' and -ic[1], used chiefly in scientific terminology in the sense of 'having an affinity, especially an abnormal affinity for' that which is specified by the combining root: **hemophilic, acrophilic, bibliophilic.** Also, **-philous.** Related forms: **-phil, -phile, -philia, -phily, -philiac, -philist, -philism, -philite.**

428 **-metallic** An adjective and an adjective-forming word-final element, derived from Greek *metall(on)* 'cave, mine, that which is found in a mine: minerals, metals' and -ic[1], used in combinations meaning 'referring or relating to, or resembling metal': **bimetallic, paleo-metallic, nonmetallic.** Related form: **-metallically.**

429 **-bolic** A word-final element, derived from Greek *ball(ein)* 'to throw;' English adjectival combinations formed from it make use of permutations of this basic meaning:
1. 'Referring to something thrown down': **catabolic.**
2. 'Referring to something thrown out': **ecbolic.**
3. 'Referring to something thrown in': **embolic.**
4. 'Referring to something thrown or set alongside': **parabolic.**
5. 'Referring to something thrown on': **epibolic.**
6. 'Referring to something thrown together': **symbolic.** Related forms: **-bola, -bole, -boly, -bolism, -bolite.**

430 **-catholic** An adjective and an adjective-forming word-final element, derived from Greek *katholik(os)* 'universal, unchanging,' used in ecclesiastical terminology in the sense of 'of, relating, or referring to the Church of Rome or its members,' as specified by the combining root: **acatholic, uncatholic, misocatholic.** Related form: **-catholicity.**

431 **-hydraulic** An adjective and an adjective-forming word-final element, derived from Greek *hydor, hydat-* (combining form *hydr-*) 'water,'

aul(os) 'pipe,' and -ic¹, with the meaning 'referring to operations effected, in whole or in part, by moving water or some other liquid (as through a pipe)': **electrohydraulic, biohydraulic, unhydraulic.** Compare **-hydria.** Related forms: **-hydraulics, -hydraulically.**

432   **-spondylic**   An adjective and an adjective-forming word-final element, derived from Greek *spondyl(os)* 'vertebra' and -ic¹, used in medical terminology in combinations meaning 'of, pertaining, or referring to the vertebrae' of a sort or with reference to a location named by the combining root: **perispondylic, diplospondylic, asterospondylic.**

433   **-ceramic**   An adjective, derived from Greek *keram(os)* 'potter's clay' and -ic¹, also used as an adjective-forming word-final element 'referring to pottery products or processes in the manufacture of pottery': **hydroceramic, odontoceramic** *(obs.)*, **photoceramic.** Related form: **-ceramics.**

434   **-demic**   An adjective-forming word-final element, derived from Greek *dēm(os)* 'settlement, populace' and -ic¹, used in its etymological sense—sometimes substantively—as qualified by the combining root:
1.   In medicine, 'of or relating to disease in a region specified by the combining root': **pandemic, epidemic, phytodemic.**
2.   'Of or relating to a region specified by the combining root': **zoanthodemic, polydemic, endemic.** Related forms: **-deme, -demically.**

435   **-academic**   An adjective and a word-final element, derived through French and Latin from *Akadēm(eia)* 'the school of Plato' and used in forming adjectives 'referring or relating to scholastic matters or to schools of literature, art, or music,' according to context: **unacademic, interacademic, pseudoacademic.** Also, **-academical.** Related form: **-academically.**

436   **-chemic**   An adjective derived from Latin *chimic(us)* 'alchemist,'—itself derived from Arabic *al* 'the' and *kimiya* 'art of transmutation,' possibly from Greek *chemia* 'Egypt'—and also used as an adjective-forming word-final element 'referring or relating to chemistry or chemical theory, usu. modern' as designated by the combining root: **metachemic, alchemic, biochemic.** The more frequently used word ending is *-chemical.* Related forms: **-chemical, -chemically, -chemist, -chemistry, -chemy.**

437   **-semic**   An adjective-forming word-final element, derived from Greek *sēm(ē)* 'sign, mark' and, by extension, 'unit of measurement,' used in

prosodic terminology in the sense of 'referring to or describing specified numbers of prosodic units in a verse': **decasemic, tetrasemic, hexasemic.** Related form: **-seme.**

438 **-(r)rhythmic** An adjective and an adjective-forming word-final element derived from Greek *rhythmik(os)* 'of or related to regular motion or pulsation,' used in combinations in its etymological sense as qualified by the combining root: **arrhythmic, monorhythmic, biorhythmic.** Related forms: **-(r)rhythm, -(r)rhythmia, -(r)rhythmical, -(r)rhythmically, -(r)rhythmics.**

439 **-mimic** A noun and a denominative verb, derived from the Greek adjective *mimile(os)* 'concerning imitation or imitators' (cf. the verb *mimēsthai* 'to imitate'), also used as an adjective-forming word-final element in combinations meaning 'referring or relating to imitation' of that which is specified by the combining root: **pantomimic, zoomimic, pathomimic.** Also, **-mimical.** Related forms: **-mime, -mimia, -mimesis, -mimetic, -mimically; -mimes, -mimeses** *(plurals).*

440 **-ophthalmic** An adjective and an adjective-forming word-final element, derived from Greek *ophthalm(os)* 'eye' and **-ic**[1], used in the sense of 'referring or relating to, near, or for the eye': **microphthalmic, exophthalmic, lagophthalmic.** Related forms: **-ophthalmos, -ophthalmia; -ophthalmias** *(plural).*

441 **-grammic** An adjective-forming word-final element, derived from Greek *gram(ma), gram(mat-)* 'that which is written (literally engraved), a letter or line of a drawing' and **-ic**[1], used to mean 'referring to a process or means of writing or drawing' specified by the combining root: **telegrammic, ideogrammic, chronogrammic.** Also, **-grammatic.** Compare **-graphic.** Related forms: **-gram, -gramme, -grammical, -grammatical, -grammically, -grammatically.**

442 **-comic** An adjective and an adjective-forming word-final element, derived from Greek *kōm(os)* 'festival' and **-ic**[1], used in the specialized sense of 'referring or relating to comedy' as specified by the combining root: **tragicomic, heroicomic, seriocomic.** Related forms: **-comical, -comically.**

443 **-gnomic** An adjective and also an adjective-forming word-final element, derived from Greek *gnōm(ē)* 'means of knowing' (cf. Greek *gnōnai* 'to know, perceive') and **-ic**[1], used in two related senses:

I. 'Referring to characteristic means of knowing' the subject denoted by the combining root: **toxignomic, pathognomic, pyrognomic.**

2. 'Referring or related to the interpretation' of the subject denoted by the combining root: **physiognomic, craniognomic** *(arch.)*, **chirognomic.** Related forms: **-gnomical, -gnomically, -gnomy, -gnomonic, -gnosia, -gnosis, -gnostic.**

444 **-economic** An adjective and an adjective-forming word-final element, derived from Greek *oikonomik(os)* 'frugal, skilled in managing a household' (from *oikos* 'house', *nomos* '**-nome**,' and **-ic¹**), used in combinations with the sense of 'referring or relating to finances and their management': **noneconomic, uneconomic, socioeconomic.** Also, **-economical.** Related forms: **-economically, -economics.**

445 **-dromic** An adjective, derived from Greek *drom(os)* 'race course' (from Greek *dramein* 'to run') and **-ic¹**, also used as an adjective-forming word-final element in several related senses:

1. 'Referring to, related to, or in the form of a race course' of the sort specified by the combining root: **hippodromic, aerodromic, monodromic.**

2. 'Referring to running in the direction or on the course' specified by the combining root: **palindromic, paradromic, exodromic.** Also, **-dromical, -dromous.** Related forms: **-drome; -dromes** *(plural).*

446 **-chromic** An adjective and an adjective-forming word-final element, derived from Greek *chrōm(a)*, *chrōm(at-)* 'color' and **-ic¹**; as a word ending it has several meanings that do not occur with the word alone. Used in forming adjectives, it means:

1. 'Referring or relating to color': **achromic, dichromic, poly-chromic.**

2. In medical terminology, 'referring to the specified number of colors seen by the eye': **dichromic, pentachromic, heptachromic.** Also, **-chromatic.**

3. In medical terminology, 'referring to a specified color of the blood to indicate the hemoglobin content': **hypochromic, normochromic.**

4. In medical terminology, 'referring to the staining ability of bacteria and tissues': **metachromic, hyperchromic, polychromic.** Also, **-chromatic.**

5. In medical terminology, 'referring to a specified skin color as indicative of disease': **xantochromic, pleiochromic, heterochromic.**

447 **-tomic** A word-final element, derived from Greek *tom(os)*, *tom(ē)*, *tom(on)* 'cut, segmented' (from the verb *temn(ein)* 'to cut') and -ic¹, used to form adjectives from nouns ending in -tomy and -tome with the sense of 'referring or related to incisions or sections of tissue' as specified by the combining root: **anatomic, microtomic, tonsillectomic.** Also, **-tomical.** Related forms: **-tomy, -tome, -tomist, -tomize, -tomous, -tomical, -tomically; -tomies** *(plural).*

448 **-atomic** An adjective and an adjective-forming word-final element, derived from Greek *atom(os), atom(ē), atom(on)* 'indivisible' (from *a*- 'un-, not' and *tom(os), tom(ē), tom(on)* 'cut, segmented,' from the verb *temn(ein)* 'to cut') and -ic¹, used in the specialized sense of 'of or referring to the atom (formerly considered to be the smallest component of matter) or to the number of atoms in a molecule': **subatomic, diatomic, triatomic.** Also, **-atomical.** Related form: **-atomically.**

449 **-pharmic** An adjective-forming word-final element, derived from Greek *pharm(akon)* 'drug, philtre, spice, remedy' and -ic¹, used in the sense of 'referring or related to drugs and medicinal remedies' as specified by the combining root: **antipharmic, alexipharmic, polypharmic.**

450 **-dermic** An adjective, derived from Greek *derm(a), derm(at-)* 'skin' and -ic¹, also used as an adjective-forming word-final element in several related senses:
   1. 'Referring or related to the skin' as designated by the combining root: **intradermic, hypodermic, epidermic.**
   2. 'Referring or related to the variety of skin' designated by the combining root: **pachydermic, sarcodermic, leptodermic.**
   3. 'Referring or related to skin ailments' named by the combining root: **leukodermic, xerodermic, toxicodermic.**
   4. 'Referring or related to creatures distinguished taxonomically by skin types': **Mycodermic, Echinodermic, Sclerodermic.**
   5. 'Referring or related to a cell division process' denoted by the combining root: **blastodermic, endodermic, ectodermic.** Also, **-dermal, -dermatic, -dermatous.** Related forms: **-derma, -derm, -dermis, -dermoid, -dermatoid.**

451 **-spermic** An adjective and an adjective-forming word-final element, derived from Greek *sperm(a), sperm(at-)* 'germ, seed, that which is sown' (from the verb *speir(ein)* 'to sow seed' and the noun-forming suffix *-ma*) and -ic¹, used in two related senses, each as specified by the combining root:
   1. 'Referring to the involvement of specified types or quantities of

seeds': **epispermic, angiospermic, aspermic.** Also, **-spermal, -spermous.**

2. 'Referring to the product of specified quantities of spermatozoa': **polyspermic, trispermic, monospermic.** Compare **-sperm.** Related form: **-spermy.**

452 **-seismic** An adjective and an adjective-forming word-final element, derived from Greek *seism(os)* 'a shaking, an earthquake' (cf. *sei(ein)* 'to shake') and -ic[1], used in combinations meaning 'referring or related to earthquakes' according to the sense of the combining root: **microseismic, bradyseismic, megaseismic.** Also, **-seismal, -seismical.** Related forms: **-seism, -seismically; -seisms** *(plural).*

453 **-cosmic** An adjective, derived from Greek *kosm(os)* 'world' and -ic[1], also used as an adjective-forming word-final element, in several related senses:
1. 'Referring to the entire universe, esp. as an orderly creation': **intracosmic, intercosmic, pancosmic.**
2. 'Referring to the material world within the solar system': **microcosmic, hypercosmic, acosmic.**
3. 'Referring to the characteristics of the cosmos, either as universe or solar system': **paleocosmic, precosmic, neocosmics.** Also, **-cosmical.** Related forms: **-cosm, -cosmically.**

454 **-volcanic** An adjective and an adjective-forming word-final element, derived through Italian and French from Latin *Volcān(us)* 'Vulcan, the god of fire' and -ic[1], used in two related senses:
1. 'Referring or relating to, characterized by, or affected by volcanoes' as denoted by the combining root: **nonvolcanic, paleovolcanic, neovolcanic.**
2. 'Resembling or characteristic of a volcano, especially concerning violence': **semivolcanic, fluviovolcanic, unvolcanic.** Related form: **-volcanically.**

455 **-organic** An adjective and an adjective-forming word-final element, derived from Greek *organik(os)* 'instrumental, referring to tools, instruments' (cf. *organon* 'tool, instrument, that which works' and *ergon* 'work'), used in several related extended senses:
1. 'Referring or related to the internal organs of the body': **psychorganic, enorganic, nonorganic.**
2. In chemistry, 'related or pertaining to, or containing carbon compounds': **inorganic, metallorganic, anorganic.**
3. 'Like an organism': **pseudorganic, cosmorganic, superorganic.** Related forms: **-organical** *(archaic)*, **-organically.**

456 **-phanic**   An adjective-forming word-final element, derived from Greek *phain(ein)* 'to appear, show (through), shine (through)' and -ic[1], used in a number of senses:

1. In chemistry, 'referring to or containing a substance with an appearance or form' specified by the combining root: **chrysophanic, tryptophanic, glaucophanic.**

2. 'Referring to a translucence' of a sort specified by the combining root: **diaphanic, lithophanic, idiophanic.** (The more common suffix is -phanous.)

3. 'Referring to a substance or substances appearing in' the substance named by the combining root in a single term: **urophanic.**

4. 'Referring to an appearance or manifestation' denoted by the combining root: **theophanic, allophanic, epiphanic.** Related forms: -phan, -phane, -phany.

457 **-manic**   An adjective, derived from Greek *manik(os)* 'of, concerning, or relating to madness' from *man(ia)* 'madness' and -ic[1], used as an adjective-forming word-final element in two related senses, each as specified by the combining root:

1. 'Referring to a specified psychosis': **poriomanic, melomanic, choromanic.**

2. 'Referring to mental states like mania': **submanic, hyomanic, melomanic.** Related forms: -mania, -mane, -maniac, -manically, -maniacally.

458 **-tetanic**   An adjective and an adjective-forming word-final element, derived from Greek *tetan(os)* 'strain, tension' (from *tein(ein)* 'to stretch') and -ic[1], used in medical terminology in the sense of 'referring or relating to, or producing tetanus or tetany' (both conditions being characterized by severe muscle contractions): **subtetanic, antitetanic, posttetanic.** Related form: -tetanically.

459 **-galvanic**   An adjective and an adjective-forming word-final element, derived from Italian *galvanic(o)*, *galvanic(a)* (after Luigi Galvani) through French, used in the sense of 'referring or relating to, resulting from, or producing a direct electrical current': **psychogalvanic, hydrogalvanic** *(archaic)*, **photogalvanic.** Related forms: -galvanically, -galvanize.

460 **-genic**   An adjective-forming word-final element, derived from Greek *gen(ea)* 'birth, growth, production' and -ic[1], and used in scientific, medical, and popular terminology in several related senses:

1. 'Causing, forming, producing' that which is named by the combining root: **hallucinogenic, carcinogenic, asthmagenic.**
2. 'Produced by or formed from' the agent or substance named by the combining root: **formagenic, nephrogenic, coccigenic.**
3. 'Referring or relating to a gene': **trigenic, polygenic, intragenic.**
4. 'Referring to suitablity for producing or reproduction by a medium' named by the combining root: **photogenic, radiogenic, telegenic.** Also, **-genous, -geneous, -genetic.** Compare **-gonic².** Related forms: **-gen, -gene, -genically, -genate, -genation, -genist, -genism, -genite, -geny.**

461 **-phrenic**   An adjective and an adjective-forming word-final element, derived from Greek *phrēn* 'midriff, diaphragm, seat of the intellect and emotions' and **-ic¹,** used in two of its etymological senses:
  1. 'Referring to the diaphragm or adjacent regions of the body' as specified by the combining root: **gastrophrenic, splenophrenic, pericardiophrenic.**
  2. 'Referring to or characteristic of a disorder of the mind' specified by the combining root: **schizophrenic, hebephrenic, cataphrenic.** Related forms: **-phrenia, -phrenically.**

462 **-technic**   An adjective and a noun, derived from Greek *techn(ē)* 'art, craft, skill' and **-ic¹/-ic²,** used as a word-final element:
  1. In adjectives, with the meaning 'of or referring to the practical art or arts' named by the combining root: **pantechnic, philotechnic, polytechnic.**
  2. In adjectives, with the meaning 'of or referring to the technical procedures, methods, or mechanics' of the area named by the combining root: **microtechnic, pyrotechnic, zootechnic.** Also, **-technical.**
  3. In nouns, as a synonym for **-technique: microtechnic, machino-technic, iatrotechnic.** Compare **-technics.** Related forms: **-technique, -technology, -technically.**

463 **-splanchnic**   An adjective and an adjective-forming word-final element, derived from Greek *splanchna* 'viscera, entrails' and **-ic¹,** used in medical terminology in its etymological sense, as qualified by the combining root: **perisplanchnic, megalosplanchnic, microsplanchnic.**

464 **-ethnic**   An adjective and an adjective-forming word-final element, derived from Greek *ethn(os)* 'a people, nation, race' and **ic¹,** used in the sense of 'referring or relating to a racial, cultural, or linguistic group' specified by the combining root: **biethnic, paleoethnic, holethnic.** Also, **-ethnical.** Related form: **-ethnically.**

465 **-morainic** An adjective and an adjective-forming word-final element, derived from French *morain(e)* 'a ridge of glacial rubble' and **-ic**[1], used in its etymological sense, as qualified by the combining root: **intramorainic, nonmorainic, extramorainal.** Also, **-morainal** *(rare).*

466 **-clinic** An adjective-forming word-final element, derived from Greek *klin(ē)* 'bed' (itself derived from Greek *klin(ein)* 'to lean, incline') and **-ic**[1], and used in both its strictly etymological sense of 'relating to a bed (specifically a sick bed)' and its more general meaning of 'leaning, inclining':

   1. 'Possessing traits and characteristics inherited from' the source denoted by the combining root: **matroclinic, patroclinic, goneoclinic.** Also, **-clinous.**

   2. In botanical terminology, 'referring to the possession of stamens and pistils by the same plant or flower or two separate flowers or plants (as in holly)': **monoclinic, diclinic, heteroclinic.** Also, **-clinous.**

   3. 'Referring to places set aside for medical treatment,' as specified by the combining root: **psychoclinic, policlinic, polyclinic.** Related forms: (meanings 1 and 2) **-cliny, -clinism; -clinies, -clinisms** *(plurals)*; (meaning 3) **-clinical, -clinically.**

467 **-conic** An adjective, derived through Latin from Greek *kon(os)* 'cone' and **-ic**[1], also used as a word-final adjective-forming element in its etymological sense:

   1. 'Referring to a cone or cones': **biconic, circumconic, obconic.**

   2. 'Resembling a cone': **breviconic, cephaloconic, euconic.** Also, **-conical.** Related forms: **-cone, -conid, -conical, -conically.**

468 **-gonic**[1] An adjective-forming word-final element, derived from Greek *gōn(ia)* 'angle' and **-ic**[1], used in the terminology of geometry to mean 'referring to a type or number of angle or angles' as denoted by the combining root: **agonic, diagonic, polygonic.** Also, **-gonal.** Related forms: **-gon; -gons** *(plural).*

469 **-gonic**[2] An adjective-forming word-final element, derived from Greek *gon(ē)* 'that which is born' (cf. Greek *genea* 'birth') and **-ic**[1], used in two related senses, each particularized by the combining root:

   1. 'Referring to agents, processes, or results of generation or reproduction, including the sexual': **theogonic, sporogonic, mythogonic.**

   2. 'Referring to theories of formation': **geogonic, cosmogonic, glottogonic.** Related forms: **-gen, -genic, -geny, -gony.**

470   **-phonic**   An adjective and also an adjective-forming word-final element, derived from Greek *phōn(ē)* 'sound' and **-ic**[1], used in a variety of related senses, each specified by the combining root:

1. 'Referring to or characterizing sound': **cacophonic, megaphonic, euphonic.**
2. 'Referring to or describing musical sound': **symphonic, polyphonic, monophonic.**
3. 'Referring to the sound produced by musical instruments and organ stops whose names end in *-phone*': **xylophonic, melophonic, keraunophonic.**
4. 'Pertaining to the sound of the human voice': **hypophonic, baryphonic, leptophonic.**
5. In medical terminology, 'referring to sounds made in a specified part of the body': **bronchiophonic, organophonic, sphygmophonic.**
6. 'Pertaining to the sounds of speech': **aphonic, homophonic, allophonic.** Related forms: **-phone, -phonia, -phony, -phonetic, -phonous, -phonically, -phonetically, -phonious.**

471   **-colonic**   An adjective and an adjective-forming word-final element, derived from **-colon** and **-ic**[1], used in medical terminology in combinations meaning 'referring, relating, or pertaining to the colon', (i.e., the part of the large intestine between the cecum and rectum) as characterized or located by the combining root: **pericolonic, ileocolonic, vesicocolonic.**

472   **-demonic**   An adjective, and also an adjective-forming word-final element, derived from Greek *daimōn* 'god, evil deity, demon' and **-ic**[1], used in two related senses:

1. 'Caused or inspired by a demon; demoniacal': **polydemonic, pandemonic, cacodemonic.**
2. 'Referring or relating to or having the traits of a demon': **superdemonic, eudaemonic, agathodaemonic.** Also, **-daemonic, -daimonic, -demonical, -daemonical.** Related forms: **-demon, -daemon, -daimon, -demoniac, -daemoniac, -demonic, -daemonic, -daimonic, -demoniacally, -daemoniacally.**

473   **-pulmonic**   An adjective and an adjective-forming word-final element, derived from Latin *pūlmō, pūlmōn-* 'lung' and **-ic**[1], used in the sense of 'referring or relating to the lungs' as specified by the combining root: **intrapulmonic, gastropulmonic, apulmonic.** Related form: **-pulmonary.**

474   **-gnomonic**   An adjective and an adjective-forming word-final element, derived from Greek *gnōmōn* 'one that knows, perceives, judges' (cf. Greek *gnōnai* 'to know, perceive') and **-ic**[1], used in medical terminology

to mean 'referring to the signs or experience in knowing or judging' the state or condition denoted by the combining root: **physiognomonic, pathognomonic, thanatognomonic.** Also, **-gnomonical.** Related forms: **-gnomic, -gnomical, -gnomonically, -gnomy, -gnosia, -gnosis, -gnostic.**

475 **-harmonic** An adjective (also used substantively), derived from Greek *harmon(ia)* 'a joining together, harmony' (from Greek *harmonizein* 'to join') and **-ic¹**, used in two senses, each particularized by the combining root:

    1. 'Referring or related to music, esp. harmonics and harmony as distinguished from rhythm and melody': **polyharmonic, subharmonic, philharmonic.**

    2. In mathematical terminology, 'referring to progressions in sine and cosine functions': **biharmonic, anharmonic, equianharmonic.** Also, **-harmonical, -harmonious.** Related forms: **-harmony, -harmonically, -harmoniously.**

476 **-pneumonic** An adjective and an adjective-forming word-final element, derived from Greek *pneumonik(os)* 'of or relating to the lungs' (cf. *pneumōn* 'lung,' *pnoē* 'air, breath,' and *pnein* 'to blow, breathe'), used in two related senses:

    1. 'Referring or related to pneumonia': **bronchopneumonic, synpneumonic, postpneumonic.**

    2. In occasional medical terms which have not been formed with *-pulmonic*, 'referring or related to the lungs': **gastropneumonic, hepatopneumonic.** Related forms: **-pneumonia; -pneumonias** *(plural)*.

477 **-chronic** An adjective, derived from Greek *chron(os)* 'time' and **-ic¹**, also used as an adjective-forming word-final element, meaning 'relating or referring to time' as specified by the combining root: **diachronic, synchronic, isochronic.** Related forms: **-chronous, -chronistic, -chronistical, -chronistically, -chrone, -chronism; -chrones, -chronisms** *(plurals)*.

478 **-electronic** An adjective, derived from Greek *elektron* 'amber' and **-ic¹**, (the rubbing of amber being among the earliest noted means of producing static electricity), and also used as an adjective-forming word-final element 'referring or relating to an electron or electrons': **isoelectronic, autoelectronic, unelectronic.**

479 **-sonic** An adjective and an adjective-forming word-final element, derived from Latin *son(us)* 'noise, sound' and **-ic¹**, used in several related senses:

1. 'Referring to the frequencies between 16 and 20,000 cps , audible to the human ear,' as specified by the combining root: **subsonic, infrasonic.**

2. 'Involving or produced by sound waves' as qualified by the combining root: **stereosonic, radiosonic, electrosonic.** Also, **-phonic.**

3. 'Referring to the speed of sound diffusion' as qualified by the combining root: **transonic, subsonic, supersonic.** Related form: **-sonically.**

480 **-tonic** A noun and an adjective, derived from Greek *ton(os)* 'that which stretches or is stretched, tension' and, by extension, 'accent, musical pitch, muscle tonus (i.e., normal contraction, tension),' and **-ic**[1]/**-ic**[2], used chiefly in forming adjectives (many of which have a substantive use) in a variety of senses:

1. In musical terminology, 'referring or relating to the number of notes in the scale' as specified by the combining root: **pentatonic, heptatonic, dodecatonic.**

2. In musical terminology, 'referring to intervals with relation to the fundamental' as specified by the combining root: **diatonic, subtonic, omnitonic.**

3. In linguistics, 'referring to phonetic units in relation to stress' as specified by the combining root: **atonic, pretonic, posttonic.**

4. In medical terminology, 'referring to or stating the quality of muscle contraction or tonus': **normotonic, hypertonic, myatonic.**

5. 'Referring to pathological conditions characterized by spasmodic or continuous contraction of muscles': **catatonic, vagotonic, holotonic.**

6. 'Referring to a substance producing or restoring a good condition' to the part of the body denoted by the combining root: **hematonic, neurotonic, peptonic.**

7. In biochemical terminology, 'referring to a solution with a concentration higher, lower, or equal to another' as specified by the combining root: **hypertonic, isotonic, hypotonic.** Related forms: **-tone, -tonia, -tony, -tonous.**

481 **-embryonic** An adjective and an adjective-forming word-final element, derived from Greek *embryon* 'that which grows inside a body, a fetus' (from *en-* 'inside' and *bry(ein)* 'to swell, grow') and **-ic**[1], used in the sense of 'of, referring, or relating to an embryo' (i.e., an organism in a fetal stage of development) in a manner specified by the combining root: **extraembryonic, pseudembryonic, postembryonic.** Related form: **-embryo.**

482   **-gynic**   An adjective-forming word-final element, derived from Greek *gyn(ē), gynaik-* 'woman' and **-ic**[1], used to mean 'referring or relating to the human female' as specifed by the combining root: **misogynic, polygynic, monogynic.** Related forms: **-gyne, -gyn, -gynous, -gynia, -gyny.**

483   **-heroic**   An adjective and an adjective-forming word-final element, derived from Greek *hērō(s)*, originally, an honorific title, later, 'an exalted, worthy person' and **-ic**[1], used in its etymological sense, as qualified by the combining root: **ultraheroic, mythoheroic, antiheroic.** Also, **-heroical.** Related forms: **-heroically, -heroicly.**

484   **-zoic**   An adjective and an adjective-forming word-final element, derived from Greek *zō(os), zō(ē), zō(on)* 'living, alive' (cf. *za(ein)* 'to live') and **-ic**[1], used in two related senses:

    1.   'Of or relating to animal life' as specified by the combining root: **azoic, celozoic, holozoic.**

    2.   'Of or relating to one or another of the geologic ages': **Eozoic, Paleozoic, Mesozoic.** Related forms: **-zoon, -zoa, -zoal, -zoan, -zoid, -zooid, -zoite.**

485   **-opic**   An adjective, derived from Greek *ops, op-* 'eye' and **-ic**[1], used as an adjective-forming word-final element in medical terminology with the sense of 'pertaining to the kind of vision or visual defect' denoted by the combining root: **hemiopic, megalopic, nyctalopic.** Also, **-opical.** Related forms: **-ope, -opia, -opy, -opically; -opias, -opies** *(plurals).*

486   **-scopic**   An adjective-forming word-final element, derived from Greek *skop(ein)* 'to look at, observe' and **-ic**[1], used in a number of related senses:

    1.   'Of or referring to viewing in a manner or from a perspective' specified by the combining root: **orthoscopic, basiscopic, acroscopic.**

    2.   'Of or referring to viewing by means of a particular instrument' specified by the combining root: **telescopic, stethoscopic, bronchoscopic.**

    3.   'Of or referring to the way something would appear when viewed in a manner, by means of an instrument, or from a perspective' specified by the combining root: **microscopic, macroscopic, telescopic.** Related forms: **-scope, -scopia, -scopy, -scopically; -scopias, -scopies** *(plurals).*

487   **-anthropic**   An adjective, derived from Greek *anthropik(os)* 'of mankind,' used also as a word ending in adjectives 'referring or relating to mankind' as qualified by the combining root: **paleoanthropic, philanthropic, misanthropic.** Also, **-anthropical.** Related forms: **-anthrope, -anthropus, -anthropism, -anthropically, -anthropoid, -anthropist, -anthropy.**

488 **-tropic** An adjective and an adjective-forming word-final element, derived from Greek *trop(os)*, *trop(ē)* 'a turning, turn, deviation, direction, mode' (from the verb *trep(ein)* 'to turn, guide') and **ic[1]**, used in several senses, all having something to do with 'turning or being turned' or, by extension, 'influencing or influenced by' that which is named by the combining root:

  1. 'Referring or relating to change or turning,' as affected by the agent named in the combining root: **heliotropic, nyctitropic, geotropic.**
  2. In ophthalmological terminology, 'referring to a turn or change in the visual axis' characterized by the combining root: **hyper-tropic, hemitropic, stereotropic.**
  3. In medical terminology, 'referring to a tendency to have an influence on, or be influenced by' that which is named by the combining root: **vagotropic, myotropic, gonadotropic.** Also, **-tropous, -tropal.** Related forms: **-trope, -tropia, -tropy, -tropism.**

489 **-typic** An adjective and an adjective-forming word-final element, derived from Greek *typ(os)* 'a blow, impression (i.e., the mark left by a blow), image, model' (from the verb *typt(ein)* 'to strike a blow') and **-ic[1]**, used in two main senses:

  1. 'Conforming or exemplifying a type or model' as specified by the combining root: **archetypic, ecotypic, paleotypic.**
  2. 'Referring or relating to, or involved in the process of printing' as specified by the combining root: **phototypic, heliotypic, stenotypic.** Also, **-typical, -typal.** Related forms: **-type, -typy, -typically, -typally.**

490 **-stearic** An adjective and an adjective-forming word-final element, derived from Greek *stear*, *steat-* 'fat, suet,' used in medical terminology to mean 'of, referring, or pertaining to fat or fat derivatives' of a sort specified by the combining root: **aleostearic, neurostearic, ketostearic.**

491 **-spheric** An adjective and an adjective-forming word-final element, derived from Greek *sphair(a)* 'ball, globe' and **-ic[1]**, used in two major senses:

  1. 'Pertaining or relating to a (spherical) enveloping layer above the earth or other celestial body' as specified by the combining root: **atmospheric, stratospheric, leucospheric.**

2. 'Pertaining or relating to a spherical shape or to its representation' as specified by the combining root: **hemispheric, megaspheric, planispheric.** Also, -**sphaeric, -spherical, -sphaerical.**
Compare -**sphere.**

492 -**generic** An adjective, derived from Latin *genus, gener-* 'birth, race,
kind, class' and -**ic**[1], also used as an adjective-forming word-final
element, used in the sense of 'referring or relating to or describing all
members of a group, class, species, or biological genus': **subgeneric,
pseudogeneric, intergeneric.** Also, -**generical** *(archaic).* Related form:
-**generically.**

493 -**nephric** An adjective, derived from Greek *nephr(oi)* 'kidneys' and -**ic**[1],
used as an adjective-forming word-final element with the meaning 'of
or referring to the kidneys': **oligonephric, pronephric, hepatonephric.**

494 -**phoric** An adjective-forming word-final element, derived from Greek
phor(ein) (the frequentative form of *pher(ein)* 'to bear, carry') and -**ic**[1],
used in two related senses:
    1. 'Possessing a tendency or bearing' specified by the combining
        root: **cetaphoric, heterophoric, anaphoric.**
    2. 'Bearing or carrying' that which is specified by the combining
        root: **gonophoric, semaphoric, metaphoric.** Also, -**phorous.**
        Related forms: -**phore, -phor, -phoria, -phoresis, -phorical,**
        -**phorically.**

495 -**chloric** An adjective, derived from Greek *chlor(os)* 'greenish yellow'
and -**ic**[1], also used as an adjective-forming word-final element used in
chemical terminology to mean 'referring to or containing chlorine' as
part of a compound named by the combining root: **hydrochloric,
perchloric, hyperchloric.** Related forms: -**chloride, -chlorine, -chlorite.**

496 -**iatric** An adjective and an adjective-forming word-final element,
derived from Greek *iatr(os)* 'physician, healer' and -**ic**[1], used to mean
'pertaining or relating to medical treatment' of the type denoted by
the combining root: **psychiatric, geriatric, pediatric.** Also, -**iatrical.**
Related forms: -**iatrics, -iatrician, -iatrist, -iatry; -iatricians, -iatrists,**
-**iatries** *(plurals).*

497 -**electric** An adjective, derived from Latin *electric(us)* 'produced by
rubbing amber' (from Greek *elektr(on)* 'amber' and -**ic**[1], the rubbing
of amber being among the earliest noted means of producing static
electricity), also used as an adjective-forming word-final element with
the sense 'concerning, relating to, produced by, or producing

electricity': **hydroelectric, thermoelectric, photoelectric.** Related forms: **-electron, -electronic, -electrical, -electrically, -electricity.**

498   **-metric**   An adjective (also used substantively), derived from Greek *metrik(os)* 'pertaining to measurement' (from Greek *metr(on)* 'measure, proportion' and -ic[1]), also used as an adjective-forming word-final element in two related senses:

    1.   'Pertaining or relating to measurement' as qualified by the combining root: **parametric, biometric, radiometric.**

    2.   'Pertaining to, employing, or obtained from a meter' specified by the combining root: **decimetric, calorimetric, cardiometric.** Related forms: **-meter, -metron, -metry, -metria[1], -metrical, -metrically, -metrist, -metrics.**

499   **-centric**   An adjective, derived through Latin from Greek *kentr(on)* 'center' and -ic[1], also used as an adjective-forming word-final element, used in either of two senses:

    1.   'Centering upon' something specified by the combining root: **egocentric, geocentric, Christocentric.**

    2.   'Possessing a kind of center or number of centers' denoted by the combining root: **concentric, allocentric, multicentric.** Related forms: **-centre, -center; -central, -centricity; -centricities** *(plural).*

500   **-gastric**   An adjective, derived from Greek *gaster, gast(e)r-* 'stomach' and -ic[1], also used as an adjective-forming word-final element designating 'a type of stomach or number of stomachs' specified by the combining root: **trigastric, paragastric, endogastric.** Related forms: **-gaster, -gastria.**

501   **-mercuric**   An adjective and an adjective-forming word-final element, derived through Middle English from Latin *Mercur(ius)* 'Mercury' (the messenger of the gods; the planet; and, later, the metallic element, named after the fleet-footed god because of its fluidity at relatively low temperatures) and -ic[1], used in the terminology of chemistry and pharmacology in combinations meaning 'pertaining to molecules of bivalent mercury or to compounds of which it is a part': **trimercuric, phenylmercuric, potassiomercuric.**

502   **-sulfuric**   An adjective and an adjective-forming word-final element, derived from Latin *sulfur (sulpur, sulphur)* 'brimstone, sulfur' and -ic[1], used in combinations meaning 'pertaining or relating to compounds containing sulfur, especially in its highest valence,' as specified by the combining root: **thiosulfuric, hyposulfuric, disulfuric.** Also, **-sulphuric** *(British).* Related forms: **-sulfurous, -sulphurous.**

503 **-telluric** An adjective and an adjective-forming word-final element, derived from Latin *tellūs*, *tellūr-* 'the earth' and -ic[1], used in its etymological sense, as qualified by the combining root: **intratelluric, extratelluric, cosmotellurian.** Also, **-tellurian.**

504 **-barbituric** An adjective and an adjective-forming word-final element, referring to an acid $CO(NHCO)_2CH_2$ (and its derivatives) used medicinally for its soporific effects: **diethylbarbituric, aminobarbituric, diallylbarbituric.** The etymology of this suffix is a matter of some debate: while agreed that it is formed of *-barbit-* and *-uric*, the latter constituent being the adjectival form of *urine* (cf. **-uria, -urea**), lexicographers have offered such disparate etymologies for *-barbit-* as *Barbara* (the name), *barbit(on)* (a musical instrument), and *(Usnea) barbata* 'bearded moss.'

505 **-basic**[1] An adjective, derived through Middle English, French, and Latin from Greek *bas(is)* 'base or step' and -ic[1], used also as a word ending in forming adjectives 'pertaining or relating to a base, a starting point, or (by extension) a minimum' according to the denotation of the combining root: **abasic, platybasic, rheobasic.** Related forms: **-base, -basis, -basically.**

506 **-basic**[2] An adjective, derived ultimately from Greek *bas(is)* 'step or base' and -ic[1], used also as a word ending in forming adjectives in chemical terminology 'pertaining or relating to, or containing alkaline compounds': **tribasic, ammonobasic, polybasic.** Related forms: **-base; -bases** *(plural).*

507 **-phasic**[1] An adjective and an adjective-forming word-final element, derived from Greek *phas(is)* 'speech, utterance' (cf. *phanai* 'to speak') and -ic[1], used chiefly in medical terminology to mean 'referring or relating to a speech disorder' as specified by the combining root: **endophasic, aphasic, paraphasic.** Also, **-phatic, -phemic.** Related forms: **-phasia, -phasy, -phasis.**

508 **-phasic**[2] An adjective and an adjective-forming word-final element, derived from Greek *phas(is)* 'an appearance' (from the verb *phainein* 'to appear, show (through),' not to be confused with *phanai* 'to speak,' whence **-phasic**[1]) and -ic[1], used in the sense of 'referring to a kind of appearance or *phase* or number of appearances or *phases*' as specified by the combining root: **monophasic, polyphasic, dikaryophasic.** Compare **-phanic.** Related form: **-phase.**

509 **-algesic** An adjective, derived from Greek *algēs(is)* 'sense of pain' and

-ic[1], also used as a word ending in adjectives 'pertaining to sensitivity to pain': **analgesic, hyperalgesic, antalgesic.** Compare **-algic.**

510 **-classic** An adjective, derived through French from Latin *classic(us)* 'of the classes of the Roman people,' used also as a word ending to form adjectives meaning, according to context, 'pertaining or relating to the first rank, the works considered part of the permanent cultural achievement of humanity, the works of ancient Greece and Rome, or their characteristics': **preclassic, neoclassic, pseudoclassic.** Also, **-classical.** Related forms: **-classicism, -classically; -classicisms** *(plural).*

511 **-tic** An adjective-forming word-final element, derived from Greek *-tik(os),* itself derived etymologically and by abstraction from past participles (marked in Greek, as in Latin, by *-t-,* cognate with English *-(e)d)* to which the adjectival suffix *-ik(os)* '**-ic**[1]' was added; from third declension nouns with oblique-case stems ending in *t-* (e.g., *sōma, sōmat-* 'body' and *hēpar, hēpat-* 'liver') plus **-ic**[1]; and from forms which in non-Attic Greek dialects end in *-s* but in Attic end in *-t,* as part of a general *s/t* alternation in Greek. Thus: **prosthetic, pancreatic, epiglottic.** (Note that **-tic** is the regular adjectival ending to nouns ending in **-sis.**) Related forms: **-sis, -tics.**

512 **-pancreatic** An adjective and an adjective-forming word-final element, derived from Greek *pankreas, pankreat-* 'sweetbread, pancreas' (literally, 'whole flesh'), used in medical terminology in the sense of 'referring or relating to the pancreas or a condition of the pancreas or adjacent organs' as specified by the combining root: **gastropancreatic, apancreatic, peripancreatic.** Related form: **-pancreatism.**

513 **-asthmatic** An adjective and an adjective-forming word-final element, derived from Greek *asthma, asthmat-* 'panting' and **-ic**[1], used to mean 'pertaining to asthma (a disease characterized by labored breathing), its symptoms, or its treatment' as specified by the combining root: **antiasthmatic, nonasthmatic, postasthmatic.** Related form: **-asthma.**

514 **-climatic** An adjective and an adjective-forming word-final element, derived from Greek *klima, klimat-* 'inclination' (from the verb *klin(ein)* 'to bend, incline' and **-ma**) and **-ic**[1], used in the meaning 'pertaining to the average weather conditions of an area measured over an extended period of time or to special and controlled conditions for experimental purposes': **paleoclimatic, bioclimatic, microclimatic.** Also, **-climatical.** Related form: **-climatically.**

515 **-grammatic** An adjective and an adjective-forming word-final element,

derived from Greek *gram(ma)*, *gram(mat-)* 'that which is written (literally, engraved), a letter or a line of a drawing' and **-ic¹**, used to mean 'pertaining to writing or to written material' specified by the combining root: **diagrammatic, epigrammatic, monogrammatic.** Also, **-grammic, -grammatical.** Related forms: **-gram, -gramme, -grammatically, -grammical, -grammically.**

516   **-diplomatic**   An adjective and an adjective-forming word-final element, derived from Greek *diplōma*, *diplōmat-* 'piece of paper folded double (from *di-* 'two-,' *-plo-* '-ple,' and **-ma**), an official document' and **-ic¹**, used in the sense of 'displaying tact, especially in an official capacity,' as specified by the combining root: **undiplomatic, preterdiplomatic, paradiplomatic.** Related forms: **-diplomatically, -diplomacy.**

517   **-chromatic**   An adjective, derived from Greek *chrōma*, *chrōmat-* 'color' and **-ia¹**, also an adjective-forming word-final element in two basic senses:
1.   Generally, 'pertaining to color': **achromatic, panchromatic, polychromatic.**
2.   In biological terminology, 'pertaining to the staining properties of tissues and microorganisms': **basichromatic, oxychromatic, lithochromatic.** Related forms: **-chrome, -chromic, -chromy, -chromatism, -chromatically.**

518   **-somatic**   An adjective and an adjective-forming word-final element, derived from Greek *sōma*, *sōmat-* 'body' and **-ic¹**, used in several related senses:
1.   In zoological taxonomy, applied to higher taxa than a genus, 'pertaining to creatures possessing the type of body denoted by the combining root': **splanchnosomatic, orthosomatic, mesosomatic.**
2.   In medical terminology, 'pertaining to the cause of effects on the body': **psychosomatic, neurosomatic, exsomatic.**
3.   In two medical terms, 'concerning a type of human body' denoted by the combining root: **eurysomatic, leptosomatic.** Related forms: **-soma, -some³, -somus, -somal, -somic, -somia, -somatia, -somatic, -somatous, -somatically, -somite.**

519   **-rheumatic**   An adjective and an adjective-forming word-final element, derived from Greek *rheuma*, *rheumat-* 'that which flows; flux, discharge' (cf. the verb *rhe(in)* 'to flow') and **-ic¹**, used in medical terminology in the sense of 'pertaining or relating to, or exhibiting traits of rheumatism': **prerheumatic, pseudorheumatic, postrheumatic.** Related form: **-rheumatically.**

520 **-cratic** An adjective-forming word-final element, derived from Greek *krat(os)* 'strength, power' and -ic[1], used in several related senses:

1. 'Pertaining to a theory of government': **democratic, gynecratic, autocratic.**
2. 'Pertaining to a political party, usually based on theories of government': **Democratic, Physiocratic, Technocratic.**
3. 'Pertaining to a dominant social class': **aristocratic, plutocratic, timocratic.**
4. In optics, 'pertaining to the qualities of lenses': **amacratic, pancratic, polycratic.**
5. In mineralogy, 'pertaining to the color of minerals' denoted by the combining root: **leucocratic, melanocratic, mesocratic.**
6. In a single term, 'referring to the self-discipline theories of the Encratites': **Encratic** (also, **encratic**).
7. In classical prosody, two terms 'pertaining to classical rhythmic systems': **first pherecratic, second pherecratic** (or **pherecratean, pherecratian**). Related forms: **-cracy, -crat, -cratically; -cracies, -crats** *(plurals).*

521 **-static** An adjective and an adjective-forming word-final element, derived from Greek *statik(os)* 'of or pertaining to standing or placement' (cf. the verb *hista(nai), stē(nai)* 'to stand, make stand'), used in two main senses:

1. 'Pertaining or relating to standing, stability, or causing to stand': **astatic, diastatic, thermostatic.**
2. 'Pertaining to the production of static electricity': **dynamostatic, electrostatic, magnetostatic.** Related forms: **-statics, -stat, -statically, -stasic, -stasis, -stasy, -state[2], -stasia.**

522 **-aquatic** An adjective and an adjective-forming word-final element, derived from Latin *aquātic(us), aquātic(a), aquātic(um)* 'of, referring, or relating to water' (cf. Latin *aqua* 'water'), used in its etymological sense, as qualified by the combining root: **transaquatic, pseudoaquatic, subaquatic.** Related forms: **-aqueous, -aquatically.**

523 **-didactic** A noun, derived from Greek *didaktik(os)* 'apt at teaching,' also used as an adjective-forming word-final element with the sense of 'concerning the ability, intention, or means to teach' as specified by the combining root: **undidactic, comicodidactic, autodidactic.** Also, **-didactical.** Related forms: **-didact, -didactically.**

524 **-practic** An adjective, derived from Greek *praktik(os)*, itself derived from the verb *prass(ein), pratt(ein)* 'to do, accomplish, perform' and

-ic[1]; also used as an adjective-forming word-final element in two extensions of its etymological sense:
1. 'Pertaining to a mode of movement or praxia' specified by the combining root: **apractic, echopractic, eupractic.**
2. 'Pertaining to a type of medical practice or praxis' named by the combining root: **chiropractic, sanipractic, radiopractic.** Also, **-praxic.** Related forms: **-praxia, -praxis, -pragia, -practics, -practice.**

525   **-tactic** An adjective and an adjective-forming word-final element, derived from Greek *taktik(os)* 'fit for arranging of, or referring to an arrangement or ordering' (from the verb *tass(ein), tatt(ein)* 'to order, arrange'), used in a number of related senses, all having to do with the idea of ordering or arranging:
1. 'Pertaining to or possessing a pattern or arrangement' specified by the combining root: **orthotactic, syntactic, paratactic.**
2. 'Exhibiting orientation or movement controlled by an agent' named by the combining root: **geotactic, phototactic, thermotactic.**
3. 'Having an arrangement or a pattern of something' named by the combining root: **phyllotactic, leukotactic, chaetotactic.** Also, **-taxic, -tactical.** Related forms: **-tactics, -taxis, -taxia, -taxy.**

526   **-deictic** An adjective and an adjective-forming word-final element, derived from Greek *deik(nunai)* 'to show' and **-tic**, used in combinations referring to a manner of 'showing,' either for rhetorical effect (**epideictic, anapodeictic**) or for purposes of diagnosis (**endeictic**).

527   **-arctic** An adjective and an adjective-forming word-final element, derived through Latin from Greek *arkt(os)* 'bear, North (i.e., where bears live)' and **-ic[1]**, used in the sense of 'of, pertaining to, or characteristic of the area near the North Pole': **periarctic, antarctic, transarctic.** Related form: **-arctically.**

528   **-etic** A word-final element, derived from Greek *-ētik(os)*, used as the equivalent of **-ic[1]** in forming adjectives, esp. from nouns ending in *-esis* (as **diuresis/diuretic**): **mimetic, kinetic, geodetic.** It has also been influential in ending terms with which it has not been associated historically, as **-rrheal, -rrheic/-rrhetic.**

529   **-logetic** An adjective-forming word-final element, derived from Greek *log(os)* 'word, speech, discourse' and **-etic**, used in combinations with the sense of 'relating to (a) speech or (b) discourse' as specified by the

combining root: **apologetic, palilogetic, paromologetic.** Related forms: **-logy, -logia, -logic, -logical, -logue, -log, -logism, -logian, -logician, -logist, -logistic, -logically, -logistically, -logetically.**

530   **-ergetic** An adjective-forming word-final element, derived from Greek *-ergētik(os)* 'of or relating to work' (cf. *-erg(ēsis)* 'act of working,' *-erg(ein)* 'to work,' *erg(on)* 'work'), used in the sense of 'working, active': **synergetic, energetic, catabolergetic.** Related forms: **-ergy, -ergetical, -ergetically.**

531   **-thetic** An adjective-forming word-final element, derived from Greek *(ti)the(nai)* 'to put, place, set' and **-tic,** used in combinations corresponding to nouns ending in **-thesis,** as:
 parenthetic: 'put off to the side, interjectory.'
 hypothetic: 'put beneath, underlying.'
 antithetic: 'put against, opposing.'
 synthetic: 'put together, made of different components.'
 prosthetic: 'replacing.' Also, **-thetical.** Compare **-thesis.**

532   **-pathetic** An adjective and an adjective-forming word-final element, derived from Greek *pathētik(os)* 'sensitive, subject to passion' (cf. *path(ein)* 'to suffer, be sensitive to'), used in combinations meaning 'pertaining to or involving emotions' as specified by the combining root: **apathetic, hyperpathetic, sympathetic.** Also, **-pathetical.** Compare **-pathic.** Related forms: **-path, -pathia, -pathy, -pathology.**

533   **-synthetic** An adjective and an adjective-forming word-final element, derived from Greek *syn(ti)the(nai)* 'to put together' and **-tic,** used in combinations corresponding to nouns ending in **-synthesis,** with the following senses:
1. 'Of, pertaining, or relating to a combination or synthesis' of a sort or in a general manner specified by the combining root: **megasynthetic, episynthetic, unsynthetic.**
2. 'Of, pertaining, or relating to a specific mode or manner of combination or synthesis' named by the combining root: **psychosynthetic, electrosynthetic, chemosynthetic.**
3. In philological terminology, 'pertaining to the putting together of elements to form words': **polysynthetic, monosynthetic, parasynthetic.** Also, **-synthetical.** Compare **-synthesis, -thesis.** Related form: **-synthetically.**

534   **-aesthetic** An adjective, derived through German and Latin from Greek *aesthētik(os)* 'of sense perception,' used also as a word ending in the forming of adjectives:

1. 'Pertaining to the beautiful or the philosophy of the beautiful': **pseudaesthetic, antiaesthetic, ethicoaesthetic.**
2. In medical terminology, usu. in the form **-esthetic**, 'pertaining to the quality of a person's sensitivity or consciousness, or to consciousness of something' named by the combining root: **anesthetic, kinesthetic, hyperesthetic.** Also, **-esthetic, -aesthetical, -esthetical.** Compare **-aesthesia.** Related forms: **-aesthetically, -esthetically.**

535 **-poietic** An adjective-forming word-final element, derived from Greek *poiētik(os)* 'capable of or referring to making, producing, creating' (cf. the verb *poi(ein)* 'to make, produce, create'), used chiefly in medical terminology in the sense of 'producing' that which is named by the combining root: **hemapoietic, uropoietic, spermatopoietic.** Also, **-poetic.** Related forms: **-poeia, -peia, -poeic, -poetical, -poietical, -poetically, -poietically, -poesis, -poiesis.**

536 **-emetic** An adjective, derived from Greek *emetik(os)* 'concerning or inclined to vomiting' (cf. Greek *emesis* 'vomit'), also used as an adjective-forming word-final element with the meaning 'pertaining to vomiting or to its inducing or control': **antiemetic, hyperemetic, hematemetic.** Also, **-emetical** *(rare).* Compare **-emesis.** Related form: **-emetically** *(rare).*

537 **-mimetic** An adjective, derived from Greek *mimētik(os)* 'skilled at or pertaining to imitation, imitative,' also used as an adjective-forming word-final element in medical terminology in combinations meaning 'pertaining to simulation of specified effects, especially because of medicinal agents,' as particularized by the combining root: **radiomimetic, progestomimetic, neuromimetic.** Related forms: **-mimesis, -mimia, -mime, -mimic, -mimical, -mimically.**

538 **-genetic** A widely used adjective-forming word-final element, derived from Greek *gen(esis)* 'origin, birth, formation' and **-etic**, employed in several related senses:
1. 'Pertaining to generation or genesis' by the agent(s) specified by the combining root: **spermatogenetic, agenetic, polygenetic.**
2. 'Producing, generating, or yielding' something specified by the combining root: **cytogenetic, hematogenetic, cyanogenetic.**
3. 'Pertaining to something produced, generated, or yielded' by an agent named by the combining root: **psychogenetic, autogenetic, ovogenetic.** Also, **-genic, -genous, -geneous.** Related forms: **-gen, -gene, -genetically, -genically, -genesis, -geny.**

539 **-magnetic** An adjective and an adjective-forming word-final element, derived through Latin from Greek *magnēs*, *magnēt* 'a Magnesian' (Magnesia being a part of Thessaly), 'a loadstone' (i.e., a Magnesian stone)' and **-ic**[1], used in a number of related senses:

1. 'Pertaining to the properties of magnets and magnetism': **diamagnetic, semimagnetic, nonmagnetic.**
2. 'Pertaining to the causing, affecting, or preventing of magnetism by an agent' named by the combining root: **radiomagnetic, ferromagnetic, thermomagnetic.**
3. 'Pertaining to a particular type of magnetism' specified by the combining root: **zoomagnetic, geomagnetic, sidero-magnetic.** Also, **-magnetical** *(archaic)*. Related forms: **-magnet, -magnetism, -magnetically.**

540 **-kinetic** An adjective, derived from Greek *kinētik(os)* 'pertaining to or skilled at motion' (compare **-kinesis** and **-etic**), also used as a combining form in adjectival compounds.

1. 'Pertaining to motion or movement': **anakinetic, hypokinetic, iridokinetic.**
2. 'Pertaining to an agent causing motion,' as named by the combining root: **telekinetic, psychokinetic, archeokinetic.**
3. In biological and medical terminology, 'referring to kinesis, either as motion or change': **catakinetic, astrokinetic, biokinetic.**
4. 'Referring to activation, by an agent, of a part of the body' named by the combining root: **gonadokinetic, cardiokinetic, glucokinetic.** Also, **-cinetic, -kinetical, -cinetical** *(all rare)*. Related forms: **-kinesia, -cinesia, -kinetically, -cinetically.**

541 **-phonetic** An adjective and an adjective-forming word-final element, derived from Greek *phōnētik(os)* 'concerning sound, speech' (cf. *phōnē* 'sound'), used in the terminology of linguistics to mean 'referring to speech sounds or their representation' as qualified by the combining root: **prephonetic, acrophonetic, nonphonetic.** Related forms: **-phone, -phonia, -phony, -phonic, -phonous, -phonious, -phonetics, -phonetical, -phonetically.**

542 **-noetic** An adjective, derived from Greek *noētik(os)* 'skilled at, relating to perception' (an adjective formed to the abstract noun *noēsis* 'perception, thought' formed to the verb *noein* 'to perceive,' itself derived from the noun *no(os)*, *no(ys)* 'mind, mood, thought'), also used as an adjective-forming word-final element with the sense of 'concerning thinking or perception' as qualified by the combining root: **anoetic, dianoetic, hypnoetic.** Related forms: **-noia, -noic, -noiac, -noid.**

543 **-poetic** An adjective and an adjective-forming element, derived from Greek *poiētik(os)* 'capable of or referring to making, producing, creating' (cf. the verb *poi(ein)* 'to make, produce, create'), used in two major senses:

    1. In medical terminology, 'capable of or referring to the production of' that which is named by the combining root: **uropoetic, oenopoetic, nosopoetic.** Also, **-poietic.**

    2. In literary terminology, 'of or referring to poetry (i.e., a literary creation)': **pseudopoetic, antipoetic, unpoetic.** Also, **-poetical.** Related forms: **-poeia, -peia, -poeic, -poetically, -poietically, -poesis, -poiesis, -poetics.**

544 **-luetic** An adjective and an adjective-forming word-final element, derived from Latin *lu(ēs)* 'plague, communicable disease' and **-tic,** used specifically to mean 'referring or pertaining to syphilis' as qualified by the combining root: **paraluetic, metaluetic, antiluetic.** Also, **-luic.** Related forms: **-lues, -luetism.**

545 **-itic** An adjective-forming word-final element, derived through French and Latin from Greek *-itik(os)*, a highly productive general adjective-forming suffix, meaning 'of, pertaining or related to' that which is specified by the combining root. In English, **-itic** is most frequently combined with nouns ending in **-ite, -itis,** or a vowel: **dendritic, phlebitic, carditic.** Related form: **-itically.**

546 **-politic** An adjective and an adjective-forming word-final element, derived from Greek *politik(os)* 'referring to a citizen or citizenry,' used in two related senses:

    1. 'Pertaining to politics or political theory': **metapolitic, geopolitic, superpolitic.** Also, **-political.**

    2. Depending upon context, 'referring to politics, to shrewdness, or to tactfulness': **impolitic, unpolitic, overpolitic.** Related forms: **-polis, -polite, -politan, -political, -politically, -politics.**

547 **-critic** A noun, derived from Greek *krit(ēs)* 'judge, decider' (from *krin(ein)* 'to separate, judge') and **-ic²,** also used as a noun-forming word-final element referring to 'the quality or rank of one who judges' as specified by the combining root: **archcritic, anticritic, supercritic.** Related forms: **-critical, -critically; -critics** *(plural).*

548 **-arthritic** An adjective, derived from Greek *arthritik(os)* 'of or relating to a disease of the joints' (from *arthr(os)* 'joint,' **-it(is),** and **-ic¹),** used also as a word ending to form adjectives 'pertaining to the extent or duration or treatment of an arthritic condition': **antiarthritic, holarthritic, postarthritic.** Also, **-arthritical.** Related form: **-arthric.**

549 **-mantic** An adjective and an adjective-forming word-final element, derived from Greek *mantik(os)* 'pertaining to or skilled at prophecy, divination,' used in combinations in its etymological sense as further specified by the combining root: **necromantic, geomantic, chiromantic.** Also, **-mantical.** Related forms: **-mancy, -mancer, -mantically.**

550 **-romantic** An adjective, derived from French *romantique* 'concerning the form of tale called a romance,' used also as a word ending in forming adjectives.
    1. 'Pertaining to the romantic tradition in literature, art, and music': **antiromantic, preromantic, proromantic.**
    2. 'Pertaining to the imaginative and emotional appeal of heroic, adventurous romances': **unromantic, tragicoromantic, superromantic.** Related forms: **-romantical, -romantically** (both sense 2 only).

551 **-odontic** An adjective-forming word-final element, derived from Greek *odous, odont-* 'tooth' and **-ic**[1], used in two major related senses:
    1. 'Pertaining to the size of teeth,' as specified by the combining root: **megadontic, microdontic, isodontic.**
    2. 'Pertaining to the type of dental treatment' denoted by the combining root: **pedodontic, periodontic, orthodontic.** Related forms: **-odontics, -odontia**[2]; **-odontias** *(plural).*

552 **-gerontic** An adjective and an adjective-forming word-final element, derived from Greek *gerōn, geront-* 'old man,' used in the sense of 'pertaining to old age' in a manner specified by the combining root: **paragerontic, ungerontic, phylogerontic.** Also, **-gerontal.**

553 **-otic**[1] An adjective and an adjective-forming word-final element, derived from Greek *ous, ōt-* 'ear' and **-ic**[1], used in medical terminology in a number of related senses:
    1. 'Pertaining or relating to a part of the ear' specified by the combining root: **epiotic, entotic, prootic.**
    2. 'Pertaining or relating to an area spatially related to the ear': **parotic, periotic, opisthotic.**
    3. 'Pertaining or relating to a bone spatially related to the ear': **prootic, sphenotic, basiotic.**

554 **-otic**[2] An adjective-forming word-final element, derived both etymologically and by abstraction from Greek *-ōtik(os)*, a general

adjectival suffix (to which *-tik(os)* '**-tic**' and *-ik(os)* '**ic**[1]' may be compared). The original suffix form was *-ik(os)*, often added to nouns with a *-t-* at the end of the combining form of the stem, which in certain phonetic environments in certain dialects of Greek appears as *-s-*. By far the most common of these alternating *t-* and *-s* forms is *-ōsis, -ōtik(os)*, in which the *-ō-* has a variety of derivations (cf. **-osis**). Thus, **-otic** appears in English in a number of different combinations:

1. 'Pertaining or relating to an action, process, or condition' specified by the combining root: **euangiotic, diotic, sialotic.**
2. In medical terminology, 'pertaining or relating to an abnormal or disease condition' specified by the combining root: **psychotic, alkalotic, aphosphorotic.**
3. 'Pertaining or relating to an increase or formation' of something specified by the combining root: **leucocytotic, zymotic, melanotic.** Related forms: **-osis, -otical, -otically.**

555 **-narcotic**   An adjective, derived from Greek *narkōtik(os)* 'benumbing' (from the verb *narkoun* 'to become numb'), also used as an adjective-forming word-final element with the sense of 'pertaining to analgesic or soporific drugs' as specified by the combining root: **subnarcotic, antinarcotic, acronarcotic.** Also, **-narcotical** *(rare).* Related forms: **-narcotically, -narcosis, -narcoticism.**

556 **-photic**   An adjective and an adjective-forming word-final element, derived from Greek *phōs, phōt-* 'light' and **-ic**[1], used in two senses:

1. 'Pertaining to the ability to see at a light level' specified by the combining root: **sthenophotic, stenophotic, euryphotic.**
2. In two terms, 'pertaining to the penetration of light under water': **aphotic, dysphotic.** Related form: **-phote.**

557 **-biotic**   An adjective-forming word-final element, derived from Greek *biōtik(os)* 'pertaining to life' (cf. *bios* 'life'), used in two main senses:

1. 'Pertaining to life' as qualified by the combining root: **antibiotic, catabiotic, ambiotic.**
2. 'Possessing or requiring a mode of life' specified by the combining root: **symbiotic, trophobiotic, aerobiotic.** Related forms: **-biosis; -bioses** *(plural).*

558 **-hypnotic**   An adjective and an adjective-forming word-final element, derived from Greek *hypnotik(os)* 'inclined or putting to sleep' (itself derived from Greek *hypn(os)* 'sleep' and **-otic**[2]), used with the meaning 'pertaining to hypnosis or hypnotism, or to susceptibility to hypnosis': **hypohypnotic, autohypnotic, posthypnotic.** Related forms: **-hypnosis, -hypnotist, -hypnotically; -hypnoses** *(plural).*

559   **-erotic**   An adjective and an adjective-forming word-final element, derived through French from Greek *erōs, erōt-* 'love, lust' and -ic[1], used in two senses:
  1. 'Of or pertaining to sexual love or desire': **anerotic** *(rare)*, **nonerotic, anterotic.**
  2. 'Of or pertaining to sexual love or desire or to its gratification' according to the mode specified by the combining root: **homoerotic, autoerotic, amphierotic.** Related forms: -**eroticism, -erotical, -erotically; -eroticisms** *(plural).*

560   **-neurotic**   An adjective, derived from Greek *neur(on)* 'sinew, fiber,' hence, 'nerve' and -otic[2], also used as an adjective-forming word-final element in two senses, the one derived from the other:
  1. In medical terminology, 'pertaining to a disease or abnormal condition of the nerves' as specified by the combining root: **trophoneurotic, angioneurotic, aponeurotic.**
  2. In medical and popular usage, 'pertaining to emotional instability or (psycho)neurosis': **psychoneurotic, unneurotic, hyperneurotic.** Compare **-neurosis.** Related form: **-neurotically.**

561   **-leptic**   An adjective-forming word-final element, derived from Greek *lēptik(os)* 'of or pertaining to taking, seizure' (from Greek *labein* 'to take, seize' and -ic[1]), used in medical terminology in combinations meaning 'of or pertaining to a seizure' of the sort specified by the combining root: **epileptic, narcoleptic, psycholeptic.** Related forms: **-lepsia, -lepsis, -lepsy.**

562   **-peptic**   An adjective-forming word-final element, derived from Greek *peptik(os)* 'of or pertaining to digestion' (from *pepsis* 'digestion,' itself from *peptein* 'to cook'), used in two related senses:
  1. 'Pertaining to or affecting digestion': **proteopeptic, kolypeptic, apeptic.**
  2. 'Pertaining to a state or condition of digestion,' as specified by the combining root: **dyspeptic, hyperpeptic, bradypeptic.** Related forms: **-pepsia, -pepsy.**

563   **-septic**   An adjective and an adjective-forming word-final element, derived from Greek *sēp(ein)* 'to rot' and -tic, used in medical terminology to mean 'of or referring to decay of a sort or due to a cause' specified by the combining root: **uroseptic, antiseptic, colyseptic.** Related form: **-sepsis.**

564   **-optic**   An adjective and an adjective-forming word-final element, derived from Greek *optik(os)* 'of or pertaining to vision or sight' (cf.

opsis 'sight, vision' and *ops, op-* 'eye'), used in its etymological sense as qualified by the combining root: **orthoptic, perioptic, holoptic.** Related forms: **-opsia, -opter, -optical, -optically.**

565 **-cathartic** An adjective and an adjective-forming word-final element, derived from Greek *kathar(euein)* 'to clean, purify' (cf. *kathar(os), kathar(a), kathar(on)* 'clean, pure') and **-sis,** used in medical terminology in the sense of 'pertaining to cleaning or clearing' as specified by the combining root: **hematocathartic, cephalocathartic, emetocathartic.** Also, **-cathartical.** Related forms: **-catharsis, -cathartically; -catharses** *(plural).*

566 **-clastic** An adjective, derived from Greek *klast(os)* 'broken' (from Greek *klān* 'to break, crush') and **-ic¹,** also used as an adjective-forming word-final element in several senses:
1. 'Pertaining to breaking and destroying' as specified by the combining root: **iconoclastic, mythoclastic, panclastic.**
2. In medical terminology, 'causing disintegration' of the substance named by the combining root: **proteoclastic, thromboclastic, glycoclastic.**
3. In geological terminology, 'consisting or composed of fragmented material' denoted by the combining root: **cryptoclastic, pyroclastic, epiclastic.** Related forms: **-clast; -clasts** *(plural).*

567 **-plastic** An adjective and an adjective-forming word-final element, derived from Greek *plastik(os)* 'able to be molded, formed' (from the verb *plass(ein), platt(ein)* 'to mold, form, shape'), used in two senses:
1. '**-ic¹**' ('of, relating to, concerning') when added to nouns ending in **-plast, -plastia, -plasm,** or **-plasty: rhinoplastic, paraplastic, oligoplastic.**
2. 'Pertaining to the development, formation, or growth' of something or in the manner named by the combining root: **osteoplastic, heteroplastic, myeloplastic.**

568 **-nastic** An adjective, also an adjective-forming word-final element, derived from Greek *nast(os)* 'pressed close, firm' and **-ic¹,** used in botanical terminology to mean 'referring to an irregular pattern of cellular growth as a result of pressure or stimulus' from that which is named by the combining root: **photonastic, thermonastic, geonastic.** (The word *gymnastic* does not contain this suffix, deriving, rather, from Greek *gymnastik(os)* 'skilled at, relating to athletic exercise' from the verb *gymnazein* 'to train, exercise (in the nude).' Cf. *gymn(os)* 'nude.') Related form: **-nasty.**

569 **-phrastic** An adjective-forming word-final element, derived from Greek *phrastik(os)* 'concerning explanation or speech' (from the verb *phrazein* 'to point out, explain, tell'), used in combinations meaning 'concerning the choice of words used in communicating' as characterized by the combining root: **paraphrastic, periphrastic, antiphrastic.** Also, **-phrastical.** Related forms: **-phrase, -phrasia, -phrastically; -phrases** *(plural)*.

570 **-mnestic** An adjective, derived from Greek *mnēst(is)* 'memory' and **-ic**[1], also used as an adjective-forming word-final element in combinations meaning 'pertaining to memory' as specified by the combining root: **amnestic, catamnestic, hypermnestic.** Also, **-mnesic.** Related forms: **-mnesia, -mnesis, -mnesiac.**

571 **-istic** An adjective-forming word-final element, derived through French and Latin from Greek *-istik(os)*, basically a combination of **-ist** and **-ic,** but used in a more general sense of 'of, pertaining, or referring to or characteristic of' that which is denoted by the combining root: **stylistic, pantheistic, parodistic.** Related forms: **-istical, -istically.**

572 **-theistic** An adjective and an adjective-forming word-final element, derived from Greek *the(os), the(a)* 'god, goddess' and **-istic,** used in the sense of 'pertaining to or involving a belief in a god or gods' as specified by the combining root: **monotheistic, henotheistic, atheistic.** Also, **-theistical.** Related forms: **-theism, -theist, -theistically; -theisms, -theists** *(plurals)*.

573 **-logistic** An adjective-forming word-final element derived from Greek *logistik(os)* 'concerning speaking, reasoning,' i.e. *log(os)* 'word, speech, discourse, reasoning,' **-ist,** and **-ic**[1], used in all of its etymological senses: **dialogistic** 'concerning the speaking of two,' **analogistic** 'concerning reasoning anew,' **paralogistic** 'concerning fallacious reasoning,' **catalogistic** 'concerning accounting, listing down.' Compare **-logic, -logetic.** Related forms: **-logistical, -logistically.**

574 **-linguistic** An adjective and an adjective-forming word-final element, derived from Latin *lingu(a)* 'tongue, language,' **-ist,** and **-ic**[1], used in combinations meaning 'pertaining to language or the knowledge or study of language' as specified by the combining root: **metalinguistic, prelinguistic, interlinguistic.** Also, **-linguistical.** Related forms: **-linguist, -linguistically; -linguists** *(plural)*.

575 **-gnostic** An adjective-forming word-final element, derived from Greek *gnōstik(os)* 'skilled at knowing, pertaining to knowledge,' used to mean 'having knowledge, pertaining to knowledge' as specified by the combining root: **agnostic, diagnostic, geognostic.** Also, **-gnostical.** Related forms: **-gnost, -gnosia, -gnosy, -gnomic, -gnomonic.**

576   **-acoustic**   An adjective and an adjective-forming word-final element, derived from Greek *akoustik(os)* 'of or relating to hearing' (cf. the verb *akou(ein)* 'to hear'), used in two related senses:

  1. In medical terminology, 'pertaining to the organs of hearing': **entacoustic, otacoustic.**
  2. 'Pertaining to sound or sound waves, natural or artificially amplified': **telacoustic, radioacoustic, micracoustic.** Also, **-acoustical.** Related form: **-acoustically.**

577   **-scorbutic**   An adjective and, in two terms, an adjective-forming word-final element, derived from Latin *scorbūt(us)* 'scurvy,' used in the sense of 'pertaining or referring to scurvy or its treatment or prevention' as specified by the combining root: **scorbutic, antiscorbutic, postscorbutic.** Also, **-scorbutical, -scorbic.** Related form: **-scorbutically.**

578   **-therapeutic**   An adjective and an adjective-forming word-final element, derived from Greek *therapeu(ein)* 'to serve, attend, take care of' and **-tic,** used in combinations meaning 'of, pertaining, or referring to the medical treatment of a disease or disorder by means or techniques' specified by the combining root: **electrotherapeutic, hemotherapeutic, chemotherapeutic.** Related forms: **-therapia, -therapy, -therapist, -therapeutics, -therapeutically.**

579   **-lytic**   An adjective-forming word-final element, derived from Greek *lytik(os)* 'able to loosen, fit for loosening' from the verb *ly(ein)* 'to loosen' and **-ic[1],** used in combinations with the sense of 'pertaining or relating to, or effecting decomposition *(lysis)*' as qualified by the combining root: **electrolytic, hydrolytic, hemolytic.** Compare **-lysis.** Related forms: **-lytical, -lytically; -lyses** *(plural).*

580   **-analytic**   An adjective and an adjective-forming word-final element, derived from Greek *analytik(os)* 'pertaining to or skilled in breaking down, taking apart' from the verb *analy(ein)* 'to take apart, loosen up' and **ic[1],** used in combinations with the meaning 'concerning the process of inspection of elements or parts' denoted by the combining root: **electroanalytic, psychoanalytic, autoanalytic.** Also, **-analytical.** Compare **-lysis, -lytic.** Related forms: **-analysis, -analytically.**

581 **-paralytic**   An adjective and an adjective-forming word-final element, derived from Greek *paralytik(os)* 'pertaining to breaking down or disabling' from the verb *paraly(ein)* 'to break down, disable' (cf. *ly(ein)* 'to loosen, break down, dissolve'), used in combinations meaning 'pertaining to paralysis (i.e. loss of muscle function) or its effects,' as specified by the combining root: **neuroparalytic, angioparalytic, preparalytic.** Also, **-paralytical.** Compare **-lysis, -lytic.** Related forms: **-paralysis, -paralytically.**

582 **-catalytic**   An adjective, derived from Greek *katalytik(os)* 'concerning dissolving,' used also as a word ending in forming adjectives 'pertaining to, involving, or causing a chemical reaction by means of an agent unchanged by the reaction': **electrocatalytic, photocatalytic, anticatalytic.** Also, **-catalytical.** Compare **-lysis, -lytic.** Related forms: **-catalysis, -catalytically.**

583 **-toxic**   An adjective and an adjective-forming word-final element, derived from Greek *tox(ikon)* 'poison,' originally, 'poison for smearing on arrows' (cf. Greek *toxa* 'bow and arrow') and **-ic**[1], used in combinations meaning 'of, pertaining, or relating to, or involving a poison or the result of poisoning' as specified by the combining root: **fungitoxic, antitoxic, neurotoxic.** Also, **-toxical.** Related forms: **-toxia, -toxy, -toxin, -toxicity, -toxism, -toxically, -toxis.**

584 **-boc**   A noun-forming word-final element, derived from Afrikaans *boc* 'male antelope,' used in borrowings from Afrikaans designating varieties of 'antelope': **Rheeboc, Kleenboc, Steenboc.** Also, **-bok.** Related form: **-bocs** *(plural).*

585 **-sarc**   A noun-forming word-final element, derived from Greek *sarx, sark-* 'flesh,' used in biomedical terminology in its etymological sense as qualified by the combining root: **perisarc, endosarc, caulosarc.** Related forms: **-sarcous; -sarcs** *(plural).*

586 **-d**[1]   An abbreviation of *-ed,* used to form the standard abbreviation of past tense verbs and past participles; it appears with and without an apostrophe: **recd., chgd., ltd.**

587 **-d**[2]   An abbreviation used after the figures 2 and 3 to mean 'second' and 'third', derived from the final letter of these two words: **2d, 3d.** Compare **-nd, -rd, -th**[1].

588 **-ad**[1]   A noun-forming suffix, derived through French and Latin from

Greek -as, -ad- 'descent from or connection with,' with a variety of modern meanings.

1. 'An epic' concerned with a topic or country denoted by the combining root: **Columbiad, Iliad, Dunciad.**
2. 'A period of time' designated by the combining root: **decad, quindecad, quinquenniad.** Also, **-ade²**.
3. 'A member of a botanical group' named by the first root: **magnoliad, acanthad, sterculiad.**
4. 'A group, unit, or aggregate' with the number of parts named by the combining root: **triad, quintad, myriad.**
5. 'An element, atom, or radical of a valence' specified by the first root: **monad, dyad, artiad.**
6. 'A plant or animal produced by or associated with a process, condition, or ecosystem' named by the combining root: **dryad, epihydriad, variad.** Related forms: **-adic; -ads** (plural).

589   **-ad²**   An adverbial suffix derived from the Latin ad 'toward' used in biological and medical terminology in its etymological sense, the terminus being denoted by the combining root: **radiad, mediad, craniad.**

590   **-head¹**   A noun, derived through Middle English from Old English hēafod 'head' (not to be confused with -head '**-hood**' from dialectal Middle English -hede), also used as a noun-forming word-final element in several related senses, most of them metaphorical or metonymic:

1. 'A head' of the type denoted by the combining root: **broadhead, bighead, Roundhead.**
2. 'A quality of intellect' as denoted by the usu. negative combining root (the majority of -head combinations): **blockhead, egghead, chucklehead.**
3. 'Hair' of the color or quantity suggested by the joining root: **towhead, barehead, redhead.**
4. 'The upper or higher end' of something named by the first root: **nailhead, spearhead, masthead.**
5. 'A tool or part of a machine': **slidehead, drivehead, spindlehead.**
6. 'The end or limit' of something named by the joining root: **railhead, tidehead, roadhead.**
7. 'A heading in printed material': **subhead, scarehead, sidehead.**
8. 'The common name or nickname of an animal or plant,' usu. based on resemblance to a head: **staghead** (tree), **fiddlehead** (fern), **greenhead** (mallard). Related forms: **-headed; -heads** (plural).

591   **-head²**   An adjective-forming word-final element, derived from Middle English *-hede* '**-hood,**' found largely in obsolete or dialectal combinations in its etymological sense of 'condition, state' of that which is specified by the combining root: **maidenhead, Godhead, youthhead.** Also, **-heid.** Compare **-hood.**

592   **-stead**   A noun and a noun-forming word-final element, derived from Old English *stede* 'place' (cognate, with **-state¹** and **-state²**), used in combinations meaning 'a location, place, or locality' of the object denoted by the combining root: **farmstead, gravestead, wellstead.** The same meaning is found in place names spelled **-sted** or **-stead: Hampstead, Winsted, Berkhamsted.** Related form: **-steads** *(plural).*

593   **-clad**   A past participle (of the verb *to clothe*), derived through Middle English *clad(d)* from Old English *(ge)claðed*, the past participle of *clad(ian)* 'to clothe,' used in two related senses:
1. 'Clothed': **beclad** *(archaic)*, **unclad, underclad.**
2. 'Sheathed or armored' by the material named in the combining root: **mailclad, tinclad, ironclad.**

594   **-ed**   A suffix derived from Middle English *-ede, -de,* from Old English *-de, -ede, -ode, -ade,* functioning as the past tense ending of regular (weak) verbs in English, those in which no vowel or form change occurs to indicate tense (*capture/captured* as against the irregular (strong) verb *ride/rode*): **jabbed, jogged, laughed.** By extension, **-ed** may also be used as an adjective-forming word-final element:
1. By addition to (weak) verbs, in what amounts to the adjectival use of the past participle: **enlisted, hyphenated, intended.**
2. By addition to nouns, with the meaning 'pertaining to the possession of something or to the characteristics of something' denoted by the combining root: **togaed, three-storied, moneyed.**

595   **-handed**   An adjective-forming word-final element, derived from **hand** and **-ed** (extended sense 2), used in general related senses:
1. 'Pertaining to a hand or hands' as qualified by the combining root: **hardhanded, barehanded, cackhanded** (i.e., **left-handed** *(dialectal)*).
2. 'Pertaining to the type of personality or behavior' denoted by the combining root: **openhanded, highhanded, underhanded.**
3. 'Pertaining to activity involving workers or actual hands': **shorthanded, singlehanded, doublehanded.** Related forms: **-handedly, -handedness.**

596   **-ceed**   A verb-forming word-final element, derived through Middle

English and French from Latin *cēd(ere)* 'to go,' used in its etymological sense, as qualified by the combining root: **succeed, proceed, exceed.** Compare **-cede** (the more common spelling of this suffix in English). Principal parts: **-ceeding, -ceeded, -ceeded.** Related forms: **-cession, -cessive** (both derived from the past participle *cess(us)*, *cess(a)*, *cess(um)* to the verb *cēd(ere)*).

597   **-feed**   A verb and a noun, derived through Middle English from Old English *fēd(an)* 'to give food to,' used also as a word-final element in noun, verb, and adjective combinations in two related senses:
  1.   'To nourish or supply': **overfeed, infeed, upfeed.** Principal parts: **-feeding, -fed, -fed.**
  2.   'Nourishment or food for livestock': **millfeed, afterfeed, winterfeed.** (The combination **upfeed** is also used as an adjective; the combinations **infeed** and **winterfeed** function either as nouns or verbs.) Related form: (sense 2) **-feeds** *(plural)*.

598   **-breed**   A verb and a deverbative noun, derived through Middle English from Old English *brēd(an)* 'to produce offspring,' also used as a word-final element in two sorts of combination:
  1.   In verb combinations, 'to improve by controlled propagation': **upbreed, crossbreed, interbreed.** Principal parts: **-breeding, -bred, -bred.**
  2.   In noun combinations, sometimes found as adjectives, 'a group of plants or animals related to a common ancestor, usu. the result of a process of controlled propagation': **crossbreed, subbreed, inbreed.** Related forms: (sense 2) **-bred, -breeding; -breeds** *(plural)*.

599   **-seed**   A noun and a noun-forming word-final element, derived through Middle English *sed, seed* from Old English *sǣd* 'that which may be sown; seed,' used in two related ways:
  1.   In the common names of seeds produced by grain grasses and other plants: **dillseed, linseed, flaxseed.**
  2.   In the common names of seed-producing plants: **fleaseed** (fleawort), **goldseed** (dog's-tail grass), **tileseed** (tree of the genus *Geissois*). Related form: **-seeds** *(plural* when seeds or plants are considered individually).

600   **-weed**   A noun and a noun-forming word-final element, derived through Middle English *wed, weed* from Old English *wēod* 'herb, grass, weed,' used extensively in common names of plants, not all considered 'weeds': **fireweed, ragweed, tickleweed.** Related form: **-weeds** *(plural)*.

601 **-shed¹** A noun and a noun-forming word-final element, derived from Middle English *shadde, shedde* 'small building for housing animals, tools' (possibly related to -shade or -shed²), used in combinations meaning 'a structure, usually roofed, but often open at the sides' for the thing or activity named by the combining root: **woodshed, washshed, cowshed.** Related form: **-sheds** *(plural).*

602 **-shed²** A verb and a word-final element, derived through Middle English *shed(en)* from Old English *scēad(an)* 'to divide, separate, lose (as of hair),' used in noun combinations with the basic meaning 'a loss' of that which is specified by the combining root: **bloodshed, watershed, snowshed.** Related form: **-sheds** *(plural).*

603 **-brained** An adjective-forming word-final element, derived from Middle English *branyd* 'having a brain' (i.e. *brain* plus -ed), used in combinations meaning 'having a quality of intelligence' specified by the (usually negative) combining root: **barmybrained, dullbrained, strongbrained.** Related forms: **-brain; -brains** *(plural).*

604 **-ped** A word-final element, derived from Latin *pēs, ped-* 'foot,' used to form both nouns and adjectives with closely related senses:

1. In nouns, 'a creature possessing or characterized by a foot or feet' of the sort or quantity specified by the combining root: **fissiped, sexiped, pinniped.**

2. In adjectives, 'possessing or characterized by a foot or feet' of the sort or quantity specified by the combining root: **taliped, palmiped, uniped.** Also, **-pede.** Compare **-pod.** Related forms: **-pedic¹, -pedia¹, -pedal; -peds, -pedes** *(plurals).*

605 **-red¹** An adjective (also used substantively) and an adjective-forming word-final element, derived from Old English *rēod* '(the color) red,' used in combinations with the sense of 'referring or pertaining to the visible spectrum at its red limit': **ultrared, infrared, extrared.**

606 **-red²** A word-ending, derived through Middle English *rede* from Old English *rǣden* 'counsel, rule, condition,' formerly used in two senses:

1. In nouns, 'a state or condition' specified by the combining root: **hatred, prehatred, kindred.**

2. In proper names, 'counsel or power' as qualified by the combining root: **Mildred, Ethelred, Eldred.** Related form: (sense 1) **-reds** *(plural).*

607 **-bred** An adjective-forming word-final element, derived from the past participle of the verb *breed* (cf. **-breed**), used in two related senses:

1. 'Pertaining to a specific breed': **crossbred, thoroughbred, inbred.**
2. 'Pertaining to quality or location of birth and rearing': **hellbred, homebred, basebred.** Related forms: **-breed, -breeding; -breeds** *(plural).*

608 **-fred** A word-final element, derived from Old High German *fridu* 'peace,' used in personal names: **Wilfred, Winifred, Alfred.**

609 **-sparred** A word-final element, derived from *spar* 'a pole, mast, yard, boom; to fit with a pole, mast, yard, boom' (from Middle English *sperre, sparre, sparr* 'pole, rafter') and **-ed,** used in adjectival combinations meaning 'having spars,' as qualified by the combining root: **undersparred, oversparred, unsparred.**

610 **-nosed** An adjective-forming word-final element, derived from **-nose** and **-ed,** used in the sense of 'having or pertaining to a shape or kind of nose' specified by the combining root: **snubnosed, crooknosed, roundnosed.** Related forms: **-nose; -noses** *(plural).*

611 **-footed** An adjective-forming word-final element, derived from **-foot** and **-ed,** used in combinations meaning 'having feet' of a sort specified by the combining root: **clubfooted, barefooted, splayfooted.** Compare **-foot.**

612 **-wed** A verb, derived through Middle English *wedden* 'to engage, pledge, marry' from Old English *weddian* 'to pledge,' also used as a word ending to form combinations acting as verbs, nouns, or adjectives according to context: **newlywed, interwed, miswed.** Principal parts: **-wedding, -wedded, -wedded.** Related form: **-weds** *(plural).*

613 **-jawed** An adjective-forming word-final element, derived from *jaw* and **-ed,** used in the sense of 'having a jaw of a sort' specified by the combining root: **gimbaljawed, underjawed, overjawed.**

614 **-eyed** An adjective-forming word-final element, derived from the word *eye* (cf. **-eye**) and **-ed,** used in the sense of 'having eyes of a sort' specified by the combining root: **popeyed, walleyed, swiveleyed.** Related forms: **-eye; -eyes** *(plural).*

615 **-sized** An adjective-forming word-final element, derived from the word *size* and **-ed,** used in combinations meaning 'of, pertaining to, or possessing a bulk or set of dimensions' specified by the combining root: **oversized, outsized, king-sized.** Also, **-size.**

616   **-id¹** A word-final element, derived from the Greek masculine
patronymic suffix *-id(ēs)*, used in two related forms:
1. In noun combinations to denote 'a person associated with a
   dynastic line' specified by the combining root: **Abassid, Fatimid,
   Sulayhid.**
2. In combinations, noun or adjective according to context,
   'pertaining to or denoting one belonging to a natural group or
   line of descent' named by the combining root: **Australid,
   Melanesid, pre-Mongolid.** Related forms: **-ida, -idae; -ids** *(plural)*.

617   **-id²** A noun-forming word-final element with no assignable general
meaning, derived from the Latin and Greek third declension noun-
forming element *-is, -id-*, appearing chiefly in two kinds of combination:
1. 'A structural element of teeth, esp. lower molars': **tritoconid,
   protoconid, trigonid.**
2. 'A body or particle' as specified by the combining root: **rhabdoid,
   cuspid, sporid.** Related form: **-ids** *(plural)*.

618   **-id³** A noun-forming word-final element, derived from the Latin suffix
-is, -id- used to indicate 'source or origin' found in English in two
kinds of combination:
1. To designate 'a meteor shower' from the celestial source named
   in the combining root: **Andromedid, Geminid, Leonid.**
2. To name 'an epic concerning the person, place, or subject' named
   in the combining root: **Aeneid, Thebaid, Achilleid.** Related form:
   -ids *(plural)*.

619   **-id⁴** A word-final element with no assignable general meaning, derived
from Latin *-id(us)*, a suffix originally used to form adjectives from
verbs, appearing in English in both adjective and noun combinations,
the latter being derived through the substantive use of the former:
horrid, florid, fluid. Related form: **-ids** *(plural)*.

620   **-id⁵** A word-final element, derived from the taxonomic suffixes **-ida**
and **-idae**, used in forming noun and adjective combinations meaning
'a member of a zoological or botanical family or other group' denoted
by the combining root or 'pertaining to such a member': **arachnid,
piscid, malacanthid.** Related form: **-ids** *(plural)*.

621   **-maid** A noun, derived by shortening of Middle English *maiden* from
Old English *maegden* 'a girl or unmarried woman' also used as a
noun-forming word-final element with the meaning 'a girl, a young or
adult woman, specifically, a female servant' whose particular

occupation or salient feature is specified by the combining root: **nursemaid, barmaid, mermaid.** Also, **-maiden** *(archaic).* Compare **-man, -woman, -girl, -boy.** Related forms: **-maids, -maidens** *(plurals).*

622   **-bid**   A verb and a verb-forming word-final element, derived through Middle English from Old English *bidd(an)* 'to entreat,' used in an extension of its etymological sense, 'to make an offer (usually, of money)': **underbid, counterbid, outbid.** Principal parts: **-bidding, -bid, -bid.**

623   **-acid**   A word, derived through French from Latin *acid(us)* 'sour,' (itself derived from Latin *ac(ere)* 'to be sour' and *-idus* '**-id**⁴'), also used as a word-final element in two types of combination:
  1.   In nouns, with the meaning 'an acid' as particularized by the combining root: **antacid, monacid, hydracid.**
  2.   In adjectives, with the meaning 'pertaining to acid' as qualified by the combining root: **subacid, semiacid, polyacid.** Related forms: **-acidity; -acids** *(plural).*

624   **-fid**   An adjective-forming word-final element, derived from Latin *-fid(us)* 'split,' the past participle to the verb *find(ere)* 'to split,' used in the sense of 'divided into parts' of a number or kind specified by the combining root: **decafid, pinnatifid, bifid.** Related form: **-fidate.**

625   **-oid**¹   A noun-forming word-final element, derived from the Greek adjective-forming suffix *-oeid(ēs)* '-like' (from the noun *eid(os)* 'form, shape, appearance'), used in the general sense of 'something resembling or having the form or shape of' something specified by the combining root: **spheroid, alkaloid, trochoid.** Compare **-ode**³. Related forms: **-oid**², **-oidal; -oids** *(plural).*

626   **-oid**²   An adjective-forming word-final element, derived from the Greek adjectival suffix *-oeid(ēs)* '-like' (from the noun *eid(os)* 'form, shape, appearance'), used extensively in combinations meaning 'possessing the form or appearance of' the thing denoted by the combining root: **anthropoid, ovoid, acanthoid.** Also, **-oidal** (esp. in adjectives formed from nouns ending in **-oid**¹). Related forms: **-oid**¹, **-oidism.**

627   **-typhoid**   An adjective and a noun, derived from Greek *typh(os)* 'stupor' and **-oid**²/**-oid**¹, used in two related senses:
  1.   In nouns, 'a form of typhus' specified by the combining root: **pleurotyphoid, meningotyphoid, nephrotyphoid.**
  2.   In adjectives, 'of, pertaining or referring to, or resembling typhus' as specified by the combining root: **paratyphoid, pretyphoid,**

posttyphoid. Also, -typhoidal. Related forms: -typhus, -typhi; -typhoids *(plural)*.

628   **-ploid** An adjective-forming word-final element, derived by abstraction from scientific Greek *haploid* and *diploid,* terms derived from Greek *hapl(os)* 'single' and *dipl(os)* 'double' (each itself a compound consisting of a numerical prefix and the suffix *-pl(os)* '-ple') and -oid, used in the terminology of genetics to mean 'having a number of chromosome sets (in an animal or plant)' specified by the combining root: **triploid, tetraploid, hexaploid.** Forms with this suffix may also be used substantively. Related forms: **-ploidy; -ploids** *(plural).*

629   **-zooid** An adjective (which may be used substantively) and an adjective-forming word-final element, derived from *zō(os), zō(ē), zō(on)* 'living, alive' (cf. the verb *za(ein)* 'to live') and -oid, used in the sense of 'of, referring or relating to, or resembling a form of animal life' specified by the combining root: **megazooid, oozooid, sporozooid.** Related forms: **-zoon, -zoa, -zoic, -zoal, -zoan, -zoid, -zoite; -zooids** *(plural).*

630   **-ald** A word-final element, derived from Old High German *walt(an)* 'to rule, wield,' used in forming personal names: **Reginald, Donald, Gerald.** Also, **-wald** *(Oswald),* **-old** *(Reynold).*

631   **-bald[1]** An adjective, derived from Middle English *ball(e)d,* itself derived from the obsolete Middle English *ball* 'white spot,' used to form two adjective combinations 'pertaining to the possession of white areas in hair or fur': **skewbald, piebald.**

632   **-bald[2]** A word-final element, derived from Late Latin *bald(us)* 'spirited, bold,' used formerly as an ending of personal names: **Archibald, Theobald, Willibald.**

633   **-geld** A noun and a noun-forming word-final element, derived from Old English *gield, geld, gild* (whence also *yield*) 'service, tax, tribute,' used in combinations meaning 'a form of tax or tribute' denoted by the combining root: **woodgeld, Danegeld, footgeld.** Related forms: **-gelds, -gelts** *(plurals).*

634   **-field** A noun and a noun-forming word-final element, derived through Middle English from Old English *feld* 'an area of open land' (akin to both *plain* and *plane*), used in two ways:

    1. In common nouns designating 'an open or cleared piece of land

used for something' specified by the combining root: **cornfield, battlefield, playfield.**

2. In personal names, originally referring to an open or cleared piece of land of a particular sort or location: **Chesterfield, Canfield, Sheffield.** Also, **-field** *(sense 2).* Related form: **-fields** *(plural, sense 1).*

635 **-veld** A noun and a noun-forming word-final element, derived from Afrikaans *velt* 'field' (with which it is cognate), used in combinations (both borrowings and partial loan-translations) designating types of 'African grassland' specified by the combining root: **bosveld, bushveld, backveld.** Also, **-veldt.** Related forms: **-velds, -veldts** *(plurals).*

636 **-gild** A verb and a verb-forming word-final element, derived through Middle English from Old English *gyld(an)* 'to cover with gold,' used in two related senses:

1. 'To cover with a thin layer of gold': **electrogild, ungild, regild.**
2. 'To embellish or gild to excess': **begild, engild, overgild.** Principal parts: **-gilding, -gilded** or **-gilt, -gilded** or **-gilt.**

637 **-fold[1]** An archaic noun and, formerly, a noun-forming word-final element, derived through Middle English from Old English *falod, falud, fald* 'pen,' used to denote 'an enclosed area for animals': **flitfold, penfold, sheepfold.** Related form: **-folds** *(plural).*

638 **-fold[2]** An adjective-forming word-final element, derived from Old English *-feald,* the past participle of the verb *fealdan* 'to fold,' (cognate with Latin *plicare* and Modern English *ply*), used in two related senses:

1. 'Multiplied by' the number forming the combining root: **threefold, tenfold, manifold.**
2. 'Having laps, parts, or layers' as specified by the combining root: **trifold, bifold, polyfold.**

639 **-fold[3]** A verb and a verb-forming word-final element, derived through Middle English from Old English *feald(an)* 'to pleat, fold,' used in combinations meaning 'to pleat or fold in a manner or for a purpose' denoted by the combining root: **backfold, infold, underfold.** Principal parts: **-folding, -folded, -folded.**

640 **-hold** A deverbative noun and a noun-forming word-final element, derived through Middle English *hold, holde* 'a hold, possession; land or property that is held' from Old English *heald* 'protection, keeping,' used in several related senses:

1. In current and feudal legal terminology, 'a possession of land or property' of a type denoted by the combining root: **freehold, leasehold, lifehold.** The terms are also used as adverbs without change in form.
2. 'A refuge or fortified place': **stronghold, fasthold, safehold.**
3. 'A storage place for cargo on a plane or ship': **afterhold, forehold, stokehold.**
4. 'Dwellers in a place' named by the first root: **household, farmhold, villeinhold.**
5. 'A grasping or possession' of a type denoted by the combining root: **handhold, anchorhold, foothold.** Related forms: **-holding** (senses 1 and 4); **holds** *(plural).*

641 **-mold** A noun (and a denominative verb), derived from Latin *modulus* 'small measure' (from *mod(us)* 'a measure' and the diminutive suffix *-ulus*), used as a word-final noun-forming element in a specialized extension of its original meaning in combinations designating 'an ornamental architectural form in a strip along the top or bottom of a wall, along a sill, or the like' of a sort specified by the combining root: **hoodmold, dripmold, neckmold.** Also, **-mould, -molding, -moulding.** Related forms: **-molds, -moulds, -mouldings, -moldings** *(plurals).*

642 **-world** A noun, derived through Middle English from Old English *wearold, woruld, worold* 'human existence, this world, age,' also used as a word ending in noun combinations concerning 'a state or place of existence' denoted by the combining root: **underworld, afterworld, dreamworld.** Related forms: **-worldly; -worlds** *(plural).*

643 **-nd** A symbol, formed by abbreviation of *second,* used after the figure 2 to form the ordinals **second** and **-second: 2nd, 22nd, 52nd.**

644 **-and** A noun-forming word-final element, derived from Latin *-and(us)* (the stem form of the future passive participle), meaning 'that which undergoes a process' specified in the combining root: **multiplicand, degradand, duplicand.** Related form: **-ands** *(plural).*

645 **-band** A noun and a noun-forming word-final element, derived through Middle English from Old English *bend* 'fetter,' used in several related senses:
1. 'A strip (as cloth) used to encircle and confine' a part of the body denoted by the combining root: **waistband, headband, bellyband.**
2. 'A strip, usually cloth, used to join two pieces of cloth together' at a location denoted by the combining root: **shirtband, neckband, wristband.**

3. 'A strip in harnesses and bridles used to join' at the location named by the combining root: **noseband, backband, witherband.**

4. 'A strip (of color, stone, or cloth) or layer' used on an object or for a purpose named by the combining root: **archband, hatband, rainband.** Related form: -bands *(plural)*.

646 **-hand**   A noun, derived from Old English *hand, hond* through Middle English, used also as a word ending in noun and adjective combinations:

1. 'A laborer' whose task or location is named by the first root: **stonehand, stagehand, foremasthand.**

2. 'A deformity of the hand' named by the combining root: **clubhand, clawhand, clefthand.**

3. 'Pertaining to the motion or position of the hand': **forehand, overhand, crosshand.**

4. 'Involving or concerning the hand': **longhand, shorthand, freehand.**

5. 'Pertaining to location, status, or time': **behindhand, secondhand, beforehand.** Related forms: (noun) -hands *(plural)*; (for some adjectives) -handed.

647 **-land**   A noun, derived through Middle English from Old English *land, lond* 'land, open land' (cf. the cognate *lawn*), also used as a word-final element in noun combinations (which may sometimes be used as adjectives):

1. In place names, 'land of' something named by the combining root: **Rhineland, Iceland, Vineland.**

2. In nicknames for localities, 'land of' something specified by the combining root: **Siestaland, Bananaland, Yankeeland.**

3. 'Land possessing a location or a geological or botanical feature' named by the combining root: **steppeland, midland, scrubland.**

4. 'An area, real or metaphorical, characterized by an activity or outlook' named by the combining root: **fableland, movieland, clubland.** Related form: -lands *(plural)*.

648 **-mand**   A word-final element, derived from Latin *mand(āre)* 'to intrust to, confide in, commission, send word by, command,' used to form verbs and deverbative nouns with an active sense of 'an order or request' as qualified by the combining root: **command, demand, remand.** Also, -mend (in *commend* and its derivatives, from *-mend(āre)*, the combining form of *mand(āre)*, not to be confused with the -mend of *mend, amend, emend,* and *remend,* which comes from Latin *mend(a)* 'fault'). Principal parts: **-manding, -manded, -manded.**

649   -stand[1]   A noun and a noun-forming word-final element, derived from
       Middle English *stand, stond* (from the verb *stand(en), stond(en)* 'to
       stand'), used in a number of related senses:
       1. 'A structure to support or act as a base' for something named by
           the combining root: **rickstand, candlestand, bookstand.**
       2. 'A structure, usu. small, for a public purpose, as selling, viewing,
           or performing' named by the combining root: **bandstand,
           newsstand, grandstand.**
       3. In two athletic terms, 'an upsidedown vertical stance, with
           support' denoted by the combining root: **headstand, handstand.**
           Related form: **-stands** *(plural).*

650   -stand[2]   A verb and a verb-forming word-final element, derived from
       Middle English and Old English *stand(en), stond(en)* 'to stand,' used
       in a number of inherited combinations:
       1. In three combinations, now archaic, illustrating the former
           English practice of preceding verbs with adverbs, 'to stand' as
           noted by the prior root: **upstand, withstand** (originally 'stand
           against'), **outstand** (originally 'contradict' or 'endure beyond').
       2. In one combination, **understand,** originally a 9th-cent. translation
           into Old English of Latin *subsist(ere)* and *substant(ia)* as
           'comprehend.' Older secondary meanings of Old English *under,*
           now obsolete, permitted the glossing of the combination as 'to
           stand among or before so as to recognize or perceive;' hence,
           'comprehend.' Principal parts: **-standing, -stood, -stood.**

651   -wand   A noun, derived through Middle English *wond, wande* from Old
       Norse *vöndr* 'slender rod or stick,' used also as a word ending in
       forming noun combinations, now archaic, meaning 'a measuring stick'
       of a size or purpose denoted by the combining root: **ellwand,
       yardwand, metewand.** Related form: **-wands** *(plural).*

652   -scend   A verb-forming word-final element, derived from the combining
       form of Latin *scand(ere)* 'to climb, go,' used in a number of common
       borrowings in its etymological senses as qualified by the combining
       root: **descend, ascend, transcend.** Principal parts: **-scending, -scended,
       -scended.** Related forms: **-scendent, -scendant, -scension.**

653   -fend   A verb, an abbreviated form of Middle English *defenden,* itself
       derived from Latin *-fend(ere)* 'to strike,' used also as a word ending in
       verb combinations meaning 'to fend, guard, act to repel' as qualified
       by the adverbial combining root: **defend, offend, forfend.** Principal
       parts: **-fending, -fended, -fended.** Related forms: **-fense, -fensive** (both

derived from *-fens(us)*, *-fens(a)*, *-fens(um)*, the past participle to Latin *-fend(ere)*.

654 **-prehend** A verb-forming word-final element, derived from Latin *prehend(ere)* 'to grasp, seize' (related to Old English *gehend(an)* 'to grasp' and Modern English *get*), used in combinations meaning 'to grasp, either physically or mentally' as qualified by the combining root: **apprehend, comprehend, reprehend**. Principal parts: **-prehending, -prehended, -prehended**. Compare **-prise**. Related forms: **-prehension, -prehensive**.

655 **-mend** A verb and a verb-forming word-final element, derived by aphesis from Latin *ēmend(āre)* 'to correct, fix' (from *ex-* 'from, out from' and *mendum* 'fault, error'), used in a few combinations, all with the basic sense of 'to repair': **amend, emend, remend**. Principal parts: **-mending, -mended, -mended**.

656 **-pend** A verb-forming word-final element, derived from Latin *pend(ere)* 'to hang, weigh, assay, pay out,' used widely in borrowed verb combinations chiefly in two of its main etymological senses:
  1. 'To hang or lean': **depend, suspend, impend**.
  2. 'To estimate, value, or pay': **compend, vilipend, expend**. Principal parts: **-pending, -pended, -pended**. Compare **-pense**.

657 **-tend** A verb and a verb-forming word-final element, derived from Latin *tend(ere)* 'to stretch,' used in a number of extensions of its etymological sense:
  1. 'To stretch out' in a manner or direction specified by the combining root: **extend, distend, subtend**.
  2. 'To "stretch" one's mental, physical, or verbal skills' in a way specified by the combining root: **intend, contend, pretend**. Principal parts: **-tending, -tended, -tended**. Related forms: **-tention[2], -tension, -tentious, -tensious, -tent, -tense, -tensine**.

658 **-bind** A noun-forming word-final element, derived from Old English *bindan* 'to tie, bind,' used in common plant nomenclature to name climbing or vining plants: **woodbind, bellbind, bearbind**. Also, **-bine**. Related form: **-binds** *(plural)*.

659 **-kind** A noun, derived through Middle English *kind, kinde* from Old English *cynd, (ge)cynde* 'nature,' related to Old English *cyn* 'kin' and cognate with **-gen**, also used as a noun-forming word-final element meaning, 'a class, group, or division' of things denoted by the combining root: **mankind, womankind, demonkind.** The combinations are usually considered collective nouns.

660   **-wind**[1]   A noun and a noun-forming word-final element, derived through Middle English from Old English *wind* 'current of air,' used to designate 'a current of air' of a type or effect named by the combining root: **whirlwind, wildwind, driftwind.** Related form: **-winds** *(plural)*.

661   **-wind**[2]   A verb, derived through Middle English from Old English *wind(an)* 'to twist, turn,' also used as a word-final element in noun combinations functioning as the common names for varieties of bindweed: **withwind, withywind, bellwind.** Related form: **-winds** *(plural)*.

662   **-mond**   A word-final element, derived from Old High German *munt* 'hand, protection,' used in forming proper names: **Raymond, Rosamond, Hammond.** Also, **-mund.**

663   **-spond**   A word-final element, derived from Latin *spond(ēre)* 'to promise, pledge,' used in forming verb combinations with the underlying meaning 'to promise or pledge' to oneself or to others as suggested by the combining root: **respond, correspond, despond.** Principal parts: **-sponding, -sponded, -sponded.** Related forms: **-spondency, -spondence, -spondent; -spondencies, -spondences, -spondents** *(plurals)*.

664   **-bund**[1]   An adjective-forming word-final element, derived from Latin *-bund(us)*, *-bund(a)*, *-bund(um)*, a suffix similar in meaning, form, and function to that which forms the present participle, used in English in learned combinations in its etymological sense or with the meaning 'prone to' that which is specified by the combining root: **furibund, moribund, ridibund.**

665   **-bund**[2]   A noun-forming word-final element, derived from German *Bund* 'association' (cf. English *bond*), used in borrowed combinations to designate 'a club, league' whose purpose is specified by the combining root: **Sängerbund, Sonderbund, plunderbund.** Related form: **-bunds** *(plural)*.

666   **-bound**[1]   A word, derived from Middle English *bound(en)* (past participle of *bind(en)* 'to bind'), used also as a word ending in adjective combinations meaning

     1. 'Limited by, surrounded by, or caught in' the substance or locale

denoted by the combining root: **snowbound, spellbound, housebound.**

2. 'Covered or bound' in the substance named by the first root: **calfbound, brassbound, clothbound.**

667   **-bound**[2] A word, derived through Middle English from Old Norse *būinn* (past participle of *būa* 'to live, dwell, make ready'), used also as a word ending in adjective combinations meaning 'planning to go, going' to the destination or in the direction denoted by the combining root: **homebound, outbound, eastbound.**

668   **-hound** A noun, derived through Middle English from Old English *hund* 'dog,' also used as a word ending in noun combinations meaning 'a dog specially trained for' the hunting or tracking task denoted by the combining root: **harehound, boarhound, draghound.** Related form: **-hounds** *(plural)*. By metaphorical extension, the form's use has been adopted colloquially to mean 'an avid pursuer or fan' of the goal or object specified by the combining noun: **candyhound, moviehound, coffeehound.**

669   **-pound** A verb-forming word-final element, derived through Middle English and Old French from Latin *pōn(ere)* 'to put, place, set,' used in a number of common combinations, all with a sense of 'put, set' as qualified by the combining prepositional prefix: **compound, impound, expound.** Principal parts: **-pounding, -pounded, -pounded.** Related forms: **-pone, -pose, -posal, -posit, -posite, -position, -positional, -positionally, -positive, -posure, -ponent, -poundable, -poundability.**

670   **-ground** A noun, derived through Middle English *ground, grund* from Old English *grund* 'earth, land, foundation,' also used as a noun-forming word-final element with the sense 'a location or place for an activity or a structure' named by the combining root: **fairground, bleachground, campground.** Related form: **-grounds** *(plural)*.

671   **-tund** A verb-forming word-final element, derived from Latin *tund(ere)* 'to beat, thump, dull,' used in its etymological sense, as qualified by the combining root: **obtund, contund, extund.** Principal parts: **-tunding, -tunded, -tunded.** Related forms: **-tuse, -tusion** (these forms are derived from the past participle *tūs(us), tūs(a), tūs(um)*).

672   **-god** A noun and a noun-forming word-final element, derived through Middle English from Old English *god* 'deity,' used in the sense of 'a deity, supernatural power' whose nature, rank, or realm is specified by

the combining root: **protogod, overgod, bridegod**. Related form: **-gods** *(plural)*.

673 **-period** A noun, derived through Middle English and Middle French from Greek *period(os)* 'way around, portion of time,' used also as a word ending in noun combinations of an essentially technical nature meaning 'a period of time involving a state or condition' named by the combining root: **thermoperiod, hydroperiod, photoperiod**. Related forms: **-periodic, -periodically, -periodicity; -periods** *(plural)*.

674 **-hood** A noun-forming word-final element, derived through Middle English *-hod, -hode* (dialectal *-hede*) from Old English *hād* 'state, rank, condition,' used extensively in combinations meaning 'a rank, condition, or occupation' named by the combining root: **widowhood, kinghood, clerkhood**. Also, **-head, -heid**. Related form: **-hoods** *(plural)*.

675 **-blood** A noun, derived through Middle English *blood* from Old English *blōd* 'blood,' used also as a word ending in noun combinations meaning 'a race, stock, or lineage' specified by the combining root: **pureblood, mixblood, gutterblood** *(Scot.)*. Related form: **-bloods** *(plural)*.

676 **-wood** A noun and a noun-forming word-final element, derived through Middle English *wode, wude* from Old English *wudu, widu* 'tree, collection of trees,' used in two related senses:
 1. 'A variety of wood (i.e. the material of which a tree is made)' specified by the combining root: **orangewood, jasminewood, ironwood**.
 2. 'A small forest' in place names and the personal names derived from them: **Norwood, Glenwood Springs, Atwood**. Related form: **-woods** *(plural)*.

677 **-pod** A word-final element, derived from Greek *pous, pod-* 'foot,' used to form both nouns and adjectives meaning '(a creature) having a type or number of feet' specified by the combining root: **gastropod, polypod, megapod**. Also, **-pode**. Compare **-ped, -pede**. Related forms: **-poda, -podia, -pus, -podial, -podium, -podal, -podous, -pody; -pods, -podes** *(plurals)*.

678 **-rd** An abbreviation, taken from the last two letters of *third*, used in combination with numbers to indicate the ordinal numbers 'third' and '-third': **3rd, 23rd, 83rd**. Also, **-d**.

679 **-ard** A word-final element, derived through Middle English and Old French from Old High German *hart* 'hard, strong,' used in two ways:
1. In personal names, 'hard, strong, powerful': **Leonard, Reynard, Richard.**
2. Generally 'a person who excessively performs, displays, or is associated with actions or qualities' specified by the conjoining root: **dullard, drunkard, sluggard.** Also, **-art.** Related forms: **-ards, -arts** *(plurals).*

680 **-card** A noun and a noun-forming word-final element, derived through Middle English *card(e)*, Middle French *cart(e)*, and Latin *chart(a)* from Greek *chart(ēs)* 'leaf of papyrus, paper,' used to denote 'a piece of paper or paperboard' of a sort or for a purpose (usually involving tallying) specified by the combining root: **timecard, scorecard, scratchcard.** Related form: **-cards** *(plural).*

681 **-board** A noun and a noun-forming word-final element, derived from Old English *bord* 'plank, piece of wood, side, border,' used in its various etymological senses:
1. 'A piece of lumber, at least originally, for a purpose' denoted by the combining root: **sideboard, dartboard, breadboard.**
2. 'Something like a board, for the purpose' stated by the combining root: **blackboard, switchboard, signboard.**
3. 'Something like a board, made of another material' named by the combining root: **pasteboard, wallboard, corkboard.** Related form: **-boards** *(plural).*

682 **-guard** A noun and a verb, derived through Middle English *garde* from Old French *guard, garde* 'protector, watcher' (from an unattested Germanic form from which the cognate *ward* is also derived), used in its etymological sense of 'protector of or from' that which is specified by the combining root: **mudguard, lifeguard, bodyguard.** Related form: **-guards** *(plural).*

683 **-ward**[1] A word-final element, derived through Middle English from Old English *-weard* 'toward,' used to form adverb and adjective combinations, many of which can function as either part of speech:
1. In adjectives, 'pertaining to moving, facing, or tending toward a direction or locale' specified by the combining root: **Americaward, cityward, homeward.**
2. In adverbs, 'in a direction toward a point or locale' specified by the combining root: **seaward, landward, sideward.**
3. In adverbs of time: **henceforward, afterward, thenceforward.** Also, **-wards** (in adverbs).

684   -ward² A noun and a noun-forming word-final element, derived through Middle English from Old English *weard* 'watchman, keeper, guard' (this last being a cognate), used in its etymological sense in two kinds of inherited word:

    1. Generally, 'a protector' as specified by the combining root: **steward, woodward** (also a personal or last name), **hogward.**

    2. In personal names, 'protector': **Edward, Heyward, Howard.** Related form: (sense 1) **-wards** *(plural).*

685   -yard A noun and a noun-forming word-final element, derived through Middle English *yard, yerd* from Old English *geard* 'enclosure, court, yard' (akin to *garden*), used in a number of related senses, each as specified by the combining root:

    1. 'An enclosed area': **backyard, churchyard, graveyard.**

    2. 'An area enclosed for an agricultural purpose': **vineyard, henyard, hogyard.**

    3. 'An area used for a commercial purpose, not necessarily enclosed': **fishyard, boatyard, coalyard.** Related form: **-yards** *(plural).*

686   -herd A noun, derived through Middle English *hierde, hirde, herde,* from Old English *hyrde, hierde* 'herdsman for an animal' specified by the combining root: **swineherd, cowherd, beeherd** *(rare).* Related form: **-herds** *(plural).*

687   -bird A noun, derived through Middle English *brid, bird* from Old English *bridd* 'young bird,' used also as a word ending in noun combinations as the common names of birds: **cowbird, kingbird, doctorbird.** Related form: **-birds** *(plural).*

688   -cord A noun, derived through Middle English, Old French, and Latin from Greek *chord(ē)* 'catgut, string, chord, cord,' also used as a noun-forming word-final element meaning 'a small rope of fiber, leather, etc.' for a purpose named by the combining root: **bedcord, ripcord, whipcord.** Compare **-chord.** Related form: **-cords** *(plural).*

689   -ford A noun and a verb, derived from Middle and Old English *ford* 'shallow area in a stream for crossing,' used also as a word ending in noun combinations that are place and personal names perhaps related to actual crossings: **Rutherford, Oxford, Bedford.**

690   -chord A noun, derived from Greek *chord(ē)* 'catgut, string, chord, cord,' used in musical terminology as a noun-forming word-final element in either of two senses:

1. 'Tones in harmony,' their number specified by the combining root: **pentachord, polychord, trichord.**
2. 'A musical instrument' of a type denoted by the first root: **harpsichord, novachord, lyrichord.** Compare **-cord.** Related form: **-chords** *(plural).*

691 **-word** A noun and a noun-forming word-final element, derived through Middle English from Old English *word* 'a spoken utterance,' used in two specialized senses:
1. 'A signal in words, sometimes a maxim': **watchword, byword, password.**
2. 'A word, of a type or origin denoted by the combining root': **loanword, swearword, catchword.** Related form: **-words** *(plural).*

692 **-bud** A noun and a denominative verb, derived from Middle English *budde* 'bud, spray, pod,' also used as a word ending in noun combinations acting as common plant names: **redbud, marybud, Junebud.** Related form: **-buds** *(plural).*

693 **-e** A word-final element used to form the feminine singular of Attic-Ionic Greek nouns of the first declension: **synecdoche, apostrophe, hyperbole.** Also, **-a⁴.**

694 **-ae¹** A word-final element, used to form the plurals of Latin nouns and adjectives of the first declension whose singulars end in *-a*. It is used in English to pluralize a variety of suffixes in taxonomic nomenclature and, in variation with **-s,** a handful of learned or semi-learned non-technical borrowings: **Columbae, Myoxidae, larvae.** Related form: **-a⁴** *(singular).*

695 **-ae²** A word-final element, derived through Latin, used to form the plurals of nouns and noun suffixes borrowed from the Greek first declension whose singulars end in *-ē* or *-a*: **basilicae, Bacchae, thecae.** Related forms: **-e, -a** *(singulars).*

696 **-ae³** A word-final element, derived from the Latin genitive singular case ending of the first declension, used chiefly in astronomical terminology to form the possessive of the names of constellations whose (nominative) singulars end in *-a:* **Aquilae, Andromedae, mensae.**

697 **-idae** A noun-forming word-final element, derived from Greek *-id(ēs)* (a patronymic suffix) and **-ae¹,** used in botanical taxonomy to name

plant subclasses and in zoological taxonomy to name animal families: **Urocoptidae, Blattidae, Heterodontidae.**

698 **-somatidae** A noun-forming word-final element, derived from Greek *sōma, sōmat-* 'body' and -idae, used in the terminology of zoological nomenclature to designate 'creatures possessing a body' of the sort specified by the combining root: **Chaetosomatidae, Loxosomatidae, Platysomatidae.** Also, -somidae. Compare -soma, -some[3], -somata.

699 **-eae** A noun-forming word-final element, derived from Latin *-e(us)*, *-e(a)*, *-e(um)* 'made of, of' and **-ae[1]**, used in botanical taxonomy to name plant tribes: **Florideae, Gramineae, Phyllantheae.**

700 **-aceae** A noun-forming word-final element, derived from Latin *-ace(us)*, *-ace(a)*, *-ace(um)* 'having the nature or qualities of' and **-ae[1]**, used in botanical taxonomy to name families of plants with the qualities or characteristics specified by the combining root: **Hydrangeaceae, Melianthaceae, Rosaceae.** Compare -acea.

701 **-phyceae** A noun-forming word-final element, derived from Greek *phyk(os)* 'seaweed' and -eae, used in the terminology of botanical nomenclature to designate classes of Algae: **Rhodophyceae, Xanthophyceae, Dinophyceae.**

702 **-oideae** A noun-forming word-final element, derived from scientific Greco-Latin -oid plus -eae, used in botanical taxonomy to name plant subfamilies: **Discoideae, Fucoideae, Coniferoideae.** Compare -oidea.

703 **-inae** A noun-forming word-final element, derived from Latin *-īn(us)*, *-īn(a)*, *-īn(um)* 'of, belonging to' and **-ae[1]**, used in botanical taxonomy to name subtribes and in zoological taxonomy to name subfamilies 'related to, like, or characterized by' that which is specified by the combining root: **Plectinae, Phyllostomatinae, Troglodytinae.** Compare -ina[2].

704 **-ferae** A noun-forming word-final element, derived from Latin *fer(re)* 'to bear, carry, produce' and **-ae[1]**, used to designate families of plants 'bearing or producing' that which is specified by the combining root: **Cruciferae, Umbelliferae, Coniferae.** Related forms: -fer, -fera, -ferous.

705 **-scribe** A verb and a verb-forming word-final element, derived from Latin *scrīb(ere)* 'to engrave, draw, write,' found in its various

etymological senses in a number of common borrowings: **ascribe, describe, inscribe.** Principal parts: **-scribing, -scribed, -scribed.** Related forms: **-scription, -scriptive.**

706   **-tribe**   A noun-forming word-final element, derived from Greek *trib(ein)* 'to rub, grind, pound,' used in medical terminology to denote 'a surgical instrument used to crush a part of the body,' the part of the body or the type of instrument being specified by the combining root: **basiotribe, omphalotribe, splanchnotribe.** Related forms: **-tripsy, -tripsis; -tribes** *(plural).*

707   **-combe**   A noun and a noun-forming word-final element, derived from Old English *cumb* 'valley,' used in combinations functioning as place names and the personal names derived from them: **Buncombe, Ilfracombe, Whitcombe.** Also, **-comb, -coombe.**

708   **-obe**   A noun-forming word-final element, derived through French *-obie* from Greek *-o-* (joining vowel) and *bi(os)* 'life,' used in combinations meaning 'a state or condition of life' as qualified by the combining root: **aerobe, microbe, dendrobe.** Compare **-bia.** Related forms: **-obic; -obes** *(plural).*

709   **-phobe**   A noun-forming word-final element, derived from Greek *phob(os)* 'fear,' used extensively in combinations designating 'one who fears' that which is specified by the combining root: **heliophobe, agoraphobe, Francophobe.** Also, **-phobiac, -phobist.** Related forms: **-phobia, -phobic, -phobism, -phobous, -phobism; -phobes, -phobiacs, -phobists** *(plurals).*

710   **-lobe**   A noun, derived from Greek *lob(os)* 'ear lobe, hanging pod,' also used as a noun-forming word-final element in combinations with the sense of 'a rounded prominence or division, as of a plant or body feature' specified by the combining root: **multilobe, sublobe, gonimolobe.** Related forms: **-lobed, -lobate; -lobes** *(plural).*

711   **-microbe**   A noun, derived from *micro(s)* 'small' and *bios* 'life,' used as a noun-forming word-final element to denote 'a small living organism, especially one that can cause disease,' of the sort specified by the combining root: **inframicrobe, ultramicrobe, aeromicrobe.** Related forms: **-microbic, -microbial, -microbian, -microbism; -microbes** *(plural).*

712   **-face**[1]   A verb-forming word-final element, derived ultimately from Latin *fac(ere)* 'to make, form, shape,' used in combinations to mean

'to affect the external appearance of something' as indicated by the combining root: **deface, efface, reface.** Principal parts: **-facing, -faced, -faced.**

713   **-face²** A noun, derived through French from Latin *faciēs* 'form, shape, face' (itself derived from the verb *fac(ere)* 'to form, shape, make'), also used as a noun-forming word-final element in several senses:
  1. 'A facial appearance' denoted by the joining root: **frogface, smockface, dollface.**
  2. 'A facial appearance as altered by makeup or a mask': **whiteface, blackface, doughface.**
  3. 'A face considered spatially': **foreface, fullface, openface.**
  4. In printing, 'the width of the lines or *face* of the type': **boldface, lightface, fullface.** Related form: **-faces** *(plural).*

714   **-lace¹** A noun, derived through Middle English *las, lace* and Old French *laz* from Latin *laeque(us)* 'snare, noose,' also used as a noun-forming word-final element in two related senses:
  1. 'A line, string, or ribbon used to encircle or draw together' the object named in the combining root: **shoelace, hairlace, staylace.**
  2. 'The result of using a thread or line, either by looping and twisting or by stringing pierced objects on the line': **bridelace, necklace.** Related form: **-laces** *(plural).*

715   **-lace²** A verb, derived through Middle English *lace(n)* and Old French *laci(er)* from Latin *laque(are)* 'to ensnare,' used also as a word ending in verb combinations meaning 'to draw a line or thread through eyelets (as in shoes) or to twist and loop to create a pattern': **interlace, enlace, relace.** Principal parts: **-lacing, -laced, -laced.** Compare **-lace¹.**

716   **-place** A noun and a noun-forming word-final element, derived through Middle English, Middle French, and Latin from Greek *plat(ys), plat(eia), plat(y)* 'flat; that which is flat; wide street,' used in combinations meaning 'a location' for that which is specified by the combining root: **workplace, farmplace, birthplace.** Related form: **-places** *(plural).*

717   **-race** A noun and a noun-forming word-final element, derived through Middle English *ras, race* from Old English *rās* 'strong current,' used in two related senses:
  1. 'A rapidly moving current of water moving through a sluice or other narrow channel': **tiderace.**
  2. 'Water, forced through a pipe or channel, for powering industrial

machines': **headrace, millrace, tailrace.** Related form: **-races** *(plural).*

718 **-brace** A noun, derived through Middle English and Middle French *brace* 'two arms' from Latin *brachia* 'arms' (singular, *brachium*), also used as a noun-forming word-final element with either of two senses:
1. 'A piece of armor for the arm': **rerebrace, vambrace, vantbrace.**
2. 'A device for swinging yardarms on a ship': **forebrace, counterbrace.** Related form: **-braces** *(plural).*

719 **-grace** A noun, derived from Latin *grātia* 'charm, favor, thanks' through Middle English and Old French, used also as a word-final element in five noun combinations concerned with 'the absence of favor, including that of God': **scapegrace, disgrace, wangrace** *(obs.),* **ungrace, malgrace** *(obs.).* Related form: **-graces** *(plural).*

720 **-piece** A noun and a noun-forming word-final element, derived through Middle English *pece, piece* from Old French *pece* and related to Italian *pezza* 'fragment of cloth, rag,' used in a variety of senses:
1. 'A portion of cloth used as a covering or as part of a costume': **neckpiece, headpiece, codpiece.**
2. 'A part of something for a purpose' involving the first root: **thumbpiece, mouthpiece, shankpiece.**
3. 'A part of something larger': **endpiece, backpiece, tailpiece.**
4. In carpentry, esp. that involved in the construction of ships and buildings, 'a piece of wood' for the purpose specified by the combining root: **hawsepiece, kingpiece, aitchpiece.**
5. 'Something constructed as a unit in itself for a purpose' named by the joining root: **altarpiece, mantelpiece, masterpiece.**
6. 'An instrument or mechanism': **timepiece, eyepiece, fieldpiece.** Related form: **-pieces** *(plural).*

721 **-ice**[1] A noun-forming word-final element, derived through Middle English *-ice, -ise* and Old French from Latin *-iti(-us, -a, -um),* an abstract-noun forming suffix, used to indicate 'a state, action, or quality' particularized by the combining root: **novice, service, prejudice.** Related form: **-ices** *(plural).*

722 **-ice**[2] A noun-forming word-final element, derived from Latin *-ix, -ic-,* a feminine agent-noun-forming suffix, used in two ways:
1. To mark nouns as having feminine agents: **aviatrice, advocatrice, mediatrice.**
2. To create feminine names: **Beatrice, Janice, Patrice.** Related form: (sense 1) **-ices** *(plural).*

723 **-fice** A word-final element, derived from Latin *-fic(are)*, a combining form of the verb *fac(ere)* 'to do, make,' and used to form both nouns and verbs with the sense of 'making or doing' that which is specified by the combining root: **benefice, sacrifice, artifice.** Principal parts (verb): **-ficing, -ficed, -ficed.** Related forms: **-fic, -ficial, -ficient, -ficate, -fication, -ficative, -fy; -fices** *(plural)*.

724 **-nice** A word-final element, derived from Greek *nikē* 'victory,' used occasionally in forming feminine proper names: **Eunice, Ber(e)nice, Aganice.**

725 **-trice** A noun-forming word-final element, derived through French from Latin *-trix, -tric-*, the feminine gender form corresponding to the masculine gender agent suffix *-tor*, found almost exclusively in borrowed combinations from French denoting 'a female who performs or is associated with an activity' named by the combining root: **advocatrice, inheritrice, monitrice.** Also, **-trix, -ess, -tress.** Related form: **-trices** *(plural)*.

726 **-practice** A verb and a noun, derived through Middle English *practis(en)* from Middle French *practis(er)*, essentially a combination of **-practic** and **-ize**, used in its etymological sense of 'a performance or accomplishment' done in a manner specified by the combining root: **malpractice, mispractice, archpractice.** Also, **-practise** *(British)*. Related forms: **-praxis, -practic, -pragia, -practical; -practices, -practises** *(plurals)*.

727 **-stice** A noun and a word-final element, derived from Latin *-stit(ium)* from *sist(ere)* 'to come to a stand, to cause to halt,' used to form nouns meaning 'a cessation or stand' as qualified by the combining root: **armistice, interstice, solstice.** Related forms: **-stitial; -stices** *(plural)*.

728 **-ance** A suffix, derived from Latin *-ant-* (the stem form of the present participle of the first conjugation) and **-ia**[1], used to form nouns from verbs and adjectives:
1. 'A quality or state': **resemblance, dependence, extravagance.**
2. 'An action or process': **avoidance, abstinence, deliverance.**
3. 'A quantity or degree': **abundance, conductance, munificence.**
Also, **-ence.** Related forms: **-ancy, -ency; -ances, -ences** *(plurals)*.

729 **-escence** A noun-forming word-final element, derived from Latin *-escentia*, that is, the ending of the present participle to verbs with the inchoative-progressive infix *-(e)sc-* plus **-ia**[1], and used to mean 'the

process or state of becoming' that which is indicated by the combining root: **pubescence, acquiescence, adolescence.** Related forms: **-esce, -escent; -escences** *(plural).*

730 **-tumescence** A noun and a noun-forming word-final element, derived from Latin *tum(ēre)* 'to swell' and **-escence,** used in a handful of inherited borrowings with the sense 'a swelling,' as qualified by the combining root: **detumescence, intumescence, extumescence.** Related forms: **-tumesce, -tumescent; -tumescences** *(plural).*

731 **-science** A noun and a noun-forming word-final element, derived through Middle English and Middle French from Latin *scientia* 'knowledge' (from *sciens, scient-*—the present participle of the verb *scīre* 'to know'—and **-ia¹**), used in two related senses:
1. 'Knowledge' of a sort specified by the combining root: **prescience, omniscience, conscience.**
2. 'A science' (i.e., a systematic body or method of knowledge) as specified by the combining root: **subscience, multiscience, interscience.** Related forms: **-scient, -scientific; -sciences** *(plural).*

732 **-valence** A noun and a noun-forming word-final element, derived from Latin *valentia* 'strength, worth' (from *valens, valent-,* the present participle of *val(ere)* 'to be healthy, be worth' and **-ia¹**), used in both inherited and technical combinations in two related senses:
1. Generally, 'power, force, quantity' as specified by the combining root: **equivalence, ambivalence, prevalence.**
2. In chemical terminology, 'the combining capacity of an atom of an element compared with that of one hydrogen atom' as indicated by the combining root: **bivalence, covalence, multivalence.** Also, **-valency.** Related forms: **-valent, -valency; -valences** *(plural).*

733 **-vince** A verb (now obsolete) and a verb-forming word-final element, derived from Latin *vinc(ere)* 'to conquer,' used chiefly in metaphorical extensions of its etymological meaning: **vince** *(obs.),* **convince, evince.** Principal parts: **-vincing, -vinced, -vinced.** Related forms: **-vincible, -vincibility.**

734 **-nounce** A verb-forming word-final element, derived through Middle English and French from Latin *nunti(āre)* 'to report, announce, declare,' used in its etymological sense as qualified by the combining root: **pronounce, denounce, announce.** Principal parts: **-nouncing, -nounced, -nounced.** Related forms: **-nouncement, -nunciate, -nunciation.**

735 **-force**   A noun and a verb, and also a verb-forming word-final element, derived through Middle English and French from Latin *fort(is)* 'strong' and **-ia¹**, used in combination to signify acts of 'compelling, strengthening, or over-powering': **enforce, deforce, overforce.** Principal parts: **-forcing, -forced, -forced.**

736 **-esce**   A verb-forming word-final element, derived from the Latin inchoative-progressive verbal infix *-(e)sc-*, used to mean 'beginning, becoming' the action or state denoted by the combining root: **acquiesce, convalesce, phosphoresce.** Principal parts: **-escing, -esced, -esced.** Related forms: **-escence, -escent, -escently.**

737 **-cresce**   A verb-forming word-final element, derived from the present stem of Latin *cresc(ere)* 'to grow,' which is itself a combination of the verbal root *cre-* (cf. English *create*) and the inchoative-progressive infix *-(e)sc-* (cf **-esce**). A number of English verbs end in *-esce*, each with the sense of 'to grow, develop' as specified by the combining root: **accresce, concresce, excresce.** Principal parts: **-crescing, -cresced, -cresced.** With these may be compared the related forms **-crete** and **-cretion** which are derived from the Latin past participle *cret(us)* to the verb *crescere*. Related forms: **-crescence, -crescent.**

738 **-duce**   A verb-forming word-final element, derived from Latin *duc(ere)* 'to lead, draw,' and used in several frequently occurring English verbs and their derivatives to mean 'lead, draw' as qualified by the combining root: **educe, introduce, seduce.** Principal parts: **-ducing, -duced, -duced.** Related forms: **-duct, -ductor, -duction, -ductive** (all from the Latin past participle of *ducere, duct(us)*); **-ducer, -ducement, -ducation.**

739 **-ade¹**   A suffix, derived through Middle English, Middle French, and Old Provencal from Latin *-at(a), -at(us)* '**ate²**,' used in noun combinations:
   1. 'An act or action': **barricade, cannonade, blockade.**
   2. 'The product or result of an action': **facade, brocade, marmalade.**
   3. 'A person or thing involved in an act or action': **comrade, brigade, tribade.**
   4. 'A liquid product, usually sweet': **lemonade, Gatorade, limeade.**
   Related form: **-ades** *(plural)*.

740 **-ade²**   See **-ad¹**.

741 **-cade**   A noun-forming word-final element, derived by abstraction from

cavalcade 'a ceremonial procession' (from Old Italian *cavalcata* 'a procession on horseback'—cf. *cavallo* 'horse'), used in two senses:
1. 'A procession' whose means of locomotion is specified by the combining root: **motorcade, cyclecade, camelcade.**
2. 'A spectacle' whose nature is suggested by the combining root: **aquacade, autocade, aerocade.** Related form: **-cades** *(plural).*

742 **-shade** A noun and a noun-forming word-final element, derived through Middle English from Old English *scead(u)* 'shadow,' used in combinations designating 'a means of protection against light' specified by the combining root: **sunshade, eyeshade, snowshade.** Related form: **-shades** *(plural).*

743 **-suade** A now-archaic verb, derived from Latin *suād(ēre)* 'to advise, urge' (cognate with the English adjective *sweet*), used as a word-final element in a number of common verb combinations in its etymological sense, as qualified by the combining root: **dissuade, assuade, persuade.** Principal parts: **-suading, -suaded, -suaded.** Related forms: **-suasive, -suasion** (both derived from the Latin past participle of *suād(ēre)*).

744 **-vade** A verb-forming word-final element, derived from Latin *vād(ere)* 'to rush, go,' used in its etymological sense, as qualified by the combining root: **invade, evade, pervade.** Principal parts: **-vading, -vaded, -vaded.** Related forms: **-vasive, -vasion** (both derived from the past participle *vās(us)*, *vās(a)*, *vās(um)*).

745 **-cede** A verb and a verb-forming word-final element, derived through Middle English and French from Latin *cēd(ere)* 'to go,' used in its etymological sense, as qualified by the combining root: **accede, recede, intercede.** Principal parts: **-ceding, -ceded, -ceded.** Compare **-ceed** (a less frequent alternate form of this suffix). Related forms: **-cedence, -cedent; -cession, -cessive** (these latter two forms being derived from the past participle *cess(us)*, *cess(a)*, *cess(um)* to the verb *cēd(ere)*).

746 **-ide** A noun-forming word-final element, derived by abstraction from the word *oxide*, (itself derived through French from a combination of *ox(ygène)* 'oxygen' and *(ac)ide* 'acid'), used in chemical terminology to name binary compounds composed of a metallic and a nonmetallic element or, by extension, a compound in which either the metallic or the nonmetallic element is replaced by a group of atoms: **carbide, iodide, sulfide.** Related form: **-ides** *(plural).*

747   **-cide**   A noun-forming word-final element, derived through Middle French from Latin *caed(ere)* 'to kill,' used in combinations to mean:
1. 'Killer': **homicide, fungicide, regicide.**
2. 'Killing': **germicide, pesticide, fratricide.** Also, **-cid.** Related forms: **-cidal, -cidally; -cides** *(plural).*

748   **-side**[1]   A noun and a noun-forming word-final element, derived from Old English *sīde* 'side, lateral surface,' used in combinations in its etymological sense and extensions of same, as qualified by the combining root:
1. 'A part of a thing, viewed from any direction': **backside, topside, underside.**
2. 'A part of a thing at one side': **hillside, cliffside, lakeside.**
3. 'A bordering district': **countryside, seaside, townside.** Related form: **-sides** *(plural).*

749   **-side**[2]   A word-final element, derived from Old English *sīde* 'side, lateral surface,' used in both prepositional and adverbial combinations in its etymological sense as qualified by the combining root: **beside, alongside, inside.** Also, *(adverb)* **-sides.**

750   **-side**[3]   A verb and a verb-forming word-final element, derived from Latin *-sīd(ēre)*, the combining form of *sed(ēre)* 'to sit, stay in one place,' used in its etymological sense as qualified by the combining root: **subside, reside, preside.** Principal parts: **-siding, -sided, -sided.**

751   **-tide**   A noun and a noun-forming word-final element, derived through Middle English *tyde, tide* from Old English *tīd* 'time,' found in a number of inherited combinations in several related senses:
1. 'A time of the day' specified by the combining root: **eventide, noontide, nighttide.**
2. 'A time or season of the year' denoted by the combining root: **summertide, wintertide, springtide.**
3. 'The time of an occasion (as a religious festival), an activity, or a state or condition,' as specified by the combining root: **Ascensiontide, schooltide, youthtide** *(archaic).* Related form: **-tides** *(plural).*

752   **-ode**[1]   A noun, derived through Middle French and Late Latin from Greek *ōid(ē)* 'song, lyric' (from the Greek verb *aeid(ein)* 'to sing'), also used as a noun-forming word-final element, in two senses:
1. 'An ode of a variety named by the combining root': **palinode, threnode, hymnode.** Also, **-ody.**

2. 'A division of a classical Greek ode': **epode, hemipode, antipode.** Related forms: **-odal; -odes, -odies** *(plurals)*.

753 **-ode²** A noun-forming word-final element, derived from Greek *(h)od(os)* 'road, path, way,' used to denote 'a type of electrical conductor' specified by the combining root: **cathode, anode, diode.** Related forms: **-odic¹, -odically; -odes** *(plural)*.

754 **-ode³** A noun-forming word-final element, derived by contraction from the Greek adjective-forming suffix *-oeid(ēs)* '-like' (itself derived from the noun *eid(os)* 'shape, form, appearance'), used in scientific terminology, esp. entomology, to form noun combinations meaning 'a thing that is like in form' the thing named by the combining root: **nematode, ostracode, placode.** Compare **-oid¹.** Related form: **-odes** *(plural)*.

755 **-lude** A word-final element, derived from Latin *lūd(us)* 'a game, sport' and Latin *lūd(ere)* 'to play,' used to form both nouns and verbs in either of two extended senses of the etymological meaning:
1. In nouns, 'an entertainment or part of an entertainment, originally athletic, then dramatic, and now also musical': **prelude, interlude, postlude.**
2. In verbs, 'to play with,' the degree of seriousness or malice being indicated by the combining root: **allude, elude, delude.** Principal parts (verb): **-luding, -luded, -luded.** Related forms: **-lusive, -lusion** (from the past participle, *lūs(us)*, of *lūd(ere)*); **-ludes** *(plural)*.

756 **-clude** A verb-forming word-final element, derived from Latin *-clūd(ere)*, the combining form of *claud(ere)* 'to close,' used in metaphorical extensions of its etymological sense as qualified by the combining root: **include, exclude, conclude.** Principal parts: **-cluding, -cluded, -cluded.** Related forms: **-clusion, -clusive** (from the past participle *-clūs(us)*, *-clūs(a)*, *-clūs(um)* to the verb *-clūd(ere)*).

757 **-trude** A verb-forming word-final element, derived from Latin *trūd(ere)* 'to push, thrust,' used in the sense of 'to push, thrust' in the manner or direction indicated by the combining root: **protrude, intrude, extrude.** Principal parts: **-truding, -truded, -truded.** Related forms: **-trusion, -trusive.** (These forms are derived from the past participle *trūs(us)*, *trūs(a)*, *trūs(um)*.)

758 **-tude** A noun-forming word-final element, derived through French from Latin *-tūd(ō)*, *-tūd(in-)*, an abstract-noun-forming suffix very

similar to English **-ness** in both meaning and grammatical usage, used in combinations denoting 'a state or condition' expressed by the combining root: **similitude, lassitude, gratitude.** Related form: **-tudes** *(plural).*

759 **-ee**[1] A word-final element, derived from French *-é* and *-ée,* the masculine and feminine endings, respectively, of the past participle of first conjugation verbs (i.e. those with infinitives in *-er*), used as a noun-forming word-final element (from the substantive use of the past participle in French) in several related senses:
1. 'A person or persons that are passive objects of the action named by the verb acting as the combining root': **divorcee, employee, nominee.**
2. 'A person or persons that are recipients of the result of an action': **amputee, biographee, selectee.**
3. 'A person furnished with' the thing named by the combining root: **custodee, patentee, mortgagee.**
4. 'A person that performs' the action named by the combining root: **escapee, salvagee, standee.** Related form: **-ees** *(plural).* In some cases (**garnishee**) the noun has been reconstructed as a verb.

760 **-ee**[2] An abstract noun- and verb-forming word-final element, with no particular assignable meaning, occurring in words which originally had endings from Latin *(-ia, -ium),* Greek *(-ia, -eia, -ion),* French *(-ie),* or German *(-ie):* **guarantee, repartee, warrantee.** Compare **-y**[2, 3], **-ie.** Related form: **-ees** *(plural).*

761 **-ee**[3] A noun-forming word-final element, possibly derived by alteration of *-ie,* used in forming combinations in three senses:
1. 'Something diminutive': **bootee, snickersnee, coatee.**
2. 'Something resembling or suggestive of' the thing named by the combining root: **goatee, cockawee, coudee.**
3. 'A person associated with' what is named by the joining root: **townee, grandee, Thuggee.** Also, **-ie.** Related form: **-ees** *(plural).*

762 **-free** An adjective and an active adjective-forming word-final element, derived through Middle English *fre, free* from Old English *frēo* 'loved, part of the family (that is, not a slave),' used in two closely related senses:
1. 'Not constrained': **carefree, ransomfree, folkfree.**
2. 'Free from, without' the thing or ingredient named by the combining root: **germfree, proteinfree, sugarfree.** Related form: **-freely.**

763   **-tree**   A noun and a noun-forming word-final element, derived through Middle English *tre*, *tree* from Old English *trēow* 'tree' (cf. Indo-Iranian *dru-* 'wood'), used in two senses:

     1.   'A kind of tree' specified by the combining root (sometimes hyphenated, more often free): **orange-tree, den-tree, pear tree.**

     2.   'A piece of wood used as a structural member' in the implement or structure named by the combining root: **axletree, rooftree, saddletree.** Related form: **-trees** *(plural).*

764   **-wife**   A noun and a noun-forming word-final element, derived through Middle English *wif* from Old English *wīf* 'woman,' used in several senses:

     1.   'A woman who sells' the commodity named by the combining root: **herbwife, fishwife, oysterwife.**

     2.   'A woman who acts as overseer or keeper': **housewife, henwife, goodwife.**

     3.   'A female worker' whose task is specified by the combining root: **washerwife, midwife, spaewife.**

     4.   'The common name of several varieties of largebellied fish': **alewife, oldwife, seawife.** Related form: **-wives** *(plural).*

765   **-age**   A word-final element, used extensively in forming nouns, derived through Middle English and Old French from the Latin adjectival suffix *-atic(um)* 'pertaining to':

     1.   'A collection or aggregate': **luggage, coinage, herbage.**

     2.   'An action or process': **pilgrimage, haulage, coverage.**

     3.   'The result of an action or process' named or implied by the combining root: **breakage, mirage, stoppage.**

     4.   'The location or house of' the person or condition named by the first root: **orphanage, harborage, parsonage.**

     5.   'A condition or rank': **peonage, bondage, parentage.**

     6.   'The amount or rate of something': **dosage, gallonage, leakage.**

     7.   'A charge for a service': **postage, towage, warehousage.** Related form: **-ages** *(plural).*

766   **-gage**   A noun and a denominative verb, derived through Middle English and Middle French from Old French *gage* (cognate with English *wage*) 'a pledge; token of a pledge,' used in noun and verb combinations as a word-final element in its etymological sense, as qualified by the combining root: **engage, mortgage, drengage.** Principal parts: **-gaging, -gaged, -gaged.** Related forms: **-gagement; -gages** *(plural).*

767   **-phage**   A noun-forming word-final element, derived from Greek

phag(os) 'eater' (cf. *phag(ein)* 'to eat'), used in biological terminology to mean 'something (as a cell or insect) that eats' the matter denoted by the combining root: **bacteriophage, xylophage, ostreophage.** Also, **-phag.** Related forms: **-phagic, -phagically, -phagous, -phagi, -phagism, -phagist, -phagy, -phagia; -phages, -phags** *(plurals).*

768   **-(r)rhage**   A noun-forming word-final element, derived from Greek *rhag(as)* 'a break, tear, bursting' (cf. the verb *rhēx(ai)* 'to burst, break, tear'), used in medical terminology in the sense of 'a rupture, an excessive fluid discharge' as specified by the combining root: **hemorrhage, phleborrhage, lymphorrhage.** Related forms: **-rrhagia, -rrhagic, -rrhagically; -rrhages** *(plural).*

769   **-massage**   A noun and a verb, which some derive from Ionic Greek *mass(ein)* 'to knead' (cf. Attic Greek *matt(ein)*) and **-age,** and others derive from Arabic *mass(a)* 'to handle, touch' and **-age,** also used as a word-final element in forming noun and denominative verb combinations denoting 'a therapeutic kneading of the body or part of the body' by a means specified by the combining root: **thermomassage, pneumomassage, vibromassage.** Principal parts: **-massaging, -massaged, -massaged.** Related form: **-massages** *(plural).*

770   **-stage**   A noun and a noun-forming word-final element, derived through Middle English from Old French *estage* 'position, place, habitation, stay' (from Latin *st(āre)* 'to stand, stay put'), used in two major extensions of its etymological sense:

1. 'A raised platform or parts thereof' as specified by the combining root: **forestage, upstage, understage.**
2. In general scientific terminology, 'a phase,' as specified by the combining root: **multistage, uredostage, aecidiostage.** Related form: **-stages** *(plural).*

771   **-edge**   A noun, derived through Middle English *egge* from Old English *ecg* 'edge, border,' used also as a word ending in noun combinations concerned with 'the point at which a material ends' and the special quality assigned by the combining root: **featheredge, razoredge, selvedge** (also, **selvage**). Related form: **-edges** *(plural).*

772   **-pledge**   A verb and a noun, derived through Middle English *plegg(en)* and Middle French *pleg(ier)* 'to guarantee, promise' from late Latin *plegium, plebium* 'a surety, guarantee, pledge,' used in its etymological sense in both nouns and verbs: **frankpledge, interpledge, repledge.** Principal parts: **-pledging, -pledged, -pledged.**

773   **-knowledge**   A noun, derived from Middle English *knaw-* or *knowlage*, *knaw-* or *knowlege*, from *knowlech(en)* 'to know,' used also as a word-final element in noun combinations meaning 'cognizance' as qualified by the combining root: **foreknowledge, interknowledge, superknowledge.** Related form: **-knowledges** *(plural).*

774   **-bridge**   A noun and a noun-forming word-final element, derived through Middle English *brigge, brugge* from Old English *brycg* 'crossway, bridge,' used in two sorts of combination:
    1. In common nouns, with the meaning 'a platform over a depression,' the style or use being denoted by the combining root: **footbridge, drawbridge, weighbridge.**
    2. In place or street names, often without reference to a specific bridge: **Stockbridge, Trowbridge, Bainbridge.** Related form: **-bridges** *(plural).*

775   **-change**   A verb and a noun, derived through Middle English and Old French from late Latin *cambi(āre)* 'to transform, change, exchange' and *cambi(um)* 'that which may be transformed, an exchange, change,' used in verb and noun combinations in its etymological sense, as qualified by the combining root: **interchange, counterchange, exchange.** Principal parts: **-changing, -changed, -changed.** Related form: **-changes** *(plural).*

776   **-range**   A noun and a word-final element, derived through Middle English and Middle French from Old French *renc, reng* 'line, row, place,' used in two major senses:
    1. In verbs, 'to set in a row, rank, place, station,' as qualified by the combining root: **arrange, derange, disarrange.**
    2. In adjectives, 'pertaining to a limit of effectiveness,' as of a projectile or radio signal: **midrange, subrange, omnirange.** Principal parts (verb): **-ranging, -ranged, -ranged.**

777   **-stringe**   A verb-forming word-final element, derived from Latin *string(ere)* 'to draw tight, compress, restrict,' used in its etymological sense as qualified by the combining root: **astringe, constringe, perstringe.** Principal parts: **-stringing, -stringed, -stringed.** Compare **-strain, -strict.** Related forms: **-stringence, -stringency, -stringent.**

778   **-charge**   A verb and a deverbative noun, derived through Middle English from Old French *charg(ier)* 'to load' (from Late Latin *carric(āre)* 'to load a wagon'), used in a variety of senses in both verb and noun combinations:

1. 'To load (with ammunition, explosives); a loading (with ammunition, explosives)': **recharge, mischarge, discharge.**
2. 'To attack; an attack': **countercharge, recharge, intercharge.**
3. 'To impose a burden, responsibility': **encharge, uncharge, intercharge.**
4. 'To impose a monetary burden, ask for payment; a monetary burden, request for payment': **undercharge, overcharge, surcharge.** Principal parts (verb): **-charging, -charged, -charged.** Related form: **-charges** *(plural).*

779   **-merge**   A verb and a verb-forming word-final element, derived from Latin *merg(ere)* 'to dip, plunge,' used in two related senses, each as qualified by the combining root:
1. 'To immerse': **submerge, immerge, emerge.**
2. 'To combine or blend': **remerge, commerge, unmerge.** Principal parts: **-merging, -merged, -merged.** Related forms: **-mergent, -mergence; -merse, -mersion** (the latter two forms being derived from the past participle *mers(us), mers(a), mers(um)*).

780   **-verge**   A verb and a verb-forming word-final element, derived from Latin *verg(ere)* 'to incline, bend, turn,' used in its etymological sense, as qualified by the combining root: **verge, converge, diverge.** Principal parts: **-verging, -verged, -verged.** Related forms: **-vergent, -vergence.**

781   **-gorge**   A noun, derived through Middle English from Latin *gurg(es)* 'whirlpool, throat' (akin to Latin *vor(are)* 'to devour'), used also as a word ending in verb combinations meaning 'to fill or stuff something, including the mouth and throat': **engorge, overgorge, disgorge.** Principal parts: **-gorging, -gorged, -gorged.** Related form: **-gorgement.**

782   **-surge**   A verb and a verb-forming word-final element, derived from Latin *surg(ere)* 'to rise,' used in a number of common borrowings and their derivatives in its etymological sense, as qualified by the combining root: **insurge, upsurge, assurge.** Principal parts: **-surging, -surged, -surged.** Related forms: **-surgent, -surgency, -surgence.**

783   **-fuge**   A noun-forming word-final element, derived from Latin *fug(ere), fug(āre)* 'to flee, put to flight,' used in both of its etymological senses:
1. 'Running away, flight': **subterfuge, refuge, transfuge** *(rare).*
2. 'That which drives away,' the object of the expulsion being denoted by the combining root: **vermifuge, febrifuge, centrifuge.** Related forms: **-fugal, -fugally; -fuges** *(plural).*

784   **-psyche**   A noun and a noun-forming word-final element, derived from

Greek *psychē* 'breath, life, mind, spirit' (from the verb *psych(ein)* 'to breathe'), used in combinations referring to 'the mind or spirit' as specified by the combining root: **metapsyche, thymopsyche, phytopsyche.** Related forms: **-psychic, -psychical, -psychically; -psyches** *(plural)*.

785 **-strophe** A noun and a noun-forming word-final element, derived from Greek *strophē* 'a turning, twisting' (from the verb *streph(ein)* 'to turn, twist'), used in two main senses:

1. In general scientific terminology, 'a turning or twisting' in a direction or of a thing specified by the combining root: **phallanastrophe, diastrophe, angiostrophe.** Also, **-strophy.**

2. In the terminology of classical rhetoric, 'a turn of phrase' as qualified by the combining root: **apostrophe, epistrophe, epanastrophe** (now called *anadiplosis*). Related forms: **-strophism, -strophic, -strophical; -strophes** *(plural)*.

786 **-ie** A highly productive noun-forming word-final element, probably derived from the (unattested) Common Romance diminutive suffix **-itt(a)*, **-ett(a)* (cf. **-et** and **-ette**), through Scottish Middle English, and used (in a variety of spellings) as a diminutive, usually affectionate: **dearie, Charlie (Charley, Charly), sweetie.** Also, **-ey, -y.**

787 **-cake** A noun and a noun-forming word-final element, derived through Middle English *cake, kake* from Old Norse *kaka* 'small (round) cake' (whence also English *cookie*, though *not*, contrary to what one might expect, English *cook*, which has a completely different etymon—cf. **-pepsia**), used in a variety of related senses, each specified by the combining root:

1. 'A thin cake, baked to have a crust on both sides': **teacake, seedcake, ashcake.**

2. 'A thin dough, usually sweetened, fried on both sides': **pancake, flapcake, carcake.**

3. 'A highly sweetened dough, baked in a special pan': **poundcake, spicecake, bridecake.**

4. 'Something solidified into a block or round shape': **soapcake, eelcake, fishcake.** Related form: **-cakes** *(plural)*.

788 **-shake** A word, derived through Middle English *shak(en)* from Old English *sceac(an)* 'to divide, part from' (perhaps by vibration or agitation), used also as a word ending in noun combinations.

1. 'An irregular, often quick, movement': **handshake, headshake, sideshake.**

2. 'A thing produced by shaking,' as a split, esp. in forestry

terminology 'fissures in annular rings caused by wind and frost': **shellshake, starshake, ringshake.** Related form: **-shakes** *(plural).*

789   **-drake**   A noun ('a small cannon;' obsolete, 'a dragon') and a noun-forming word-final element, derived through Middle English *drake* and Old English *drac(a)* from Latin *drac(ō)*, *drac(ōn-)* 'dragon, serpent,' used in at least two combinations designating 'a type of dragon': **firedrake, earthdrake.** Etymologists assert the influence of the term upon the name of the plant *mandrake,* but the connection is not direct. The male of a duck, called a *drake,* is apparently from a different etymon. Related form: **-drakes** *(plural).*

790   **-take**   A verb (and a deverbative noun), derived through Middle English *tak(en)* from Old English *tac(an)* 'to seize, grasp with the hands' and related to Gothic *tek(an)* 'to touch,' also used as a word-final element:

    1. In verb combinations, in the basic meaning 'to take in hand': **partake, overtake, undertake.** Principal parts: **-taking, -took, -taken.**

    2. In noun combinations, 'an apparatus for conveying, as for filling or emptying': **intake, uptake, outtake.** Related form (noun): **-takes** *(plural).*

791   **-stake**   A verb of uncertain origin—possibly from a specialized use of the noun *stake* 'a post or stick driven into the ground'—with the meaning 'to wager,' also used as a noun and a noun-forming word-final element with the meaning 'that which is wagered, hazarded for loss or gain': **sweepstake, grubstake, alestake.** Related form: **-stakes** *(plural).*

792   **-quake**   A verb, derived through Middle English *quak(en)* from Old English *cwac(ian)* and related to Old English *cwecc(an)* 'to shake, tremble,' also used as a word-final element in noun combinations meaning 'trembling, vibration, or concussion caused by or resembling seismic effects': **earthquake, waterquake, icequake.** Related form: **-quakes** *(plural).*

793   **-like**   A word—variously parsed as a preposition, an adjective, and an adverb—derived through Middle English *lik, ilik* from Old English *gelic* 'like, alike,' used also as a very productive word ending in adjective combinations meaning 'similar to' the thing denoted by the combining root: **madonnalike, cagelike, gooselike.**

794   **-stroke**   A noun and a verb, derived from Middle English *stroke, strake* 'the act of striking a blow' (from Old English *strīc(an)* 'to strike'), used in several extensions of its etymological meaning:

1. 'An effort and movement' of the kind denoted by the combining root: **handstroke, backstroke, midstroke.**
2. 'A sudden action or process': **seastroke, thunderstroke, windstroke.**
3. 'A condition caused by or resembling an apoplectic stroke': **sunstroke, heatstroke, bloodstroke.** Related form: **-strokes** *(plural).*

795 **-voke** A verb-forming word-final element, derived from Latin *voc(āre)* 'to call' (cf. *vōx, vōc-* 'sound, voice'), used in its etymological sense, as qualified by the combining root: **provoke, evoke, convoke.** Principal parts: **-voking, -voked, -voked.** Compare **-vocalic.** Related forms: **-vocation, -vocative, -vocable.**

796 **-le¹** A noun-forming word-final element, derived through Middle English *-el* and Old English *-il* from the Latin and Late Latin diminutive suffixes *-ell(us), -ell(a), -ell(um)* and **-ill(us), *-ill(a), *-ill(um)*, preserved in its etymological sense: **dimple, nipple, steeple.** Compare **-el, - il².** Related form: **-les** *(plural).*

797 **-le²** A noun-forming word-final element, derived through Middle English *-el* from Old English *-ol, -ul*, used in the sense of 'an instrument or agent' of the sort specified by the combining root: **bridle, ladle, thimble.** Related form: **-les** *(plural).*

798 **-le³** An adjective-forming word-final element, variously derived through Middle English *-el* from Old English *-ol*, and through French *-le* from Latin *-il(is)* '**-ile²**,' all used in the general sense of 'having a tendency towards' the quality or state specified by the combining root: **brittle, stable, nimble.**

799 **-le⁴** A verb-forming word-final element, derived through Middle English *-len* from Old English *-lian*, used in combinations expressing 'a repeated (frequentative) action or state' denoted by the combining root: **rumple, trample, grapple.** Principal parts: **-ling, -led, -led.**

800 **-dale** A noun and a word-final element, derived through Middle English from Old English *dæl* 'valley,' used also in noun combinations meaning 'vale, valley, especially a river valley' in place and personal names, often used to name products of the area: **Airedale, Clydesdale, Chippendale.** Related form: **-dales** *(plural).*

801   **-hale**   A verb-forming word-final element, derived from Latin *hal(are)* 'to breathe,' and used in its etymological sense as qualified by the combining root, in two basic combinations and their derivatives in English: **inhale, exhale.** Principal parts: **-haling, -haled, -haled.** Related forms: **-halant, -halent, -halation.**

802   **-pale**   A noun and a denominative verb-forming word-final element, derived through Middle English *pāl* (cf. Modern English *pole*) from Latin *pāl(us)* 'stake, rod, pole,' used in the sense of 'to insert, enclose with, or place on stakes': **forepale, impale, repale.** Principal parts: **-paling, -paled, -paled.**

803   **-wale**   A noun, derived through Middle English from Old English *wal(u)* 'weal, ridge,' used also as a word ending in shipbuilding terminology denoting 'strakes or strips of lumber in the sides of a wooden ship,' the combining root indicating the precise location: **inwale, outwale, gunwale.** Related form: **-wales** *(plural).*

804   **-able**   A very active suffix, derived through Middle English and Middle French from Latin *-abil(is)*, *-ibil(is)* (from *-bil(is)* 'suitable, fit for a purpose'), used in the formation of adjective combinations.
   1.   'Capable of or fit for' the action denoted in the combining root: **amicable, readable, visible.**
   2.   'Tending to or given to' the state or action named in the first root: **perishable, changeable, curable.** Also, **-ible.** Compare **-abilia.** Related forms: **-ably, -ability, -ibly, -ibility.**

805   **-syllable**   A noun and a noun-forming word-final element, derived through Anglo-Norman *sillable* from Greek *syllab(ē)* 'that which may be taken together, that which holds together' (from *syn-* 'together, with' and *lab(ein)* 'to take'), used in the specialized sense of 'a group of sounds (or, for the early Greeks, letters) which, when taken together, form a single phonological entity,' the number of such entities being specified by the combining root: **monosyllable, disyllable, polysyllable.** Related forms: **-syllabic, -syllabical, -syllabically, -syllabicate, -syllabication; -syllables** *(plural).*

806   **-semble**   A verb-forming word-final element, derived through French from Latin *simul(āre)* 'to copy (literally, 'to make similar'), represent, unite' (cf. *similis* 'similar, as one'), used in its etymological senses of 'make, be similar; bring together (as a collection of similar constituents)' as qualified by the combining root: **resemble, dissemble, assemble.** Principal parts: **-sembling, -sembled, -sembled.** Related forms: **-semblance, -similate.**

807 **-noble** An adjective, derived from Latin *nōbil(is)* 'known, famous, high-born,' used as a word-final element in two ways:

1. In adjective combinations, 'pertaining to illustriousness in character or deeds': **prenoble, ignoble, unnoble.**

2. In verb combinations, 'to raise to the rank of a nobleman or to the level of the illustrious': **ennoble, disennoble.** Principal parts: **-nobling, -nobled, -nobled.** Related forms: **-nobled, -noblement, -nobility.**

808 **-soluble** An adjective and an adjective-forming word-final element, derived from Latin *solv(ere)* 'to loosen' and the adjective-forming suffix *-bil(is)* (cf. **-able**), used in the sense of 'able to be dissolved,' the combining root functioning either as an adverb or as the name of the dissolving agent: **acetosoluble, dissoluble, resoluble.** Related forms: **-solve, -solution, -solvable, -solubility, -solvability.**

809 **-sicle** A noun-forming word-final element, derived by abstraction from *icicle* (itself derived from Middle English *īsgicel*, a compound of *īs* 'ice' and *gicel* 'icicle'), used to designate varieties of 'flavored ices' served on a stick: **Popsicle, fudgesicle, creamsicle.** Related form: **-sicles** *(plural).*

810 **-cycle** A noun, derived through French and Latin from Greek *kykl(os)* 'circle, ring, wheel' and used as a word-final noun-forming element in several related senses:

1. 'A completion of steps or stages in a process': **biocycle, ontocycle, subcycle.**

2. 'Something circular in arrangement': **epicycle, pericycle, hemicycle.**

3. 'A recurrence of events or a repetition of stages over a period of time': **teracycle, supercycle, multicycle.**

4. 'A vehicle, often described in terms of wheel count': **unicycle, bicycle, motorcycle.**

5. 'A unit involving a quantity of cycles per second,' denoted by the combining root: **megacycle, kilocycle, kilomegacycle.** Related forms: **-cyclic, -cyclically; -cycles** *(plural).*

811 **-saddle** A noun and a verb, derived through Middle English *sadel* from Old English *sadol, sadul* 'seat for a rider; to affix a seat for a rider, to load' (cf. Latin *sed(ēre)* 'to sit'), used in a variety of combinations:

1. As a verb, 'to place a specially designed seat upon a horse, mule, or pony': **upsaddle, unsaddle, offsaddle** *(British).*

2. As a noun, the name of 'a variety of the standard saddle': **sidesaddle, packsaddle.**

3. As a noun, 'a cut of meat for roasting, consisting of the loins and nearby areas': **foresaddle, hindsaddle.** Principal parts: **-saddling, -saddled, -saddled.** Related form (noun): **-saddles** *(plural).*

812 **-handle** A verb and a noun, both derived through Middle English *handel(en)* from Old English *handl(ian)* 'to take or feel with the hands' (cf. **-hand**), used also as both a verb- and noun-forming word-final element in several related senses, each particularized by the combining root:

1. 'To touch with the hands, manipulate': **prehandle, rehandle, overhandle.**

2. 'To manage with the hands or through physical force': **manhandle, mishandle.**

3. In an extended sense, 'to beg, though ablebodied,' from a literal reaching out, perhaps while holding a beggar's bowl: **panhandle.** Principal parts: **-handling, -handled, -handled.**

4. In nouns 'the handle (i.e., part you put your hand on) of a thing' specified by the combining root: **valvehandle, knife-handle, broom handle.** (Usage varies when it comes to running together, hyphenating, or separating the components of this type of combination.)

813 **-cele¹** A noun-forming word-final element, derived from Greek *kēlē* 'tumor, swelling,' used in medical terminology to denote 'a tumor or swelling' of a sort or in an area of the body specified by the combining root: **cephalocele, enterocele, oscheocele.** Related forms: **-celic; -celes** *(plural).*

814 **-cele²** A noun-forming word-final element, derived through Latin from Greek *koil(os)* 'belly, hollow, cavity,' often written *-coele,* and used in biomedical terminology to refer to a cavity in an organism or region of the body as specified by the combining root: **blastocele, gastrocele, hemocele.** Also, **-coele, -coel.**

815 **-angle** A noun and a noun-forming word-final element, derived from Latin *angul(us)* 'corner, angle' (from an Indo-European root meaning 'to bend,' whence also English *ankle*), used in mathematical terminology in two closely related senses:

1. 'An angle' of a type denoted by the combining root: **semiangle, recipiangle, equiangle.**

2. 'A geometric figure containing angles,' the number or type being

stated by the combining root: **rectangle, pentangle, triangle.** Related forms: **-angular, -angularly, -angularity; -angles** *(plural).*

816 **-mingle** A verb and a verb-forming word-final element, derived through Middle English from Old English *meng(an)* 'to mix, blend,' used in combinations meaning 'to combine without loss of separate identities': **intermingle, commingle, mismingle.** Principal parts: **-mingling, -mingled, -mingled.**

817 **-ile¹** A noun-forming word-final element, derived by analogy to the final suffix in Latin *quartil(is)*, used in noun combinations to mean 'a part or segment in a frequency distribution of a size' denoted by the combining root: **centile, decile, tredecile.** Also, **-il¹** (sense 2). Related form: **-iles** *(plural).*

818 **-ile²** An adjective-forming word-final element, derived through Middle English and Middle French from Latin *-il(is)*, a general adjective-forming suffix, used in two main senses:
1. 'Of, pertaining, or appropriate to' that which is specified by the combining root: **virile, infantile, senile.**
2. 'Capable of' that which is specified by the combining root: **visile, mobile, contractile.** Also, **-il.** Related form: **-ility.**

819 **-labile** An adjective and an adjective-forming word-final element, derived from Latin *labil(is)* 'able or apt to fall away, loosen' (from the verb *lab(āre)* 'to fall away, loosen' and *-abil(is)* '**-able**'), used in biomedical terminology to mean 'unstable, subject to change as a result of variation in haptic stimulus or the passage of time' as specified by the combining root: **thermolabile, hydrolabile, tempolabile.** Related form: **-lability.**

820 **-stabile** An adjective and an adjective-forming word-final element, derived from Latin *stabil(is)* 'steadfast,' literally, 'able to stand fast' (from the verb *st(āre)* 'to stand, stay in place' and *-abil(is)* '**-able**'), used in biomedical terminology to mean 'stable, resistant to change as a result of variation in haptic stimulus or the passage of time' as specified by the combining root: **frigostabile, siccostabile, thermostabile.** Related forms: **-stability, -stabilize.**

821 **-mobile¹** A noun and a noun-forming word-final element, derived from the substantive use of the English adjective *mobile* (cf. **-mobile²**), used in two related senses:
1. 'A vehicle propelled' by the means specified by the combining

root: **automobile, locomobile** (also *cap.* as brand name), **electromobile.**

2. 'A vehicle for a purpose' named by the combining root: **bloodmobile, bookmobile, snowmobile.** Related form: **-mobiles** *(plural).*

822 **-mobile²** An adjective, derived through French from Latin *mōbil(is)* 'capable of moving,' also used as an adjective-forming word-final element in two frequently occurring combinations in its etymological sense: **mobile, immobile, nonmobile.** Compare **-mobile¹.** Related form: **-mobility.**

823 **-phile** A word-final element, derived from Greek *phil(ein)* 'to love, have an affinity for,' used to form both nouns and adjectives in the etymological sense of 'loving, love of' that which is named by the combining root: **homophile, ornithophile, bibliophile.** Compare **-phil.** Related forms: **-philia, -phily, -philous, -philiac, -philism, -philist, -philite; -philes, -phils** *(plurals).*

824 **-while** A word, derived through Middle English *whil, while* from Old English *hwil* 'time,' used also as a word ending in noun, adverb, and conjunction combinations concerned with 'a period of time, usually short': **awhile, handwhile** *(Scottish),* **meanwhile.**

825 **-febrile** An adjective and an adjective-forming word-final element, derived from Latin *febr(is)* 'fever' and **-ile²,** used in the sense of 'of, pertaining, or relating to fever' as specified by the combining root: **antefebrile, antifebrile, postfebrile.**

826 **-motile** An adjective, derived from Latin *mōt(us),* the past participle of the verb *mōv(ēre)* 'to move,' and the adjective-forming suffix *-il(is)* '**-ile²,**' also used as an adjective-forming word-final element in combinations meaning 'capable of movement' in a manner or by a means specified by the combining root: **nonmotile, hypermotile, irritomotile.** Also, **-mobile².** Related forms: **-move, -motility, -motive, -motor¹, -motor², -motored, -motorial, -motoric, -motorially.**

827 **-fertile** An adjective and an adjective-forming word-final element, derived from Latin *fertil(is)* 'fruitful, productive' (cf. Latin *ferre* 'to bear'—whence **-fer**—and **-ile²**), used in its etymological sense, as qualified by the combining root: **infertile, interfertile, overfertile.** Related forms: **-fertilely, -fertility, -fertilize.**

828 **-elle** A noun-forming word-final element, derived from French *-elle,*

itself from Latin *-ella*, the feminine singular form of the Latin diminutive suffix *-ellus*, *-ella*, *-ellum*, used in its etymological sense, in direct borrowings from French: **nacelle, sarcelle, rondelle.** Compare **-el, -ella.** Related form: **-elles** *(plural).*

829   **-ille**   A noun-forming word-final element, derived from Modern French *-ille*, itself derived from the feminine form of the Late Latin diminutive suffix *-ill(us)*, *-ill(a)*, *-ill(um)*, found in borrowings from French, in some of which at least its etymological sense is preserved: **chenille, pastille, vanille.** Compare **-il², -elle.** Related form: **-illes** *(plural).*

830   **-ville**   A word-final element derived through Middle English and Old French from Latin *vīll(a)* 'farm, village,' used in two related ways:

1.   In place names, usually for small communities; or in family names: **Knoxville, Unionville, Baskerville.**

2.   In terms resembling place names, for places or conditions of a nature (usually pejorative) expressed by the combining root: **squaresville, hicksville, dullsville.** Related form: **-villes** *(plural).*

831   **-ole¹**   A noun-forming word-final element, derived from the Latin diminutive suffix *-ol(us)*, *-ol(a)*, *-ol(um)*, used in two senses:

1.   As a diminutive naming 'a small one' of the sort specified by the combining root: **nucleole, aureole, arteriole.**

2.   As a taxonomic suffix in biological terminology, often without diminutive force, to name genera: **Glareole, Pheidole, Collembole.** Also, **-ola.** Related form: **-oles** *(plural).*

832   **-ole²**   A noun-forming word-final element, derived from Latin *ole(um)* 'oil,' used as a less frequent variant of **-ol²** in combinations meaning 'an oil or oil-like material' specified by the combining root: **benzole, tetrole, pyrrole.** Compare **-ol².** Related forms: **-oleic; -oles, -ols** *(plurals).*

833   **-cole**   A noun-forming word-final element, derived from Latin *col(ere)* 'to inhabit,' used in botanical and biological terminology to denote a plant or organism 'having or characterized by a habitat' specified by the combining root: **arboricole, calcicole, arenicole.** Compare **-cola.** Related forms: **-colid, -colous; -coles** *(plural).*

834   **-hole**   A noun, derived through Middle English *hole* 'hollow place, hole, hold of a ship' from Old English *hol* 'hollow, cave,' also used as a noun-forming word-final element in several related senses:

1.   'A hollow or depression': **sinkhole, chuckhole, pitchhole.**

2. 'An opening,' its purpose either named or hinted at by the combining root: **armhole, buttonhole, manhole.**
3. 'A storage place': **cuddyhole, coalhole, pigeonhole.** (Some of the terms have additional meanings.)
4. 'A place, usu. of small size': **cubbyhole, stokehole, hellhole.** Related form: **-holes** *(plural).*

835   **-pole**[1]   A noun, derived through Middle English from Old English *pāl* 'stake, pole,' also used as a noun-forming word-final element in the meaning 'a pole, stake, timber' placed or used for a purpose as specified by the combining root: **flagpole, ridgepole, forepole.** Related form: **-poles** *(plural).*

836   **-pole**[2]   A noun-forming word-final element, derived from Middle English *pol, polle* 'hair of the head, head,' used in the sense of 'head' as qualified by the combining root: **tadpole, philotadpole, rantipole.** Compare **-poll.** Related form: **-poles** *(plural).*

837   **-pole**[3]   A noun-forming word-final element, derived from Greek *pōl(ein)* 'to exchange, sell,' used to designate 'one who engages in commerce in a manner or of a sort' specified by the combining root: **bibliopole, monopole, duopole.** Also, **-polist.** Related forms: **-poly, -polist, -polistic, -polism; -poles** *(plural).*

838   **-pole**[4]   A noun, derived through Middle English *pool* and Latin *pol(us)* from Greek *pol(os)* 'pivot, axle,' used also in the terminology of physics, radio, and electrical engineering to form noun combinations having to do with 'the flow of electrons along a wire or antenna bar in electrical or radio signal transmission, the flow taking place from the area (pole) of higher potential to the lower': **dipole, multipole, interpole.** Related forms: **-polar, -polarity; -poles** *(plural).*

839   **-sole**   A noun and a noun-forming word-final element, derived through Middle English and Middle French from Latin *sole(a)* 'sandal, slipper, sole,' used in combinations differentiating among the layers of material between the bottom of a shoe and the foot of its wearer, as specified by the combining root: **slipsole, insole, intersole.** Related form: **-soles** *(plural).*

840   **-stole**   A noun-forming word-final element, derived from Greek *-stolē,* one of the combining forms of the verb *stell(ein)* 'to set in place, bring together, contract' and the noun-forming suffix *-ē,* used in biomedical terminology in a handful of borrowed combinations referring to the contraction, retraction, or dilation of various organs, as specified by

the combining root: **diastole, peristole, systole.** Compare **-stalsis.** Related forms: **-stolic; -stoles** *(plural).*

841   **-diastole**   A noun and a noun-forming word-final element, derived from Greek *diastolē* 'dilation' (specifically, of the heart and arteries), used in biomedical terminology differentiating among 'types and locations of the lower blood pressure measurement': **hypodiastole, bradydiastole, peridiastole.** Compare **-stole, -stalsis.** Related forms: **-diastolic; -diastoles** *(plural).*

842   **-systole**   A noun and a noun-forming word-final element, derived from Greek *systolē* 'contraction' (specifically, of the heart and arteries), used in biomedical terminology differentiating among 'types and locations of the higher blood pressure measurement': **hyposystole, extrasystole, sphygmosystole.** Compare **-stole, -stalsis.** Related forms: **-systolic; -systoles** *(plural).*

843   **-ple**   A word-final element, derived from the Latin suffix *-pl(us), -pl(a), -pl(um)* '**-fold**[2]' (from the Indo-European root **pel-, *ple-,* whence the Latin verbs *plectere* and *plicāre* 'to fold'), used in learned combinations acting as adjectives or nouns without change in form to indicate 'quantity' as multiplied by the number named by the first root: **duple, octuple, centuple.** Compare **-plicate, -ply, -plex.** Related forms: **-plication; -ples, -plications** (noun plurals).

844   **-people**   A noun (and a denominative verb), derived through Middle English and Old French from Latin *popul(us)* 'nation, body of citizens, people,' used in forming both noun and verb combinations:

1.   In nouns, 'human beings of a location or sort of social organization' specified by the combining root: **tribespeople, townspeople, countrypeople.**
2.   In nouns, 'human beings of an occupation' specified by the combining root: **tradespeople, fisherpeople, salespeople.**
3.   In verbs, 'to supply with humans' (originally, 'to conquer, subjugate, take over'): **outpeople, repeople, unpeople.** Principal parts: **-peopling, -peopled, -peopled.** Compare **-person.** Related form: **-peoples** *(plural).*

845   **-title**   A noun and a denominative verb, derived through Middle English *titel(en)* and *titel* from Old French and from Latin *titul(us)* 'title, inscription, label,' used also as a word-final element in verb combinations to mean 'to give a name to a work of art or a designation of office, rank, or relationship to a person': **betitle, subtitle, mistitle.** Principal parts: **-titling, -titled, -titled.**

846   **-castle**   A noun, derived through Middle English *castel* from Old English and Old French *castel* 'castle, i.e., a walled or otherwise fortified dwelling' from Latin *castell(um)* 'fort, refuge,' used as a word-final element in noun combinations describing the location of 'an elevated structure on the deck of earlier wooden sailing vessels': **forecastle, sterncastle, summercastle.** Related form: **-castles** *(plural).*

847   **-bottle**   A noun and a noun-forming word-final element, derived through Middle English *botel* and Middle French *boteille, bouteille* from late Latin *butticula* 'small cask,' used in a number of ways:
  1. To denote 'a person who drinks': **suckbottle, blowbottle, hidebottle.**
  2. In the common names of insects: **bluebottle, greenbottle, cornbottle.**
  3. In the common names of plants: **harebottle, whitebottle, knapbottle.** Related form: **-bottles** *(plural).*

848   **-ule**   A noun-forming word-final element, derived through French from the Latin diminutive suffix *-ul(us), -ul(a), -ul(um),* used in its etymological sense of 'small one' of a sort specified by the combining root: **vestibule, globule, tubule.** Compare **-cule.** Related forms: **-ula[1], -ula[2], -ulus, -ulum, -uli, -ulae, -ular, -ulate, -ulous, -ulic; -ules** *(plural).*

849   **-cule**   A word-final element, derived through French from the common Latin noun- and adjective-forming diminutive suffix *-culus, -cula, -culum,* used in English to form nouns with a diminutive sense, physical or metaphoric, of the combining root: **molecule, animalcule, ridicule.** Also, **-cle.** Compare **-ule.** Related forms: **-culus, -cula, -culum** (masculine, feminine, neuter *singulars*); **-culi, -culae, -cula** (masculine, feminine, neuter *plurals*); **-cular, -cularly, -culate** (i.e., **-cule** and **-ate[3]**); **-cules** *(plural).*

850   **-condyle**   A noun and a noun-forming word-final element, derived from Greek *kondyl(os)* 'knuckle,' used in medical terminology to designate 'a knucklelike projection on a bone' of a sort specified by the combining root: **epicondyle, ectocondyle, entocondyle.** Also, **-condylus.** Related forms: **-condyloid, -condylic, -condylian; -condyli, -condyles** *(plurals).*

851   **-style**   A noun, derived from Greek *styl(os)* 'pillar,' also used as a word-final element in forming noun and adjective combinations of two major sorts:
  1. In the vocabulary of classical architecture, 'having pillars' of a

size, location, or quantity specified by the combining root: **decastyle, peristyle, polystyle.**

2. In biomedical terminology, 'a bone attached to an internal supporting structure or the structure itself' as specified by the combining root: **zygostyle, pygostyle, axostyle.** Related forms: **-stylous, -stylic, -stylar; -styles** *(plural).*

852 **-dame** A noun and a noun-forming word-final element, derived through Middle English and Old French *dame* from Latin *domina* 'mistress, lady,' used (archaically) in the specialized sense of 'female parent' of a sort specified by the combining root: **stepdame, granddame, gudame** *(Scot.).* Also, **-dam** (chiefly in terms designating animal parents). Related forms: **-dames, -dams** *(plurals).*

853 **-fame** A noun, derived through Middle English *fam(a)* 'public opinion, reputation,' used also as a word ending in verb combinations meaning 'to make highly regarded or renowned' as qualified by the combining root: **befame, defame, outfame.** Principal parts: **-faming, -famed, -famed.** Related forms: **-famous, -famously.**

854 **-name** A noun and a denominative verb, derived through Middle English *name* and *nam(en)* from Old English *nama* and *nam(ian)* 'name' and 'to name,' used as a word-final element in noun and verb combinations in its etymological sense, as qualified by the combining root:

  1. In nouns: **forename, agname, surname.**
  2. In verbs: **bename, prename, misname.** Principal parts: **-naming, -named, -named.** Related form (noun): **-names** *(plural).*

855 **-frame** A verb and a noun, derived from Middle English *fram(ian)*, *fram(ien)* 'to benefit, comfort, construct' and Old English *fram(ian)*, *from(ian)* 'to avail, make progress, benefit,' used also as a word ending in two limited senses:

  1. As a verb, 'to devise, formulate, or construct, both mentally and physically': **enframe, reframe, misframe.**
  2. As a noun, 'a structure,' the purpose or location named by the combining root: **bedframe, doorframe, airframe.** Principal parts: **-framing, -framed, -framed.** Related form (noun): **-frames** *(plural).*

856 **-eme** A noun-forming word-final element, derived from French *-ème* (from Greek *-ēma*), an abstract noun-forming suffix with the meaning 'thing, unit,' and used chiefly in linguistic terminology to designate 'a basic contrastive unit' at the level of language designated by the

combining root: **phoneme, morpheme, semateme.** Related forms: **-emic; -emes** *(plural).*

857 **-reme** A noun-forming word-final element, derived from Latin *rēm(us)* 'oar,' used in terms for 'ships of Classical times powered by ranks of oars,' the number of ranks being specified by the combining root: **bireme, trireme, quinquereme.** Related form: **-remes** *(plural).*

858 **-seme** A noun-forming word-final element, derived from Greek *sēmē* 'sign, mark,' and, by extension, 'unit of measurement,' used in two major senses:

1. In the terminology of prosody, 'a line containing a number of prosodic units' specified by the combining root: **tetraseme, hexaseme, decaseme.**

2. In optometry, '(one) having an orbital index of less than 84, more than 89, or in between' as specified by the combining root: **megaseme, mesoseme, microseme.** Related forms: **-semic; -semes** *(plural).*

859 **-lime** A noun, derived through Middle English *lim* from Old English *līm* 'calcium oxide,' used also as a word ending in noun combinations identifying 'calcium carbonate products': **hydralime, quicklime, nitrolime.** Related form: **-limes** *(plural).*

860 **-mime** A noun, derived from Greek *mim(os)* 'an imitator' (cf. Greek *mimēsthai* 'to imitate'), also used as a noun-forming word-final element in combinations meaning 'an actor who communicates solely through bodily and facial gestures' as qualified by the combining root: **pantomime, archimime.** *Pantomime* and *mime* may also be used as verbs, each with the sense 'to perform in the style of a mime.' Related forms: **-mimia, -mimic, -mimesis, -mimetic, -mimical, -mimically; -mimes** *(plural).*

861 **-time** A noun and a productive noun-forming word-final element, derived through Middle English *time, tyme* from Old English *tīma* 'period, time,' used in the sense of 'a season, occasion, or appointed hour' for that which is specified by the combining root: **seedtime, harvesttime, suppertime.** Compare **-tide.** Related form: **-times** *(plural).*

862 **-nome** A noun-forming word-final element, derived from Greek *nom(os)*, a term with a variety of related senses: originally, 'that which is distributed, shared,' then, by extension, 'custom, convention, law, body of received knowledge.' In modern combinations, two senses predominate:

1. 'One who engages in or is versed in the customs or knowledge of a field' named by the combining root: **antinome, agronome, gastronome.**
2. 'A device that gives a standard measure' specified by the combining root: **metronome, rheonome, octodianome.** Related forms: **-nomy, -nomic, -nomical, -nomous, -nomian, -nomist; -nomes** *(plural).*

863 **-drome** A word-final element, derived through Middle French and Latin from Greek *drom(os)* 'race course' (from Greek *dramein* 'to run'), used in several related senses:
1. 'A large place, prepared for an activity' named by the combining root: **aerodrome, picturedrome, velodrome.**
2. 'A race course,' the racers or vehicles being named by the first root: **hippodrome, motordrome, autodrome.**
3. In medical and rhetorical forms, 'that which runs' in a way specified by the combining root: **heterodrome, palindrome, syndrome.** Related forms: **-dromic, -dromical, -dromous; -dromes** *(plural).*

864 **-chrome**[1] An adjective-forming word-final element, derived from Greek *chrōma, chrōmat-* 'color, thing with color,' used in combinations to mean 'colored' as specified by the combining root: **monochrome, polychrome, stereochrome.** Also, **-chromic, -chromatic.** Related forms: **-chromatically, -chromy.**

865 **-chrome**[2] A noun-forming word-final element, derived from Greek *chrōma, chrōmat-* 'color, thing with color,' used in combinations to mean 'a coloring substance within a cell or a chemical compound': **endochrome, bathochrome, lipochrome.** Related forms: **-chromatic, -chromatically; -chromes** *(plural).*

866 **-chrome**[3] A noun and a noun-forming word-final element, derived by abbreviation from *chromium* (French *chrome* and Latin *-ium*), used also as a word ending in noun combinations distinguishing 'chromium alloys': **Nichrome** (trademark), **nicochrome, topchrome.** Compare **-chrome**[1, 2].

867 **-some**[1] An adjective-forming word-final element, derived through Middle English *-som* from Old English *-sum* 'same,' used in the sense of 'characterized by an action, state, or quality' named by the combining root: **awesome, lonesome, troublesome.** Related forms: **-someness, -somely.**

868   -some² A noun-forming word-final element, derived through Middle English -*som* from Old English *sum*, a pronoun meaning 'one, a certain one, one of a group' (whence Modern English *some*), used in combinations denoting 'a group of members' whose number is specified by the combining root: **twosome, foursome, fivesome.** Related form: -**somes** *(plural)*.

869   -some³ A noun-forming word-final element, derived from Greek *sōma, sōmat-* 'body,' used in biomedical terminology to designate 'a body or an organism having a body' of a sort specified by the combining root: **metasome, megasome, sarcosome.** Related forms: -**soma, -somus, -somia, -somal, -somic, -somatic, -somatous, -somatically, -somite;** -**somes** *(plural)*.

870   -tome A noun-forming word-final element, derived from Greek *tomē* 'a cutting' (from the verb *temn(ein)* 'to cut'), used in medical terminology in two extensions of its etymological sense:
   1.   'An instrument for cutting' of a sort or for use in operating on a part of the body specified by the combining root: **labiotome, osteotome, rachiotome.**
   2.   'A segment, region' of that which is specified by the combining root: **viscerotome, myotome, dermatome.** Related forms: -**tomy, -tomic, -tomize, -tomous;** -**tomes** *(plural)*.

871   -fume A noun and a verb, derived through Middle English *fum(en)* and Middle French *fum(er)* 'to smoke, expose to fumes' from Latin *fum(āre)* 'to smoke,' used also as a word ending in verb combinations meaning 'to expose to fumes': **befume, perfume, reperfume.** Principal parts: -**fuming, -fumed, -fumed.**

872   -plume A noun, derived through Middle English and Middle French from Latin *plūma* 'feather,' used also as a word ending in noun combinations differentiating among shapes and types of 'feathers': **corniplume, pennoplume, pulviplume.** Related form: -**plumes** *(plural)*.

873   -sume A verb-forming word-final element derived from Latin *sūm(ere)* 'to take, take up' (from **sub-* plus *em(ere)* 'to buy'), used in its etymological sense (often metaphorically), as qualified by the combining root: **assume, presume, consume.** Principal parts: -**suming, -sumed, -sumed.** Related forms: -**sumable, -sumably, -sumptive, -sumption** (the last two forms being derived from the Latin past participle to the verb *sūm(ere)*).

874   -zyme A noun-forming word-final element, derived from Greek *zymē*

'leavening, i.e., an agent which causes fermentation,' used in biochemical terminology to denote 'a ferment or enzyme' as specified by the combining root: **microzyme, vitazyme, cytozyme**. Related forms: **-zymic; -zymes** *(plural)*.

875   **-ne**   A word-final element in French nouns and adjectives of feminine gender, added to the corresponding masculine-gender forms ending in *-n*, found in English in a number of borrowings from French designating feminine agents: **comedienne, equestrienne, tragedienne**. Related form: **-nes** *(plural)*.

876   **-ane**   A chemical suffix, derived by analogy to **-ine** and **-ene**, and used to designate hydrocarbons of the paraffin series: **ethane, methane, propane**. Related forms: **-anic; -anes** *(plural)*.

877   **-bane**   A noun and a noun-forming word-final element, derived through Middle English *bane* from Old English *ban(a)* 'murderer,' used in combinations to mean 'that which destroys life, especially a poison':
1. In the names of plants that are poisonous or thought to be poisonous or harmful to the animal named by the combining root: **mousebane, henbane, cowbane**.
2. By extension, in the names of plants thought to repel the insects named by the combining root: **fleabane, bugbane, flybane**.
3. By extension or because of folklore, in the names of harmless plants: **houndsbane (horehound), goatsbane, foxbane**. Related form: **-banes** *(plural)*.

878   **-phane**   A noun-forming word-final element, derived from Greek *phain(ein)* 'to appear, show (through), shine (through),' used to mean 'a thing which has the appearance or quality' of that which is named by the combining root: **uranophane, rhabdophane, cellophane**. Also, **-phan**. Related forms: **-phanic, -phanous, -phany; -phanes, -phans** *(plurals)*.

879   **-plane**[1]   An adjective, derived from Latin *plān(us)* 'flat, level, even,' used as a noun and a noun-forming word-final element in mathematical terminology in the sense of 'a level or flat surface' as specified by the combining root: **hemiplane, hyperplane, nonplane**. Related forms: **-planula, -planular; -planes** *(plural)*.

880   **-plane**[2]   A word-final element, derived from Greek *plan(os)* 'a wandering, going astray' (cf. the verb *planein* 'to lead astray, go astray, wander'), used largely by analogy to its occurrence in the word

aeroplane (airplane) to designate 'an airplane or an action connected with flying' specified by the combining root: **monoplane, seaplane, deplane.** Related forms: **-plania, -planetary; -planes** *(plural).*

881   **-mane**   A noun-forming word-final element, derived from French *-mane* 'one dressed with, or inordinately fond of' that which is named by the combining root. The French suffix *-mane* is itself derived from Greco-Latin *-mania* 'obsession or preoccupation' (from general Indo-European **men-* 'mind' and **-ia¹**). In English, **-mane** appears in borrowings from French with the sense of 'a person obsessed by or inordinately fond of' that which is named by the combining root: **bibliomane, balletomane, Anglomane.** Related forms: **-mania, -maniac, -manic, -maniacal, -manically, -maniacally; -manes** *(plural).*

882   **-montane**   An adjective-forming word-final element, derived through French from Latin *montān(us)* 'of or referring to a mountain or mountains' (from Latin *mons, mont-* 'hill, mountain' and the adjectival suffix *-ān(us), -ān(a), -ān(um)* '**-an¹**'), used in combinations, especially in botanical terminology, meaning 'of, pertaining, or referring to a mountain or mountains' as specified by the combining root: **cismontane, intermontane, submontane.**

883   **-ene**   A noun-forming word-final element, derived from Greek *-ēnē*, a suffix designating origin or source (as specified by the combining root), used in chemical terminology in naming hydrocarbons: **benzene, eth(yl)ene, naphthalene.**

884   **-cene**   A noun-forming word-final element, derived from Greek *kain(os), kain(ē), kain(on)* 'fresh, new,' used in the sense of 'recent' in naming geological eras: **Neocene, Eocene, Pleistocene.**

885   **-phene**   A noun-forming word-final element, derived from Greek *phain(ein)* 'to appear, show (through), shine (through),' used chiefly in chemical terminology to denote members of the phenol group and other derivatives from coal-tar (originally observed as by-products of illuminating gases): **penthiophene, hexachlorophene, benzothiophene.** Also, **-phen.** Related forms: **-phenol, -phenyl; -phenes, -phens** *(plurals).*

886   **-vene**   A verb-forming word-final element, derived from Latin *ven(īre)* 'to come,' used in its etymological sense, as qualified by the combining root: **intervene, convene, subvene.** Principal parts: **-vening, -vened, -vened.** Related forms: **-venient, -vention, -vent.**

887   **-ine¹**   A noun-forming word-final element, derived through French *-ine*

from Latin *-in(us)*, *-in(a)*, *-in(um)* 'of, belonging to,' used in chemical terminology in several senses:

1. 'A chemical substance, usually basic': **chlorine, quinine, pyrroline.**
2. 'A mixture of hydrocarbons': **gasoline, kerosine, aribine.**
3. In the names of commercial chemical products: **glassine, Visine, Murine.** Also, (sense 2) **-ene.** Compare **-in.** Related form: **-ines** *(plural).*

888 **-ine²** A noun-forming word-final element, derived through Middle English *-ina*, *-ine*, *-in* (an ending used in female given names) and Old English *-in(a)* from Latin *-in(a)*, used in combinations to mean 'a female person': **chorine, Josephine, undine.** Compare **-ina¹.**

889 **-ine³** An adjective-forming word-final element, derived through Middle English *-ine*, *-in* from Middle French *-in(e)*, Latin *-īn(us)*, *-īn(a)*, *-īn(um)*, and Greek *-in(os)*, *-in(ē)*, *-in(on)* 'of, belonging to,' used in two major senses as qualified by the combining root:

1. 'Of, belonging, or relating to': **marine, Sabine, alpine.**
2. 'Made of': **gabardine, opaline, bombazine.**

890 **-caine** A word-final noun-forming element, derived by abstraction from *cocaine* (from Quechua *kuka* 'coca plant' and **-ine¹**), an alkaloid used as a local anesthetic, used in combinations naming a variety of related synthetic alkaloid anesthetics: **Novocaine, procaine, dibucaine.** Related form: **-caines** *(plural).*

891 **-vaccine** A noun and a noun-forming word-final element, derived from Latin *vaccīn(us)*, *vaccīn(a)*, *vaccīn(um)* 'of or pertaining to cows' (cf. *vacca* 'cow' and **-ine¹**), used to differentiate by type, origin, or purpose 'a preparation containing microorganisms for the purpose of producing immunity to a particular disease' as specified by the combining root: **dermovaccine, neurovaccine, bovovaccine.** Related forms: **-vaccinate, -vaccination; -vaccines** *(plural).*

892 **-fine** A verb-forming word-final element, derived through Middle English *fin(en)* and Middle French *fin(er)* from Latin *fin(īre)* 'to bound, limit, restrain, prescribe, end, complete,' used in borrowed verb combinations based upon the etymological meanings: **define, refine, confine.** Principal parts: **-fining, -fined, -fined.** Related forms: **-finition, -finement.**

893 **-(r)rhine** An adjective-forming word-final element, derived from Greek *rhis, rhin-* 'nose,' used in combinations (which may be used substantively) in medical terminology with the meaning 'having a

nose' of the sort specified by the combining root: **monorhine, oxyrhine, platyrrhine.** Related form: **-(r)rhinia.**

894 **-line**[1] A noun-forming word-final element, derived through Middle English *line* from Latin *līn(um)* 'flax' (cf. English *linen*), used in combinations naming fabrics: **crinoline, silkaline, mousseline.** Related form: **-lines** *(plural)*.

895 **-line**[2] A noun, derived through Middle English *line* and Old English *līne* 'rope made of flax, cord; stroke, mark; row, guiding rule' from Latin *līne(us)* 'made of flax or linen,' used also in noun combinations in a variety of meanings:

1. 'A rope or wire used for a purpose' named by the combining root: **clothesline, fishline, towline.**
2. 'A rope or wire used on sailing ships': **bowline, buntline, ratline.**
3. 'A path that a line, usually imagined, would take': **bloodline, beeline, crossline.**
4. 'An imagined line on the human body marking an area rather than a precise location': **neckline, waistline, eyeline.**
5. In publishing, 'material arranged in lines': **headline, sideline, printline.**
6. 'A line, sometimes metaphoric, marking a limit of some kind': **hemline, borderline, deadline.** Compare **-line**[1]. Related form: **-lines** *(plural)*.

896 **-line**[3] A verb and a verb-forming word-final element, derived from Middle English *lin(en)* 'to cover the inner surface of,' used in combinations meaning 'to put something on an inner or interior surface': **interline, reline, unline.** Principal parts: **-lining, -lined, -lined.** Compare **-line**[1, 2].

897 **-alkaline** An adjective and an adjective-forming word-final element, derived from *alkali* (from Arabic *al-* 'the' and *galīy* 'ashes') 'an acid-neutralizing hydroxide of one of the alkali metals (potassium, lithium, et al.)' and **-ine**[3], used in combinations meaning 'of or referring to alkali' of a type or degree designated by the combining root: **subalkaline, vegetoalkaline, silicoalkaline.** Related forms: **-alkalinity, -alkalinize.**

898 **-cline** A word-final element, derived from Greek *klin(ein)* 'to lean, incline,' used in forming verbs and nouns:

1. In verbs and nouns, meaning 'to slope, a slope': **incline, decline, recline** (verb only).
2. In nouns, meaning 'a gradient layer': **thermocline, heterocline,**

syncline. Principal parts (verb): -clining, -clined, -clined. Related forms: -clinal, -clinic, -clinous, -clination; -clines *(plural)*.

899   **-one**   A noun-forming word-final element, derived, ultimately from Greek *-ōnē*, a feminine patronymic suffix, used in chemical terminology to designate organic compounds: **acetone, ketone, quinone.** Related form: **-ones** *(plural)*.

900   **-bone**   A noun, derived through Middle English *boon, bon* from Old English *bān* 'bone,' used also as a word ending in noun combinations that act as common names of bones in human and animal bodies: **shinbone, collarbone, aitchbone.** Related forms: **-boned; -bones** *(plural)*.

901   **-phone**   A noun and a noun-forming word-final element, derived from Greek *phōn(ē)* 'sound,' used in combinations in several related extensions of its etymological sense, each as specified by the combining root:
1. 'A musical instrument': **xylophone, saxophone, sousaphone.**
2. 'A device for transmitting sound': **telephone, megaphone, earphone.**
3. 'A device for the recording or reproduction of sound': **dictaphone, gramophone, graphophone.**
4. 'A device for monitoring the sounds of the body': **stethophone, cardiophone, sphygmophone.** Related forms: **-phonia, -phony, -phonic, -phonetic, -phonous, -phonically, -phonetically, -phonious, -phoniously; -phones** *(plural)*.

902   **-cyclone**   A noun, also used as a noun-forming word-final element, derived from Greek *kykl(os)* 'circle, ring, wheel' and either the neuter adjectival ending *-on* or the agentive suffix *-ōn*, used in meteorological terminology to designate 'a storm or wind system rotating around an area of low atmospheric pressure': **anticyclone, pericyclone, precyclone.** Related forms: **-cyclonic; -cyclones** *(plural)*.

903   **-hormone**   A noun and a noun-forming word-final element, derived from Greek *hormōn, hormon-*, the present participle of the verb *hormaein* 'to excite, set in motion,' used in biomedical terminology to denote 'a chemical substance, produced either in the body or by synthesis, possessing a regulatory effect on organic activity':
1. Classified according to source: **parahormone, zoohormone, phytohormone.**
2. Classified according to the area or organic activity affected:

proteohormone, neurohormone, parathormone. Related forms: -hormonic, -hormonal, -hormonally; -hormones *(plural)*.

904 **-pone**   A verb-forming word-final element, derived from Latin pōn(ere) 'to put, place, set,' used in its etymological sense, as qualified by the preposition acting as the combining root: **depone** 'put down,' **postpone** 'put after,' **propone** 'put forward or before,' **compone** 'put together.' Principal parts: **-poning, -poned, -poned.** Related forms: **-ponent, -ponement, -ponency.**

905 **-tone**   A noun and a word-final element, derived from Greek *ton(os)* 'that which stretches or is stretched, tension, accent, pitch' (from the verb *tein(ein)* 'to stretch'), used in a number of extensions of its etymological sense:
  1. In verbs, from its secondary meaning of 'accent, musical pitch,' 'to utter or chant': **entone, intone, betone** *(archaic)*.
  2. In nouns, in musical terminology, from its sense as 'musical pitch,' 'a pitch or interval': **semitone, ditone, subtone.**
  3. In nouns, in printing, 'a color quality or value': **doubletone, middletone, halftone.** Related forms: **-tonic, -tony, -tonia, -tonous; -tones** *(plural)*.

906 **-stone**   A noun and a widely-used noun-forming word-final element, derived through Middle English *stan, ston, stoon* from Old English *stān* 'rock, stone,' used in a variety of related senses:
  1. 'A stone, usually dressed, used for a purpose' named by the combining root: **tombstone, curbstone, whetstone.**
  2. 'A common name for stone or minerals': **sandstone, lodestone, freestone.**
  3. 'A variety of stone classified by shape or appearance': **woodstone, slabstone, birdstone.**
  4. 'A semiprecious stone': **bloodstone, jadestone, moonstone.**
  5. By extension or analogy, 'a common name for a calculus in a human organ or duct': **gallstone, bilestone, wombstone.**
  6. As a final element in personal or place names: **Gladstone, Firestone, Whitestone.** Related form (senses 1-5): **-stones** *(plural)*.

907 **-borne**   A word-final element, derived through Middle English *bourne* from Old English *burn(a)* 'stream, brook, fountain,' used in the formation of place names and the personal names derived from them: **Claiborne, Swanborne, Sherborne.** Also, **-bourne, -born, -burn.**

908 **-odyne**   A word-final element, derived from Greek *odyn(ē)* 'pain,' used to form adjectives (frequently employed substantively) with the sense of 'referring to, treating pain': **anodyne, acesodyne, biodyne.** Related forms: **-odynia, -odynic; -odynes** *(plural).*

909   -gyne   A noun-forming word-final element, derived from Greek *gyn(ē)*, *gynaik-* 'woman,' used to designate 'a creature or plant with female characteristics' or 'female characteristics,' as specified by the combining root: **androgyne, trichogyne, epigyne.** Also, **-gyn.** Related forms: **-gynia, -gynic, -gynous, -gyny, -gynist; -gynes, -gyns** *(plurals).*

910   -toe   A noun and a noun-forming word-final element, derived through Middle English *ta, to, too* from Old English *tā, take* 'toe, digit of the foot,' used in two senses:
  1. 'A deformity of the toes': **hammer toe.** (Compare **pigeon-toed, ding-toed,** referring to an irregularity of stance.)
  2. 'The common name of a plant': **pussytoe, crowtoe.** (The name *mistletoe* is now regarded as a misinterpretation of Old English *misteltān,* in which the final element means 'twig,' a sense lost by Middle English times.) Related form: **-toes** *(plural).*

911   -scape   A noun-forming word-final element, derived from the last element of Dutch *landscap* 'region of land,' used in combinations meaning 'a view or a photograph or painting of a view' specified by the combining root: **seascape, cloudscape, moonscape.** Related form: **-scapes** *(plural).*

912   -pipe   A noun and a noun-forming word-final element, derived through Middle English *pipe* and Old English *pīpa* 'tube' from Latin *pīp(āre)* 'to chirp, peep' (presumably from the noise made by blowing through a tube, *pīp(āre)* itself being onomatopoeic in origin), used in a variety of senses, all related to the meaning 'tube':
  1. 'A length of pipe' for a purpose stated by the combining root: **stovepipe, tailpipe, hawsepipe.**
  2. 'A cylinder resembling a pipe': **windpipe, standpipe, swallowpipe.**
  3. 'A musical instrument involving small pipes or a pipe on a musical instrument': **bagpipe, panpipe, dronepipe.**
  4. A word-final element in the common names of plants and animals: **toadpipe, snakepipe, swinepipe.** Related form: **-pipes** *(plural).*

913   -ope   A noun-forming word-final element, derived from Greek *ops, op-* 'eye, face, voice,' (the earliest sense being that of *voice*, then *face*, as the locus of the voice, and then, by extension, the *eye*), used in combinations designating 'a person having a defect of the eye' specified by the combining root: **myope, presbyope, amblyope.** Related forms: **-opic, -opia, -opy; -opes** *(plural)*.

914 **-scope**   A noun and a noun-forming word-final element, derived from Greek *skop(ein)* 'to look at, observe,' used in combinations meaning 'a mechanism or instrument for observing or viewing with the eye': **telescope, microscope, periscope.** The basic meaning has been transferred to instruments that observe in other ways: **stethoscope, radiotelescope, phonendoscope.** Related forms: **-scopia, -scopic, -scopical, -scopist, -scopy, -scopically; -scopes** *(plural)*.

915 **-trope**   A word-final element, derived from Greek *trop(os)*, *trop(ē)* 'a turning, turn, direction, means, mode' (from the verb *trep(ein)* 'to turn, guide'), used in medical terminology as a noun-forming element in a number of combinations, some of which may be used adjectivally, all of which have something to do with 'turning or being turned,' often in the metaphorical sense of 'influencing or influenced by' as specified by the combining root: **rheotrope, heliotrope, gonadotrope.** Related forms: **-tropia, -tropy, -tropic, -tropal, -tropism, -tropous; -tropes** *(plural)*.

916 **-thorpe**   A word-final element, derived through Middle English from Old English *-thorp* 'farm, village,' used in forming noun combinations in place names and surnames derived from them: **Oglethorpe, Woolsthorpe, Althorpe.** Also, **-thorp.**

917 **-type**   A noun and a noun-forming word-final element, derived from Greek *typ(os)* 'a blow, impression (i.e., the mark left by a blow), image, model' (from the verb *typt(ein)* 'to strike a blow'), used in a number of its etymological senses:
1. Generally, 'a representative form or class' as specified by the combining root: **archetype, orthotype, prototype.**
2. 'An impressed, stamped, or printed object' as specified by the combining root: **tintype, electrotype, hyalotype.**
3. 'A machine on which printed messages may be produced': **Linotype, Monotype, Teletype.** Related forms: **-typic, -typical, -typically, -typal, -typy; -types** *(plural)*.

918 **-fare**[1]   A noun and a noun-forming word-final element, derived through Middle English *fare* from Old English *far(u)* 'journey' (from Old English *faran* 'to go, travel'), used to mean 'a journey or passage,' whether actual or metaphoric, as specified by the combining root: **seafare, warfare, welfare.** Related forms: **-fare**[2]; **-fares** *(plural)*.

919 -fare² An archaic verb and verb-forming word-final element, derived through Middle English *far(en)* from Old English *far(an)* 'to travel, go,' used in its etymological sense: **forthfare, wayfare, misfare.** Principal parts: **-faring, -fared, -fared.**

920 -mare An obsolete noun and a noun-forming word-final element, derived through Middle English from Old English *mare* 'a goblin' supposed to produce bad dreams by sitting on the dreamer, preserved as a free form and in two combinations meaning 'bad dream': **mare, nightmare, daymare.** Related form: **-mares** *(plural).*

921 -ware A noun and a noun-forming word-final element, derived through Middle English from Old English *war(u)* 'a thing of care,' used in the sense of 'manufactured merchandise,' its raw material or use being specified by the combining root: **silverware, leatherware, dinnerware.** The combinations are collectives and not ordinarily pluralized.

922 -here A word-final element, derived from Latin *haer(ēre)* 'to stick, cling,' used in borrowed verb combinations meaning 'to affix, stick, cling': **adhere, cohere, inhere.** Principal parts: **-hering, -hered, -hered.** Related forms: **-herence, -herent, -herency.**

923 -sphere A noun and a noun-forming word-final element, derived from Greek *sphair(a)* 'ball, globe,' used in a variety of related senses:
1. 'A representation of spherical lines and bodies': **planisphere, hemisphere, perisphere.**
2. In astronomical and geological terminology, 'an enveloping layer, as about the earth, spherical in shape': **geosphere, leucosphere, atmosphere.**
3. In biological terminology, especially in botany, 'a spherical mass forming a body': **chondriosphere, archisphere, coccosphere.**
4. In biological terminology, 'a realm, in which life support is available' for the species or class named by the combining root: **biosphere, zoosphere, vivosphere.** Also, **-sphaere, -sphaera.** Related forms: **-spheric, -sphaeric, -spherical, -sphaerical, -spherically, -sphaerically, -spherite, -sphaerite, -sphericity, -sphaericity; -spheres, -sphaeres, -sphaerae** *(plurals).*

924 -there A noun-forming word-final element, derived through scientific Latin *ther(ium)* from Greek *thēr(ion)* 'wild beast,' used to designate 'a mammal (usually prehistoric)' of a sort specified by the combining root: **megathere, palaeothere, dinothere.** Also, **-therium.** Related forms: **-therian, -therioid, -theroid; -theres, -theria** *(plurals).*

925 **-iere** A word-final noun-forming element, derived from French *-ière,* the feminine-gender form of *-ier,* from the Latin agentive suffix *-ari(us, -a, -um),* used in borrowed words from French to designate 'a female (or grammatically feminine) agent' as specified by the combining root: **costumiere, boulevardiere, boutonniere.** Compare **-ier, -eer, -er[1], -er[2].** Related form: **-ieres** *(plural).*

926 **-mere** A noun and a noun-forming word-final element, derived through Middle English from Old English *mere* 'sea, pool,' used in place names in the sense of 'arm of the sea, inlet, lake': **Ellesmere, Grasmere, Windermere.** This suffix is not to be confused with **-mere,** the variant spelling of **-mer** (from Greek *mer(os)* 'part').

927 **-aire** A word ending, derived from French *-aire* '**-ary[2],**' used in forming noun and adjective combinations:
1. Nouns meaning 'a thing, place, or person connected with' something named by the combining root: **reliquaire, millionaire, concessionaire.**
2. Nouns naming devices: **luminaire, Frigidaire, veuglaire.**
3. In borrowed adjectives meaning 'of or connected with': **debonaire, doctrinaire.** Compare **-ary[1, 2].** Related forms: (noun) **-aires** *(plural);* (adjective) **-airly.**

928 **-shire** A noun and a word-final element, derived through Middle English *shir, shire* from Old English *scir* 'district, province,' also used in its etymological sense in noun combinations acting as the names of 'administrative districts,' especially in British county names: **Buckinghamshire, New Hampshire, Oxfordshire.** Related form: **-shires** *(plural).*

929 **-spire** A verb-forming word-final element, derived from Latin *spīr(āre)* 'to breathe,' used in a number of common borrowings and their derivatives in its etymological sense, as qualified by the combining root: **aspire, conspire, transpire.** Principal parts: **-spiring, -spired, -spired.** Related forms: **-spiration, -spirational, -spirationally.**

930 **-tire** A verb, derived through Middle English *tyr(en), tyer(en)* from Old English *tyr(ian), tēor(ian)* 'to become weary,' used also as a word-final element in verb combinations meaning 'to weary': **overtire, outtire, untire.** Principal parts: **-tiring, -tired, -tired.**

931 **-quire** A verb-forming word-final element, derived from Latin *quaer(ere)* 'to seek, ask, investigate,' used in a number of common borrowings and their derivatives, all with a basic sense of 'ask about,

ask for, demand': **inquire, require, acquire.** Principal parts: **-quiring, -quired, -quired.** Related forms: **-quirement, -quirable; -quisition, -quisitive** (from the non-rhotacized form of the verbal root, *quaes-*, as in *quest, question*, and the like).

932 **-fore** A word and a word ending, derived through Middle English and Old English *fore* 'before,' used in forming combinations in two senses:
  1. In adverbs, 'prior in time': **heretofore, theretofore, herebefore.** The combinations are considered archaic because of their limited occurrence in modern usage.
  2. In adverbs and prepositions, 'prior in space, in front of': **before, afore** *(dialectal)*, **pinafore. Before** can be used in both senses.

933 **-phore** A noun-forming word-final element, derived from Greek *phor(ein)* (the frequentative form of *pher(ein)* 'to bear, carry'), used in the sense of 'a bearer, carrier, possessor' of that which is specified by the combining root: **semaphore, carpophore, osteophore.** Also, **-phor.** Compare **-fer, -pher.** Related forms: **-phora, -phorae, -phori, -phoria, -phorous, -phoric; -phores, -phors, -fers, -phers** *(plurals)*.

934 **-plore** A verb-forming word-final element, derived from Latin *plōr(āre)*, 'to flow, cause to flow, weep, bewail,' used in three common verbs and numerous derivatives: **implore** 'to beseech (with tears)': **deplore** 'to bemoan, weep over': **explore** 'to seek out, investigate' (originally, 'cause to flow forth'). Principal parts: **-ploring, -plored, -plored.** Related forms: **-plorable, -ploration, -plorer, -ploringly;** for **explore** only: **-ploratory.**

935 **-pore** A noun and a noun-forming word-final element, derived from Greek *por(os)* 'a means of passage, passage-way,' used in general scientific terminology to designate 'a passage-way or pore' of a sort specified by the combining root, or 'a creature possessing or producing passageways or pores': **megalopore, gonopore, millepore.** Related forms: **-poric, -porous, -pora; -pores** *(plural)*.

936 **-spore** A noun and a noun-forming word-final element, derived from Greek *spor(os)* 'a sowing, a seed' (from the verb *speir(ein)* 'to sow seed,' whence also **-sperm**), used to denote 'a reproductive element or body, a seed' of a sort specified by the combining root: **zygospore, oospore, ascospore.** Related forms: **-spora, -sporic, -sporous; -spores** *(plural)*.

937 **-vore** A noun-forming word-final element, derived from Latin *vor(āre)* 'to swallow, swallow up, eat' (whence English *devour*), used to

designate 'a creature who eats something' specified by the combining root: **carnivore, herbivore, insectivore.** Related forms: **-vorous; -vores, vora** *(plurals).*

938 **-ure** A noun-forming word-final element, derived from Latin *-ūra,* a feminine-gender abstract-noun-forming suffix, meaning 'a state, process, condition' of that which is named by the combining root: **verdure, procedure, pleasure.** Compare **-ture.** Related forms: **-ural, -urally; -ures** *(plural).*

939 **-cure** A noun and a noun-forming word-final element, derived from Latin *cūr(a)* 'care, attention, worry,' used in its etymological senses, as specified by the combining root: **pedicure, manicure, sinecure.** Related form: **-cures** *(plural).*

940 **-neure** A noun, derived from Greek *neur(on)* 'sinew, tendon, fiber,' hence, 'nerve,' used as a noun-forming word-final element in bio-medical terminology with the meaning 'a nerve cell' as specified by the combining root: **zygoneure, chitoneure, rhizoneure.** Also, **-neuron.** Related forms: **-nuria, -nuric, -neural, -neurotic, -neurosis, -neuroma; -neures** *(plural).*

941 **-figure** A verb and a noun, derived from Latin *figūr(āre)* 'to form, fashion, devise' and *figūr(a)* 'a form, manner' (from *fing(ere)* 'to touch, form, arrange'), used as a word-final element in both verb and noun combinations in two senses:
1. In verbs, 'to compute or reckon' in a manner specified by the combining root: **misfigure, refigure, outfigure.**
2. In verbs and nouns, 'to give shape to something' or 'the result of giving shape to something' as specified by the combining root: **transfigure, disfigure, forefigure.** Principal parts: **-figuring, -figured, -figured.** Related forms: **-figuration; -figures** *(plural).*

942 **-posure** A noun-forming word-final element, derived from **-pos(e)** and **-ure,** used in combinations sharing the basic meaning 'the act, process, or condition of placement' specified by the combining root: **exposure, composure, interposure** *(archaic).* Related forms: **-pose, -pound, -posal, -posite, -posit, -position, -positely, -positional, -positionally; -posures** *(plural).*

943 **-ture** A noun-forming word-final element, derived from two Latin sources, *-tūr(us), -tūr(a), -tūr(um)* (the ending of the future participle, itself a combination of the past participle plus the abstract-noun-forming suffix *-ūr(us), -ūr(a), -ūr(um)*—cf. **-ure**) and *-tūr(a),* an

abstract-noun-forming suffix, felt to be related to the agentive suffix *-tor* (cf. **-or, -ator**), used in three senses reflecting both derivations:

1. 'An action, process, or state' specified by the combining root: **investiture, culture, signature.**
2. 'An office or rank' specified by the combining root: **judicature, prelature, prefecture.**
3. 'A group assembled for an activity' named by the combining root: **legislature, jointure, nunciature.** Compare **-ure.** Related forms: **-tural, -turally; -tures** *(plural).*

944 **-ature** An abstract noun-forming word-final element, derived from **-ate**[1, 3] and **-ure: ligature, armature, legislature.**

945 **-facture** A noun and a noun-forming word-final element derived from the Latin future participle *factūr(us)* 'to be done, made' to the Latin verb *fac(ere)* 'to do, make, shape,' used in combinations to mean 'the act or process of creating with the substance' denoted by the joining root: **metallifacture, vitrifacture, machinofacture.** The last combination was developed as the antonym of the verb **manufacture** (literally, 'to make by hand'), itself derived, as was *factur(a)*, from the Latin *fac(ere)* 'to make.' The verb also acts as the word-final element in verb combinations: **remanufacture, semimanufacture, premanufacture.** The terms also act as nouns. Principal parts: **-facturing, -factured, -factured.** Related forms: **-facient, -faction, -factive, -factory, -fect, -(i)fic, -(i)fy; -factures** *(plural).*

946 **-phyre** A noun-forming word-final element, derived by abbreviation of the word *porphyry* (from Greek *porphyr(os)* 'purple, purple stone, stone embedded with fine crystals'), used in the terminology of mineralogy to denote 'a rock containing feldspar crystals or of the consistency of porphyry' as specified by the combining root: **melaphyre, granophyre, vitrophyre.** Related forms: **-phyric, -phyritic; -phyres** *(plural).*

947 **-ase** A suffix in chemical terminology, derived by abstraction of the *-ase* of the word *diastase* (which is actually a combination of *dia-* and *-stase*), used in naming enzymes: **protease, oxidase, amylase.** Related form: **-ases** *(plural).*

948 **-phrase** A noun and noun-forming word-final element, derived from Greek *phrasis* 'a speaking, a way of speaking (from the verb *phrazein* 'to point out, show, tell, explain'), found in several borrowings (all of which may also be used as verbs), all sharing a basic sense of 'stating or restating': **paraphrase** 'stating in other words; a free restatement';

metaphrase 'stating or restating literally'; **periphrase** 'restating in a roundabout manner'; **holophrase** 'stating or restating a complex of ideas in a single word.' Principal parts: **-phrasing, -phrased, -phrased.** Related forms: **-phrastic, -phrastically; -phrases** *(plural)*.

949   **-ese** A word-final element, derived through modern Romance *-es(e)* from Vulgar Latin *-es(is)* from Latin *-ens(is)*, an adjectival suffix indicating origin, used in forming adjectives and nouns with a number of related senses:

1. Adjective combinations meaning 'pertaining or relating to or originating in a place or country' specified by the combining root: **Tyrolese, Siamese, Chinese.**
2. Nouns meaning 'a native or resident of a place or country' named by the joining root: **Japanese, Lebanese, Genoese.**
3. Nouns meaning 'speech, literary style, or diction': **stagese, Brooklynese, journalese.** The plurals and singulars of the noun combinations have identical forms.

950   **-prise** A verb-forming word-final element, derived through French from the past participle of the Latin verb *prehend(ere)* 'to grasp, seize,' used in combinations meaning 'to take' as qualified by the combining root: **reprise** 'take back'; **comprise** 'take together'; **enterprise** 'undertake.' Principal parts: **-prising, -prised, -prised.** Many of the **-prise** verbs function as nouns without change in form. Compare **-prehend.**

951   **-vise** A verb-forming word-final element, derived from Latin *vīs(us)*, *vīs(a)*, *vīs(um)*, the past participle to the verb *vid(ēre)* 'to see,' used in a number of common borrowings with the basic meaning of 'to see, observe': **revise** 'to look back or again'; **televise** 'to show visually at a distance'; **supervise** 'to look over'. Several related forms share this ending, but changes in meaning obscure the etymological sense: **improvise** 'to react to the unforeseen'; **advise** 'to see, recognize, and inform'. Principal parts: **-vising, -vised, -vised.** Related forms: **-vision, -visional, -visionally.**

952   **-wise** An adverb-forming word-final element, derived through Middle English from Old English *wīs(e)* 'manner, means,' used extensively in combinations with the following senses:

1. 'In the manner of' that which is specified by the combining root: **crabwise, sardinewise, likewise.**
2. 'In the direction or position of' what is named by the combining root: **edgewise, churchwise, clockwise.**
3. 'With regard to' something named by the combining root: **problemwise, teamwise, umbrellawise.** Compare **-ways.**

953 **-pulse** A verb (also used as a noun) and a verb-forming word-final element, derived from Latin *puls(us)*, *puls(a)*, *puls(um)*, the past participle of the verb *pell(ere)* 'to push, drive,' used in a number of common borrowings in its etymological sense as qualified by the combining root: **repulse, impulse, expulse.** Principal parts: **-pulsing, -pulsed, -pulsed.** Related forms: **-pel, -pulsion, -pulsive.**

954 **-pense** A verb-forming word-final element, derived from Latin *pens(us)*, *pens(a)*, *pens(um)*, the past participle to the verb *pend(ere)* 'to hang, weigh, assay, pay out,' used in a number of borrowed verb combinations, most of which may also be used as nouns, generally in its etymological sense of 'to pay': **recompense, dispense, expense.** Principal parts: **-pensing, -pensed, -pensed.** Compare **-pend.** Related forms: **-pensate, -pensation, -pensive, -pension.**

955 **-sense** A noun and a noun-forming word-final element, derived through French *-sens* from Latin *sēns(us)* 'an understanding, feeling, perception' (from the verb *sent(īre)* 'to perceive, feel, understand'), used in combinations denoting 'an understanding or receptiveness, or the capability or result of understanding or receptiveness' as specified by the combining root: **nonsense, foresense, lacksense.** Related forms: **-sensical, -sensitive, -sensically, -sensitivity, -sensicality, -sensicalness.**

956 **-ose**[1] An adjective-forming word-final element, derived through Middle English from Latin *-ōs(us)*, *-ōs(a)*, *-ōs(um)*, an adjectival suffix meaning 'full of,' used in English in the sense of 'abounding in, having the qualities or characteristics of, tending to' that which is specified by the combining root: **verbose, bulbose, bellicose.** Compare **-ous.** Related forms: **-osic, -osity, -osely.**

957 **-ose**[2] A noun-forming word-final element, derived by abstraction from French *glucose*, itself derived from Greek *gleukos* 'sweet wine' (cf. *glykys* 'sweet'), used in chemical terminology in two senses:
  1. 'A carbohydrate, especially sugar': **fructose, glycose, sorbose.**
  2. 'A primary product of hydrolysis': **proteose, caseose, apiose.**
     Related form: **-oses** *(plural).*

958 **-close** A verb and a verb-forming word-final element, derived through Middle English *clos(en)* from Old French *clos-* (a stem form of the verb *clo(re)*) from Latin *claus(us)*, *claus(a)*, *claus(um)*, the past participle to the verb *claud(ere)* 'to bring to an end, cut off, close,' used in its etymological sense, as qualified by the combining root: **enclose, foreclose, disclose.** Principal parts: **-closing, -closed, -closed.**

959   **-nose**   A noun (and a denominative verb), derived through Middle English from Old English *nos(u)* 'nose,' used as a word-final element in noun and adjective combinations:

1. As a noun naming 'a condition or shape of a human nose': **saddlenose, hooknose, coppernose.**
2. As a noun characterizing 'a personality trait': **snipnose, nebnose, bluenose.**
3. As a noun acting as the common name of plants and animals: **bottlenose, butternose, sheepnose.**
4. As an adjective, possibly derived by contraction of the participle *nosed*, 'pertaining to the shape found at the ends of tools': **roundnose, bullnose, needlenose.** Related form (noun): **-noses** *(plural).*

960   **-goose**   A noun, derived through Middle English *goos, gos* from Old English *gōs* 'goose, ducklike bird of the *Anatidae* family,' used also as a word-final element in noun combinations that act as the common names of four bird species similar to geese only in possessing webbed feet: **skelgoose** (sheldrake), **cargoose** (grebe), **embergoose** (loon), **niggergoose** (cormorant). Note that the word *mongoose* (a variety of ferret) does not contain this element, being derived instead from Marathi *mangūs*. Related form: **-geese** *(plural).*

961   **-pose**   A verb, derived through Middle English *pos(en)* from Middle French *pos(er)* 'to put, place,' a verb derived from the past of Latin *pōn(ere)* 'to put, place' (cf. **-pone**), also used as a verb-forming word-final element in combinations that share the fundamental sense 'to put, place,' often with modern extensions allowing the placement to be mental or verbal as well as physical: **oppose, interpose, transpose.** Principal parts: **-posing, -posed, -posed.** Compare **-pound.** Related forms: **-posal, -posit, -posite, -position, -positional, -positionally, -positive, -posure, -ponent.**

962   **-lapse**   A noun and a verb, both derived from Latin *laps(us)* 'a slip, mistake' (itself derived from the verb *lābī* 'to slip, slide'), also used as a noun- and verb-forming word-final element in its etymological sense as qualified by the combining root: **collapse, relapse, interlapse.** Principal parts: **-lapsing, -lapsed, -lapsed.** Related form: **-lapses** *(plural).*

963   **-merse**   A verb-forming word-final element, derived from Latin *mers(us)*, the past participle of the verb *mergere* 'to dip, plunge,' used in a handful of frequently occurring combinations, all with the sense of 'to place in water or some other fluid medium' as specified by the

combining root: **immerse, submerse, emerse.** Principal parts: **-mersing, -mersed, -mersed.** Related forms: **-merge, -mersion.**

964 **-sperse** A verb-forming word-final element, derived from Latin *-spers(us)*, *-spers(a)*, *-spers(um)*, the past participle of *-sperg(ere)*, the combining form of *sparg(ere)* 'to scatter, strew,' used in its etymological sense, as qualified by the combining root, in a number of borrowings: **asperse, disperse, intersperse.** Principal parts: **-spersing, -spersed, -spersed.** Related form: **-spersion.**

965 **-verse** A word-final element, derived from Latin *vers(āre)* 'to turn, bend, incline' (from *vers(us)*, *vers(a)*, *vers(um)*, the past participle of the verb *vert(ere)* 'to turn'), used in several related senses:
1. In borrowed nouns meaning 'the result of turning' or 'a turn of something' as specified by the combining root: **universe, multiverse, anniverse** *(obsolete).*
2. In borrowed verbs meaning 'to turn': **traverse, reverse, tergiverse.**
3. In borrowed adjectives (which function as nouns without change in form) meaning 'turned, changed' as qualified by the joining root: **inverse, reverse, obverse.**
4. In borrowed adjectives meaning 'turned, changed': **adverse, averse, perverse.** Principal parts: **-versing, -versed, -versed.** Compare **-vert.** Related forms: **-versary, -version, -versation; -verses** *(plural).*

966 **-horse** A noun, derived through Middle English from Old English *hors* 'horse,' used in a number of combinations reflecting its etymological sense:
1. 'A horse' whose function is described by the combining root: **bathorse, workhorse, studhorse.**
2. 'A frame or support' for a purpose specified by the combining root: **clotheshorse, sawhorse, drawhorse.**
3. 'An imaginary horse or horselike toy': **hobbyhorse, cockhorse.** Related form: **-horses** *(plural).*

967 **-fuse** A verb-forming word-final element, derived through the Middle English past participle *fused* 'poured,' itself derived through Middle French *fus* from Latin *fus(us)*, the past participle to the verb *fund(ere)* 'to pour,' used in borrowed combinations meaning 'to pour or flow' as qualified by the combining root: **confuse, effuse, transfuse.** Principal parts: **-fusing, -fused, -fused.** Related forms: **-fusion, -fusal.**

968 **-house** A noun and a productive noun-forming word-final element, derived through Middle English *house* from Old English *hūs* 'shelter, house,' used in combinations designating 'a shelter or house' for that which is specified by the combining root: **playhouse, gatehouse, henhouse.** Related form: **-houses** *(plural).*

969   **-mouse**   A noun and a noun-forming word-final element, derived through Middle English *mous* from Old English *mūs* 'mouse, i.e., small rodent of the *Muridae* family,' used in three ways:
    1. In the common names of 'mice and mice-like animals': **creep-mouse, shrewmouse, dormouse.**
    2. In three epithets for 'bat': **rattlemouse** *(obsolete),* **reremouse** *(archaic),* **flittermouse.**
    3. In the common names of certain birds: **titmouse, tomtitmouse, coalmouse.** Related form: **-mice** *(plural).*

970   **-tuse**   A word-final element, derived through Middle French *tus(er)* from Latin *tūs(us), tūs(a), tūs(um),* the past participle of the verb *tund(ere)* 'to beat, thump, dull,' used in borrowed combinations in two senses:
    1. In two adjectives meaning, basically, 'dull or blunt': **obtuse, retuse.**
    2. In two verbs meaning, basically, 'to beat or thrust': **contuse, pertuse.** Principal parts: **-tusing, -tused, -tused.** Related forms: **-tusion, -tund.**

971   **-ate**[1]   An adjective-forming word-final element, derived from the past participle ending of the first conjugation of Latin (see the discussion under **-ata**), used in both native combinations and learned borrowings, often substantively:
    1. 'Acted upon, brought into or being in a state' indicated by the combining root: **expatriate, degenerate, appropriate.**
    2. 'Possessing, characterized by possessing' something specified by the joining root: **foliate, floreate, cuspidate.** Related forms: **-ately, -ation.**

972   **-ate**[2]   A noun-forming word-final element, originating in Latin as an application of **-ate**[1] to nouns without change in form, used in borrowed and native noun combinations.
    1. 'A rank or official position': **delegate, laureate, advocate.**
    2. 'Persons filling an office': **episcopate, pontificate, diaconate.**
    3. 'A person or thing acted upon': **retardate, initiate, distillate.** Also, **-at.** Related forms: **-ation; -ates** *(plural).* Terms like **episcopate** are usu. considered collective nouns and lack **-ation** and **-ates** forms.

973   **-ate³**   A verb-forming word-final element, originating in the causative use of **-ate¹**, and found widely in both native and semi-learned combinations:

1.   'To act upon' in a way specified by the combining root: **venerate, medicate, probate.**
2.   'To act' in a way indicated by the joining root: **adjudicate, placate, deprecate.**
3.   'To cause to be affected or modified by' something indicated in the combining root: **detoxicate, pollinate, abbreviate.**
4.   'To cause to be in a state or condition' named by the combining root: **eradicate, activate, authenticate.**
5.   'To furnish with' something specified by the combining root: **substantiate, populate, chloridate.** Principal parts: **-ating, -ated, -ated.** Related forms: **-ation, -ative.**

974   **-ate⁴**   A chemical suffix, derived from a specialized use of **-ate¹**, and used in two basic senses:

1.   'A chemical compound derived from an element or compound' named by the first root: **silicate, sulfate, opiate.**
2.   'An acid compound derived from an acid ending in *-ic* but not beginning with *hydro-*': **acetate, carbonate, salicylate.** Related form: **-ates** *(plural)*.

975   **-bate**   A verb-forming word-final element, derived through Middle English *batt(en)* and Middle French *bat(re)* from Latin *batt(ere)* 'to beat, hit,' used in a handful of borrowings in various metaphorical extensions of its etymological sense, as qualified by the combining root: **rebate, debate, abate.** Some of the combinations (for example, **rebate**) function as nouns without change in form. Also, **-bat.** Principal parts: **-bating, -bated, -bated.** Related forms: **-bats, -bates** *(plurals)*.

976   **-ficate**   A verb-forming word-final element, derived from the causative use of the past participle of the Latin verb *-fic(are)*, a combining form of the verb *fac(ere)* 'to do, make,' used to mean 'do or make or make into' that which is specified by the combining root: **petrificate, falsificate, vivificate.** (Note that this suffix is preceded in combination by the joining vowel *-i-*). Also, (by apocope) **-(i)cate.** Compare **-fy.** Related forms: **-(i)fication, -(i)ficative.**

977   **-plicate**   A word-final element, derived from Latin *plicāt(us), plicāt(a), plicāt(um)*, the past participle to the verb *plicāre* 'to fold' (itself derived from the combining form of the verb *plactere* 'to fold'), used in a variety of borrowed combinations:

1. In verbs, in extensions of its etymological sense as qualified by the combining root: **duplicate, complicate, explicate.**
2. In verbs, nouns, and adjectives, in the sense of English *-fold* (cf. *-fold*[2]), 'to copy, a copy, pertaining to a copy' in the number specified by the combining root: **duplicate, triplicate, quadruplicate.** Principal parts: **-plicating, -plicated, -plicated.** Compare **-ply, -plex, -ple.** Related forms: **-plication; -plicates** *(plural).*

978　**-locate**　A verb and a verb-forming word-final element, derived from Latin *loc(us)* 'a place' and *-ate*[3], used in its etymological sense of 'to place,' as qualified by the combining root: **dislocate, relocate, collocate.** Principal parts: **-locating, -located, -located.** Related form: **-location.**

979　**-create**　A verb and a verb-forming word-final element, derived through Middle English *creat(en)* from Latin *cre(āre)* 'to beget, produce' and *-ate*[3], used in combinations with the meaning 'cause to exist': **cocreate, procreate, intercreate.** Principal parts: **-creating, -created, -created.** Related forms: **-creation, -creative, -creatively.**

980　**-gregate**　A verb-forming word-final element, derived from Latin *greg(are)* 'to collect' (from Latin *grex, greg-* 'herd, flock') and *-ate*[3], used in its sense of 'collect' as qualified by the combining root: **segregate, congregate, aggregate.** Principal parts: **-gregating, -gregated, -gregated.** Related form: **-gregation.**

981　**-rogate**　A verb-forming word-final element, derived from Latin *rog(āre)* 'to ask, call for a vote, propose' and *-ate*[3], used in a number of common borrowings and their derivatives in its etymological senses and in extensions of same, as specified by the combining root:
1. 'To ask': **interrogate.**
2. 'To propose' is the basic meaning of other borrowed terms; the modern meaning is 'to act on a proposal, personal or from an outside source': **surrogate, subrogate, abrogate.** Principal parts: **-rogating, -rogated, -rogated.** Related forms: **-rogation, -rogatory.**

982　**-nunciate**　A verb-forming word-final element, derived from Latin *nunti(āre)* 'to report, announce, declare' and *-ate*[3], used in its etymological sense of 'to make a report, announcement, declaration' as qualified by the combining root: **enunciate, denunciate, annunciate.** Compare **-nounce.** Principal parts: **-nunciating, -nunciated, -nunciated.** Related forms: **-nounce, -nouncement, -nunciation.**

983　**-sociate**　A verb-forming word-final element, derived from Latin *soci(āre)* 'to share' (compare *soci(us)* 'sharer, companion') and -ate³, used in a number of common borrowings in the sense of 'to share, join together' as qualified by the combining root: **associate, consociate, dissociate.** Principal parts: **-sociating, -sociated, -sociated.** Related forms: **-social, -sociation, -sociative.**

984   **-alate**   An adjective and an adjective-forming word-final element, derived from Latin *āl(a)* 'wing' and -ate¹, used to mean 'referring or relating to wings, having wings' as specified by the combining root: **bialate, trialate, subalate.**

985   **-flate**   A verb-forming word-final element, derived from Latin *flat(us)*, the past participle to the verb *fla(re)* 'to blow, puff,' and used in borrowed combinations to mean 'letting air in or out (often in a metaphoric sense),' of that which is specified by the combining root: **inflate, conflate, deflate.** Principal parts: **-flating, -flated, -flated.** Related forms: **-flatable, -flation.**

986   **-ambulate**   A word-final element, derived from Latin *ambulat(us)*, past participle of *ambul(are)* 'to walk,' used in borrowed and learned verb combinations in its etymological sense: **circumambulate, somnam-bulate, perambulate.** Principal parts: **-ambulating, -ambulated, -ambulated.** Related forms: **-ambulation, -ambulator, -ambulatory, -ambulance, -ambulant, -ambulic, -ambulism, -ambulist.**

987   **-mate**   A noun and a noun-forming word-final element, derived from Middle English *mate*, related to Middle English *mette* from Old English *gemett(a)* 'guest, messmate' (cf. English *meat*), used in combinations with the basic meaning of 'a person with whom one shares a close relationship' as qualified by the combining root:

   1.   'A partner in love or marriage': **lovemate, bedmate, couchmate.**
   2.   'A friend or buddy': **tablemate, housemate.**
   3.   'An associate': **clubmate, stablemate, watchmate.**
   4.   'A relative, perhaps a twin': **cradlemate, birthmate.** Related form: **-mates** *(plural)*.

988   **-climate**   A noun and a noun-forming word-final element, derived from Greek *klima, klimat-* 'inclination' (from the verb *klin(ein)* 'to lean'—whence **-cline**—and **-ma**), used in combinations in the specialized sense of 'the prevailing temperature, humidity, and atmospheric conditions in a place' named by the combining root: **macroclimate, microclimate, hydroclimate.** Related forms: **-climatic, -climatical, -climatically; -climates** *(plural)*.

989 **-ordinate** A noun, derived from the substantive use of Latin
     ordināt(us), the past participle of the verb *ordināre* 'to put in order,'
     also used as a word-final element in verb and adjective combinations:
     1. As a verb meaning 'to order': **coordinate, subordinate, reordinate.**
     2. As an adjective meaning 'pertaining to order or rank': **inordinate,
         semiordinate, insubordinate.** Principal parts: **-ordinating,
         -ordinated, -ordinated.** Related forms: **-ordination, -ordinatingly,
         -ordinative.**

990 **-seminate** A verb and a verb-forming word-final element, derived
     from Latin *sēmin(āre)* 'to sow, produce' (cf. *sēmen* 'seed') and **-ate³**,
     used in combinations in its etymological sense as qualified by the
     combining root: **inseminate, reseminate, disseminate.** Principal parts:
     -seminating, -seminated, -seminated. Related forms: **-semination,
     -seminative.**

991 **-criminate** A verb-forming word-final element, derived from Latin
     crīmin(ārī) 'to accuse' (from Latin *crīmen* 'crime') and **-ate³**, used in
     its etymological sense, as qualified by the combining root: **incriminate,
     excriminate, recriminate.** Principal parts: **-criminating, -criminated,
     -criminated.** Related forms: **-crimination, -criminatory.**

992 **-pennate** An adjective and an adjective-forming word-final element,
     derived from Latin *penn(a)* 'feather' and **-ate¹**, used to mean 'having
     feathers' of a quantity or sort specified by the combining root:
     bipennate, longipennate, brevipennate. These forms may also be used
     substantively. Related form: **-pennates** *(plural).*

993 **-pinnate** An adjective and an adjective-forming word-final element,
     derived from late Latin *pinn(a)* 'feather' and **-ate¹**, used in botanical
     terminology with the meaning 'having featherlike parts' as specified
     by the combining root: **tripinnate, paripinnate, ramosopinnate.** These
     forms may also be used substantively. Related form: **-pinnates**
     (plural).

994 **-carnate** A word-final element, derived from Latin *car(ō)*, *carn-* 'flesh,
     body' and **-ate¹/-ate³**, used in a handful of forms meaning 'embody,
     embodied,' as qualified by the combining root: **incarnate, discarnate,
     postcarnate.** Principal parts: **-carnating, -carnated, -carnated.** Related
     form: **-carnation.**

995 **-pate** A noun and a noun-forming word-final element, derived from
     Middle English *pate* 'head, crown of the head,' used in largely
     obsolescent forms in two related senses:

1. 'A person with a head of a sort' specified (as to baldness) by the combining root: **baldpate, smoothpate, shagpate.**
2. 'A person with an intellect' of a sort specified by the combining root—virtually always with a pejorative sense: **rattlepate, clodpate, addlepate.** Compare **-head.** Related forms: **-pated; -pates** *(plural).*

996 **-culpate** A verb-forming word-final element, derived from Latin *culp(a)* 'fault, blame, crime' and **-ate**[3], used in a number of common borrowings in its etymological sense, as qualified by the combining root: **inculpate, disculpate, exculpate.** Principal parts: **-culpating, -culpated, -culpated.** Related forms: **-culpation; -culpations** *(plural).*

997 **-secrate** A verb-forming word-final element, derived from Latin *-secr(āre)*—the combining form of *sacr(āre)* 'to make sacred' (cf. *sacer* 'holy, sacred')—and **-ate**[3], used in borrowed combinations in its etymological sense as qualified by the combining root: **consecrate, desecrate, execrate.** Related forms: **-secrative, -secration; -secrations** *(plural).*

998 **-generate** A verb, derived from Latin *generat(us)*, past participle of *gener(are)* 'to beget, create,' used also as a word ending in borrowed verb combinations that function as adjectives (and sometimes as nouns); the combinations retain the etymological senses: **progenerate, regenerate, ingenerate.** Principal parts: **-generating, -generated, -generated.** Compare **-gen, -generic.** Related forms: **-generacy, -generately, -generative, -generation; -generations** *(plural).*

999 **-literate** An adjective, derived from Latin *litterāt(us)* 'lettered, i.e., able to read and write' (from Latin *litterae* 'letters, writing' and *-āt(us)*, *-āt(a)*, *-āt(um)* '**-ate**[1]'), also used as both an adjective-forming word-final element (with **-ate**[1]) and a verb-forming word-final element (with **-ate**[3]):
1. In verbs, with the meaning 'to perform an action involving the letters of the alphabet' as specified by the combining root: **transliterate, alliterate, obliterate.** Principal parts: **-literating, -literated, -literated.**
2. In adjectives, sometimes used substantively, with the meaning 'pertaining to the ability to use letters, to reading and writing': **illiterate, semiliterate, preliterate.** Related forms: **-literacy, -literation; -literations** *(plural).*

1000 **-florate** An adjective-forming word-final element, derived from Latin *flōs, flōr-* 'flower' and **-ate**[1], used in combinations meaning 'possessing flowers' of the type or quantity specified by the combining root: **biflorate, diversiflorate, calyciflorate.**

1001 **-dentate** An adjective (which may be used substantively) and an adjective-forming word-final element, derived from Latin *dens, dent-* 'tooth' (cf. Greek *odous, odont-*) and **-ate¹**, also a noun-forming word-final element with **-ate²**, used in the sense of 'possessing teeth or toothlike projections' of a number or type indicated by the combining root: **bidentate, curvidentate, serratodentate.** Compare **-odon.** Related forms: **-dental, -dentata; -dentates** *(plural).*

1002 **-state¹** A verb and a verb-forming word-final element, derived from Latin *stat(us), stat(a), stat(um),* the past participle of the verb *st(āre)* 'to stand, make stand' (cf. Greek *hista(nai), stē(nai),* whence **-state²**), used in a number of common combinations with the meaning of 'say,' i.e. 'set forth' as qualified by the combining root: **understate, misstate, restate.** Principal parts: **-stating, -stated, -stated.** Related forms: **-statement.**

1003 **-state²** A noun-forming word-final element, derived from Greek *stat(os),* the past participle of the verb *hista(nai), stē(nai)* 'to stand, make stand,' used in medical terminology to denote 'the result of an anabolic, catabolic, or metabolic process' as specified by the combining root: **anastate, catastate, mesostate.** Related forms: **-static, -stat, -static, -stasis, -stasy, -stasic, -stasia; -states** *(plural).*

1004 **-costate** An adjective and an adjective-forming word-final element, derived from Latin *cost(a)* 'rib' and **-ate¹**, used in combinations meaning 'having a rib or ribs' of a sort or quantity specified by the combining root: **tricostate, fissicostate, multicostate.** Related form: **-costal.**

1005 **-ite¹** A highly productive noun-forming word-final element in both technical and everyday English, derived through Middle English, Old French, and Latin from Greek *-it(ēs),* an adjective-forming suffix meaning 'of, belonging or related to,' used substantively in a variety of combinations, more or less in its etymological sense, as qualified by the combining root:

  1. 'A person associated with a group or organization as member, supporter, or devotee': **cosmopolite, laborite, Krishnaite.**
  2. 'A native of an area; a resident of a place or accommodation': **Israelite, New Hampshirite, trailerite.**
  3. 'A mineral or fossil': **granulite, ceratite, corallite.**
  4. 'An explosive': **cordite, dynamite, Cyclonite.**

5. In chemical terminology, 'compounds, esp. salts of acids whose names end in *-ous*': **sulfite, phosphite, nitrite.**

6. 'A pharmaceutical or commercial product, usually serving as a trademark': **Jennite, Bakelite, Alemite.**

7. 'A member or part of a body': **somite, zonite, sternite.** Related forms: -itic, -itically; -ites *(plural)*.

1006 **-ite²** A word-final element with no assignable general meaning, derived from Latin *īt(us)*, *īt(a)*, *-īt(um)*, the inflected ending of the past participle of the fourth conjugation, found chiefly in Latinate borrowed noun and adjective combinations: **composite, opposite, tripartite.** Also, -itus, -ita, -itum. Compare -ate¹, -ate². Related forms: -ition, -itely, -itious, -itive; -ites *(plural)*.

1007 **-zoite** A noun-forming word-final element, derived from Greek *zō(on)* 'living being, animal' (cf. the verb *za(ein)* 'to live') and -ite¹, used in zoological terminology to designate 'a simple organism' of a sort specified by the combining root: **sporozoite, saprozoite, merozoite.** Related forms: -zoon, -zoa, -zoic, -zoan, -zoal, -zoid, -zooid; -zoites *(plural)*.

1008 **-site** A noun-forming word-final element, derived from Greek *sit(os)* 'grain, food,' used in biomedical terminology to designate 'an organism living on or inside another from which it derives its sustenance,' location on or inside the host organism being named by the combining root: **parasite, cenosite.** Related forms: -sitia, -sitic, -sitism; -sites *(plural)*.

1009 **-posite** An adjective-forming word-final element, derived from Latin *posit(us)*, *posit(a)*, *posit(um)*, the past participle of the verb *pōn(ere)* 'to put, place' (cf. **-pone**), used in combinations borrowed from Latin but familiar enough to English speakers to act themselves as word-final elements in enlarged combinations. The compounds share the basic meaning 'put or placed': **composite** 'together'; **apposite** 'near'; **opposite** 'against.' Related forms: -pose, -posal, -posit, -position, -positioned, -positionally, -posure, -pound.

1010 **-partite** An adjective-forming word-final element derived from Latin *partīt(us)*, *partīt(a)*, *partīt(um)*, the past participle to the verb *partīre* 'to divide into parts' (cf. *pars, part-* 'part, portion'), used in combinations meaning 'having the number of parts or divisions' specified by the combining root: **bipartite, multipartite, tripartite.**

1011 **-ette** A noun-forming word-final element, derived through Old French

-ete from the (unattested) Common Romance feminine diminutive suffix **-itta*, **-etta*, used in several types of combination:

1. 'A female agent' whose activity is named by the combining root: **usherette, majorette, suffragette.**
2. In masculine names made feminine by this suffix: **Jeannette, Claudette, Bernardette.**
3. A diminutive meaning 'little thing' specified by the first root: **dinette, novelette, cigarette.**
4. A diminutive meaning 'little' in feminine names: **Annette, Suzette, Lisette.**
5. 'An imitation' of something named by the first root: **leatherette, plushette, flannelette.** Compare **-et.** Related forms: **-etta; -ettas, -ettes** *(plurals).*

1012   **-volute**   An adjective and a noun, derived from Latin *volūt(us), volūt(a), volūt(um),* the past participle to the verb *volv(ere)* 'to roll, turn around,' used as a verb-forming word-final element in its etymological sense and, in homographic adjectives, in the sense of 'resulting from the process' described by those verbs or like verbs ending in **-volve: convolute, involute, obvolute.** Principal parts: **-voluting, -voluted, -voluted.** Related forms: **-volve, -volution.**

1013   **-pute**   A verb-forming word-final element, derived from Latin *put(āre)* 'to think, consider, reckon,' used in a number of common borrowings, each emphasizing one or another of the etymological senses: **compute** 'reckon;' **dispute** Latin 'discuss,' now 'argue;' **repute** Latin 'think again,' now 'hold in thought;' **depute** 'consider, assign;' **impute** 'reckon about, ascribe to' (usu. something discreditable). Two of the terms (**dispute, repute**) act as nouns without change in form; all form nouns with *-ation.* Principal parts: **-puting, -puted, -puted.** Related forms: **-putedly, -putation, -putative.**

1014   **-cyte**   A noun-forming word-final element, derived from Greek *kyt(os)* 'vessel, hollow, cavity, cell' (from *ky(ein)* 'to hold'), widely used in biomedical terminology to designate 'a cell' as specified by the combining root: **lemnocyte, chromocyte, monocyte.** Related forms: **-cytal, -cytic, -cytosis; -cytes** *(plural).*

1015   **-phyte**   A noun-forming word-final element, derived from Greek *phyt(os)* (the past participle to the verb *phyein* 'to grow, make grow, produce,' used in the specific sense of 'that which has been grown, produced; a plant'), used chiefly in botanical terminology to designate 'a plant which grows in or on or produces' that which is specified by the combining root: **spermaphyte, geophyte, lithophyte.** Related forms: **-phyta, -phytal, -phytic, -phytism, -physis, -physite, -physics, -physical, -physial, -physeal; -phytes** *(plural).*

1016   **-lyte**   A noun-forming word-final element, derived from Greek *lyt(os)* 'that which may be loosened' from the verb *ly(ein)* 'to loosen,' used in scientific terminology to form combinations meaning 'a substance capable of or resulting from undergoing lysis or decomposition' as specified by the combining root: **electrolyte, hydrolyte, cytolyte.** Compare **-lysis.** Related forms: **-lytic; -lytes** *(plural).*

1017   **-tongue**   A noun and a noun-forming word-final element, derived through Middle English from Old English *tunge* 'tongue,' used in a number of related senses:
  1. 'The common names of illnesses affecting the tongue by discoloration or tumor': **bluetongue, frogtongue, blacktongue.**
  2. 'The common names of certain fungi resembling tongues': **beeftongue, earthtongue, oaktongue.**
  3. 'As part of the common names of plants having parts resembling tongues': **hartstongue, beardtongue, goosetongue.** Related form: **-tongues** *(plural).*

1018   **-agogue**   A noun-forming word-final element, derived through French and Late Latin from Greek *-agōg(os)* 'drawing forth, leading,' used in forming noun combinations:
  1. 'A leader,' the follower identified by the combining root: **demagogue, pedagogue, psychagogue.**
  2. 'An agent promoting the expulsion of a substance' named by the joining root: **cholagogue, hemagogue, lithagogue.** Also, **-agog, -agoge.** Related forms: **-agogic, -agogical, -agogically, -agoguery, -agogy; -agogues, -agogs** *(plurals).*

1019   **-logue**   A noun-forming word-final element, derived through Middle English *-loge, -logue,* Old French, and Latin from Greek *log(os)* 'word, speech, discourse' from Greek *leg(ein)* 'to put in order, speak, read (aloud),' used in a variety of combinations with related senses:
  1. 'A talk, conversation, discourse' as specified by the combining root: **dialogue, decalogue, monologue.**
  2. 'A performance or recital, or a part thereof,' as specified by the combining root: **pianologue, prologue, travelogue.**
  3. 'A student of or specialist in a field' named by the combining root: **musicologue, Assyriologue, theologue.** Also, **-log.** Compare **-lexia.** Related forms: **-logy, -logia, -logic, -logical, -logetic, -logism, -logian, -logician, -logist, -logistic, -logically, -logistically, -logetically; -logues, -logs** *(plurals).*

1020   **-ique**   A noun-forming word-final element, derived from French *-ique* '-ic²', used in borrowings from French (virtually all of Greek origin) in its etymological sense: **technique, physique, critique.** Compare **-ic¹,** **-ic².** Related form: **-iques** *(plural).*

1021   **-technique**   A noun and a noun-forming word-final element, derived from French *technique,* itself derived from Greek *techn(ē)* 'art, craft' and **-ic¹/-ic²,** used in combinations denoting 'the (artful or skillful) way in which something is done,' the area or means of endeavor being specified by the combining root: **microtechnique, machinotechnique, iatrotechnique.** Also, **-technic.** Related forms: **-technics, -techny, -technology, -technical, -technically; -techniques, -technics** *(plurals).*

1022   **-esque**   A word-final element, derived through French *-esque* and Italian *-esc(o),* perhaps from Old High German *-isc,* used in forming adjective and noun combinations:
   1.   'In the style or manner of' a person or fashion named by the first root: **Zolaesque, statuesque, picaresque.**
   2.   'A style or something created in a style' specified by the combining root: **arabesque, burlesque, humoresque.** Compare **-ish.** Related form (noun): **-esques** *(plural).*

1023   **-'ve**   A contraction of *have* used after present and present perfect tense verbs in speech and increasingly in writing: **I've, we've, would've.** (Its use in speech with modals like *would, should,* and *must* causes it to be mistakenly considered to be *of.*)

1024   **-grave**   A word-final element, derived through Middle English from Old English *grǣf(a)* 'bush, thicket,' used in combinations functioning as place names and the personal names derived from them: **Hargrave, Musgrave, Wargrave.** Also, **-greave, -grove.**

1025   **-ive**   A word-final element, derived through Middle English and French *-if, -ive* from Latin *-īv(us), -īv(a), -īv(um),* an adjective-forming suffix, denoting 'a tendency or disposition for the action or effect' specified by the combining root, virtually always a verb. In English, **-ive** has two major uses, to form adjectives with either of two related senses, and to form nouns (through the substantive use of adjectives):
   1.   'Possessing a tendency, disposition' for an action or effect named by the combining root: **active, corrective, abrasive.**
   2.   'Tending to perform' an action named by the combining root, usu. lastingly: **divorcive, educative, coercive.**
   3.   'Something that performs or tends to perform' an action specified

by the combining root: **sedative, directive, correlative.** Compare **-ative, -itive.** Related forms: **-ively, -ivity; -ives, -ivities** *(plurals).*

1026   **-ceive**   A verb-forming word-final element, derived through Middle English *-ceiv(en)* and Old Norman French *(re)ceiv(re)* from Latin *-cip(ere)* (from Latin *capere* 'to take'), used in a few verbs of high frequency of occurrence in English in their rough etymological sense of 'to take, seize' as modified by the combining root: **receive, deceive, perceive.** Principal parts: **-ceiving, -ceived, -ceived.** Related forms: **-cept, -ception, -ceptible.**

1027   **-tive**   An adjective-forming word-final element, derived from Latin *-tīv(us), -tīv(a), -tīv(um),* that is, the past participle marker *-t-* plus *-īv(us), -īv(a), -īv(um)* '**-ive,**' used in the same way as **-ive, -itive,** and **-ative** to mean 'relating to, having a disposition towards, or tending towards performing' that which is specified by the combining root: **conjunctive, productive, perceptive.** Compare **-ive, -ative, -itive.** Related form: **-tivity.**

1028   **-ative**   An adjective-forming word-final element, derived from Latin *-ātīv(us), -ātīv(a), -ātīv(um),* i.e., the ending of the Latin past participle of the first conjugation (cf. **-ata**) and the adjective-forming suffix *-īv(us)* (cf. **-ive**). In English, **-ative** is used extensively to form adjectives largely, though not exclusively, from verbs which end in *-ate* (cf. **-ate**[3]):

1. 'Something tending to perform an action' or 'tending toward an action' named by the combining root: **correlative, purgative, fugitive.**
2. 'Pertaining to or connected with' something stated by the joining root: **authoritative, definitive, normative.** Compare **-itive, -tive, -ive.** Related forms: (adjective) **-atively;** (noun) **-atives** *(plural).*

1029   **-factive**   An adjective and an adjective-forming word-final element, derived from Latin *fact(us), fact(a), fact(um),* the past participle of *fac(ere)* 'to do, make,' and **-ive,** used in the sense of 'making' that which is specified by the combining root: **liquefactive, chylifactive, putrefactive.** Also, **-fying.** Related forms: **-faction, -factory, -facture, -facient, -(i)fic, -fect, -(i)fy.**

1030   **-itive**   An adjective-forming word-final element, derived from Latin *-ītīv(us), -ītīv(a), -ītīv(um),* that is, the ending of the past participle of the Latin fourth (and, in some instances, the third) conjugation (cf. **-ite**[2]) and the adjective-forming suffix *-īv(us)* (cf. **-ive**), found in its etymological sense of 'relating to, having a disposition towards, or tending towards performing' that which is specified by the combining root: **cognitive, positive, definitive.** Related form: **-itivity.**

1031   **-valve**   A noun and a noun-forming word-final element, derived from Latin *valva* 'folding door,' used in the sense of 'a thing that regulates the flow of air or water (or some other gas or liquid)' of a sort or quality specified by the combining root: **pseudovalve, bivalve, quadrivalve.** Related form: **-valves** *(plural).*

1032   **-solve**   A verb and a verb-forming word-final element, derived from Latin *solv(ere)* 'to loosen, set loose, accomplish,' used in a number of common borrowings in its etymological senses and extensions thereof, as qualified by the combining root: **absolve, resolve, dissolve.** Principal parts: **-solving, -solved, -solved.** Related forms: **-solution, -soluble, -solubility.**

1033   **-volve**   A verb-forming word-final element, derived from Latin *volv(ere)* 'to roll, turn around,' used in various extensions of its etymological sense, as specified by the combining root: **evolve, revolve, circum-volve.** Principal parts: **-volving, -volved, -volved.** Related forms: **-volute, -volution** (from the past participle *volūt(us)*, *volūt(a)*, *volūt(um)*).

1034   **-prove**   A verb and a verb-forming word-final element, derived through Middle English *prov(en)* and Middle French *-prov(er)* from Latin *prob(āre)* 'to commend, demonstrate,' used in a number of borrowed combinations in its etymological senses as qualified by the combining roots: **approve, counterprove, disprove.** This ending also appears in two combinations in which the basic sense is 'to condemn, disapprove': **reprove, improve.** The negative sense of the second is now obsolete except in Scottish law terminology. (The current sense of **improve,** 'to make better,' has a very different etymology.) Principal parts: **-proving, -proved, -proved.** Related forms: **-proof, -proval, -provable.**

1035   **-serve**[1]   A verb and a verb-forming word-final element, derived through Middle English and French from Latin *serv(īre)* 'to serve' (not to be confused with *serv(āre)* 'to protect, guard,' whence **-serve**[2]), used in its etymological sense as qualified by the combining root: **subserve, misserve, deserve.** Principal parts: **-serving, -served, -served.**

1036   **-serve**[2]   A verb and a verb-forming word-final element, derived through Middle English and French from Latin *serv(āre)* 'to protect, guard' (not to be confused with *serv(īre)* 'to serve,' whence **-serve**[1]), used in its etymological sense as qualified by the combining root: **reserve, preserve, observe.** Principal parts: **-serving, -served, -served.** Related forms: **-servation, -servative.**

1037   **-eye**   A noun and a noun-forming word-final element, derived through Middle English *eie, eye, eighe* from Old English *ēage,* used in a variety of related senses:

     1.   'An appearance or condition of human eyes' denoted by the combining root: **walleye, cockeye, bungeye.**

     2.   'A quality of glance or vision' named by the joining root: **fisheye, hawkeye, gladeye.**

     3.   'A quality or appearance of or like an eye' in the common names of fish, plants, and gems: **sockeye, oxeye, tigereye.**

     4.   In the common names of some birds, 'the color of the eye or its surrounding plumage': **pinkeye, goldeneye, silvereye.**

     5.   'An opening in a structure or instrument resembling an eye': **kilneye, poteye, deadeye.** Related forms: **-eyes** *(plural);* (senses 1 and 2) **-eyed.**

1038   **-ize**   A highly productive and still active verb-forming word-final element, derived through Middle English *-is(en),* Old French *-is(er),* and Late Latin *-iz(āre)* from Greek *-iz(ein),* added chiefly to adjectives and some nouns to form several kinds of combination:

     1.   'To act upon, treat, make, or affect' as indicated by the combining root: **Americanize, brutalize, theorize.**

     2.   'To engage in an activity' specified by the combining root: **botanize, evangelize, poeticize.**

     3.   'To give support or, usu., to spread a doctrine' specified by the combining root: **Judaize, Slavicize, democratize.** Also, **-ise.** In America, the more common spelling of this suffix is *-ize;* in Britain, following the derivation from French *-is(er),* the more common till recently has been *ise.* But exceptions occur: the British spell most words derived from Greek (from *-izein*) with *-ize,* and Americans spell **advise, compromise, surprise,** and others with *-ise,* though in these words, the *s* is etymological, the original Latin forms from which they were derived having *s.* Principal parts: **-izing, -ized, -ized.** Related forms: **-izer, -iser, -ization, -isation.**

1039   **-lyze**   A verb-forming word-final element, derived from Greek *ly(sis)* 'a loosening, breaking down' (from the verb *ly(ein)* 'to loosen') and **-(i)ze,** used chiefly in scientific terminology to mean 'to produce *lysis,* decomposition, or destruction' as specified by the combining root: **catalyze, hydrolyze, analyze.** Also, **-lyse** *(chiefly British).* Compare

-lysis. Principal parts: -lyzing, -lyzed, -lyzed; -lysing, -lysed, -lysed. Related forms: -lyzation, -lysation, -lyzer, -lyser, -lysand.

1040   -leaf   A noun and a noun-forming word-final element, derived through Middle English *leef* from Old English *lēaf* 'leaf, that which with others constitutes the foliage of a plant,' used in its etymological sense in common names of plants: **bloodleaf, laceleaf, dollarleaf**. Related forms: **-leafs, -leaves** *(plurals)*.

1041   -proof   A noun and a word-final element, derived through Middle English *proof, prove* and Old French *preuve* from Latin *proba* 'a test,' used in two ways:
1. In a few nouns, with the condemnatory sense of the corresponding verbs ending in *-prove* (**-prove**): **reproof, improof, disproof**.
2. In many adjectives, 'able to withstand or repel' that which is named by the combining root: **burglarproof, waterproof, fireproof**. Some of the combinations concern rather curious guarantees of resistance: **praiseproof, loveproof, sermonproof, smutproof, kissproof, joyproof**. Compare **-prove**.

1042   -g   An abbreviation, developed through shortening of *-ing*, used in standard abbreviations for the present participle: **actg** (acting), **acctg** (accounting), **dwg** (drawing).

1043   -leg   A noun and a noun-forming word-final element, derived through Middle English *leg, legge* from Old Norse *leggr* 'leg, bone,' used in several ways:
1. In common names for some diseases: **whiteleg, bigleg, blackleg**.
2. In the common names for two varieties of bird: **redleg, roughleg**.
3. In generally deprecatory terms designating people: **blueleg, blackleg, jackleg**. Related form: **-legs** *(plural)*.

1044   -wig   A noun and a noun-forming word-final element, derived by abbreviation of *periwig*, itself an alteration of French *perruque* 'peruke, hairpiece,' used in a handful of combinations:
1. In recognition of the popularity of wigs through the 18th cent., 'a wig' of a type or size specified by the first root: **buzzwig, tiewig, bagwig**.
2. An early, now archaic, name for 'a tadpole,' perhaps because its tail resembled the back of a peruke: **polliwig** (pollywog). Related form: **-wigs** *(plural)*.

1045   -ing[1]   A word-final element, derived through Middle English *-inge* from Old English *-ende*, used in forming verb and adjective combinations:

1. As the present participle suffix of all English verbs: **walking, robbing, scrubbing.**
2. With few exceptions, the present participle forms can be used, without change in form, as adjectives: **weeping, bleeding, singing.**
3. The suffix is also added to nouns to form adjectives meaning 'pertaining to or resembling': **hulking, drinking, printing.** Related form: **-ingly.**

1046   -ing² A noun-forming word-final element, derived through Middle English *-inge* from Old English *-ing, -ung*, used chiefly to form nouns from verbs or nouns:

1. 'An action or process' named by the combining root: **dancing, dicing, coughing.**
2. 'The product of' an action or process named by the combining root: **painting, icing, beading.**
3. 'Something used' in the action or process specified: **plumbing, latticing, studding.**
4. In nouns formed from nouns, 'an action or process involving something' specified by the combining root: **berrying, terracing, roofing.**
5. In a few cases, **-ing²** is used to form nouns from prepositions: **toing, froing, offing.** Related form: **-ings** *(plural)*.

1047   -ing³ A noun-forming word-final element, derived through Middle English from Old English *-ing, -ung* 'one belonging to, descended from, of the kind of,' used in the sense 'one of a particular kind' specified by the combining root: **wilding, gelding, farthing.** Related form: **-ings** *(plural)*.

1048   -ing⁴ A suffix, once a word, derived from either Old English *-ing* 'place, river,' or Old Norse *-eng* 'meadow,' used in forming place names in the singular (**Reading**) or the plural (**Hastings**), in the latter case referring to Old English clan names: **Doulting, Ealing, Worthing.**

1049   -ling A noun-forming word-final element, probably etymologically a double suffix: the dimunitive **-el** and/or **-il²** and **-ing³**, used to form combinations of several sorts, each with a diminutive—and sometimes pejorative—sense:

1. 'One belonging to or associated with a group, condition, or quality' named by the combining root: **darling, hatchling, weakling.**
2. 'One belonging to a breed or group, named by the combining root, with a diminutive force added': **gosling, pigling, oysterling.**
3. 'One belonging to a group or activity' named by the combining

root, with some diminutive force and definite pejorative force added: **hireling, roqueling, underling**. Related form: **-lings** *(plural)*.

1050   **-wing**   A noun and a noun-forming word-final element, derived through Middle English *winge, wenge* from Old Norse *vaengr* 'wing, i.e., organ of flight in birds,' used in two ways:
  1. As the common names of birds, identified in the combining root by the color or other qualities of their wings: **sapphirewing, bronzewing, whistlewing**.
  2. As the common names of moths and butterflies, described in the combining root by the qualities of their wings: **scalewing, lacewing, gauzewing**. Related form: **-wings** *(plural)*.

1051   **-phthong**   A noun-forming word-final element, derived from Greek *phthong(os)* 'voice, sound, utterance,' used in the terminology of linguistics to designate 'a monosyllabic sequence of vowel sounds' the number of which is specified by the combining root: **monophthong, diphthong, triphthong**. Related forms: **-phthongize, -phthongization, -phthongia; -phthongs** *(plural)*.

1052   **-berg**   A noun-forming word-final element, derived by abstraction from the word *iceberg*, a partial loan translation of Danish *isberg* (*is-* 'ice' and *-berg* 'mountain'), used in combinations denoting 'something mountainlike' specified by the combining root: **floeberg, snowberg, inselberg**. Related form: **-bergs** *(plural)*.

1053   **-burg**   A noun (informally, 'a town or city,' historically, 'a fortified town or city') and, more frequently, a (proper) noun-forming word-final element, derived through Middle English *burgh* from Old English *burg, burh* 'fortified town, fortress,' used in place names: **Fitchburg, Ogdensburg, Pittsburg**. Also, **-burgh**. Compare **-boro, -borough, -bury, -by**.

1054   **-stich**   A noun and a noun-forming word-final element, derived from Greek *stix(os)* 'a row, line, line of verse' (from the verb *steix(ein)* 'to go in order, in line'), used in the terminology of poetics, especially classical, to denote 'a verse or stanza having the number of lines' specified by the combining root: **distich, hemistich, hexastich**. Related forms: **-stichal, -stichic; -stichs** *(plural)*.

1055   **-finch**   A noun and a noun-forming word-final element, derived through Middle English from Old English *finc* 'sparrow, finch,' used in combinations functioning as the common names of small birds, usually identified with the families *Fringillidae* and *Ploceidae*: **goldfinch, chaffinch, hawfinch.** Related form: **-finches** *(plural).*

1056 **-troch** A noun-forming word-final element, derived from Greek *troch(os)* '(circular) race course, wheel, hoop,' used in zoological terminology to mean 'ciliated band' of a sort specified by the combining root: **metatroch, telotroch, cephalotroch.** Related forms: **-trocha, -trochal; -trochs** *(plural).*

1057 **-arch** A noun suffix, derived through Middle English *-arke, -arche,* Old French, and Latin from Greek *-arch(ōn)* 'leader,' used in combinations to designate 'a ruler or leader' as specified by the joining root: **monarch, patriarch, ecclesiarch.** Related forms: **-archate, -archic, -archical, -archically, -archist, -archistic, -archism, -archy; -archs** *(plural).*

1058 **-leigh** A word-final element, once a noun, derived through Middle English from Old English *hlēow* 'sheltered place,' used in place names to mean 'glade on the side of a hill': **Raleigh, Budleigh, Northleigh.**

1059 **-borough** A noun and a (proper) noun-forming word-final element, derived through Middle English *burgh, burwe, borugh* from either Old English *burg* 'fortified place' or *byrig* 'borough;' the double descent is reflected in the Middle English meanings. As a word ending, the term is found in place names and the personal names derived from them: **Marlborough, Glassboro, Gainsborough.** Also, **-boro.** Compare **-burg, -burgh, -bury, -by.**

1060 **-graph** A noun and a noun-forming word-final element, derived from Greek *graph(ē)* 'a marking with lines, writing' (from Greek *graph(ein)* 'to write,' literally, 'to engrave'), used in two related senses:
  1. 'The product of writing or drawing' as specified by the combining root: **epigraph, holograph, cryptograph.**
  2. 'A machine or instrument for making or for reproducing or transmitting something written or drawn': **telegraph, Mimeograph, phonograph.** Compare **-gram.** Related forms: **-graphic, -graphist, -grapher, -grapha, -graphia, -graphy, -graphal, -graphical, -graphous.**

1061 **-taph** A noun-forming word-final element, derived from Greek *taph(os)* 'funeral rites, burial, tomb,' found in its etymological sense in three terms: **cenotaph, epitaph, tritaph.** It is also the last element of a word forming a learned joke: **bibliotaph** 'one who hides books, as by burying them.' Related forms: **-taphic; -taphs** *(plural).*

1062 **-lymph** A noun and a noun-forming word-final element, derived from Latin *lymph(a)* 'water, clear water,' used in medical terminology to designate 'a clear fluid produced by the body' as specified by the combining root: **endolymph, hydrolymph, neurolymph.** Related forms: **-lymphatic; -lymphs** *(plural).*

1063 **-troph** A noun-forming word-final element, derived from Greek *troph(os)* 'that which feeds' (from the verb *treph(ein)* 'to feed'), used in medical terminology in two senses:
1.   'That which feeds or nourishes an embryo': **hemotroph, histotroph, embryotroph.**
2.   'An organism that gets its food or nourishment from a source' specified by the combining root: **metatroph, heterotroph, autotroph.** Related forms: **-trophy, -trophic, -trophous; -trophi, -trophs** *(plurals).*

1064 **-morph** A noun derived from Greek *morph(ē)* 'form, shape,' used in general scientific terminology as a noun-forming word-final element in combinations designating 'something or someone possessing or characterized by a form or shape' as specified by the combining root: **allomorph, ectomorph, polymorph.** Related forms: **-morphia, -morphy, -morphic, -morphous, -morphically, -morphously, -morphism, -morphosis; -morphs, -morphae, -morphi** *(plurals).*

1065 **-ish[1]** A highly productive and still active adjective-forming word-final element, derived through Middle English from Old English *-isc*, used in combinations with a variety of related senses, each qualified by the combining root:
1.   'Belonging to': **Finnish, Swedish, English.**
2.   'After the manner of': **boyish, childish, amateurish.**
3.   'Characteristic or typical of': **snobbish, backwoodish, modish.**
4.   'Somewhat or rather': **baldish, sickish, reddish.**
5.   Of age or time, 'approximately': **twentyish, sixish, fortyish.** Compare **-esque.** Related form: **-ishly.**

1066 **-ish[2]** A verb-forming word-final element with no assignable meaning in English, found in borrowings from French from the second *(-ir)* conjugation with its present stem ending *-iss-* (from the Latin inchoative-progressive infix *-(e)sc-*): **finish, establish, impoverish.** Principal parts: **-ishing, -ished, -ished.** Compare **-esce.** Related forms: **-ishment, -isher.**

1067 **-fish** A noun and a noun-forming word-final element, derived through Middle English from Old English *fisc* 'fish, i.e., cold-blooded aquatic vertebrate,' used in hundreds of combinations functioning as the common names of different types of fish: **bluefish, swordfish, catfish.**

1068   **-bush** A noun and a noun-forming word-final element, derived from Middle English *bush, bosh, busk* 'shrub, small tree,' used in combinations functioning as the common names of large plants, shrubs, and small trees: **hopbush, elderbush, rosebush.** Related form: **-bushes** *(plural).*

1069   **-th¹** An adjective-forming word-final element, derived from Middle English *-(e)the, -te* from Old English *-(o)tha, -(o)the,* used in the formation of ordinal numbers other than *1, 2,* and *3* or ending in other than *1, 2,* or *3:* **fifth, 6th, twelfth.** Cf. **-nd, -rd, -st.** Also, **-eth** in numbers ending in *-y:* **eightieth, twentieth, ninetieth.**

1070   **-th²** An abstract noun-forming word-final element, derived through Middle English *-th(e)* from Old English *-th(o), -th(u), -th,* used in combination with adjectives to mean 'a condition, quality, or action' specified by the combining root: **warmth, width, breadth.** Related form: **-ths** *(plural).*

1071   **-math** A noun-forming word-final element, derived from Greek *math(ein)* 'to learn,' used to denote 'a person who learns in a manner or has an attitude towards learning' expressed by the combining root: **opsimath, misomath, polymath.** Related forms: **-mathy, -mathic; -maths** *(plural).*

1072   **-path¹** A noun-forming word-final element, derived from Greek *path(ein)* 'to suffer, be sensitive to,' used in medical terminology in two senses:

    1. 'One who suffers from an illness' specified by the combining root: **psychopath, erotopath, neuropath.**

    2. 'One who treats the ill by means of a system of medicine' specified by the combining root: **osteopath, allopath, homeopath.** Related forms: **-pathia, -pathy, -pathetic, -pathic, -pathology.**

1073   **-path²** A noun and a noun-forming word-final element derived from Old English *paeth* 'a trodden way, road' (cf. Greek *pat(ein)* 'to tread'), used in its etymological sense as qualified by the combining root: **trekpath, footpath, towpath.** Related form: **-paths** *(plural).*

1074   **-eth** A verb suffix, derived through Middle English from Old English *-eth, -ath, -th,* formerly used as the ending of verbs in the 3rd person singular present indicative: **goeth, taketh, bringeth.** The suffix is to be found in the King James Bible, in some current religious materials, and as a relic in certain dialects of English.

1075   **-lith**   A noun-forming word-final element, derived from Greek *lith(os)* 'stone,' used to form noun combinations of several meanings:
1. 'A structure or implement of stone': **monolith, rhabdolith, glyptolith.**
2. In medical terminology, 'a calculus' formed in the part of the body named by the combining root: **angiolith, nephrolith, phlebolith.**
3. 'A mineral or fossil in stone': **coccolith, zoolith, phytolith.** Also (sense 3), **-lite.** Related forms: **-lithic, -lithically; -liths, -lites** (sense 3) *(plurals).*

1076   **-smith**   A noun and a noun-forming word-final element, derived from Old English *smið* 'craftsman,' used in a number of related senses:
1. 'A worker in a metal' named by the combining root: **goldsmith, tinsmith, blacksmith.**
2. 'A worker on or with' something denoted by the combining root: **locksmith, stonesmith, ropesmith.**
3. 'A producer of' something named by the combining root: **adsmith, jokesmith, tunesmith.** Related forms: **-smithy** (especially sense 1); **-smiths** *(plural).*

1077   **-anth**   A noun-forming word-final element, derived from Greek *anth(os)* 'flower,' used in combinations to mean 'a kind of flower' or 'part of a flower' as specified by the combining root: **amaranth, perianth, hydranth.** Related forms: **-anthic, -anthous; -anthes, -anths** *(plurals).*

1078   **-acanth**   A noun-forming word-final element, derived from Greek *akanth(os)* 'thorn, spine,' used largely in botanical nomenclature to designate plants with thorns or spines of a sort specified by the combining root: **tragacanth, coelacanth, anacanth.** Related forms: **-acanthid, -acanthous; -acanths** *(plural).*

1079   **-helminth**   A noun and a noun-forming word-final element, derived from Greek *helmin(s), helminth-* 'worm,' used in zoological taxonomy to designate members of the 'worm' group as specified by the combining root: **trochelminth, nemathelminth, platyhelminth.** Also, **-elminth.** (Like other Greek roots beginning with *h*, *helminth* often loses its initial *h* in combination as a word-final element.) Related forms: **-helminthic, -elminthic; -helminths, -elminths, -helminthes, -elminthes** *(plurals).*

1080 **-cloth**   A noun and a noun-forming word-final element, derived through Middle English from Old English *clāth* 'garment, clothing, fabric,' used to designate 'fabric of a sort or for a purpose' specified by the combining root: **washcloth, cerecloth, loincloth.** Related forms: **-clothy; -cloths** *(plural).*

1081 **-worth**   A word ending, derived from Old English *worð* 'courtyard, enclosure,' used in personal and place name combinations: **Kenilworth, Epworth, Butterworth.**

1082 **-mouth**   A noun and a noun-forming word-final element, derived from Old English *mūð* 'mouth, oral opening,' used in two sorts of combination:
   1. In place names, with the meaning 'mouth of a river' (**Tweedmouth**) or 'harbor entrance' (**Plymouth**): **Yarmouth, Tynemouth, Bournemouth.**
   2. In the common names of certain animals: **pipemouth, frogmouth, cottonmouth.** Related form: **-mouths** *(plural).*

1083 **-i¹**   A word-final element, used to form the plurals of masculine nouns and adjectives of the Latin second declension whose singulars end in -us. In English, this element is used to form the plurals of two kinds of Latinate borrowings:
   1. Native and later scientific Latin words: **alumni, foci, fungi.**
   2. Technical or scientific terms derived through Latin from Greek: **thalami, Isospondyli, hippopotami.** (The original Greek plural would have been **-oi**, and the corresponding singular, **-os**.) The homographic outcome of this element in modern Italian may be observed in a handful of borrowings: **libretti, zucchini, graffiti.** Related forms: **-us, -os, -o** *(singulars).*

1084 **-i²**   A word-final element, used to form the genitive (possessive) singular of masculine nouns and adjectives of the second declension of Latin. In English, this element is used in the nomenclature of zoological and botanical taxonomy in naming subspecies after their discoverers: **Burcelli, Williamsi, Wolfi.**

1085 **-oi**   A word-final element used to form the plurals of masculine nouns of the second declension of Greek (whose singulars end in -os), found exclusively in learned borrowings from Greek: **polloi, catanephroi, auloi.** Also, **-i¹.** Related form: **-os** *(singular).*

1086 **-jack**   A noun and also a noun-forming word-final element, derived from Middle English *jacke* 'man, fellow' (possibly from the French proper name *Jacques*, to which the Modern American use of *john* from *John* may be compared), used in three senses:

1. Used literally, 'a man,' described by the combining root in terms of his manner (**skipjack** 'jockey'), his deserts (**whipjack** 'rogue'), or the raw material of his work (**lumberjack**).
2. Used metaphorically and indefinitely for 'food' or 'drink': **flapjack, crackerjack, applejack**.
3. Used metaphorically and indefinitely in the common names of plants, animals, and esp. fish: **skipjack, natterjack, bluejack**. Related form: **-jacks** *(plural)*.

1087 **-sack** A noun and a word-final element, derived though Middle English *sac* 'sack, bag, sackcloth,' from Old English *sæcc*, both from Latin *sacc(us)* 'sack, bag, sackcloth,' used in forming noun combinations differentiating among types of carrying cases: **packsack, haversack, rucksack**. Related form: **-sacks** *(plural)*.

1088 **-beck** A noun, derived through Middle English *bek, becc* from Old Norse *bekkr* 'stream, brook,' used as a word-final element in place names: **Caldbeck, Wisbeck, Rhinebeck**. Also, **-bech**.

1089 **-stick** A noun and a noun-forming word-final element, derived through Middle English *stikke, stik* from Old English *sticc(a)* 'stick, stake, slender piece of wood,' used in two senses:

1. 'A slender piece of wood' used for a purpose identified by the combining root: **yardstick, matchstick, broomstick**.
2. 'An object shaped like a stick, but made of a material other than wood': **toothstick, lipstick, joystick**. Related form: **-sticks** *(plural)*.

1090 **-wick** A noun and a word-final element, derived from Old English *wīc* 'dwelling, village, farm; bay, creek, inlet' (by influence of Icelandic *vīk* 'creek'), used in several senses:

1. In common nouns, 'an area of a farm' specified by the combining root: **herdwick, berewick**.
2. In common nouns, 'an area of power or authority' specified by the combining root: **Constablewick, Sheriffwick, bailiwick**. Related forms: **-wicks** *(senses 1 and 2)*.
3. In place names, in various of its etymological senses: **Borthwick, Berwick, Southwick**. Also, **-wich, -wic, -wyke, -vick**.

1091 **-ock**[1] A noun-forming word-final element, derived through Middle English *-oc, -ok* from Old English *-oc, -uc*, used in forming diminutives: **hillock, bullock, ballock**. Also, **-ick**. Related form: **-ocks** *(plural)*.

1092   **-ock²**   A word-final element, derived through Middle English *ook* from Old English *āc* 'oak,' used in forming place name combinations, sometimes in the plural: **Sevenoaks, Greenock, Barnack.** Also, **-oak, -ack.**

1093   **-stock**   A word-final element, derived through Middle English *stoc* from Old English *stocc* 'a tree stump, holy meeting-place,' preserved in a number of English place names: **Woodstock, Shustoke, Tavistock.** Also, **-stoke.**

1094   **-chik**   A noun-forming word-final element, derived from a Russian masculine diminutive ending, used in borrowed and native noun combinations to mean 'small one': **apparatchik, golubchick, boychik.** Also, **-zhik, -jik** (**muzhik, moujik**).

1095   **-nik**   A noun-forming word-final element, derived from Eastern European Yiddish *-nik* 'someone connected with, involved in, or characterized by' that which is specified by the combining root: **nudnik, beatnik, refusenik.** Also, **-nick.** Related forms: **-niks, -nicks** *(plurals)*.

1096   **-folk**   A noun, derived through Middle English *folk* from Old English *folc* 'tribe or clan,' preserved as a word ending in its etymological sense in the names of two English shires: **Norfolk, Suffolk.** Historically, both were divisions of the Old English kingdom of East Anglia, with power and wealth concentrated in the south.

1097   **-brook**   A noun and a word-final element, derived from Middle English *brook, broke* and Old English *brōec* 'stream,' used to form noun combinations functioning as place names and the personal names derived from them: **Seabrook, Centerbrook, Old Saybrook.**

1098   **-work**   A noun and a much-used noun-forming word-final element, derived through Middle English *werk, work* from Old English *werc, weorc, worc* 'labor, the product of labor,' used in both of its etymological senses:

   1.   'Labor involving a material, or the results of that labor,' as specified by the combining root: **woodwork, brickwork, tilework.**
   2.   'A kind of labor' specified by the combining root: **scratchwork, headwork, brushwork.** These combinations are generally construed as collectives and so do not ordinarily have corresponding plural forms. Most may be used as adjectives or verbs with no change in form. Related forms: **-worker, -works.**

1099   **-hawk**   A noun and a noun-forming word-final element, derived through Middle English *hauk* from Old English *hafoc, heafoc* 'falcon, hawk,' used in two ways:
1. In names differentiating among the varieties of the order *Falcones*: **mousehawk, sparhawk, goshawk.**
2. In names of hawklike birds of other species: **dorhawk, molly-hawk, nighthawk.** Related form: **-hawks** *(plural).*

1100   **-al¹**   A very productive adjectival suffix, derived through Middle English and old French *-al, -el* from Latin *-al(is)*, meaning 'pertaining to, relating to, characterized by' that which is specified by the combining root (or root plus suffix): **tribal, judgmental, educational.** Also, in many medical terms, **-eal,** thus creating such doublets as **esophagal** and **esophageal.** Also, **-ale.** Related forms: **-ally, -ality, -alism, -alist, -alistic, -alize.**

1101   **-al²**   A very common noun-forming word-final element, derived through Middle English and Old French *-aille* from Latin *-al(ia)*, used in combinations made from verbs and other nouns to mean 'a process or action': **bestowal, dismissal, ceremonial.**

1102   **-al³**   A suffix in chemical terminology, derived from an abbreviation of the word *aldehyde*, designating a compound containing a member of the aldehyde group: **benzal, chloral, ethanal.**

1103   **-ical**   A double suffix, combining **-ic¹** and **-al²**; existent since Middle English times and derived from Late Latin *-ical(is)*, it is used to form adjective combinations of two types:
1. From nouns: **algebraical, farcical, anthological.**
2. From nouns already possessing an adjectival form ending in *-ic*, to provide either a synonym of the original adjective or a new adjective with somewhat wider implications: **poetical, scientifical, economical.** Related form: **-ically.**

1104   **-physical**   An adjective and an adjective-forming word-final element, derived from Greek *physik(os)* 'natural' (from the verb *phyein* 'to grow, make grow, produce'), used in a variety of etymologically related senses specified by the combining root: **paraphysical, metaphysical, geophysical.** Related forms: **-physis, -physics, -phyte.**

1105   **-grammatical**   An adjective and an adjective-forming word-final element, derived from Greek *grammatik(os)* 'one skilled in writing, grammar' (from *gram(ma)*, *gram(mat-)* 'that which is written'), used to mean 'pertaining to language, grammar, writing' as specified by the combining root: **agrammatical, ungrammatical, neogrammatical.** Also, **-grammatic.** Related forms: **-gram, -gramme, -grammic, -grammically, -grammatically.**

1106 **-meal**[1] An adverb-forming word-final element, derived through Middle English *-mele* from Old English *māel(um)*, a combining form of *mael* 'appointed time, occasion, measure,' used in the sense of 'by a measure or portion of time' specified by the combining root: **piecemeal, inchmeal, limbmeal.**

1107 **-meal**[2] A noun and a noun-forming word-final element, derived through Middle English *mele* from Old English *melu* 'ground grain' (cf. modern English *mill*), used in its etymological sense, the kind of grain or the manner of its milling being specified by the combining root: **oatmeal, wheatmeal, poundmeal.**

1108 **-lecithal** An adjective and an adjective-forming word-final element, derived from Greek *lekith(os)* 'egg yolk' and **-al**[1], used in combinations describing 'a yolk': **megalecithal, tropholecithal, centrolecithal.**

1109 **-ial** An adjective-forming word-final element, derived through Middle English from Middle French *-iel*, *-ial* and ultimately from Latin *-ial(is)*, used to create combinations meaning 'pertaining or relating to, or characterized by' whatever is stated by the first root: **managerial, racial, financial.** Compare **-ian.** Related form: **-ially.** Despite appearances, many English terms ending in *-ial* contain the suffix **-al**[1] rather than **-ial.** The explanation: the combining roots end etymologically in *i*, to which **-al**[1] has been added. Example: English **official** equals Latin *offici(um)* plus **-al**[1].

1110 **-labial** An adjective and an adjective-forming word-final element, derived from Latin *labi(a)* 'lips' and **-al**[1], used chiefly in medical terminology in the sense of 'of, pertaining, or referring to lips' of a sort or with reference to a location specified by the combining root: **bilabial, maxillolabial, vaginolabial.**

1111 **-social** An adjective and an adjective-forming word-final element, derived from Latin *sociāl(is)* 'of, pertaining, or relating to companionship' (cf. the noun *soci(us)* 'sharer, companion' and the verb *soci(āre)* 'to share'), used in the sense of 'of, pertaining, or relating to fellowship or community or participation therein' as specified by the combining root: **antisocial, psychosocial, ethicosocial.** Related forms: **-sociate, -socially, -sociative, -sociation.**

1112   **-ennial**   An adjective-forming word-final element, derived from Latin *-enni(um)* 'period of time reckoned in years' (cf. *annus* 'year') and **-al¹**, used in combinations meaning 'at intervals of years' the number of which is specified by the combining root: **decennial, biennial, centennial**. Related form: **-ennium.**

1113   **-normal**   An adjective and an adjective-forming word-final element, derived from Latin *nōrm(a)* 'rule, measure, standard' and **-al¹**, used in combinations meaning 'relating or conforming to an established norm, rule, or principle': **abnormal, paranormal, subnormal**. Related forms: **normalcy, -normality, -normally.**

1114   **-sternal**   An adjective and an adjective-forming word-final element, derived from Greek *stern(on)* and Latin *stern(um)* 'breast-bone' and **-al¹**, used in biomedical terminology to mean 'of, pertaining, relating, or referring to the sternum (and any adjoining bones),' as specified by the combining root: **infrasternal, episternal, costosternal**. Related forms: **-sternum, -sternia.**

1115   **-carpal**   An adjective, derived through Latin from Greek *karp(os)* 'wrist'—not to be confused with the homographic Greek *karp(os)* 'fruit' (cf. **-carp**)—and **-al¹**, used in medical terminology to refer to the wrist as specified in the combining root: **metacarpal, midcarpal, carpocarpal**. Related forms: **-carpus; -carpals** (*plural*).

1116   **-cerebral**   An adjective and an adjective-forming word-final element, derived from Latin *cerebr(um)* 'brain' and **-al¹**, used in medical terminology in its etymological sense, as qualified by the combining root: **extracerebral, pericerebral, corticocerebral.**

1117   **-vertebral**   An adjective and an adjective-forming word-final element, derived from Latin *vertebra* 'joint, thing that something turns on or by' (cf. the verb *vert(ere)* 'to turn') and **-al¹**, used in the specialized sense of 'of, relating, or referring to the bones of the spinal column' as specified by the combining root: **intravertebral, basivertebral, lumbovertebral.**

1118   **-ventral**   An adjective and an adjective-forming word-final element, derived from Latin *venter, ventr-* 'stomach, womb' and **-al¹**, used in the sense of 'of, pertaining, or referring to the stomach or abdominal region' as specified by the combining root: **subventral, dorsoventral, anteroventral.**

1119   **-neural**   An adjective, derived through Latin from Greek *neur(on)* 'sinew, tendon, fiber,' hence, 'nerve' and -al[1], also used as an adjective-forming word-final element in biomedical combinations meaning 'of, relating to a nerve or nerves' as specified by the combining root: **trineural, stereoneural, spinoneural.** Also, **-neuric.** Related forms: **-neure, -neuron, -neuria, -neurotic, -neurosis, -neuroma.**

1120   **-dorsal** An adjective and an adjective-forming word-final element, derived from Latin *dors(um)* 'back' and -al[1], used in combinations referring to 'the back or part of the back of something (usually, the body)' or to 'the back' and some other part of the body, as specified by the combining root: **middorsal, lumbodorsal, iliodorsal.**

1121   **-el** A noun-forming word-final element, derived through Middle English *-el* and Old French *-el, -ele* from Latin *-ell(us), -ell(a), -ell(um)*, a diminutive ending, used in noun combinations with the meaning 'small one': **satchel, roundel, citadel.** Compare **-elle, -ella.**

1122   **-mel** A noun-forming word-final element, derived from Latin *mel, mellis* 'honey' and Greek *meli, melit-* 'honey' (with which English *mead* is cognate), used in the sense of 'a honey-sweet solution' specified by the combining root: **caramel, philomel, oxymel.** Related forms: **-melic, -melitic; -mels** *(plural).*

1123   **-pel** A verb-forming word-final element, derived through French from Latin *pell(ere)* 'to push, drive,' used widely in borrowed verb combinations in its etymological sense as qualified by the combining root: **expel, compel, dispel.** Principal parts: **-pelling, -pelled, -pelled.** Related forms: **-pulse, -pulsion, -pulsive.** (These forms are all derived from *puls(us), puls(a), puls(um)*, the past participle to *pell(ere)*.)

1124   **-il**[1] A noun-forming word-final element, derived through German *-il* and French *-ile* from Latin *-il(is)*—an adjective-forming suffix—used in learned combinations meaning 'a substance related to another' named by the combining root: **uracil, benzil, uramil.** Also, **-ile.** Related forms: **-ils, -iles** *(plurals).*

1125   **-il**[2] A noun-forming word-final element, derived through French from the late Latin (masculine) diminutive suffix *-ill(us)*, used as a diminutive in combinations, often technical in nature: **bulbil, focil, pencil.** Compare **-ille, -el, -elle.** Related form: **-ils** *(plural).*

1126   **-phil** A word-final element, derived from Greek *phil(ein)* 'to love, have an affinity for,' used in forming both nouns and adjectives in bio-medical terminology, with the meaning '(of or referring to) that which readily combines with, absorbs, or is stained by' that which is specified by the combining root: **hydrophil, acidophil, basophil.** Also, **-philic, -philous.** Compare **-phile.** Related forms: **-phila, -philia, -phily, -philiac, -philism, -philist, -philite; -phils, -philes** *(plurals).*

1127   **-foil**   A noun-forming word-final element, derived from Latin *foli(um)* 'leaf,' and used to mean 'a plant having a sort or number of leaves' as specified by the combining root: **multifoil, trefoil, quadrifoil.** Related forms: **-folia, -foliate; -foils** *(plural).*

1128   **-fall**   A verb and a noun, derived through Middle English *fall* from Old English *feall,* used in forming noun combinations:
   1.   'A descent caused by gravity': **snowfall, waterfall, pratfall.**
   2.   'An apparent or metaphoric descent': **nightfall, dewfall, landfall.** Related form: **-falls** *(plural).*

1129   **-hall**   A noun, derived through Middle English *halle* from Old English *heall* 'shelter, corner, hall,' used as a word ending in personal, place, and house names: **Vauxhall, Rivenhall, Worminghall.**

1130   **-stall**   A noun and a noun-forming word-final element, derived through Middle English *stal* from Old English *steall* 'place, standing,' used in combinations meaning 'a place for something, a place to put something' named by the combining root: **fingerstall, footstall, whipstall.** Related form: **-stalls** *(plural).*

1131   **-bell**   A noun and a noun-forming word-final element, derived through Middle English from Old English *belle* 'bell, i.e., a hollow instrument struck with a clapper or hammer to make a musical sound' (akin to English *bellow* and *bawl*), used in two main senses:
   1.   'A bell' of a sort specified by the combining root: **doorbell, mortbell, cowbell.**
   2.   In common plant names, 'a bell-shaped flower': **harebell, bluebell, rockbell.** Related form: **-bells** *(plural).*

1132   **-hill**   A noun and a noun-forming word-final element, derived through Middle English *hil, hul* from Old English *hyll* 'hill, natural elevation,' used in two ways:
   1.   In combinations designating a type of hill: **molehill, dunghill, foothill.**
   2.   In place names and the personal names derived from them: **Churchill, Gadshill, Thornhill.** Related form: **-hills** *(plural).*

1133   **-coll**   A noun-forming word-final element, derived from Greek *koll(a)* 'glue,' used in chemical terminology to designate 'a glue or resin' as specified by the combining root: **glycocoll, phenocoll, saprocoll.** Related form: **-colls** *(plural)*.

1134 **-poll** A noun and a verb, derived from Middle English *pol, polle* 'hair of the head, head,' also used as a word-final element in several related senses:
 1. In nouns, 'a quality of intelligence, (usually low)' specified by the combining root: **clodpoll, stunpoll** ('dunce'), **doddypoll.**
 2. In the common names of two bird species, 'the feathers of the head' identified by color: **redpoll, blackpoll.**
 3. In a single verb + noun combination, **pitchpoll,** meaning literally 'a head throw;' functioning as either a verb or a noun, the term since the 17th cent. has meant 'somersault.' Principal parts (verb): **-polling, -polled, -polled.** Compare **-pole².** Related form (noun): **-polls** *(plural)*.

1135 **-phyll** A noun-forming word-final element, derived from Greek *phyll(on)* 'leaf,' used in two related senses:
 1. 'A leaf' as specified by the combining root: **cataphyll, hypophyll, sclerophyll.**
 2. 'A variety of coloring matter found in plants' as specified by the combining root: **chlorophyll, chromophyll, chrysophyll.** Also, **-phyl.** Related forms: **-phyllum, -phyllic, -phyllous, -phylline, -phylly; -phylls, -phyls** *(plurals)*.

1136 **-ol¹** A noun-forming word-final element, derived by abbreviation of Arabic *al koh'l*, originally, 'antimony sulfide,' then, any powder that could be purified by vaporisation and subsequent condensation, then, any 'spirit,' i.e., pure liquid that could be obtained by distillation, most notably, *alcohol*; now used in chemical terminology to denote a member of the alcohol group, that is, a compound made of one or more hydroxyl groups joined to a hydrocarbon group: **naphthol, ethanol, methanol.** Related forms: **-olic; -ols** *(plural)*.

1137 **-ol²** A noun-forming word-final element, derived from Latin *ol(eum)* 'oil,' used as a frequent variant of **-ole²** in combinations meaning 'an oil or oillike material' as specified by the combining root: **benzol, petrol, furol.** Also, **-ole².** Related forms: **-ols, -oles** *(plurals)*.

1138 **-sol** A noun and a noun-forming word-final element, derived by abbreviation of the word *solution*, used in chemical terminology to denote 'a colloidal solution' in which the solids are suspended in a medium named by the combining root: **aerosol, hydrosol, sylnasol.** Related form: **-sols** *(plural)*.

1139   **-girl**   A noun, derived from Middle English *gyrle, girle* (of unsure origin) 'a child, a female child, an unmarried woman,' also used as a noun-forming word-final element in the sense of 'a female child, a young or adult woman, specifically, a female servant or menial' whose occupation or salient characteristic is named by the combining root: **goosegirl, schoolgirl, shopgirl.** Compare **-man, -woman, -maid, -boy.** Related form: **-girls** *(plural)*.

1140   **-ful¹**   A noun-forming word-final element, derived through Middle English *-ful* from Old English *-ful, full,* used in combinations to indicate 'a quantity or number that fills': **handful, mouthful, bucketful.** Also, **-full** *(rare)*. Related forms: **-fuls, -fulls** *(plurals)*. If the container name is plural, the ending remains singular (**bagsful**), but if the quantity is pluralized, the plural suffix is placed on the last root (**bagfuls**).

1141   **-ful²**   An adjective-forming word-final element, derived as was **-ful¹,** used in forming combinations of several meanings:
   1.   'Full of' whatever is named by the combining root: **eventful, dreadful, unhealthful.**
   2.   'Characterized by a quality' named by the first root: **beautiful, graceful, tasteful.**
   3.   'Resembling, possessing the qualities of' something denoted by the joining root: **masterful, useful, successful.**
   4.   'Tending to, causing' something named by the first root: **tactful, harmful, pitiful.** Related forms: **-fulness, -fully.**

1142   **-yl**   A noun-forming word-final element, derived from Greek *hyl(ē)* 'wood, the material of which things are made,' used in chemical terminology to form the names of radicals: **hydroxyl, ethyl, benzoyl.** Related forms: **-ylate, -ylation, -ylene; -yls** *(plural)*.

1143   **-dactyl**   A noun, more frequently a noun-forming word-final element, derived from Greek *daktyl(os)* 'digit, i.e., finger or toe,' used in zoological terminology to denote 'a creature possessing or characterized by fingers, toes, or—by extension—hands or feet' as specified by the combining root: **tetradactyl, zygodactyl, polydactyl.** Related forms: **-dactyla, -dactylia, -dactylic, -dactylism, -dactyly, -dactyloid, -dactylous; -dactyls** *(plural)*.

1144   **-ham**   A word-final element, derived through Middle English from either Old English *hamm* 'enclosed land' or Old English *hemm* 'border,' used in combinations functioning as place names and the personal names derived from them with the original sense of 'homestead, grassland': **Birmingham, Twickenham, Dedham.**

1145   **-gram**   A noun and a noun-forming word-final element, derived from Greek *gram(ma)*, *gram(mat-)* 'that which is written (literally, engraved), a letter or line of a drawing' (from Greek *graph(ein)* 'to write,' originally, 'to carve or engrave' and the noun-forming suffix **-ma**), used in two senses, each as particularized by the combining root:

1. 'A drawing, record, piece of writing': **telegram, diagram, program** (British **programme**).
2. 'A weight equal to 1/1000 kilogram': **decagram** (or **-gramme**), **microgram, myriagram.** (This usage derives from a specialized meaning of Greek *gramma* as 'a small weight, a basic unit of measurement' by extension from the meaning 'a letter of the alphabet.') Also, **-gramme.** Compare **-graph.** Related forms: **-grammic, -grammical, -grammically, -grammatic, -grammatical, -grammatically; -grams, -grammes** *(plurals).*

1146   **-im**   A word-final element, used in Hebrew and in Hebraic Yiddish to form the plurals of nouns, found in English exclusively in plural noun borrowings from Hebrew and Yiddish: **cherubim, sephardim, goyim.**

1147   **-holm**   A word-final element, derived through Middle English from Old Norse *hōlmr* 'islet,' used in combinations functioning as place names with the meanings 'small island in a river or lake' or 'flat land by a river': **Langholm, Chisholm, Priestholm.** Also, **-holme.**

1148   **-dom**   A noun-forming word-final element, derived through Middle English from Old English *dōm* 'judgment;' the combinations using it are based upon an abstract meaning of 'condition, state, dignity':

1. 'An office or position' denoted by the combining root: **dukedom, czardom, wifedom.**
2. A collective noun for 'persons having an office, occupation, interest, or character' denoted by the joining root: **moviedom, officialdom, dogdom.**
3. 'A realm': **Christendom, kingdom, kaiserdom.**
4. 'A state, condition, or fact of being': **freedom, boredom, martyrdom.** Also, **-dome.** Related forms: **-doms, -domes** *(plurals).*

1149   **-derm**   A noun-forming word-final element, derived through French *-derme* and Latin *-dermis* from Greek *derma, dermat-* 'skin,' used to mean 'a skin or covering' of a type denoted by the combining root: epiderm, pachyderm, periderm. Related forms: -derma, -dermis, -dermal, -dermic, -dermoid, -dermatoid, -dermatic, -dermatous; -derms *(plural)*.

1150   **-therm**   A noun-forming word-final element, derived from Greek *therm(ē)* 'heat,' used in the terminologies of several of the sciences in related extensions of its etymological sense:

1.   'A plant requiring a kind of heat' specified by the combining root: **xerotherm, microtherm, mesotherm.**

2.   'An animal possessing a body temperature' specified by the combining root: **ectotherm, endotherm, hematherm.**

3.   With the prefix *iso-* 'equal,' 'a line connecting areas of equal temperature' specified by the combining root: **isotherm, isogeotherm, isobathytherm.** Related forms: **-thermic, -thermal, -thermous, -thermy; -therms** *(plural)*.

1151   **-sperm**   A noun and a noun-forming word-final element, derived from Greek *sperm(a)*, *sperm(at-)* 'germ, seed, that which is sown' (from the verb *speir(ein)* 'to sow seed' and the noun-forming suffix -ma), used in its etymological sense to refer to the seed of both plants and animals as specified by the combining root: **angiosperm, zoosperm, zygosperm.** Related forms: **-sperma, -spermal, -spermic, -spermous, -spermia, -spermy, -spermatism; -sperms, -spermata** *(plurals)*.

1152   **-form**   A noun, derived through Middle French *-forme* from Latin *form(a)* 'shape,' used in creating adjective combinations meaning 'having the form or shape of' whatever is denoted by the combining root: **paraform, linguiform, torulaform.** Also, **-forme.** Compare **-iform.** Related forms: **-formic, -formity, -formation; -forms** *(plural)*.

1153   **-iform**   An adjective-forming word-final element, derived through Middle French *-iforme* from Latin *-iform(a)*, a combining form of Latin *forma* 'form, shape,' used with the meaning 'in the form or shape of' whatever is designated by the combining root: **cubiform, cuneiform, crystalliform.** Compare **-form.** Related forms: **-formic, -formity.**

1154   **-asm**   A noun-forming word-final element, found in a number of borrowings from Greek, in which the original *-(a)sm(os)* represented a noun-forming suffix applied to verbs to make combinations denoting 'the result or condition of an action' expressed by the combining root: **chasm, enthusiasm, orgasm.** Compare **-ism.** Related forms: **-asmus, -astic, -astically; -asms** *(plural)*.

1155   **-plasm**   A noun-forming word-final element, derived from Greek *plasm(a)* 'a thing that is molded or formed' (from the verb *plass(ein)*, *platt(ein)* 'to mold, form, shape' and the abstract noun-forming suffix **-ma**), used in combinations meaning 'the substance of a cell or tissue, either formative or formed' as specified by the combining root: **protoplasm, cytoplasm, ooplasm.** Also, **-plasma.** Related forms: **-plasis, -plasia, -plasy, -plastia, -plasty, -plastic, -plasmic, -plasmatic; -plasms, -plasmas, -plasmata** *(plurals)*.

1156   **-spasm**   A noun and a noun-forming word-final element, derived from Greek *spasm(a)* 'a convulsion' (from the verb *sp(ān)* 'to push, pull, wrench, convulse' and the noun-forming suffix **-ma**), used in medical terminology to designate 'a convulsion' of a sort or in a part of the body specified by the combining root: **paraspasm, esophagospasm, logospasm.** Related forms: **-spastic, -spasmodic; -spasms** *(plural)*.

1157   **-ism**   A common noun-forming word-final element, derived through Middle English and French *-ism(e)* from Greek *-(i)sm(os)*, a noun-forming suffix, originally applied to verbs and later extended in usage to form combinations with nouns and adjectives as well, with several related senses, each specified by the combining root:

　　1. 'An action or practice': **idealism, snobbism, Dadaism.**
　　2. 'A state or condition': **phobism, exoticism, alcoholism.**
　　3. 'Principles, doctrines, or beliefs, or an organization founded to support them'; **monotheism, Bahaism, communism.**
　　4. 'A linguistic usage or characteristic': **Anglicism, archaism, Yiddishism.** Compare **-asm.** Related forms: **-ismus, -ise, -ize, -ist, -istic, -istically, -ismic, -ismically; -isms** *(plural)*.

1158   **-acism**   A double noun-forming suffix, derived from **-ac** and **-ism,** and used in medicine and linguistics to denote 'a tendency to overuse or misarticulate' the sound specified by the combining root: **lambdacism, iotacism, rhotacism.** Related form: **-acisms** *(plural)*.

1159   **-theism**   A noun and a noun-forming word-final element, derived from Greek *the(os)*, *the(a)* 'god, goddess' and **-ism,** used in combinations meaning 'a belief in a god or gods' as specified by the combining root: **monotheism, atheism, zootheism.** Related forms: **-theist, -theistic, -theistically; -theisms** *(plural)*.

1160   **-seism**   A noun and a noun-forming word-final element, derived from Greek *seism(os)* 'a shaking, an earthquake' (cf. the verb *sei(ein)* 'to shake'), used in combinations denoting 'earth tremors and other seismic movements' as specified by the combining root: **megaseism,** bathyseism, microseism. Related forms: -seismic, -seismal, -seismically, -seismical; -seisms *(plural)*.

1161 **-morphism**   A noun-forming word-final element, derived from Greek *morph(ē)* 'form, shape' and **-ism,** used in combinations naming 'the condition or state of having a form or shape' specified by the combining root: **dimorphism, neomorphism, zoomorphism.** Related forms: **-morph, -morphia, -morphy, -morpha, -morphae, -morphi, -morphic, -morphous, -morphically, -morphously, -morphosis; -morphisms** *(plural)*.

1162 **-tropism**   A noun and a noun-forming word-final element, derived from Greek *trop(os), trop(ē)* 'a turning, turn, direction, influence' (from the verb *trep(ein)* 'to turn, guide') and **-ism,** used in medical terminology in the sense of 'a condition of having an affinity for something' specified by the combining root: **trophotropism, vagotropism, stereotropism.** Also, **-tropy.** Related forms: **-trope, -tropia, -tropic, -tropal, -tropous; -tropisms, -tropies** *(plurals)*.

1163 **-cosm**   A noun-forming word-final element, derived through Middle English *-cosme,* Middle French, and Latin from Greek *kosm(os)* 'world,' used in its etymological sense as modified by the combining root: **megacosm, microcosm, macrocosm.** Related forms: **-cosmos, -cosmic, -cosmical, -cosmically, cosmology; -cosms** *(plural)*.

1164 **-um**   A word-final element, used to mark the nominative singular of Latin neuter nouns and adjectives of the second declension, found in Latinate scientific terminology and learned borrowings: **quantum, cerebellum, dextrum.** Compare **-ium.** Related forms: **-ums, -a** *(plurals)*.

1165 **-ium**   A noun-forming word-final element, derived by abstraction from Latin *-ium,* the neuter singular ending for nouns and adjectives of the second declension, many of which are merely Latinized borrowings from Greek, in which the corresponding ending is *-ion* (cf. **-ion**[3]), used extensively in chemical terminology to name metallic elements: **sodium, radium, aluminium** *(British)*. Compare **-um.** Related forms: **-iums, -ia** *(plurals)*.

1166 **-thecium**   A noun-forming word-final element, derived from Greek *thēk(ē)* 'case, container, receptacle' and **-ium,** used in botanical terminology to designate 'a sack or container' specified by the combining root: **perithecium, endothecium, epithecium.** Compare **-theca.** Related forms: **-thecial; -thecia, -theciums** *(plurals)*.

1167   **-idium**   A noun-forming word-final element, derived from Latin *-idium*, a diminutive suffix derived from the Greek diminutive suffix *-idion*, found in its etymological sense in general Latinate scientific terminology: **ascogonidium, basidium, nephridium.**

1168   **-podium**   A noun-forming word-final element, derived through Latin from Greek *pous, pod-* 'foot' and *-ion*, a diminutive suffix, used in general scientific terminology in the sense of 'something footlike' specified by the combining root: **pseudopodium, phyllopodium, axiopodium.** Related forms: **-pod, -pode, -pus, -poda, -podia, -podial, -podal, -podous, -pody; -podiums, -podia** *(plurals)*.

1169   **-sporangium**   A noun and a noun-forming word-final element, derived through scientific Latin from Greek *spor(os)* 'seed' (cf. **-spore**) and *angeion* 'vessel, capsule,' used to designate 'an encasement of spores' of a sort or quantity specified by the combining root: **megasporangium, monosporangium, gynosporangium.** Related forms: **-sporangiums, -sporangia** *(plurals)*.

1170   **-pterygium**   A noun and a noun-forming word-final element, derived through Latin from Greek *pterygion* 'wing, winglike growth, fin' (from *pteryx, pteryg-* 'wing, winglike growth' and the diminutive *-ion*), used in two senses:
   1.   In zoological terminology, 'a fin or bone or cartilage to which a fin is attached': **archipterygium, basipterygium, chiropterygium.**
   2.   In medical terminology, 'an abnormality of the conjunctiva (after its winglike shape)' specified by the combining root: **pseudopterygium, pimelopterygium, symblepharopterygium.** Related forms: **-pter, -pteron, -pteryx; -pterygiums, -pterygia** *(plurals)*.

1171   **-brachium**   A noun, borrowed from Latin *brachium* 'arm,' also used as a noun-forming word-final element used in medical terminology to designate a part of the arm or an armlike growth as specified by the combining root: **antebrachium, restibrachium, myelobrachium.** Related form: **-brachia** *(plural)*.

1172   **-thelium**   A noun and a noun-forming word-final element, derived from Greek *thēl(ē)* 'nipple' and **-ium**, used in biomedical terminology in the extended sense of 'a layer of cellular tissue' of a sort specified by the combining root: **epithelium, perithelium, endothelium.** Related forms: **-thelia, -theliums** *(plurals)*.

1173   **-cranium**   A noun, also used as a noun-forming word-final element, derived from Latin *cranium* 'skull,' and used in biomedical terminology to mean 'referring to the skull (or, more specifically, the brain pan)' as specified by the combining root: **epicranium, osteocranium, otocranium.** Related forms: **-cranic, -cranial; -crania** *(plural)*.

1174 -ennium A noun-forming word-final element, derived from Latin *-ennium* 'period of time reckoned in years' (cf. *annus* 'year'), used in borrowed combinations designating 'a period of years' of a number specified by the combining root: **biennium, millennium, triennium.** Compare **-ennial.** Related forms: **-enniums, -ennia** *(plurals)*.

1175 -arium A noun-forming word-final element, derived from Latin *-ārium*, '-ary,' meaning 'a place containing or related to' that which is specified by the combining root: **aquarium, solarium, planetarium.** Compare **-orium, -ary, -ory.** Related forms: **-ariums, -aria** *(plurals)*.

1176 -orium A noun-forming word-final element, derived from the Latin suffix *-ōrium*, used in its two main etymological senses:
1. 'A place for an activity' denoted by the combining root: **auditorium, sanatorium, lubritorium.**
2. 'An instrument or thing used' for an action denoted by the combining root: **ostensorium, suppositorium, inductorium.** Compare **-arium, -ary, -ory.** Related forms: **-oriums, -oria** *(plurals)*.

1177 -phyllum A noun-forming word-final element, derived through Latin from Greek *phyll(on)* 'leaf' and **-um,** used in botanical taxonomy to designate genera of plants 'having leaves' of a sort specified by the combining root: **Podophyllum, Xerophyllum, Brachyphyllum.** Compare **-phyll.**

1178 -ulum A noun-forming word-final element, derived from the neuter singular form of the Latin diminutive *-ul(us)*, *-ul(a)*, *-ul(um)*, found in scientific terminology and learned borrowings in its etymological sense of 'small one' of a sort specified by the combining root: **speculum, ovulum, scutulum.** Also, **-ule.** Related forms: **-ula[1], -ulus, -uli, -ulae, -ulic, -ular, -ulous; -ulums, -ula[2]** *(plurals)*.

1179 -sternum A noun and a noun-forming word-final element, derived through scientific Latin *sternum* from Greek *stern(on)* 'chest, breastbone' and **-um,** used in biomedical terminology to designate 'a region of or near the breastbone (sternum)' specified by the combining root: **midsternum, episternum, xiphosternum.** Related forms: **-sternia, -sternal; -sterna, -sternums** *(plurals)*.

1180 **-onym** A noun-forming word-final element, derived from Aeolian Greek *onyma, onymat-* 'name' (cf. Attic-Ionic *onoma, onamat-*), used in combinations meaning 'a name, word' of a sort specified by the combining root: **synonym, antonym, pseudonym.** Related forms: **-onymy, -onymous, -onymously, -onymic, -onymically; -onyms** *(plural).*

1181 **-an**[1] A word-final element, most frequently occurring as *-ian* and, in technical terminology, *-ean*, derived from Latin *-(i)an(us)*, and used to form adjectives often used substantively:
1. 'Pertaining or belonging to': **Cuban, urban, Wesleyan.**
2. 'Resembling or characteristic of': **Proustian, Nietzschean, Alaskan.**
3. 'Pertaining or belonging to a geological period' identified by the combining root: **Cambrian, Devonian, Permian.**
4. 'A person of, from, or belonging to' whatever the combining root denotes: **American, Illinoisian, Mediterranean.**
5. 'A person versed in a specialty (esp. one ending in *-ic* or *-ics*)': **statistician, veterinarian, logician.**
6. 'A creature belonging to a zoological group' named by the combining root: **crustacean, Osteostraean, Dinosaurian.** Also, **-ian, -ean.** Compare **-ana.** Related forms: **-anly, -ianly, -eanly; -ans, -ians, -eans** *(plurals).*

1182 **-an**[2] A suffix, derived from abbreviation of the word *anhydride*, used in chemical terminology to designate polysaccharides as specified by the combining root: **pentosan, dextran, fructosan.** Related form: **-ans** *(plural).*

1183 **-ian** A word-final element, used to form adjectives (often used substantively), derived from Latin *-ian(us)*, which may itself be analyzed variously as **-i(a**[1]**)** and *-an(us)*, **-i(a**[2]**)** and *-an(us)*, the joining vowel *-i-* and *-an(us)*, or the stem vowel *-i-*, that is, the last phonological and orthographic element in a stem, and *-an(us)*, all with the sense of 'belonging to, derived from, or characteristic of a class, condition, place, person, or thing' specified by the combining root: **mammalian, Tunisian, Mendelian.** Compare **-an**[1], **-ana.** Related forms: **-ianly, -ianism, -ianist.**

1184 **-ician** A double suffix, derived from Latin *-ic(us)* (cf. **-ic**[1]) and *-ian(us)* (cf. **-ian**), used to form nouns designating 'a specialist or practitioner in a field' specified by the combining root: **theoretician, beautician, statistician.** Related form: **-icians** *(plural).*

1185 **-arian** A suffix, derived from Latin *-ari(us)* '-ary' and -an, used in combination to form nouns and adjectives:

1. 'A believer or advocate; pertaining to a believer or advocate or to the doctrine involved': **millenarian, equalitarian, Latitudinarian.**
2. 'A person who produces' whatever is named by the combining root, or 'pertaining to the producer or his product': **legendarian, platitudinarian, grammarian.**
3. 'A person who is or is part of' what the joining root denotes, or 'pertaining to his state or condition': **nonagenarian, seminarian, librarian.** Related form: **-arians** *(plural)*.

1186 **-man** A noun, derived through Middle English from Old English *man(n)* 'adult male human, person,' also commonly used as a noun-forming word-final element with the meaning 'an adult person—usually, though not always, understood to be male—who is characteristically associated with' that which is named by the combining root. Two kinds of combination, of approximately equal frequency of occurrence and no discernible difference in sense, are possible with nouns:

1. That in which **-man** is added to a plain noun: **horseman, chairman, gagman.**
2. That in which **-man** is added to a noun with a possessive ending: **marksman, swordsman, kinsman.** This suffix may also be added to adjectives, usually referring to a place of origin: **Welshman, Scotsman, Dutchman.** All three kinds of combination are still productive in English. Compare **-woman, -maid, -boy, -girl.** Related forms: **-manship; -men** *(plural)*.

1187 **-woman** A noun and a noun-forming word-final element, derived from Old English *wīfman* (i.e., *wīf* 'woman' and *man* 'adult human') 'adult female,' used in the sense of 'an adult female characteristically associated with that which is specified by the combining root.' Two kinds of combination (with no discernible difference in meaning) are possible with nouns:

1. That in which **-woman** is added to a plain noun: **horsewoman, applewoman, councilwoman.**
2. That in which **-woman** is added to the possessive form of a noun: **herdswoman, stateswoman, kinswoman.** This suffix may also be added to adjectives, usually designating a place of origin: **Welshwoman, Scotswoman, Irishwoman.** Compare **-man, -boy, -girl, -maid.** Related forms: **-womanship; -women** *(plural)*.

1188 **-pan** A noun and a noun-forming word-final element, derived through

Middle English from Old English *panne* 'dish, vessel' used in a number of related senses:

1. Most commonly, 'a vessel or dish used chiefly for domestic purposes': **saucepan, dishpan, piepan.**
2. 'A hollow or depression': **brainpan, kneepan, harnpan** *(Scottish).*
3. In flintlock guns, two terms describing the hollow in which powder ignited by the flint was placed: **touchpan, flashpan** (the part meant by *flash in the pan,* when a gun misfired, causing the powder to flash without moving the bullet). Related form: **-pans** *(plural).*

1189 **-en**[1] A word-final element, derived through Middle English *-en* from Old English, formerly used to form adjectives from nouns with the meanings 'made of, consisting of, resembling': **oaken, leaden, golden.** Also, **-n** when the joining noun ends in *-e.* Related form: **-(e)nly.**

1190 **-en**[2] A word-final element derived through Middle English *-nen* from Old English *-n(ian),* used to form verbs from adjectives and nouns:

1. Transitive verbs meaning 'to cause to be of a condition or quality' denoted by the combining adjective: **sharpen, embolden, deaden.**
2. In transitive verbs made from nouns, 'to cause to have the quality' named: **lengthen, strengthen, heighten.**
3. Intransitive verbs made from adjectives meaning 'to become': **steepen, darken, brighten.**
4. Intransitive verbs made from nouns meaning 'to have': **leafen, breadthen, hearten.** Also, **-n** in combination with roots ending in *-e.* Principal parts: **-ening, -ened, -ened.**

1191 **-en**[3] A word-final element formerly widely used to form the plurals of nouns, now preserved in the tenacious trio: **oxen, children, brethren.** All three words illustrate three obsolete methods of forming the plural in older stages of English:

1. The *-n* plural: **ox** and **-(e)n.**
2. The *-r* plural: **child** and **-(e)r** (the **-n** is a second plural).
3. Vowel change: **brother/breth(e)r** and **-(e)n,** which may be a second plural.

1192 **-en**[4] A suffix, comparable to **-ed**[1], derived through Middle and Old English as the way of forming the past participles of strong verbs (for an explanation of *strong verb,* see **-ed**[1]); the ending survives in many current strong verbs and has spread to a few weak verbs and those having both strong and weak forms: strong: **taken, gotten, ridden;**

weak: **proven** (also **proved**), **swollen** (also **swelled**), **strewn** (also **strewed**).

1193   **-en**[5]   An obsolete diminutive noun-forming word-final element, derived from Middle and Old English *-en* acting as a neuter of **-en**[1]; like all diminutives, the basic meaning of the suffix is 'small one,' but the diminutive force is not always strongly felt: **kitten, maiden, haven.**

1194   **-een**[1]   A word-final element, perhaps derived from the *-ine* of *bombazine* and *crinoline*, used to form noun combinations meaning 'an inferior fabric, in appearance like a better fabric named in the joining root': **sateen, velveteen, damaskeen.** Related form: **-eens** *(plural)*.

1195   **-een**[2]   A word-final element, derived from Irish *-in* 'small one,' used as a diminutive in Anglo-Irish noun combinations in its etymological sense, often with either an affectionate or a contemptuous overtone: **girleen, mavourneen, poteen.** Also, **-in.** Related form: **-eens** *(plural)*.

1196   **-gen**   A noun-forming word-final element, derived through French *-gène* from Greek *gen(ea)* 'birth, production, growth,' used in general scientific terminology in two related senses, each qualified by the combining root:
1. 'That which generates': **halogen, carcinogen, pathogen.**
2. 'That which is generated or produced': **immunogen, antitoxigen, hydrogen.** Also, **-gene.** Related forms: **-genic, -genically, -genist, -genism, -genous, -geneous, -genate, -genation, -genite, -geny; -gens, -genes** *(plurals)*.

1197   **-men**   A noun-forming word-final element with no particular meaning, derived from the Latin suffix *-men, -min-* (cognate with Greek *-ma* '-ma'), found in a number of Latin borrowings originally denoting 'a condition or the result of an action' specified by the combining root: **flumen, lumen, semen.** Related forms: **-minal; -mens, -mina** *(plurals)*.

1198   **-haven**   A noun and a noun-forming word-final element, derived through Middle English *haven* from Old English *haefen, haefene* 'sea inlet, harbor,' used in combinations functioning as place names: **Strathhaven, New Haven, Motthaven.** Many combinations in contemporary spelling note the last root as separate. In most cases, however, earlier spelling conventions show the place names as solid compounds.

1199   **-in**   A noun-forming word-final element, derived through French *-in(e)* from Latin *-in(a)* 'of or belonging to,' used in forming combinations of an essentially technical nature.

1. 'An antibiotic': **penicillin, streptomycin, bacitracin.**
2. 'A pharmaceutical product, often a trademark': **aspirin, Empirin, niacin.**
3. 'A chemical compound, neither basic nor acidic': **albumin, gelatin, palmitin.**
4. 'An enzyme': **emulsin, pepsin, myrosin.** Also, **-ine**[1], esp. in sense 3. Related form: **-ins** (plural).

1200 **-strain** A verb-forming word-final element, derived through Middle English and Old French from Latin *string(ere)* 'to draw tight, compress, restrict,' used in a handful of common borrowings in its etymological sense as qualified by the combining root: **constrain, restrain, overstrain.** Principal parts: **-straining, -strained, -strained.** Compare **-stringe, -strict.** Related form: **-straint.**

1201 **-tain** A verb-forming word-final element, derived through Middle English and French from Latin *ten(ēre)* 'to hold,' used in a number of inherited combinations that have retained their etymological meaning despite modern modifications: **obtain** 'to hold completely'; **maintain** literally, 'to hold in the hand'; **detain** 'to hold away, from'; **retain** 'to hold back'; **contain** 'to hold together'; **sustain** 'to hold up'; **abstain** 'to withhold, hold out'; **entertain** 'to hold between, maintain.' (Although similar in form, **pertain** 'to reach to, belong' and **attain** 'to touch, reach' are derived from Latin *tang(ere)* 'to touch, reach.') Principal parts: **-taining, -tained, -tained.** Related forms: **-tainment, -tention**[1]; **-tenance, -tinence.**

1202 **-kin** A word-final element, derived from the Middle English diminutive suffix *-kin* (cognate with Modern German *-chen*), formerly used in two kinds of combination preserved in English:
1. In its etymological sense, as a noun-forming suffix meaning 'small (or inferior) one' of the sort specified by the combining root: **lambkin, ciderkin, maidkin.** Also, **-kins** (possibly **-kin** and **-s**[2]).
2. In combination with the patronymic suffix **-s** (found in such names as **Jones, Adams,** and **Roberts**), as a surname-forming word-final element: **Jenkins, Atkins, Dawkins.**

1203 **-skin** A noun and a noun-forming word-final element, derived through Middle English from Old Norse *skinn* 'tegument,' used in its etymological sense and extensions thereof, as qualified by the combining root:
1. 'The skin of an animal': **pigskin, deerskin, sheepskin.**

2. 'The skin of an animal prepared for a purpose' denoted by the joining root, often for storage: **waterskin, wineskin, ribskin.**
3. 'The covering layer of something, usually outermost': **grapeskin, onionskin, silverskin.**
4. 'In the names of fabrics, some of which are manufactured to resemble an animal skin': **doeskin, sharkskin, oilskin.**
5. 'A kind of paper': **sheepskin, onionskin.**

1204 **-lysin** A noun and a noun-forming word-final element, derived from Greek *-lys(is)* 'a loosening, breaking down' (v. **-lysis**) and **-in,** used in biochemical terminology to denote 'an antibody that dissolves cells' of a sort or in a part of the body specified by the combining root: **endolysin, proteolysin, lymphatolysin.** Compare **-lysis.** Related forms: **-lysine; -lysins** *(plural).*

1205 **-quin** A noun-forming word-final element, ultimately derived from Quechua *kina* 'bark (of a tree),' specifically, 'bark of the cinchona,' from which the alkaloid quinine (an antimalarial agent) is derived; used in pharmaco-medical terminology to name antimalarial medicinal compounds derived from quinine, as specified by the combining root: **pamaquin, pentaquin, plasmoquin.** Also, **-quine.** Related forms: **-quins, -quines** *(plurals).*

1206 **-toxin** A noun and a noun-forming word-final element, derived from Greek *tox(ikon)* 'poison' and **-in,** used in biomedical terminology to designate 'a poison produced in or by or affecting' that which is named by the combining root: **lymphotoxin, hemotoxin, bufotoxin.** Related forms: **-toxia, -toxy, -toxic, -toxism, -toxis, -toxicity, -toxical, -toxically; -toxins** *(plural).*

1207 **-on** A word-final element, used to form the neuter singular of Greek nouns of the second declension with plurals ending in *-a* (cf. **-a²**), used in direct borrowings from Greek (e.g., **parhelion, neuron,** and **encephalon**) as well as modern combinations denoting 'a basic or elementary unit,' most notably in the terminology of physics and chemistry:
1. 'An elementary atomic particle': **nucleon, proton, electron.**
2. 'A unit or quantum': **photon, magneton, phonon.**
3. 'A (nonmetallic) chemical element': **carbon, silicon, krypton.**

1208 **-odon** A noun-forming word-final element, derived from Greek *odous, odont-* 'tooth,' used in zoological taxonomy to name genera 'having or characterized by teeth' of a sort specified by the combining root: **Mastodon, Glyptodon, Dicynodon.** Also, **-odus, -odont.** Related forms:

-odonic, -odontic, -odontia[1], -odontia[2], -odontoid; -odons, -odonts, -odontes *(plurals)*.

1209   **-osteon**   A noun-forming word-final element, derived from Greek *osteon* 'bone,' and used in medical terminology to designate 'a bone or area near a bone' as specified by the combining root: **malacosteon, pleurosteon, otosteon.** Also, **-osteum.** Related forms: **-osteal, -osteoid, -osteoma; -ons, -a** *(plurals)*.

1210   **-gon**   A noun-forming word-final element, derived from Greek *gōn(ia)* 'angle,' used in the terminology of geometry to designate 'a geometric figure possessing angles' in the quantity stated by the combining root: **hexagon, decagon, tetragon.** Related forms: **-gonic[1], -gonal, -gonally; -gons** *(plural)*.

1211   **-thon**   A productive noun-forming word-final element, derived by abstraction from the word *marathon* (itself derived from the place name Marathon, the site of a prolonged battle between the Greeks and the Persians), used in the sense of 'a long-lasting, demanding activity' of a sort specified by the combining root (generally a verb or verb derivative): **telethon, talkathon, walkathon.** Related form: **-thons** *(plural)*.

1212   **-ion[1]**   A noun-forming word-final element, derived through Middle English *-ioun, -ion, -iun* and Old French *-ion, -iun* from Latin *-iō, -iōn-*, a very productive abstract noun-forming suffix, used to form combinations from adjectives and verbs with one or another of the following senses:

   1.   'An act or process' specified by the combining root: **rebellion, initiation, coercion.**
   2.   'The result of an action or process,' specified by the combining root: **destruction, confection, revision.**
   3.   'A thing acted upon or conditioned' as specified by the combining root: **ambition, suspicion, passion.**
   4.   'A state or condition' denoted by the combining root: **confusion, possession, aversion.** Related form: **-ions** *(plural)*.

1213   **-ion[2]**   A noun and a noun-forming word element, derived from Greek *iōn, iousa, ion,* the present participle of the verb *ienai* 'to go,' used in the terminology of physics and chemistry to denote 'an electrically charged particle which may be set in motion when an electrical force is applied to it': **ion, anion, cation.** Related forms: **-ionic, -ionically; -ions** *(plural)*.

1214   **-ion**[3] A noun-forming word-final element, derived from Greek *-ion* (cf. Latin **-ium**), the neuter singular ending for nouns and adjectives of the second declension whose stems end in *-i*. The retention of this suffix (in learned words and general scientific terminology) owes something to the productivity of the suffixes **-ia**[1] and **-ia**[2], to which *-ion* is the logical, if not always the true, corresponding singular: **parhelion, endognathion, osteopedion.** Compare **-ium.** Related form: **-ia** *(plural).*

1215   **-chorion** A noun, derived from Greek *chorion* 'leather, skin, membrane,' also used as a noun-forming word-final element in medical terminology to designate 'a membrane' as qualified by the combining root: **omphalochorion, epichorion, mallochorion.** Related forms: **-chorioid, -choric; -choria, -coria** *(plurals).* Note that the plural form **-coria** (to Latin **-corium** from Greek **-chorion**) is not to be confused with **-coria**[1] or **-coria**[2].

1216   **-pulsion** A noun-forming word-final element, derived from Latin *puls(us), puls(a), puls(um)*—the past participle of the verb *pell(ere)* 'to push, drive'—and **-ion**[1], used in a number of common borrowings, all sharing a basic meaning of 'the action, process, or condition of pushing or driving': **propulsion, compulsion, expulsion.** Related forms: **-pel, -pulse, -pulsive; -pulsions** *(plural).*

1217   **-tion** A noun-forming word-final element, derived through Middle English and French from Latin *-tiō, -tiōn-*, that is, the past participle marker *-t-* plus the abstract-noun-forming suffix *-iō, -iōn-*, '**-ion**[1],' used synonymously with **-ion**[1]: **diminution, emendation, absorption.** Compare **-ion**[1]. Related form: **-tions** *(plural).*

1218   **-ation** A noun-forming word-final element, derived from Latin *-ātiō, -ātiōn-*, itself derived from the Latin past participle of the first conjugation (cf. **-ata**) and the abstract-noun-forming suffix *-iō, -iōn-* (cf. **-ion**[1]). English **-ation** is used extensively to form nouns largely, though not exclusively, from verbs which end in *-ate* (cf. **-ate**[3]), in two major senses:
1. 'An action or process': **classification, personification, implication.**
2. 'The result, effect, or product of a process or action': **civilization, perspiration, vaporization.** Compare **-ition, -tion, -ion**[1].

1219   **-faction** A noun-forming word-final element, derived through Middle English *-faccioun* from Latin *fac(ere)* 'to make, shape, do,' and used in combinations which have as their initial element verbs ending in **-fy** (q.v.):

1. 'An act or process of causing to become or making' as denoted by the combining root: **liquefaction, petrifaction, vitrifaction.**
2. 'A result or state of an action or process': **satisfaction, stupefaction, olfaction.** Related forms: -facient, -factive, -factory, -facture, -(i)fic, -fect, -(i)fy; -factions *(plural)*.

1220 **-ition** A noun-forming word-final element, derived from Latin *-itiō*, *-itiōn-*, itself derived from the Latin past participle of the fourth conjugation (cf. **-ite²**) *-it(us)* and the abstract-noun-forming suffix *-iō*, *-iōn-* (cf. **-ion¹**), used synonymously with **-ation** in learned and semi-learned borrowings: **perdition, lenition, cognition.** Compare **-ation, -tion, -ion¹.** Related forms: -ite, -itious, -itive, -itively; -itions *(plural)*.

1221 **-position** A noun and a noun-forming word-final element, derived from Latin *posit(us), posit(a), posit(um)*—the past participle of *pōn(ere)* 'to put, set in place'—and **-ion¹**, used in forming noun combinations from verbs ending in *-pose* and *-posit*, or adjectives ending in *-posite*. The etymological sense is basic to all the combinations: **exposition, composition, supposition.** Related forms: **-pose, -posit, -posite, -positely, -positional, -positionally.**

1222 **-tention¹** A noun-forming word-final element, derived from Latin *tent(us), tent(a), tent(um)*, the past participle of the verb *ten(ēre)* 'to hold,' and **-ion¹**, used in inherited combinations made from verbs ending in **-tain: abstention, detention, contention.** Related forms: **-tain, -tainment, -tenance, -tinence; -tentions** *(plural)*.

1223 **-tention²** A noun-forming word-final element, derived from Latin *tent(us), tent(a), tent(um)*, the original past participle—later replaced by *tēns(us), tēns(a), tēns(um)*—to the verb *tend(ere)* 'to stretch' and **-ion¹**, used in inherited combinations made from verbs ending in **-tend: contention, intention, attention.** Also, **-tension,** from the later form of the past participle: **extension, pretension, intension.** Related forms: **-tend, -tent, -tense, -tensive, -tentious, -tensious; -tentions, -tensions** *(plurals)*.

1224 **-colon** A noun and a noun-forming word-final element, derived from Greek *kōlon* 'limb, member; the part of the large intestine between the cecum and rectum' or from Greek *kolon* 'food; the part of the large intestine between the cecum and rectum,' used in medical terminology in combinations referring to 'the part of the large intestine between the cecum and rectum' as specified by the combining root: **macro-colon, dolichocolon, mesocolon.** Related forms: **-colonic; -colons, -cola** *(plurals)*.

1225 **-stemon** A noun-forming word-final element, derived from Greek *stēmōn, stēmon-* 'stamen,' originally, 'warp of a standing loom' (cf. the verb *hista(nai), stē(nai)* 'to stand, make stand'), used in botanical taxonomy in naming typical genera of plants 'having a stamen or stamens' of a sort specified by the combining root: **Podostemon, Odostemon, Pterostemon.** Related form: **-stemonous.**

1226 **-zoon** A noun and a noun-forming word-final element, derived from Greek *zōon* 'living being, animal' (cf. the verb *za(ein)* 'to live'), used in zoological terminology to designate 'a living being, an individual member of a complex organism': **spermatozoon, protozoon, microzoon.** Related forms: **-zoal, -zoan, -zoic, -zoid, -zooid, -zoite; -zoa** *(plural)*.

1227 **-hedron** A noun-forming word-final element, derived as a back-formation to Greek *hedr(a)* 'seat, (i.e. something flat to sit on),' meaning 'a geometrical figure or a crystal possessing surfaces or a form' indicated by the combining root: **decahedron, polyhedron, octahedron.** Related forms: **-hedroid, -hedral, -hedric; -hedrons, -hedra** *(plurals)*.

1228 **-dendron** A noun, also a noun-forming word-final element, derived from Greek *dendron* 'tree,' used in scientific terminology in several related senses:
  1. Especially in generic names, 'a tree': **Rhododendron, Philodendron, Phoradendron.**
  2. In neurological terminology, 'a treelike formation': **neurodendron, telodendron.**
  3. 'A stem or part of a stem': **Calamodendron, anodendron, Schizodendron.** Related forms: **-dendrite, -dendritic; -dendra, -dendrons** *(plurals)*.

1229 **-pteron** A noun-forming word-final element, derived from Greek *pteron* 'feather, wing,' used in combinations meaning 'a creature or man-made vehicle with wings' of a sort specified by the combining root: **dipteron, trichopteron, ornithopteron.** Also, **-pter.** Related forms: **-ptera, -pteryx; -pters, -pterons, -ptera** *(plurals)*.

1230 **-tron** A noun-forming word-final element, derived from Greek *-tron*, a noun-forming suffix denoting, chiefly, 'an instrument or means,' used in technical combinations in two main senses:
  1. 'A type of vacuum tube' designated by the combining root: **megatron, dynatron, klystron.**

2. 'A complex device for manipulating subatomic particles': **cyclotron, betatron, bevatron.** Related form: **-trons** *(plural)*.

1231 **-person** A noun and, increasingly, a noun-forming word-final element, derived through French from Latin *persōna* 'mask, character, role, role in life,' and, by extension, 'player of such a role, i.e., a person,' used as a "nonsexist" substitute for **-man** and **-woman** in combinations which have heretofore ended in one or the other of these sex-specific suffixes: **chairperson, salesperson, tradesperson.** Related forms: **-persons, -people** *(plurals)*.

1232 **-ton** A word-final element, derived through Middle English from Old English *tūn* 'farmstead, settlement,' used in place names and the personal names derived from them in the sense 'settlement, town': **Washington, Hamilton, Boston.** Also, **-town.**

1233 **-corn** A word-final element, derived from Latin *corn(u)* 'horn' used in forming nouns and adjectives meaning 'a creature possessing a type of horn or number of horns' or 'possessing a horn or horns' as designated by the combining root: **unicorn, Capricorn, nasicorn.** Related forms: **-cornia; -corns** *(plural)*.

1234 **-town** A noun and a word-final element, derived through Middle English from Old English *tūn* 'enclosure, farmstead, settlement, village,' used in forming place name combinations and the personal names derived from them: **Voluntown, Germantown, Newtown.** Also, **-ton.**

1235 **-o[1]** A noun-forming word-final element, probably derived from the Portuguese-Spanish-Italian masculine noun ending *-o*, with reinforcement from **-o[2]**, used in two senses in current spoken English:
   1. 'A person associated with' something named by the combining root: **medico, politico, bucko.**
   2. 'A person who is or has the qualities of' something denoted by the combining root: **jocko, boyo, magnifico.** Related form: **-os** *(plural)*.

1236 **-o[2]** An interjectory suffix, perhaps derived from *oh*, added to other parts of speech to form combinations essentially imitative or onomatopoetic in character: **cheer(i)o, righto, smacko.**

1237 **-io** A highly productive noun-forming suffix in Latin, added to the past participles of verbs with the sense of 'an action or result of an action' named by the combining root; found in medical terminology in borrowings from Latin: **perspiratio, injectio, defluxio.** Compare **-ion[1],** **-tion.** Related form: **-iones** *(plural).*

1238 **-illo** A noun-forming word-final element, derived from the masculine form of the Spanish diminutive suffix *-illo,* itself derived from the late Latin diminutive suffix *-ill(us),* from earlier Latin *-ell(us),* found in English in borrowings from Spanish: **cigarillo, frijolillo, armadillo.** Compare **-il[2].** Related form: **-illos** *(plural).*

1239 **-mo** A noun-forming word-final element, derived by abstraction from the word *duodecimo* 'a book size in which each sheet of paper used is folded so as to form twelve leaves' *(duodecimo* being derived from Latin *in duodecimō* 'in a twelfth'), used in the terminology of book manufacture after numerals or their names to indicate the number of leaves made by folding a sheet of paper: **16mo, eighteenmo, 32mo.** Related form: **-mos** *(plural).*

1240 **-embryo** A noun and a noun-forming word-final element, derived from Greek *embryo(n)* 'that which grows inside a body, a fetus' (from *en-* 'inside' and *bry(ein)* 'to swell, grow'), used to designate 'an organism in a fetal stage of development' specified by the combining root: **pseudembryo, hemiembryo, typembryo.** Related forms: **-embryonic; -embryos** *(plural).*

1241 **-trap** A noun (and a verb) and a noun-forming word-final element, derived through Middle English *trap, trappe* from Old English *treppe, traeppe* 'snare, trap,' used in several related senses:
1. 'A device for capturing destructive or game animals': **mousetrap, springtrap.**
2. By extension, 'something (as a structure, device, or location) offering possible entrapment or danger': **firetrap, deathtrap, fevertrap.**
3. By relation to *trap* as 'device' or to Middle English *trappe* 'cloth ornament' (modern **trappings**) or 'personal belongings' (modern **traps**), in two combinations meaning 'something of low value': **rattletrap, clattertrap** (both also used as adjectives). Related form: **-traps** *(plural).*

1242 **-ship** A noun-forming word-final element, derived through Middle English *-schipe, -shipe, -ship* from Old English *-scipe* 'nature, condition, quality,' used in combinations in several related senses, specified by the combining root:
1. 'An office or occupation': **judgeship, lectureship, lordship.**
2. 'A skill or art': **craftsmanship, horsemanship, marksmanship.**

3. 'A state or condition': **hardship, apprenticeship, husbandship.**
4. 'A quality of character or behavior': **friendship, rogueship, lackeyship.**
5. 'A state of relationship': **fathership, grandmothership, sonship.** Related form: **-ships** *(plural).*

1243   **-manship**   A noun-forming word-final element, derived from the combination of **-man** and **-ship**, used in the sense of 'the art of' that which is named by the combining root, often with the implication of artfulness: **horsemanship, penmanship, gamesmanship.**

1244   **-carp**   A noun-forming word-final element, derived from Greek *karp(os)* 'fruit,' used in botanical terminology to refer to the fruit or fruit-bearing parts of plants as specified in the combining root: **pericarp, sporocarp, mesocarp.** Related forms: **-carpus, -carpic, -carpous, -carpium; -carps** *(plural).*

1245   **-ar**[1]   An adjective-forming suffix, derived from Latin *-ar(is)*, used in combinations made from nouns:
1. 'Pertaining or belonging to': **polar, vehicular, linear.**
2. 'Existing,' as specified by the combining root: **rectangular, velar, spectacular.**
3. 'Resembling': **mammilar, oracular, annular.** The suffix *-ar* continues a practice in Latin of alternating with *-al* when the first root ended in *-l*. Current English practice affects words ending in *-l* or *-le*; the ending is changed to *-ul* before *-ar* is added: **triangle/triangular.** Also, **-are.** Related forms: **-arly, -arity.**

1246   **-ar**[2]   See **-er**[1].

1247   **-bar**   A noun-forming word-final element, derived from Greek *bar(os)* 'weight, heaviness,' used in meteorological terminology to denote 'atmospheric pressure' as specified by the combining root: **kilobar, millibar, isobar.** Related forms: **-baric; -bars** *(plural).*

1248   **-nuclear**   An adjective and an adjective-forming word-final element, derived from Latin *nuc(u)le(us)* 'kernel, core' (cf. *nux, nuc-* 'nut') and **-ar**[1], used chiefly in biomedical terminology in the sense of 'of, referring, or relating to the nucleus (i.e., central element) in a cell,' as qualified by the combining root: **intranuclear, binuclear, bulbonuclear.** Related forms: **-nucleic, -nucleate.**

1249   **-ular**   An adjective-forming word-final element, derived from Latin *-ulār(is)* (from *-ul(us), -ul(a), -ul(um)* '**-ule**' and *-ār(is)* '**-ar**[1]'), used in forming combinations with Latin and native nouns ending in *-ule*, *-ula*, *-ûlus*, and *-ulum*, as **tubule/tubular, uvula/uvular, oculus/ocular, vestibulum/vestibular,** in either of two senses:

1. 'Pertaining or relating to' that which is specified by the combining root: **vascular, nebular, fibular.**
2. 'Resembling' that which is specified by the combining root: **tabular, perpendicular, modular.** Related form: **-ularly.**

1250   **-spar**   A noun and a noun-forming word-final element, derived by abstraction from *spar-stone* from Old English *spaerstān* 'gypsum,' used in combinations designating 'a lustrous crystalline mineral' of a sort specified by the combining root: **feldspar, fluorspar, calcspar.** Related form: **-spars** *(plural).*

1251   **-er^1**   An extremely productive noun-forming word-final element, derived through Middle English *-ere, -er* from Old English *-ere*, used to form combinations with several related meanings:

1. As the principal agentive suffix in English, it serves to identify persons by the object of their labors or occupations: **baker, tinner, hatter.**
2. 'A person who is a native': **New Yorker, Londoner, Southerner.**
3. 'A person associated with' something specified by the combining root: **highschooler, choirsinger, do-gooder.**
4. 'A person identified by a characteristic' named by the combining root: **six-footer, gladhander, teetotaler.**
5. 'A thing that has' a specific characteristic named by the combining root: **sidewheeler, two-decker, threewheeler.**
6. As a suffix added to verbs, 'a person or device that produces or yields': **slicer, fryer, bearer.** Also, **-ar^2**, perhaps an analogy to Latin *vicar*: **liar** (sense 4), **scholar** (sense 3), **beggar** (sense 6). Related form: **-ers** *(plural).*

1252   **-er^2**   A noun-forming word-final element, derived through Middle English *-ere, -er, -ier* and Anglo-French *-er, -ere* and Old French *-ier* from Latin *-arius* '**-ary^1**,' used to form combinations:

1. 'A person associated with an occupation': **jailer, furrier, soldier.**
2. 'A person who does or performs an action': **sawyer, robber, winebibber.** Also, **-ier, -yer.**

1253   **-er^3**   A word-final element, derived through Middle English *-er, -ere, -re* from Old English, used to form the comparative degree in adjectives and adverbs:

1. In adjectives, derived from Old English *-ra, -re*: **drier, fatter, skinnier.**

2. In adverbs, derived from Old English *-or*: **sooner, faster, quicker.** By convention, the suffix is used chiefly with one-syllable words, sometimes with two-syllable words, and never with those of three or more syllables. In adverbs and adjectives of two or more syllables, the convention is to precede the modifying word (unchanged) with *more*: **soon/sooner, magically/more magically.**

1254   **-er**[4] A word-final element, derived through Middle English from Old English *-r-*, used to form frequentative verbs (those concerned with repeated actions): **flicker, twitter, stutter.** Principal parts: **-ering, -ered, -ered.**

1255   **-eer** A noun-forming word-final element, derived through Middle French *-ier(e)* from Latin *-arius, -aria, -arium* '**-ary**[1],' used to form combinations in two senses:
   1. 'A person who is concerned professionally with, or deals in, or produces' something denoted by the combining root: **munitioneer, mountaineer, engineer.**
   2. 'A contemptible person' in the activity denoted by the first root: **patrioteer, sermoneer, fictioneer.** Compare **-ary**[1]. Related form: **-eers** *(plural).*

1256   **-fer** A word-final element, derived through French *-fère* and Latin *-fer-* from Latin *fer(re)* 'to bear, carry,' used in forming two types of combination:
   1. Verbs, with the meaning, generally metaphoric, of 'carry' as qualified by the combining root: **defer, transfer, refer.** Principal parts: **-ferring, -ferred, -ferred** (in verbs in which the suffix is stressed) and (in verbs in which the stress falls on the syllable preceding the suffix) **-fering, -fered, -fered.**
   2. Nouns, with the meaning 'a creature or thing that bears or carries something' specified by the combining root: **conifer, crucifer, aquifer.** (Note that in nouns and their derivatives formed with **-fer**, the joining vowel *-i-* precedes the suffix). Compare **-phore.** Related forms: **-ference, -ferent, -ferently, -ferential, -(i)ferous, -fera, -ferae; -fers** *(plural).*

1257   **-monger** A noun and a noun-forming word-final element, derived through Middle English *monger(e)* and Old English *manger(e)* from Latin *mang(ō), mang(ōn-)* 'commercial dealer, slave-trader,' used in two senses:
   1. 'A person who sells goods' denoted by the combining root (the usage is essentially British): **ironmonger, clothesmonger, cheesemonger.**

2. 'A person active with something in a petty or contemptible way':
scandalmonger, rumormonger, scaremonger. Related forms:
-mongering; -mongers *(plural).*

1258 **-burger** A noun-forming word-final element (used informally as a
word), derived by abstraction of the *-burger* of the word *hamburger*
(which is actually a combination of *hamburg* i.e., Hamburg, and the
German adjectival suffix *-er*), used in two related but distinct senses:
1. 'A patty of a type' specified by the combining root: **buffaloburger, nutburger, turkeyburger.**
2. 'A sandwich made with a patty of ground beef with an added
ingredient,' usually specified: **cheeseburger, deluxeburger, bacon-
burger.** Related form: **-burgers** *(plural).*

1259 **-pher** A noun-forming word-final element, derived from Greek
pher(ein) 'to carry, bear,' used in combinations designating 'one who
or that which carries or bears something' named by the combining
root: **chronopher, Christopher, telpher.** Also, **-phor, -phore.** Compare
-fer. Related forms: **-phers, -phors, -phores** *(plurals).*

1260 **-grapher** A noun-forming word-final element, derived from Greek
graph(ein) 'to write' (literally, 'to engrave') and **-er**[1], used in the sense
of 'a person who writes about something or writes in a manner'
specified by the combining root: **lexicographer, stenographer,
calligrapher.** Related forms: **-graph, -graphist, -graphic, -graphous,
-graphical, -graphically, -graphy; -graphers** *(plural).*

1261 **-ier** A noun-forming word-final element, derived through French *-ier*
from Latin *-ari(us)*, used in borrowed and native noun combinations
as a suffix of agency meaning 'a person engaged in or connected with'
whatever is denoted by the combining root: **boulevardier, collier,
gondolier.** Compare **-eer, -iere.** Related form: **-iers** *(plural).*

1262 **-mer** A noun-forming word-final element, derived from Greek *mer(os)*
'part, portion,' used in its etymological sense in scientific terminology
as qualified by the combining root: **polymer, isomer, monomer.** Also,
-mere. Related forms: **-meric, -meral, -merous, -merism, -meria,
-meron, -meride, -merite; -mers, -meres** *(plurals).*

1263 **-later** A noun-forming word-final element, derived through Middle
English *-latrer* from Greek *latr(is)* 'servant, especially a servant of
God' and **-er**[1], used in combinations to identify 'a person who
worships or shows intense devotion' to something denoted by the

combining root: **bardolater, bibliolater, heliolater.** Related forms: **-latria, -latry, -latrous; -laters** *(plural).*

1264 **-meter**   A noun, derived through French *mètre* from Greek *metr(on)* 'a measure, that by which a thing may be measured, a proportion,' also used actively in forming noun combinations meaning 'an instrument measuring the quantity, extent, degree, etc.' of something named by the combining root: **dynameter, thermometer, odometer.** Also, **-metre** *(chiefly British).* Related forms: **-metron, -metry, -metria[1], -metric, -metrical, -metrically, -metrics, -metrist; -metra, -meters, -metres** *(plurals).*

1265 **-pter**   A noun-forming word-final element, derived from Greek *pter(on)* 'feather, wing,' used in combinations meaning 'a creature or man-made vehicle with wings' of a sort specified by the combining root: **hymenopter, helicopter, dipter.** (Note: **-pter** is frequently preceded by the joining vowel *-o-* in combinations and should not be confused with **-opter**, in which the *-o-* is an original, integral part of the suffix.) Also, **-pteron.** Related forms: **-pteryx, -ptera; -pters** *(plural).*

1266 **-opter**   A noun-forming word-final element derived from Greek *optēr* 'one who looks' (from *ops*, *op-* 'eye' and the agent-noun suffix *-tēr*), used in medical terminology to refer to 'an instrument, means, or measurement of vision' as specified by the combining root: **diopter, phoropter, oxyopter.** Related forms: **-optic, -opsis, -ope; -opters** *(plural).*

1267 **-ster**   A noun-forming word-final element, derived through Middle English *-ster*, *-stere*, *-estere* from Old English *-estre*, a feminine-gender agent-noun-forming suffix, now used in forming non-gender-specific combinations (though cf. the strictly feminine-gender-expressing suffix **-stress,** from **-ster** and **-ess**):

1. 'A person who handles or operates' something specified by the first root: **teamster, swordster, webster.**
2. 'A person who makes or uses' whatever the combining root denotes: **songster, jester, rimester.**
3. 'A person associated with' something named by the joining root: **mobster, oldster, clubster.** This suffix also appears in numerous English surnames (derived from agent nouns) and place names (derived from surnames derived from agent nouns): **Sangster, Brewster, Webster City.** Related forms: **-stress; -sters** *(plural).*

1268 **-aster[1]**   A noun-forming word-final element, derived from Greek *astēr*, *astr-* 'star,' used in combinations designating 'something star-shaped' specified by the combining root: **amphiaster, Goniaster, spiraster.** Related form: **-asters** *(plural).*

1269   **-aster**^{2} A noun-forming word-final element, derived from Latin *-aster,* a suffix denoting (with distinctly pejorative overtones) 'a partial resemblance' to that which is specified by the combining root: **criticaster, poetaster, philosophaster.** Related forms: **-ast, -astery; -asters** *(plural).*

1270   **-chester**   A word-final element, derived through Old English *caester* from Latin *castr(a)* 'fort, settlement,' used in forming place name combinations, all meaning 'fortified or walled town':
  1. In the primary spelling: **Winchester, Dorchester, Rochester.**
  2. In variant spellings: **Gloucester, Lancaster, Exeter.**

1271   **-minster**   A word-final element, derived through Middle English and Old English *mynster* from Late Latin *monaster(ium),* used to form place name combinations meaning 'location of a monastery church or cathedral' (often, historically, one and the same): **Westminster, Leominster, Axminster.**

1272   **-buster**   A noun and a noun-forming word-final element, derived from the verb *bust* 'burst, break' and **-er**^{2}, used in combinations meaning 'a person or thing that breaks or breaks up something' named by the combining root: **sodbuster, broncobuster, bellybuster.** Related form: **-busters** *(plural).*

1273   **-or**^{1} A noun-forming word-final element, derived through Middle English *-or, -our* and Old French *-eor, -eur* from the Latin agentive suffix *-or, -ātor,* used to denote 'a person or thing that performs an action' specified by the combining root: **councillor, sailor, elevator.** Related form: **-ors** *(plural).*

1274   **-or**^{2} A noun-forming word-final element, derived through Middle English *-or, -our* and Old French *-eur* from the Latin abstract-noun-forming suffix *-or,* used in combinations denoting 'an action, state, condition, result, quality, or characteristic' specified by the combining root: **labor, candor, misdemeanor.** Also, **-our** *(British).* Related form: **-ors** *(plural).*

1275   **-color**   A noun and a noun-forming word-final element, derived through Middle English and Old French *colour* from Latin *color* 'hue, tint, complexion, color,' used in combinations of two sorts:

1. In common nouns, 'a quantity of hues' specified by the combining root: **bicolor, polycolor, multicolor.** Also, **-colour** *(British).*
2. In the copyrighted names of processes involving color film: **Technicolor, Agfacolor, Dufaycolor.** These nouns may all be used adjectivally, in attributive position. Compare **-chrome[1], -chrome[2].** Related forms: **-colored, -coloured; -colors, -colours** *(plurals).*

1276   **-moor**   A noun and a noun-forming word-final element, derived through Middle English *mor* from Old English *mōr* 'unenclosed waste ground,' used in place names: **Dartmoor, Exmoor, Sherramoor.** Also, **-muir.** Related form: **-moors** *(plural).*

1277   **-ator**   A noun-forming word-final element, derived from Latin *-ator*, itself derived from the past participle of the Latin first conjugation (cf. *-ata*) and the agentive suffix *-or* (cf. **-or[1]**). In English, **-ator** is used extensively to denote 'a person or thing that performs an action' specified in the combining root: **adjudicator, mediator, vociferator.** Also, **-ater.** Related forms: **-atory, -atorial, -atorially; -ators** *(plural).*

1278   **-motor[1]**   A noun and a noun-forming word-final element, derived from Latin *mōt(us)*, the past participle of the verb *mōv(ēre)* 'to move' and the agentive suffix **-or[1]**, used in its basic etymological meaning of 'a mover' in combinations designating 'an engine or other motion-creating mechanism' specified by the combining root: **dynamotor, telemotor, pedomotor.** Related forms: **-move, -mobile[1], -mobile[2], -motile, -motility, -mobility, -motive, -motorial, -motoric, -motorially, -motored; -motors** *(plural).*

1279   **-motor[2]**   An adjective-forming word-final element, derived from the adjectival use of the noun and noun-forming suffix **-motor[1]** (from Latin *mōt(us)*, the past participle of the verb *mōv(ēre)* 'to move' and the agent-noun suffix **-or[1]**), used in two related senses:
1. In medical terminology, 'pertaining to the effects of activity produced by or in a part of the body' named by the combining root: **vasomotor, psychomotor, viscerimotor.**
2. 'Pertaining to the number of motors in a device, esp. an airplane': **bimotor, trimotor, multimotor.** Compare **-motor[1].**

1280   **-saur**   A noun-forming word-final element, derived from Greek *saur(os)*, *saur(a)* 'lizard,' used to designate 'an extinct reptile' of a sort specified by the combining root: **brachiosaur, dinosaur, ichthyosaur.** Also, **-saurus.** Related forms: **-sauria, -saurian; -saurs** *(plural).*

1281   **-'s**   A word-final element, derived through Middle English *-s*, *-es* from Old English *-es*, used to form the possessive of nouns:
1. Singular nouns (no matter what they end in): **girl's, boy's, Max's.**
2. Plural nouns not ending in *-s* (**-s¹** or **-es¹**): **men's, children's, geese's.** Compare **-s'.**

1282   **-s'**   A word-final element, derived through Middle English *-s* from Old English *-es*, used to form the plural possessive of virtually all nouns whose singulars do not end in a sibilant (*s*, *sh*, *z*, *ch*, or *x*) or post-consonantal *y*: **girls', boys', lemmas'.** Compare **-es'.**

1283   **-s¹**   A word-final element, derived through Middle English *-es*, *-s* from Old English *-as*, used to form the plurals of virtually all nouns except those ending in a sibilant (*s*, *sh*, *z*, *ch*, or *x*) or post-consonantal *y* (for which, see **-es¹**): **books, cats, boys.**

1284   **-s²**   A proper noun-forming word-final element of uncertain origin, used to give a diminutive sense to the combining root, which may be either a noun, an adjective, or a verb: **Moms, Fats, Cuddles.**

1285   **-s³**   A word-final element, derived from Middle English *-es*, used to form the third person singular present indicative of verbs not ending in a sibilant (*s*, *sh*, *z*, *ch*, or *x*) or post-consonantal *y* (for which, see **-es²**): **walks, runs, sleeps.**

1286   **-s⁴**   A word-final element, derived from Middle and Old English *-es* (a genitive ending), used in the formation of adverbs: **backwards, always, unawares.** See also **-ways, -wards.**

1287   **-mas**   A noun-forming word-final element, derived through the shortening of English *mass*, used in liturgical terminology to name 'a feast day or festival, or the time of its occurrence' specified by the combining root: **Christmas, Candlemas, Lammas.** Related form: **-mases** *(plural)*.

1288   **-tas**   A highly productive noun-forming suffix in Latin with much the same meaning and grammatical function as English **-hood** and **-ness**, found in medical terminology in a number of borrowings from Latin: **extremitas, sanitas, obesitas.** Compare **-ty¹.** Related form: **-tates** *(plural)*.

1289   **-ics**   A noun-forming word-final element, derived from **-ic²** and **-s¹**, used in two kinds of combination:

1. With the sense of 'the systematic formulation of a body of knowledge concerning a science or art, or the science or art itself,' as specified by the combining root: **optics, physics, electronics.** (Combinations of this kind are construed as singulars.)

2. With the sense of 'characteristic actions, activities, or phenomena associated with something' specified by the combining root: **polemics, gymnastics, hysterics.** (Combinations of this kind are generally construed as plurals.) The origin of this double, singular-plural usage is this: first, nouns ending in -ic² came into the language as a result of the substantive use of adjectives which, in Latin and Greek, had been inflected in both the singular and plural to agree with the nouns that they modified. Subsequently, -s¹ was added to -ic³ in nouns derived from neuter plurals in Greek and Latin to mark their etymological plurality, though they remained singular in grammatical usage, partly by association with -ic¹ and -ic², and partly because of their generally collective meanings. The modern vacillation in usage reflects a traditional discomfort with the grammatical number of collectives, exacerbated by the presence of the final -s.

1290   **-technics**   A noun and a noun-forming element, derived from Greek *techn(ē)* 'art, craft' and -ics, used in combinations meaning 'the art, craft, or mechanics' of that which is named by the combining root: **biotechnics, eutechnics, polytechnics.** Also, **-technology, -techny.** Related forms: **-technique, -technic, -technical, -technically.**

1291   **-iatrics**   A noun-forming word-final element, derived from Greek *iatrik(o)s* 'pertaining to or skilled in healing, medical treatment', or, Greek *iatr(os)* 'healer, physician' and -ics, used in English to mean 'medical treatment, healing, or the science of medical treatment or healing' specified by the combining root: **dermiatrics, geriatrics, pediatrics.** Usage varies as to the grammatical construction—singular, plural, or collective—of nouns ending in **-iatrics.** Related forms: **-iatric, -iatry, -iatrically.**

1292   **-physics**   A noun and a noun-forming word-final element, derived from Greek *phys(is)* (the abstract resultative noun formed from the verb *phy(ein)* 'to grow') and -ics, used in the sense of 'the science of the basic matter or nature of' that portion of the natural universe named by the combining root: **biophysics, chemicophysics, iatrophysics.** Related forms: **-physis, -physical, -physial, -physeal, -phyte, -phytal, -phytic, -physite, -phytism.**

1293   **-statics** A noun and a noun-forming word-final element, derived from Greek *stat(ikē)* 'the study of things at rest' (cf. the verb *hista(nai)*, *stē(nai)* 'to stand, make stand') and **-ics**, used to mean 'the study of things in a state of equilibrium in relation to each other,' the general medium of equilibrium being specified by the combining root: **hydrostatics, aerostatics, electrostatics.** Related forms: **-static, -stat, -stasis, -stasy, -stasia, -stasic, -state**[2].

1294   **-therapeutics** A noun and a noun-forming word-final element, derived from *therapeut(ic)* 'of, pertaining, or referring to the treatment of disease' (from Greek *therapeu(ein)* 'to attend, care for' and **-tic**) and **-ics,** used in the sense of 'the art or science of medical treatment by means or techniques' specified by the combining root: **pharmacotherapeutics, mechanotherapeutics, hydrotherapeutics.** Related forms: **-therapia, -therapy, -therapist, -therapeutic, -therapeutically.**

1295   **-es'** A word-final element, derived through Middle English *-es* from Old English *-as*, used to form the plural possessive of nouns ending in a sibilant (*s, sh, z, ch,* or *x*) or post-consonantal *y* (which changes to *i* in combination): **churches', dresses', bodies'.** Related form: **-s'.**

1296   **-es**[1] A word-final element, derived through Middle English *-es, -s* from Old English *-as*, used to form the plural of nouns ending in a sibilant (*s, sh, z, ch,* or *x*), post-consonantal *y* (which changes to *i* in combinations, or, in some cases, post-consonantal *f* (which changes to *v* in combination): **dishes, babies, calves.** Related form: **-s**[1]. The plural ending **-es** also appears in nouns borrowed from the third declensions of Greek and Latin, recapitulating the original nominative/accusative plural endings *-es* (in Greek) and *-ēs* (in Latin): **Galliformes, Serpentes, syntheses.**

1297   **-es**[2] A word-final element, derived from Middle English *-es*, used to form the third person singular present indicative of verbs ending in a sibilant (*s, sh, z, ch,* or *x*) or post-consonantal *y* (which changes to *i* in combination): **misses, washes, defies.** Related form: **-s**[3].

1298   **-myces** A noun-forming word-final element, derived from Greek *mykēs, mykēt-* 'fungus,' used largely in the terminology of botanical nomenclature to designate 'a fungus' of the sort specified by the combining root: **Coccomyces, Discomyces, Chondromyces.** Related forms: **-mycetic, -mycetous, -mycosis, -mycin; -mycetes** *(plural).*

1299   **-alis** An adjective-forming word-final element in Latin, meaning 'pertaining to, related to, characterized by' that which is specified by the combining root (cf. -al¹). The use of this suffix in English is essentially restricted to learned borrowings from Latin and scientific names, generally substantive (cf. -al²): **digitalis, cornealis, cardinalis.** Related forms: **-alia, -ales** *(plurals).*

1300   **-polis**   A noun-forming word-final element, derived from Greek *polis* 'city, state, citizenry,' used in the sense of 'city' as qualified by the combining root: **cosmopolis, megalopolis, metropolis.** Related forms: **-polite, -politan, -politic, -politics, -political, -politically; -polises** *(plural).*

1301   **-dermis**   A noun, derived from Latin *dermis* 'skin' (compare Greek *derma, dermat-*), also used as a noun-forming word-final element denoting 'a layer of tissue or skin' in a location or of a type specified by the combining root: **epidermis, hypodermis, osteodermis.** Related forms: **-derm, -derma, -dermal, -dermic, -dermatic, -dermoid, -dermatoid, -dermatous; -derms, -dermata, -dermises** *(plurals).*

1302   **-sis**   A noun-forming word-final element, derived from Greek *-sis*, an abstract noun-forming suffix denoting 'an action, process, or result' of that which is specified by the combining root—most often, a verb: **analysis, stasis, catalepsis.** Compare **-asis, -iasis, -esis, -osis, -lysis** (all derived originally or by abstraction from forms ending in a thematic, stem, or joining vowel plus **-sis**). Related forms: **-sic, -tic; -ses** *(plural).*

1303   **-asis**   A noun-forming word-final element, derived from Greek *-āsis*, that is, the verbal theme/stem vowel *-ā-* and **-sis**, found in a number of borrowed combinations made from Greek verbs and the noun-forming suffix **-sis** with the basic meaning of 'an action, process, or result' of that which is specified by the combining root: **stasis, basis, allophasis.** Related forms: **-asic, -atic; -ases** *(plural).*

1304   **-phasis**   A noun-forming word-final element, derived from Greek *phasis* 'speech, utterance' (cf. *phanai* 'to speak'), used in its etymological sense as qualified by the combining root: **emphasis, allophasis, heterophasis.** Also, **-phasia, -phasy.** Related forms: **-phatic, -phasic¹; -phases, -phasias, -phasies** *(plurals).*

1305   **-iasis**   A noun-forming word-final element, derived from **-ia¹** and **-sis**, used widely in medical terminology in two related senses, each an extension of the basic meaning, 'a diseased state or condition':

             1. 'A disease produced' as specified by the combining root **amoebiasis, trichiasis, nematodiasis.**

2. 'A disease possessing characteristics' stated by the joining root: **psoriasis, elephantiasis, lithiasis**. Related forms: **-iasic; -iases** *(plural)*.

1306   **-stasis**   A noun and a noun-forming word-final element, derived from Greek *stasis* 'a standing, placement, position' (from the verb *hista(nai)*, *stē(nai)* 'to stand, make stand' and the noun-forming suffix **-sis**), used largely in biomedical terminology in the sense of 'a standing still, stoppage, inhibition' of a sort specified by the combining root: **metastasis, cytostasis, mycostasis**. Related forms: **-stasy, -stasic, -stasia, -state², -static, -statics, -stat; -stases** *(plural)*.

1307   **-esis**   A noun-forming word-final element, derived from Greek *-ēsis*, that is, the verbal theme/stem vowel *-ē-* and **-sis**, found in a number of borrowed combinations made from Greek verbs and the noun-forming suffix **-sis** with the basic meaning of 'an action, process, or result' of that which is specified by the combining root: **enuresis, mimesis, synthesis**. Related forms: **-esic, -etic; -eses** *(plural)*.

1308   **-thesis**   A noun and a noun-forming word-final element, derived from Greek *(ti)the(nai)* 'to put, place, set' and **-sis**, used in a variety of extensions of its etymological sense, as qualified by the combining root: **parenthesis** 'something put off to the side, an aside'; **hypothesis** 'something put underneath, a basis for argument or explanation'; **metathesis** 'the transposition of sounds or letters'; **antithesis** 'something set against something else, an opposite'; **synthesis** 'something made by putting things together'; **prosthesis** 'the replacement of something by something else.' Related forms: **-thetic, -thetical, -thetically; -theses** *(plural)*.

1309   **-synthesis**   A noun and a noun-forming element, derived from Greek *syn(ti)the(nai)* 'to put together' (from *syn-* 'with' and *(ti)the(nai)* 'to put, place, set') and **-sis**, used in a number of extensions of its etymological sense, as: **osteosynthesis** 'the suturing back together of broken bones'; **biosynthesis** 'the formation of a chemical compound in a living creature'; **photosynthesis** 'the formation of a chemical compound in plants through the absorption of light.' Related forms: **-synthetic, -synthetical, -synthetically; -syntheses** *(plural)*.

1310   **-poiesis**   A noun and a noun-forming word-final element, derived from Greek *poiēsis* 'a making, producing' (from the verb *poi(ein)* 'to make, produce, create' and **-sis**), used chiefly in medical terminology to mean 'the creation or production' of that which is named by the combining root: **biopoiesis, leucopoiesis, hormopoiesis**. Also, **-poesis**.

Related forms: -poeia, -peia, -poeic, -poietic, -poetic, -poietical, -poetical, -poietically, -poetically; -poieses, -poeses *(plurals)*.

1311 **-mimesis** A noun, derived from Greek *mimēsis* 'imitation' (from the verb *mimē(sthai)* 'to imitate' and **-sis**), also used as a noun-forming word-final element in medical terminology with the meaning 'simulation, imitation' of that which is named by the combining root: **pathomimesis, necromimesis, neuromimesis.** Related forms: -mimia, -mime, -mimic, -mimetic, -mimical, -mimically; -mimeses *(plural)*.

1312 **-kinesis** A noun, derived from Greek *kinēsis* 'motion' (from Greek *kin(ein)* 'to move' and the abstract noun-forming suffix **-esis**), also used as a noun-forming word-final element in biomedical terminology in two senses:
   1. 'An activation,' its source stated by the combining root: **psychokinesis, akinesis, chemokinesis.**
   2. 'A division, esp. of cells': **diakinesis, catakinesis, heterokinesis.** Also, -cinesis, -kinesia, -cinesia. Related forms: -kinetic, -cinetic, -kinesic, -kinetically, -cinetically; -kineses, -cineses, -kinesias, -cinesias *(plurals)*.

1313 **-phoresis** A noun and a noun-forming word-final element, derived from Greek *phorēsis* 'a bearing or carrying' (cf. *phorein*, the frequentative form of *pherein* 'to bear, carry'), used in the sense of 'a movement or carrying in a medium or in a manner' specified by the combining root: **anaphoresis, pathophoresis, photophoresis.** Related forms: -phore, -phor, -phoric, -phorous, -phoria; -phoreses *(plural)*.

1314 **-stalsis** A noun-forming word-final element, derived from Greek *stalsis* 'contraction' (from the verb *stell(ein)* 'to set in place, bring together, contract' and the noun-forming suffix **-sis**), used in biomedical terminology to refer to 'a contraction in the alimentary canal' whose directionality is specified by the combining root: **diastalsis, anastalsis, peristalsis.** Compare -stole. Related forms: -staltic; -stalses *(plural)*.

1315 **-osis** A noun-forming word-final element, derived both etymologically and by abstraction from Greek *-ōsis*, variously, the theme vowel *-ō-* (of contract verbs with infinitives ending in *-oun*) or the (lengthened) stem vowel *-ō-* of second declension masculine and neuter nouns and adjectives, and the noun-forming suffix **-sis**, used in two senses, the first etymological, the second abstracted:
   1. 'An action, process, or result' specified by the combining root: **hypnosis, metamorphosis, symbiosis.**

2. In medical terminology, 'a pathological condition' specified by the combining root: **cirrhosis, tuberculosis, acidosis.** Related forms: **-otic²; -oses, -osises** *(plurals).*

1316 **-psychosis** A noun and a noun-forming word-final element, derived from Greek *psych(ē)* 'mind, spirit' and **-osis,** used in medical terminology to designate 'a serious mental or emotional disorder' of a sort specified by the combining root: **geriopsychosis, hypopsychosis, neuropsychosis.** Related forms: **-psyche, -psychotic, -psychic; -psychoses** *(plural).*

1317 **-morphosis** A noun-forming word-final element, derived from Greek *morphōsis* 'a forming or shaping' (from the verb *morphoun* 'to form, shape'—itself from the noun *morph(ē)* 'form, shape'—and **-sis,** a suffix denoting the action or result of an action named by the combining verbal root), used in biomedical terminology to denote 'a development or change,' either in something specified or in a manner described by the combining root: **metamorphosis, zoomorphosis, chemomorphosis.** Related forms: **-morph, -morphic, -morphous, -morphism; -morphoses** *(plural).*

1318 **-biosis** A noun-forming word-final element, derived from Greek *biōsis* 'mode of life,' itself derived from *bios* 'life' and **-sis,** used in its etymological sense as specified by the combining root: **aerobiosis, microbiosis, symbiosis.** Related forms: **-biotic, -biotical; -bioses** *(plural).*

1319 **-gnosis** A noun-forming word-final element, derived from Greek *gnosis* 'knowledge, knowing' (cf. Greek *gnōnai* 'to know, perceive'), and used in the sense of 'knowledge, cognition, recognition' of something denoted by the combining root: **prognosis, diagnosis, geognosis.** Related forms: **-gnosia, -gnosy, -gnostic; -gnoses** *(plural).*

1320 **-neurosis** A noun and a noun-forming word-final element, derived from Greek *neur(on)* 'sinew, fiber,' hence, 'nerve' and **-osis,** used in medical terminology to denote 'a disease or abnormal process of the nerves' of a sort specified by the combining root: **toponeurosis, vasoneurosis, myoneurosis.** By abbreviation of one such combination, **psychoneurosis, -neurosis** has taken on the more specific sense, in both medical and popular usage, of 'a mental disorder' usually specified by a preceding noun or adjective: **anxiety neurosis, gastric neurosis, war neurosis.** Related forms: **-neure, -neuron, -neuria,-neuric, -neural, -neurotic, -neurotically, -neuroma; -neuroses** *(plural).*

1321   **-ptosis**   A noun and a noun-forming word-final element, derived from
Greek *ptōsis* 'a fall' (from the verb *pipt(ein)* 'to fall down' and -osis),
used in medical terminology in combinations designating 'a prolapse
or downward displacement of an organ or organs' specified by the
combining root: **laryngoptosis, cardioptosis, panoptosis.** Related
form: **-ptoses** *(plural).*

1322   **-sepsis**   A noun and a noun-forming word-final element, derived from
Greek *sēpsis* 'putrefaction, rotting' (from the verb *sēp(ein)* 'to rot' and
-sis), used in medical terminology in combinations denoting 'decay of
a sort or due to a cause' specified by the combining root: **sarcosepsis,
encephalosepsis, urosepsis.** Related forms: **-septic; -sepses** *(plural).*

1323   **-lipsis**   A noun-forming word-final element, derived from Greek
lip(ein) 'to leave, fail, omit' and -sis, used in a small number of
important technical terms in its rough etymological meaning as
qualified by the combining root: **ellipsis, eclipsis, menolipsis.** Also,
-lipse. Related forms: **-liptic, -liptical, -liptically, -lipsoid; -lipses**
(plural).

1324   **-tripsis**   A noun and a noun-forming word-final element, derived from
Greek *tripsis* 'a rubbing, grinding' (from the verb *trib(ein)* 'to rub,
grind, pound' and -sis), used in medical terminology to denote,
variously, 'a massaging, chafing, friction, wearing away' as specified
by the combining root: **anatripsis, biotripsis, xerotripsis.** Related
forms: **-tribe, -tripsy, -triptic; -tripses** *(plural).*

1325   **-opsis**   A noun-forming word-final element, derived from Greek *opsis*
'vision, appearance' (cf. *ops, op-* 'eye'), used in taxonomic nomenclature to name genera of plants and animals 'having or characterized
by the appearance' of that which is named by the combining root:
Ampelopsis, Fasciolopsis, Scopulariopsis.

1326   **-ysis**   A noun-forming word-final element, derived from Greek *-ysis*,
that is, the verbal stem vowel *-y-* and -sis, found in a number of
borrowed combinations made from Greek verbs and the noun-forming
suffix **-sis** with the basic meaning of 'an action, process, or result' of
that which is specified by the combining root: **lysis, physis, ptysis.**
Related forms: **-ysic, -ytic; -yses** *(plural).*

1327   **-physis**   A noun and a noun-forming word-final element, derived from
Greek *physis*, that is, the verb *phy(ein)* 'to bring forth, produce, make
grow' and the abstract resultative noun-forming suffix -sis, used in
general scientific terminology to denote 'a growth or growing' of a

sort specified by the combining root: **diaphysis, symphysis, zygapophysis.** Related forms: **-physeal, -physial, -physics, -physical, -physite, -phyta, -phyte, -phytal, -phytic, -phytism; -physes** *(plural).*

1328　**-lysis**　A noun and a noun-forming word-final element, derived from Greek *lysis* 'a loosening' from the verb *ly(ein)* 'to loosen' and the abstract-noun-forming suffix *-sis*, used in a variety of combinations, all with the sense—sometimes metaphoric—of 'a breaking down, loosening, decomposition, detachment' of or by means of that which is specified by the combining root: **electrolysis, dialysis, analysis.** Related forms: **-lyse, -lysation, -lyser, -lyze, -lyzation, -lyzer, -lyst, -lysin, -lyte, -lytic, -lytical, -lytically; -lyses** *(plural).*

1329　**-ptysis**　A noun-forming word-final element, derived from Greek *ptysis* 'a spitting' (from the verb *pty(ein)* 'to spit' and *-sis*), used in medical terminology to designate 'a spitting of matter' specified by the combining root: **hemoptysis, albuminoptysis, pyoptysis.** Related form: **-ptyses** *(plural).*

1330　**-itis**　A noun-forming word-final element, derived through Latin from Greek *-itis*, the feminine form of the adjective-forming suffix *-it(ēs)* 'of, belonging or related to' (cf. **-ite**[1]). In English, this suffix has two closely related meanings, both abstracted from the substantive use of adjectives with this ending in Greek used specifically to modify the word *nosos* 'disease':

　　1. 'An inflammation of an organ' specified by a combining root: **bronchitis, phlebitis, appendicitis.**
　　2. 'An abnormal state or condition, or obsession, usually not pathological': **baseballitis, accidentitis, televisionitis.** Related forms: **-itic, -itically; -ites, -itides** *(plurals).*

1331　**-cystitis**　A noun, and frequently a noun-forming word-final element, derived from Greek *kyst(is)* 'sack, bladder' and **-itis**, used in bio-medical terminology to denote 'an inflammation of the bladder or cyst' as specified by the combining root: **cystitis, paracystitis, cholecystitis.** Compare **-cyst.**

1332　**-praxis**　A noun and a noun-forming word-final element, derived from Greek *prāxis* 'a doing, deed, business' (from the verb *prass(ein)*, *pratt(ein)* 'to do, accomplish' and *-sis*), used chiefly in medical terminology in combinations denoting 'a therapeutic treatment involving a method or agent' specified by the combining root: **orthopraxis, chiropraxis, radiopraxis.** Related forms: **-praxia, -pragia, -praxic, -practic, -practics, -practice; -praxises, -praxes** *(plurals).*

1333   **-taxis**   A noun-forming word-final element, derived from Greek *taxis* 'an ordering, arrangement' (from the verb *tass(ein), tatt(ein)* 'to order, arrange' and the noun-forming suffix **-sis**), used in biomedical terminology in two related senses:
   1. 'An order or arrangement' of a nature specified by the combining root: **homotaxis, heterotaxis, biotaxis.**
   2. 'A movement of a simple organism in response to a stimulus' denoted by the combining root: **chemotaxis, heliotaxis, thermotaxis.** Also, **-taxia, -taxy.** Related forms: **-taxic, -tactic; -taxes** *(plural).*

1334   **-(r)rhexis**   A noun and a noun-forming word-final element, derived from Greek *rhēxis* 'a break, tear, bursting' (from the verb *rhēx(ai)* 'to burst, break, tear' and **-sis**), used in medical terminology to denote 'a rupture of a part of the body' specified by the combining root: **gastrorrhexis, hepatorrhexis, hysterorrhexis.** Related forms: **-(r)rhage, -(r)rhagia, -(r)rhagenic; -(r)rhexes** *(plural).*

1335   **-pexis**   A noun and a noun-forming word-final element, derived from Greek *pēxis* 'a making fast, a fastening' (from *pēxesthai* 'to make fast, fasten'), used in medical terminology to denote 'a surgical fixation or a neutralization' of that which is specified by the combining root: **calcipexis, toxicopexis, viropexis.** Also, **-pexy, -pexia.** Related forms: **-pexic; -pexes, -pexias, -pexies** *(plurals).*

1336   **-mixis**   A noun-forming word-final element, derived from Greek *mixis* 'a mingling,' used in biomedical terminology to denote 'a means of mating or conjugation' specified by the combining root: **amphimixis, apomixis, endomixis.** Also, **-mixia, -mixy,** and **-mixie** *(rare).* Related forms: **-mixias, -mixies,** *(plurals).*

1337   **-works**   A noun and a noun-forming word-final element, derived from the plural of *work* (cf. **-work**), though generally construed as a singular in combinations, used in two related senses:
   1. 'A place where work is done, resulting in a product' named by the combining root: **gasworks, sugarworks, ironworks.**
   2. 'The totality of parts that make up a mechanism' named by the combining root: **clockworks, watchworks.**

1338   **-ans**   A word-final element, derived from Latin *-ans* (the nominative singular stem form of the present participle of the first conjugation, to which the oblique case stem *-ant-* may be compared), and used exclusively in learned borrowings, largely in medical terminology, with the meaning '-ing': **communicans, infestans, perforans.** Compare *-ens.* Related form: **-ant.**

1339   **-kins** A word-final element, derived from Middle English *-kin* (a diminutive ending) and *-s* (a patronymic suffix, found in **Adams, Roberts, Jones**), used in forming surnames still current today: **Jenkins, Atkins, Dawkins.**

1340   **-os** A word-final element used to form the masculine singular of Greek nouns of the second declension, found exclusively in technical and learned borrowings from Greek: **megophthalmos, hepatomphalos, megaloceros.** Compare **-us.** Related form: **-oi** *(plural).*

1341   **-ess** A noun-forming word-final element, derived through Middle English and Old French *-esse* from Latin and Greek *-issa* 'a female agent,' used in combinations to denote 'an occupation or status held by a female': **abbess, stewardess, poetess.** Also, **-esse** in borrowed French nouns (**duchesse**). When the ending is added to an agent noun ending in *-er*, the *e* is often syncopated: **porter/portress** or **porteress.** Related form: **-esses** *(plural).*

1342   **-less** An adjective-forming word-final element, derived through Middle English *-les, -lesse* from Old English *-lēas* (from Old English *lēas* 'devoid'), used very commonly to form combinations with two related senses:
1. 'Without something' specified by the combining root: **childless, homeless, timeless.**
2. In adjectives derived from verbs, 'failure or inability to perform or have performed' that which is specified by the combining root: **countless, measureless, priceless.** Related forms: **-lessness, -lessly.**

1343   **-ness**[1] A noun-forming word-final element, derived through Middle English *-nes, -ness, -nesse* from Old English *-nes, -ness, -nyss, -nys,* used extensively to form combinations meaning 'a state, condition, quality, or degree' denoted by the adjective, past participle, or adverb acting as the combining root: **sickness, affectedness, earliness.** Related form: **-nesses** *(plural).*

1344   **-ness**[2] A noun, derived through Middle English *naisse, nasse* from Old English *naessa, naess, nes* 'cape, headland' (compare English *nose*), used also as a word ending in place names with the meaning 'cape, headland, promontory': **Inverness, Strathkinness, Skipness Point.** The usage is chiefly Scots.

1345 **-someness** *See* **-some**[1] and **-ness**[1].

1346 **-fulness** *See* **-ful**[2] and **-ness**[1].

1347 **-stress** A noun-forming word-final element, derived from **-ster** (originally, a feminine-gender agent-noun-forming suffix) and **-ess** (another feminine-gender agent-noun-forming suffix), used in combinations designating 'an occupation or status held by a female,' as specified by the combining root: **songstress, seamstress, impostress.** Related form: **-stresses** *(plural).*

1348 **-us** A word-final element, used to mark the nominative singular of Latin masculine nouns of the second declension, found in scientific terminology and learned borrowings: **stimulus, tonus, bacillus.** Related form: **-i** *(plural).*

1349 **-coccus** A noun, derived through Latin from Greek *kokkos* 'grain, berry,' also used as a noun-forming word-final element in botanical and biological terminology:
   1. 'A plant possessing berries or seeds' of a kind specified by the combining root: **Pterococcus, Oxycoccus, Coelococcus.**
   2. 'A berry-shaped organism' (esp. in the generic names of algae and bacteria): **Staphylococcus, Pneumococcus, asterococcus.** Related form: **-coccic, -coccous, -coccoid; -cocci** *(plural).*

1350 **-pithecus** A noun-forming word-final element, derived from Greek *pithēk(os)* 'ape' and Neo-Latin **-us**, used in zoological nomenclature to designate 'an ape or primate' of the sort specified by the combining root: **Nyctipithecus, Australopithecus, Archeopithecus.** Related forms: **-pithecan, -pithecoid.**

1351 **-ulus** A noun-forming word-final element, derived from the masculine singular form of the Latin diminutive *-ul(us)*, *-ul(a)*, *-ul(um)*, found in scientific terminology and learned borrowings in its etymological sense of 'small one' of a sort specified by the combining root: **globulus, homunculus, modulus.** Also, **-ule.** Related forms: **-ula**[1], **-ulum, -ula**[2], **-ulae, -ulous, -ulic, -ular; -uli, -uluses** *(plurals).*

1352 **-somus** A noun-forming word-final element, derived through scientific Latin from Greek *sōma, sōmat-* 'body' and **-us**, used in medical terminology to designate 'a fetus, especially a fetal monster, with a body' of the sort specified by the combining root: **nanosomus, platysomus, celosomus.** Related forms: **-soma, -some**[3], **-somia, -somal, -somic, -somatic, -somatous, -somatically, -somite; -somi** *(plural).*

1353   **-didymus**   A noun and a noun-forming word-final element, derived through scientific Latin from Greek *didym(os)* 'twin' and **-us**, used in medical terminology in two related senses:

    1.   'A pair of twins joined at a part of the body' specified by the combining root: **gastrodidymus, Xiphodidymus, thoracodidymus.**

    2.   'A fetal monster having a supernumerary organ or supernumerary organs' specified by the combining root: **opodidymus, pygodidymus, atlodidymus.** Related forms: **-didymi, -didymuses** *(plurals).*

1354   **-ous**   An adjective-forming word-final element, derived through Middle English and Old French *-ous* from Latin *-ōs(us)*, *-ōs(a)*, *-ōs(um)* '**-ose**[1],' used extensively in both borrowed and native combinations in a variety of senses:

    1.   'Full of, characteristic of something' specified by the combining root: **wondrous, nervous, dangerous.**

    2.   In chemical terminology, 'an element or compound with a valence lower than the corresponding one ending in *-ic*': **ferrous, cuprous, hypochlorous.** Also, **-eous.** Compare **-ious, -ose**[1]. Related forms: **-ously, -ousness, -osity.**

1355   **-mucous**   An adjective and an adjective forming word-final element, derived from Latin *mūcōsus* 'slimy, runny, snotlike' (from Latin *mūc(us)* 'snot' and the adjectival suffix *-ōs(us)*, *-ōs(a)*, *-ōs(um)* 'full of, endowed with'), used in medical terminology to mean 'containing or composed of mucus' as specified by the combining root: **semimucous, fibromucous, seromucous.** Related forms: **-mucus, -mucic, -mucoid.**

1356   **-cladous**   An adjective-forming word-final element, derived from Greek *klad(os)* 'shoot, small branch' and **-ous**, used in botanical terminology to describe plants 'having shoots or branches' of a sort specified by the combining root: **macrocladous, acanthocladous, orthocladous.**

1357   **-eous**   An adjective-forming word-final element, derived from Latin *-eus* 'composed of, having the qualities or nature of,' used in the sense of 'like, resembling, of the nature of' that which is specified by the combining root: **aqueous, vitreous, sulfureous.**

1358   **-aceous**   An adjective-forming word-final element, derived from Latin *-aceus* 'having the qualities or nature of,' used in two related senses:

    1.   In technical terminology, esp. biological, combinations meaning 'pertaining or belonging to, of the nature of, or characterized by' whatever is denoted by the combining root: **sebaceous, herbaceous, bulbaceous.**

2. In taxonomy, used for forming adjectives from generic names ending in *-acea* and *-aceae:* **Pleurococcaceous, Orchidaceous, Polypodiaceous.** Compare **-acea, -aceae.**

1359   **-ious**   An adjective-forming word-final element, variously derived by abstraction from French and Latinate adjectives ending in *-cious*, *-tious*, and etymological *-ious*, i.e., **-ice**[1] and **-ous, -ice**[2] and **-ous, -tious,** and etymological **-i(us), -i(a),** or **-i(um)** and **-ous.** All combinations have the sense of 'of, pertaining or relating to, or resembling' that which is named by the combining root: **impecunious, parsimonious, bilious.** Compare **-ous, -ose**[1]. Related forms: **-iousness, -iously.**

1360   **-tious**   An adjective-forming word-final element, derived through Middle English and French from Latin *-tiōs(us)*, *-tiōs(a)*, *-tiōs(um)*, that is, the abstract-noun-forming suffix *-tiō* '**-tion**' plus the adjective-forming suffix *-ōs(us)*, *-ōs(a)*, *-ōs(um)* '**-ose**[1],' used in combinations with the sense of 'of, pertaining or relating to, or resembling' that which is specified by the combining root: **infectious, surreptitious, ostentatious.** Compare **-ious, -ous, -ose**[1].

1361   **-itious**   A common adjective-forming word-final element, variously derived (through French) from Latin *-iti(us)*, *-iti(a)*, *-iti(um)* (cf. **-ice**[1]) and **-ous;** Latin *-ici(us)*, *-ici(a)*, *-ici(um)* (cf. **-ice**[2]) and **-ous;** Latinate nouns ending in **-ition** in combination with **-ous;** and Latinate verbs, adjectives, and nouns ending in *-ite* (cf. **-ite**[1] and **-ite**[2]) in combination with **-(i)ous.** All of these combinations retain a roughly etymological sense of 'of, pertaining or relating to, or resembling' that which is named in the combining root: **expeditious, repetitious, ambitious.** Related forms: **-itiously, -itiousness.**

1362   **-philous**   An adjective-forming word-final element, derived from Greek *phil(ein)* 'to love, have an affinity for' and **-ous,** used chiefly in bio-medical terminology in the sense of 'having an affinity, often, an abnormal affinity, for' that which is named by the combining root: **calciphilous, heliophilous, anthrophilous.** Compare **-philic.** Related forms: **-phil, -phile, -philia, -phily, -philiac, -philist, -philism, -philite.**

1363   **-ulous**   An adjective-forming word-final element, derived from Latin *-ulōs(us)*, *-ulōs(a)*, *-ulōs(um)*, a suffix derived from the combination of the diminutive suffix *-ul(us)*, *-ul(a)*, *-ul(um)* (cf. **-ule**) and the augmentative suffix *-ōs(us)*, *-ōs(a)*, *-ōs(um)* (cf. **-ose, -ous**), used in combinations with the sense of 'tending towards a state or condition' specified by the combining root: **credulous, ridiculous, miraculous.** Related forms: **-ulously, -ulousness.**

1364   **-genous** An adjective-forming word-final element, derived from Greek *gen(ea)* 'birth, production, growth' and **-ous**, used in both the active and passive senses 'producing' and 'produced by' that which is specified by the combining root: **hydrogenous, ignigenous, dermatogenous.** Compare **-genic.**

1365   **-venous** An adjective and an adjective-forming word-final element, derived from Latin *vēn(a)* 'vein, artery' and **-ous**, used in medical terminology in the sense of 'of, relating, or referring to veins' of a sort or in a manner specified by the combining root: **pyelovenous, intravenous, paravenous.** Related form: **-venously.**

1366   **-clinous** An adjective-forming word-final element, derived from Greek *klin(ein)* 'to bend, incline' and **-ous**, used in forming adjectives meaning 'pertaining to ancestry' in biological terminology, either, in terms of human inheritance, **matroclinous** or **patroclinous,** or, in terms of botanical inheritance, from stamens and pistils on the same flower (**monoclinous**) or on separate flowers (**diclinous**). Related form: **-cliny.**

1367   **-gynous** An adjective-forming word-final element, derived from Greek *gyn(ē), gynaik-* 'woman' and **-ous**, used in two related senses:
1. 'Pertaining to a quantity of females or to female characteristics' as specified by the combining root: **polygynous, misogynous, androgynous.** Also, **-gynic.**
2. In the terminology of botany, 'pertaining to or possessing female organs' as specified by the combining root: **hexagynous, protogynous, perigynous.** Related forms: **-gyne, -gyn, -gynia, -gyny.**

1368   **-parous** An adjective-forming word-final element, derived from Latin *par(ere)* 'to produce (children)' and **-ous**, used in combinations meaning 'pertaining to the quantity of offspring produced at one time or to the method of gestation' as specified by the combining root: **viviparous, multiparous, oviparous.** Related forms: **-para, -parity, -parously.**

1369   **-fibrous** An adjective, derived from Latin *fibr(a)* 'fiber' and **-ous**, also used in medical terminology as an adjective-forming word-final element meaning 'composed of fibrous tissue and that which is named by the combining root': **mucofibrous, osteofibrous, serofibrous.**

1370   **-androus** An adjective-forming word-final element, derived from Greek *anēr, andr-* 'man' and **-ous**, used chiefly in botanical terminology to mean 'having a stamen or stamens' of a sort or quantity specified by the combining root: **monandrous, heptandrous, polyandrous.** Related forms: **-ander, -andric, -andrism, -andra, -andrian, -andry, -andria.**

1371   **-cerous**   An adjective-forming word-final element, derived from Greek *ker(os)* 'horn' and **-ous,** used in the sense of 'having a horn' of a sort specified by the combining root: **brachycerous, cladocerous, cryptocerous.** Related forms: **-cera, -ceran, -ceratoid.**

1372   **-ferous**   An adjective-forming word-final element, derived through French from Latin *fer(re)* 'to bear, carry' and **-ous,** used to mean 'producing, bearing, carrying' that which is specified by the combining root: **herbiferous, somniferous, lactiferous.** (Note that the joining vowel *-i-* precedes this suffix in combination.) Related forms: **-fer, -fera, -ferae, -ference, -ferent, -ferently, -ferential.**

1373   **-gerous**   An adjective-forming word-final element, derived from Latin *ger(ere)* 'to bear, carry, sustain' and **-ous,** used synonymously with the more frequently occurring **-ferous** in general scientific terminology to form combinations meaning 'bearing, possessing, or characterized by' that which is specified by the combining root: **peltigerous, dentigerous, cystigerous.** Related form: **-ger.**

1374   **-florous**   An adjective-forming word-final element, derived from Latin *flōs, flōr-* 'a blossom, flower' and **-ous,** used in the sense of 'having blossoms or flowers' of a sort specified by the combining root: **tubiflorous, pluriflorous, anomaloflorous.** Related forms: **-flora, -florate.**

1375   **-vorous**   An adjective-forming word-final element, derived from Latin *vor(āre)* 'to swallow, swallow up, eat' and **-ous,** used in the sense of 'of or referring to feeding on' that which is specified by the combining root: **herbivorous, carnivorous, omnivorous.** Related forms: **-vore, -vora.**

1376   **-pus**   A noun-forming word-final element, derived from Greek *pous, pod-* 'foot,' used in a few forms designating 'a creature having a type or number of feet' specified by the combining root: **dipus, octopus, platypus.** Compare **-pod, -pode, -ped, -pede.** Related forms: **-podal, -podial, -podous; -puses, -pi, -pods, -podes** *(plurals).*

1377   **-anthropus**   A noun-forming word-final element, derived from Greek *anthrōp(os)* 'man, person' and **-us,** used to form the generic names of primates: **Pithecanthropus, Africanthropus, Meganthropus.** Related forms: -anthrope, -anthropic, -anthropically, -anthropoid, -anthropism, -anthropist, -anthropy.

1378 **-hippus** A noun and a noun-forming word-final element, derived through Linnaean Latin from Greek *hipp(os)* 'horse' and **-us,** used in zoological taxonomies to designate members of the 'horse' group as specified by the combining root: **Eohippus, Pliohippus, Mesohippus.**

1379 **-saurus** A noun-forming word-final element, derived through Latin from Greek *saur(os), saur(a)* 'lizard' and **-us**[1], used to designate 'an extinct reptile or class of extinct reptiles' as specified by the combining root: **brontosaurus, Brontosaurus, megalosaurus.** Related forms: **-saur, -sauria, -saurian; -sauruses, -sauri** *(plurals).*

1380 **-ways** An adverb-forming word-final element, derived from Middle English *way(e)s, wey(e)s,* the genitive case form of *wey(e)* 'path, road' and, by extension, 'means, manner,' used in the sense of 'in the direction, course, way, or manner' specified by the combining root: **endways, longways, always.** Compare **-wise** (which, while similar in usage and phonetic composition, is etymologically unrelated to **-ways**).

1381 **-t** A word-final element, derived by the process of regular phonetic change from **-ed,** used to mark the past tense and past participle of some 'strong' verbs which end (or, historically, ended) in a voiceless consonant: **slept, left, fought.** By and large, **-ed** is the past marker in all but the most conservative English verbs, no matter what their phonetic shape. Related form: **-ed.**

1382 **-chat** A verb and a noun, derived through Middle English *chatt(en)* from *chatter(en)* 'to chatter,' used as a noun ending in forming common names for birds: **woodchat, whinchat, stonechat.** Related form: **-chats** *(plural).*

1383 **-throat** A noun and a noun-forming word-final element, derived through Middle English *throte* from Old English *throte, throtu* 'throat, i.e., the part of the alimentary canal between the mouth and the esophagus, or its outer covering,' used in the latter sense in combinations functioning as the common names of birds: **starthroat, ashthroat, bluethroat.** Related form: **-throats** *(plural).*

1384 **-crat** A noun-forming, word-final element, derived through French *-crate* from Greek *krat(os)* 'strength, power,' used in several related senses:

1. 'An advocate of a theory of government' specified by the joining root: **theocrat, democrat, sociocrat.**
2. 'A member or supporter of a political party': **Dixiecrat, Democrat, Technocrat.**
3. 'A member of a group or social class' specified by the first root: **aristocrat, autocrat, bureaucrat.** Also, **-crate.** (As with other suffixes beginning with a consonant cluster, **-crat** is preceded by a joining vowel, usually *-o-*, in combination.) Related forms: **-cratic, -cratism, -cracy; -crats** *(plural).*

1385   **-stat**   A noun-forming word-final element, derived from Greek *stat(os)*, the past participle of the verb *hista(nai)*, *stē(nai)* 'to stand, make stand,' used in several related senses:
1. 'An apparatus or device for keeping stationary' something denoted by the combining root: **gyrostat, barostat, cryostat.**
2. 'An instrument for the regulation of' something named by the combining root: **thermostat, humidistat, hemostat.**
3. 'An apparatus for the reflection in a single direction of' something specified by the combining root: **heliostat, siderostat, coelostat.**
4. 'A device for studying in a state of rest' something denoted by the combining root: **hydrostat, orbitostat, microstat.**
5. 'An agent inhibiting or stopping the growth of' that which is named by the combining root: **fungistat, mycostat, bacteriostat.** Related forms: **-state², -static, -statics, -statically, -stasia, -stasic, -stasis, -stasy; -stats** *(plural).*

1386   **-tract**   A verb-forming word-final element, derived from Latin *tract(us)*, *tract(a)*, *tract(um)*, the past participle to the verb *trah(ere)* 'to haul, drag, draw,' used in a number of common verbs and their derivatives, all with the basic sense of 'draw, pull,' (generally metaphorically) in a direction indicated by the combining root: **extract, attract, retract.** Principal parts: **-tracting, -tracted, -tracted.** Related forms: **-tractive, -traction.**

1387   **-fect**   A word-final element, derived from the past participle of *-fic(ere)*, a combining form of Latin *fac(ere)* 'to do, make, shape,' used in its etymological sense, as qualified by the combining root, to form both verbs and (deverbative) nouns: **infect, effect, affect.** Related forms: **-fex, -fective, -fectious, -fection, -fecture, -fectory, -facient, -factory, -faction, -facture, -(i)fic, -(i)fy.**

1388   **-ject**   A verb-forming word-final element, derived from Latin *-ject(us)*, the past participle to the combining form of the verb *jac(ere)* 'to throw,' used in a number of borrowed verbs of high frequency of occurrence in English with some sense of 'throw' qualified by the combining root:

1. 'To throw' in the manner or direction indicated by the first root: **eject** 'throw out'; **reject** 'throw back'; **inject** 'throw in'; **deject** 'throw down'; **interject** 'throw between'; **disject** 'throw about, scatter'; **traject** 'throw across'; **subject** 'bring or cast under.'
2. In one combination, 'to speak' in the sense of 'to speak against': **object**. Principal parts: **-jecting, -jected, -jected**. Related forms: **-jection, -jector, -jectory**.

1389 **-flect** A verb-forming word-final element, derived through Middle English *-flect(en)* from Latin *flect(ere)* 'to bend, turn, flex,' used in borrowed verb combinations familiar for several centuries. Each combination makes use of part of the etymological meaning.

1. 'To turn': **deflect** 'turn down or aside'; **reflect** 'turn back'; **inflect** 'turn in' (one modern meaning).
2. In two terms from medical terminology, 'to bend': **anteflect** 'bend forward'; **circumflect** 'bend around.' Also, **genuflect** 'bend the knee.' Principal parts: **-flecting, -flected, -flected**. Related forms: **-flex, -flexion, -flection, -flective, -flector**.

1390 **-spect** A word-final element, derived from Latin *spect(āre)* 'to look at, observe, watch,' used in borrowed combinations often acting as nouns or verbs without any distinction in basic form: **aspect, inspect, prospect**. The word ending also yields one adjective combination: **circumspect**. Principal parts: **-specting, -spected, -spected**. Related forms: **-spectful, -spection, -spective**.

1391 **-sect** A verb-forming word-final element, derived from Latin *sect(us)*, *sect(a)*, *sect(um)*, the past participle of the verb *sec(āre)* 'to cut, divide,' used in its etymological sense as qualified by the combining root: **dissect, resect, vivisect**. Principal parts: **-secting, -sected, -sected**. Related forms: **-section, -sectional, -sectionally**.

1392 **-strict** A verb-forming word-final element, derived from Latin *strict(us)*, *strict(a)*, *strict(um)*, the past participle of the verb *string(ere)* 'to draw tight, compress, restrict,' used in a number of common borrowings and their derivatives in its etymological sense as qualified by the combining root: **restrict, constrict, astrict**. Principal parts: **-stricting, -stricted, -stricted**. Compare **-stringe, -strain**. Related forms: **-striction, -strictive**.

1393 **-struct** A verb-forming word-final element, derived from Latin *strŭct(us), strŭct(a), strŭct(um)*, the past participle of the verb *stru(ere)* 'to place together, arrange, build,' used in a number of common borrowings and their derivatives in its etymological sense, as qualified by the combining root: **construct, obstruct, superstruct.** Principal parts: **-structing, -structed, -structed.** Related forms: **-structure, -struction, -structive.**

1394   **-et**   A noun-forming word-final element, derived through Middle English *-et* and Old French *-et, -ete* from the (unattested) common Romance masculine diminutive suffix **-itto, *-etto*, used in two types of combination:
   1. As a diminutive: **giblet, ringlet, floweret.**
   2. To denote 'a group,' the size being specified by the first root: **quartet, septet, duet.** Also, **-etto.** Compare **-ette.** Related form: **-ets** *(plural).*

1395   **-let**   A noun-forming word-final element, derived through Middle English and Middle French *-let, -lette* from Old French *-el* (cf. **-el**) and *-et, -ette* (cf. **-et, -ette**), used in two senses, each reflecting the etymological diminutive meaning of this double suffix:
   1. As a diminutive suffix: **gablet, bulblet, booklet.**
   2. As a denotation of 'an article worn on a part of the body' specified by the combining root: **wristlet, anklet, corselet.** Related form: **-lets** *(plural).*

1396   **-uret**   A noun-forming word-final element, derived from scientific Latin *-uretum*, formerly used in chemical terminology to designate a binary compound (cf. the more modern and widely used **-ide**): **sulphuret, phosphuret, carburet.** Related forms: **-uretize, -uretic; -urets** *(plural).*

1397   **-set**   A word ending, derived from Old English *sǣta* 'a holding of land,' used in place of name combinations with the meaning 'pasture': **Somerset, Dorset, Basset.**

1398   **-craft**   A noun and a noun-forming word-final element, derived through Middle English from Old English *cræft* 'strength, skill,' used in a number of senses:
   1. 'A skill, especially a manual skill, or art, or the product of that skill or art,' the medium or means used therein being specified by the combining root: **woodcraft, leathercraft, handicraft.**
   2. 'A nonmanual skill or art, or its product,' the medium or means being specified by the combining root: **wordcraft, statecraft, witchcraft.**
   3. An extension, apparently, of the 17th-century nautical usage

'small craft' (a boat that could be handled without any great skill) to name sea-going and, in more modern times, air-going vehicles: **aircraft, spacecraft, Hovercraft.** Related forms: **-craftsman, -craftswoman, -craftsmanship; -crafts** (*plural, chiefly sense 1*).

1399 **-thrift** A noun and a noun-forming word-final element, derived in its present form through Middle English from Old Norse with the meaning 'prosperity, success': it is used in verb-noun combinations in which **thrift** is the object of a transitive verb and the total meaning is condemnatory: **spendthrift, wastethrift, wantthrift.** Related form: **-thrifts** (*plural*).

1400 **-right** A word and a word ending, derived through Middle English *riht, right* from Old English *riht*, cognates of words in many languages from the Indo-European root **reg* 'to move in a straight line,' used in forming adjective combinations meaning 'in accord with fitness, justice, honesty': **upright, forthright, downright.** Related forms: **-rightness, -rightly.**

1401 **-wright** A noun and a noun-forming word-final element, derived through Middle English *wright, wrighte* from Old English *wyrhta, wryhta* 'worker, maker' (cf. *wyrc(an)* 'to work,' *worhte* 'worked'), used in a number of related senses, each specified by the combining root:

   1. 'A worker in wood': **shipwright, wainwright, woodwright.**

   2. 'A worker in other materials': **candlewright, tilewright, butterwright.**

   3. 'A producer of things requiring intellectual rather than manual skills': **playwright, versewright, songwright.** Related form: **-wrights** (*plural*).

1402 **-posit** A verb and a verb-forming word-final element, derived from Latin *posit(us), posit(a), posit(um)*, the past participle of the verb *pōn(ere)* 'to put, place, set,' used in combinations sharing the basic sense of 'set down, set forth': **contraposit, deposit, oviposit.** Principal parts: **-positing, -posited, -posited.** Related forms: **-pose, -posal, -posite, -position, -positional, -positionally, -positive, -posure, -pound.**

1403 **-n't** A word ending, formed by contraction of *not*, used chiefly after modal auxiliaries in forming negative combinations: **didn't, mustn't, haven't.** Also, **-nt** (chiefly British).

1404 **-ant** A word-final element, derived from Latin *-ant-* (the oblique case stem form of the present participle of the first conjugation), used to form adjectives, often used substantively:

1. 'Performing an action' named by the combining root: **dessicant, intoxicant, attendant.**
2. 'Promoting an action or process' named by the joining root: **febricant, retardant, petrificant.**
3. 'In a state or condition' labeled by the first root: **vacant, significant, communicant.**
4. 'Something used for a purpose or that performs an action' named by the combining root: **denudant, deodorant, lubricant.**
5. 'Something that promotes an action' named by the joining root: **dessicant, eradicant, vesicant.**
6. 'Something or someone acted upon' in a manner noted by the first root: **confidant, anesthesiant, geldant.** Compare -ent. Note that many English words ending in -*ant* and -*ent* (and -*ance* and -*ence*) have come from Latin via French in which these suffixes happen to be homophonous, as they are in English, which has resulted in some measure of confusion in the match between orthography and etymology. Related forms: **-antly, -ently, -ancy, -ency; -ants, -ents** *(plurals).*

1405   **-ent**   A word-final element, derived from Latin -*ens*, -*ent*- (the stem form of the Latin present participle of verbs of the second and third conjugations), used in English to form two related combinations:

1. In nouns, with the sense of 'something or someone that performs an action' specified by the combining root (generally a verb from the second or third conjugation of Latin): **resident, student, intransigent.**
2. In adjectives, often used substantively, with the sense of 'behaving as, or doing' that which is specified by the combining root: **absorbent, incumbent, somnolescent.** Compare -ant. Related forms: **-ence, -ance, -ency, -ancy, -ential, -antial, -entially, -antially.**

1406   **-jacent**   An (obsolete) adjective, and an adjective-forming word-final element, derived from Latin *jacens, jacent*-, the present participle of the verb *jac(ēre)* 'to lie,' used in the sense of 'lying' in a place or position specified by the combining root: **adjacent, circumjacent, interjacent.**

1407   **-escent**   An adjective-forming word-final element, derived from the Latin present participle ending **-escens, -escent**- to verbs with the inchoative-progressive infix -*(e)sc*-, used in two senses:

1. 'Beginning to be, slightly': **pubescent, adolescent, somnolescent.**

2. 'Emitting or reflecting light in a manner' stated by the combining root: **opalescent, incandescent, fluorescent.** Related forms: **-esce, -escence, -escently.**

1408   **-lucent**   An adjective and an adjective-forming word-final element, derived from Latin *lūcens, lūcent-* 'shining,' the present participle of the verb *lūcēre* 'to shine' (from *lūx, lūc-* 'light'), used in the specific sense of 'light-admitting' as qualified by the combining root: **translucent, radiolucent, omnilucent.** Related form: **-lucence.**

1409   **-scient**   An adjective-forming word-final element, derived from Latin *sciens, scient-*, the present participle of the verb *scīre* 'to know,' used in a number of borrowings in its etymological sense as qualified by the combining root: **nescient, omniscient, parviscient.** Related forms: **-science, -sciently.**

1410   **-valent**   An adjective-forming word-final element, derived from Latin *valens, valent-*, the present participle to the verb *val(ere)* 'to be healthy, be worth,' used in two senses:
   1. Generally, 'having a power, force, or worth' specified by the combining root: **equivalent, ambivalent, prevalent.**
   2. In chemical terminology, 'having a valency (i.e., a combining power)' of a magnitude specified by the combining root: **monovalent, divalent, trivalent.** Related forms: **-valence, -valency.**

1411   **-ulent**   An adjective-forming word-final element, derived from Latin *-ulent(us), -ulent(a), -ulent(um)*, an adjective-forming suffix meaning 'full of, characterized by' that which is specified by the combining root, used in its etymological sense: **turbulent, fraudulent, virulent.** Related form: **-ulency.**

1412   **-ment**   A word-final element, derived through Middle English and French from the Latin suffix *-ment(um)*, originally used to form agent and action nouns from verbs, now used to form nouns and denominative verbs in several related senses:
   1. 'An action, process, or skill' denoted by the combining root: **rearmament, tournament, management.**
   2. 'A result, object, or agent of an action' named by the joining root: **entombment, enthrallment, agreement.**
   3. 'The means or instrument of an action': **implement, medicament, reinforcement.**
   4. 'The place of an action' named by the first root: **battlement, ambushment, settlement.**
   5. 'A state or condition' specified by the first root: **bewilderment,**

predicament, bereavement. The verb combinations show no change in basic form: cement, compliment, lament. Principal parts: -menting, -mented, -mented. Related forms: -mentum *(singular)*; -menta, -menti, -ments *(plurals)*.

1413   -current   An adjective and an adjective-forming word-final element, derived from Latin *currens, current-*, the present participle of the verb *curr(ere)* 'to run,' used in the sense of 'running, flowing, happening,' as qualified by the combining root: concurrent, recurrent, occurrent. Related forms: -cur, -currence.

1414   -potent   An adjective and an adjective-forming word-final element, derived from Latin *potens, potent-*, the present participle of the verb *posse* 'to be able,' used in the sense of 'able to act in a way or do something' specified by the combining root: omnipotent, viripotent, alymphopotent. Related forms: -potence, -potency, -potential.

1415   -fluent   An adjective and also an adjective-forming word-final element, derived from the Latin present participle *fluens, fluent-* of the verb *flu(ere)* 'to flow,' used, often metaphorically, to mean 'flowing' in a manner or direction specified by the combining root: refluent, mellifluent, circumfluent. Related forms: -fluct, -flux, -fluction (from the past participle), -fluence.

1416   -loquent   An adjective and an adjective-forming word-final element, derived from Latin *loquens, loquent-* 'speaking, saying,' the present participle to the verb *loquī* 'to speak, say,' used in combinations in its etymological sense, as qualified by the combining root: eloquent, pauciloquent, breviloquent. Related forms: -loquence, -loquently.

1417   -vent   A word-final element, derived from Latin *vent(us), vent(a), vent(um)*, the past participle to the verb *ven(īre)* 'to come,' used in a handful of common words:
   1.   In nouns, 'a coming, coming to pass, coming together': advent, event, convent.
   2.   In two verbs and their derivatives, 'to come upon, to keep from coming to pass': invent, prevent. Principal parts: -venting, -vented, -vented. Related forms: -vene, -ventive, -vention.

1418   -mont   A word-final element, derived through Middle English *monte, munte* and Old English *munt* from Latin *mons, mont-* 'hill, mountain,' used in both borrowed and native place names: Vermont, Sawmont, Strathmont. Also, -mount.

1419   **-glot**   A word-final element, derived from Attic Greek *glot(ta)* (cf. Ionic Greek *glossa*) 'tongue,' used to form adjective combinations, usually used substantively, with the meaning 'possessing knowledge of or able to make use of a language or languages,' the number being specified by the combining root: **monoglot, polyglot, tetraglot.** Related forms: **-glottic, -glottal, -glossa, -glossal; -glots** *(plural)*.

1420   **-foot**   A noun and a word-final element, derived through Middle English from Old English *fōt* 'foot,' originally, 'the organ attached to the bottom of the leg at the ankle,' now having many extended senses as well, some of which are found in combinations:

  1.   In adjectives, 'being twelve inches (or a multiple thereof) long,' the multiple being specified by the combining root: **one-foot, two-foot, ten-foot.**
  2.   In nouns, 'an animal having a foot' of a sort specified by the combining root: **webfoot, duckfoot, finfoot.**
  3.   In nouns, 'a kind of foot or a condition of the feet' specified by the combining root: **flatfoot, clubfoot, skewfoot.**
  4.   In nouns, a word-final element in combinations functioning as the common names of plants: **pigeonfoot, harefoot, nettlefoot.**
  Related forms: **-footed; -feet, -foots** *(plurals)*.

1421   **-root**   A noun and a noun-forming word-final element, derived through Middle English from Old English *rōt* 'root, i.e., the part of a plant that grows underground,' used in combinations functioning as the common names of plants and tubers: **arrowroot, bloodroot, snakeroot.** Compare **-wort** (ultimately from the same etymon). Related form: **-roots** *(plural)*.

1422   **-pot**   A noun, a denominative verb, and a noun-forming word-final element, derived from Middle English *pott* 'a (small) vessel or container,' used in its etymological sense, as qualified by the combining root: **gluepot, tosspot, crackpot.** Compare **-pan.** Related form: **-pots** *(plural)*.

1423   **-rupt**   A verb-forming word-final element, derived from Latin *rupt(us)*, *rupt(a)*, *rupt(um)*, the past participle of the verb *rump(ere)* 'to break, tear, burst,' used in a number of common borrowings and their derivatives in its etymological sense (sometimes metaphorical) as qualified by the combining root: **erupt, corrupt, bankrupt.** Principal parts: **-rupting, -rupted, -rupted.** Related form: **-ruption.**

1424   **-vert**   A word-final element, derived from Latin *vert(ere)* 'to turn,' used in its etymological sense in two kinds of combination:

1. In verbs, 'to turn (often metaphorically)' in a direction specified by the combining root: **convert, revert, invert.**
2. In nouns, 'a person who has turned (metaphorically)' in a direction specified by the combining root: **animadvert, pervert, convert.** Principal parts: **-verting, -verted, -verted.** Related forms: **-verse, -version; -verts** *(plural)*.

1425   **-port**   A noun and a word-final element, derived through French from Latin *port(a)* 'gateway, passageway, entranceway,' used in two ways:
1. In plain noun combinations, 'an entranceway, shelter,' of a sort specified by the combining root: **carport, airport, seaport.**
2. In place names, in its etymological sense of 'entranceway, haven': **Newport, Westport, Newburyport.** Related form: **-ports** *(plural)*.

1426   **-wort**   A noun and a noun-forming word-final element, derived through Middle English *wurt, wort, wert* from Old English *wyrt* 'root, plant, herb,' used widely in combinations designating 'a herbaceous plant' of a sort specified by the combining root: **garlicwort, beewort, buglewort.** Related form: **-worts** *(plural)*.

1427   **-st**[1]   A word-final element, derived through Middle English from Old English *-est, -ast, -st*, used formerly to mark the second person singular indicative of verbs: **wast, hast, canst.** Also, **-est**[1].

1428   **-st**[2]   A word ending, derived from *-est* (the superlative suffix), used as a symbol to mark an ordinal number after the figure *1*: **1st, 21st, 31st.**

1429   **-ast**   A noun suffix, derived through Middle English *-aste* from Latin and Greek *-ast(es)* (equivalent to English **-ist**[1]), used to form combinations meaning 'a person connected with an activity' specified by the combining root: **enthusiast, gymnast, utopiast.** Related form: **-asts** *(plural)*.

1430   **-blast**   A noun-forming word-final element, derived from Greek *blast(os)* 'germ, bud, shoot,' used extensively in scientific—and especially medical—terminology to denote 'a germinal or embryonic stage of development' as specified by the combining root: **endoblast, myeloblast, zygotoblast.** Related form: **-blasts** *(plural)*.

1431   **-clast**   A noun-forming word-final element, derived from Greek *klast(ēs)* 'one who breaks, crushes' (from Greek *klān* 'to break, crush'), used in its etymological sense:
1. 'A person who breaks or destroys' something designated by the combining root: **mythoclast, biblioclast, iconoclast.**

2. In medical terminology, 'something that breaks or destroys, esp. a tool for breaking' something specified by the joining root: **osteoclast, lithoclast, odontoclast.** Related forms: **-clastic, -clasis, -clasia, -clase; -clasts** *(plural).*

1432 **-plast** A noun-forming word-final element, derived from Greek *plast(os),* the past participle of the verb *plassein, plattein* 'to mold, form, shape,' used largely in medical terminology to denote 'a primitive cell, a substantial mass within a cell' as specified by the combining root: **endoplast, sarcoplast, leukoplast.** Compare **-plasm.** Related forms: **-plastic, -plastia; -plasts** *(plural).*

1433 **-est**[1] An archaic word-final element, derived through Middle English from Old English *-est, -ast, -st,* used formerly to mark second person singular indicative verbs: **biddest, enoblest, diddest** (also **didst**). Also, **-st**[1]. The usage is still found in the King James Bible and certain liturgical works.

1434 **-est**[2] A word-final element, derived through Middle English from Old English *-st, -est, -ost,* used to mark the superlative degree of adjectives and adverbs of one syllable: **biggest, soonest, oldest.** The ending is used with some two-syllable words: **oftenest, luckiest, remotest.** More common with words of two or more syllables is the use of **most** before the base form of the adjective or adverb.

1435 **-fest** A noun-forming word-final element, derived from German *Fest* 'festival, holiday,' and used in two related senses:
    1. 'A festive gathering, often for competition': **Oktoberfest, song-fest, sängerfest.**
    2. 'A session, usu. informal, for an activity' specified by the joining root: **gabfest, beerfest, slugfest.** Related form: **-fests** *(plural).*

1436 **-ist** A highly productive agent-noun-forming word-final element, derived through Middle English and Old French *-iste* and Latin *-ist(a)* from the Greek agentive suffix *-ist(ēs),* used in several related senses:
    1. 'A doer or performer' as specified by the combining root: **pianist, monologist, archivist.**
    2. 'A student or practitioner of an art or science' named by the combining root: **pharmacist, physicist, gynecologist.**
    3. 'A supporter of a doctrine, theory, system, or policy' denoted by the combining root: **classicist, Communist, Methodist.**
    4. 'A person identified by qualities' specified by the combining root: **sadist, Anglophobist, pessimist.** Related forms: **-ism** *(senses 1, 3, 4),* **-istic, -istically; -ists** *(plural).*

1437   **-theist**   A noun and a noun-forming word-final element, derived from Greek *the(os)*, *the(a)* 'god, goddess' and **-ist**, used in the sense of 'one who believes in a god or gods' of a sort or in a quantity specified by the combining root: **atheist, monotheist, zootheist.** Related forms: **-theism, -theistic, -theistically; -theists** *(plural)*.

1438   **-iatrist**   A noun-forming word-final element, derived, in a rather roundabout way, from Greek *iatr(os)* 'physician, healer' and **-ist** (through *iatr(y)* and **-ist**, *iatr(y)* itself being derived from *iatr(os)* and **-y³**), used to mean 'a physician or healer' of a type specified by the combining root: **podiatrist, psychiatrist, physiatrist.** Also, **-iatrician.** Related forms: **-iatry, -iatric, -iatrical, -iatrics; -iatrists** *(plural)*.

1439   **-sist**   A verb-forming word-final element, derived from Latin *sist(ere)*, the reduplicated form of *st(āre)* 'to stand, remain, be,' used in a number of common borrowings in its etymological sense as qualified by the combining root: **consist, subsist, exist.** Principal parts: **-sisting, -sisted, -sisted.** Related forms: **-sistent, -sistence, -sistency.**

1440   **-linguist**   A noun and a noun-forming word-final element, derived from Latin *lingu(a)* 'tongue, language' and **-ist**, used in combinations denoting 'a person accomplished in language or languages' as specified by the combining root: **polylinguist, bilinguist, monolinguist.** Related forms: **-linguistic, -linguistical, -linguistically; -linguists** *(plural)*.

1441   **-most**   An adjective, derived from Middle English *mast*, *most*, the superlative to 'many, much; more,' also used as an adjective-forming word-final element in its etymological sense of 'the superlative degree' of that which is specified by the combining root, usually a word designating position or location: **uttermost, leftmost, hindmost.**

1442   **-gnost**   A noun-forming word-final element, derived as a back formation from Greek *gnōstikos* 'one skilled at knowing, judging' (itself derived from *gnōs(is)* 'knowledge' and **-ic¹**, from Greek *gnōnai* 'to know'), used to mean 'one who knows,' the field of specialty being noted by the combining root: **geognost, bibliognost, siderognost.** Related forms: **-gnosia, -gnosy, -gnosis, -gnostic, -gnostically; -gnosts** *(plural)*.

1443   **-hurst**   A word ending, derived through Middle English *hurst* from Old English *hyrst* 'wooded hill,' used in forming place names and the surnames derived from them: **Bensonhurst, Lakehurst, Sissinghurst.**

1444   **-cyst**   A noun, derived through Latin from Greek *kyst(is)* 'bag, bladder,' used widely in biomedical terminology as a noun-forming word-final element to denote 'a pouch, sack, or bladder' as specified by the combining root: **ovicyst, fibrocyst, hematocyst.** Also, **-cystis.** Related forms: **-cystic; -cysts** *(plural).*

1445 **-naut** A noun-forming word-final element, derived from Greek *naut(ēs)* 'sailor' (cf. Greek *naus* 'ship'), used to designate 'a traveler in a manner or by means' named by the combining root: **Argonaut, astronaut, aeronaut.** Related forms: **-nautical, -nautics; -nauts** *(plural).*

1446 **-shaw** A word-final element, derived through Middle English *shawe* from Old English *scaga* 'small wood,' used in forming place name combinations and the surnames derived from them: **Bradshaw, Crashaw, Robertshaw.**

1447 **-dew** A noun and a noun-forming word-final element, derived through Middle English from Old English *dēaw* 'dew, i.e., condensed moisture from the air,' used in a handful of combinations denoting 'deposits or excretions of moisture resembling dew, or that which produces same': **honeydew, mildew, sundew.** Related form: **-dews** *(plural).*

1448 **-bow** A noun and a noun-forming word-final element, derived through Middle English *bowe* from Old English *boga* 'arch, bow,' used in several related senses, all sharing the basic meaning of 'something bent into a simple curve':
1. 'A weapon (shaped like an arch)': **handbow, longbow, crossbow.**
2. 'Something shaped like an arch': **elbow, saddlebow, oxbow.**
3. 'An arch-shaped phenomenon caused by light shining on water droplets': **rainbow, mistbow, frostbow.** Related form: **-bows** *(plural).*

1449 **-low** A word ending, derived from Old English *hlāw, hlǣw* 'hill, mound,' used in forming place name combinations and the surnames descended from them: **Winslow, Ludlow, Marlowe.** Also, **-lowe.**

1450 **-stow** A word-final element, derived through Middle English *stowen* 'to put in a place' from Old English *stow* 'a place,' used in forming place name combinations meaning 'a place': **Elstow, Netherstow, Chepstow.**

1451 **-x** A word-final element, used to mark the plurals of certain masculine nouns and adjectives in French, found exclusively in borrowings from French: **beaux, plateaux, adieux.** For many of these nouns, -s[1] serves as an alternate plural marker.

1452 **-plex**   A word-final element used to form adjectives and nouns, derived from Latin *plex(us)*, *plex(a)*, *plex(um)*, the past participle of the verb *plect(ere)* 'to fold, braid' (whence **-plicate** and **-ply**), used in several related senses, all having something to do with folding, layering, or braiding:

    1. Generally, 'having many or few layers or strands' as specified by the combining root: **complex, simplex, duplex.**

    2. In the field of communications, 'of or pertaining to a system allowing messages to be transmitted and received simultaneously': **simplex, diplex, multiplex.**

    3. In medical terminology, 'a network' of a sort specified by the combining root: **cerviciplex, brachiplex, veniplex.** Also, **-plexus.** Compare **-plicate, -ply, -ple.** Related forms: **-plexity, -plectic; -plexes, -plexus, -plexuses** *(plurals).*

1453 **-thrix**   A noun-forming word-final element, derived from Greek *thrix*, *trich-* 'hair,' used in zoological and botanical taxonomy to name lower orders of animals and plants that are hairlike, inhabit hair or hairlike structures, as specified by the combining root: **Cladothrix, Endothrix, Thiothrix.** Also, **-trichum.** Related forms: **-tricha, -trichia, -trichan, -trichic, -trichous; -thrices, -tricha** *(plurals).*

1454 **-trix**   A noun-forming word-final element, derived from Latin *-trix*, *-tric-*, the feminine gender form corresponding to the masculine gender agent suffix *-tor*, used in two quite different senses:

    1. 'A female who performs or is associated with an activity' named by the combining root: **aviatrix, mediatrix, executrix.**

    2. In the terminology of geometry, 'a straight line' of a type specified by the combining root: **matrix, bisectrix, tractrix.** Also, *(sense 1)* **-trice, -ess.** Related form: **-trices** *(plural).*

1455 **-mastix**   A noun-forming word-final element, derived from Greek *mastix*, *mastig-* 'whip,' used in zoological taxonomy to designate 'flagellates' of a sort specified by the combining root: **Helkesimastix, Trichomastix, Copromastix.** Compare **-mastigina, -flagellata.**

1456 **-pteryx**   A noun-forming word-final element, derived from Greek *pteryx*, *pteryg-* 'wing, winglike growth,' used in botanical and zoological taxonomy to name plants and animals 'having wings or winglike parts' as specified by the combining root: **Aphanapteryx, Dipteryx, Micropteryx.** Compare **-ptera.** Related forms: **-pter, -pteron, -pterygium.**

1457 **-y**[1]   A highly productive adjective-forming word-final element, derived through Middle English from Old English *-ig*, used in combinations in several senses, each as specified by the combining root:

1. 'Characterized by or composed of': **muddy, clayey, juicy.**
2. 'Resembling': **folksy, smeary, fleecy.**
3. 'Tending or inclined to': **sleepy, nebby, hungry.**

1458 $-y^2$ A noun-forming word-final element, derived through Middle English and Anglo-Norman *-ie* from Latin *-i(um)*, used to form combinations, usually from verbs, meaning 'an instance of an action' specified by the combining root: **entreaty, perfidy, subsidy.** Related form: **-ies** *(plural)*.

1459 $-y^3$ A noun-forming word-final element, derived through Middle English and Old French *-ie* from Latin and Greek *-ia* and, in some forms, Greek *-ē*, used in three major senses:

1. 'An activity or place of business' characterized by the goods or service noted in the first root: **grocery, bakery, laundry.**
2. In combinations involving initial roots from French, Latin, or Greek, 'a specified state, condition, or quality': **monogamy, appendectomy, democracy.**
3. 'A whole body or group' (usually construed as plural): **clergy, soldiery, episcopacy.** Related form: **-ies** *(plural)*.

1460 $-y^4$ A noun-forming word-final element, probably derived from the (unattested) Common Romance diminutive suffix **-itt(a)*, **-ett(a)* (cf. **-et** and **-ette**), used more or less interchangeably with **-ie** as a diminutive ending, usually affectionate: **Betsy, Charly** (also **Charley, Charlie**), **lovey.** Compare **-ie.**

1461 **-bay** A noun and a word-final element, derived through Middle English *baye* from Middle French *baie* 'sea inlet,' used in forming place name combinations: **Boothbay Harbor, Torbay, Falmouth Bay.** In contemporary spellings, combinations using *-bay* are often two words, esp. if the bay is not part of the place or city itself —**Torbay,** a city; **Tor Bay,** a large bay to the south of the city.

1462 **-lay** A verb and a verb-forming word-final element, derived through Middle English *lay(en)*, *legg(en)* from Old English *lecg(an)* 'to cause to lie,' used in its etymological sense, as qualified by the combining root: **inlay, overlay, mislay.** Principal parts: **-laying, -laid, -laid.** (Note: the *-lay* of *delay* and *relay* (as in *relay race*) is derived from a different etymon, namely, Latin *lax(āre)* 'to loosen, leave, let go' through Old French.)

1463 **-way** A noun and a noun-forming word-final element, derived through Middle English *wey(e)* from Old English *weg* 'path, road,' used in its etymological sense, the kind of 'path' or 'road' being specified by the combining root: **highway, floodway, seaway.** This suffix also appears in the adverb **away** (from Old English *aweg* 'on the way') and its derivative (by shortening) *way.* Compare **-ways.** Related form: **-ways** *(plural).*

1464 **-by** A (proper) noun-forming word-final element, derived from Old English *bȳ* 'farm, village,' and akin to or borrowed from various Scandinavian terms (Danish and Swedish *by* and Icelandic *bȳr*), used extensively in place name combinations meaning 'town or village': **Whitby, Ashby, Appleby.** Many of the place names were used as surnames in medieval times and after. Compare **-boro, -borough, -burg, -burgh, -bury.**

1465 **-cy** A noun-forming word-final element, derived by abstraction from nouns like *residency* (from the Latin present participle *resident-* and **-ia**[1]), *advocacy* (from the Latin past participle *advocat-* and **-ia**[1]), *democracy* (from Greek *demokrat(os)* and **-ia**[1]), and *fallacy* (from Latin *fallacia,* from *fallac-* and **-ia**[1]). This element is now generally used to form abstract nouns with the meaning 'a state, condition, office, or act of' that which is specified by the combining root, usually, though not always, a verb or adjective ending in *-t* or *-te:* **bankruptcy, celebacy, captaincy.** Compare **-acy, -y**[3]. Related form: **-cies** *(plural).*

1466 **-acy** A noun-forming suffix, derived from the Latin word endings *-ācia* and *-ātia,* denoting 'a state or quality' specified by the combining root: **legacy, diplomacy, primacy.** Related form: **-acies** *(plural).*

1467 **-cracy** A noun-forming word-final element, derived through French *-cratie* and Latin *-cratia* from Greek *krat(os)* and **-ia**[1], used in several related senses:
  1. A form of government' specified by the combining root: **democracy, hagiocracy, mobocracy.**
  2. 'A political or social class' denoted by the combining root **aristocracy, gerontocracy, bureaucracy.**
  3. 'A social or political theory': **theocracy, technocracy, isocracy.** Related forms: **-crat, -cratic, -cratism, -cratically; -cracies** *(plural).*

1468 **-ancy** An abstract noun-forming suffix, derived from Latin *-ant-* (the stem form of the present participle of the first conjugation) and **-ia**[1], used in forming combinations concerned with condition or agency. All are formed from adjectives ending in *-ant*.

1. 'A state or quality' denoted by the combining root: **blatancy, militancy, vagrancy.**
2. 'An example of a quality or state': **expectancy, exorbitancy, exultancy.** Related forms: **-ance, -ence, -ency; -ancies** *(plural)*.

1469 **-mancy** A noun-forming word-final element, derived through Middle English *-mancie, mauncie,* Old French *-mancie,* and Latin *-mantia* from Greek *manteia* 'divination, prophecy,' used to form combinations meaning 'divination in a manner, through a medium, or by a means' specified by the combining root: **geomancy, bibliomancy, chiromancy.** Also, **-mantia.** Related forms: **-mancer, -mantic, -mantical, -mantically; -mancies, mantias** *(plurals)*.

1470 **-ency** An abstract noun-forming suffix, derived from Latin *-ent-* (the stem form of the present participle of the second and third conjugations) and **-ia**[1], used in forming combinations concerned with conditions or agency. All are formed from adjectives ending in *-ent*:

1. 'A quality or state' indicated by the joining root: **decency, absorbency, dependency.**
2. 'A person or thing possessing a quality or being in a state' indicated by the first root: **residency, superintendency, latency.**
3. 'An instance of a quality or state': **emergency, contingency, regency.** Also, **-ence, -ance, -ancy.** Related forms: **-ent, -ant, -ential, -entially; -encies, -ancies** *(plurals)*.

1471 **-ploidy** A noun and a noun-forming word-final element, derived from **-ploid** and **-y**[3], used in the terminology of cytobiology to mean 'the condition of having a number of chromosome sets' specified by the combining root: **diploidy, amphidiploidy, triploidy.** Compare **-ploid.**

1472 **-ey** A word-final element, derived from Old English *ieg* 'islet,' used in forming place names with the extended meaning 'water, river; island': **Fowey, Nether Stowey, Sawrey.**

1473 **-ley** A word-final element, derived through Middle English *lee, leye* from Old English *lēah* 'pasture,' used to form place name combinations in its etymological sense: **Alderley, Sedgeley, Northleigh.** Also, **-leigh.**

1474 **-fy** A verb-forming word-final element, derived through French *-fi(er)* from Latin *-fic(are),* a combining form of the verb *fac(ere)* 'to do, make,' used in two related senses:

1. 'To form into or make into something' specified by the joining root: **casefy, liquefy, mummify.**
2. 'To make similar to, to give the attributes of something' indicated by the first root: **Yankeefy, calcify, Frenchify.** Also, **-ify.** The first form follows initial roots ending in a vowel; the second, historically the same as the first with the addition in Latin times of the infix *-i-*, is used when initial roots end in a consonant or, sometimes, *-y* (**person/personify; mummy/mummify**). Thus, the adjective **rare** becomes **rarefy.** But the influence of the other form has also permitted the creation of **rarify** and **casify,** making the **-fy** form become rare. Principal parts: **-ifying, -ified, -ified.** Related forms: **-(i)fic, -(i)fice, -(i)ficient, -(i)ficial, -(i)ficate, -(i)fication, -(i)ficative.**

1475 **-phagy** A noun-forming word-final element, derived from Greek *phag(ein)* 'to eat' and **-y**[3], used in biomedical terminology to mean 'the act or practice of eating' that which is named by the combining root: **anthropophagy, cytophagy, geophagy.** Also, **-phagia.** Related forms: **-phag, -phage, -phagi, -phagic, -phagically, -phagism, -phagist, -phagous; -phagias, -phagies** *(plurals).*

1476 **-logy** A noun-forming word-final element, frequently preceded by the joining vowel *-o-*, derived through Middle English and Old French *-logie* from Latin *-logia* from Greek *log(os)* 'word, speech, discourse' (from the verb *leg(ein)* 'to put in order, speak, read (aloud), reason') and **-ia**[1], used in several related combinations, the particular meaning of each being specified by the combining root:
1. 'An oral or written work or action': **trilogy, necrology, apology.**
2. 'A science, or a body of information, knowledge, or doctrine': **psychology, archaeology, theology.**
3. 'A discourse or treatise': **methodology, chronology, eulogy.** Also, **-logia.** Related forms: **-logue, -log, -logic, -logical, -logetic, -logism, -logian, -logician, -logist, -logistic, -logically, -logistically, -logetically; -logies, -logias** *(plurals).*

1477 **-ergy** A noun-forming word-final element, derived from Greek *erg(on)* 'work' and **-y**[3], used in the following senses:
1. 'An action, instance of work': **synergy, energy, bionergy.**
2. 'An effect or result': **allergy, anergy, anabolergy.** Related forms: **-ergic, -ergetic, -ergetical, -ergetically; -ergies** *(plural).*

1478 **-urgy** A noun-forming word-final element, derived through Latin from Greek *-ourg-*, a combining form of *erg(on)* 'work,' and **-y**[3], used to mean 'the art or technique of working in a manner or with a tool or material' named by the combining root: **thaumaturgy, metallurgy, dramaturgy**. Compare **-ergy**. Related forms: **-urge, -urgist, -urgic, -urgical, -urgically; -urgies** *(plural)*.

1479   **-machy**   A noun-forming word-final element, derived from Greek *mach(ē)* 'battle, fight' and -y³, used in combinations meaning 'warfare or contest between opponents or by means of agents' specified by the combining root: **psychomachy, tauromachy, logomachy**. Also, **-machia**. Related forms: **-mach, -machic, -machist, -machical; -machies, -machias** *(plurals)*.

1480   **-(r)rhaphy**   A noun-forming word-final element, derived from Greek *rhaph(ē)* 'a seam, stitch' and -y³, used in medical terminology to denote 'a suturing in place' of an organ specified by the combining root: **orchidorrhaphy, perineorrhaphy, laryngorrhaphy**. Also, **-(r)rhaphia**. Compare **-pexis**. Related forms: **-(r)rhaphias, -(r)rhaphies** *(plurals)*.

1481   **-graphy**   A noun-forming word-final element, derived from Greek *graph(ē)* 'a marking with lines, writing' (from Greek *graph(ein)* 'to write,' originally, 'to engrave') and -y³, used in two senses, the one an extension of the other:
   1. 'A kind or process of writing or printing' denoted by the combining root: **stenography, lithography, photography**.
   2. 'A descriptive art or science' specified by the combining root: **oceanography, lexicography, epigraphy**. Related forms: **-graph, -grapher, -graphist, -graphia, -graphic, -graphous, -graphical, -graphically; -graphies** *(plural)*.

1482   **-trophy**   A noun-forming word-final element, derived from Greek *troph(os)* 'that which feeds, food, nourishment' (from the verb *treph(ein)* 'to feed') and -y³, used in medical terminology to denote 'a condition of nutrition, nurture, nourishment, or growth' specified by the combining root: **eutrophy, atrophy, chemotrophy**. Also, **-trophia**. Related forms: **-troph, -trophic, -trophous, -trophically; -trophies, -trophias** *(plurals)*.

1483   **-strophy**   A noun-forming word-final element, derived from Greek *stroph(ē)* 'a turning, twist' (from the verb *streph(ein)* 'to turn, twist') and -y³, used in medical terminology to denote 'a twisting or turning' of an organ or in a manner specified by the combining root: **exstrophy, angiostrophy, syringosystrophy**. (Note that the word *dystrophy* and its derivatives do not contain this suffix being, rather, combinations of *dys-* and **-trophy.**) Also, **-strophe.** Related forms: **-strophic; -strophies, -strophes** *(plurals).*

1484   -sophy A noun-forming word-final element, derived from Greek *soph(os)* 'wise, clever, skilled' and -y^3, used in the sense of 'a body of received wisdom, knowledge, or theory' about that which is specified by the combining root: **theosophy, pantosophy, psychosophy.** Related forms: **-sophic, -sophical, -sophically; -sophies** *(plural).*

1485   -pathy A noun-forming word-final element, derived from Greek *path(ein)* 'to suffer, be sensitive to' and -y^3, used in two major senses:
1. 'A suffering, sensitivity, or illness' of a sort specified by the combining root: **cardiopathy, sympathy, telepathy.**
2. 'A therapy or system of therapy for suffering' as specified by the combining root: **osteopathy, homeopathy, allopathy.** Also, (*sense 2*) **-pathology.** Related forms: **-path, -pathia, -pathic, -pathetic, -pathize; -pathies, -pathias** *(plurals).*

1486   -worthy An adjective and an adjective-forming word-final element, derived through Middle English from Old English *wyrðe,* a dialectal form of *weorth, weorð(e)* 'of value,' used in the sense of 'fit for' that which is named by the combining root: **seaworthy, praiseworthy, noteworthy.**

1487   -sky A noun-forming word-final element, derived from Slavic *-ski* (a diminutive suffix used with masculine proper names), used in both borrowed and native combinations, usually with a humorous connotation: **drosky, marrowsky, buttinsky.** Also, **-ski.** Related forms: **-skies, -skis** *(plurals).*

1488   -ly[1] An adjective-forming word-final element, derived through Middle English *-lich, -ly, -li* from Old English *-līc, -lic,* used in combination with nouns and adjectives in two major senses:
1. 'Like' that which is specified by the combining root: **teacherly, manly.**
2. 'Repeated or recurring at an interval' specified by the combining root: **hourly, yearly.**

1489   -ly[2] An adverbial suffix, derived from Middle English *-liche, -ly, -li* and taken from the Old English adjectival forms *-līc* and *-lic* and the adverbial marker *-e*; apart from grammatical suffixes like those marking tense, **-ly[2]** is the most active suffix in English. It adds the meaning 'in the manner specified' to the combining root, which is usually an adjective: **quickly, improbably, submissively.**

1490 **-megaly**   A noun-forming word-final element, derived from Greek *meg(as)*, *megal-* 'great, large' and **-y³**, used in medical terminology to denote 'an enlargement of a part of the body' specified by the combining root: **adrenomegaly, splenomegaly, nephromegaly.** Also, **-megalia.** Related forms: **-megalies, -megalias** *(plurals)*.

1491 **-cephaly**   A noun-forming word-final element, derived from Greek *kephal(ē)* 'head' and **-y³**, used in medical terminology to denote 'a condition of the head' as specified by the combining root: **cymbocephaly, strophocephaly, nanocephaly.** Also, **-cephalia.** Related forms: **-cephalic, -cephalism; -cephalies, -cephalias** *(plurals)*.

1492 **-phily**   A noun-forming word-final element, derived from Greek *phil(ein)* 'to love, have an affinity for' and **-y³**, used in two closely related senses:

   1. 'A fondness for something' named by the combining root: **bibliophily, iconophily, ornithophily.**
   2. In biochemical terminology, 'an affinity for something' named by the combining root: **photophily, xerophily, hydrophily.** Compare **-philia.** Related forms: **-phil, -phile, -philiac, -philous, -philism, -philist, -philite, -philic; -philies, -philias** *(plurals)*.

1493 **-arily**   See **-ary²** and **-ly²**.

1494 **-orily**   See **-ory²** and **-ly²**.

1495 **-ally**   An adverbial compound suffix, composed of **-al¹** and **-ly²**, used to form adverbs from adjectives ending in *-ic*. These usually do not have alternative forms in *-ical*. **Judaically, nomadically, aerobically.**

1496 **-ically**   See **-ical** and **-ly²**.

1497 **-ially**   See **-ial** and **-ly²**.

1498 **-urally**   See **-ure, al¹,** and **-ly²**.

1499 **-fully**   See **-ful²** and **-ly²**.

1500 **-enly**   See **-en¹** and **-ly²**.

1501 **-poly**   A noun-forming word-final element, derived from Greek *pōl(ein)* 'to exchange, sell,' and **-y³**, used in the terminology of economics and other learned vocabularies to describe varieties of 'ownership or control of goods for sale' as specified by the combining root: **monopoly, oligopoly, bibliopoly.** Related forms: **-pole³, -polist, -polistics, -polistically; -polies** *(plural).*

1502 **-ply** A verb and a verb-forming word-final element, derived through French *plier* from Latin *plic(āre)* 'to fold' (itself derived from the combining form of the verb *plect(ere)* 'to fold'), used in a small number of frequently occurring borrowings in various extensions of its etymological sense: **reply, apply, multiply.** This suffix may also be used in its etymological sense in adjectival combinations meaning 'having folds or layers' in a number specified by the combining root: **two-ply, three-ply, four-ply.** Principal parts: **-plying, -plied, -plied.** Compare **-plicate, -plex, -ple.** Related forms: **-plice, -plicity, -plication.**

1503 **-gamy** A noun-forming word-final element, derived from Greek *gam(os)* 'marriage' and **-ia¹,** used in several related senses:
1. 'A type of marriage' specified by the first root: **bigamy, monogamy, endogamy.**
2. 'A union for propagation': **microgamy, syngamy, hologamy.**
3. 'Possession of organs for reproduction' as indicated by the combining root: **cleistogamy, homogamy, dichogamy.** Related forms: **-gamist, -gametism, -gamic, -gamous, -gamistic; -gamies** *(plural).*

1504 **-nomy** A noun-forming word-final element, derived through Middle English and Old French *-nomie,* from Greco-Latin *-nomia,* from Greek *nom(os)* 'customs, law, body of received knowledge' and **-ia¹,** used in the sense of 'the body of laws or received knowledge of a field' specified by the combining root: **agronomy, taxonomy, economy.** Related forms: **-nome, -nomic, -nomous, -nomical, -nomically; -nomies** *(plural).*

1505 **-gnomy** A noun-forming word-final element, derived from Greek *gnōm(ē)* 'means of knowing' (cf. Greek *gnōnai* 'to know, perceive') and **-y³,** used to mean 'the art, science, or means of judging' something specified by the joining root: **physiognomy, chirognomy, pathognomy.** Related forms: **-gnomic, -gnomical, -gnomically, -gnomonic, -gnosia, -gnosis, -gnostic.**

1506 **-tomy** A noun-forming word-final element, derived from Greek *tom(ē)* 'a cutting' and **-y³,** used in medical terminology to denote 'a surgical incision' in a part of the body named by the combining root: **osteotomy, craniotomy, phlebotomy.** Related forms: **-tome, -tomize, -tomist, -tomic, -tomical, -tomically, -tomous; -tomies** *(plural).*

1507 **-ectomy** A noun-forming word-final element, derived from Greek *ektomē* 'a cutting out' (from Greek *ek* 'out' and *temnein* 'to cut'), used in medical terminology to designate 'the surgical removal' of that which is named by the combining root: **tonsillectomy, appendectomy, thyroidectomy.** Related forms: **-ectome, -ectomize; -ectomies** *(plural).*

1508 **-stomy** A noun-forming word-final element, derived from Greek *stom(a), stom(at-)* 'mouth,' hence, 'opening' and **-y³**, used in medical terminology to denote 'a surgical opening' made in an organ specified by the combining root: **hepatostomy, ovariostomy, colostomy.** (Note that this suffix is to be distinguished from the etymologically unrelated suffix **-tomy**, which refers to surgical incision.) Related form: **-stomies** *(plural).*

1509 **-thermy** A noun-forming word-final element, derived from Greek *therm(ē)* 'heat' and **-y³**, used in medical terminology in two senses:
1. 'The state of body temperature' specified by the combining root: **hypothermy, endothermy, hyperthermy.**
2. 'The generation of body heat' as specified by the combining root: **diathermy, radiothermy, photothermy.** Also, **-thermia.** Related forms: **-thermic, -thermal, -thermous, -therm; -thermies, -thermias** *(plurals).*

1510 **-onymy** A noun-forming word-final element, derived from Aeolian Greek *onym(a), onym(at-)* 'name' (cf. Attic-Ionic *onoma, onomat-*) and **-y³**, used in two related senses:
1. 'A type of word or name' specified by the combining root: **homonymy, synonymy, antonymy.**
2. 'The study of a type of words or names' denoted by the combining root: **polyonymy, eponymy, paedonymy.** Related forms: **-onym, -onymous, -onymously, -onymic, -onymically; -onymies** *(plural).*

1511 **-phany** A noun-forming word-final element, derived from Greek *phain(ein)* 'to appear, show (through), shine (through)' and **-y³**, used largely in the terminology of theology to mean 'an appearance, manifestation' as specified by the combining root: **epiphany, theophany, christophany.** Related forms: **-phan, -phane, -phanic, -phanous; -phanies** *(plural).*

1512 **-botany** A noun and a noun-forming word-final element, derived from Greek *botan(ē)* 'grass, herbs' and **-y³**, used in combinations differentiating among specialized areas in 'the science of plant life': **geobotany,**

paleobotany, ethnobotany. Related forms: -botanic, -botanical, -botanically; -botanies *(plural)*.

1513   **-geny**   A noun-forming word-final element, derived from Greek *gen(eia)* 'birth, growth, production' and -ia[1], used in general scientific terminology to mean 'production, generation, origin' as specified by the combining root: **biogeny, ontogeny, eugeny.** Compare **-gony.** Related forms: **-gen, -gene, -genic, -genous, -geneous, -genically, -genate, -genite, -genist, -genism; -genies** *(plural)*.

1514   **-techny**   A noun-forming word-final element, derived from Greek *techn(ē)* 'art, craft' and -y[3], used in combinations referring to 'the art, craft, or mechanics' of the area named by the combining root: **zootechny, hydrotechny, pyrotechny.** Also, **-technology, -technics.** Related forms: **-technique, -technic, -technical, -technically; -technies, -technologies, -technics** *(plurals)*.

1515   **-gony**   A noun-forming word-final element, derived from Greek *gon(ē)* 'that which is born' (cf. Greek *genea* 'birth') and -y[3], used largely in bio-medical terminology to denote 'birth or origin' from the source specified by the combining root: **bibliogony, gamogony, andromerogony.** Related forms: **-gen, -genic, -gonic, -geny; -gonies, -genies** *(plurals)*.

1516   **-phony**   A noun-forming word-final element, derived from Greek *phōn(ē)* 'sound' and -y[3], used in two related senses:
   1. 'Sound, both musical and natural': **cacophony, antiphony, euphony.**
   2. 'A speech disorder' of a type specified by the joining root: **aphony, kinesiphony, tracheophony.** Also, **-phonia.** Related forms: **-phone, -phonic, -phonous, -phonious, -phonetic; -phonies, -phonias** *(plurals)*.

1517   **-tony**   A noun-forming word-final element, derived from Greek *ton(os)* 'that which stretches or is stretched, tension' (whence scientific Latin *tonus*) and -y[3], used in medical terminology to denote 'a condition or degree of tonus or motor control of a sort or in a region of the body' specified by the combining root: **typhlatony, nephratony, vagotony.** Also, **-tonia.** Related forms: **-tone, -tonic, -tonous; -tonies, -tonias** *(plurals)*.

1518   **-boy**   A noun, derived from Middle English *boi*, *boy* 'male child, male servant, knave,' used as a noun-forming word-final element with the meaning 'a male child, adolescent,' or, occasionally, 'an adult engaged in an activity' metonymically named by the combining root: **gooseboy** 'a boy who tends geese'; **choirboy** 'a boy who sings in a choir'; **houseboy** 'a male hired to perform a variety of duties about a house or hotel'; rarely a 'boy' but, rather, a young man or adult male. Compare **-man, -woman, -maid, -girl**. Related form: **-boys** *(plural)*.

1519 **-therapy** A noun and a noun-forming word-final element, derived from Greek *therapeia* 'a service done to someone, especially to a sick person' (from the verb *therapeu(ein)* 'to serve, attend, take care of'), used in two related senses, each specified by the combining root:
1. 'Medical treatment of a disease or disorder' by means or techniques specified by the combining root: **chemotherapy, hypnotherapy, pyretotherapy.**
2. 'Medical treatment of a disorder or area of the body' specified by the combining root: **psychotherapy, oncotherapy, pyretotherapy.** Also, **-therapia** *(archaic)*. Related forms: **-therapist, -therapeutic, -therapeutics; -therapies, therapias** *(plurals)*.

1520 **-epy** A word-final element, derived from Greek *ep(os)* 'speech, word' and -y[3], used in forming noun combinations concerning 'pronunciation' of a type specified by the combining root: **cacoepy, orthoepy, heteroepy.** Related forms: **-epist; -epies** *(plural)*.

1521 **-scopy** A noun-forming word-final element, derived from Greek *skop(ein)* 'to look at, observe' and -y[3], used in combinations meaning 'the art or process of observation in a manner, by means of an instrument, or from a perspective' specified by the combining root: **microscopy, fluoroscopy, telescopy.** Related forms: **-scope, -scopist, -scopia, -scopic, -scopical, -scopically; -scopies** *(plural)*.

1522 **-tropy** A noun-forming word-final element, derived from Greek *trop(os)*, *trop(ē)* 'a turning, turn, deviation, direction, mode' (from the verb *trep(ein)* 'to turn, guide') and -y[3], used mostly in the sense of 'influenced by, or having an affinity for or influence upon' that which is named by the combining root: **geotropy, organotropy, lipotropy.** Also, **-tropism**. Related forms: **-trope, -tropia, -tropic, -tropal, -tropous; -tropies, -tropisms** *(plurals)*.

1523 **-ary**[1] A noun suffix, derived through Middle English *-arie* and Old French *-arie, -aire* from Latin *-ari(us)*, used to form combinations meaning 'a thing or person that is connected with or belongs to' that which is specified by the combining root: **herbary, lapidary, judiciary.** Related forms: **-arium, -aria; -aries** *(plural)*.

1524 **-ary²** A suffix derived from -ary¹ used in developing adjective
combinations without any change in form; the meaning is 'pertaining
or belonging to, or connected with' that which is specified by the
combining root: **legendary, secondary, fiduciary**. Related form: **-arily.**

1525 **-ery** A highly productive noun-forming word-final element, derived
from Middle English *-erie* from Old French *-ier* '-**er¹**', and '-**y³**'; it has
been very active in forming combinations involving several meanings:

    1. 'Qualities considered collectively, character': **prudery, lechery,
comradery.**

    2. 'An art, practice, or trade': **jobbery, sorcery, midwifery.**

    3. 'A place of activity or selling' as specified by the initial root:
bakery, grocery, slumbery.

    4. 'A collection of something' denoted by the combining root:
greenery, perfumery, sprucery.

    5. 'A state or condition' denoted by the joining root: **savagery,
slavery, gimcrackery.** Related form: **-eries** *(plural).*

1526 **-surgery** A noun and a noun-forming word-final element, derived
through Middle English, French, and Latin from Greek *cheirourgia*
'handiwork, work done by hand' (from *cheir* 'hand' and *-ourgia*
'-**urgy**'), now used in a specialized sense, in the terminology of
medicine, to mean 'the treatment of illness or deformity by manual or
instrumental operation,' the illness or operative means being specified
by the combining root: **psychosurgery, electrosurgery, macrosurgery.**
Also, **-chirurgia** *(obsolete).* Related forms: **-surgeon, -surgical;
-surgeries** *(plural).*

1527 **-ory¹** A noun-forming word-final element, derived through Middle
English *-orie* from Latin *-ori(um)*, used in its two main etymological
senses:

    1. 'A place used for an activity' specified by the combining root:
laboratory, observatory, operatory.

    2. 'Something—especially an instrument—used for a purpose'
specified by the combining root: **ostensory, accessory, respon-
sory.** Also, **-orium.** Compare **-ary¹, -arium.** Related forms: **-orial;
-ories** *(plural).*

1528 **-ory²** An adjective-forming word-final element, derived through Middle
English and French *-orie, -oire* from the Latin adjectival suffix
-ōri(us), -ōri(a), -ōri(um), used in three of its etymological senses:

    1. 'Pertaining or relating to, or characterized by' the action
described by the combining root: **sensory, exclusory, infusory.**

2. 'Conveying, involving, or containing' something named by the combining root: **vapory, advisory, compulsory.**
3. 'Maintaining, producing, or serving for' whatever the combining root indicates: **classificatory, stimulatory, incensory.** Compare **-orium.** Related forms: **-orial, -orily.**

1529   **-atory**   An adjective-forming word-final element, derived from the combination of **-ate**[3] and **-ory**[2], used in two major senses, each specified by the combining root:
1. 'Pertaining to, or belonging to, or connected with': **perspiratory, aleatory, migratory.**
2. 'Tending to or serving' an action or state indicated by the first root: **amendatory, explanatory, commendatory.** Related forms: **-ator, -atorily.**

1530   **-factory**   A word-final element, derived from Latin *fact(us)* (past participle of *fac(ere)* 'to make, do') and **-ory**[1] 'an instrument or agent,' used in adjective combinations meaning 'pertaining to an agent or instrument for making' whatever is denoted by the joining root: **benefactory, olfactory, malefactory.** Related forms: **-factive, -facture, -(i)fic, -fect, -faction, -(i)fy.**

1531   **-iatry**   A noun-forming word-final element, derived from Greek *iatreia* 'the art or action of healing,' or, Greek *iatr(os)* 'healer, physician' and **-y**[3], used in English to name 'a type of medical treatment or healing' specified by the combining root: **psychiatry, podiatry, gyniatry.** Also, **-iatria.** Related forms: **-iatric, -iatrical, -iatrician, -iatrist, -iatrics; -iatries, -iatrias** *(plurals).*

1532   **-latry**   A noun-forming word-final element, derived through Middle English *-latrie* and late Latin *-latria* from Greek *latr(eia)* 'service, worship' (cf. Greek *latris* 'servant'), used in combinations to mean 'devotion to or worship of' an object denoted by the combining root: **idolatry, bibliolatry, diabolatry.** Related forms: **-latria, -latrous, -later; -latrias, -latries** *(plurals).*

1533   **-metry**   A noun-forming word-final element, derived through Middle English and French *-metrie* and Latin *metria* from Greek *metr(on)* 'a measure, proportion' and **-ia**[1], used to name 'the process, art, or science of measuring something' specified by the combining root: **calorimetry, thermometry, psychometry.** Also, **-metria**[1]. Related forms: **-meter, -metron, -metrical, -metrically, -metrist, -metrics; -metra, -metrias, -metries** *(plurals).*

1534   **-bury**   A (proper) noun-forming word-final element of uncertain etymology, used very actively in British place names. Although one meaning, 'fortified place,' is closely related to that for **-burg**, it is also related to *-borg*, a word for *-borough* taken from Danish and used in early medieval times to denote a borough in those areas under the control of the Danes during the 9th and 10th centuries. The term could also mean 'manor house,' for in earlier times it would have been a fortified place. Whatever the precise meaning (and only local history can clarify it), the term was widely used in Britain and in the United States through the 18th century: **Canterbury, Aylesbury, Simsbury.** Compare **-boro, -borough, -burg, -burgh, -by.**

1535   **-sy**   A noun-forming word-final element of uncertain origin, possibly from a combination of $-s^2$ and $-y^4$, used as a diminutive, usually affectionate: **popsy, poopsy, Betsy.** Also, **-sie.**

1536   **-lepsy**   A noun-forming word-final element, derived through Middle French *-lepsie* and Latin *-lepsia* from Greek *lēpsia* 'act of taking, seizure' (from Greek *labein* 'to take, seize' and *-ia¹*), used in medical terminology to denote 'a seizure' of the sort specified by the combining root: **epilepsy, narcolepsy, catalepsy.** Also, **-lepsia, -lepsis.** Related forms: **-leptic; -lepsies, -lepsias, -lepses** *(plurals).*

1537   **-tripsy**   A noun-forming word-final element, derived from Greek *trips(is)* 'a rubbing, grinding' (from the verb *trib(ein)* 'to rub, grind, pound' and *-sis*) and $-y^3$, used in medical terminology to denote 'a crushing of a part of the body by means of a surgical instrument,' the part of the body or the type of instrument being specified by the combining root: **angiotripsy, neurotripsy, histotripsy.** Related forms: **-tribe, -tripsis, -triptic; -tripsies** *(plural).*

1538   **-ty¹**   A noun-forming word-final element, derived through Middle English and Old French from Latin *-tās, -tāt-*, a productive abstract-noun-forming suffix with much the same meaning and grammatical function as English **-hood** or **-ness**, used to form combinations with adjectives of Latin origin with the meaning 'a quality, state, condition' of that which is specified by the combining root: **nicety, subtlety, poverty.** Compare **-ity.** Related form: **-ties** *(plural).*

1539   **-ty²**   A noun-forming word-final element, derived through Middle English *-ty, -ti* from Old English *-tig*, used to mark multiples of ten: **twenty, thirty, sixty.** Related form: **-ties** *(plural).*

1540   **-ity**   A common abstract-noun-forming word-final element, derived through French -*ité* from Latin -*itās*, -*itātis*, a very productive abstract-noun-forming suffix, used in combination with adjectives to designate 'a quality, state, or degree' of that which is specified by the combining root: **opacity, veracity, publicity.** Compare -**ty**[1]. Related form: -**ities** *(plural)*.

1541   -**ability**   See -**able** and -**ity**.

1542   -**ibility**   See -**able** and -**ity**.

1543   -**motility**   A noun, derived from Latin *mōt(us)*, the past participle of the verb *mōv(ēre)* 'to move,' -**ile**[2], and -**ity**, used largely in medical terminology to mean 'the condition or state of being motile, i.e., capable of movement,' of the sort or in the manner specified by the combining root: **neurimotility, nervimotility, hypomotility.** Also, -**mobility.** Related forms: -**motile, -motive, -mobile**[1], -**mobile**[2], -**move, -motor**[1], -**motor**[2], -**motorial, -motored, -motorially, -motoric.**

1544   -**plasty**   A noun-forming word-final element, derived from Greek *plast(os)* (the past participle of the verb *plass(ein)*, *platt(ein)* 'to mold, form, shape') and -**y**[3], used in medical terminology to denote 'a surgical shaping or molding, i.e., plastic surgery' on a part of the body or by a means specified by the combining root: **dermoplasty, thoracoplasty, osteoplasty.** Related forms: -**plastic, -plastia, -plast, -plasia, -plasy, -plasis; -plasties** *(plural)*.

1545   -**nasty**   A noun-forming word-final element, derived from Greek *nast(os)* 'pressed close, firm' and -**y**[3], used in botanical terminology to denote 'an irregular pattern of cellular growth in a direction, of a kind, or because of pressure or stimulus from' that which is named by the combining root: **photonasty, nyctinasty, geonasty.** Related forms: -**nastic; -nasties** *(plural)*.

Index

Index

agnostic 575
-agog 1018
-agoge 1018
-agogic 1018
-agogical 1018
-agogically 1018
-agōg(os) 1018
-agogue 1018
-agoguery 1018
-agogy 1018
agonic 468
agoraphobe 709
agoraphobia 40
-agra 355
agrammatical 1105
agrapha 33.1
agreement 1412.2
agronome 862.1
agronomy 1504
agrypnocoma 301.2
agyria 196
-aille 1101
'air' 24, 476
'air, let in or out of' 985
aircraft 1398.3
-aire 1523
-aire 927
Airedale 800
airframe 855.2
airplane 880
airport 1425.1
aisthēs(is) 212
aitchbone 900
aitchpiece 720.4
Akadēm(eia) 435
akanth(os) 1078
akinesis 1312.1
aknephascopia 160
ako(ē) 154
-ak(os) 378
akou(ein) 576
akous(is) 231
akoustik(os) 576
-akusis 231
-al 436, 897, 1100, 1245
-al¹ 1100, 1109, 1495
-al² 1101
-al³ 1102
āl(a) 984
Alaskan 1181.2
-alate 984
albumin 195, 1199.3
albuminoptysis 1329
albuminuria 190.1,
-albuminuria 195
alchemic 436

'alchemist' 436
alcohol 1136
alcoholemia 96.2
alcoholic 383.2
alcoholism 1157.2
alcoholophilia 88.2
-ald 630
aldehyde 1102
Alderley 1473
-ale 1100
aleatory 1529.1
Alemite 1005.6
aleostearic 490
alestake 791
aleukemia 102
alewife 764.4
Alexandra 4.1
alexia 248
alexipharmic 449
Alfred 608
'Algae, class of' 701
'algae, threadlike' 288.4
algarobilla 265.1
algebraical 1103.1
-algesia 210
-algesic 210, 509
algēs(is) 210, 509
-algetic 210
-algia 55, 405
-algic 55, 405
algogenesia 213.2
algolagnia 138
alg(os) 55, 405
-algy 55, 405
Alhambraic 383.1
-al(ia) 1101
-alia 76
-alian 76
'alike' 793
'alimentary canal,
   contraction in' 1314
-al(is) 1100,
-alis 1299
-alism 1100
-alist 1100
-alistic 1100
-ality 1100
'alive' 484, 629
-alize 1100
alkali 897
'alkaline' 506,
-alkaline 897
-alkalinity 897
-alkalinize 897
alkaloid 625
alkalotic 554.2

al koh'l 1136
allergic 407.2
allergy 1477.2
alliterate 999.1
allocentric 499.2
allochiria 182.2
allomorph 1064
allopath 1072.2
allopathic 419.3
allopathy 1485.2
allophanic 456.4
allophasis 1303, 1304
allophonic 470.6
allorhythmia 110
Allotheria 38.2, 178
allude 755
-ally 1100, 1495
alongside 749
alpine 889.1
altarpiece 720.5
Althorpe 916
alumina 4.2
aluminium 1165
alumni 1083.1
always 1286, 1380
alymphopotent 1414
amacratic 520.4
amaranth 1077
amastia 244
amateurish 1065.2
'amber' 478, 497
ambiotic 557.1
ambition 1212.3
ambitious 1361
ambivalence 732.1
ambivalent 1410.1
amblyope 913
amblyopia 158
-ambulance 986
-ambulant 986
ambul(are) 986
-ambulate 986
-ambulation 986
-ambulator 986
-ambulatory 986
ambulat(us) 986
-ambulic 986
-ambulism 986
-ambulist 986
ambushment 1412.4
'a measuring stick' 651
-ameba 5
-ameban 5
-amebic 5
-amebid 5
-ameboid 5

-amebous 5
amend 648, 655
amendatory 1529.2
amenia 134
amentia 239
American 1181.4
Americana 341
Americanize 1038.1
Americaward 683.1
Ametabola 270
ametria 188
ametropia 164
amicable 804.1
amimia 111
aminoacidemia 99
aminobarbituric 504
ammonobasic 506
Ammophila 260
amnesia 215
amnestic 570
amoeba 4.2,
-amoeba 5
-amoeban 5
amoebiasis 1305.1
-amoebic 5
-amoebid 5
-amoeboid 5
-amoebous 5
amoib(ē) 5
amorphia 72
'amount' 765.6
Ampelopsis 1325
amphiaster 1268
Amphibia 37.4
amphiblastula 279
Amphibola 269.2
amphidiploidy 1471
amphierotic 559.2
amphimixis 1336
amphimorula 277
amphitrocha 32
Amphochaeta 371
amphodiplopia 161
amphoterodiplopia 161
amputee 759.2
amylase 947
amyostasia 209.1
amyosthenia 131
amyotaxia 247.1
an- 105, 162, 227
-an¹ 1181
-an² 1182
-ana 341
-ān(a) 882
anabolergy 1477.2
anacanth 1078

anacousia 231
anadiplosis 785.2
anadipsia 225
-anaemia 105
anaerobia 39
anaesthesia 212
anaglyphic 417.1
anakinetic 540.1
analgesia 210
analgesic 509
'analgesic drugs' 555
analogistic 573
analy(ein) 580
analysis 580, 1302, 1328
-analytic 580
-analytical 580
-analytically 580
analytik(os) 580
analyze 1039
ananastasia 209.1
anaphia 69
anaphoresis 1313
anaphoric 494.1
anaphrodisia 219
anaphrodisiac 382
Anaplasma 335.2
anaplastia 243
Anaplocephala 257
anapodeictic) 526
anastalsis 1314
anastate 1003
Anatidae 960
anatomic 447
anatripsis 1324
anatropia 163
Anaxonia 148
-ance 728, 1405, 1468,
    1470
'ancestry' 1366
anchorhold 640.5
-ancy 728, 1405, 1468,
    1470
Ancylodactyla 280
-and 644
-ander 174, 1370
-andra 174, 1370
-andria 174, 1370
-andrian 174, 1370
-andric 174, 1370
-andrism 174, 1370
androgyne 909
androgynous 1367.1
Andromedae 696
Andromedid 618.1
andromerogony 1515
-androus 174, 1370

-andry 174, 1370
-and(us) 644
-ane 876
-anemia 96.1, 105
-anemic 105
anēr 174, 1370
anergy 1477.2
anerotic 559.1
anesthesiant 1404.6
anesthetic 534.2, 890
angeion 306, 1169
'angel' 425
-angelic 425
-angelical 425
-angelically 425
angel(os) 425
ang(ere) 346
-angina 346
-anginal 346
'angina pectoris' 346
angiochondroma 321
angiofibroma 320
angioglioma 310
angiolipoma 319
angiolith 1075.2
angiolymphoma 305
-angioma 306
-angiomatous 306
angiomyxoma 332
angioneurotic 560.1
angioparalytic 581
angiospasmodic 396
angiosperm 1151
angiospermic 451.1
angiosthenia 132
angiostrophe 785.1
angiostrophy 1483
angiotripsy 1537
'angle' 468, 815.1, 1210
-angle 815
'angles, figure containing'
    815.2
Anglicism 1157.4
Anglomane 881
Anglomania 127.2
Anglophobic 386.1
Anglophobist 1436.4
angophrasia 207
-angular 815
-angularity 815
-angularly 815
angul(us) 815
anharmonic 475.2
anhedonia 143
anhydride 1182
-anic 876

animadvert 1424.2
'animal' 348, 912.4,
  959.3, 1007, 1082.2,
  1086.3, 1226
animalcule 849
animalia 38.2
'animal life' 347, 629
'animal live' 484.1
'animals' 19
'animals, related' 598.2
anion 1213
anisochela 258
anisochromia 114
ankle 815
anklet 1395.2
ankylocheilia 87
Ankylosauria 191
ankylotia 242
-anly 1181
Annette 1011.4
anniverse 965.1
'announce' 734, 982
'announcement, make an'
  982
annually 1488.2
annular 1245.3
annunciate 982
annus 1112, 1174
anode 753
anodendron 1228.3
anodic 393.2
anodyne 908
anoetic 542
anoia 155
anomaloflorous 1374
anomia 113
Anomodontia 240
-anopia **162**, 227
-anopic 162
-anopsia 162, 226, **227**
anorexia 250
anorganic 455.2
anosmia 122
anosphrasia 216
anovaria 173
anoxemia 107
anoxia 252
-ans **1338**
-ant 728, 1338, **1404,**
  1468, 1470
antacid 623.1
antalgesic 509
antaphrodisiac 382
Antarctalia 76.1
antarctic 527
antebrachium 1171

antefebrile 825
anteflect 1389.2
'antelope' 584
'antelope, male' 584
anterotic 559.1
anteroventral 1118
-anth **1077**
-anthema **287**
anthēma 287
-anthic 1077
anthological 1103.1
Anthophila 260
anth(os) 1077
-anthous 7, 1077
-anthrope 487, 1377
anthrophilous 1362
-anthropic **487,** 1377
-anthropical 487
-anthropically 487, 1377
anthropik(os) 487
-anthropism 487, 1377
-anthropist 487, 1377
-anthropoid 487, 626,
  1377
anthropomorphic 416
anthropopathic 419.4
anthropophagy 1475
anthrōp(os) 1377
-anthropus 487, **1377**
-anthropy 487, 1377
antiaesthetic 534.1
-antial 1405
-antially 1405
antianemia 105
antiaphrodisiac 382
antiarthritic 548
antiasthmatic 513
'antibiotic' 557.1, 1199.1
'antibody' 1204
anticatalytic 582
anticritic 547
anticyclone 902
antiemetic 536
antifebrile 825
antiheroic 483
antiluetic 544
'antimalarial agent' 1205
antimicrobic 387
'antimony sulfide' 1136
antimythic 421
antinarcotic 555
antinome 862.1
antipathic 419.2
antipharmic 449
antiphony 1516.1
antiphrastic 569

antipode 752.2
antipoetic 543.2
antipyretic 383.8
antiromantic 550.1
antiscientific 401
antiscorbic 388
antiscorbutic 577
antiseptic 563
antisocial 1111
antispasmodic 384.4, 396
antitetanic 458
antithesis 1308
antithetic 531
antitoxic 583
antitoxigen 1196.2
-antly 1404
antonomasia 203
antonym 1180
antonymy 1510.1
-ān(um) 882
Anura 362
-anus 236, 370, 1181,
  1183
-ān(us) 882
anxiety 1320
aortectasia 208
apancreatic 512
apathetic 532
'ape' 1350
apeptic 562.1
aphagia 50.2
aphakia 74
Aphanapteryx 1456
aphasia 199
'aphasia involving names'
  113
aphasic 507
aphemia 100
-aphia **69**
aphonic 470.6
aphony 1516.2
aphosphorotic 554.2
aphotic 556.2
-aphrodisia **219,** 382
-aphrodisiac 219, **382**
'Aphrodite' 219, 382
-aphroditic 219, 382
aphthongia 57
apiose 957.2
Aplodontia 240
apodema 285
apogamia 94
apologetic 529
apology 1476.1
apomixis 1336
aponeurotic 560.1

arthroempyema 291
arthrophyma 340
Arthropoda 16
arthr(os) 548
Arthrostraca 6
arthr(oun) 181
artiad 588.5
'articulate' 181
artifice 723
Artiodactyla 280
'art of' 1243
'art of judging' 1505
-ary 169
-ary¹ **1523**
-ary² **1524**
as 4, 588, 1245.1, 1295,
  1296
ascend 652
Ascensiontide 751.3
Ascetta 373
ascogonidium 1167
ascorbic 388
ascospore 936
ascribe 705
'ascribe to' 1013
-ase **947**
Ashby 1464
ashcake 787.1
'ashes' 897
ashthroat 1383
asialia 79
-asic 1303
-asis 1302, **1303**
-āsis 1303
asitia 237
'ask' 931, 981, 981.1
'ask about' 931
'ask for' 931
-asm **1154**
-(a)sm(os) 1154
-asmus 1154
aspect 1390
aspermic 451.1
asperse 964
asphygmia 109
Aspidosperma 334
aspire 929
aspirin 1199.2
asplenia 133
'assay' 656, 954
assemble 806
'assembly' 76
'assign' 1013
associate 983, 987.3
'associated with' 383.5
'association' 665

assuade 743
assume 873
'assumption' 296
assurge 782
Assyriologue 1019.3
-ast 1269, 1427, **1429**,
  1433
astasia 209.1
astatic 521.1
-aster 1269
-aster¹ **1268**
-aster² **1269**
astēr 1268
asternia 151
asterococcus 1349.2
asterospondylic 432
-astery 1269
-ast(es) 1429
-asthenia **132**
-asthenic 132
asthenocoria 184
asthenoxia 252
-asthma **294**, 513
asthmagenic 460.1
-asthmatic 294, **513**
-astic 1154
-astically 1154
'astray, go' 880
'astray, lead' 880
astrict 1392
astringe 777
astrokinetic 540.3
astronaut 1445
Astylospongia 58
asymbolia 89
asynechia 61
asyntaxia 247.2
'at' 136, 972
-ata **364**, 739
-āt(a) 999
-atae 364
ataraxic 383.8
ataxia 247.1
ataxiophemia 100
-ate 364, 1028, 1218
-ate¹ **971**
-ate² **972**
-ate³ **973**
-ate⁴ **974**
atelencephalia 78
-ately 971
-ater 1277
-ath 1074
atheism 1159
atheist 1437
atheistic 572

athelia 83
'athletic exercise' 568
athyrea 28
-ati 364
-ātia 1466
-atic 1303
-atic(um) 765
-atiō 1218
-ation 1013
-ation 971, 972, 973,
  1218
-ātīv(a) 1028
-ative 973, **1028**
-atively 1028
-ātīv(um) 1028
-ātīv(us) 1028
Atkins 1202.2, 1339
atlodidymus 1353.2
atmosphere 923.2
atmospheric 491.1
'atmospheric conditions'
  988
'atmospheric pressure'
  1247
'atom' 448, 588.5
atom(ē) 448
-atomic **448**
-atomical 448
-atomically 448
'atomic particle' 1207.1
atom(on) 448
atom(os) 448
'atoms, ring of' 424.5
atonic 480.3
atopognosia 221
-ator **1277**, 1529
-ātor 1273
-atorial 1277
-atorially 1277
-atorily 1529
-atory 1277, **1529**
atresia 217,
-atresia **218**
-atresic 218
-atretic 218
atretoblepharia 170
atretometria 188
atretorrhinia 139
-atrophia 71
-atrophic 71
atroph(os) 71
atrophy 71, 1482
'attack' 778.2
'attend' 157, 578, 1294,
  1519
attendant 1404.1

basiotic 553.3
basiotribe 706
basipterygium 1170.1
basis 197, 505, 506, 1303
basiscopic 486.1
'basis for argument' 1308
basivertebral 1117
Baskerville 830.1
basophil 1126
Bassalia 76.1
Basset 1397
-bat 197, 969.2, 975
-bate 975
-bath 418
-bathic 418
bathochrome 865
bathorse 966.1
bath(os) 418
bathypelagic 403
bathyseism 1160
-batic 197
bat(re) 975
batt(en) 975
batt(ere) 975
'battle' 409, 1479
battlefield 634.1
battlement 1412.4
bawl 1131
'bay' 1090,
-bay 1461
baye 1461
-bdella 264
Bdellostoma 330
'be' 1439
beading 1046.2
'beak' 31
'bear' 185, 352, 357, 494,
 527, 704, 827, 933,
 1256, 1259, 1313,
 1372, 1373
beardtongue 1017.3
bearer 933, 1251.6,
 1256.2, 1259
'bearing' 352, 494.1,
 494.2, 704, 1313, 1372
'beast, wild' 178, 924
'beat' 671, 970, 970.2,
 975
beatnik 1095
Beatrice 722.2
beautician 1184
beautiful 534.1, 1141.2
beaux 1451
becc 1088
-bech 1088
-beck 1088

beclad 593.1
'become' 1190.3
'becoming' 729, 736
'bed' 324, 466
bedcord 688
'bed covering' 324
Bedford 689
bedframe 855.2
bedmate 987.1
beeftongue 1017.2
beeherd 686
beeline 895.3
beerfest 1435.2
beewort 1426
befame 853
'before' 932, 932.2
beforehand 646.5
befume 871
'beg' 812.3
'beget' 979, 998
beggar 1251
begild 636.2
'beginning' 736
'beginning to be' 1407.1
'behaving as' 1405.2
'behavior' 595.2, 1242.4
behindhand 646.5
'being' 230, 348
'being, fact of' 1148.4
'being, living' 1007, 1226
bek 1088
bekkr 1088
'belief in a god or gods'
 1159
'beliefs' 1157.3
'believer' 1185.1
'believer in god' 1437
-bell 1131
bellbind 658
belle 1131
bellicose 956
bellow 1131
'bell-shaped flower'
 1131.2
bellwind 661
'belly' 189, 814
bellyband 645.1
bellybuster 1272
'belong' 1201
'belongings, personal'
 1241.3
'belonging to' 343, 703,
 887, 889, 889.1, 1005,
 1065.1 1181.1, 1183,
 1199, 1245.1, 1330,
 1358.1, 1524, 1529.1

'belt' 149
'bemoan' 934
bename 854.2
'bend' 514, 645, 780,
 815, 965, 1366, 1389,
 1389.2 5
'bend forward' 1389.2
'bend the knee' 1389
benefactory 1530
benefice 723
'benefit' 855
Bensonhurst 1443
'benumbing' 555
benzal 1102
benzene 883
benzil 1124
benzol 1137
benzole 832
benzothiophene 885
benzoyl 1142
'bereave' 245
bereavement 1412.5
Ber(e)nice 724
berewick 1090.1
-berg 1052
Berkhamsted 592
Bernardette 1011.2
Beroida 14
'berry' 7, 1349, 1349.1
berrying 1046.4
'berry-shaped organism'
 1349.2
Berwick 1090.3
berylia 4.2
'beseech' 934
beside 749
bestowal 1101
betatron 1230.2
betitle 845
betone 905.1
Betsy 1460, 1535
'better, make' 1034
bevatron 1230.2
'bewail' 934
bewilderment 1412.5
-bia 39
bialate 984
-bian 39
biblioclast 1431.1
bibliognost 1442
bibliogony 1515
bibliolater 1263
bibliolatry 1532
bibliomancy 1469
bibliomane 881
bibliomania 127.2

bibliophile 823
bibliophilic 427
bibliophily 1492.1
bibliopole 837
bibliopoly 1501
bibliotaph 1061
bibliotaphic 413
bibliotheca 4.2
bicolor 1275.1
biconic 467.1
bicycle 810.4
bicyclic 424.2
-bid 622
bidd(an) 622
biddest 1433
bidentate 1001
bidermoma 315
biennial 1112
biennium 1174
biethnic 464
bifid 624
biflorate 1000
bifold 638.2
bigamy 1503.1
biggest 1434
bighead 590.1
bigleg 1043.1
biharmonic 475.2
bilabial 1110
'bile' 90
bilestone 906.5
bilinguist 1440
bilious 1359
-bil(is) 804, 808
bimetallic 428
bimotor 1279.2
-bind 658, 666
bindan 658
bind(en) 666
-bine 658
binuclear 1248
biochemic 436
bioclimatic 514
biocycle 810.1
biodyne 908
biogeny 1513
biographee 759.2
biographia 70.1
biohydraulic 431
biokinetic 540.3
biometric 498.1
-bion 39
bionergy 1477.1
-biont 39
biophysics 1292
biopoiesis 1310

biorhythmic 438
bios 39, 557, 708, 711,
  1318
-biosis 557, 1318
biōsis 1318
biosphere 923.4
biosynthesis 1309
biotaxis 1333.1
biotechnics 1290
-biotic 557, 1318
-biotical 1318
biōtik(os) 557
biotripsis 1324
bipartite 1010
bipennate 992
bird 969.3, 1037.4,
  1043.2, 1050.1, 1134.2,
  1382, 1383
-bird 687
'bird, hawklike' 1099.2
'bird, young' 687
birdstone 906.3
bireme 857
Birmingham 1144
'birth' 43, 213, 460, 469,
  492, 538, 1196, 1364,
  1513,1515
'birth and rearing' 607.2
birthmate 987.4
birthplace 716
bisectrix 1454.2
-bium 39
-bius 39
bivalence 732.2
blackboard 681.2
blackface 713.2
blackleg 1043.1, 1043.3
blackpoll 1134.2
blacksmith 1076.1
blacktongue 1017.1
'bladder' 331, 1331, 1444
'bladder, inflammation
  of' 1331
'blame' 996
-blast 1430
-blastema 290
blastēma 290
-blastemal 290
-blastematic 290
-blastemic 290
blastocele 814
blastodermic 450.5
blastographia 70.1
'blastomeres' 277
blast(os) 279, 1430
blastostroma 324

blastula 272,
-blastula 279
-blastular 279
blatancy 1468.1
Blattidae 697
bleachground 670
bleeding 1045.2
'blend' 779.2, 816
blennorrhagic 402
-blepharal 170
-blepharia 170
Blepharocera 351
blepharocoloboma 300
blephar(on) 170
-blepsia 223
bleps(is) 223
-blepsy 223
'block' 787.4
blockade 739.1
blockhead 590.2
blōd 675
'blood' 96, 97, 98, 101,
  102, 105, 328,
-blood 675
'blood, acid in' 99
'blood, carbon dioxide in
  the' 150
'blood, color of' 446.3
'blood, hemoglobin in'
  104
'blood, red cell
  deficiency in' 105
'blood, swelling
  containing' 328
'blood, toxin in' 108
bloodleaf 1040
bloodline 895.3
bloodmobile 821.2
'blood oxygen' 107
'blood pressure
  measurement' 841, 842
bloodroot 1421
bloodshed 602
bloodstone 906.4
bloodstroke 794.3
'blood sugar' 98
'blood vessels, tumor of'
  306
'blossom' 1374
'blow' 53, 249, 476, 489,
  917, 985
blowbottle 847.1
bluebell 1131.2
bluebottle 847.2
bluefish 1067
bluejack 1086.3

blueleg 1043.3
bluenose 959.2
bluethroat 1383
bluetongue 1017.1
'blunt' 970.1
-board 681
boarhound 668
boatyard 685.3
-boc 584
bodies' 1295
'body' 115, 232, 285,
    326, 368, 511, 518,
    617.2, 698, 869, 994,
    1352
'body build' 285
bodyguard 682
'body member' 1005.7
'body part' 1005.7
'body region' 814
'body walls of insects'
    274
boga 1448
boi 1518
-bola 269, 429
'bold' 632
boldface 713.4
-bole 429
-bolic 269, 429
-bolism 429
-bolite 429
-boly 429
bombazine 889.2, 1194
bon 900
'bond' 336, 665
bondage 765.5
'bone' 1043, 1209, 304,
    56,
-bone 900
-boned 900
'bone marrow' 85
'bone tumor' 304
booklet 1395.1
bookmobile 821.2
books 1283
'books, hider of' 1061
'book size' 1239
bookstand 649.1
'boom' 609
boon 900
bootee 761.1
Boothbay 1461
bord 681
'border' 681, 771, 1144
borderline 895.6
boredom 1148.4
-borg 1534

boric 383.2
'born' 469, 907, 1515
-borne 907
-boro 1059
-borough 1059, 1534
Borthwick 1090.3
borugh 1059
bosh 1068
Boston 1232
bosveld 635
botan(ē) 1512
-botanic 1512
-botanical 1512
-botanically 1512
botanize 1038.2
-botany 1512
boteille 847
botel 847
-bottle 847
bottlenose 959.3
boul(ē) 91
boulevardier 1261
boulevardiere 925
-boulia 91
-boulic 91
'bound' 666.2, 892
-bound¹ 666
-bound² 667
bound(en) 666
bourne 907
Bournemouth 1082.1
bouteille 847
boutonniere 925
bovovaccine 891
-bow 1448
'bow and arrow' 253,
    583
bowe 1448
bowline 895.2
-boy 1518
boychik 1094
boyish 1065.2
boyo 1235.2
boy's 1281.1, 1282, 1283
-brace 718
-brachia 60, 718
brachi(on) 60
brachiosaur 1280
brachiplex 1452.3
-brachium 718, 1171
brachybasia 197
brachycerous 1371
brachymetropia 164
brachyphalangia 56
Brachyphyllum 1177
Bradshaw 1446

bradyarthria 181
bradycardia 48.1
bradydiastole 841
bradyecoia 154
bradyglossia 228.1
bradykinesia 214
bradylalia 80
bradylexia 248
bradypepsia 224
bradypeptic 562.2
bradyphagia 50.1
bradyphasia 199
bradyphemia 100
bradyphrasia 207
bradypragia 52
bradyseismic 452
bradysphygmia 109
bradytocia 43.1
'braid' 1452
'brain' 78, 603, 1116
-brained 603
'brain pan' 1173, 1188.2
'branch' 65, 365, 1356
'branch, small' 1356
branchi(a) 365
-branchia 65
-branchial 65, 365
-branchiata 65, 365
-branchiate 65, 365
'branching of nerve
    fibers' 175
branyd 603
brassbound 666.2
breadboard 681.1
breadth 1070
breadthen 1190.4
'break' 51, 200, 402, 566,
    768, 1272, 1334, 1423,
    1431
'break down' 581
'breaker' 1272, 1431.1,
    1431.2
'breaking' 200, 566.1
'breaking down' 580,
    1039, 1204, 1328
'breaking tool' 1431.2
'breaking up' 200
'breast' 244, 255
'breast-bone' 151, 1114,
    1179
'breast-plate' 390
'breath' 24, 476, 784
'breathe' 476, 784, 801,
    929
'breathing' 24
'breathing, labored' 294

-bred 598, **607**
brēd(an) 598
-breed **598**, 607, 607.1
-breeding 598, 607
brethren 1191
breviconic 467.2
breviloquent 1416
brevipennate 992
Brewster 1267.3
brickwork 1098.1
brid 687
bridd 687
bridecake 787.3
bridegod 672
bridelace 714.2
-bridge **774**
'bridging' 336
bridle 797
brigade 739.3
brigge 774
brighten 1190.3
'brimstone' 502
'bring about, tending to'
    383.8
bringeth 1074
'bring forth' 1327
'bring to an end' 958
'bring together' 806, 840,
    1314
'bring under' 1388.1
'bristle' 371
brittle 798
broadhead 590.1
brocade 739.2
brōec 1097
broke 1097
'broken' 566
bronchiophonic 470.5
bronchitis 1330.1
broncobuster 1272
bronchopneumonia 145
bronchopneumonic 476.1
bronchoscopic 486.2
brontosaurus 1379
bronzewing 1050.1
'brook' 907, 1088,
-brook **1097**
Brooklynese 949.3
broom 812.4
broomstick 1089.1
brother/breth(e)r 1191.3
brugge 774
brushwork 1098.2
brutalize 1038.1
brycg 774
bry(ein) 481, 1240

būa 667
bubonic 383.7
bucketfull 1140
Buckinghamshire 928
bucko 1235.1
'bud' 279, 1430
-bud **692**
budde 692
Buddleia 37.2
'buddy' 987.2
Budleigh 1058
buffaloburger 1258.1
bufotoxin 1206
bugbane 877.2
buglewort 1426
'build' 1393
'building, small' 601
būinn 667
bulbaceous 1358.1
bulbil 1125
bulblet 1395.1
bulbonuclear 1248
bulbose 956
'bulge' 299
-bulia **91**
-bulic 91
'bulk' 615
bullnose 959.4
bullock 1091
Buncombe 707
Bund 665
-bund¹ **664**
-bund² **665**
-bund(a) 664
-bund(um) 664
-bund(us) 664
bungeye 1037.1
buntline 895.2
Burcelli 1084
'burden, impose' 778.3
bureaucracy 1467.2
bureaucrat 1384.3
burg 1059
-burg **1053**
-burger **1258**
burgh 1053, 1059
burglarproof 1041.2
burh 1053
'burial' 413, 1061
burlesque 1022.2
-burn **907**
burn(a) 907
'burst' 51, 402, 768,
    1272, 1334
'bursting' 51, 402, 768,
    1334

burwe 1059
-bury **1534**
'bush' 1024,
-bush **1068**
bushveld 635
'business' 1332
busk 1068
bust 1272
-buster **1272**
'butterfly' 1050.2
butternose 959.3
Butterworth 1081
butterwright 1401.2
butticula 847
buttinsky 1487
buttonhole 834.2
'buy' 873
buzzwig 1044.1
-by **1464**
bȳr 1464
byrig 1059
Byrobia 39
byword 691.1

C

cackhanded 595.1
cacochroia 156
cacochymy 124
cacodemonic 472.1
cacoepy 1520
cacogeusia 229
cacomelia 84
cacophonic 470.1
cacophony 1516.1
cacosmia 122
cacostomia 116
cacothanasia 205
-cade **741**
caed(ere) 747
caester 1270
cagelike 793
-caine **890**
'cake, flat' 372
'cake, small' 787
'cake, thin' 787.1
-cake **787**
Calamodendron 1228.3
calcicole 833
calcify 1474.2
calciorrhachia 59
calcipenia 135
calcipexis 1335
calciphilous 1362
calciprivia 245

'calcium carbonate
  products' 859
'calcium oxide' 859
calcspar 1250
'calculus' 906.5, 1075.2
Caldbeck 1088
calfbound 666.2
'call' 203, 795
Calligrapha 33.2
calligrapher 1260
caloric 383.10
calorimetric 498.2
calorimetry 1533
calves 1296
calyciflorate 1000
Calystegia 54
cambi(āre) 775
cambi(um) 775
Cambrian 1181.2
camelcade 741.1
-camera 353
-campa 349
Campanularia 169
campground 670
camptocormy 121
Candlemas 1287
candlestand 649.1
candlewright 1401.2
candor 1274
Canfield 634.2
'cannon, small' 789
cannonade 739.1
canst 1427
Canterbury 1534
'capable of' 86, 804.1,
  818.2
'cape' 1344
capere 1026
-capnia 150
-capnial 150
-capnic 150
Capricorn 1233
'capsule' 1169
captaincy 1465
'capturing device' 1241.1
Carambola 269.2
caramel 1122
carbide 746
carbocyclic 424.5
'carbohydrate' 957.1
carbon 1207.3
carbonate 974.2
'carbon compounds'
  455.2
'carbon dioxide in the
  blood' 150

carburet 1396
carcake 787.2
carcinogen 1196.1
carcinogenic 460.1
-carcinoma 318
-carcinomatoid 318
-carcinomatous 318
-card 680
card(e) 680
-cardia 48, 379
cardiac 378
-cardiac 48, 379
cardiasthenia 132
cardinalis 1299
cardioasthma 294
cardiokinetic 540.4
cardiometric 498.2
cardiopathic 419.1
cardiopathy 1485.1
cardiophone 901.4
cardioplegia 53
cardioptosis 1321
carditic 545
'care' 939
'care, thing of' 921
'care for' 1294
carefree 762.1
'cargo, storage place for'
  640.3
cargoose 960
-carnate 994
-carnation 994
Carnivora 361
carnivore 937
carnivorous 1375
car(ō) 994
-carp 1244
-carpal 1115
-carpic 1244
-carpium 1244
carpocarpal 1115
carpophore 933
carport 1425.1
-carpous 1244
-carpus 1115, 1244
carric(āre) 778
'carrier' 933, 1256.2,
  1259
'carry' 185, 352, 357,
  494, 704, 933, 1256,
  1256.1, 1259,1313,
  1372, 1373
'carrying case' 1087
cart(e) 680
'cartilage' 176, 176.2, 321

'cartilage of rib-cage'
  176.2
'cartilaginous tumor' 321
'carve' 35, 417, 1145
'carving' 417.1, 417.2
'case' 8, 1166
'case, carrying' 1087
casefy 1474.1
caseose 957.2
casify 1474
'cask, small' 847
'cast' 269, 269.1, 269.2
castel 846
castell(um) 846
-castle 8464
'cast off' 269, 269.2
castr(a) 1270
'cast under' 1388.1
catabiotic 557.1
catabolergetic 530
catabolic 429.1
catakinesis 1312.2
catakinetic 540.3
catalepsis 1302
catalepsy 1536
catalogistic 573
-catalysis 582
-catalytic 582
-catalytical 582
-catalytically 582
catalyze 1039
catamnestic 570
catanephroi 1085
cataphoria 185.1
cataphrenia 137
cataphrenic 461.2
cataphyll 1135.1
catastate 1003
catatonia 147
catatonic 480.5
catatropia 163
catchword 691.2
-cate 976
'caterpillar' 349
catfish 1067
'catgut' 17, 688, 690
-catharsis 565
-cathartic 565
-cathartical 565
-cathartically 565
'cathedral' 1271
cathode 753
cathodic 393.2
-catholic 430
-catholicity 430
cation 1213

cats 1283
'caught in' 666.1
caulosarc 585
'causation' 400
'cause to be' 973.4,
 1190.1
'cause to grow' 374
'cause to have' 1190.2
'causing' 460.1, 1141.4
'causing to become'
 1219.1
cavalcade 741
cavalcata 741
cavallo 741
'cave' 428, 834
'cavity' 814, 1014
'cavity in an organism'
 814
-cede 745
-cedence 745
-cedent 745
cēd(ere) 596, 745
cedilla 265.2
Cediopsylla 267
-ceed 596
-ceive 1026
-ceiv(en) 1026
-cel 263
-cele¹ 813
-cele² 814
celibacy 1465
-celic 813
'cell' 101, 1014
'cell, mass within a'
 1432
'cell, primitive' 1432
-cella 263
-cellate 263
'cell division' 1312.2
'cell division process'
 450.5
Cellepora 359
'cell nucleus' 1248
cellophane 878
'cells in the blood' 101
'cell substance' 1155
'cellular growth,
 irregular' 568
'cellular tissue, tumor in'
 307
'cellular tissue layer' 307,
 1172
celosomia 115
celosomus 1352
celozoic 484.1
cement 22, 1412

-cene 884
cenocite 1008
cenotaph 1061
cenotaphic 413
centennial 1112
-center 499
'center' 499
Centerbrook 1097
'centering upon' 499.1
centile 817
-central 499
-centre 499
-centric 499
-centricity 499
centrifuge 783.2
centrolecithal 1108
centuple 843
-cephala 7, 257
cephalagra 355
-cephalan 77, 257
cephalhematoma 328
-cephalia 77, 257, 423,
 1491
-cephalic 77, 257, 423,
 1491
-cephalism 77, 423, 1491
cephalocathartic 565
cephalocele 813
Cephalochorda 17
cephaloconic 467.2
cephalodymia 123
-cephaloid 257, 77
cephaloplegic 404.1
cephalotroch 1056
cephalotrocha 32
-cephalous 77, 257
-cephalus 257
-cephaly 77, 257, 423,
 1491
-cept 1026
-ceptible 1026
-ception 1026
cer- 351
-cera 351, 1371
-ceramic 433
-ceramics 433
-ceran 351, 1371
ceratite 1005.3
-ceratoid 351, 1371
-ceratosis 351
-cerca 12
-cercal 12
cercaria 169
Cercospora 360
cerebellum 1164
-cerebral 1116

'cerebral cortex' 196
cerebr(um) 1116
cerecloth 1080
ceremonial 1101
ceria 4.2
-cerite 351
-ceros 351
-cerous 1371
'certain one' 868
cerviciplex 1452.3
cess(a) 596, 745
'cessation' 727
-cession 596, 745
-cessive 596, 745
cess(um) 596, 745
cess(us) 596, 745
cetaphoric 494.1
Cetarea 19
-chaeta 371
-chaete 371
chaetognatha 36
Chaetosomatidae 698
chaetotactic 525.3
chaffinch 1055
'chafing' 1324
chairman 1186.1
chairperson 1231
chait(ē) 371
'chamber' 353
'change' 5, 488.1, 540.3,
 1317
-change 775
'changeable' 270, 804.2
'changed' 965.3, 965.4
'chant' 905.1
'character' 383.1, 1231,
 1242.4, 1525.1
'characteristic of' 383.4,
 571, 1065.3, 1181.2,
 1183, 1354.1
'characterized by' 383.7,
 703, 867, 1100, 1109,
 1141.2, 1299, 1358.1,
 1373, 1411, 1457.1,
 1528.1
'charge for' 765.7
charg(ier) 778
Charley 786, 1460
Charlie 786, 1460
Charly 786, 1460
'charm' 719
chart(a) 680
chart(ēs) 680
chasm 1154
-chat 1382
chatt(en) 1382

'chatter' 1382
chatter(en) 1382
'cheek' 172, 266
'cheerfulness' 143
cheer(i)o 1236
cheeseburger 1258.2
cheesemonger 1257.1
-cheilia 87
cheil(os) 87
cheir 182, 1526
-cheiria 182
Cheiroglossa 363
cheirourgia 1526
-chela 258
-chelate 258
chēl(ē) 258
Chelura 362
chemia 436
-chemic 436
-chemical 436
'chemical compound'
   1199.3
-chemically 436
'chemical theory' 436
chemicophysics 1292
chemisorb 377
-chemist 436
'chemistry' 436
chemokinesis 1312.1
chemomorphosis 1317
chemosynthetic 533.2
chemotaxis 1333.2
chemotherapeutic 578
chemotherapy 1519.1
chemotrophic 414
chemotrophy 1482
chemurgic 408.2
-chemy 436
-chen 1202
chenille 829
Chepstow 1450
Cherubim 1146
-chesia 256
'chest' 151, 390, 1179
-chester 1270
Chesterfield 634.2
-chete 371
chez(ein) 256
-chezia 256
chgd 586
-chik 1094
'child' 45, 1139, 1191.2
'child, male' 1518
childish 1065.2
childless 1342.1
children 1191

'children, pregnancies
   producing' 350.1
children's 1281.2
-chilia 87
chimic(us) 436
Chinese 949.1
Chiococca 7
Chippendale 800
-chiria 182
chirognomic 443.2
chirognomy 1505
chiromancy 1469
chiromantic 549
chiropractic 524.2
chiropraxis 1332
chiropterigium 1170.1
'chirp' 912
-chirurgia 1526
Chisholm 1147
chitoneure 940
chloral 1102
chlorenchyma 339
chlorhistechia 62
-chloric 495
chloridate 973.5
-chloride 495
'chlorine' 495, 887.1
-chlorite 495
chloromyeloma 312
chloronoma 312
chlorophyll 1135.2
chloropsia 226
chlor(os) 495
chlorosarcomyeloma 312
Chlorostigma 293
choirboy 1518
choirsinger 1251.3
cholagogue 1018.2
chol(ē) 90
cholecystitis 1331
-choleic 90
cholestasia 209.2
cholesterohistechia 62
-cholia 90
-choliac 90
choliamb 376
-cholic 90
-cholically 90
-cholily 90
-choliness 90
-cholish 90
-cholist 90
-cholize 90
-choly 90
-chondria 176
chondriosphere 923.3

chondroconia 142
-chondroma 321
-chondromatous 321
Chondromyces 1298
chondr(os) 176, 321
chondrosteoma 304
'chord' 17, 688,
-chord 690
-chorda 17
'Chordata' 17, 364
-chordate 17, 364
chord(ē) 17, 688, 690
-chorea 26
-choreal 26
-choreatic 26
choreia 26
-choreic 26
choriamb 376
-choric 1215
chorine 888
chorioadenoma 317
chorioepithelioma 308
-chorioid 1215
-chorion 1215
choromanic 457.1
Christendom 1148.3
Christmas 1287
Christocentric 499.1
christophany 1511
Christopher 1259
-chroia 156
-chroic 156
-chroism 156
chrōma 104, 114, 204,
   446, 517, 864, 865
-chromasia 204
chrōmat- 204
chromata 2.2, 364
-chromatic 114, 204, 446,
   517, 864, 865
-chromatically 204, 517,
   864, 865
-chromatism 114, 204,
   517
chromatophilia 88.1
-chrome 114, 204, 517,
   866
-chrome[1] 864
-chrome[2] 865
-chrome[3] 866
-chromemia 104
-chromia 114, 204
-chromic 114, 446, 517,
   864
chromium 866
'chromium alloys' 866

chromocyte 1014
chromophobic 386.2
chromophyll 1135.2
'chromosomes, threadlike'
    288.3
'chromosome sets' 628,
    1471
-chromous 114
-chromy 114, 204, 517,
    864
'chronaxy' 146.2
-chrone 146, 477
-chronia **146**
-chronic 146, 383.7, **477**
-chronism 146, 477
-chronistic 477
-chronistical 477
-chronistically 477
chronogrammic 441
chronology 1476.3
chronopher 1259
chron(os) 146, 477
-chronous 477
chro(os) 156
-chroous 156
chrōs 156
-chrous 156
Chrysomonadina 344
chrysophanic 456.1
chrysophill 1135.2
chuckhole 834.1
chucklehead 590.2
churches' 1295
Churchill 1132.2
'Church of Rome' 430
churchwise 952.2
churchyard 685.1
'chyle' 92
-chylia **92**
chylifactive 1029
chyl(os) 92
-chymia **124**
chym(os) 124, 339
-chymy 124
-cid 747
-cidal 747
-cidally 747
-cide **747**
ciderkin 1202.1
cigarette 1011.3
cigarillo 1238
'ciliated band' 32
'ciliation' 30
Cilioflagellata 366
'cinchona bark' 1205
cinecamera 353

cinemascopia 160
Cinerama 283
-cinesia 214, 540, 1312
-cinesis 214, 1312
-cinetic 214, 540, 1312
-cinetical 540
-cinetically 540, 1312
-cious 1359
-cip(ere) 1026
'circle' 424, 424.4, 810,
    902
'circular race track' 32
'circular thing' 810.2
circumambulate 986
circumconic 467.1
circumflect 1389.2
circumfluent 1415
circumjacent 1406
circumspect 1390
circumvolve 1033
cirrhosis 1315.2
Cirripedia 44
cismontane 882
citadel 1121
'citizen' 546
'citizenry' 546, 1300
'citizens' 844
'city' 1053, 1267.3, 1300
cityward 683.1
civilization 1218.2
-clad **593**
clad(d) 593
clad(ian) 593
Cladocera 351
cladocerous 1371
Cladothrix 1453
-cladous **1356**
Claiborne 907
'clan' 1096
-clase 200, 1431
-clasia **200,** 1431
-clasis 200, 1431
'class' 37, 492, 659
'class, social or political'
    520.3, 1467.2
'classes, Roman' 510
-classic **510**
-classical 510
-classically 510
-classicism 510
classicist 1436.3
classic(us) 510
classification 1218.1
classificatory 1528.3
-clast 200, 566, **1431**
-clastic 200, **566,** 1431

clāth 1080
clattertrap 1241.3
claud(ere) 756, 958
Claudette 1011.2
claus(a) 958
claustrophobia 40
claus(um) 958
claus(us) 958
'claw' 68, 258
clawhand 646.2
'clay, potter's' 433
clayey 1457.1
-cle 849
'clean' 565
'cleaning' 565
'clearing' 565
'clear water' 1062
clefthand 646.2
cleistogamy 1503.3
clergy 1459.3
clerkhood 674
'clever' 1484
'clever person' 415
cliffside 748.2
-climate **988**
-climatic **514,** 988
-climatical 514, 988
-climatically 514, 988
'climb' 652
-clinal 898
-clination 898
-cline **898**
'cling' 922
-clinic **466,** 898
-clinism 466
-clinous 466, 898, **1366**
-cliny 466, 1366
clockwise 952.2
clockworks 1337.2
clodpate 995.2
clodpoll 1134.1
clonal 144
clone 144
-clonia **144**
-clonic 144
-clonism 144
-clonus 144
clo(re) 958
clos- 958
'close' 756,
-close **958**
clos(en) 958
'cloth, fragment' 720
-cloth 720.1, **1080**
clothbound 666.2
clothe 593

'clothed' 593.1
clotheshorse 966.2
clothesline 895.1
clothesmonger 1257.1
'clothing' 1080
'cloth ornament' 1241.3
-clothy 1080
cloudscape 911
'club' 665
clubfoot 1420.3
clubfooted 611
clubhand 646.2
clubland 647.4
clubmate 987.3
clubster 1267.3
-clude 756
-clūd(ere) 756
-clūs(a) 756
-clusion 756
-clusive 756
-clūs(um) 756
-clūs(us) 756
Clydesdale 800
-cnemia 106
-cnemial 106
-cnemic 106
-cnemy 106
coagula 273
coalhole 834.3
coalmouse 969.3
'coal-tar derivative' 885
coalyard 685.3
coatee 761.1
cocaine 890
'coca plant' 890
-cocca 7
-coccic 1349
Coccidiomorpha 34
coccigenic 460.2
coccobacteria 180
-coccoid 1349
coccolith 1075.3
Coccomyces 1298
coccosphere 923.3
-coccous 1349
-coccus 7, 1349
cockawee 761.2
cockeye 1037.1
cockhorse 966.3
cocreate 979
codpiece 720.1
-coel 814
coelacanth 1078
-coele 814
'coelenterate, flattened
    larva of' 275

Coelococcus 1349.1
coeloplanula 275
coelostat 1385.3
coenobia 39
coercion 1212.1
coercive 1025.2
cognition 1220, 1319
cognitive 1030
'cognizance' 773
coinage 765.1
-cola 271
-cole 833
col(ere) 271, 833
-colid 833
-coll 1133
collapse 962
collarbone 900
'collect' 980
'collection' 37, 765.1,
    1525.4
Collembole 831.2
collenchyma 339
collier 1261
collocate 978
'colloidal solution' 1138
-coloboma 300
-colon 471, 1224
-colonic 471, 1224
colonorrhagia 51
'color' 104, 114, 156,
    204, 446, 517, 864,
    865,
-color 1275
'coloration' 156
-colored 864, 1275
'coloring matter' 1135.2
'coloring substance' 865
'color of blood' 446.3
'color of minerals' 520.5
'color of the skin' 156
'color quality or value'
    905.3
'colors' 446.2
'color vision, defective'
    162, 227.2
colostomy 1508
colour 1275
-colour 1275
-colous 833
Columbae 694
Columbiad 588.1
colyseptic 563
-coma¹ 301
-coma² 302
-comatose 301

-comb 707
-combe 707
'combination' 533.1,
    533.2
'combine' 779.2, 816
combining 1245.1
'come' 886, 1417
comedienne 875
'comedy' 442
'come upon' 1417.2
'comfort' 855
-comic 442
-comical 442
-comically 442
comicodidactic 523
'coming' 1417.1
'coming together' 1417.1
'coming to pass' 1417.1
-comma 298
'command' 648
'commend' 1034
commendatory 1529.2
'commerce' 837
'commercial area' 685.3
commerge 779.2
commingle 816
'commission' 648
communicans 1338
communicant 1404.3
communism 1157.3
Communist 1436.3
'community' 1111
'companion' 983, 1111
'companionship' 1111
'compare' 89
compel 1123
'compelling' 735
compend 656.2
'competition' 1435.1
'complete' 892
complex 1452.1
'complexion' 1275
complicate 977.1
compliment 1412
compone 904
'components, made of
    different' 531
'composed of' 1357,
    1457.1
composite 1006, 1009
composition 1221
'composition for the
    stage' 282.1
composure 942
compound 669
'comprehend' 650.2, 654

correlative 1025.3, 1028.1
correspond 663
Corrigiola 268.1
corrupt 1423
corselet 1395.2
corticocerebral 1116
-cosm 453, **1163**
-cosme 1163
-cosmic **453**, 1163
-cosmical 453, 1163
-cosmically 453, 1163
cosmogonic 469.2
cosmology 1163
cosmopolis 1300
cosmopolite 1005.1
cosmorganic 455.3
-cosmos 453.3, 1163
cosmotellurian 503
cost(a) 1004
-costal 1004
-costate **1004**
costosternal 1114
costumiere 925
cottonmouth 1082.2
couchmate 987.1
coudee 761.2
coughing 1046.1
councillor 1273
councilwoman 1187.1
'counsel' 606, 606.2
counterbid 622
counterbrace 718.2
counterchange 775
counterprove 1034
countless 1342.2
countrypeople 844.1
countryside 748.3
'county' 928
'course' 445.2, 1380
'court' 685
'courtyard' 1081
covalence 732.2
'covenant' 89
'cover' 54
coverage 765.2
'covered' 666.2
'covering' 8, 333.1, 1149
'covering layer' 1203.3
'cow' 891
cowbane 877.1
cowbell 1131.1
cowbird 687
cowherd 686
cowshed 601
'crab' 318
crabwise 952.1

crackerjack 1086.2
crackpot 1422
-cracy 520, 1384, **1467**
cradlemate 987.4
craeft 1398
'craft' 462, 1021, 1290,
  1514
-craft **1398**
'craft, small' 1398.3
'craftsman' 1076, 1398
craftsmanship 1242.2,
  1398
-craftswoman 1398
-crania **128**
craniad 589
-cranial 128, 1173
-cranic 128, 1173
craniognomic 443.2
craniotomy 1506
-cranium 128, **1173**
Crashaw 1446
-crasia **206**
-crasic 206
-crat 520, **1384**, 1467
-crate 1384
-cratia **234**, 1467
-cratic **520**, 1384, 1467
-cratically 520, 1467
-cratie 1467
-cratism 1384, 1467
'craze' 127.2
cre- 737
creamsicle 809
cre(āre) 979
'create' 49, 399, 535,
  543, 737, 998, 1310
-create **979**
creat(en) 979
'creating' 535, 543
'creating with' 945
'creation' 399, 979, 1310
-creative 979
-creatively 979
'creature' 1181.6
'creatures' 14, 23
'creatures related to' 169
credulous 1363
'creek' 1090
creepmouse 969.1
-cresce **737**
crescence 737
-crescent 737
cresc(ere) 737
cret(us) 737
'crime' 991, 996
crīmen 991

crīmin(ārī) 991
-criminate **991**
-crimination 991
-criminatory 991
-crine 140
-crinia **140**
-crinism 140
crinoline 894, 1194
-crisia **220**
critic 384.1,
-critic **547**
-critical 547
-critically 547
criticaster 1269
critique 1020
'crocodile' 67
crooknosed 610
crossbow 1448.1
crossbred 607.1
crossbreed 598.1, 598.2
crosshand 646.3
'crossing in stream' 689
crossline 895.3
'crossway' 774
'crown of the head' 995
crowtoe 910.2
crucifer 1256.2
Cruciferae 704
'crush' 566, 1431
'crushing' 200
'crushing, surgical' 1537
'crushing instrument,
  surgical' 706
Crustacea 19
crustacean 1181.6
cryostat 1385.1
Cryptobranchia 65.1
cryptocerous 1371
cryptoclastic 566.3
Cryptogamia 37.4, 38.2
Cryptogramma 295
cryptograph 1060.1
Cryptomeria 179.1
cryptomnesia 215
Cryptomonadina 344
Cryptostegia 54
Cryptostomata 369
Cryptozonia 149
crystalliform 1153
'crystalline mineral' 1250
Cryptogamia 94
Cuban 1181.1
cubbyhole 834.4
cubiform 1153
Cuddles 1284
cuddyhole 834.3

'declaration, make a' 982
'declare' 734, 982
decline 898.1
'decline of part of body'
  71
'decomposition' 579,
  1016, 1039, 1328
Decynodontia 240
Dedham 1144
'deed' 282, 1332
deerskin 1203.1
deface 712
defame 853
'defecate' 256
'defecation' 256
defend 653
defenden 653
defer 1256.1
'deficiency' 135
defies 1297
define 892
definitive 1028.2, 1030
deflate 985
deflect 1389.1
defluxio 1237
deforce 735
degenerate 971.1
degradand 644
'degree' 728.3, 1343,
  1540
-deictic 526
deik(nunai) 526
'deity' 672
'deity, evil' 472
deject 1388.1
delay 1462
delegate 972.1
deliverance 728.2
delude 755
deluxeburger 1258.2
-dema 285
demagogue 1018.1
demand 648, 931
dem(as) 285
-deme 434
'dementia' 186, 239
-demic 434
-demically 434
democracy 1459.2, 1465,
  1467.1
democrat 1384.1, 1384.2
democratic 520.1, 520.2
democratize 1038.3
demographic 412.2
demokrat(os) 1465
'demon' 472

-demoniac 472
'demoniacal' 472.1
-demoniacally 472
-demonic 472
-demonical 472
demonkind 659
'demonstrate' 1034
dēm(os) 285, 434
-dendria 175
-dendrite 1228
-dendritic 545, 1228
dendrobe 708
Dendrogaea 18
-dendron 175, 1228
denounce 734
dens 1001
-dental 1001
'dental treatment' 551.2
-dentate 1001
dentigerous 1373
den-tree 763.1
denudant 1404.4
denunciate 982
deodorant 1404.4
depend 656.1
dependence 728.1
dependency 1470.1
deplane 880
deplore 934
depone 904
deposit 1402
deprecate 973.2
deprementia 239
'depression' 834.1, 1188.2
'deprivation' 245
'depth' 418
depute 1013
deranencephalia 78
derange 776.1
'derived from' 1183
-derm 118, 333, 450,
  1149, 1301
derma 118, 315, 450,
  1301
-derma **333**, 1149
-dermal 118, 333, 450,
  1149, 1301
-dermatic 118, 333, 450,
  1149, 1301
Dermatobia 39
dermatogenous 1364
-dermatoid 118, 333, 450,
  1149, 1301
dermatome 870.2
dermatopathic 419.1

-dermatous 118, 333,
  450, 1149, 1301
-derme 1149
-dermia **118**
dermiatrics 1291
-dermic 118, 333, **450,**
  1149, 1301
-dermis 118, 333, 450,
  1149, **1301**
-dermoid 118, 333, 450,
  1149, 1301
-dermoma **315**
dermoplasty 1544
dermovaccine 891
Derotremata 367
descend 652
'descent' 23, 616.2, 1128,
  1128.2
'descent from' 588
describe 705
desecrate 997
deserve 1035
designata 364
'desire' 250
'desire, sexual' 559.1,
  559.2
-desm 336
-desma **336**
desmectasia 208
-desmic 336
Desmognatha 36
desm(os) 336
despond 663
dessicant 1404.1, 1404.5
'destroyer' 1431.1, 1431.2
'destroying' 566.1
'destruction' 1039, 1212.2
'detachment' 1328
detain 1201
detention 1222
detoxicate 973.3
detumescence 730
deuteranopsia 227.2
Deuterostomia 117
'develop' 737
'development' 567.2,
  1317
'development, abnormal'
  202
'development of cells or
  tissue' 243
'deviation' 126, 163, 488,
  1522
'device' 927.2, 1241.3,
  1251.6

'device giving measure'
862.2
'devise' 855.1, 941
'devoid' 1342
Devonian 1181.2
'devotee' 1005.1, 1263
'devotion to' 1532
devour 361, 781, 937
-**dew 1447**
dextran 1182
dextrocardia 48.1
dextrogastria 189
dextrum 1164
di- 516
dia- 947
diabolatry 1532
diachronic 477
diaconate 972.2
Diadema 285
diadochokinesia 214
diagnosis 220.1, 1319
diagnostic 575
diagonic 468
diagrammatic 515
diakinesis 1312.2
diallylbarbituric 504
dialogic 406.1
dialogistic 573
dialogue 1019.1
dialysis 1328
diamagnetic 539.1
diamb 376
dianoetic 542
diaphanic 456.2
'diaphragm' 137, 461,
461.1
diaphragma 292
diaphysis 1327
diarrhea 21
diastalsis 1314
diastase 947
diastatic 521.1
diastole 840,
-**diastole 841**
diastolē 841
-**diastolic** 841
diastomyelia 85
diastrophe 785.1
diataxia 247.1
diatela 259
diathermia 119.2
diathermy 1509.2
Diatoma 327
diatomic 448
diatonic 480.2
diblastula 279

dibrachia 60
dibucaine 890
dichogamy 1503.3
dichromic 446.1, 446.2
dicing 1046.1
diclinic 466.2
diclinous 1366
dicoria 184
dictaphone 901.3
'diction' 949.3
dicyclic 424.3
Dicynodon 1208
-**didact** 523
-**didactic 523**
-**didactical** 523
-**didactically** 523
didaktik(os) 523
diddest 1433
didermoma 315
didn't 1403
didst 1433
didym(os) 123, 1353
-**didymus 1353**
diethylbarbituric 504
'difficult' 202
Digenea 23
'digested food, partly'
124
'digestion' 224, 562
'digestive juices' 92
'digit' 93, 1143
digitalis 1299
Digitigrada 13
'digit of the foot' 910
diglossia 228.2
'dignity' 1148
digynia 153
dikaryophasic 508
'dilation' 208, 841
'dilation of organs' 840
dilemma 296
dillseed 599.1
'dimensions' 615
dimetria 188
diminution 1217
'diminutive' 262, 265,
272, 273, 761.1, 796,
829, 831, 849, 1011.3,
1011.4, 1049.2, 1049.3,
1091, 1094, 1121,
1125, 1167, 1168,
1178, 1193, 1195,
1202, 1238, 1284,
1339, 1351, 1363,
1394.1, 1395.1, 1460,
1487, 1535

dimorphism 1161
dimple 796
dinette 1011.3
ding-toed 910.1
dinnerware 921
Dinoflagellata 366
Dinophyceae 701
dinornithic 420
dinosaur 1280
Dinosauria 191
Dinosaurian 1181.6
dinothere 924
diode 753
Dioecia 42
diopter 1266
dioramic 383.1
diotic 554.1
'dip' 779, 963
Dipetalonema 288.1
diphthong 1051
diphthongia 57
Dipladenia 129.2
Diplocardia 48.2
diploid 628
diploidy 1471
diplōma 516
diplomacy 516, 1466
-**diplomatic 516**
-**diplomatically** 516
diplonema 288.3
diplopia 158,
-**diplopia 161**
-**diplopic** 161
dipl(os) 628
diplosomatia 232
diplospondylic 432
diplo(us) 161
dipodia 47
dipole 838
dip(sa) 225
-**dipsia 225**
dipsomaniac 381.2
-**dipsy** 225
dipter 1265
Diptera 354
dipteron 1229
Dipteryx 1456
dipus 1376
'direction' 445.2, 488,
915, 1162, 1380, 1522
'direction of, in the'
952.2
directive 1025.3
'disability' 10
'disable' 581
'disapprove' 1034

disarrange 776.1
discarnate 994
'discharge' 519, 778.1
'discharge, excessive fluid' 51, 402, 768
'discharge, fluid' 11, 397
disclose 958
discoblastula 279
Discoideae 702
Discomyces 1298
discoplacenta 372
Discoplacentalia 81
'discourse' 406, 529, 573, 1019, 1019.1, 1476
'discourse' 'treatise' 1476.3
'discourse, written' 406.3
disculpate 996
'discuss' 1013
'disease' 37, 554.2, 1305.1, 1305.2, 1330
'disease, communi- cable' 544
'disease, treatment of' 1294
'diseased condition' 1305
'diseased state' 1305
'disease in a region' 434.1
disennoble 807.2
disfigure 941.2
disgorge 781
disgrace 719
'dish' 1188, 1188.1
dishes 1296
dishpan 1188.1
'disintegration' 566.2
disject 1388.1
dislocate 978
dismissal 1101
dispel 1123
dispense 954
disperse 964
'displacement' 167
'displacement of organ' 1321
'disposition' 1025, 1025.1, 1027, 1030
disproof 1041.1
disprove 1034
dispute 1013
dissect 1391
dissemble 806
disseminate 990
dissociate 983
dissoluble 808

dissolve 581, 1032
'dissolved, able to be' 808
'dissolving' 582
dissuade 743
distend 657.1
'distension' 208
distich 1054
distichia 64
distillate 972.3
Distocardia 48.2
'distributed' 862
'district' 748.3, 928
'district, administrative' 928
disulfuric 502
disyllable 805
ditone 905.2
Ditrocha 32
diuresis/diuretic 528
diuretic 383.8, 384.4
divalent 1410.2
diverge 780
diversiflorate 1000
'divide' 602, 788, 1010, 1391
'divided into parts' 624
'divination' 238, 549, 1469
'division' 659
'division, rounded' 710
'division (of cells)' 1312.2
'divisions' 1010
divorcee 759.1
divorcive 1025.2
Dixiecrat 1384.2
'do' 52, 246, 400, 524, 723, 945, 976, 1029, 1219, 1332, 1387, 1474, 1530
doctorbird 687
doctrinaire 927.3
'doctrine' 1476.2
'doctrines' 1157.3
doddypoll 1134.1
dodecatonic 480.1
'doer' 1436.1
doeskin 1203.4
'dog' 668
dogdom 1148.2
do-gooder 1251.3
'doing' 723, 1332, 1405.2
dolichocolon 1224
Dolichosoma 326.1
dollarleaf 1040

dollface 713.1
-dom 1148
dōm 1148
-dome 1148
domina 852
Donald 630
'door, folding' 1031
doorbell 1131.1
doorframe 855.2
doormouse 969.1
-dora 356
Dorchester 1270.1
dorhawk 1099.2
dor(on) 356
-dorsal 1120
Dorset 1397
Dorsibranchiata 365
dorsoventral 1118
dors(um) 1120
dosage 765.6
'double' 161, 628
doublehanded 595.3
doubletone 905.3
'double vision' 161
'dough, sweet baked' 787.3
'dough, thin fried' 787.2
doughface 713.2
Doulting 1048
downright 1400
drac(a) 789
drac(ō) 789
'drag' 1386
draghound 668
'dragon' 789
-drake 789
drama 281,
-drama 282
-dramatic 282
-dramatically 282
dramaturgic 408.2
dramaturgy 1478
dramein 445, 863
'draw' 705, 738, 1386
drawbridge 774.1
drawhorse 966.2
'drawing' 441, 1042, 1060.1, 1145.1
'drawing forth' 1018
'draw tight' 777, 1200
'dread' 40
dreadful 1141.1
'dream, bad' 920
dreamworld 642
drengage 766
dresses' 1295

drier 1253.1
driftwind 660
'drink' 1086.2
'drinker' 847.1
drinking 1045.3
dripmold 641
'drive' 953, 1123, 1216
'drive away' 783.2
'driving' 1216
-drome 445, **863**
-dromic **445**, 863
-dromical 445, 863
drom(os) 445, 863
-dromous 445, 863
dronepipe 912.3
drosky 1487
dru- 763
'drug' 449
drunkard 679.2
dryad 588.6
-ducation 738
-duce **738**
-ducement 738
-ducer 738
duc(ere) 738
duchesse 1341
duckfoot 1420.2
'ducklike bird' 960
-duct 738
-duction 738
-ductive 738
-ductor 738
duct(us) 738
duet 1394.2
Dufaycolor 1275.2
dukedom 1148.1
'dull' 186, 671, 970,
970.1
dullard 679.2
dullbrained 603
dullsville 830.2
'dunce' 1134.1
Dunciad 588.1
dunghill 1132.1
duodecimo 1239
'duodenum' 124
duopole 837
duple 843
duplex 1452.1
duplicand 644
duplicate 977.1, 977.2
'dust' 142
Dutchman 1186.2
'dwell' 667
'dwellers' 640.4
'dwelling' 42, 1090

dwg 1042
dyad 588.5
-dymia 123
-dymus 123
dynameter 1264
-dynamia **95**
-dynamic 95
dynam(is) 95
dynamite 1005.4
dynamostatic 521.2
dynamotor 1278
-dynamy 95
'dynastic line' 616.1
dynatron 1230.1
-dyne 95
dys- 202, 1483
dysanagnosia 222
dysaphia 69
dysarthria 181
dysbasia 197
dyschezia 256
dyschiria 182.2
dysdipsia 225
dysecoia 154
dysgenesia 213.2
dysgnosia 221
dysgraphia 70.2
dyslalia 80
dyslexia 248
dysmenorrhoeica 11
dysmetria 187
dysmimia 111
dysnomia 113
dyspepsia 224
dyspeptic 562.2
dysphasia 199
dysphoria 185.2
dysphotic 556.2
dysphrasia 207
dysplasia 201,
-dysplasia **202**
-dysplastic 202
dyssomnia 141
dyssymbolia 89
dystocia 43.1
dystrophy 1483

E

-e **693**, 695
-é 759
-ē 695, 840
-ea 20, 699
-eae **699**
ēage 1037
-eal 1100

Ealing 1048
-ean 1181
-eanly 1181
'ear' 242, 553
earliness 1343
'ear lobe' 710
earphone 901.2
'earth' 18, 503, 670
earthdrake 789
'earthquake' 452, 792,
1160
earthtongue 1017.2
earwig 1044.2
eastbound 667
'eat' 29, 50, 361, 767,
937, 1375, 1475
'eater' 767, 937
'eating' 50.1, 1375, 1475
ecbolic 429.2
ecclesiarch 1057
ecg 771
ech(ein) 61, 62
-echia **61**
Echinodermic 450.4
echolalia 80
echomimia 111
echopractic 524.1
echopraxia 246
-ecian 42
-ecious 42
-ecism 42
-ecium 42
eclipsis 1323
-ecoia **154**
ecologic 406.2
-economic **444**
economical 444, 1103.2
-economically 444
-economics 444
economy 1504
ecotypic 489.1
-ectasia **208**
-ectasis 208
-ectasy 208
-ectatic 208
ectocondyle 850
ectocornea 25
ectodermic 450.5
-ectome 1507
-ectomize 1507
ectomorph 1064
-ectomy **1507**
-ectopia **167**
-ectopic 167
ectoplacenta 372
ectoplasm 335.1

-ectopy 167
ectotherm 1150.2
ectromelia 84
ectypia 168
-ed 364, 586, **594,** 1381
-ede 594
-edema 286
-edematous 286
-edemic 286
-edge 771
edgewise 952.2
educabilia 86
'education' 45, 392.2
educational 1100
educative 1025.2
educe 738
Edward 684.2
-ée 759
-ee[1] **759**
-ee[2] **760**
-ee[3] **761**
eelcake 787.4
-een[1] **1194**
-een[2] **1195**
-eer 1255, 1261
efface 712
'effect' 1218.2, 1387,
    1477.2
'effecting' 384.4
effuse 967
'egg' 173, 350.2
'egg-yolk' 1108
egge 771
egghead 590.2
egocentric 499.1
egomaniac 381.2
'Egypt' 436
-eia 760
eid(os) 625, 626, 754
eie 1037
eighe 1037
eighteenmo 1239
eightieth 1069
Einsteinia 37.3
eisanthema 287
eject 1388.1
ek 156, 1507
ektas(is) 208
ektein(ein) 208
ektomē 1507
-el 262, 796, 797, 798,
    1100, 1395
-el 262, 796, **1121,** 1395
elbow 1448.2
elderbush 1068
Eldred 606.2

-ele 1121
-electric 497
-electrical 497
'electrical conductor' 753
'electrical current, direct'
    459
-electrically 497
'electricity' 497
'electricity, static' 521.2
electric(us) 497
electroanalytic 580
electrocatalytic 582
'electrode' 393.2
electrogild 636.1
electrohydraulic 431
electrolysis 1328
electrolyte 1016
electrolytic 579
electromobile 821.1
electron 478, 497, 1207.1
-electronic 478, 497
electronics 1289.1
electrophonic 383.6
electrosonic 479.2
electrostatic 521.2
electrostatics 1293
electrosurgery 1526
electrosynthetic 533.2
electrothanasia 205
electrotherapeutic 578
electrotype 917.2
elektron 478, 497
'element' 588.5, 1207.3
elephantiasis 1305.2
elevator 1273
-ell(a) 796, 828, 1121
-ella 262
-elle 262, **828**
Ellesmere 926
ellipsis 1323
-ell(um) 262, 796, 828,
    1121
-ell(us) 262, 796, 828,
    1121, 1238
ellwand 651
-elminth 1079
-elminthic 1079
eloquent 1416
Elstow 1450
elude 755
-ēma 856
'embellish' 636.2
embergoose 960
'embodied' 994
'embody' 994
embolden 1190.1

embolic 429.3
-embryo 481, **1240**
embryo(n) 481, 1240
-embryonic 481, 1240
'embryonic stage' 278,
    279, 1430
embryotocia 43.2
embryotroph 1063.1
-eme 856
-ème 856
emend 648, 655
ēmend(āre) 655
emendation 1217
em(ere) 873
emerge 779.1
emergency 1470.3
emerse 963
emesis 536
-emetic 536
-emetical 536
-emetically 536
emetik(os) 536
emetocathartic 565
-emia 96
-emic 96, 856
'emitting light' 1407.2
'emotional disorder' 1316
'emotional instability'
    560.2
'emotional state' 185.2
'emotions' 419.2, 532
'emotions, seat of' 137,
    176.2, 461
empathic 419.2
emphasis 1304
Empirin 1199.2
employee 759.1
-empyema 291
empyēma 291
-empyemic 291
-empyesis 291
emulsin 1199.4
-en 481, 1189, 1191.1,
    1191.3, 1193, 1240
-en[1] **1189**
-en[2] **1190**
-en[3] **1191**
-en[4] **1192**
-en[5] **1193**
enanthema 287
-ence 728, 1405, 1468,
    1470
-encephalia 78
encephalodysplasia 202
encephalon 1207
encephalosepsis 1322

-encephalous 78
-encephalus 78
-encephaly 78
encharge 778.3
ench(ein) 339
enchondroma 321
-enchyma **339**
-enchyme 339
enclose 958
'enclosed agricultural
   area' 685.2
'enclosed area' 685.1
'enclosed area for
   animals' 637
'enclosed land' 1144
'enclose with stakes' 802
'enclosure' 685, 1081,
   1234
Encratic 520.6
'Encratites' 520.6
-ency 728, 1405, 1468,
   1470
encyclic 424.4
encyclopedic 392.2
'end' 426, 590.6, 892,
   959.4
'end, bring to an' 958
'end, upper or higher'
   590.4
-ende 1045
endeictic 526
endemic 434.2
endo- 309
endoblast 1430
endochrome 865
endocrine 140
'endocrine secretion' 140,
   220.2
endocuticula 274
endodermic 450.5
endogamy 1503.1
endogastric 500
endognathion 1214
endolymph 1062
endolysin 1204
endomixis 1336
endophasic 507
endoplasma 335.1
endoplast 1432
endopsychic 411.1
endosarc 585
endothecium 1166
'endothelial tumor' 309
endothelioma 307,
-endothelioma **309**
endothelium 309, 1172

endotherm 1150.2
endothermy 1509.1
Endothrix 1453
'endowed with' 1355
endpiece 720.3
'endure beyond' 650.1
endways 1380
-ene **883**, 887
-ēnē 883
energetic 530
energy 1477.1
enforce 735
enframe 855.1
-eng 1048
'engage' 612, 766
'engage in' 1038.2
engild 636.2
'engine' 1278
engineer 1255.1
English 1065.1
engorge 781
'engrave' 33, 705, 1060,
   1145, 1260, 1481
enkephal(os) 78
enlace 715
'enlargement' 1490
enlisted 594.1
-enly 1189, **1500**
-ennial **1112**
-enni(um) 1112,
-ennium **1174**
ennoble 807.2
enoblest 1433
enorganic 455.1
-ens 1405
-ens(is) 949
'ensnare' 715
Ensuchia 67
-ent **1405**, 1470
entacoustic 576.1
enterocele 813
enteroproctia 236
enterprise 950
'entertainment' 755.1
enthrallment 1412.2
enthusiasm 1154
enthusiast 1429
-ential 1405, 1470
-entially 1405, 1470
-ently 1404
entocondyle 850
Entoloma 311
entombment 1412.2
entone 905.1
Entoprocta 370
entotic 553.1

'entrails' 463
'entranceway' 1425
'entreat' 622
entreaty 1458
enunciate 982
enuresis 1307
'enzyme' 874, 1199.4
Eocene 884
Eohippus 1378
-eor 1273
-eous 1354, **1357**
Eozoic 484.2
epanastrophe 785.2
epi- 308
epiblastema 290
epibolic 429.5
'epic' 588.1, 618.2
epichorion 1215
epiclastic 566.3
epicondyle 850
epicranium 1173
epicuticula 274
epicycle 810.2
epicyclic 424.1
epideictic 526
epidemic 434.1
epiderm 1149
epiderma 333.1
epidermic 450.1
epidermis 1301
epiglottic 511
epigrammatic 515
epigraph 1060.1
epigraphy 1481.2
epigyne 909
epihydriad 588.6
epilepsy 1536
epileptic 561
epinephroma 323
epiotic 553.1
epiphanic 456.4
epiphany 1511
epipubic 389
episcopacy 1459.3
episcopate 972, 972.2
epispermic 451.1
-epist 1520
episternal 1114
episternum 1179
epistrophe 785.2
episynthetic 533.1
epitaph 1061
epitaphic 413
epitela 259
epithecium 1166

'epithelial tumor' 308,
313
'epithelial tumor,
malignant' 318
epithelioma 307,
-epithelioma **308**
epithelium 308, 1172
epode 752.2
eponychia 68
eponymy 1510.2
ep(os) 1520
Epworth 1081
-**epy 1520**
'equal' 1150.3
equalitarian 1185.1
equestrienne 875
equiangle 815.1
equianharmonic 475.2
equivalence 732.1
equivalent 1410.1
-er 759, 1191.2, 1251,
1252, 1253, 1258, 1341
-**er¹ 1251**
-**er² 1252**
-**er³ 1253**
-**er⁴ 1254**
'era, geological' 884
eradicant 1404.5
eradicate 973.4
-ere 1251, 1252, 1253
-**ergasia 198**
-**ergastic** 198
ergaz(esthai) 198
-erg(ein) 530
-erg(ēsis) 530
-**ergetic** 407, **530,** 1477
-**ergetical** 407, 530, 1477
-**ergetically** 407, 530,
1477
-ergētik(os) 530
-**ergic 407,** 1477
erg(on) 407, 408, 455,
530, 1477, 1478
-**ergy** 407, 530, **1477**
-erie 1525
Eriglossa 363
erōs 559
-**erotic 559**
-**erotical** 559
-**erotically** 559
-**eroticism** 559
erotomania 127.1
erotopath 1072.1
erotopathic 419.4
'error' 655
erupt 1423

'eruption' 287
-**ery 1525**
-es 1281, 1282, 1283,
1285, 1286, 1295,
1296, 1297
-**es' 1282, 1295**
-**es¹** 1281, 1283, **1296**
-**es² 1285, 1297**
-ēs 1296
-(e)sc- 729, 736, 737,
1066, 1407
escapee 759.4
-**esce** 729, **736,** 737, 1407
-**escence 729,** 736, 1407
-**escens** 1407
-**escent** 729, 736, **1407**
-escentia 729
-**escently** 736, 1407
-esc(o) 1022
escobilla 265.1
-**ese 949**
-**esic** 1307
-**esis** 528, 949, 1302,
1307
-ēsis 1307
esophagal 1100
esophageal 1100
esophagospasm 1156
-**esque 1022**
-**ess** 725, **1341,** 1454
-esse 1341
'essence' 230
-est 1427, 1428, 1433,
1434
-**est¹** 1427, **1433**
-**est² 1434**
establish 1066
estage 770
-estere 1267
-**esthesia** 212
-**esthetic** 212, 534
-**esthetical** 534
-**esthetically** 534
'estimate' 656.2
-**et** 373, **1394,** 1395, 1460
-ete 1011, 1394
-**eth** 1069, **1074**
ethanal 1102
ethane 876
ethanol 1136
-(e)the 1069
Ethelred 606.2
ethicoaesthetic 534.1
ethicosocial 1111
-**ethnic 464**
-**ethnical** 464

-**ethnically** 464
ethnobotany 1512
ethnoflora 358.1
ethn(os) 464
ethyl 1142
eth(yl)ene 883
-**etic 528,** 1307
-ētik(os) 528
-**etta 373,** 1011
*-etta 373, 786, 1011
*-ett(a) 1460
-**ette** 373, **1011,** 1395,
1460
-**etto** 1394
*-etto 1394
etymologic 406.2
euangiotic 554.1
eucapnia 150
euconic 467.2
eucrasia 206.1
eucyclic 424.3
eudaemonic 472.2
eugeny 1513
eulogy 1476.3
-e(um) 20, 699
Eunice 724
eupepsia 224
euphonic 470.1
euphony 1516.1
euphoria 185.2
eupractic 524.1
eupyrexia 251
-eur 1273, 1274
eurhythmia 110
eurybathic 418
euryphotic 556.1
eurysomatic 518.3
Eurytrema 289.2
-eus 20, 699, 1357
eusitia 237
Euspongia 58
eutechnics 1290
euthanasia 205
eutrophy 1482
evade 744
evangelize 1038.2
'even' 879
event 1417.1
eventful 1141.1
eventide 751.1
'evil deity' 472
evince 733
evoke 795
evolve 1033
ex 655
'exalted person' 483

'finances' 444
financial 1109
'fin bone' 1170.1
finc 1055
'fin cartilage' 1170.1
-finch **1055**
find(ere) 624
-fine **892**
-finement 892
fin(en) 892
fin(er) 892
finfoot 1420.2
'finger' 93, 280, 1143
'finger bones' 56
fing(ere) 941
'fingers' 280
fingerstall 1130
fin(īre) 892
finish 1066
-finition 892
Finnish 1065.1
'fire' 251
firedrake 789
fireproof 1041.2
Firestone 906.6
firetrap 1241.2
fireweed 600
'firm' 568, 1545
'first' 1428
'first rank' 510
fisc 1067
fish 1037.3, 1086.3
-fish **1067**
'fish, largebellied' 764.4
fishcake 787.4
fisherpeople 844.2
fisheye 1037.2
fishline 895.1
fishwife 764.1
fishyard 685.3
fissicostate 1004
fissiped 604.1
Fissipeda 3
Fissipedia 44
'fit' 804
Fitchburg 1053
'fit for' 86, 804.1, 1486
'fitness' 1400
fivesome 868
'fix' 655
'fixation, surgical' 1335
-flagellata **366**
'flagellate' 1455
flagell(um) 366
flagpole 835
'flanks' 380

flannelette 1011.5
flapcake 787.2
flapjack 1086.2
fla(re) 985
flashpan 1188.3
'flat' 75, 275, 372, 716,
    879
-flatable 985
'flat cake' 372
-flate **985**
flatfoot 1420.3
-flation 985
'flattened larva' 275
flat(us) 985
'flax' 894
'flax, made of' 895
'flax rope' 895
flaxseed 599.1
'flea' 267
fleabane 877.2
fleaseed 599.2
-flect **1389**
-flect(en) 1389
flect(ere) 1389
-flection 1389
-flective 1389
-flector 1389
'flee' 783
fleecy 1457.2
'flesh' 303, 585, 994
'flesh, whole' 512
'fleshy growth' 303
'flex' 1389
-flexion 1389
flicker 1254
'flight' 783.1
'flight, put to' 783
flitfold 637
flittermouse 969.2
'flock' 980
floeberg 1052
floodway 1463
-flora **358**, 1374
-florate 358, **1000**, 1374
floreate 971.2
florid 619
Florideae 699
-florous 358, **1374**
flos 358
flōs 1000, 1374
'flow' 11, 21, 397, 519,
    934, 967, 1415
'flow, cause to' 934
'flower' 358, 1000, 1077,
    1374

'flower, bell-shaped'
    1131.2
'flowering' 287
'flowering plant' 358
'flowers' 358.2
'flowing' 1413, 1415
-fluct 1415
-fluction 1415
-fluence 1415
fluens 1415
-fluent **1415**
flu(ere) 1415
fluid 619
'fluid, clear body' 1062
'fluid, place in' 963
'fluid discharge' 11, 21,
    397
'fluid discharge,
    excessive' 51, 402, 768
'fluid in cytoplasm or
    protoplasm' 335.1
'fluid in the body' 177
flumen 1197
fluor 1415
fluorescent 1407.2
fluoride 1415
fluorine 1415
fluoroscopy 1521
fluors 1415
fluorspar 1250, 1415
fluviovolcanic 454.2
-flux 519, 1415
'fly' 254
flybane 877.2
'flying' 880
foci 1083.1
focil 1125
-foil **1127**
folc 1096
'fold' 638, 639, 843, 977,
    977.2, 1452, 1502
-fold¹ **637**
-fold² **638**
-fold³ **639**
'folding door' 1031
-folia 1127
'foliage' 1040
-foliate 971.2, 1127
foli(um) 1127
-folk **1096**
folkfree 762.1
folksy 1457.2
'folly' 186
'fondness for' 1492.1
'fond of, person
    inordinately' 881

'food' 71, 237, 414, 1008,
1063.2, 1086.2, 1224,
1482
'food, desire for' 50
'food, give' 497
'food for livestock' 597.2
'foot' 16, 44, 47, 391,
604, 677, 1168, 1376,
1420.2, 1420.3
-foot 1420
-footed 611, 1420
footgeld 633
foothill 1132.1
foothold 640.5
footpath 1073
footstall 1130
for 870.1
'force' 732.1, 1410.1
-force 735
-ford 689
-fore 932
forebrace 718.2
forecastle 846
foreclose 958
foreface 713.3
forefigure 941.2
forehand 646.3
forehold 640.3
foreknowledge 773
foremasthand 646.1
forename 854.1
forepale 802
forepole 835
foresaddle 811.3
foresense 955
'forest, small' 676.2
forestage 770.1
forfend 653
'form' 34, 72, 201, 202,
243, 383.1, 416, 456.1,
567, 625, 626, 712,
713, 754, 941, 1064,
1155, 1161, 1317,
1432, 1544
form(a) 1152, 1153
formagenic 460.2
-formation 201, 213,
213.1, 469.2, 538,
567.2, 1152, 1309
'formation of chemical
compound' 1309
-forme 1152
'formed' 335, 335.2
'formed from' 460.2
-formic 1152, 1153
'forming' 460.1, 1317

'form into' 1474.1
-formity 1152, 1153
forms 1180
'formulate' 855.1
'fort' 846, 1270
forthfare 919
forthright 1400
'fortified city' 1053
'fortified place' 640.2,
1059, 1534
'fortified town' 1053,
1270
fort(is) 735
'fortress' 1053
fortyish 1065.5
'fossil' 1005.3
'fossil in stone' 1075.3
fōt 1420
fought 1381
'foundation' 670
'fountain' 907
four-ply 1502
foursome 868
Fowey 1472
foxbane 877.3
'fragment' 298
'fragmented material'
566.3
-frame 855, 966.2
fram(ian) 855
fram(ien) 855
Francomania 127.2
Francophobe 709
frankpledge 772
fratricide 747.2
fraudulent 1411
fre 762
-fred 608
-free 762
freedom 1148.4
'free from' 762.2
freehand 646.4
freehold 640.1
-freely 762
freestone 906.2
Frenchify 1474.2
frēo 762
'fresh' 884
'friction' 1324
fridu 608
'friend' 987.2
friendship 1242.4
Frigidaire 927.2
frigostabile 820
frijolillo 1238
'fringe' 311

Fringillidae 1055
frogface 713.1
frogmouth 1082.2
frogtongue 1017.1
froing 1046.4
from 655
from(ian) 855
frostbow 1448.3
fructosan 1182
fructose 957.1
'frugal' 444
'fruit' 1115, 1244
'fruitful' 827
fryer 1251.6
Fuchsia 37.2
Fucoideae 702
fudgesicle 809
-fugal 783
-fugally 783
fug(āre) 783
-fuge 783
fug(ere) 783
fugitive 1028.1
-ful 1140
-ful¹ 1140
-ful² 1141
full 1140
fullface 713.3, 713.4
'full of' 956, 1141.1,
1354.1, 1355, 1411
-fully 1141, 1499
-fulness 1141, 1346
fum(āre) 871
-fume 871
fum(en) 871
fum(er) 871
'fumes, expose to' 871
fund(ere) 967
'funeral rites' 1061
fungi 1083.1
fungicide 747.1
'fungi like tongues'
1017.2
fungistat 1385.5
fungitoxic 583
'fungus' 75, 1298
furibund 664
'furnish with' 973.5
furol 1137
furrier 1252.1
fus 967
-fusal 967
-fuse 967
fused 967
-fusion 967
fus(us) 967

-fy 400, 723, 945, 1029, 1219, 1387, **1474,** 1530
-fying 1029

G

-g **1042**
gabardine 889.2
gabfest 1435.2
gablet 1395.1
gadoleic 398.2
Gadshill 1132.2
-gaea **18**
-gaean 18
-gaeic 18
-gage **766**
-gagement 766
gagman 1186.1
gaia 18
Gainsborough 1059
gala 235
-galactia **235**
galīy 897
Galliformes 1296
gallonage 765.6
gallstone 906.5
-galvanic **459**
-galvanically 459
galvanic(o) 459
-galvanize 459
-gam 94
-gamae 94
'game' 755
-gametism 94, 1503
-gamia **94**
-gamic 94, 1503
-gamist 94, 1503
gamistic 94, 1503
gamogony 1515
gam(os) 94, 1503
-gamous 94, 1503
-gamy 94, **1503**
ganglioma 310
ganglioneuroma 325
'gangrene' 316
garde 682
garden 685
garlicwort 1426
'garment' 1080
garnishee 759
gasoline 887.2
gaster 189, 278, 500
-gastria **189,** 500
-gastric 189, **500**
gastric neurosis 320
gastrocamera 353

gastrocele 814
gastrodidymus 1353.1
gastromalacia 41
gastronome 862.1
gastropancreatic 512
gastrophrenic 461.1
gastroplegia 53
gastropneumonic 476.2
gastropod 677
Gastropoda 16
gastrorrhexis 1334
Gastrotricha 30
-gastrula **278**
-gastrular 278
gasworks 1337.1
gatehouse 968
'gateway' 1425
gatophilia 88.2
Gatorade 739.4
gauzewing 1050.2
-gea 18
-gean 18
geard 685
(ge)claðed 593
(ge)cynde 659
-geène 1196
geese's 1281.2
gehend(an) 654
-geic 18
Geissois 599.2
gelatin 1199.3
'gelatinous medium' 22
-geld **633**
geldant 1404.6
gelding 1047
gelic 793
'gem' 1037.3
gemett(a) 987
Geminid 618.1
-gen 460 469, 538, **1196,** 1513, 1515
-genate 460, 1196, 1513
-genation 460, 1196
-gene 340, 460.3, 538, 1196, 1513
gen(ea) 460, 469, 1196, 1364, 1515
-genea **23**
genealogic 406.3
gen(eia) 1513
-geneous 23, 460, 538, 1196, 1513
genera 1.2
-generacy 998
gener(are) 998
-generate **998**

'generated' 538.3, 1196.2
-generately 998
'generating' 538.2
'generation' 469.1, 538.1, 998, 1513
-generative 998
'generator' 1196.1
generat(us) 998
-generic **492**
-generical 492
-generically 492
-genesia **213**
genes(is) 213, 538, 538.1
-genetic 213, 460, **538**
-genetically 538
-genia **130**
-genic **460,** 469, 538, 1196, 1513, 1515
-genically 460, 538, 1196, 1513
-genism 460, 1196, 1513
-genist 460, 1196, 1513
'genitalia' 389
-genite 460, 1196, 1513
Genoese 949.2
gen(os) 23
-genous 460, 538, 1196, **1364,** 1513
gentianophobic 386.2
genuflect 1389
'genus' 37.2, 76, 492
-geny 1196, 213, 460, 469, 538, 1196, **1513,** 1515
gen(ys) 130
geobotany 1512
geocentric 499.1
geocyclic 424.4
geodetic 528
geognosis 1319
geognost 1442
geognostic 575
geogonic 469.2
'geologic ages' 484.2
'geological period' 1181.2
geomagnetic 539.3
geomancy 1469
geomantic 549
'geometric figure' 1210, 1227
geomorphic 416
geonastic 568
geonasty 1545
geophagia 50.1
geophagy 1475
geophysical 1104

geophyte 1015
geopolitic 546.1
Georgia 4.1
georgic 384.1
geosphere 923.2
geotactic 525.2
geotropic 488.1
geotropy 1522
-ger 1373
Gerald 630
ger(ere) 1373
geriatric 496
geriatrics 1291
geriopsychosis 1316
'germ' 120, 334, 451,
    1151, 1430
Germantown 1234
germfree 762.2
germicide 747.2
'germinal stage' 1430
gerodermia 118
gerōn 552
-gerontal 552
-gerontic 552
gerontocracy 1467.2
-gerous 1373
'gestation' 1368
'gestures' 111
get 654
geuein 229
-geusia 229
-geusic 229
geus(is) 229
-geustia 229
gicel 809
gield 633
'gift' 356
gild 633,
-gild 636
'gills' 65, 365
gimbaljawed 613
gimcrackery 1525.5
'girdle' 149
-girl 621, 1139
girle 1139
girleen 1195
girl's 1281.1, 1282
'given to' 804.2
'glacial rubble, ridge of'
    465
'glade on hill' 1058
gladeye 1037.2
gladhander 1251.4
Gladiola 268.1
Gladstone 906.6
'glance' 1037.2

'gland' 129, 317
'gland, shield-shaped' 28
glandilemma 297
Glareole 831.2
Glassboro 1059
glassine 887.3
Glaucionetta 373
glaucophanic 456.1
-glea 22
-gleic 22
Glenwood 676.2
gleukos 957
glia 22, 310
-glial 22
-glioma 310
-gliomatous 310
glioneuroma 325
'globe' 491, 923
Globicephala 257
globin 194
'globin in urine' 194
-globinuria 194
globule 848
globulus 1351
glob(us) 194
-gloea 22
-gloeal 22
gloia 22, 310
glossa 228, 1419
-glossa 228, 363, 1419
glōssa 363
-glossal 228, 363, 1419
-glossia 228, 363
glossomantia 238
Glossophaga 29
glossotrichia 63.2
-glot 228, 363, 1419
glot(ta) 228, 1419
glōtta) 363
-glottal 228, 363, 1419
-glottic 228, 363, 1419
glottogonic 469.2
Gloucester 1270.2
glucoascorbic 388
glucokinetic 540.4
glucose 957
'glue' 22, 310, 1133
gluepot 1422
gluk(us) 98
-glycaemia 98
-glycemia 98
-glycemic 98
glycoclastic 566.2
glycocoll 1133
glycohistechia 61, 62
glycorrachia 59

glycose 957.1
glycosialia 79
glycotrophic 414
glykys 957
-glyph 35, 417
-glypha 35
glyph(ein) 35, 417
-glyphic 35, 417
-glyphous 35
Glyptodon 1208
glyptolith 1075.1
-gnath 36, 73
-gnatha 36, 73
-gnathae 36, 73
-gnathan 36, 73
-gnathi 36, 73
-gnathia 73
-gnathic 36, 73
gnath(os) 36, 73
Gnathostoma 330
Gnathostomata 369
-gnathous 73
-gnathus 36, 73
gnōm(ē) 443, 1505
-gnomic 221, 443, 474,
    575, 1505
-gnomical 443, 474, 1505
-gnomically 443, 1505
gnōmōn 474
-gnomonic 221, 443, 474,
    575, 1505
-gnomonical 474
-gnomonically 474
-gnomy 443, 474, 1505
gnōnai 221, 443, 1319,
    1442, 1505
-gnosia 221, 443, 474,
    575, 1319, 1442, 1505
-gnosis 221, 443, 474,
    1319, 1442, 1505
gnōs(is) 221, 222, 1442
-gnost 575, 1442
-gnostic 221, 443, 474,
    575, 1319, 1442, 1505
-gnostical 575
-gnostically 1442
gnōstikos 575, 1442
-gnosy 221, 575, 1319,
    1442
'go' 596, 652, 744, 745,
    918, 919, 1213
'go astray' 880
goatee 761.2
goatsbane 877.3
'goblin' 920

'god' 472, 572, 1159,
1437
-god 672
'god, belief in' 1159
'god, believer in' 1437
'goddess' 572, 1159, 1437
Godhead 591
'god of fire' 454
goeth 1074
'going' 667
'going astray' 126, 880
'gold, cover with' 636
golden 1189
goldeneye 1037.4
goldfinch 1055
goldseed 599.2
goldsmith 1076.1
golubchick 1094
-gon 468, 1210
gonacratia 234.2
gonadokinetic 540.4
gonadotrope 915
gonadotropic 488.3
-gonal 468, 1210
-gonally 1210
gondolier 1261
gon(ē) 469, 1515
goneoclinic 466.1
gōn(ia) 468, 1210
Goniaster 1268
-gonic 1515
-gonic¹ 468, 1210
-gonic² 469
gonimolobe 710
gonophoric 494.2
gonopore 935
gonorrhea 21
gonorrheic 397
gonorrhoeica 11
gonotrema 289.1
-gony 469, 1515
goodwife 764.2
goos 960
-goose 960
gooseboy 1518
goosegirl 1139
gooselike 793
goosetongue 1017.3
-gorge 781
-gorgement 781
Gorgonacea 19
gos 960
gōs 960
goshawk 1099.1
gosling 1049.2
Gothic 384.3

gotten 1192
'government' 1467.1
'government, advocate
of' 1384.1
'government, theory of'
520.1, 520.2, 1467.3
goyim 1146
-grace 719
-grada 13
-grade 13
grad(us) 13
grǣf(a) 1024
graffiti 1083
'grain' 7, 176, 237, 314,
321, 1008, 1349
'grain, ground' 1107
-gram 441, 515, 1105,
1145
Gramineae 699
gram(ma) 441, 515, 1105,
1145
-gramma 295
'grammar' 1105
grammarian 1185.2
-grammatic 441, 515,
1105, 1145
-grammatical 441, 515,
1105, 1145
-grammatically 441, 515,
1105, 1145
grammatik(os) 1105
-gramme 441, 515, 1105,
1145
-grammic 441, 515, 1105,
1145
-grammical 441, 515,
1145
-grammically 441, 515,
1105, 1145
gramophone 901.3
granddame 852
grandee 761.3
grandiflora 358.2
grandmothership 1242.5
grandstand 649.2
granophyre 946
'granulation tissue' 314
'granules' 142
'granules in cells' 176.1
granulite 1005.3
-granuloma 314
-granulomatous 314
grānul(um) 314
grapeskin 1203.3
-graph 70, 412, 1060,
1260, 1481

-grapha 33, 1060
-graphal 33, 1060
graph(ē) 1060, 1481
graph(ein) 33, 70, 412,
1060, 1145, 1260, 1481
-grapher 33, 70, 412,
1060, 1260, 1481
-graphia 33, 70, 1060,
1481
-graphic 33, 70, 412,
1060, 1260, 1481
-graphical 33, 70, 412,
1060, 1260, 1481
graphically 70, 412, 1260,
1481
-graphist 33, 70, 412,
1060, 1260, 1481
graphophone 901.3
-graphous 33, 70, 412,
1060, 1260, 1481
-graphy 33, 70, 412,
1060, 1260, 1481
grapple 799
Grasmere 926
'grasp' 69, 654, 950
'grasping' 640.5
'grasp with the hands'
790
'grass' 1512, 600
'grassland' 1144
'grassland, African' 635
grastrophia 71.2
grātia 719
gratitude 758
-grave 1024
graveful 1141.2
gravestead 592
graveyard 685.1
-gravida 15
-gravidic 15
gravid(us) 15
'great' 1490
-greave 1024
'grebe' 960
'Greece, ancient' 510
Greek 1038
greenbottle 847.2
greenery 1525.4
greenhead 590.8
'greenish yellow' 495
Greenock 1092
greg(are) 980
-gregate 980
-gregation 980
grex 980
'grind' 706, 1324, 1537

'grinding' 1324, 1537
'gristle' 176, 321
grocery 1459.1, 1525.3
'groin' 380
'grooved fangs' 35
'grope' 211
-ground 670
'ground grain' 1107
'group' 76, 492, 588.4,
   659, 943.3, 1394.2,
   1459.3
'group, botanical' 588.3
'group, natural' 616.2
'group, zoological or
   botanical' 620
'group of members' 868
-grove 1024
'grow' 374, 481, 737,
   1015, 1104, 1240,
   1292, 1327
'grow, make' 1015
'growing' 1327
'grown' 1015
'growth' 460, 567.2,
   1196, 1327, 1364,
   1482, 1513
'growth, fleshy' 303
'growth, irregular
   cellular' 1545
'growth inhibitor' 1385.5
grubstake 791
grund 670
guarantee 760, 772
'guard' 653, 684, 1036
-guard 682
gudame 852
'guest' 987
'guide' 488, 915, 1162,
   1522
'gullet' 284
gunwale 803
gurg(es) 781
gutterblood 675
gyld(an) 636
Gymnadenia 129.2
gymnast 1429
gymnastic 568
gymnastics 1289.2
gymnastik(os) 568
gymnazein 568
Gymnema 288.5
gymnobacteria 180
Gymnolaema 284
gymnopedic 392.1
-gyn 153, 482, 909, 1367
Gynandria 174

gynatresia 218
-gyne 153, 482, **909,**
   1367
gyn(ē) 153, 482, 909,
   1367
gynecologist 1436.2
gynecomastia 244
gynecomazia 255
gynecratic 520.1
-gynia **153,** 482, 909,
   1367
gyniatry 1531
-gynic 153, **482,** 909,
   1367
-gynious 153
-gynist 909
Gynocardia 48.3
gynosporangium 1169
-gynous 153, 482, 909,
   1367
-gyny 153, 482, 909,
   1367
'gypsum' 1250
-gyria **196**
-gyric 196
gyrle 1139
gyr(os) 196
gyrostat 1385.1

H

'habitat' 271, 833
'habitation' 770
hād 674
hæfen 1198
hæfene 1198
-haemia 96
-haemic 96
haer(ēre) 922
hafoc 1099
hagiocracy 1467.1
hagiographa 33.1
hagiographic 412.2
haim(a) 96, 98, 105, 328
'hair' 30, 63, 63.1, 302,
   371, 590.3
'hairiness' 63.2
hairlace 714.1
'hair of the head' 836,
   1134
'hairpiece' 1044
-halant 801
hal(are) 801
-halation 801
-hale **801**
-halent 801

halftone 905.3
halia 76
-hall 1129
halle 1129
hallucinogenic 460.1
halogen 1196.1
'halt' 727
-ham 1144
hamburg 1258
hamburger 1258
Hamilton 1232
hamm 1144
hammer toe 910.1
Hammond 662
Hampstead 592
'hand' 182, 595.1, 646.3,
   646.4, 656, 662, 812,
   1526
-hand 646
'hand deformity' 646.2
-handed 595, 646, 812
-handedly 595
-handedness 595
handel(en) 812
handful 1140
handhold 640.5
handicraft 1398.1
'handiwork' 1526
'handle' 769, 812.4
-handle 812
'handler' 1267.1
handl(ian) 812
'hands' 182.1, 280, 595.3,
   1143
handshake 788.1
handstand 649.3
handstroke 794.1
handwhile 824
'hang' 656.1, 954
'hanging pod' 710
haphalgesia 210
haph(ē) 69
-haphia 69
haploid 628
hapl(os) 628
'happening' 1413
haptein 69
-haptic 69
'harbor' 1198, 1461
harborage 765.4
'harbor entrance' 1082.1
'hard' 322, 679, 679.1
'hardening' 322
hardhanded 595.1
hardship 1242.3
harebell 1131.2

harebottle 847.3
harefoot 1420.4
harehound 668
Hargrave 1024
harmful 1141.4
harmon(ia) 475
-harmonic **475**
-harmonical 475
-harmonically 475
'harmonics' 475.1
-harmonious 475
-harmoniously 475
harmonizein 475
'harmony' 475
harnpan 1188.2
harpsichord 690.2
hart 679
hartstongue 1017.3
harvesttime 861
hast 1427
Hastings 1048
hatband 645.4
hatchling 1049.1
hatred 606.1
hatter 1251.1
hauk 1099
'haul' 1386
haulage 765.2
have 61, 1023, 1190.4
haven 1193, 1425.2
-haven **1198**
haven't 1403
haversack 1087
hawfinch 1055
-hawk **1099**
hawkeye 1037.2
hawsepiece 720.4
hawsepipe 912.1
'head' 77, 128, 257, 423,
  590, 590.1, 590.8, 674,
  836, 995, 995.1
-head² **591**
headband 645.1
'headedness' 257
'heading' 590.7
'headland' 1344
headline 895.5
headpiece 720.1
headrace 717.2
headshake 788.1
headstand 649.3
'head throw' 1134.3
headwork 1098.2
heafoc 1099
hēafod 590
heald 640

'healer' 496, 1291, 1438,
  1531
'healing' 1291, 1531
heall 1129
'healthy, be' 732, 1410
'hear' 576
'hearing' 154, 231, 576,
  1373
'hearing organs' 576.1
'heart' 48, 379
'heart ailment patients'
  379.2
'heart ailments' 379.1
'heartbeat' 110
hearten 1190.4
'heat' 119, 1150, 1150.1,
  1509
'heat, body' 119, 1509.2
heatstroke 794.3
'heaviness' 1247
'heavy' 15
hebephrenic 461.2
Hebraic 383.3
-*hede* 590, 591, 674
hēdon(ē) 143
-hedonia **143**
-hedonic 143
hedr(a) 1227
-hedral 1227
-hedric 1227
-hedroid 1227
-hedron **1227**
-heid 591, 674
heighten 1190.2
helicopter 1265
helicotrema 289.1
heliolater 1263
heliophilous 1362
heliophobe 709
heliostat 1385.3
heliotaxis 1333.2
heliotrope 915
heliotropic 488.1
heliotypic 489.2
Helkesimastix 1455
hellbred 607.2
hellhole 834.4
helmin(s) 1079
-helminth **1079**
-helminthic 1079
Heloderma 333.3
'hem' 311
hemagogue 1018.2
hemamoeba 5
hemangioma 306
hemapoietic 535

hematemetic 536
hematherm 1150.2
hematocathartic 565
hematochezia 256
hematocyst 1444
hematogenetic 538.2
-hematoma **328**
hematomyelia 85
hematonic 480.6
Hemerocampa 349
-hemia 96
hemianopia 162.1
hemianopsia 227.1
-hemic 96
hemicephalia 77
Hemichorda 17
hemicycle 810.2
hemicyclic 424.3
hemiembryo 1240
Hemimetabola 270
hemiopic 485
hemiosmia 122
hemiplane 879
hemiplegic 404.1
hemipode 752.2
hemisphere 923.1
hemispheric 491.2
hemistich 1054
hemitropic 488.2
hemline 895.6
hemm 1144
hemocele 814
hemocite 1008
hemoconia 142
hemocrine 140
'hemoglobin' 104
'hemoglobin, protein in'
  194
hemoglobinuria 190.1,
  194
hemolytic 579
hemophilic 427
hemoproctia 236
hemoptysis 1329
hemorraphilia 88.1
hemorrhage 768
hemorrhagic 402
hemostasia 209.2
hemostat 1385.2
hemotherapeutic 578
hemotoxin 1206
hemotroph 1063.1
henbane 877.1
henceforward 683.3
henhouse 968
henotheistic 572

henwife 764.2
henyard 685.2
hēpar 233, 511
-hepatia **233**
-hepatic 233
Hepaticola 271
hepatomphalos 1340
hepatonephric 493
hepatopneumonic 476.2
hepatorrhexis 1334
hepatostomy 1508
heptachromic 446.2
heptandrous 1370
heptatonic 480.1
'herb' 600, 1426
herbaceous 1358.1
herbage 765.1
herbary 1523
herbiferous 1372
Herbivora 361
herbivore 937
herbivorous 1375
'herbs' 1512
herbwife 764.1
-herd **686, **980
herde 686
'herdsman' 686
herdswoman 1187.2
herdwick 1090.1
-here **922**
herebefore 932.1
-herence 922
-herency 922
-herent 922
heretofore 932.1
hermoglyphic 417.2
-heroic **483**
-heroical 483
-heroically 483
-heroicly 483
heroicomic 442
hērō(s) 483
herpangina 346
hesperanopia 162.1
heterochromic 446.5
heterochronia 146.3
heterocline 898.2
heteroclinic 466.2
Heterodontidae 697
heterodrome 863.3
heteroepy 1520
heterokinesis 1312.2
heterometropia 164
heteroousia 230
heterophasis 1304
heterophoric 494.1

heterophthalmia 112
heterophthongia 57
heteroplasia 201
heteroplastic 567.2
heterotaxia 247.2
heterotaxis 1333.1
heterotopia 166
heterotroph 1063.2
hexachlorophene 885
hexacoralla 261
hexadactylia 93
hexagon 1210
hexagynous 1367.2
hexaploid 628
hexaseme 858.1
hexasemic 437
hexastich 1054
hexastichic 410
Heyward 684.2
hicksville 830.2
hidebottle 847.1
hierde 686
hieroglyphic 383.2, 417.2
'high-born' 807
'higher end' 590.4
highhanded 595.2
highschooler 1251.3
highway 1463
hil 1132
'hill, wooded' 1443
-hill 882, **1132, **1418,
1449
hillock 1091
hillside 748.2
'hill, wooded' 1443
hindmost 1441
hindsaddle 811.3
'hip joint' 66
hippodrome 863.2
hippodromic 445.1
hippopotami 1083.2
hipp(os) 1378
-hippus **1378**
hirde 686
hireling 1049.3
hista(nai) 209, 521, 1002,
1003, 1225, 1293,
1306, 1385
histohydria 177
Histoplasma 335.2
hist(os) 62
histotripsy 1537
histotroph 1063.1
'hit' 975
hlǽw 1449
hlāw 1449

hlēow 1058
hobbyhorse 966.3
-*hod* 674
-*hode* 674
hodos 393, 395, 753
hogward 684.1
hogyard 685.2
hol 834
holarthritic 548
'hold' 61, 62, 1014, 1201,
1222
-hold **640**
'hold back' 1201
holde 640
'holding' 61, 640.1, 640.4
'holding of land' 1397
'hold of a ship' 834
'hold out' 1201
'hold together' 1201
'hold up' 1201
'hole' 218, 289, 367,
-hole **834**
holethnic 464
'holiday' 1435
'hollow' 101, 1014,
1188.2, 814, 834, 834.1
'hollowed fangs' 35
'hollow place' 834
-holm **1147**
-holme 1147
hōlmr 1147
hologamy 1503.2
holograph 1060.1
holophrase 948
holoptic 564
Holosomata 368
holotonic 480.5
holozoic 484.1
'holy' 997
'holy meeting-place' 1093
homebound 667
homebred 607.2
homeless 1342.1
homeopath 1072.2
homeopathy 1485.2
'homestead' 1144
homeward 683.1
homicide 747.1
homoerotic 559.2
homogamy 1503.3
homoiousia 230
homonymy 1510.1
homoousia 230
homophagia 50.1
homophile 823
homophonic 470.6

homoplasia 201
homotaxis 1333.1
homunculus 1351
hond 646
'honesty' 1400
'honey' 1122
honeydew 1447
'honey-sweet solution'
1122
-hood **674**
hoodmold 641
hooknose 959.1
'hoop' 32, 1056
hopbush 1068
horāma 283
horā(n) 283
horehound 877.3
hormaein 903
hormochromasia 204.2
hormōn 903
-hormonal 903
-hormonally 903
-hormone **903**
-hormonic 903
hormonoprivia 245
hormopoiesis 1310
'horn' 25, 351, 1233,
1371
'horn of plenty' 159
'horny' 25
'horny skin layer' 274
horrid 619
hors 966
'horse' 741, 966.1, 1378
-horse **966**
'horseback procession'
741
'horse mackerel' 191
horseman 1186.1
horsemanship 1242.2,
1243
horsewoman 1187.1
-hound **668**
houndsbane 877.3
'hour, appointed' 861
hourly 1488.2
'house' 42, 444,
-house **968**
housebound 666.1
houseboy 1518
household 640.4
housemate 987.2
'house of' 765.4
housewife 764.2
Hovercraft 1398.3
Howard 684.2

'hue' 1275, 1275.1
hul 1132
hulking 1045.3
'human beings' 844.1,
844.2
'humans, supply with'
844.3
humidistat 1385.2
humoresque 1022.2
hund 668
hungry 1457.3
-hurst **1443**
hūs 968
husbandship 1242.3
'husk' 297
hwil 824
hyaloplasma 335.1
Hyalospongia 58
hyalotype 917.2
hydor 431
hydōr 177
hydr- 177
hydracid 623.1
hydralime 859
Hydrangeaceae 700
hydranth 1077
-hydraulic **431**
-hydraulically 431
-hydraulics 431
-hydria **177**
hydro- 974.2
'hydrocarbons' 883
'hydrocarbons, mixture
of' 887.2
'hydrocarbons, paraffin'
876
hydroceramic 433
hydrochloric 495
hydroclimate 988
hydrocyclic 424.2
hydroelectric 497
hydrogalvanic 459
hydrogen 177, 1196.2
hydrogenous 1364
hydrolabile 819
hydrolymph 1062
hydrolyte 1016
hydrolytic 579
hydrolyze 1039
hydroperiod 673
hydrophil 1126
hydrophily 1492.2
hydroplanula 275
hydroponic 383.6
hydrosol 1138
hydrostat 1385.4

hydrostatics 1293
hydrotechny 1514
hydrotherapeutics 1294
-hydrous 177
hydroxyl 1142
hyl(ē) 1142
Hylemyia 254
hyll 1132
hymenopter 1265
hymnode 752.1
hyomanic 457.2
hypacidemia 99
hypaphrodisia 219
hyperacousia 231
hyperalgesic 509
hyperbola 269.1
hyperbole 693
hyperbulia 91
hyperchloric 495
hypercholia 90
hyperchromic 446.4
hypercoria 183
hypercosmic 453.2
hypercrisia 220.2
hyperemetic 536
hyperemia 96.1
hyperendocrisia 220.2
hyperesthetic 534.2
hypergalactia 235
hyperhedonia 143
hyperhepatia 233
hypermetria 187
hypermnestic 570
hypermotile 826
hypernephroma 323
hyperneurotic 560.2
hyperovaria 173
hyperoxemia 107
hyperpathetic 532
hyperpeptic 562.2
hyperphagia 50.2
hyperplane 879
hyperpnea 24
hyperpraxia 246
hyperpselaphesia 211
hyperpyrexia 251
hypersplenia 133
hypersthenia 131
hypertelic 426
hyperthermia 119.1
hyperthermy 1509.1
hyperthyrea 28
hypertonic 480.4, 480.7
hypertrophic 414
hypertropia 163
hypertropic 488.2

hypervolemia 103
hyphedonia 143
hyphenated 594.1
hypnoetic 542
hypnoia 155
hypn(os) 558
hypnosis 558, 1315.1
hypnotherapy 1519.1
-hypnotic **558**
-hypnotically 558
hypnotik(os) 558
'hypnotism' 558
-hypnotist 558
hypo- 176.2
hypoadenia 129.1
hypocapnia 150
hypochlorous 1354.2
hypochondria 176.2
hypochromasia 204.1
hypochromemia 104
hypochromic 446.3
hypochylia 92
hypocrine 140
hypodermic 450.1
hypodermis 1301
hypodiastole 841
hypodynamia 95
hypoendocrisia 220.2
hypoergasia 198
hypogeusia 229
hypoglycemia 96.2, 98
hypohypnotic 558
hypokinetic 540.1
hypometria 187
hypomotility 1543
hypophonic 470.4
hypophoria 185.1
hypophyll 1135.1
hypopselaphesia 211
hypopsychosis 1316
hyposphresia 216
hyposthenuria 193
hypostoma 329
hypostomia 116
hyposulfuric 502
hyposystole 842
hypothermia 119.1
hypothermy 1509.1
hypothesis 1308
hypothetic 531
hypothyrea 28
hypotonia 147
hypotonic 480.7
Hypotremata 367
hypotrichia 63.1
hypovaria 173

hypovolemia 103
hypoxemia 107
hypoxia 252
hyrde 686
hyrst 1443
hysteria 37.1
Hystericomorpha 34
hysterics 1289.2
hysterorrhexis 1334

I

-i 1214
-i¹ **1083**, 1085
-i² **1084**
-ia 38.1, 760
-ia¹ **37**
-ia² **38**
-ia -ā 1459
-ial 37, 38, **1109**
-ial(is) 1109
-ially 1109, **1497**
-iamb **376**
-iambic 376
-iambically 376
iamb(os) 376
iambus 376
-ian 37, 38, 1181,
-ian **1183**
-(i)ana 341
-ianism 1183
-ianist 1183
-ianly 1181, 1183
-ianus 1181, 1183, 1184
-iasic 1305
-iasis 1302, **1305**
iatreia 1531
-iatria 1531
-iatric **496**, 1291, 1438,
  1531
-iatrical 496, 1438, 1531
-iatrically 1291
-iatrician 496, 1438, 1531
-iatrics 496, **1291**, 1531
iatrik(o)s 1291
-iatrist 496, **1438**, 1531
iatrophysics 1292
iatr(os) 496, 1291, 1438,
  1531
iatrotechnic 462.3
iatrotechnique 1021
-iatry 496, 1291, 1438,
  1531
-ibil(is) 804
-ibility 804, **1542**
-ible 804

-ibly 804
-ic 383, 722, 974.2,
  1103.2, 1181.5, 1495
-ic¹ **383**
-ic² **384**
-ica¹ **9**
-ica² **10**
-ical 383, **1103**, 1495
-ical(is) 1103
-ically 383, 1103, **1496**
-icate 383, 976
-ication 383
'ice' 721, 809, 1052
'ice, flavored' 809
-ice¹ **721**
-ice² **722**
iceberg 1052
Iceland 647.1
Icelandic 383.3
icequake 792
ichthyomorphic 416
ichthyosaur 1280
-ician **1184**
icicle 809
icing 1046.2
-icism 383
-icist 383
-icity 383
-ici(us) 1361
-icize 383
-ick 383, 1091
-icly 383
iconoclast 1431.1
iconoclastic 566.1
iconophily 1492.1
-ics 1181.5, **1289**
-ic(us) 9, 10, 383, 384,
  1184
-id¹ 14, **616**
-id² **617**
-id³ **618**
-id⁴ **619**
-id⁵ 14, **620**
-ida 14, 616
-idae 14, 616, **697**
-idan 14
-ide **746**
idealism 1157.1
ideaphoria 185.2
ideogrammic 441
-id(es) 14
-id(ēs) 616, 697
-idion 1167
idiopathic 419.4
idiophanic 456.2
-idium **1167**

idolatry 1532
-id(us) 619, 623
-ie 760, 761, 1458, 1459
-ie 786
ieg 1472
-iel 1109
ienai 1213
-ier 1252, 1525
-ier 1261
-ier(e) 1255
-iere 925, 1261
-ière 925
-if 1025
-iferous 1256
-ific 401, 945, 1029,
 1219, 1387, 1474, 1530
-ificate 1474
-ification 976, 1474
-ificative 976, 1474
-ifice 1474
-ificial 1474
-ificient 1474
-iform 1153
-iform(a) 1153
-iforme 1153
-ify 945, 1029, 1219,
 1387, 1474, 1530
-ig 1457
ignigenous 1364
ignoble 807.1
-ik 383
-ik(os) 9, 10, 383, 384,
 511, 554
-il 796, 818, 1124
-il¹ 1124
-il² 1125
-ile 1124
-ile¹ 817
-ile² 818
-ileal 380
ileocolonic 471
Ilfracombe 707
īli(a) 380
iliac 378,
-iliac 380
Iliad 588.1
ilik 793
iliodorsal 1120
-il(is) 798, 818, 826, 1124
ilium 380
-illa 265, 829
*-ill(a) 796
-ille 829
Illinoisian 1181.4
illiterate 999.2
'illness' 419.1, 1485.1

-illo 1238
-ill(um) 829
*-ill(um) 796
-ill(us) 829, 1125, 1238
*-ill(us) 796
'illustrious' 807.2
'illustriousness' 807.1
-im 1146
'image' 489, 917
'imitate' 439, 860, 1311
'imitation' 439, 537,
 1011.5, 1311
'imitative' 537
'imitator' 860
'imitators' 439
immerge 779.1
'immerse' 779.1, 963
immobile 822
'immunity' 891
immunogen 1196.2
impale 802
impecunious 1359
impend 656.1
'imperfection' 300
implement 1412.3
implication 1218.1
implore 934
impolitic 546.2
impostress 1347
impound 669
impoverish 1066
'impressed object' 917.2
'impression' 489, 917
improbably 1489
improof 1041.1
improve 1034
improvise 951
impulse 953
impute 1013
-in 415, 888, 889
-in 1195, 1199
-in(a) 342, 887, 888,
 1199
-ina¹ 342
-ina² 343
-īn(a) 703, 889
'inability' 1342.2
-inae 703
inbred 607.1
inbreed 598.2
incandescent 1407.2
incarnate 994
incensory 1528.3
inchmeal 1106
'incision, surgical' 1506,
 1508

'incisions of tissue' 447
'inclination' 514, 988
'incline' 466, 514, 780,
 898, 898.1, 965, 1366
'inclined to' 1457.3
'inclining' 466
include 756
'incontinence' 234.2
'increase or formation'
 554.3
incriminate 991
inculpate 996
incumbent 1405.2
incunabula 273
'indivisible' 448
inductorium 1176.2
'induration' 322
-ine 342, 887, 888, 889,
 1194, 1199
-ine¹ 887, 1199
-ine² 888
-ine³ 889
-in(ē) 889
infantile 818.1
'infatuation' 127.2
infect 1387
infectious 1360
infeed 597.1
'inferior one' 1202.1
infertile 827
infestans 1338
'inflammation' 1330.1
inflate 985
inflect 1389.1
'influence' 488, 488.3,
 1162
'influenced by' 915, 1522
'influencing' 915, 1522
infold 639
'inform' 951
'information, body of'
 1476.2
inframicrobe 711
infrared 605
infrascientific 401
infrasonic 479.1
infrasternal 1114
infrathoracic 390
'in front of' 932.2
'infuse' 339
'infusion' 339
infusory 1528.1
-ing 1042, 1046, 1047,
 1048, 1338
-ing¹ 1045
-ing² 1046

-ing³ **1047**
-ing⁴ **1048**
-inge 1045, 1046
ingenerate 998
-ingly 1045
'inhabit' 271, 833
inhale 801
'inherited characteristics'
    466.1
inheritrice 725
'inhibition' 209, 1306
'inhibitor' 1385.5
initiate 972.3
initiation 1212.1
inject 1388.1
injectio 1237
'injury' 338
inlay 1462
'inlet' 926, 1090
'inner surface of, cover'
    896
inocomma 298
-inoma 320
-in(on) 889
inordinate 989.2
inorganic 455.2
-in(os) 889
inquire 931
inscribe 705
'inscription' 845
'insect' 847.2, 1044.2
Insectivora 361
insectivore 937
inselberg 1052
inseminate 990
'insert stakes' 802
'inside' 481, 749, 1240
insole 839
insomnia 141
insomniac 378
inspect 1390
'inspection' 580
'instrument' 455, 720.6,
    797, 870.1, 1176.2,
    1230, 1412.3, 1527.2,
    1530
'instrumental' 455
'instruments, musical'
    470.3
insubordinate 989.2
insurge 782
intake 790.2
'intellect' 590.2, 995.2
'intellect, seat of' 137,
    461
'intelligence' 603, 1134.1

intend 657.2
intended 594.1
intension 1223
intention 1223
interacademic 435
interbreed 598.1
intercede 745
interchange 775
intercharge 778.3
intercosmic 453.1
intercreate 979
interelectrodic 393.1,
    393.2
'interest, inordinate' 381
interfertile 827
intergeneric 492
interjacent 1406
interject 1388.1
'interjectory' 531
interknowledge 773
interlace 715
interlapse 962
interline 896
interlinguistic 574
interlude 755.1
intermaxilla 266
intermingle 816
intermontane 882
interpledge 772
interpole 838
interpose 961
interposure 942
'interpret' 89
'interpretation' 443.2
interrogate 981.1
interscience 731.2
intersole 839
intersperse 964
interstice 727
'interval' 905.2
'interval of time' 395
'intervals, musical' 480.2
intervene 886
intervocalic 422
interwed 612
'intestine, large' 1224
intone 905.1
intoxicant 1404.1
intracosmic 453.1
intradermic 450.1
intragenic 460.3
intramorainic 465
intransigent 1405.1
intranuclear 1248
intratelluric 503
intravenous 1365

intravertebral 1117
introduce 738
intrude 757
'intrust to' 648
intumescence 730
-in(um) 342, 887
-īn(um) 703, 889
-in(us) 342, 343, 887
-īn(us) 703, 889
invade 744
invent 1417.2
Inverness 1344
inverse 965.3
invert 1424.1
'investigate' 931, 934
investiture 943.1
involute 1012
'involving' 1528.2
inwale 803
-io **1237**
-iō 1212, 1217, 1218,
    1220
iodide 746
iodoamoeba 5
-ion 38, 38.1, 760, 1165,
    1168, 1170, 1212,
    1213, 1214
-ion² **1213**
-ion³ **1214**
-iōn 1212, 1213
-iōn- 1217, 1218
-ionic 1213
-ionically 1213
-ios 38, 38.2
iotacism 1158
-ioun 1212
-ious **1359**
iousa 1213
-iously 1359
-iousness 1359
-ique **1020,** 383, 384
-ir 1066
iridocoloboma 300
iridokinetic 540.1
'iris, absence or defect
    of' 300
Irishwoman 1187.2
ironclad 593.2
ironmonger 1257.1
ironwood 676.1
ironworks 1337.1
'irregular cellular growth'
    1545
irritomotile 826
is- 38.2, 617, 618, 1052
īs 809

Isadora 356
-isation 1038
isberg 1052
-isc 1022, 1065
ischemia 96.1
-ischia **66**
-ischiac 66
-ischian 66
-ischiatic 66
ischiodymia 123
ischi(on) 66
ischiopubica 9
ischogyria 196
-ise 721, 1038, 1157
-is(en) 1038
-is(er) 1038
īsgicel 809
-ish¹ **1065**
-ish² **1066**
-isher 1066
-ishly 1065
-ishment 1066
'island' 1472
'island in river or lake'
  1147
'islet' 1147, 1472
-ism **1157**, 1436
-ism(e) 1157
-ismic 1157
-ismically 1157
-(i)sm(os) 1157
-ismus 1157
iso- 1150.3
isobar 1247
isobathic 418
isobathytherm 1150.3
Isocardia 48.3
isochela 258
isochronia 146.3
isochronic 477
isocracy 1467.3
isodontic 551.1
isoelectronic 478
isogeotherm 1150.3
isohydria 177
Isoloma 311
isomer 1262
Isospondyli 1083.2
isosthenuria 193
isotherm 1150.3
isotonic 480.7
Israelite 1005.2
-issa 1341
-issi 1066
-ist 1157, **1436**
-ist(a) 1436

-iste 1436
-ist(ēs) 1436
-istic **571**, 1157, 1436
-istical 571
-istically 571, 1157, 1436
-istik(os) 571
-ita 1006
īt(a) 1006
-itās 1540
-itātis 1540
-ite¹ **1005**, 1361
-ite² **1006,** 1220, 1361
-ité 1540
-itely 1006
-it(ēs) 1005, 1330
-itia 721
-itic **545**, 1005, 1330
-itically 545, 1005, 1330
-itik(os) 545
-itiō 1220
-ition 1006, **1220**
-itious 1006, 1220, **1361**
-itiously 1361
-itiousness 1361
-itis **1330**
-itium 721
-iti(us) 721, 1361
-ītīv(a) 1030
-itive 1006, **1030,** 1220
-itively 1220
-itivity 1030
-ītīv(um) 1030
-ītīv(us) 1030
*-itta 373, 786, 1011,
  1460
*-itto 1394
-itum 1006
-īt(um) 1006
-itus 1006, 1220
īt(us) 1006
-ity **1540**
-ium 38, 760, 866, **1165,**
  1458
-iun 1212
-ius 38, 38.2
-īv(a) 1025, 1027
I've 1023
-ive **1025**
-ively 1025
-ivity 1025
-īv(um) 1025, 1027
-īv(us) 1025, 1027, 1028,
  1030
-ix 722
-iz(āre) 1038
-ization 1038

-ize **1038**, 1157
-iz(ein) 1038
-izer 1038

J

jabbed 594
jacens 1406
-jacent **1406**
jac(ere) 1388
jac(ēre) 1406
-jack **1086**
jacke 1086
jackleg 1043.3
Jacques 1086
jadestone 906.4
jailer 1252.1
Janice 722.2
Japanese 949.2
jasminewood 676.1
'jaw' 36, 73, 130, 266,
  613
-jawed **613**
Jeannette 1011.2
-ject **1388**
-jection 1388
-jector 1388
-jectory 1388
-ject(us) 1388
Jenkins 1202.2, 1339
Jennite 1005.6
jester 1267.2
-jik 1094
jobbery 1525.2
'jockey' 1086.1
jocko 1235.2
jogged 594
john 1086
'join' 475
'joining together' 475
'joint' 548, 1117
'join together' 983
'joints, disease of' 548
jointure 943.3
jokesmith 1076.3
Jones 1202.2, 1339
Josephine 888
journalese 949.3
'journey' 918
joyproof 1041
joystick 1089.2
Judaica 9
Judaically 1495
Judaize 1038.3
'judge' 140, 220, 474,
  547

-leg 82, **1043**
legacy 1466
'leg below knee' 106
leg(ein) 248, 1019, 1476
'legend' 421
legendarian 1185.2
legendary 1524
legere 248
legge 1043
legg(en) 1462
leggr 1043
legislature 943.3, 944
-leigh **1058,** 1473
lekith(os) 1108
lemma 297
-lemma¹ **296**
-lemma² **297**
lēmma 296
-lemmal 297
lemmas' 1282
lemnocyte 1014
lemonade 739.4
-len 799
lengthen 1190.2
lenition 1220
'lens' 74
'lenses' 520.4
'lentil' 74
Leominster 1271
Leonard 679.1
Leonid 618.1
Lepidoptera 354
Lepidosperma 334
-lepsia 561, 1536
lēpsia 1536
-lepsie 1536
-lepsis 561, 1536
-lepsy 561, **1536**
-leptic 561, 1536
lēptik(os) 561
Leptocardia 48.2
leptochymia 124
leptodermic 450.2
leptonema 288.3
leptophonic 470.4
leptoprosopia 165
leptosomatic 518.3
Leptostraca 6
-les 1342
-less **1342**
-lesse 1342
-lessly 1342
-lessness 1342
-let **1395**
'let go' 1462
lethologica 10

-lette 1395
'letter' 295, 441, 515,
  1145, 1145.2
'lettered' 999
'letters' 999
-leucaemia 102
leucaemic 102
-leucemia 102
leucemic 102
Leucetta 373
leucocratic 520.5
leucocytotic 554.3
leucoderma 333.2
leucopoiesis 1310
leucosphere 923.2
leucospheric 491.1
-leukaemia 102
-leukaemic 102
-leukemia **102**
-leukemic 102
'leukocytes' 102
leukocythemia 101
leukocytoplania 126
leukoderma 118
leukodermic 450.3
leukonychia 68
leukoplakia 75
leukoplast 1432
leuk(os) 102
leukotactic 525.3
'level' 879
-lexia **248**
-lexic 248
lexicographer 1260
lexicographic 412.2
lexicography 1481.2
lex(is) 248
-ley **1473**
leye 1473
-li 1488, 1489
-lian 799
liar 1251
librarian 1185.3
libretti 1083
-lic 1488, 1489
-līc 1488, 1489
-lich 1488
-liche 1489
'lie' 248, 1406
lie, cause to' 1462
'life' 39, 557, 708, 711,
  784, 1318
'life, animal' 629
'life, mode of' 1318
lifeguard 682
lifehold 640.1

'ligament' 336
ligature 944
'light' 556, 1408
'light, arch of' 1448.3
'light, emitting or
  reflecting' 1407.2
'light, protection against'
  742
'light-admitting' 1408
lightface 713.4
'light penetration' 556.2
lik 793
'like' 703, 754, 1357,
  1488.1
-like **793**
likewise 952.1
'liking, abnormal' 88
lim 859
līm 859
'limb' 84
limbmeal 1106
-lime **859**
limeade 739.4
'limit' 590.6, 892, 895.6
'limited by' 666.1
'limit of effectiveness'
  776.2
'line' 64, 295, 410, 616.1,
  714.1, 776, 894, 895,
  1054
'line, go in a' 410
'line, straight' 1454.2
-line¹ **894**
-line² **895**
-line³ **896**
līne 895
'lineage' 675
linear 1245.1
linen 894, 896
'linen, made of' 895
'line of a drawing' 295,
  441, 515, 1145
'line of battle' 56
'line of verse' 410, 858.1,
  1054
'line on body' 895.4
'lines, marking with'
  1481
līne(us) 895
-ling **1049**
lingu(a) 574, 1440
linguiform 1152
-linguist 574, **1440**
-linguistic 574, 1440
-linguistical 574, 1440
-linguistically 574, 1440

'linguistic characteristic'
1157.4
'linguistic group' 464
'linguistic usage' 1157.4
linoleic 398.1
Linotype 917.3
linseed 599.1
līn(um) 894
'lip' 87
lip(ein) 1323
-lipid 319
lipochondria 176.1
lipochrome 865
lipogranuloma 314
-lipoid 319
-lipoma **319**
-lipomatous 319
lip(os) 319
lipotropy 1522
'lips' 1110
-lipse 1323
-lipsis **1323**
-lipsoid 1323
lipstick 1089.2
-liptic 1323
-liptical 1323
-liptically 1323
liquefaction 1219.1
liquefactive 1029
liquefy 1474.1
'liquid' 339
'liquid product' 739.4
'liquid that nourishes
tissue' 339
Lisette 1011.4
Lissoflagellata 366
lissotrichia 63.1
'listing down' 573
-lite 1075
-literacy 999
'literary style' 949.3
-literate **999**
-literation 999
-lith **1075**
lithagogue 1018.2
lithiasis 1305.2
-lithic 1075
-lithically 1075
lithochromatic 517.2
lithoclast 1431.2
lithodesma 336
lithoglyphic 417.1
lithography 1481.1
Lithophaga 29
lithophanic 456.2
lithophyte 1015

lith(os) 1075
litterae 999
litterāt(us) 999
'little' 1011.4
'little thing' 1011.3
'live' 348, 484, 629, 667,
1007, 1226
'liver' 233, 511
'living' 484, 629
'living substance' 290
'lizard' 191, 1280, 1379
'load' 778, 778.1, 811
'load a wagon' 778
'loading' 778.1
'loadstone' 539
loanword 691.2
-lobate 710
-lobe **710**
-lobed 710
lob(os) 710
'locality' 592
-locate **978**
'location' 166, 592,
646.5, 670, 716, 978
'location of' 765.4
locksmith 1076.2
locomobile 821.1
loc(us) 978
lodestone 906.2
-log 406, 529, 1019, 1476
logagnosia 222
-loge 1019
-logetic **529**, 1019, 1476
-logetically 529, 1019,
1476
-logia 406, 529, 1019,
1476
-logian 406, 529, 1019,
1476
-logic **406**, 529, 1019,
1476
-logical 406, 529, 1019,
1476
-logically 406, 529, 1019,
1476
-logician 406, 529, 1019,
1181.5, 1476
-logie 1476
logik(os) 406
-logism 406, 529, 1019,
1476
-logist 406, 529, 1019,
1476
-logistic 529, **573**, 1019,
1476
-logistical 573

-logistically 529, 573,
1019, 1476
logistik(os) 573
logoclonia 144
logomachic 409
logomachy 1479
logopedia 45
log(os) 406, 529, 573,
1019, 1476
logospasm 1156
-logue 406, 529, **1019**,
1476
-logy 406, 529, 1019,
1476
loincloth 1080
-loma **311**
lōm(a) 311
lond 647
Londoner 1251.2
lonesome 867
longbow 1448.1
longhand 646.4
longipennate 992
longways 1380
'look again' 951
'look at' 160, 486, 914,
1390, 1521
'look back' 951
'looker' 1266
'look over' 951
'loon' 960
'loop' 714.2, 715
'loose' 1032
'loosen' 579, 581, 808,
819, 1016, 1032, 1039,
1328, 1462
'loosen up' 580
-loquence 1416
loquens 1416
-loquent **1416**
-loquently 1416
loquī 1416
lordship 1242.1
'lose' 602
'loss' 245, 602
'loss of control' 206.2
'love' 88, 260, 419.4,
427, 559, 823, 1126,
1362, 1492
'love, sexual' 559.2
'loved' 762
lovemate 987.1
'love of' 823
loveproof 1041
lovey 1460
'loving' 823

-low **1449**
-lowe 1449
Loxosomatidae 698
ltd 586
lubricant 1404.4
lubritorium 1176.1
-lucence 1408
lūcens 1408
-lucent **1408**
lūcēre 1408
luckiest 1434
-lude **755**
lūd(ere) 755
Ludlow 1449
lūd(us) 755
-lues 544
lu(ēs) 544
-luetic **544**
-luetism 544
luggage 765.1
-luic 544
'lumber, piece of' 681.1
'lumber in side of ship'
   803
lumberjack 1086.1
lumbodorsal 1120
lumboiliac 380
lumbovertebral 1117
lumen 1197
lumina 1.2
luminaire 927.2
'lung' 145
'lung inflammation' 145
'lungs' 473, 476, 476.2
-lusion 755
-lusive 755
'lust' 138, 559
lūs(us) 755
lūx 1408
-*ly* 1488, 1489
-ly¹ **1488**
-ly² **1489**, 1495
lycorexia 250
ly(ein) 579, 581, 1016,
   1039, 1328
'lying' 1406
-lymph **1062**
lymph(a) 305, 1062
lymphadenia 129.1
lymphadenoma 317
lymphangioendothelioma
   309
lymphangioma 306
-lymphatic 1062
lymphatolysin 1204
lymphedema 286

lymphepithelioma 308
'lymphoid tissue,
   neoplastic disorder of'
   305
'lymphoid tissue, tumor
   of' 305
lymphoidtoxemia 108
-lymphoma **305**
lymphomyxoma 332
lymphopenia 135
lymphorrhage 768
lymphosarcoma 303
lymphotoxin 1206
lymphsarcoleukemia 102
'lymph vessels, tumor of'
   306
'lyric' 752
lyrichord 690.2
-lysand 1039
-lysation 1039, 1328
-lyse 1039, 1328
-lyser 1039, 1328
-lysin **1204**, 1328
-lysine 1204
lysis 579, 1039, 1204,
   1328
'lysis' 1016
-lysis 579, 1016, 1039,
   1204, 1302, 1326, **1328**
-lyst 1328
-lyte **1016**, 1328
-lytic **579**, 1016, 1328
-lytical 579, 1328
-lytically 579, 1328
lytik(os) 579
lyt(os) 1016
-lyzation 1039, 1328
-lyze **1039**, 1328
-lyzer 1039, 1328

M

-m 281
-*m* 281
-*ma* 451, 1197
-ma **281**, 1197
-mach 409, 1479
mach(ē) 409, 1479
-machia 1479
-machic **409**, 1479, **409**
-machical 409, 1479
'machine part' 590.5
machinofacture 945
machinotechnic 462.3
machinotechnique 1021
-machist 409, 1479

-machy 409, **1479**
macramoeba 5
Macrobdella 264
macroblepharia 170
macrobrachia 60
macrocheilia 87
macrocladous 1356
macroclimate 988
macrocnemia 106
macrocolon 1224
macrocosm 1163
macrodontia 241
macroglossia 228.1
macroplastia 243
macrorhinia 139
macroscelia 82
macroscopic 486.3
macrosomatia 232
macrostereognosia 221
macrosurgery 1526
'made of' 699, 889.2,
   1189
'madness' 127, 381, 457
madonnalike 793
mægden 621
mæl 1106
mæl(um) 1106
magic 384.1
magnēs 539
'Magnesian' 539
-magnet 539
magnēt 539
-magnetic **539**
-magnetical 539
-magnetically 539
-magnetism 539, 539.1,
   539.2, 539.3
magneton 1207.2
magnetostatic 521.2
'magnets' 539.1
magnifico 1235.2
magnoliad 588.3
-maid **621**
maiden 621, 1193
maidenhead 591
maidkin 1202.1
mailclad 593.2
'maim' 300
maintain 1201
'maintaining' 1528.3
majorette 1011.1
'make' 49, 399, 400, 535,
   543, 712, 713, 723,
   945, 976, 1029, 1038.1,
   1219, 1310, 1387,
   1474, 1530

'make fast' 1335
'make into' 976, 1474.1
'maker' 1267.2, 1401
'make similar to' 1474.2
'make stand' 209
'making' 49, 535, 543,
   723, 1029, 1219.1,
   1310
'making fast' 1335
malacanthid 620
-malacia **41**
Malacobdella 264
malacoplakia 75
Malacosoma 326.1
malacosteon 1209
malakia 41
malak(os) 41
'male child' 1518
malefactory 1530
'male human, adult'
   1186
'males, adult' 389
'male servant' 1518
malgrace 719
mallochorion 1215
'malnutrition' 71.1
malpractice 726
'mammal' 924
Mammalia 37.4, 38.2
mammalian 1183
'mammalian taxa' 178
mammilar 1245.3
'man' 174, 1086, 1370,
   1377,
-man **1186,** 1187, 1518
'manage' 812.2
management 1412.1
managerial 1109
-mancer 238, 549, 1469
-*mancie* 1469
-mancy 238, 549, **1469**
-mand **648**
mand(āre) 648
mandrake 789
-mane 381, 457, **881**
manger(e) 1257
mangifera 352
mang(ō) 1257
mangūs 960
manhandle 812.2
manhole 834.2
-mania **127,** 381, 457,
   457.2, 881
-maniac 127, 378, **381,**
   457, 881
-maniacal 127, 381, 881

-maniacally 127, 381,
   457, 881
-manic 127, 381, 383.10,
   457, 881
-manically 127, 381, 457,
   881
manicure 939
'manifestation' 456.4,
   1511
manifold 638.1
manik(os) 457
'manipulate' 812.1
'mankind' 487, 659
manly 1488.1
man(n) 1186
'manner' 941, 952,
   1022.1, 1380, 1489
'manner of' 952.1, 1065.2
'manor house' 1534
-manship 1186, **1243**
manteia 238, 1469
mantelpiece 720.5
-*mantia* 1469
-mantia **238**
-mantic 238, **549, 1469**
-mantical 549, 1469
-mantically 549, 1469
mantik(os) 549
manufacture 945
'manufactured
   merchandise' 921
'many' 1441
marathon 1211
-mare **920**
marginalia 38.2
marine 889.1
'mark' 33, 293, 437, 858,
   895
'marking' 293
'markings' 33.2
'marking with lines'
   1060, 1481
marksman 1186.2
marksmanship 1242.2
Marlborough 1059
Marlowe 1449
marmalade 739.2
'marriage' 94, 1503,
   1503.1
'marrow' 85, 312
marrowsky 1487
'marrow tumor' 312
'marry' 612
martyrdom 1148.4
marybud 692
Marylandia 37.3

-mas **1287**
'mask' 1231
mass 1287
mass(a) 769
-massage **769**
'massaging' 1324
mass(ein) 769
mast 609, 1441
masterful 1141.3
masterpiece 720.5
masthead 590.4
-mastia **244,** 255
-mastigina **345**
-mastigine 345
-mastix 345, **1455**
mastocarcinoma 318
Mastodon 1208
-mastoid 244
mastoplastia 243
mast(os) 244
-masty 244, 255
matchstick 1089.1
-mate **987**
'material' 412.2, 1142
-math **1071**
math(ein) 1071
-mathic 1071
-mathy 1071
-matic 281
-matical 281
-matically 281
-maticist 281
'mating' 1336
-matism 281
matrix 1454.2
matroclinic 466.1
matroclinous 1366
matt(ein) 769
mauncie 1469
-maxilla **266**
-maxillar 266
-maxillary 266
maxillolabial 1110
'maxim' 691.1
Max's 1281.1
-mazia 244, **255**
maz(os) 255
-*me* 281
mead 1122
'meadow' 1048
-meal[1] **1106**
-meal[2] **1107**
'means' 915, 952, 1230,
   1380, 1412.3
meanwhile 824

'measure' 164, 187, 498, 641, 1106, 1113, 1264, 1533
'measure, small' 641
'measure, by a' 1106
measureless 1342.2
'measurement' 498
'measurement, unit of' 437, 858
'measurement of muscular acts' 187
'measuring' 1533
'measuring instrument' 1264
meat 987
'meat, loin' 811.3
'mechanics' 1290, 1514
'mechanism' 720.6, 1337.2
mechanotherapeutics 1294
media 38.1
mediad 589
mediator 1277
mediatrice 722.1
mediatrix 1454.1
'medical care' 157
'medical practice or praxis' 524.2
'medical treatment, place for' 466.3, 496, 578, 1291,1294, 1519.1, 1519.2, 1531
medicate 973.1
'medicinal remedies' 449
medico 1235.1
Mediterranean 1181.4
'meeting place, holy' 1093
megacosm 1163
megacycle 810.5
megadontic 551.1
Megalaema 284
megalecithal 1108
-megalia 1490
megaloceros 1340
megalocornea 25
megalodactylia 93
megalohepatia 233
megalomelia 84
megalopic 485
megalopodia 47
megalopolis 1300
megalopore 935
megalosaurus 1379
megalosplanchnic 463
megalosplenia 133

-megaly 1490
Meganthropus 1377
megaphone 901.2
megaphonic 470.1
megapod 677
meg(as) 1490
megaseism 1160
megaseismic 452
megaseme 858.2
megasome 869
megaspheric 491.2
megasporangium 1169
megasynthetic 533.1
megathere 924
megatron 1230.1
megazooid 629
megophthalmos 1340
-mel 1122
melancholia 90
Melanesid 616.2
melanocratic 520.5
melanoma 299
melanoplakia 75
melanotic 554.3
melaphyre 946
Melastoma 330
-mele 1106, 1107
meli 1122
-melia 84
Melianthaceae 700
-melic 84, 1122
Melicocca 7
-melitic 1122
mellifluent 1415
mellis 1122
melodrama 282.1
melomanic 457.1, 457.2
melophonic 470.3
melopoeic 399
mel(os) 84
melotia 242
melu 1107
-melus 84
'member' 298, 1005.1
'membrane' 1215
'membrane, confining' 297
memorabilia 38.2, 86
'memory' 215, 570
-men 1197
*men- 881
-mend 648, 655
mend(a) 648
-mend(āre) 648
Mendelian 1183
mendum 655

mēnē 134
meng(an) 816
-menia 134
mēn(iaia) 134
mēniaion 134
mēniaios 134
meninghematoma 328
meningotyphoid 627.1
menolipsis 1323
menorrhagic 402
menorrheic 397
Menorrhyncha 31
men(os) 127
men's 239, 1281.2
mensae 696
'menses' 134
'menstrual activity' 134
-ment 1412
'mental disorder' 127.1, 137, 461.2, 1316, 1320
-mentia 239
-mential 239
-ment(um) 1412
-mer 1262
-meral 179, 1262
'merchandise, manufactured' 921
mercuric 383.9,
-mercuric 501
Mercur(ius) 501
'Mercury' 501
-mere 926, 1262
-merge 779, 963
-mergence 779
-mergent 779
merg(ere) 779, 963
-meria 179, 1262
-meric 179, 1262
-meride 1262
-merism 1262
-merite 1262
mermaid 621
meroacrania 128
-meron 1262
mer(os) 179, 926, 1262
-merous 1262
merozoite 1007
mers(a) 779
-merse 779, 963
-mersion 779, 963
mers(um) 779
mers(us) 779, 963
mesoblastema 290
mesocarp 1244
mesocolon 1224
mesocratic 520.5

mesoglea 22
Mesohippus 1378
mesonephroma 323
mesophragma 292
mesoseme 858.2
mesosoma 326.2
mesosomatic 518.1
mesostate 1003
mesostroma 324
Mesosuchia 67
mesothelioma 307
mesotherm 1150.1
Mesozoic 484.2
'messenger' 425
'messenger of God' 425
'messmate' 987
Metabola 269.2
-metabola **270**
-metabolic 270
-metabolism 270
metabol(os) 270
-metaboly 270
metacarpal 1115
metachemic 436
metachromasia 204.1,
  204.2
metachromic 446.4
metagastrula 278
'metal, worker in' 1076.1
metalinguistic 574
-metallic **428**
-metallically 428
metallifacture 945
metall(on) 428
metallorganic 455.2
metallurgic 408.2
metallurgy 1478
'metals' 428
metaluetic 544
metamorphosis 1315.1,
  1317
'metamorphosis of
  insects' 270
metaphoric 494.2
metaphrase 948
metaphysical 1104
metapolitic 546.1
metapsyche 784
metapsychic 411.2
metasome 869
metastasis 1306
metatela 259
Metatheria 178
metathesis 1308
metatroch 1056
metatroph 1063.2

metatrophia 71.1
Metazoa 348
'meteor shower' 618.1
-meter 498, **1264,** 1533
metewand 651
methane 876
methanol 1136
methemoglobinuria 194
Methodist 1436.3
methodology 1476.3
mētr(a) 188
metratrophia 71.1
-metre 1264
mètre 1264
metria 1533
-metria[1] **187,** 498, 1264,
  1533
-metria[2] **188**
-metric **498,** 1264
-metrical 498, 1264, 1533
'metrical foot' 376
-metrically 498, 1264,
  1533
-metrics 498, 1264, 1533
-metrie 1533
metrik(os) 498
-metrist 498, 1264, 1533
-metrium 188
metr(on) 164, 187, 498,
  1264, 1533
metronome 862.2
-metropia **164**
-metropic 164
-metropical 164
metropolis 1300
-metropy 164
-metry 498, 1264, **1533**
mette 987
'mice' 969.1
micracoustic 576.2
microbe 708,
-microbe **711**
'microbes' 387
-microbial 387, 711
-microbian 387, 711
-microbic **387,** 711
microbiosis 1318
-microbism 711
microcheiria 182.1
microclimate 988
microclimatic 514
microcoria 184
microcosm 1163
microcosmic 453.2
microcythemia 101
microdontic 551.1

microfauna 347
microfilaria 171
microflora 358.1
microgamy 1503.2
microgastria 189
microgenia 130
micrognathia 73
microgram 1145.2
microhepatia 233
Micromeria 179.1
micromyelia 85
microphakia 74
microphthalmic 440
micropodia 47
Micropteryx 1456
micro(s) 711
microscope 914
microscopic 486.3
microscopy 1521
microseism 1160
microseismic 452
microseme 858.2
microsomatia 232
microsphygmia 109
microsplanchnic 463
microstat 1385.4
microtechnic 462.2, 462.3
microtechnique 1021
microthelia 83
microtherm 1150.1
microtomic 447
microtrauma 338
microzoon 1226
microzyme 874
midcarpal 1115
middletone 905.3
middorsal 1120
midland 647.3
midrange 776.2
'midriff' 137, 461
midsternum 1179
midstroke 794.1
midwife 764.3
midwifery 1525.2
migratory 1529.1
mildew 1447
Mildred 606.2
Milford 1198
Miliola 268.1
militancy 1468.1
'milk' 235
mill 1107
millenarian 1185.1
millennium 1174
Millepora 359
millepore 935

millfeed 597.2
millibar 1247
millionaire 927.1
millrace 717.2
-mime 111, 439, 537,
860, 1311
mimeograph 1060.2
-mimesis 111, 439, 537,
860, 1307, **1311**
mimēsis 1311
mimē(sthai) 439, 860,
1311
-mimetic 111, 439, 528,
537, 860, 1311
mimētik(os) 537
-mimia **111**, 111, 439,
537, 860, 1311
-mimic 111, **439**, 537,
860, 1311
-mimical 111, 439, 537,
860, 1311
-mimically 111, 1311,
439, 537, 860
'mimicry' 111
mimile(os) 439
mimodrama 282.1
mim(os) 860
-min- 1197
-minal 1197
'mind' 125, 127, 155,
239, 411, 542, 784,
881, 1316
'mineral' 1005.3
'mineral, crystalline' 1250
'mineral in stone' 1075.3
'minerals' 428, 906.2
-mingle **816**
'mingling' 1336
'minimum' 505
-minster **1271**
miopragia 52
miraculous 1363
mirage 765.3
misanthropic 487
'misarticulate, tendency
to' 1158
mischarge 778.1
misdemeanor 1274
misfare 919
misfigure 941.1
misframe 855.1
mishandle 812.2
mislay 1462
mismingle 816
misname 854.2
misocatholic 430

misogynic 482
misogynous 1367.1
misomath 1071
mispractice 726
misserve 1035
misses 1297
misstate 1002
'mistake' 962
mistbow 1448.3
misteltān 910.2
mistitle 845
mistletoe 910.2
'mistress' 852
miswed 612
mitochondria 176.1
mitogenesis 213.1
'mix' 816
mixblood 675
'mixed' 206
-mixia 1336
-mixis **1336**
mixoscopia 160
'mixture' 206, 206.1
-mixy 1336
-mnesia **215**, 570
-mnesiac 215, 570
-mnesic 215, 570
-mnesis 215, 570
mnēs(is) 215
-mnestic 215, **570**
mnēst(is) 570
-mo **1239**
mobile 818.2, 822
-mobile¹ **821**, 1278, 1543
-mobile² **822**, 826, 1278,
1543
mōbil(is) 822
-mobility 822, 1278, 1543
mobocracy 1467.1
mobster 1267.3
'mode' 488, 915, 1522
'model' 168, 489, 489.1,
917
'modified by' 973.3
modish 1065.3
modular 1249.2
modulus 1351
mod(us) 641
mogiarthria 181
'moisture' 1447
'mold' 201, 243, 567,
1155, 1432, 1544
-mold **641**
'molded' 335
'molding' 201, 641
'molding, surgical' 1544

molecule 849
'molecule, atoms in a'
448
molehill 1132.1
Molluscoidea 20
mollyhawk 1099.2
Moluccella 262.3
Moms 1284
monacid 623.1
monad 344, 588.5
Monadina 343
-monadina **344**
monandrous 1370
monarch 1057
monarchomachic 409
Monardella 262.3
monaster(ium) 1271
'monastery church' 1271
-mond **662**
monergic 407.1
moneyed 594.2
-monger **1257**
monger(e) 1257
-mongering 1257
mongoose 960
monitrice 725
mon(o) 344
monoblepsia 223
monochrome 864
monoclinic 466.2
monoclinous 1366
monocyclica 10
monocytangina 346
monocyte 1014
monodermoma 315
monodiplopia 161
monodrama 282.1
monodromic 445.1
Monoecia 42
monogamy 1459.2, 1503.1
Monogenea 23
monoglot 1419
monogrammatic 515
monogynic 482
monolinguist 1440
monolith 1075.1
monologist 1436.1
monologue 1019.1
monomer 1262
monomicrobic 387
monomoria 186
monophasic 508
monophonic 470.2
monophthong 1051
monoplane 880
monoplegic 404.2

monopole 837
monopoly 1501
Monorchotrema 289.2
monorhine 893
monorhythmic 438
monospermic 451.2
monosporangium 1169
monosyllabic 385
monosyllable 805
monosynthetic 533.3
monotheism 1157.3, 1159
monotheist 1437
monotheistic 572
Monotremata 367
Monotrocha 32
Monotype 917.3
monovalent 1410.2
mons 1418, 882
'monster, fetal' 1352, 1353.2
-mont **1418**
-montane **882**
montān(us) 882
monte 1418
'monthly' 134
'mood' 542
'moon' 134
moonscape 911
moonstone 906.4
-moor **1276**
mor 1276
mōr 1276
mōr(a) 186
-morainal 465
morain(e) 465
-morainic **465**
more 1253.2, 1441
-moria **186**
mōria 186
moribund 664
mōr(on) 186
mōr(os) 186
-morph 72, 416, **1064,** 1161, 1317
-morpha **34,** 416, 1161
-morphae 72, 416, 1161
morph(ē) 34, 72, 416, 1064, 1161, 1317
morpheme 856
-morphi 72, 416, 1161
-morphia **72,** 416, 1064, 1161
-morphic 72, **416,** 1064, 1161, 1317
-morphically 72, 416, 1064, 1161

-morphism 72, 416, 1064, **1161,** 1317
-morphosis 72, 416, 1064, 1161, **1317**
morphōsis 1317
morphoun 1317
-morphous 72, 416, 1064, 1161, 1317
-morphously 72, 416, 1064, 1161
-morphy 72, 416, 1064, 1161
mortbell 1131.1
mortgage 766
mortgagee 759.3
-morula **277**
-morular 277
mōr(us) 277
Mosaic 383.5
'moss, bearded' 504
most 1434,
-most **1441**
'moth' 1050.2
-motile **826,** 1278, 1543
-motility 826, 1278, **1543**
'motion' 214, 540, 540.1, 540.2, 540.3, 1312
'motion, regular' 110, 438
'motion-creating mechanism' 1278
-motive 826, 1278, 1543
'motor' 1279.2
-motor[1] 826, **1278,** 1543
-motor[2] 826, **1279,** 1543
motorcade 741.1
'motor control' 1517
motorcycle 810.4
motordrome 863.2
-motored 826, 1278, 1543
-motorial 826, 1278, 1543
-motorially 826, 1278, 1543
-motoric 826, 1278, 1543
mōt(us) 826, 1278, 1279, 1543
moujik 1094
-mould 641
-moulding 641
'mound' 1449
-mount 1418
'mountain' 882, 1052, 1418
mountaineer 1255.1
'mountainlike' 1052
mous 969

-mouse **969**
mousebane 877.1
mousehawk 1099.1
mousetrap 1241.1
mousseline 894
-mouth 116, 117, 329, 330, 369, **1082,** 1508
mouthful 1140
'mouth of a river' 1082.1
mouthpiece 720.2
'move' 826, 1278, 1279, 1312, 1543
'movement' 214, 525.2, 540.1, 794.1, 1313
'movement, capability of' 1543
'movement, capable of' 826
'movement, irregular' 788.1
'movement, mode of' 524.1
'movement of simple organism' 1333.2
'movements' 246
'mover' 1278
mōv(ēre) 826, 1278, 1279, 1543
moviedom 1148.2
movieland 647.4
'moving, capable of' 822
Mozarabic 383.5
'much' 1441
-mucic 1355
mucofibrous 1369
-mucoid 1355
mūcōsus 1355
-mucous **1355**
'mucus' 1355
mūc(us) 1355
mūð 1082
muddy 1457.1
mudguard 682
-muir 1276
'mulberry' 277
müllerianoma 316
multicentric 499.2
multicolor 1275.1
multicostate 1004
multicycle 810.3
multiflora 358.2
multifoil 1127
multilobe 710
multimotor 1279.2
multiparous 1368
multipartite 1010

multiplicand 644
'multiplied by' 638.1
multiply 1502
multipole 838
multiscience 731.2
multistage 770.2
multivalence 732.2
multiverse 965.1
mummy/mummify 1474
-mund 662
munificence 728.3
munitioneer 1255.1
munt 662, 1418
munte 1418
'murderer' 877
Muridae 969
Murine 887.3
mūs 969
'muscle contraction' 147,
    480
'muscles, abnormal
    function of' 480.5
'muscle tonus' 480
'muscular acts,
    measurement of' 187
Musgrave 1024
music 384.2, 475.1
'musical instrument' 342
'musical instrument,
    pipe' 912.3
'musical instruments'
    470.3, 690.2, 901.1
'musical intervals' 480.2
'musical pitch' 480,
    905.1, 905.2
'musical sound' 470.2
musicologue 1019.3
must 1023
mustn't 1403
muzhik 1094
'muzzles' 31
myatonic 480.4
-myces **1298**
-mycetic 1298
-mycetous 1298
-mycin 1298
Mycoderma 333.3
Mycodermic 450.4
-mycosis 1298
mycostasis 1306
mycostat 1385.5
myctipelagic 403
myectopia 167
-myeletic 85
-myelia **85**
-myelic 85

myeloblast 1430
myelobrachium 1171
myelocythemia 101
myelodysplasia 202
-myeloma **312**
-myelomatoid 312
-myelomatous 312
myelomenia 134
myeloplastic 567.2
myelorrhagia 51
myel(os) 85, 312
-myia **254**
mykēs 1298
mynster 1271
myocardiac 379.2
myoclonia 144
myocomma 298
myoglobinuria 194
myoneurosis 1320
myope 913
myopia 158
myosteoma 304
myostroma 324
myotome 870.2
myotropic 488.3
Myoxidae 694
myriad 588.4
myriagram 1145.2
myrosin 1199.4
-myth 421
-mythic **421**
-mythical 421
-mythically 421
mythoclast 1431.1
mythoclastic 566.1
mythogonic 469.1
mythoheroic 483
mythopoeic 399
myth(os) 421
'myths' 421
myx(a) 332
myxofibroma 320
myxoinoma 320
-myxoma **332**
myxopapilloma 313

N

-n 875, 1190, 1191
naess 1344
naessa 1344
nailhead 590.4
'nails' 68
naisse 1344
nama 854

'name' 113, 203, 845,
    1180, 1510
-name **854**
nam(en) 854
'names, study of' 1510.2
nam(ian) 854
nanocephaly 1491
nanocormia 121
nanosomia 115
nanosomus 1352
naphthalene 883
naphthol 1136
narcolepsy 1536
narcoleptic 561
narcoma 301.1
narcomaniac 381.1
-narcosis 555
narcosomania 127.1
-narcotic **555**
-narcotical 555
-narcotically 555
-narcoticism 555
narkōtik(os) 555
narkoun 555
'nasal slime' 332
nascelle 828
nasicorn 1233
nasse 1344
-nastic **568**, 1545
nast(os) 568, 1545
-nasty 568, **1545**
'nation' 464, 844
'native' 949.2, 1005.2,
    1251.2
natterjack 1086.3
'natural' 1104, 1292
'nature' 659, 700, 1242,
    1357, 1358, 1358.1
naturopathic 419.3
naus 1445
-naut **1445**
naut(ēs) 1445
-nautical 1445
-nautics 1445
navicella 263
-nd **643**
-ne **875**
'near' 136, 1009
nebby 1457.3
nebnose 959.2
nebular 1249.1
neckband 645.2
necklace 714.2
neckline 895.4
neckmold 641
neckpiece 720.1

necrology 1476.1
necromantic 549
necromimesis 1311
necrophilia 88.2
necrophobic 386.1
needlenose 959.4
-nema **288**
nēma 288
nemathelminth 1079
nematode 754
'nematode, threadlike'
  288.1
'nematodes, filamentous'
  171
nematodiasis 1305.1
nematospermia 120
-neme 288
-nemia 105
Nemophila 260
Neocene 884
neoclassic 510
neocosmics 453.3
neogrammatical 1105
neomorphism 1161
'neoplasm, malignant'
  303
'neoplastic disorder of
  lymphoid tissue' 305
Neotoma 327
neovolcanic 454.1
nephradenoma 317
nephratony 1517
-nephric **493**
nephridium 1167
nephrogenic 460.2
nephr(oi) 493
nephrolith 1075.2
nephroma 299,
-nephroma **323**
nephromegaly 1490
nephr(os) 323
nephrotyphoid 627.1
'nerve' 192, 325, 560,
  940, 1119, 1320
'nerve cell' 940
'nerve fibers, branching
  of' 175
nervimotility 1543
nervous 26, 1354.1
'nervous disease' 560.1,
  1320
'nervous tumor' 325
-nes 1343, 1344
nescient 1409
-ness[1] **1343**
-ness[2] **1344**

-nesse 1343
Netherstow 1450
nettlefoot 1420.4
'network' 1452.3
neuradynamia 95
-neural 940, **1119**, 1320
neuralgia 55
neuralgic 405
neurasthenia 132
neuratrophia 71.2
-neure **940**, 1119, 1320
neurectopia 167
neurergic 407.1
-neuria **192**
-neuric 1119, 1320
neurimotility 1543
neurocardiac 379.2
neurocrine 140
neurodendron 1228.2
neurodynia 152
neuroepithelioma 308
'neuroglia tumor' 310
neurohormone 903.2
neurolemma 297
neurolymph 1062
-neuroma **325**, 940, 1119,
  1320
neuromimesis 1311
neuromimetic 537
neur(on) 192, 325, 560,
  940, 1119, 1207, 1320
neuroparalytic 581
neuropath 1072.1
neuropsychic 411.1
neuropsychosis 1316
-neurosis 560.2, 940,
  1119, **1320**
neurosomatic 518.2
neurostearic 490
-neurotic **560**, 940, 1119,
  1320
-neurotically 560, 1320
neurotonic 480.6
neurotoxia 253
neurotoxic 583
neurotrauma 338
neurotripsy 1537
neurovaccine 891
neururgic 408.1
'neutralization' 1335
new 884
Newburyport 1425.2
newlywed 612
Newport 1425.2
newsstand 649.2
Newtown 1234

niacin 1199.2
-n(ian) 1190
-nice **724**
nicety 1538
Nichrome 866
-nick 1095
nicochrome 866
Nietzschean 1181.2
niggergoose 960
nighthawk 1099.2
nightmare 920
nighttide 751.1
-nik **1095**
nikē 724
nimble 798
ninetieth 1069
'nipple' 83, 307, 313,
  796, 1172
nitrite 1005.5
nitrolime 859
nōbil(is) 807
-nobility 807
-noble **807**
-nobled 807
'nobleman' 807.2
-noblement 807
noctalbuminuria 195
noein 542
noēsis 542
-noetic 155, **542**
noētik(os) 542
-noia **155,** 542
-noiac 155, 542
-noic 155, 542
-noid 155, 542
'noise' 479
-noma **316**
nomadically 1495
-nome **862**, 1504
nom(ē) 316
-nomia **113,** 1504
-nomian 862
-nomic 113, 862, 1504
-nomical 862, 1504
-nomically 1504
-nomie 1504
nominee 759.1
-nomist 862
nom(os) 444, 862, 1504
-nomous 862, 1504
-nomy 862, **1504**
nonagenarian 1185.3
nonasthmatic 513
noneconomic 444
nonerotic 559.1
nonmagnetic 539.1

nonmetallic 428
nonmobile 822
nonmorainic 465
nonmotile 826
nonorganic 455.1
nonphonetic 541
nonplane 879
nonpsychic 411.2
nonsense 955
nonvolcanic 454.1
noontide 751.1
no(os) 155, 542
'noose' 714
Norfolk 1096
'norm' 1113
nōrm(a) 1113
-normal **1113**
normalcy 1113
-normality 1113
-normally 1113
normative 1028.2
normochromic 446.3
normoglycemia 98
normosthenuria 193
normothermia 119.1
normotonic 480.4
normotopia 166
normovolemia 103
'North' 527
Northleigh 1058, 1473
'North Pole, area near'
  527
Norwood 676.2
'nose' 139, 893, 959
nose 1344
-nose 610, **959**
noseband 645.3
-nosed **610**, 959.4
nosos 1330
nos(u) 959
not 1403
'not' 71, 218, 448
notabilia 86
notancephalia 77
'notes in scale' 480.1
noteworthy 1486
'notochord' 17
-nounce **734,** 982
-nouncement 734, 982
'nourish' 597.1
'nourishment' 414,
  1063.2, 1482
'nourishment for embryo'
  1063.1
nova 4.1
novachord 690.2

novelette 1011.3
novice 721
Novocaine 890
no(ys) 155, 542
-n't **1403**
-nuclear **1248**
-nucleate 1248
-nucleic 1248
nucleole 831.1
nucleon 1207.1
'nucleus in a cell' 1248
nuc(u)le(us) 1248
nudiflora 358.2
nudnik 1095
nullipara 350.1
'numb' 555
-nunciate 734, **982**
-nunciation 734, 982
nunciature 943.3
nunti(āre) 734, 982
-nuria 940, 1119, 1320
-nuric 940
nursemaid 621
'nurture' 1482
'nut' 1248
nutburger 1258.1
'nutrition' 414, 1482
nux 1248
nyctalbuminuria 195
nyctalopic 485
nyctinasty 1545
Nyctipithecus 1350
nyctitropic 488.1
-nys 1343
-nyss 1343

O

-o 1083
-*o* 1235
-o¹ **1235**
-o² **1236**
'oak' 1092
oaken 1189
oaktongue 1017.2
'oar' 857
'oared ship' 857
oatmeal 1107
obconic 467.1
-obe **708**
obesitas 1288
-obic 708
-*obie* 708
object 1388.2, 1412.2
'object of action' 759.1
obliterate 999.1

'observation' 160, 1521
observatory 1527.1
observe 160, 486, 914,
  951, 1036, 1390, 1521
'obsession' 881, 1330.2
obstruct 1393
obtain 1201
obtund 671
obtuse 970.1
obverse 965.3
obvolute 1012
-*oc* 1091
ocarina 342
'occasion' 861, 1106
'occlusion' 218
'occupation' 674, 1242.1
occurrent 1413
oceanography 1481.2
ochlophobia 40
-ock¹ **1091**
-ock² **1092**
octacorallia 261
octahedron 1227
octodianome 862.2
octogynia 153
octopus 1376
octuple 843
'ocular tissue, absence or
  defect of' 300
oculus/ocular 1249
-odal 752
'ode, division of' 752.2
-*ode* 594, 752.1
-ode¹ **752**
-ode² **753**
-ode³ **754**
-odic¹ **393**, 753
-odic² **394**
-odically 393, 394, 753
odometer 1264
-odon **1208**
-odonic 1208
-odont 1208
odontalgia 55
-odontia¹ **240**, 1208
-odontia² **241**, 551, 1208
-odontic 241, **551**, 1208
-odontics 241, 551
odontoceramic 433
odontoclast 1431.2
-odontoid 1208
odontotherapia 157
'odor' 122, 337
odorific 400
odos 393, 395
Odostemon 1225

odous 240, 241, 551,
   1001, 1208
-odus 1208
-ody 752
-odyne 152, **908**
odyn(ē) 152, 908
-odynia **152,** 908
-odynic 152, 908
-oecia **42**
-oecian 42
-oecious 42
-oecism 42
-oecium 42
-oedema 286
-oeid(ēs) 396, 625, 626,
   754
'of' 20, 343, 383.3, 470.6,
   545, 567.1, 571, 578,
   699, 703, 818.1, 887,
   889, 889.1, 927.3,
   1005, 1023, 1199,
   1330, 1359, 1360, 1361
offend 653
offenest 1434
'offer' 622
'office' 943.2, 1148.1,
   1242.1, 1465
'office, persons filling an'
   972.2
official 1109
officialdom 1148.2
'official position' 972.1
offici(um) 1109
offing 1046.4
offsaddle 811.1
'offspring' 290, 350.2,
   1368
'offspring, produce' 598
Ogdensburg 1053
Oglethorpe 916
oh 1236
-oi **1085**
-oid¹ **625,** 626
-oid² 625, **626**
-oida 20
-oidal 625, 626
ōid(ē) 394, 752
-oidea **20**
-oideae **702**
-oidei 20
oidēma 286
-oides 20
-oidism 626
oikonomik(os) 444
oik(os) 42, 444

'oil' 398, 398.1, 832,
   1137
oilskin 1203.4
-oire 1528
-ok 1091
Oktoberfest 1435.1
-ol 797, 798
-ol¹ **1136**
-ol² **1137**
-ola **268,** 831
'old age' 552
oldest 1434
'old man' 552
Old Saybrook 1097
oldster 1267.3
oldwife 764.4
-ole¹ **831**
-ole² **832,** 1137
Oleacina 343
-oleic **398,** 832
'oleic acid' 398.2
oleogranuloma 314
ol(eum) 398, 832, 1137
olfaction 1219.2
olfactory 1530
-olic 1136
oligergasia 198
Oligochaeta 371
oligochromemia 104
oligochylia 92
oligochymia 124
oligodendria 175
oligogalactia 235
oligohydria 177
oligonephric 493
oligoplastic 567.1
oligopnea 24
oligopoly 1501
oligosialia 79
oligotrichia 63.1
Olisiocampa 349
-ol(um) 831
-ol(us) 831
-oma **299**
-omatoid 299
-ome 299
'omit' 1323
omnilucent 1408
omnipotent 1414
omnirange 776.2
omniscience 731.1
omniscient 1409
omnitonic 480.2
omnivorous 1375
omphalochorion 1215
omphalotribe 706

'on' 308
-on 902, **1207**
ōn 230
-ōn 902
Onchocerca 12
oncotherapy 1519.2
'one' 344, 868
'one, as' 806
-one **899**
-ōnē 899
one-foot 1420.1
'one of a group' 868
oneupmanship 1243
onionskin 1203.3, 1203.5
onkōma 299
onko(un) 299
(o)nom(a) 113, 203, 1180,
   1510
-onomasia **203**
onomatopoeia 49
onomatopoeic 399
onomaz(ein) 203
ontocycle 810.1
ontocyclic 424.1
ontogeny 1513
-onychia **68**
onych(ion) 68
-onychium 68
-onym **1180,** 1510
onyma 1180, 1510
-onymic 1180, 1510
-onymically 1180, 1510
-onymous 1180, 1510
-onymously 1180, 1510
-onymy 1180, **1510**
ooglea 22
ook 1092
ooplasm 1155
Oospora 360
oospore 936
oozooid 629
opacity 1540
opalescent 1407.2
opaline 889.2
-ope 158, 485, **913,** 1266
Opegrapha 33.2
openface 713.3
openhanded 595.2
'opening' 289.1, 289.2,
   834.2, 1037.5, 1508
'opening, surgical' 1508
opera 1.2
'operative treatment'
   1526
'operator' 1267.1
operatory 1527.1

operetta 373
ophid- 46
-ophidia **46**
ophiotoxemia 108
ophis 46
ophthalmagra 355
-ophthalmia **112, 440**
-ophthalmic 112, **440**
ophthalmodynia 152
ophthalm(os) 112, 440
-opia **158,** 226, 485, 913
opiate 974.1
-opic 158, **485,** 913
-opical 158, 485
-opically 158, 485
opisthogenia 130
Opisthoglypha 35
Opisthoparia 172
opisthotic 553.2
opodidymus 1353.2
oppose 961
'opposing' 531
opposite 1006, 1009,
    1308
ops 158, 161, 162, 226,
    227, 485, 564, 913,
    1266, 1325
opsimath 1071
-opsis 226, 227, 564,
    1266, **1325**
opsoclonia 144
-opsy 158, 226
-opter 564, **1266**
-optic 226, **564,** 1266
-optical 226, 564
optically 226, 564
optics 1289.1
optik(os) 564
-opy 158, 226, 485, 913
-or 1253.2, 1273, 1274,
    1277
-or¹ **1273**
-or² **1274**
oracular 1245.3
'oral opening' 1082
'oral work or action'
    1476.1
-orama **283**
-oramic 283
orange-tree 763.1
orangewood 676.1
orbitostat 1385.4
orchichorea 26
Orchidaceous 1358.2
orchidorrhaphy 1480
orchiomyeloma 312

'order' 37, 247, 525, 648,
    989, 1333
'order, go in' 410, 1054
'order, put in' 989, 1019
'ordering' 247, 247.2,
    1333
'ordinal' 643, 678, 1069,
    1428
ordināre 989
-ordinate **989**
-ordinatingly 989
-ordination 989
-ordinative 989
ordināt(us) 989
-orectic 250
oregein 250
-oretic 250
-orexia **250**
-orexic 250
orex(is) 250
'organ, displaced' 167
-organic **455**
-organical 455
'organically' 455
organik(os) 455
'organism' 455.3
'organism, simple' 344,
    1007
'organism, small' 711
'organismic functioning'
    198
'organization' 1157.3
organon 455
organophonic 470.5
organotropy 1522
'organs, body' 455.1
'organs, placement of'
    166
orgasm 1154
-ōri(a) 1528
-orial 1527, 1528
-orie 1527, 1528
'orientation' 525.2
'orifice' 289.1, 367
'origin' 213, 538, 618,
    1513, 1515
'originating in' 949.1
-orily **1494,** 1528
-orium **1176,** 1527
-ōrium **1176**
-ōri(um) 1528
-ōri(us) 1528
ornis 420
-ornithes 420
-ornithic **420**
Ornithischia 66

-ornithoid 420
ornithophile 823
ornithophily 1492.1
ornithopteron 1229
orphanage 765.4
orthocladous 1356
orthocrasia 206.1
orthodontia 241
orthodontic 551.2
orthoepy 1520
orthognathia 73
orthomorphia 72
orthopedia 45
orthopedic 383.6, 392.1
orthopraxis 1332
orthoptic 564
orthoscopic 486.1
orthosomatic 518.1
orthotactic 525.1
orthotype 917.1
-ory¹ **1527**
-ory² **1528**
-os 1083, 1085, **1340**
-ōs(a) 956
oscheocele 813
-ose¹ **956**
-ose² **957**
-osely 956
-osic 956
-osis 554, 1302, **1315**
-ōsis 554, 1315
-osity 956, 1354
-osma **337**
osm(ē) 122, 337
-osmia **122**
-osmic 122
osmiophobic 386.2
-osphrasia 216
osphrāsia 216
-osphresia **216**
-osphresis 216
osphrēsis 216
-osphretic 216
-ost 1434
-osteal 1209
osteectopia 167
ostensorium 1176.2
ostensory 1527.2
ostentatious 1360
osteoclast 1431.2
osteocomma 298
osteocranium 1173
osteocystoma 331
osteodermis 1301
osteofibrous 1369
-osteoid 1209

osteolipoma 319
-osteoma **304**, 1209
osteomalacia 41
-osteomatoid 304
-osteomatous 304
-osteon 304, **1209**
osteopath 1072.2
osteopathic 419.3
osteopathy 1485.2
osteopedion 1214
osteophore 933
osteophyma 340
osteoplastic 567.2
osteoplasty 1544
osteosarcoma 303
Osteostraean 1181.6
osteosynthesis 1309
osteotome 870.1
osteotomy 1506
-osteum 304, 1209
-ostraca **6**
-ostracan 6
ostracode 754
Ostracoidea 20
ostrak(on) 6
ostreophage 767
-ōs(um) 956
-ōs(us) 956, 1354, 1355,
   1360, 1363
Oswald 630
otacoustic 576.1
otalgic 405
-(o)tha 1069
-(o)the 1069
othematoma 328
-otia **242**
-otic¹ **553**
-otic² **554**, 1315
-otical 554
-otically 554
-ōtik(os) 554
otocranium 1173
otosteon 1209
-oun 1315
-our 1273, 1274
our(a) 362
-ourg- 408, 1478
-ourgia 1526
our(on) 27, 190
-ous 242, 553, 1005.5,
-ous **1354**
ous(a) 230
-ousia **230**
-ousian 230
-ously 1354
-ousness 1354

'out' 167, 1507
outbid 622
outbound 667
outfame 853
outfigure 941.1
'out from' 655
'out of' 167
outpeople 844.3
outsized 615
outstand 650.1
outtake 790.2
outtire 930
outwale 803
-ovaria **173**
-ovarial 173
ovariodysneuria 192
ovariostomy 1508
-ovarism 173
ōvāri(um) 173
'ovary' 173
overangelic 425
overcharge 778.4
overfeed 597.1
overfertile 827
overforce 735
overgild 636.2
overgod 672
overgorge 781
overhand 646.3
overhandle 812.1
overjawed 613
overlay 1462
overpolitic 546.2
'over-powering' 735
oversized 615
oversparred 609
overstrain 1200
overtake 790.1
overtire 930
'overuse, tendency to'
   1158
ovicyst 1444
oviparous 1368
oviposit 1402
ovogenetic 538.3
ovoid 626
ovovivipara 350.2
ovula 273
ovulum 1178
ōvum 173
'ownership of goods for
   sale' 1501
ox 1191.1
oxalylurea 27
oxbow 1448.2
-oxemia **107**

-oxemic 107
oxen 1191
oxeye 1037.3
Oxford 689
Oxfordshire 928
-oxia **252**
-oxic 252
oxidase 947
'oxide' 4.2, 746
oxyblepsia 223
Oxycardia 48.3
oxychromatic 517.2
Oxycoccus 1349.1
oxyecoia 154
ox(ygen) 252, 746
'oxygenation' 252
oxygène 252, 746
'oxygen in the blood'
   107
oxymel 1122
oxyopter 1266
oxyosphresia 216
oxyrhine 893
Oxyrrhyncha 31
oxy(s) 252
oxytocia 43.1
Oxytricha 30
oysterling 1049.2
oysterwife 764.1

P

'pace' 13
pachyderm 1149
pachydermic 450.2
pacific 400
packsack 1087
packsaddle 811.2
-paedia 45
-paedic 45, 392
-paedics 45
-paedist 45
paedonymy 1510.2
paeovolcanic 454.1
pæth 1073
pagoplexia 249
paideia 45
'pain' 55, 152, 210, 355,
   405, 509, 908
'pain, sensitivity to' 210
'painful seizure' 355
painting 1046.2
pais 45, 392
pāl 802, 835
Palaeogaea 18
palaeothere 924

-pale 802
paleoanthropic 487
paleobotany 1512
paleoclimatic 514
paleocosmic 453.3
paleoethnic 464
paleofauna 347
paleometallic 428
paleotypic 489.1
Paleozoic 484.2
palilogetic 529
palindrome 863.3
palindromic 445.2
palingraphia 70.2
palinode 752.1
palinodic 394
palmiped 604.2
palmitin 1199.3
palmitoleic 398.1
pāl(us) 802
pamaquin 1205
-pan 1188
pancake 787.2
panchromatic 517.1
panclastic 566.1
pancosmic 453.1
pancratic 520.4
'pancreas' 512
pancreatic 511,
-pancreatic 512
-pancreatism 512
pandemic 434.1
pandemonic 472.1
Pandora 356
panhandle 812.3
pankreas 512
panne 1188
panoptosis 1321
panorama 283
panpipe 912.3
panpsychic 411.2
pansophic 415
pantatrophia 71.1
pantechnic 462.1
pantencephalia 78
pantheistic 571
'panting' 294, 513
pantomime 860
pantomimic 439
pantosophy 1484
'paper' 1203.5, 680
'paper, folded' 516
'paperboard' 680
papill(a) 313
-papilloma 313
-papillomatous 313

'papyrus, leaf of' 680
-para 350, 1368
parabola 269.1
parabolic 429.4
parabranchia 65.2
parabulia 91
paracardiac 379.1
parachroia 156
paracystitis 1331
paradiplomatic 516
paradromic 445.2
'paraffin hydrocarbons'
 876
paraform 1152
paragastric 500
paragenesia 213.1
paragerontic 552
paragranuloma 314
parahormone 903.1
paralogistic 573
paraluetic 544
paraly(ein) 581
'paralysis' 53, 404, 581
'paralysis sufferer' 404.2
-paralytic 581
-paralytical 581
-paralytically 581
paralytik(os) 581
paramenia 134
parametric 498.1
paranephroma 323
paranoia 155
paranomia 113
paranormal 1113
paraphasic 507
paraphrase 948
paraphrastic 569
paraphysical 1104
paraplastic 567.1
paraplegia 53
paraplegic 383.7, 384.3,
 404.2
parasite 1008
parasomnia 141
paraspasm 1156
Parasuchia 67
parasynthetic 533.3
paratactic 525.1
parathormone 903.2
parathymia 125
paratyphoid 627.2
paravenous 1365
parei(a) 172
'parent, female' 852
parentage 765.5
parentheses 1308

parenthetic 531
par(ere) 350, 1368
parhelion 1207, 1214
-paria 172
-parian 172
-pariid 172
paripinnate 993
parisyllabic 385
-parity 350, 1368
parodistic 571
paromologetic 529
paronomasia 203
paronychia 68
parorexia 250
parotic 553.2
-parous 350, 1368
-parously 350, 1368
pars 1010
parsimonious 1359
parsonage 765.4
'part' 179, 720.2, 720.3,
 748.1, 748.2, 817,
 926, 1010, 1262
'part from' 788
'particle' 314, 617.2
'particle, atomic' 1207.1
'particle, charged' 1213
'particles' 142
partīre 1010
-partite 1010
'partner' 987.1
'parts' 638.2, 1010
'parturition' 43.1, 43.2
paruria 190.2
parviscient 1409
'passage' 359, 918
'passage, means of' 935
'passageway' 359, 935,
 1425
passion 1212.3
'passion, subject to' 532
password 691.1
pasteboard 681.3
pastille 829
'pasturage' 316
'pasture' 1397, 1473
-pate 995
-pated 995
pat(ein) 1073
patentee 759.3
'path' 393, 419, 532, 753,
 895.3, 1380, 1463,
 1485
-path¹ 1072
-path² 1073

periophthalmia 112
perioptic 564
periosteoma 304
periotic 553.2
peripancreatic 512
periphrase 948
periphrastic 569
peripneumonia 145
perisarc 585
periscope 914
perishable 804.2
perisphere 923.1
perisplanchnic 463
perispondylic 432
Perissodactyla 280
peristalsis 1314
peristole 840
peristyle 851.1
perithecium 1166
perithelium 1172
peritrema 289.1
Peritricha 30
periwig 1044
Permian 1181.2
perpendicular 1249.2
perruque 1044
'person' 1095, 1181.4,
 1181.5, 1185.3, 1186,
 1235.1, 1235.2, 1251.3,
 1251.4, 1251.6, 1252.1,
 1252.2, 1255, 1261,
 1267.3, 1377, 1429,
 1436.4, 1523
-person **1231**
persōna 1231
'personality' 595.2
'person associated with'
 761.3
'person furnished with'
 759.3
personification 1218.1
person/personify 1474
'persons' 1148.2
'persons filling an office'
 972.2
perspiratio 1237
perspiration 1218.2
perspiratory 1529.1
perstringe 777
persuade 743

'pertaining to' 545, 571,
 765, 818.1, 949.1,
 1028.2, 1045.3, 1100,
 1109, 1181.1, 1249.1,
 1299, 1358.1, 1359,
 1360, 1361, 1524,
 1528.1, 1529.1
'peruke' 1044
pervade 744
perverse 965.4
pervert 1424.2
pēs 44, 391, 604
pessein 224
pessimist 1436.4
pesticide 747.2
Petricola 271
petrificant 1404.2
petrificate 976
petrification 1219.1
petroglyphic 417.1
petrol 1137
pēxesthai 1335
-pexia 1335
-pexic 1335
-pexis **1335**
pēxis 1335
-pexy 1335
pezza 720
Phacella 262.2
-phag 29, 50, 767, 1475
-phaga **29**
-phage 29, 50, **767,** 1475
phag(ein) 29, 50, 767,
 1475
-phagi 29, 50, 767, 1475
-phagia 29, **50,** 767, 1475
-phagic 29, 50, 767, 1475
-phagically 29, 50, 767,
 1475
-phagism 29, 50, 767,
 1475
-phagist 29, 50, 767,
 1475
phag(os) 767
-phagous 29, 50, 767,
 1475
-phagy 29, 50, 767, **1475**
phain(ein) 456, 508, 878,
 885, 1511
-phakia **74**
phak(os) 74
-phalangia **56**
-phalangism 56
phalanx 56
phallanastrophe 785.1
-phan 456, 878, 1511

phanai 199, 507, 508,
 1304
-phane 456, **878,** 1511
Phanerogamia 94
Phanerozonia 149
-phanic 1511, **456,** 878
-phanous 1511, 878
phantasmatomoria 186
-phany 456, 878, **1511**
'pharmaceutical product'
 1199.2
pharmacist 1436.2
pharmacologic 406.3
pharmacopedia 45
pharmacopedic 392.2
pharmacopoeia 49
pharmacotherapeutics
 1294
pharm(akon) 449
-pharmic **449**
pharyngoscleroma 322
-phase 508, 770.2
-phasia **199,** 507, 1304
-phasic¹ 199, **507,** 1304
-phasic² **508**
-phasis 199, 507, 507,
 508, **1304**
-phasy 199, 507, 1304
-phatic 199, 507, 1304
Pheidole 831.2
phēm(a) 100
-phemia **100,** 199
-phemic 100, 507
-phen 885
-phene **885**
phenocoll 1133
-phenol 885
'phenol group member'
 885
phenomena 2.1
-phenyl 885
phenylmercuric 501
-pher **1259**
pherecratean 520.7
pherecratian 520.7
pherecratic 520.7
pher(ein) 185, 357, 494,
 933, 1259, 1313
-phil 88, 427, **1126,** 1362,
 1492
-phila **260,** 1126
philanthropic 487
-phile 88, 427, **823,**
 1362, 1492
phil(ein) 88, 260, 427,
 823, 1126, 1362

philharmonic 475.1
-philia **88**, 427, 823,
  1126, 1362, 1492
-philiac 88, 427, 823,
  1126, 1362, 1492
-philic **427**, 1126, 1362,
  1492
-philism 88, 427, 823,
  1126, 1362, 1492
-philist 88, 427, 823,
  1126, 1362, 1492
-philite 88, 427, 823,
  1126, 1362, 1492
Philodendron 1228.1
philomel 1122
philosophaster 1269
philotadpole 836
philotechnic 462.1
-philous 88, 427, 823,
  1126, **1362**, 1492
'philtre' 449
-phily 88, 427, 823, 1126,
  1362, **1492**
phlebangioma 306
phlebitic 545
phlebitis 1330.1
phlebolith 1075.2
phleborrhage 768
phlebostasia 209.2
phlebotomy 1506
-phobe 40, 386, **709**
phobia 37.1
-phobia **40**, 386, 709
phobiac 40, 378, 386,
  709
-phobic 40, **386**, 709
-phobically 40
phobism 40, 386, 709,
  1157.2
-phobist 40, 386, 709
phob(os) 40, 386, 709
-phobous 40, 386, 709
pholornithic 420
-phone 470, 470.3, 541,
  901, 1516
phōn(ē) 470, 541, 901,
  1516
phoneme 856
phonendoscope 914
-phonetic 470, **541**, 901,
  1516
-phonetical 541
-phonetically 470, 541,
  901
-phonetics 541
phōnētik(os) 541

-phonia 470, 541, 901,
  1516
-phonic **470**, 479, 541,
  901, 1516
-phonically 470, 901
-phonious 470, 541, 901,
  1516
-phoniously 901
phonograph 1060.2
phonon 1207.2
-phonous 470, 541, 901,
  1516
-phony 470, 541, 901,
  1516
-phor 185, 357, 494, 933,
  1259, 1313
-phora 185, **357**, 933
Phoradendron 1228.1
-phorae 357, 933
-phore 185, 357, 494,
  933, 1259, 1313
phorein 185, 357, 494,
  933, 1313
-phoresis 494, **1313**
phorēsis 1313
-phori 357, 933
-phoria **185**, 357, 494,
  933, 1313
-phoric 185, 357, **494**,
  933, 1313
-phorical 494
-phorically 494
phoropter 1266
-phorous 185, 357, 494,
  933, 1313
phōs 556
phosphite 1005.5
phosphoresce 736
phosphuret 1396
-phote 556
-photic **556**
photocatalytic 582
photoelectric 497
photogalvanic 459
photogenic 460.4
photographic 412
'photographic device' 353
photography 1481.1
photon 1207.2
photonastic 568
photonasty 1545
photoperiod 673
photoperiodic 395
photophily 1492.2
photophoresis 1313
photosynthesis 1309

phototactic 525.2
photothermy 1509.2
phototypic 489.2
-phragm 292
-phragma **292**
-phrase 207, 569, **948**
phraseologic 406.1
-phrasia **207**, 569
phras(is) 207, 948
-phrastic 207, **569**, 948
-phrastical 569
-phrastically 569, 948
phrastik(os) 569
phrazein 207, 569, 948
phrēn 137, 461
-phrenia **137**, 461
-phrenic 137, **461**
-phrenically 137, 461
phreniclasia 200
-phthong 57, **1051**
-phthongia 57, 1051
-phthongization 1051
-phthongize 1051
phthong(os) 57, 1051
-phyceae **701**
phyein 374, 1015, 1104,
  1292, 1327
phyk(os) 701
-phyl 1135
Phylactolaema 284
-phyll **1135**
Phyllantheae 699
-phyllic 1135
-phylline 1135
phyll(on) 1135, 1177
phyllopodium 1168
Phyllostomatinae 703
phyllotactic 525.3
-phyllous 1135
-phyllum 1135, **1177**
-phylly 1135
phylogerontic 552
-phyma **340**
-phymatic 340
-phyre **946**
-phyric 946
-phyritic 946
-physeal 1015, 1292,
  1327
-physial 1015, 1292, 1327
physiatrist 1438
-physical 1015, **1104**,
  1292, 1327
'physician' 496, 1291,
  1438, 1531
physicist 1436.2

plastochondria 176.1
plast(os) 243, 1432, 1544
-plasty 201, 567.1, 1155,
1544
-plasy 201, 1155, 1544
plateaux 1451
plat(eia) 716
'platform' 770.1
'platform over a
depression' 774.1
platitudinarian 1185.2
'Plato, school of' 435
platt(ein) 201, 243, 1155,
1432, 1544
plat(y) 716
platybasic 505
platycephalic 423
platycnemia 106
platyhelminth 1079
platymeria 179.2
platypus 1376
platyrrhine 893
plat(ys) 716
Platysomatidae 698
platysomus 1352
plax 75, 372
'play' 755
playfield 634.1
playhouse 968
'play with' 755
playwright 1401.3
-ple **843**
*ple- 843
'pleasure' 143, 938
'pleat' 639
plebium 772
plect(ere) 843, 1452, 1502
-plectic 249, 404, 1452
Plectinae 703
'pledge' 612, 663, 766,
-pledge **772**
plēgē 53, 249
plegg(en) 772
pleg(ia) 404
-plegia **53**
-plegic 53, **404**
pleg(ier) 772
plegium 772
-plegy 53, 404
pleiochromic 446.5
Pleistocene 884
'plenty' 159
'plenty, horn of' 159
pleomastia 255
pleonotia 242
plēss(ein) 249

plētt(ein) 249
Pleurococcaceous 1358.2
Pleuronema 288.2
pleuropneumonia 145
pleurosteon 1209
Pleurostigma 293
pleurotyphoid 627.1
-plex **1452**
-plexia **249**, 404
-plexic 249, 404
plēx(is) 249
-plexity 1452
plex(us) 1452
-plexy 249, 404
plic(āre) 638, 843, 977,
1502
plicāt(a) 977
-plicate **977**
-plication 843, 977, 1502
plicāt(um) 977
plicāt(us) 977
-plice 1502
-plicity 1502
plier 1502
Pliohippus 1378
-plo- 516
Ploceidae 1055
-ploid **628**
-ploidy 628, **1471**
-plorable 934
plōr(āre) 934
-ploration 934
-ploratory 934
-plore **934**
-plorer 934
-ploringly 934
-pl(os) 628
-pl(um) 843
plūma 872
plumbing 1046.3
-plume **872**
plunderbund 665
'plunge' 779, 963
pluriflorous 1374
pluripara 350.2
-pl(us) 843
plushette 1011.5
plutocratic 520.3
-ply **1502**
Plymouth 1082.1
-pnea 24
-pneic 24
pnein 476
Pneumococcus 1349.2
pneumocrania 128
pneumoempyema 291

pneumomalacia 41
pneumomassage 769
pneumōn 145, 476
-pneumonia 37.1, **145**,
476
-pneumonic 145, **476**
pneumonik(os) 476
pneumosepticemia 97
pnoē 24, 476
-pnoea 24
-pnoeic 24
pnoiē 24
'pod, hanging' 710
-pod 16, 47, **677**, 692,
1168, 1376
-poda **16**, 47, 677, 1168
-podal 16, 47, 677, 1168,
1376
podalgia 55
Podaxonia 148
-pode 16, 47, 677, 1168,
1376
-podia 16, **47**, 677, 1168
-podial 16, 47, 677, 1168,
1376
podiatrist 1438
podiatry 1531
-podium 16, 47, 677,
1168
podobranchia 65.2
Podophyllum 1177
Podosomata 368
Podostemon 1225
-podous 16, 47, 677,
1168, 1376
-pody 16, 47, 677, 1168
-poeia **49**, 399, 535, 543,
1310
-poeic 49, **399**, 535, 543,
1310
'poem' 394
-poesis 49, 399, 535, 543,
1310
poetaster 1269
poetess 1341
-poetic 49, 399, 535, **543**,
1310
poetical 49, 399, 535,
543, 1103.2, 1310
-poetically 49, 399, 535,
543, 1310
poeticize 1038.2
-poetics 543
'poetry' 543.2
poi(ein) 49, 399, 535,
543, 1310

-poiesis 49, 399, 535, 543, **1310**
poiēsis 1310
-poietic 49, 399, **535,** 543, 1310
-poietical 49, 399, 535, 1310
-poietically 49, 399, 535, 543, 1310
poiētik(os) 535, 543
'point out' 569, 948
'poison' 108, 253, 583, 877, 1206
'poison for arrows' 253, 583
'poisonous plant' 877.1
pol 836, 1134
polar 838, 1245.1
-polarity 838
'pole' 609, 802, 835
-pole[1] **835**
-pole[2] **836**
-pole[3] **837**, 1501
-pole[4] **838**
pōl(ein) 837, 1501
polemics 1289.2
policlinic 466.3
-polis 546, **1300**
-polism 837
-polist 837, 1501
-polistic 837
-polistically 1501
-polistics 1501
-politan 546, 1300
-polite 546, 1300
-politic **546,** 1300
-political 546, 1300
-politically 546, 1300
'political party' 520.2
'political party, member of' 1384.2
'political theory' 546.1, 1467.3
politico 1235.1
-politics 546, 1300
politik(os) 546
-poll **1134**
polle 836, 1134
pollinate 973.3
polliwig 1044.3
polloi 1085
pollywog 1044.3
pol(os) 838
pol(us) 838
-poly 837, **1501**
polyacid 623.2

Polyandria 174
polyandrous 1370
polybasic 506
polychord 690.1
polychromatic 517.1
polychrome 864
polychromemia 104
polychromic 446.1, 446.4
polyclinic 466.3
polycolor 1275.1
polycratic 520.4
polydactyl 1143
polydemic 434.2
polydemonic 472.1
polyfold 638.2
polygenetic 538.1
polygenic 460.3
polyglot 1419
polygonic 468
polygynic 482
polygynous 1367.1
polyharmonic 475.1
polyhedron 1227
polylemma 296
polylinguist 1440
polymastia 244
Polymastigina 345
polymath 1071
polymer 1262
polymeria 179.2
polymicrobic 387
polymorph 1064
polymythic 421
polyonymy 1510.2
polypapilloma 313
polypeptidorrhachia 59
polyphagia 50.2
polypharmic 449
polyphasic 508
polyphonia 38.1
polyphonic 470.2
polyplegic 404.1
polypnea 24
polypod 677
Polypodiaceous 1358.2
polyscelia 82
polysomia 115
polyspermia 120
polyspermic 451.2
polystichia 64
polystyle 851.1
polysyllable 805
polysynthetic 533.3
polytechnic 462.1
polytechnics 1290
polythelia 83

polytrichia 63.2
polyuria 190.2
-pone 669, **904**
-ponement 904
-ponency 904
-ponent 669, 904, 961
pōn(ere) 669, 961, 1009, 1221, 1402
pontificate 972.2
pool 838, 926
poopsy 1535
popeyed 614
Popsicle 809
popsy 1535
'populace' 285, 434
populate 973.5
popul(us) 844
-pora **359,** 935
-pore 359, **935**
'pores' 359
-poric 359, 935
poriomanic 457.1
por(os) 359, 935
-porous 359, 935
porphyr(os) 946
porphyry 946
-port **1425**
port(a) 1425
porteress 1341
porter/portress 1341
'portion' 179, 1010, 1262
portunalia 76.2
-posal 669, 942, 961, 1009, 1402
-pose 669, 942, **961,** 1009, 1221, 1402
pos(en) 961
pos(er) 961
-posit 669, 942, 961, 1009, 1221, **1402**
posit(a) 1009
-posite 669, 942, 961, **1009,** 1221, 1402
-positely 942, 1221
'position, official' 972.1
-position´ 669, 770, 942, 961, 1009, 1148.1, **1221,** 1306, 1402
-positionally 669, 942, 961, 1009, 1221, 1402
-positioned 1009
positive 669, 961, 1030, 1402
posit(um) 1009
posit(us) 1009, 1221, 1402

posse 1414
'possessing' 594.2, 971.2, 1373
possession 640, 1212.4
'possession of land or property' 640.1
'possessor' 933
'post' 791
postage 765.7
postarthritic 548
postasthmatic 513
postcardiac 379.2
postcarnate 994
postcephalic 423
postembryonic 481
postfebrile 825
posthypnotic 558
postlude 755.1
postpneumonic 476.1
postpone 904
postrheumatic 519
postscorbutic 577
postspasmodic 396
posttetanic 458
posttonic 480.3
posttyphoid 627.2
-posure 669, **942**, 961, 1009, 1402
-pot 1422
potassiomercuric 501
poteen 1195
-potence 1414
-potency 1414
potens 1414
-potent 1414
-potential 1414
poteye 1037.5
pott 1422
'pottery' 433
'pouch' 1444
-pound 669, 706, 942, 1009, 1324, 1402, 1537
-poundability 669
-poundable 669
poundcake 787.3
poundmeal 1107
'pour' 967
'poured' 967
'pour in' 339
pous 16, 47, 677, 1168, 1376
'poverty' 135, 1538
'power' 95, 131, 234, 520, 606.2, 732.1, 1384, 1410.1

-practic 246, 52, **524,** 726, 1332
-practical 726
'practical art' 462.1
'practice' 52, 246, 524, 1157.1, 1332, 1525.2
-practice 726
'practice, medical' 524.2
'practicer' 1436.2
-practics 52, 246, 524, 1332
-practise 726
practis(en) 726
practis(er) 726
-pragia 52, 246, 524, 726, 1332
pragmatagnosia 222
praiseproof 1041
praiseworthy 1486
praktik(os) 524
prass(ein) 52, 246, 524, 1332
pratfall 1128.1
pratt(ein) 52, 246, 524, 1332
-praxia 52, **246**, 524, 524.1, 1332
-praxic 52, 246, 524, 1332
'praxis, medical' 524.2
-praxis 52, 246, 524, 726, **1332**
prāxis 1332
preclassic 510
precosmic 453.3
precyclone 902
predicament 1412.5
prefecture 943.2
'preferring' 260
'pregnancies' 15
'pregnancies producing children' 350.1
'pregnant woman' 15
prehandle 812.1
prehatred 606.1
-prehend 654
prehend(ere) 654, 950
-prehension 654
-prehensive 654
'prehistoric mammal' 924
prejudice 721
prelature 943.2
prelinguistic 574
preliterate 999.2
prelude 755.1
premanufacture 945

premaxilla 266
pre-Mongolid 616.2
prename 854.2
prenoble 807.1
'preoccupation' 881
preparalytic 581
prephonetic 541
prephragma 292
prerheumatic 519
preromantic 550.1
presbyacousia 231
presbyope 913
prescapula 276
prescience 731.1
'prescribe' 892
preserve 1036
preside 750
'pressed close' 568, 1545
'pressure, atmospheric' 1247
'pressure-influenced growth' 1545
presume 873
pretend 657.2
pretension 1223
preterdiplomatic 516
pretonic 480.3
pretyphoid 627.2
preuve 1041
prevalence 732.1
prevalent 1410.1
prevent 1417.2
prevocalic 422
priceless 1342.2
Priestholm 1147
primacy 1466
'primate' 1350
primigravida 15
primipara 350.1
'principle' 1113
'principles' 1157.3
'printed material' 412
'printed object' 917.2
printing 489.2, 1045.3, 1481.1
'printing machine' 917.3
printline 895.5
'prior in space' 932.2
'prior in time' 932.1
-prise 950
prīv(āre) 245
prīv(ātus) 245
-privia 245
-privic 245
-privous 245
proba 1041

psoriasis 1305.2
psychagogue 1018.1
psychanopsia 227.1
-psyche 411, **784, 1316**
psych(ē) 411, 784, 1316
psych(ein) 784
psychiatric 496
psychiatrist 1438
psychiatry 1531
-psychic 384.2, **411,** 784, 1316
-psychical 411, 784
-psychically 411, 784
-psychist 411
psychoanalytic 580
psychoclinic 466.3
psychodrama 282.2
psychogalvanic 459
psychogenetic 538.3
psychokinesis 1312.1
psychokinetic 540.2
psycholeptic 561
psychology 1476.2
psychomachy 1479
psychometry 1533
psychomotor 1279.1
'psychoneurosis' 560.2, 1320
psychoneurotic 560.2
psychopath 1072.1
psychopathic 419.1
psychorganic 455.1
-psychosis 457.1, **1316**
psychosocial 1111
psychosomatic 518.2
psychosophy 1484
psychosurgery 1526
psychosynthetic 533.2
psychotherapy 1519.2
'psychotic' 381, 554.2
-psylla **267**
-pter 354, 1170, 1229, **1265,** 1456
-ptera **354,** 1229, 1265
Pteridophyta 374
Pterococcus 1349.1
-pteron 354, 1170, **1229,** 1229, 1265, 1265, 1456
Pterosauria 191
Pterostemon 1225
pterostigma 293
pterygion 1170
-pterygium **1170,** 1456
Pterygogenea 23
pteryx 1170

-pteryx 354, 1170, 1229, 1265, **1456**
-ptosis **1321**
ptōsis 1321
Ptychoparia 172
Ptychosperma 334
pty(ein) 1329
ptysis 1326,
-ptysis **1329**
pūb(ēs) 389
pubescence 729
pubescent 1407.1
pubic 383.10,
-pubic **389**
'pubis' 389
publicity 1540
'public opinion' 853
'puff' 985
'pull' 1156, 1386
pūlmō 473
pulmobranchia 65.2
pulmocardiac 379.1
-pulmonary 473
-pulmonic **473,** 476.2
puls(a) 953, 1123
'pulsation' 438
'pulse' 109, 110
-pulse **953,** 1123, 1216
-pulsion 953, 1123, **1216**
-pulsive 953, 1123, 1216
puls(um) 953, 1123
puls(us) 953, 1123, 1216
pulviplume 872
pupa 4.1
'pupil' 184
pupipara 350.2
'pure' 565
pureblood 675
purgative 1028.1
'purify' 565
'purple' 946
'purple stone' 946
'purpose' 426
-pus 16, 47, 291, 677, 1168, **1376**
'push' 757, 953, 1123, 1156, 1216
'pushing' 1216
pussytoe 910.2
'put' 531, 669, 904, 961, 1009, 1221, 1308, 1309, 1402
put(āre) 1013
-putation 1013
-putative 1013
'put before' 904

'put down' 904
-pute **1013**
-putedly 1013
'put forward' 904
'put in a place' 1450
'put in order' 1476
'putrefaction' 97, 1322
putrefactive 1029
'putrified' 97
'putting together' 1308
'put together' 89, 531, 533, 904, 1309
pyelovenous 1365
Pygobranchiata 365
pygodidymus 1353.2
pygostyle 851.2
Pyncnocoma 302
pyochezia 256
pyoptesis 1329
pyorrhea 21
pyosepticemia 97
pyr 251
pyress(ein) 251
pyretos 251
pyretotherapy 1519.1, 1519.2
pyrett(ein) 251
-pyrexia **251**
pyroclastic 566.3
pyrognomic 443.1
pyromania 127.1
pyrotechnic 462.2
pyrotechny 1514
pyrrole 832
pyrroline 887.1
pyuria 190.2

Q

quadrantanopia 162.1
quadrantanopsia 227.1
quadrifoil 1127
quadriplegic 404.2
quadrivalve 1031
quadruplicate 977.2
quaer(eré) 931
quaes- 931
-quake **792**
quak(en) 792
'qualities' 700, 956, 1357, 1358, 1525.1
'quality' 721, 728.1, 878, 1070, 1242, 1343, 1459.2, 1466, 1468.1, 1468.2, 1470.1, 1470.2, 1470.3, 1538, 1540

quantum 1164, 1207.2
quartet 1394.2
quartil(is) 817
quest 931
question 931
quicker 1253.2
quicklime 859
quickly 1489
-quin 1205
quindecade 588.2
-quine 1205
quinine 887.1
quinone 899
quinquenniad 588.2
quinquereme 857
quintad 588.4
-quirable 931
-quire 931
-quirement 931
-quisition 931
-quisitive 931

R

-r 1191.2
-ra 1253.1
'race' 23, 464, 492, 675,
-race 717
'race course' 445, 863,
   1056
rachiotome 870.1
racial 1109
'racial group' 464
radiad 589
'radical' 588.5
radioacoustic 576.2
radiogenic 460.4
radiographic 412
radiolucent 1408
radiomagnetic 539.2
radiometric 498.1
radiomimetic 537
radiopractic 524.2
radiopraxis 1332
radiosonic 479.2
radiotelescope 914
radiothermy 1509.2
radium 1165
ræden 606
'rafter' 609
'rag' 720
'rage' 127
ragweed 600
railhead 590.6
rainband 645.4
rainbow 1448.3

Raleigh 1058
ramosopinnate 993
-range 776
'rank' 674, 765.5, 943.2,
   972.1, 989.2
ransomfree 762.1
rantipole 836
rare 1474
rarefy 1474
ras 717
rās 717
'rash' 287
'rate' 765.6
'rather' 1065.4
ratline 895.2
rattlemouse 969.2
rattlepate 995.2
rattletrap 1241.3
Raymond 662
razoredge 771
-rd 678
-re 1253
'reach for' 250
'reach to' 1201
'reaction, chemical' 582
'read' 1019
readable 804.1
'read (aloud)' 248, 1476
Reading 999.2, 1048
'reading impairment' 248
'ready, make' 667
'realm' 923.4, 1148.3
'realm, biogeographic' 76
'rearing' 607.2
rearmament 1412.1
'reason' 1476
'reasoning' 406, 573
'reasoning, fallacious'
   573
'reasoning anew' 573
rebate 975
rebellion 1212.1
recd 586
recede 745
receive 1026
'received thing' 296
(re)ceiv(re) 1026
'recent' 884
'receptacle' 8, 1166
'receptiveness' 955
recharge 778.1
recipiangle 815.1
'recipient of result of
   action' 759.2
'recital' 1019.12
'reckon' 941.1, 1013

'reckon about' 1013
recline 898.1
'recognition' 1319
'recognize' 951
'recognizing, faculty of'
   221
recompense 954
'record' 1145.1
recriminate 991
rectangle 815.2
rectangular 1245.1
'recurrence of events'
   810.3
recurrent 1413
'recurring at an interval'
   1488.2
'red' 605
-red¹ 605
-red² 606
redbud 692
reddish 1065.4
rede 606
redhead 590.3
redleg 1043.2
redpoll 1134.2
reface 712
refer 1256.1
'referring to' 571
refigure 941.1
refine 892
reflect 1389.1
'reflecting light' 1407.2
'reflection apparatus'
   1385.3
refluent 1415
'refraction of the eye'
   164
reframe 855.1
'refuge' 640.2, 783.1, 846
refusenik 1095
*reg 1400
'regard to, with' 952.3
regency 1470.3
regenerate 998
regicide 747.1
regild 636.1
Reginald 630
'region' 434.2, 870.2
'region, disease in a'
   434.1
'region of land' 911
'regular motion' 110, 438
'regulator' 1031, 1385.2
'regulatory substance'
   903
rehandle 812.1

'rheumatism' 519
rhēx(ai) 51, 402, 768, 1334
402,
-rhexis 1334
rhēxis 1334
-rhine 139, 893
Rhinebeck 1088
Rhineland 647.1
893
-rhinia 139
rhinoplastic 567.1
rhinoscleroma 322
rhis 139, 893
-rhiza 375
-rhizal 375
Rhizomastigina 345
rhizoneure 940
Rhododendron 1228.1
Rhodophyceae 701
-rhoea 11, 21, 397
-rhoeic 21, 397
-rhoeica 11
Rhopalocera 351
rhotacism 1158
-rhyncha 31
rhynch(os) 31
-rhyncous 31
-rhythm 438
-rhythmia 110
rhythmic 110
-rhythmical 110, 438
-rhythmically 438
-rhythmics 438
rhythmik(os) 438
rhythm(os) 110
'rib' 1004
'ribbon' 714.1
ribskin 1203.2
Richard 679.1
ricinoleic 398.1
rickstand 649.1
ridden 1192
'ridge' 803
ridgepole 835
ridibund 664
ridicule 849
ridiculous 1363
-right 1400
-rightly 1400
-rightness 1400
righto 1236
riht 1400
rimester 1267.2
'rind' 297
'ring' 196, 424, 810, 902

'ring of atoms' 424.5
ringshake 788.2
ripcord 688
'rise' 782
Rivenhall 1129
'river' 1048, 1472
'river mouth' 1082.1
'river valley' 800
'road' 393, 395, 753, 1073, 1380, 1463
roadhead 590.6
'rob' 245
robber 1252.2
robbing 1045.1
Roberta 4.1
Roberts 1202.2, 1339
Robertshaw 1446
Rocella 263
Rochester 1270.1
'rock' 906
rockbell 1131.2
'rod' 180, 802
'rod, slender' 651
rog(āre) 981
-rogate 981
-rogation 981
-rogatory 981
'rogue' 1086.1
rogueship 1242.4
'role' 1231
'roll' 1012, 1033
'romance' 550, 550.2
'Roman classes' 510
-romantic 550
-romantical 550
-romantically 550
'romantic tradition' 550.1
romantique 550
'Rome, ancient' 510
'Rome, Church of' 430
rondelle 828
'roof' 54
roofing 1046.4
rooftree 763.2
'room' 353
'root' 375, 1426
-root 1421
'rope' 895.1, 895.2
'rope, small' 688
'rope made of flax' 895
ropesmith 1076.2
roqueling 1049.3
Rosaceae 700
Rosamond 662
rosebush 1068
roseola 4.1

'rot' 97, 563, 1322
rōt 1421
'rotting' 1322
roughleg 1043.2
'rounded prominence or division' 710
roundel 1121
Roundhead 590.1
roundnose 959.4
roundnosed 610
'row' 64, 410, 776, 895, 1054
-(r)rhachia 59
-rrhachitic 59
-rrhage 402, 768, 1334
-rrhagenic 1334, 51
-rrhagia 51, 402, 768, 1334
-(r)rhagic 51, 402, 768
-rrhagically 768
-rrhaphia 1480
-(r)rhaphy 1480
-rrhapsy 1480
-rrhea 11, 21, 397
-rrheal 21, 397, 528
-rrhecis 51
-rrheic 21, 397
-rrheic/-rrhetic 528
-rrhetic 21, 397
-(r)rhexis 402, 1334
-rrhine 139, 893
-(r)rhinia 139, 893
-(r)rhiza 375
-rrhizal 375
-rrhoea 11, 21, 397
-rrhoeic 397
-(r)rhoeica 11, 21, 397
-(r)rhoia 21
-(r)rhyncha 31
-rrhynchous 31
-(r)rhythm 438
-(r)rhythmia 110, 438
-(r)rhythmic 110, 438
-(r)rhythmical 110, 438
-(r)rhythmically 438
-(r)rhythmics 438
'rub' 706, 1324, 1537
'rubbing' 1324, 1537
rucksack 1087
'rule' 606, 630, 1113
'rule, guiding' 895
'ruler' 1057
rumormonger 1257.2
rump(ere) 1423
rumple 799
'run' 445, 863, 1413

'runners' 32
'running' 1413
'running away' 783.1
'runny' 1355
runs 1285
-rupt **1423**
-ruption 1423
'rupture' 768, 1334
rupt(us) 1423
'rush' 744
Rutherford 689

S

-'s **1281**
-s' **1282**, 1295
-s 1282, 1283, 1339
-s¹ **1283**, 1296
-s² 1202, **1284**
-s³ **1285**, 1297
-s⁴ **1286**
Sabine 889.1
sac 1087
saccharocoria 183
Saccorhiza 375
sacc(us) 1087
sacer 997
-sack 331, **1087**, 1166,
   1331, 1444
'sackcloth' 1087
sacr(āre) 997
'sacred' 997
'sacred, make' 997
sacrifice 723
sacroiliac 380
-saddle **811**
saddlebow 1448.2
saddlenose 959.1
saddletree 763.2
sadel 811
sadist 1436.4
sadol 811
sadul 811
sæcc 1087
sǣd 599
sǣta 1397
safehold 640.2
sailor 1273, 1445
salespeople 844.2
salesperson 1231
salicylate 974.2
'saliva' 79
salvagee 759.4
'same' 867
sanatorium 1176.1
'sandal' 839

sandstone 906.2
'sandwich, patty' 1258.2
Sängerbund 665
sängerfest 1435.1
sanipractic 524.2
sanitas 1288
sapphirewing 1050.1
saprocoll 1133
saprozoite 1007
-sarc 303, **585**
sarcelle 828
sarcocarcinoma 318
Sarcocca 7
sarcoderma 333.1
sarcodermic 450.2
sarcolemma 297
-sarcoma **303**
-sarcomatoid 303
-sarcomatous 303
sarcoplast 1432
Sarcopsylla 267
sarcosepsis 1322
sarcosome 869
sarcotheca 8
-sarcous 585
sardinewise 952.1
sarkōma 303
sarx 303, 585
satchel 1121
sateen 1194
'satiety' 183
satisfaction 1219.2
saucepan 1188.1
-saur 191, **1280**, 1379
-sauria **191**, 1280, 1379
-saurian 191, 1280, 1379
Saurischia 66
sauroderma 333.1
saur(os) 191, 1280, 1379
-saurus 191, 1280, **1379**
savagery 1525.5
sawhorse 966.2
Sawmont 1418
Sawrey 1472
sawyer 1252.2
saxophone 901.1
'say' 248, 1002, 1416
'saying' 1416
scaga 1446
scalewing 1050.2
scandalmonger 1257.2
scand(ere) 652
-scape **911**
scapegrace 719
-scapula **276**
-scapular 276

scapulothoracic 390
scarehead 590.7
scaremonger 1257.2
'scatter' 964, 1388.1
sceac(an) 788
scēad(an) 602
scead(u) 742
-scelia **82**
-scend **652**
-scendant 652
-scendent 652
'scene' 283
-scension 652
schemata 2.2
-schipe 1242
Schistocerca 12
schistocormia 121
schistosternia 151
Schizodendron 1228.3
schizogyria 196
Schizomeria 179.1
'Schizomycetes' 180
schizophrenia 137
schizophrenic 461.2
schizoprosopia 165
schizothymia 125
scholar 1251
schoolgirl 1139
schooltide 751.3
'science' 401, 731.2,
   1289.1, 1292, 1409,
   1476.2
-science **731**
'science, descriptive'
   1481.2
'science of judging' 1505
sciens 401, 731, 1409
-scient 401, 731, **1409**
scientia 731
-scientific **401**, 731
'scientifical 401, 1103.2
-scientifically 401
-sciently 1409
-scioe 1242
scir 928
scire 401, 731, 1409
sclerocornea 25
Sclerodermic 450.4
-scleroma **322**
sclerophyll 1135.1
-scope 160, 486, **914**,
   1521
-scopia **160**, 486, 914,
   1521
-scopic 160, **486**, 914,
   1521

-scopical 160, 914, 1521
-scopically 160, 486, 914, 1521
-scopist 160, 914, 1521
Scopulariopsis 1325
-scopy 486, 914, **1521**
-scorbic **388,** 577
-scorbutic 388, **577**
-scorbutical 388, 577.
-scorbutically 388, 577
scorb(ūtus) 388, 577
scorecard 680
Scorpionida 3, 14
Scotsman 1186.2
Scotswoman 1187.2
scratchcard 680
scratchwork 1098.2
-scribe **705**
scrīb(ere) 705
-scription 705
-scriptive 705
scrubbing 1045.1
scrubland 647.3
'sculpture' 417.1, 417.2
'scurvy' 388, 577
scutulum 1178
'sea' 403, 926
Seabrook 1097
seafare 918
'sea inlet' 1198, 1461
'seam' 1480
seamstress 1347
seaplane 880
seaport 1425.1
seascape 911
seaside 748.3
'season' 861
'season of the year' 751.2
seastroke 794.2
'seat' 1227
'seat for a rider' 811
seaward 683.2
seaway 1463
'seaweed' 701
seawife 764.4
seaworthy 1486
sebaceous 1358.1
seborrhagia 51
seborrheic 397
seborrhoeica 11
sec(āre) 1391
'second' 587, 643
secondary 1524
secondhand 646.5
-secr(āre) 997

-secrate **997**
-secration 997
-secrative 997
-sect **1391**
-section 1391
-sectional 1391
-sectionally 1391
'sections of tissue' 447
sect(us) 1391
secundigravida 15
secundipara 350.1
sed 599
sedative 1025.3
sed(ēre) 750, 811
Sedgely 1473
seduce 738
'see' 283, 951
'see, ability to' 556.1
'seed' 120, 334, 360, 451, 599.1, 936, 990, 1151, 1169, 1349.1
-seed **599**
'seed-producing plant' 599.2
'seeds' 451.1
seedtime 861
'seek' 931
'seek out' 934
'segment' 817, 870.2
'segmentation' 327
'segmented' 327, 447, 448
segregate 980
sei(ein) 452, 1160
-seism 452, **1160**
seismaesthesia 212
-seismal 452, 1160
-seismic **452**, 1160
-seismical 452, 1160
-seismically 452, 1160
'seismic movement' 1160
'seismic trembling' 792
seism(os) 452, 1160
'seize' 296, 561, 654, 790, 950, 1026, 1536
'seizure' 355, 561, 1536
'seizure, painful' 355
selectee 759.2
selenoplexia 249
'sell' 837, 1501
'seller' 1257.1
'selling place' 1525.3
selvage 771
selvedge 771
semaphore 933
semaphoric 494.2

semateme 856
-semblance 806
-semble **806**
-seme 437, **858**
sēm(ē) 437, 858
semen 1197
sēmen 990
semiacid 623.2
semiangle 815.1
-semic **437**, 858
semicoma 301.1
semiliterate 999.2
semimagnetic 539.1
semimanufacture 945
semimucous 1355
sēmin(āre) 990
seminarian 1185.3
-seminate **990**
-semination 990
-seminative 990
semiordinate 989.2
semitone 905.2
semivocalic 422
semivolcanic 454.2
'send word by' 648
senile 818.1
-sens 955
'sensation' 212
-sense **955**
-sensical 955
-sensicality 955
-sensically 955
-sensicalness 955
'sensitive' 532, 955
'sensitive to' 419, 532, 1485
'sensitive to, be' 1072
'sensitivity' 534.2, 955, 1485.1
sensory 1528.1
sēns(us) 955
sent(īre) 955
'separate' 140, 220, 547, 602
'separation' 220
sēp(ein) 563, 1322
Sephardim 1146
-sepsis 563, **1322**
sēpsis 97, 1322
septet 1394.2
-septic **563**, 1322
-septicaemia 97
-septicaemic 97
-septicemia **97**
-septicemic 97
septic(us) 97

'similar, make' 806
'similar to' 793
'similar to, make' 1474.2
-similate 806
similis 806
similitude 758
simplex 1452.1
Simsbury 1534
simul(āre) 806
'simulation' 537, 1311
sinecure 939
'sinew' 192, 325, 560,
 940, 1119, 1320
'sing' 752
singing 1045.2
'single' 344, 628
singlehanded 595.3
sinkhole 834.1
-sis 511, **1302**
Sissinghurst 1443
-sist **1439**
-sistence 1439
-sistency 1439
-sistent 1439
sist(ere) 727, 1439
'sit' 750, 811
-site **1008**
-sitia **237**, 1008
-sitic 1008
-sitism 1008
sit(os) 237, 1008
six-footer 1251.4
sixish 1065.5
sixty 1539
size 615
-sized **615**
skeletopia 166
skelgoose 960
skel(os) 82
skewbald 631
skewfoot 1420.3
-*ski* 1487
'skill' 462, 1242.2, 1398,
 1412.1
'skilled' 1484
'skilled person' 415
'skin' 118, 274, 315, 333,
 450, 450.1, 1149, 1215,
 1301
-skin **1203**
'skin, animal' 1203.1,
 1203.2
'skin color' 156, 446.5
skinn 1203
skinnier 1253.1
'skin surface' 156

'skin tumor' 315
'skin types' 450.4
'skin variety' 450.2
skipjack 1086.1, 1086.3
Skipness Point 1344
sklēr(os) 322
skop(ein) 160, 486, 914,
 1521
-*skopia* 160
'skull' 128, 1173
-sky **1487**
slabstone 906.3
slavery 1525.5
'slave-trader' 1257
Slavicize 1038.3
'sleep' 141
'sleep, deep' 301
sleeps 1285
sleepy 1457.3
slept 1381
slicer 1251.6
'slide' 962
'slightly' 1407.1
'slime, nasal' 332
'slimy' 1355
'slip' 962
'slipper' 839
slipsole 839
'slope' 898.1
slugfest 1435.2
sluggard 679.2
slumbery 1525.3
smacko 1236
'small' 711, 1094, 1178
'small one' 262.1, 262.2,
 262.3, 265, 265.1,
 265.2, 268.1, 272, 373,
 831.1, 848, 1094, 1121,
 1178, 1193, 1195,
 1202.1, 1351
smeary 1457.2
'smell' 122, 216, 337
'smelling' 216
smið 1076
-smith **1076**
-smithy 1076
smockface 713.1
'smoke' 150, 871
smoothpate 995.1
smutproof 1041
'snake' 46
snakepipe 912.4
snakeroot 1421
'snakes, venomous' 35,
 46
'snare' 714, 1241

snickersnee 761.1
snipnose 959.2
snobbish 1065.3
snobbism 1157.1
'snot' 1355
'snotlike' 1355
'snout' 31
snowberg 1052
snowbound 666.1
snowfall 1128.1
snowmobile 821.2
snowshade 742
snowshed 602
snubnosed 610
'soak up' 377
soapcake 787.4
-social **1111**
sociāl(is) 1111
-socially 1111
soci(āre) 983, 1111
-sociate **983**, 1111
-sociation 983, 1111
-sociative 983, 1111
sociocrat 1384.1
sociodrama 282.2
socioeconomic 444
soci(us) 983, 1111
sockeye 1037.3
sodbuster 1272
sodium 1165
'soft' 41
'softening' 41
'softness' 41
-sol **1138**
solarium 1175
'solar system' 453.3
soldier 1252.1
soldiery 1459.3
-sole **839**
sole(a) 839
Solenoglypha 35
solstice 727
-solubility 808, 1032
-soluble **808**, 1032
-solution 808, 1032, 1138
-solvability 808
-solvable 808
-solve 808, **1032**, 808
solv(ere) 808, 1032
-som 867, 868
-soma 115, 232, **326**,
 518, 869, 1352
sōma 115, 232, 326, 368,
 511, 518, 698, 869,
 1352
somata 2.2

-spermia 120, 1151
-spermic 120, 451, 1151
-spermous 120, 451, 1151
-spermy 1151, 120
sperre 609
-spers(a) 964
-sperse 964
-spersion 964
-spers(um) 964
-spers(us) 964
-sphaera 923
-sphaere 923
-sphaeric 491, 923
-sphaerical 491, 923
-sphaerically 923
-sphaericity 923
-sphaerite 923
sphair(a) 491, 923
sphenotic 553.3
sphenotresia 217
-sphere 923
-spheric 491, 923
-spherical 491, 923
-spherically 923
'spherical shape' 491.2
-sphericity 923
-spherite 923
spheroid 625
sphilophyma 340
-sphygmia 109
-sphygmic 109
sphygmophone 901.4
sphygmophonic 470.5
sphygm(os) 109
sphygmosystole 842
'spice' 449
spicecake 787.3
'spinal column' 1117
'spinal cord' 85
'spinal fluid' 59
'spine' 59, 1078
spinoneural 1119
spīr(āre) 929
spiraster 1268
-spiration 929
-spirational 929
-spirationally 929
-spire 929
'spirit' 125, 411, 784,
    1136, 1316
'spirited' 632
spirivalve 1031
Spirocerca 12
'spit' 1329
'spitting' 1329
'spittle' 79

splanchna 463
-splanchnic 463
splanchnosomatic 518.1
splanchnotribe 706
splayfooted 611
'spleen' 133
splēn 133
-splenia 133
-splenic 133
-splenism 133
splenomegaly 1490
splenophrenic 461.1
'split' 624
'spoken utterance' 691
-spond 663
-spondence 663
-spondency 663
-spondent 663
spond(ēre) 663
-spondylic 432
spondyl(os) 432
'sponge' 58
-spongia 58
-spongiae 58
-spongium 58
Spongospora 360
-spora 360, 936
sporangia 38.1
-sporangium 1169
-spore 936
'spores' 360
'spores, encasement of'
    1169
-sporic 936
sporid 617.2
sporocarp 1244
sporogonic 469.1
spor(os) 360, 936, 1169
-sporous 936
Sporozoa 348
sporozoite 1007
sporozooid 629
'sport' 755
'spray' 692
'spread' 316, 1038.3
springtide 751.2
springtrap 1241.1
'sprout' 279
sprucery 1525.4
Squamata 46
squaresville 830.2
squireen 1195
-st 1427, 1428, 1433,
    1434
-st¹ 1427, 1433
-st² 1428

-stabile 820
stabil(is) 820
'stability' 521.1, 820
-stabilize 820
stable 798, 820
stablemate 987.3
-stage 770
'stage action' 282
'stage composition' 282.1
stagehand 646.1
'stages, completion of'
    810.1
'stages, repetition of'
    810.3
stagese 949.3
staghead 590.8
'stainability' 204.2
'staining properties'
    446.4, 517.2
'stake' 802, 835, 1089
-stake 791
'stakes, enclose with' 802
'stakes, insert' 802
'stakes, place on' 802
stal 1130
-stall 1130
-stalsis 1314
-staltic 1314
'stamen' 1225, 1370
'stamens' 174, 466.2
'stamens and pistils'
    1366
'stamped object' 917.2
stan 906
stān 906
'stance, upsidedown'
    649.3
'stand' 209, 521, 649,
    650, 727, 770, 820,
    1002, 1003, 1225,
    1293, 1306, 1385,
    1439.2
-stand¹ 649
-stand² 650
'stand against' 650.1
'standard' 1113
standee 759.4
stand(en) 649, 650
'standing' 521, 1130,
    1306
'standing still' 209, 1306
standpipe 912.2
'stanza' 1054
staphyledema 286
staphyloangina 346
Staphylococcus 1349.2

'star' 1268
st(āre) 770, 820, 1002, 1439
starshake 788.2
'star-shaped' 1268
starthroat 1383
'starting point' 505
-stase 947
-stasia **209**, 521, 1003, 1293, 1306, 1385
-stasic 209, 521, 1003, 1293, 1306, 1385
stasimorphia 72
-stasis 209, 521, 1003, 1293, 1302, 1303, **1306,** 1385
-stasy 209, 521, 1003, 1293, 1306, 1385
-stat 209, 521, 1003, 1293, 1306, **1385**
stat(a) 1002
'state' 37, 281, 591, 606.1, 642, 674, 721, 728.1, 758, 799, 938, 943.1, 971.1, 1148, 1157.2, 1212.4, 1219.2, 1242.3, 1300, 1343, 1404.3, 1412.5, 1459.2, 1465, 1466, 1468.1, 1468.2, 1470.1, 1470.2, 1470.3, 1525.5, 1538, 1540
-state[1] 1002
-state[2] 209, 521, **1003,** 1293, 1306, 1385
statecraft 1398.2
stateswoman 1187.2
-static 209, **521,** 1003, 1293, 1306, 1385
-statically 521, 1385
'static electricity' 521.2
-statics 209, 521, 1003, **1293,** 1306, 1385
stat(ikē) 1293
statik(os) 521
'stating' 948
'stating in other words' 948
'stating literally' 948
'stationary, device for keeping' 1385.1
statistician 1181.5, 1184
statoconia 142
stat(os) 1003, 1385
statuesque 1022.1
stat(um) 1002

stat(us) 646.5, 1002
'stay' 770
'stay in one place' 750
'stay in place' 820
staylace 714.1
'stay put' 770
-stead 592
'steadfast' 820
steall 1130
stear 490
-stearic **490**
stede 592
Steenboc 584
steepen 1190.3
steeple 796
steg(e) 54
-stegia 54
Stegomyia 254
Steironema 288.5
steix(ein) 410, 1054
stell(ein) 840, 1314
'stem' 1228.3
-stemon **1225**
stēmōn 1225
-stemonous 1225
stē(nai) 209, 521, 1002, 1003, 1225, 1293, 1306, 1385
stenographer 1260
stenography 1481.1
stenophotic 556.1
stenostomia 116
stenotypic 489.2
'step' 13, 197, 505, 506
stepdame 852
Stephanofilaria 171
steppeland 647.3
'steps, completion of' 810.1
-ster **1267**
sterculiad 588.3
-stere 1267
stereochrome 864
stereoneural 1119
stereoplanula 275
stereornithic 420
stereosonic 479.2
stereotropic 488.2
stereotropism 1162
-sternal 151, **1114,** 1179
sterncastle 846
-sternia **151,** 1179
sternite 1005.7
sternodymia 123
stern(on) 151, 1114, 1179
stern(um) 151, 1114,

-sternum **1179**
stethophone 901.4
stethoscope 914
stethoscopic 486.2
steward 684.1
stewardess 1341
stewed 1192
sthen(es) 132
sthen(ēs) 131
-sthenia **131**
-sthenic 131
sthenophotic 556.1
sthen(s) 193
-sthenuria **193**
sticc(a) 1089
-stice **727**
-stich 410, **1054**
-stichia **64**
-stichic **410,** 1054
-stichically 410
stichomythic 421
-stichous 64
'stick, measuring' 651
'stick, slender' 651
-stick 180, 922, **1089**
stigma 281,
-stigma **293**
-stigmal 293
-stigmatic 293
-stigmatism 293
stik 1089
stikke 1089
stimulatory 1528.3
stimulus 1348
'stimulus and its perception' 182.2
'stinger' 366
'stitch' 1480
-stitial 727
-stit(ium) 727
stix(os) 64, 410, 1054
stoc 1093
stocc 1093
-stock 675, **1093**
Stockbridge 774.2
-stoke 1093
stokehold 640.3
stokehole 834.4
-stole **840,** 1314
-stolē 840
-stolic 840
stom(a) 116, 117, 329, 330, 369, 1508
-stoma[1] **329**
-stoma[2] 329, **330**

'stomach' 189, 278, 500, 1118
-stomata 330, **369**
-stomate 329
stomatographia 70.1
-stomatous 329
-stome 329
-stomia¹ **116,** 329
-stomia² **117,** 329
-stomous 329
-stomum 329
-stomus 329
-stomy 329, **1508**
ston 906
stond 649
stond(en) 649, 650
'stone' 906.1, 906.2, 906.3, 1075, 1075.1
-stone **906**
'stone, mineral or fossil in' 1075.3
'stone, purple' 946
'stone, semiprecious' 906.4
stonechat 1382
stonehand 646.1
stonesmith 1076.2
stoon 906
'stoppage' 209, 209.2, 765.3, 1306
'storage place' 640.3, 834.3
'story' 421
stovepipe 912.1
-stow **1450**
stowen 1450
'straight, move' 1400
-strain 458, **1200**
-straint 1200
strake 794
'strands' 1452.1
'strangle' 346
strata 1.1
Strathhaven 1198
Strathkinness 1344
Strathmont 1418
stratospheric 491.1
'stream' 907, 1088, 1097
'street wide' 716
'strength' 95, 127, 131, 132, 193, 234, 234.1, 520, 732
'strengthening' 735
streph(ein) 785, 1483
strephosymbolia 89
strepsinema 288.3

streptomycin 1199.1
-stress 480.3, 1267, **1347**
'stretch' 250, 458, 480, 657, 905, 1223
'stretched' 147, 905, 1517
'stretches' 1517
'stretching out' 208
'stretch out' 208, 657.1
'stretch out one's hand' 250
'strew' 964
strewn 1192
strīc(an) 794
-strict **1392**
-striction 1392
-strictive 1392
strict(us) 1392
'strike' 249, 269, 653, 794
'strike a blow' 489, 917
'striking' 794
strikingly 1488.1
'string' 17, 688, 690, 714.1, 714.2
-stringe **777**
-stringence 777
-stringency 777
-stringent 777
string(ere) 777, 1200, 1392
'strip' 645.1, 645.2, 645.3, 645.4
'strip, architectural' 641
'stroke' 53, 249, 895
-stroke **794**
-stroma 324
strōma 324
-stromal 324
-stromatal 324
-stromatic 324
'strong' 679, 679.1, 735
strongbrained 603
stronghold 640.2
-strophe **785,** 1483
stroph(ē) 785, 1483
-strophic 785, 1483
-strophical 785
-strophism 785
strophocephaly 1491
-strophy 785, **1483**
-struct **1393**
-struction 1393
-structive 1393
'structure, supporting' 649.1

-structure 601, 649.2, 855.2, 1393
'structure on deck' 846
strŭct(us) 1393
stru(ere) 1393
studding 1046.3
student 1405.1, 1436.2
'student of' 1019.3
studhorse 966.1
'stuff' 781
'stump, tree' 1093
stunpoll 1134.1
'stunt' 300
stupefaction 1219.2
'stupid' 186
'stupor' 627
stutter 1254
-stylar 851
'style' 1022.1, 1022.2
-style **851**
-stylic 851
stylistic 571
styl(os) 851
-stylous 851
-suade **743**
suād(ēre) 743
-suasion 743
-suasive 743
*sub- 873
subacid 623.2
subalate 984
subalkaline 897
subaquatic 522
subatomic 448
subbreed 598.2
subchela 258
subcycle 810.1
subflora 358.1
subgeneric 492
subharmonic 475.1
subhead 590.7
subject 1388.1
'subjugate' 844.3
sublobe 710
submanic 457.2
submerge 779.1
submerse 963
submissively 1489
submontane 882
subnarcotic 555
subnormal 1113
subordinate 989.1
subplacenta 372
subpubic 389
subrange 776.2
subrogate 981.2

subscience 731.2
subserve 1035
subside 750
subsidy 1458
subsist 1439
subsist(ere) 650.2
subsonic 479.1, 479.3
'sub-species' 1084
'substance' 230, 290
substant(ia) 650.2
substantiate 973.5
subtend 657.1
subterfuge 783.1
subtetanic 458
subthoracic 390
subtitle 845
subtlety 1538
subtone 905.2
subtonic 480.2
subvene 886
subventral 1118
succeed 596
'success' 1399
successful 1141.3
-suchia 67
-suchian 67
suckbottle 847.1
'suet' 490
'suffer' 419, 532, 1072, 1485
'sufferer' 1072.1
'suffering' 1485.1
Suffolk 1096
suffragette 1011.1
'sugar' 957.1
sugarfree 762.2
'sugar in the blood' 98
sugarworks 1337.1
'suggestive of' 761.2
'suitable' 804
Sulayhid 616.1
sulfate 974.1
sulfite 1005.5
sulfourea 27
sulfur 502
sulfureous 1357
-sulfuric 502
-sulfurous 502
sulphide 746
sulpholeic 398.2
sulphur 502
sulphuret 1396
-sulphuric 502
-sulphurous 502
sulpur 502
-sum 867, 868

-sumable 873
-sumably 873
-sume **873**
sūm(ere) 873
summercastle 846
summertide 751.2
-sumption 873
-sumptive 873
sundew 1447
sunshade 742
sunstroke 794.3
supercritic 547
supercycle 810.3
superdemonic 472.2
'superfamily' 20
superintendency 1470.2
superknowledge 773
'superlative' 1434, 1441
'supernatural power' 672
superorganic 455.3
superpolitic 546.1
superromantic 550.2
supersonic 479.3
superstruct 1393
supervise 951
suppertime 861
'supply' 597.1
'support' 966.2, 1038.3
'supporter' 1005.1, 1436.3
'supporting tissue' 324
supposition 1221
suppositorium 1176.2
'suppuration' 291
supramaxilla 266
suprapubic 389
suprascapula 276
surcharge 778.4
'surface, level or flat' 879
'surface of the skin' 156
-surge **782**
-surgence 782
-surgency 782
-surgent 782
-surgeon 1526
surg(ere) 782
'surgery, plastic' 1544
-surgery **1526**
-surgical 1526
surname 854.1
surprise 1038
surreptitious 1360
surrogate 981.2
'surrounded by' 666.1
suspend 656.1
suspicion 1212.3

'sustain' 1373
'suturing' 1480
'suturing of broken bones' 1309
Suzette 1011.4
'swallow' 361, 937, 1375
swallowpipe 912.2
'swallow up' 361, 937, 1375
Swanborne 907
swearword 691.2
Swedish 1065.1
sweepstake 791
sweet 98, 743, 957
'sweetbread' 512
sweetie 786
'sweet wine' 957
'swell' 299, 481, 730, 1240
swelled 1192
'swelling' 286, 299, 340, 730, 813
'swelling containing blood' 328
swineherd 686
swinepipe 912.4
switchboard 681.2
swiveleyed 614
swollen 1192
swordfish 1067
swordsman 1186.2
swordster 1267.1
-sy **1535**
syllab(ē) 385, 805
-syllabic **385,** 805
-syllabical 385, 805
-syllabically 385, 805
-syllabicate 385, 805
-syllabication 385, 805
-syllabification 385
-syllabify 385
-syllable 385, **805**
sylnasol 1138
symball(ein) 89
symbiosis 1315.1, 1318
symbiotic 557.2
symblepharopterygium 1170.2
-symbolia **89**
symbolic 429.6
symbol(on) 89
'symbols' 89
-symboly 89
sympathetic 532
sympathic 419.2
sympathy 1485.1

symphalangia 56
symphonic 470.2
symphysis 1327
syn- 805, 1309
synchiria 182.2
synchronia 146.3
synchronic 477
syncline 898.2
synecdoche 693
synechia 61
synergetic 530
synergic 407.1
synergy 1477.1
syngamy 1503.2
syngenesis 213.2
synonym 1180
synonymy 1510.1
synophthalmia 112
synpneumonic 476.1
syntactic 525.1
syntheses 1296
synthesis 533.1, 533.2,
   1307, 1308
-synthesis **1309**
-synthetic 531, **533**, 1309
-synthetical 533, 1309
-synthetically 533, 1309
syn(ti)the(nai) 533, 1309
'syphilis' 544
Syriac 378
syringocystoma 331
syringosystrophy 1483
systole 840,
-systole **842**
systolē 842
-systolic 842

T

-t- 1217
-t **1381**
ta 910
tā 910
tablemate 987.2
tabloidia 37.3
tabular 1249.2
tac(an) 790
tachycardia 48.1
tachypragia 52
'tact, displaying' 516
tactful 1141.4
'tactfulness' 546.2
-tactic 247, **525**, 1333
-tactical 525
-tactics 525
'tactile sense' 211

'tadpole' 836, 1044.3
'tail' 12, 362
tailpiece 720.3
tailpipe 912.1
tailrace 717.2
-tain **1201**, 1222
-tainment 1201, 1222
'take' 296, 561, 805, 873,
   910, 950, 1026, 1536
-take **790**
'take back' 950
'take care of' 157, 578,
   1519
'take in hand' 790.1
taken 790, 1192
'taken thing' 296
'take over' 844.3
taketh 1074
'take together' 950
'take up' 873
'taking' 1536, 561
'taking apart' 580
taktik(os) 525
taliped 604.2
talipedic 391
'talk' 1019.1
talkathon 1211
-taph 413, **1061**
taph(ē) 413
-taphic **413**, 1061
taph(os) 1061
tapinocephalic 423
-tas **1288**
-tās 1538
tass(ein) 247, 525, 1333
'taste' 229
tasteful 1141.2
-tāt- 1538
tatt(ein) 247, 525, 1333
'tattoo' 293
tauromachic 409
tauromachy 1479
tautologic 406.1
Tavistock 1093
'tax' 633
taxa 2.1
-taxia **247**, 525, 1333
-taxic 247, 525, 1333
-taxis 247, 525, **1333**
taxonomy 1504
-taxy 247, 525, 1333
-te 1069
teacake 787.1
'teach' 523
teacherly 1488.1
'teaching, apt at' 523

teamster 1267.1
teamwise 952.3
'tear' 51, 402, 768, 1334,
   1423
-tec 8
-teca 8
techn(ē) 462, 1021, 1290,
   1514
-technic **462**, 1021, 1290,
   1514
-technical 462, 1021,
   1290, 1514
-technically 462, 1021,
   1290, 1514
'technical procedures'
   462.2
Technicolor 1275.2
-technics 1021, **1290**,
   1514
technique 462, 1020,
   1290, 1514
-technique **1021**
technocracy 1467.3
Technocrat 1384.2
Technocratic 520.2
-technology 462, 1021,
   1290, 1514
-techny 1021, 1290, **1514**
'teeth' 240, 241
'teeth, element of' 617.1
'teeth, size of' 551.1
teetotaler 1251.4
'tegument' 1203
tein(ein) 458, 905
tek(an) 790
-tela **259**
tēla 259
telacoustic 576.2
telecamera 353
telegenic 460.4
telegram 1145.1
telegrammic 441
telegraph 1060.2
telekinetic 540.2
telemotor 1278
telepathy 1485.1
telephone 901.2
telergic 407.2
telescope 914
telescopic 486.2, 486.3
telescopy 1521
telethon 1211
Teletype 917.3
televise 951
televisionitis 1330.2
-telic **426**

-telical 426
-telically 426
'tell' 207, 569, 948
'telling' 421
-tellurian 503
-telluric **503**
tellūs 503
telodendria 175
telodendron 1228.2
telokinesia 214
tel(os) 426
telotroch 1056
telotrocha 32
telpher 1259
temnein 447, 448, 870,
1507
'temperature' 1150.3
'temperature, body' 119,
1150.2, 1509.1
tempolabile 819
'ten, multiples of' 1539
-tenance 1201, 1222
-tend **657**, 1223
'tendency' 88.1, 494.1,
185.2, 1025, 1025.1
'tendency towards' 798
tend(ere) 657, 1223
'tending' 1025.2, 1028.1,
1529.2
'tending to' 804.2, 956,
1141.4, 1457.3
'tending towards' 1363
'tending towards
performing' 1027, 1030
'tendon' 192, 940, 1119
ten(ēre) 1201, 1222
tenfold 638.1
ten-foot 1420.1
-tense 657, 1223
-tensine 657
-tension 147, 458, 480,
657, 905, 1223, 1517
-tensious 657, 1223
-tensive 1223
tēns(us) 1223
-tent 657, 1223
-tention[1] 1201, **1222**
-tention[2] 657, **1223**
-tentious 657, 1223
tent(us) 1222, 1223
tēor(ian) 930
-tēr 1266
teracycle 810.3
Terebella 262.2
tergiverse 965.2
terracing 1046.4

'test' 1041
-tetanic **458**
-tetanically 458
tetan(os) 458
'tetanus' 458
'tetany' 458
tetartanopia 162.2
Tetrabranchia 65.1
tetracoralla 261
tetradactyl 1143
tetraglot 1419
tetragon 1210
tetralemma 296
tetramazia 255
Tetrandria 174
tetraploid 628
tetraseme 858.1
tetrasemic 437
tetrastichic 410
Tetraxonia 148
tetrole 832
th 1069, 1070, 1074
-th[1] **1069**
-th[2] **1070**
thalami 1083.2
thalm(os) 125
-thanasia **205**
-thanasic 205
thanatognomonic 474
thanatophidia 46
thanat(os) 205
'thanks' 719
thaumaturgic 408.1
thaumaturgy 1478
-th(e) 436, 897, 1070,
1245.1
the(a) 572, 1159, 1437
Thebaica 9
Thebaid 618.2
-thec 8
-theca **8**
thecae 695
-thecal 8
-thecial 8, 1166
-thecium 8, **1166**
Thecophora 357
Thecosomata 368
-theism 572, **1159**, 1437
-theist 572, 1159, **1437**
-theistic **572**, 1159, 1437
-theistical 572
-theistically 572, 1159,
1437
thēk(ē) 8, 1166
thēl(ē) 83, 1172
-thelia **83**

-thelioma **307**
-theliomatous 307
-thelism 83
-thelium 307, 308, 309,
1172
thelytocia 43.2
thenceforward 683.3
Theobald 632
theocracy 1467.3
theocrat 1384.1
Theodora 356
theogonic 469.1
theologic 406.2
theologue 1019.3
theology 1476.2
theomaniac 381.2
theophanic 456.4
theophany 1511
'theorem' 296
theoretician 1184
theorize 1038.1
'theory' 1484
'theory, social or
political' 1467.3
the(os) 572, 1159, 1437
theosophic 415
theosophy 1484
therapeia 157, 1519
therapeu(ein) 157, 578,
1294, 1519
therapeut(ic) 157, 1294,
1519
-therapeutic **578**
-therapeutically 578, 1294
-therapeutics 157, 578,
1294, 1519
'therapeutic treatment'
1332
-therapia **157,** 578, 1294,
1519
-therapist 157, 578, 1294,
1519
-therapy 157, 578, 1294,
1485.2, **1519**
-there 178, **924**
theretofore 932.1
-theria **178**
-therian 924
-theridae 178
-therioid 924
thēr(ion) 178, 924
-therium 178, 924
-therm 119, **1150**, 1509
-thermal 119, 1150, 1509
thermalgesia 210
therm(ē) 119, 1150, 1509

'toes, deformity of' 910.1
togaed 594.2
'together' 805, 1009
toing 1046.4
'token' 89
'token of a pledge' 766
-tokia 43
tok(os) 43
-toky 43
-toma 327
'tomb' 1061
tombstone 906.1
-tome 447, **870,** 1506
tom(ē) 327, 447, 448, 870, 1506
-tomic 327, **447,** 870, 1506
-tomical 447, 1506
-tomically 447, 1506
-tomist 447, 1506
-tomize 447, 870, 1506
tom(on) 327, 447, 448
tom(os) 327, 447, 448
-tomous 447, 870, 1506
tomtitmouse 969.3
-tomy 447, 870, **1506,** 1508
-ton **1232**
-tone 147, 480, **905,** 1517
'tones in harmony' 690.1
-tongue 228, 363, 574, **1017,** 1419, 1440
'tongue illness' 1017.1
-tonia **147,** 480, 905, 1517
-tonic 147, **480,** 905, 1517
ton(os) 147, 480, 905, 1517
-tonous 147, 480, 905, 1517
tonsillectomic 447
tonsillectomy 1507
tonus 147, 1348, 1517
-tony 147, 480, 905, **1517**
too 910
'tool' 455, 590.5
'tooth' 240, 241, 551, 1001, 1208
toothstick 1089.2
topchrome 866
-topia **166**
-topic 166
-topism 166
toponeurosis 1320
top(os) 166, 167

topside 748.1
-topy 166
-tor 725, 943, 1454, 1461
Torbay 1461
'torpor' 301.2
torulaform 1152
tosspot 1422
'touch' 69, 211, 769, 790, 941
'touching' 211
touchpan 1188.3
'touch with the hands' 812.1
tournament 1412.1
towage 765.7
'toward' 589, 683, 683.1, 683.2
towhead 590.3
towline 895.1
'town' 1053, 1232, 1464
-town **1234**
townee 761.3
'town, fortified or walled' 1270
townside 748.3
townspeople 844.1
towpath 1073
toxa 253, 583
-toxaemia 108
toxaemic 108
-toxemia **108**
-toxemic 108
-toxia **253,** 583, 1206
-toxic 253, **583,** 1206
-toxical 253, 583, 1206
-toxically 253, 583, 1206
-toxicity 253, 583, 1206
toxicoderma 333.2
toxicodermic 450.3
toxicomaniac 381.1
toxicopexis 1335
toxicophidia 46
-toxicosis 253
toxignomic 443.1
tox(ikon) 108, 253, 583, 1206
-toxin 253, 583, **1206**
'toxin in the blood' 108
toxiphrenia 137
-toxis 253, 583, 1206
-toxism 253, 583, 1206
Toxoplasma 335.2
-toxy 253, 583, 1206
tracheophony 1516.2
Trachybdella 264
-tract **1386**

-traction 1386
-tractive 1386
tractrix 1454.2
tract(us) 1386
'trade' 1525.2
tradespeople 844.2
tradesperson 1231
træppe 1241
tragacanth 1078
tragedienne 875
tragicomic 442
tragicoromantic 550.2
trah(ere) 1386
trailerite 1005.2
'train' 568
'trait' 959.2
traject 1388.1
trample 799
transaquatic 522
transarctic 527
transcend 652
transfer 1256.1
transfigure 941.2
'transform' 775
transfuge 783.1
transfuse 967
transiliac 380
translatrix 1454.1
transliterate 999.1
'translucence' 456.2
translucent 1408
'transmitted material' 412
'transmutation' 436
transonic 479.3
transpire 929
transpose 961
'transposition of sounds or letters' 1308
transthermia 119.2
trap 1241
-trap **1241**
trappe 1241
trappings 1241.3
traps 1241.3
-trauma **338**
-traumatic 338
-traumatically 338
'travel' 918, 919
'traveler' 1445
travelogue 1019.12
traverse 965.2
tre 763
'tread' 1073
'treat' 1038.1
'treater' 1072.2

'tuber' 1421
tuberculosis 1315.2
tubiflorous 1374
tubule 848
tubule/tubular 1249
Tubulibranchiata 365
tubulifera 352
-tude **758**
-tūd(in-) 758
-tūd(ō) 758
tum(ēre) 730
-tumesce 730
-tumescence **730**
-tumescent 730
'tumor' 286, 299, 340, 813
'tumor, bone' 304
'tumor, cartilaginous' 321
'tumor, cystic' 331
'tumor, endothelial' 309
'tumor, epithelial' 308, 313
'tumor, fatty' 319
'tumor, fibrous' 320
'tumor, kidney' 323
'tumor, malignant epithelial' 318
'tumor, marrow' 312
'tumor, nervous' 325
'tumor, neuroglial' 310
'tumor, skin' 315
'tumor in cellular tissue' 307
'tumorlike granulation tissue' 314
'tumor of blood and lymph vessels' 306
'tumor of connective tissues' 332
'tumor of lymphoid tissue' 305
'tumult' 144
tūn 1232, 1234
-tund **671**, 970
tund(ere) 671, 970
Tunisian 1183
tunesmith 1076.3
tunge 1017
-tūr(a) 943
-tural 943
-turally 943
turbulent 1411
-ture **943**
turkeyburger 1258.1

'turn' 163, 488, 661, 780, 785, 915, 965 1117, 1162, 1389, 1389.1, 1424, 1483, 1522
'turn aside' 1389.1
'turn back' 1389.1
'turn down' 1389.1
'turned' 965.3, 965.4
'turn in' 1389.1
'turning' 163, 488, 488.1, 785, 785.1, 915, 965.1, 1162, 1483, 1522
-tūr(um) 943
-tūr(us) 943
tūs(a) 671, 970
-tuse 671, **970**
tus(er) 970
-tusion 671, 970
tūs(um) 671, 970
tūs(us) 671, 970
Tweedmouth 1082.1
twelfth 1069
'twelve inches' 1420.1
twentieth 1069
twenty 1539
twentyish 1065.5
Twickenham 1144
'twig' 144, 910.2
'twin' 123, 987.4 1353
'twins, joined' 123, 1353.1
'twist' 661, 715, 785, 1483
'twisting' 785, 785.1, 1483
twitter 1254
'two-' 516
two-decker 1251.5
two-foot 1420.1
two-ply 1502
twosome 868
-ty 1539
-ty¹ **1538**
-ty² **1539**
tyde 751
tyer(en) 930
tyme 861
Tynemouth 1082.1
-typal 168, 489, 917
-typally 489
'type' 168, 489, 489.1,
-type **917**
'type, width of' 713.4
typembryo 1240
-typhi 627
typhlatony 1517

typhloempyema 291
-typhoid **627**
-typhoidal 627
typh(os) 627
-typhus 627, 627.1, 627.2
-typia **168**
-typic **489**, 917
-typical 489, 917
-typically 489, 917
'typical of' 1065.3
-typism 168
typologic 406.3
typ(os) 168, 489, 917
typt(ein) 489, 917
-typy 489, 917
tyr(en) 930
tyr(ian) 930
Tyrolese 949.1

U

-uc 1091
-ul 797, 1245
-ul(a) 272, 273, 848, 1178, 1249
-ula¹ **272**, 273, 848 1178, 1351
-ula² 272, **273**, 848, 1351
-ulae 273, 848, 1178, 1351
-ular 272, 848, 1178, **1249**, 1351
-ulār(is) 1249
-ularly 1249
-ulate 272, 848
'ulceration' 346
-ule 272, 273, **848**, 1178, 1249, 1351
-ulency 1411
-ulent **1411**
-ulent(us) 1411
-uli 272, 273, 848, 1178
-ulic 272, 848, 1178, 1351
-ulōs(us) 1363
-ulous 272, 848, 1178, 1351, **1363**
-ulously 1363
-ulousness 1363
ultraheroic 483
ultramicrobe 711
ultrared 605
-ulum 272, 273, 848, **1178**, 1249, 1351
ul(us) 272, 273, 641, 848, 1178, 1249, 1363

-ulus 1351
-um 1.1,
-um 1164
Umbelliferae 704
umbrellawise 952.3
'un-' 448
unacademic 435
unawares 1286
uncatholic 430
'unchanging' 430
uncharge 778.3
unclad 593.1
'unconsciousness' 301.1
under 650.2
underbid 622
undercharge 778.4
underclad 593.1
underfold 639
'undergoing' 644
underhanded 595.2
underjawed 613
underling 1049.3
'underlying' 531
underside 748.1
undersparred 609
understage 770.1
understand 650.2, 955
'understanding' 955
understate 1002
undertake 790.1, 950
underworld 642
undidactic 523
undine 888
undiplomatic 516
uneconomic 444
unelectronic 478
'unfed' 71
'unforeseen, react to the'
    951
-ung 1046, 1047
ungerontic 552
ungild 636.1
ungrace 719
ungrammatical 1105
unhealthful 1141.1
unhydraulic 431
unicorn 1233
unicycle 810.4
unimeographic 412
'union for propagation'
    1503.2
Unionville 830.1
uniped 604.2
'unit' 588.4, 856, 1207.2
'unit, basic' 1207
'unite' 806

'unit of language' 856
'unit of measurement'
    437, 858, 1145.2
'universal' 430
'universe' 453.1, 453.3,
    965.1
unline 896
unmerge 779.2
unneurotic 560.2
unnoble 807.1
unpeople 844.3
unperiodic 395
unpoetic 543.2
unpolitic 546.2
unromantic 550.2
unsaddle 811.1
unsparred 609
'unstable' 819
unsynthetic 533.1
untire 930
unvolcanic 454.2
upbreed 598.1
upfeed 597.1
'upper end' 590.4
upright 1400
upsaddle 811.1
upstage 770.1
upstand 650.1
upsurge 782
uptake 790.2
-ura 362
-ūra 938, 943
uracil 1124
uracrasia 206.2
uracratia 234.2
-ural 938
-urally 938, 1498
uramil 1124
uranophane 878
urban 1181.1
-ure 938
-urea 27
-ureal 27
uredostage 770.2
uremia 96.2
-uret 1396
-uretic 1396
-uretize 1396
-uretum 1396
-urge 408, 743, 1478
-urgia 408
-urgic 408, 1478
-urgical 408, 1478
-urgically 408, 1478
-urgist 408, 1478
-urgy 408, 1478

-uria 27, 190
uriacidemia 99
-uric 27, 190, 504
uricotelic 426
-uridae 362
'urination' 193
'urine' 27, 190, 193, 195,
    504
'urine, globin or proteins
    in' 194
'urine, serum proteins in'
    195
Urocoptidae 697
urocrisia 220.1
-uroid 362
urolagnia 138
uromantia 238
Uronema 288.2
urophanic 456.3
uroplania 126
uropoietic 535
urosepsis 1322
uroseptic 563
urotoxia 253
-ūr(um) 943
-urus 362
-ūr(us) 943
-us 1083, 1348
useful 1141.3
'user' 1267.2
usherette 1011.1
Usnea 504
-us(us) 1351
'uterus' 188
'utilizing' 383.6
utopiast 1429
'utter' 100, 905.1
'utterance' 57, 100, 199,
    507, 1051, 1304
'utterance, spoken' 691
'utter distinctly' 181
uttermost 1441
uvula/uvular 1249

V

vacant 1404.3
vacca 891
vaccīn(a) 891
-vaccinate 891
vaccination 891
-vaccine 891
vacciniola 268.2
vaccīn(um) 891
vaccīn(us) 891
'vacuum tube' 1230.1